Sixth Palenque Round Table, 1986

The Palenque Round Table Series, Volume 8

Sixth Palenque Round Table, 1986

Merle Greene Robertson, General Editor

Virginia M. Fields, Volume Editor

University of Oklahoma Press : Norman and London

Library of Congress Cataloging-in-Publication Data

Palenque Round Table (6th : 1986)
   Six Palenque Round Table, 1986 / Merle Greene
Robertson, general editor ; Virginia M. Fields, volume
editor. — 1st ed.
      p.   cm. — (The Palenque Round Table series ; v. 8)
   "The Sixth Palenque Round Table Conference was held
from June 8–14, 1986, at Palenque, Chiapas, Mexico"—
Pref.
   Includes bibliographical references.
   ISBN 0-8061-2277-3
   1. Palenque Site (Mexico)—Congresses.   2. Mayas—
Antiquities—Congresses.   3. Indians of Mexico—Antiq-
uities—Congresses.   4. Indians of Central America—
Antiquities—Congresses.   I. Title.   II. Series: Palenque
Round Table. Palenque Round Table series ; v. 8
F1435.1.P2P26   1990
972'.75—dc20   90-12171
                                   CIP

Published with the assistance of the National Endowment for
the Humanities, a federal agency which supports the study of
such fields as history, philosophy, literature, and languages.

To the memory of
Dra. Marta Foncerrada de Molina
1928–1988
who contributed to the Palenque conferences
since the very beginning in 1973. Marta was a
dear friend and colleague of us all and will be
sorely missed.

Contents

ix   Preface

xi   Editor's Introduction
MERLE GREENE ROBERTSON

3   Historical Notes on the Discovery of the Ruins,
the Founding of the Town, and the Origin and
Significance of the Name of Palenque
ARNULFO HARDY GONZÁLEZ, M.D.

6   The Demotion of Chac-Zutz': Lineage
Compounds and Subsidiary Lords at Palenque
LINDA SCHELE

12   The Narrative Structure of Hieroglyphic Texts
at Palenque
J. KATHRYN JOSSERAND

32   Cycles of Time: Caracol in the Maya Realm
ARLEN F. CHASE

43   Dedication Ceremonies at Chichén Itzá:
The Glyphic Evidence
RUTH KROCHOCK

51   The Great Ball Court Stone from Chichén Itzá
LINNEA H. WREN

59   Symbolism of the Maya Ball Game at Copán:
Synthesis and New Aspects
JEFF KARL KOWALSKI and WILLIAM L. FASH

68   Lineage Patrons and Ancestor Worship Among
the Classic Maya Nobility: The Case of Copán
Structure 9N-82
WILLIAM L. FASH

81   The Cross Pattern at Copán: Forms, Rituals,
and Meanings
CLAUDE F. BAUDEZ

89   Lifeline to the Gods: Ritual Bloodletting at Santa
Rita Corozal
DIANE Z. CHASE

97   Tlalocs at Uxmal
RUBEN MALDONADO C. and BEATRIZ REPETTO TIO

102   The Period-Ending Stelae of Yaxchilán
CAROLYN TATE

110   The Structure 8 Tablet and Development of the
Great Plaza at Yaxchilán
RAMÓN CARRASCO V.

118   Damming the Usumacinta: The Archaeological
Impact
S. JEFFREY K. WILKERSON

135   The Teotihuacán-Kaminaljuyu-Tikal
Connection: A View from the South Coast
of Guatemala
FREDERICK J. BOVE

143   Olmec Bloodletting: An Iconographic Study
ROSEMARY A. JOYCE, RICHARD EDGING, KARL
LORENZ, and SUSAN D. GILLESPIE

151   Olmec Iconographic Influences on the Symbols
of Maya Rulership: An Examination of Possible
Sources
F. KENT REILLY, III

167   The Iconographic Heritage of the Maya
Jester God
VIRGINIA M. FIELDS

175   The Bearer, the Burden, and the Burnt:
The Stacking Principle in the Iconography
of the Late Preclassic Maya Lowlands
DAVID A. FREIDEL, MARIA MASUCCI, SUSAN
JAEGER, and ROBIN A. ROBERTSON

184   Beyond Rainstorms: The Kawak as an Ancestor,
Warrior, and Patron of Witchcraft
JOANNE M. SPERO

194   Aspects of Impersonation in Classic Maya Art
ANDREA STONE

203   The Maya "Posture of Royal Ease"
ANNE-LOUISE SCHAFFER

217   The "Holmul Dancer" Theme in Maya Art
DORIE REENTS-BUDET

223   An Investigation of the Primary Standard
Sequence on Classic Maya Ceramics
NIKOLAI GRUBE

233   A Study of the Fish-in-Hand Glyph, T714: Part 1
DIANE WINTERS

246   Jaws II: Return of the *Xoc*
TOM JONES

255   Classic and Modern Relationship Terms and the
"Child of Mother" Glyph (TI:606.23)
NICHOLAS A. HOPKINS

266   Prepositions and Complementizers in the Classic
Period Inscriptions
MARTHA J. MACRI

273   Aspects of Polyvalency in Maya Writing:
Affixes T12, T229, and T110
DIETER DÜTTING

285 Faunal Offerings in the Dresden Codex
VICTORIA R. BRICKER

293 A Text from the Dresden New Year Pages
BRUCE LOVE

303 Codex Dresden: Late Postclassic Ceramic
Depictions and the Problems of Provenience
and Date of Painting
MERIDETH PAXTON

309 The Real Venus-Kukulcan in the Maya
Inscriptions and Alignments
ANTHONY AVENI

322 Artificial Intelligence Meets Maya Epigraphy
JORGE L. OREJEL OPISSO

333 Bibliography

357 Index

Preface

The Sixth Palenque Round Table Conference was held from June 8–14, 1986, at Palenque, Chiapas, Mexico. The Palenque conferences, specializing in the Maya but including Maya contact, exchange, and influence groups, began with a small conference at La Cañada, Palenque, over the Christmas holidays in 1973. Subsequent conferences were held in December 1974 and in June 1978, 1980, and 1983. The First Palenque Round Table Conference had only thirty-five participants from thirteen universities in the United States and Mexico. The conference in 1980 and all of those following accommodated over two hundred persons. The sixth conference had 235 registrants from twelve countries—the United States, Mexico, Guatemala, Honduras, Belize, Canada, England, Australia, France, Germany, Switzerland, and Holland.

The Palenque Conference has come to be recognized as the foremost Maya conference in the world, and the proceedings are quoted in just about every volume published on Maya art, iconography, dynastic history, and epigraphy. The conferences started on a small scale, the participants hoping to learn everything possible about Palenque, but the scale soon grew to include other areas relating to Maya art, dynastic history, and epigraphy. The First Palenque Round Table Conference actually generated the wholesale study of Maya epigraphy, and since then each conference has built upon the others. Scholars from many universities and backgrounds, both from the Americas and Europe, meet for a week to share new data and to discuss differences in their findings.

These conferences have become the place to look for new approaches, new problems, and new discoveries, and although all is not completely agreed upon, ideas are shared and opened for discussion. With each new volume we have seen a wider range of related subjects, a wider viewpoint, and a common agreement on many aspects that would not have been dealt with had it not been for the open discussions of the Palenque conferences, which have forced each of us to listen to our neighbor. This is what the Palenque Round Table conferences are all about—sharing and discussing ideas.

Without the dedicated efforts of a capable staff, the Sixth Palenque Round Table Conference would simply not have happened. We sincerely thank George Stuart, Chair of Speaker Sessions, for taking on a difficult, and at times trying, job. To our co-Chairs of Local Affairs, Kathryn Josserand and Nicholas Hopkins, we all owe a debt. And, of course, we could not have had these meetings at all had Kathy Keith not gone through the daily grind of running the projector. Finance Officer Annette Metzler took on the unbelievable task of trying to keep up with the daily exchange of the peso. Ever helpful Key Sanchez took care of hotel reservations and kept all of the hotels happy, a demanding job. Our bus transportation was handled by Jeff Wilkerson and Arnulfo Hardy, with drivers Jim Metzler and Carlos Carmona. We thank you all for the long, and at times unpredicted, hours.

Two other people who kept the unseen electrical and mechanical portion of the conference going were Alfonso Morales and Chencho (Aucencio Guzman). Tom Jones, Expediter, was kept busy trying to let people know what was taking place and where. Sales, always a busy and trying task, were handled by Virginia Fields, Carolyn Tate, John Bowles, Kent Reilly, and Vickie Velasco. The Hospitality Committee—whose members included Augusto Molina, Marta Molina, Claudine Marken, Don Marken, and Beatrice de la Fuente—was also kept busy. And we must not forget the Mailing Committee—Leroy Cleal, Joyce Livingston, Elayne Marquis, Claudine Marken, Patricia Amlin, and Barbara Verby—all of whom we thank for performing the monotonous task of mailing.

We had a wonderful Patrons Committee made up of citizens of Palenque who had been working all year making plans that would assure this conference of being the best ever. We owe all of you a tremendous applause— Miguel Angel Sanchez, Ofelia Morales de Sanchez, Carlos Morales, Moises Morales, Mario Leon Tovilla, Amalia Leon, Manuel Leon Tovilla, Efren Elias B., Arnulfo Hardy Gonzales, David Morales Timbres, Sonia Morales, Manuel Leon Perez, Zacarias Hardy, and Marco Antonio Morales Timbres. We salute all of you.

We also thank all of the citizens of Palenque, the

mayor, the bankers, the police officers, the tourism group, everyone, for the hospitality extended to the participants at this conference. You have all become endeared to each of us.

I want especially to acknowledge the large amount of work done by Don Benke, who took on the difficult task of registering all of the participants of this conference. Don passed away in September 1986. We extend our heartfelt sympathy to Lois and to his son, Tim McGill.

It is another sad duty for me to announce that our very dear friend and colleague Marta Foncerrada Molina passed away in May 1988. Marta was a participant in every Palenque Round Table conference and a brilliant contributor. She was awarded her doctorate just before she died. We all extend our sympathy to Augusto and to her three sons, Miguel, Pedro, and Augusto, Jr.

MERLE GREENE ROBERTSON

San Francisco, California

Editor's Introduction

MERLE GREENE ROBERTSON

Our knowledge of the ancient Maya and their related neighbors has increased tremendously in the past twenty years, with the focus being upon hieroglyphic inscriptions, art, iconography, dynastic history, demography, and linguistics. No longer are allegations by early scholars taken for granted and accepted as fact when new evidence indicates discrepancies in the earlier data or when recent investigations using scientific equipment not available in earlier work point to an entirely different approach than was previously known. Palenque, the great center on the western periphery of the Maya realm, is a case in point. Seventeen years ago we did not know who the rulers of the city were or what their relationships were to each other and to outsiders. We did not know that kings were ballplayers, nor did we know that some works of art were actually signed by their artist.

The First Palenque Round Table Conference, held in 1973, opened new vistas into our knowledge of the Maya at Palenque as well as at other sites. It was here at Palenque that the few of us attending this small conference, including Floyd Lounsbury, Linda Schele, Peter Mathews, Jeffrey Miller, and Michael Coe, came up with the names and dates of rulership of the kings of Palenque. This moment was tremendously exciting and of uppermost significance in the minds of all of us there. No longer were rulers unknown beings, but suddenly they had become real people, real kings who lived and ruled the city where we had come to study. The citizens of Palenque and the surrounding area were so excited when they learned that we knew the names of people who ruled the city ages ago that one community near the railroad station even renamed its town Pacal Na (home of Pacal).

This first meeting was held at Na Chan-Balam, the home of Merle and Bob Robertson at Palenque. We took pictures off the walls and hung black cloth over the windows to allow the white wall to be used as a projector screen. We sat on chairs, cushions, and beds or draped ourselves over tables during meetings, and a pot of coffee sat ready for people to help themselves. When Floyd Lounsbury, Jeffrey Miller, Linda Schele, and Peter Mathews found the name glyphs of the rulers, we had to decide what to refer to them by—English names, Spanish names, or something else? Moises Morales said, "Why are we discussing English or Spanish names? These rulers were Chol Maya. Why do we not give them the Chol names for their glyphs?" So it came to be. They were given Chol Maya names, although we knew that our names were not the ones by which they were called in ancient times.

Just a short time later, however, Michael Coe and Floyd Lounsbury found that indeed Pacal, the greatest ruler of Palenque, who ruled from the age of twelve years until he died at age eighty (from 9.9.2.4.8 [A.D. 615] to 9.12.11.5.18 [A.D. 683]), would undoubtedly have been called by that name. Pacal or Chimal ("Shield") would have been his personal name and his lineage name also would have been "Shield" (certainly pronounced *Pacal*). The title *Mah K'ina*, the superfix on the left glyph and spelled out phonetically on his right glyph, is a title also known in the highlands and in use throughout the sixteenth century.

Since then work on deciphering the hieroglyphs has proceeded by leaps and bounds. Groups from all over the United States and Europe, including scholars in archaeology and linguistics, have studied the hieroglyphs. The whole field of Mesoamerican study has become interdisciplinary. It was not so long ago that we knew nothing about the impressive size and grandeur of the Late and Early Preclassic site of Mirador, the early sites of Cerros and Colha in Belize, the vast hydraulic system of canals and reservoirs of Edzna, or the dense population of the entire Yucatán peninsula during Classic times. We have now begun to rethink the Toltec question at Chichén Itzá and the sociopolitical system of these peoples and their connection to other groups in Mesoamerica. In other words, with every year a wealth of knowledge has opened up to us on the entire Maya-Mesoamerica question. The 1986 Sixth Palenque Round Table Conference addressed many of these questions and brought up new ones as well.

The 1986 conference papers start out by anchoring us in time and space. Dr. Arnulfo Hardy, a medical doctor living in Palenque, introduces this volume by bringing to light the little-known history of the town of Palenque and its famous bell. Such a study should have been done long ago but was always overlooked. Dr. Hardy's timely work documents information about Palenque that few know anything about and that soon would have been lost forever. In keeping with having Palenque serve as our introduction, Linda Schele discusses the demotion of an important noble at Palenque, Chac Zutz', who was previously thought to have been a king of Palenque but now, with the ability to decipher the pertinent glyphs, is believed to have been a *cahal*, or war chief, a high-ranking war lord under Chaacal III. J. Kathryn Josserand enlarges on Palenque's history by dealing with the inscriptions that relate to dynastic histories and their mythological legitimization. She points out how at Palenque they are told in "story form" as literary narratives, another aspect of Maya history that was not known before.

At the Third Palenque Round Table, in 1978, it became apparent that it was necessary to include other sites besides Palenque if we were to understand what was taking place in the Maya area affecting Palenque, and so neighboring Bonampak was included and, from a further distance, Cacaxtla and Yucatán. This pattern has been followed from then on. We cannot isolate Palenque if we are to understand what was going on in Preclassic or Classic Mesoamerica. Thus numerous other areas are represented in this volume. Arlen F. Chase's paper on the cycles of Caracol proves to be a good example of the importance of directional and cyclical time in the Lowland Maya area. Caracol, like Palenque, was a boundary site for the Maya realm, Caracol in the east and Palenque on the west.

Ruth Krochock goes to Chichén Itzá in Yucatán and opens up an extraordinary range of new interpretations for the iconography and hieroglyphic inscriptions at that site. She brings out new interpretations for the child-of-mother glyph and, combining new information from elsewhere with that from Chichén Itzá, she offers possible readings for the bird-in-mouth and hand-crossed bands verbs. Linnea H. Wren discusses for the first time the stone ball carved with many figures found in the Great Ball Court at Chichén Itzá.

Jeff Karl Kowalski and William L. Fash introduce new material from Copán directly from the field. Burials found in association with earlier buildings are found to support the premise that fusion of ancestors with deities was the same at Copán as at Palenque for the Late Classic Maya. Claude F. Baudez comments on Structure 11, probably the most ambitious representation of the universe built at Copán.

Bloodletting among the Maya is probably the single most discussed topic of the practices of these ancient people, and although a great deal of material has been published on the subject, each new aspect only reinforces that it was indeed the foremost ritual practice in their society. Diane Z. Chase demonstrates that bloodletting rites carry over from the Early Classic and Classic Periods to the Postclassic, as evidenced by her study at Santa Rita Corozal, and that these rites, now known to play an important role in Maya dynastic history, were ceremonies well known to the Maya over their entire span of time and space.

Three of the papers in this volume—Ruben Maldonado and Beatriz Repetto Tio's, Carolyn Tate's, and Ramón Carrasco's—analyze art styles and iconography. Iconography in the art of Mesoamerica has come to the forefront only in recent years. George Kubler's definitive *Studies in Classic Maya Iconography*, published in 1969, led scholars to take on this long-overlooked aspect of Maya art. Ruben Maldonado and Beatriz Repetto Tio discuss Tlaloc symbolism at Uxmal, and Carolyn Tate undertakes the study of art at the large center at Yaxchilán, while Ramón Carrasco investigates the pattern of construction activity and dynastic patterns at Yaxchilán.

S. Jeffrey K. Wilkerson takes on the critical situation of the Usumacinta River hydroelectric dam project, pointing out the great loss not only to archaeology but to the ecology of the entire region if the dam proceeds. As we now know, the dam has been abandoned, at least for the present.

Frederick J. Bove takes us to the Teotihuacán-Kaminaljuyu-Tikal connection in southern Mesoamerica, illuminating again that Pre-Columbian Mesoamerica was made up of numerous interacting polities with widespread social, political, demographic, and economic dislocations and restructuring. Large-scale population dislocations are seen along the Pacific Coast of Guatemala as well as in the Guatemala Highlands and northern Yucatán. During the same period on the Pacific slopes, Bove finds fortifications at Edzna, Becan, and Tikal-Uaxactún. Widespread trade has been understood for a long time, but now warfare is much more widely accepted as a way of life and probably as an accompaniment of trade amongst the Maya and their neighbors than was suspected in earlier studies.

At this point it is necessary to bring the Olmec into these studies. In their study of Olmec bloodletting practices, Rosemary A. Joyce and her coauthors refer to iconography similar to that discussed by Diane Chase at Santa Rita Corozal and suggest that the practice of bloodletting adds substance to the argument that Maya bloodletting imagery was the expression of a long-established Mesoamerican cosmological system. F. Kent Reilly shows that the origins of Classic Maya civilization are pushed further back into the Formative period, and suggests direct Olmec influence on Classic Maya iconography. Copán, a Classic site, reveals pottery incised with Olmec motifs in a grave carbon dated to 1000 B.C. lying under the earliest identifiable Maya deposits on the site. Recent work at Cerros reinforces this hypothesis.

Each successive volume of the Palenque Round Table proceedings has investigated further the iconography of the Maya and their neighbors. Several papers in this volume deal mainly with this subject. Virginia M. Fields reinforces the Olmec connecton in her examination of the Jester God prototype appearing on a Cerros Preclassic building. David A. Freidel, Maria Masucci, Susan Jaeger, and Robin A. Robertson also suggest Preclassic connections in their examination of Cerros iconography, specifically the "stacking principle" found in Classic Maya iconography with its early form showing up at Cerros. Joanne M. Spero, using ethnographic sources, writes about a multidimensional image of the Pre-Columbian "Cauac" monster, an underworld god. Ancestors and the underworld are shown to belong to the same realm as guardians of the community. Andrea Stone examines the functions of rulership and suggests that rulers, women, and captives are equated with one another within a structured visual system. Anne-Louise Schaffer brings out the iconography of seated figures, suggesting that only gods and lords are permitted to be elevated above ground. Dorie Reents-Budet takes on polychrome pottery workshops, indicating that there were workshops for pottery as there were workshops or "schools," as suggested by Marvin Cohodas, for Yaxchilán.

Following the advances made in deciphering hieroglyphs at the First Palenque Round Table Conference, in 1973, a series of conferences arranged by Elizabeth Benson was held at Dumbarton Oaks, in Washington, D.C., where Floyd Lounsbury, David Kelly, Tatiana Proskouriakoff, Linda Schele, Peter Mathews, George Kubler, Merle Greene Robertson, and Joyce Marcus deciphered hieroglyphs late into the night. These conferences led to yearly Texas Hieroglyphic Workshops from 1978 through 1989, arranged by Nancy Troike and led by Linda Schele. Other workshops on hieroglyphs have taken place across the country, including the University of Pennsylvania Maya Weekend, where "hands-on" computer workshops are carried out, these starting in 1983, arranged by Christopher Jones and Elin Danien.

Work on deciphering Maya hieroglyphs has been underway since the last quarter of the nineteenth century. Today's work builds upon the initial identifications recorded by Diego de Landa in his *Relación de los Cosas de Yucatan* (Tozzer 1941) from information taken down from his Yucatecan informant. Other key early hieroglyphic researchers and their accomplishments include Heinrich Berlin (1950–1958), who first identified the personal name glyphs and Emblem Glyphs and noted that principal cities each had their own identifying glyph. Berlin also presented the hypothesis that the Temple of the Cross, the Temple of the Foliated Cross, and the Temple of the Sun at Palenque were each associated with a particular deity and specific glyphs. David Kelly (1965) found that the inscriptions on the Cross Group tablets at Palenque refer to the birth of the gods, GI, GII, and GIII. The Russian Yuri Knorozov (1952) proposed that the approach to decipherment of the hieroglyphs was through the assignment of morphemic and phonetic values to its various signs. Günter Zimmerman,

from Germany, published a catalog in 1956 of Maya hieroglyphs confined to the three Maya codices, and in 1962, J. Eric S. Thompson published his *Catalogue of Maya Hieroglyphs*, which added to the known signs, those on stelae, altars, lintels, etc., an efficient system of recording main signs and affixes. Thompson's exhaustive study, *Maya Hieroglyphic Writing: An Introduction* (1950), is still used as a source book by everyone studying the Maya, as is his *Catalogue of Maya Hieroglyphs*. Tatiana Proskouriakoff (1960, 1963, 1964) opened a whole new vista of meanings and understandings when she made the notable discovery that texts on stone monuments named individual rulers, with dates indicating birth, accession, death, warfare, and events in the lives of these people. She identified glyphs referring to birth, inauguration, death, bloodletting, and capture, and showed where women played a role in the Maya hierarchy.

Then for some time there was no real advancement in the decipherment of hieroglyphs, but in the last fifteen years phenomenal progress has been made, with the leaders in the field being Floyd Lounsbury, Linda Schele, Peter Mathews, Victoria Bricker, David Stuart, and Nikolai Grube.

Three papers in this volume—those of Nikolai Grube, Diane Winters, and Tom Jones—deal with hieroglyphic interpretation. Grube's investigation, based upon the study of the Primary Standard Sequence (PSS), first discovered by Michael Coe (1973), indicates that among the three hundred vessels with the PSS studied, there are various styles memorized by artists of different workshops, and that numerous substitution patterns in PSS have monumental parallels. Winters discusses the fish-in-hand glyph with references to different meanings.

Jones gives an exciting interpretation of the *xoc* glyph, which has been read as "count" and turns up numerous times as a mythological fish in Maya art with features of the "count" glyph and has been labeled the "*xoc* fish." Drawing from ethnohistorical sources and hieroglyphic inscriptions, Jones proposes to link the word "*xoc*" with "shark."

Linguistics have now taken an important and necessary place in understanding the Maya. Nicholas A. Hopkins argues new interpretations for another glyph, the son/daughter glyph, which he proposes should be read as "nephew/niece." Martha J. Macri takes the computer data-base approach and examines the Chol, Chontal, Chorti, and older Acalán and Chol texts as well as modern Yucatecan texts. Dieter Dütting examines yet another glyph, the fire glyph, proposing new readings for graphemes.

Three authors in this volume discuss the Dresden Codex. Victoria R. Bricker discusses faunal offerings in the Dresden as presented in the two ritual almanacs of 260 days, with each clause referring to the motion of the rain god Chac toward the four cardinal directions—east, north, west, and south—and to some faunal offering—turtle, fish, iguana, turkey, or deer. Bruce Love presents an analysis of the texts in the New Year pages of the same codex, while Meredith Paxton proposes that the Dresden was a Late Classic production probably made during the occupation of Mayapán rather than in the vicinity of Chichén Itzá as proposed by Thompson.

The last two papers deal with different subject matter. Anthony Aveni's astronomical paper deals with the planet Venus and with what the Maya could actually have seen in the sky. He finds that Venus did not always disappear for eight days before morning heliacal rise, but could remain invisible for up to twenty days. On the other hand there were instances when Venus did not disappear at all but could remain visible as both morning and evening stars on the same day.

Jorge L. Orejel Opisso applies his research project on artificial intelligence techniques to decipherment of hi-

eroglyphic inscriptions and presents a schema-based interpretive system.

The proceedings of the Sixth Palenque Round Table Conference thus present new material on many facets of the civilization of the Maya and their neighbors. Presenting material previously unavailable has always been the intent of the Palenque Round Table conferences and will continue to be so. So much is being done today in the fields of archaeology, epigraphy, linguistics, dynastic history, and the art and iconography of Mesoamerica that by bringing a group of scholars together from many parts of the world, discussions such as those presented here can be openly aired, discussed, and then published, so that the new information is available to everyone.

Sixth Palenque Round Table, 1986

Historical Notes on the Discovery of the Ruins, The Founding of the Town, and the Origin and Significance of the Name of Palenque

ARNULFO HARDY GONZALEZ, M.D.
(translated by J. Kathryn Josserand)

A consideration of the discovery of Palenque has been an obligatory theme for investigators who have taken on the task of clarifying the historical past of this great cultural legacy of the Maya civilization. One early historian, Manuel Larráinzar, mentions in his "Historia de Chiapa y Guatemala" (a chapter in his five-volume study, 1875–1878) that the ruins of Palenque were discovered in 1740 by the priest of Palenque and Tumbalá, Don Antonio Solís. But the majority of the early sources attributed the discovery of the ruins of Palenque to the canon of Chiapas, Ramón Ordoñez y Aguiar.

In 1773, Ordoñez sent a letter to the president of the Real Audiencia (Royal High Court) of Guatemala, to whose jurisdiction Chiapas belonged, stating that he "had knowledge of a town in ruins"; this constitutes the first official notice we have of Palenque. But the research of Beatriz de la Fuente indicates that "Ordoñez never had the opportunity to know Palenque personally, [and] all his information was given to him by his uncle, Antonio de Solís" (de la Fuente 1968:15).

Furthermore, much earlier than the earliest historical mention of the ruins of Palenque, during the Spanish conquest in the sixteenth century, there was another person whose activities are important to the clarification of this historical overview of Palenque: Fray Pedro Lorenzo de la Nada.

The Founding of Palenque

In the year 1560, at the invitation of Fray Domingo de Azcona, Fray Pedro Lorenzo de la Nada came to the royal capital (today San Cristóbal de las Casas) from San Estéban de Salamanca (Spain), to work in the Indian towns. In 1561, he began his missionary work by learning the Tzotzil and Tzeltal languages. By 1564, he had resettled the Pochutla Indians in the town of Ocosingo and had similarly resettled in Yaxalum (today Yajalón) the Tzeltal Indians who previously lived in Ocot. Those who lived to the north of Ocosingo were resettled in the town of Bachajón. He also collected the dispersed Chol Indians and settled them into the towns of Tumbalá and Tila, and it was in these last towns that he "became enamored of the sonorous sound of the Chol language" (de Vos 1980:24). Fray Pedro Lorenzo de la Nada was probably the first missionary to approach the Chol Indians in their own language, and he also became familiar with their life and culture, as well as their history. It is his commentary on the history of the Chols that states that they themselves "mention some abandoned temples and palaces at the foot of the range of hills which borders the plain of Tabasco, near the River Chacamáx" (de Vos 1980:24–25).

Later on, Fray Pedro Lorenzo learned of the Lacandón Indians and soon made a trip to Lacantún to invite them to join in the peace which had been established with their allies, the Pochutecs, the Tzeltals, and the Chols. But the Lacandóns categorically rejected his offer,

so Fray Pedro walked towards the north of the Lacandón Jungle, where he discovered many Chol families still living in small hamlets according to their ancient customs. These families he gently invited to leave their huts in order to follow him to a new town which he had prepared for them near the River Chacamáx, at the foot of a range of hills where some ruins of singular beauty were situated. With the Indians who accepted his invitation, Fray Pedro founded, by the year 1567, the town of Palenque, giving homage with this name to the ancient "palenque" ["fenced site, fortified place, walled city"] whose vestiges he had encountered at a short distance from the new site. [de Vos 1980:34]

Thus, Fray Pedro not only founded the town of Palenque, but so named the town because of the nearby ruins. That is, he knew of the ruins almost 200 years before the "discovery" of Palenque according to the early historians cited above.

The Bells of Palenque

Between the years of 1567 and 1573, Fray Pedro Lorenzo made two trips to Spain to arrange for the legal foundation of the town of Palenque; almost certainly on his last

Fig. 1   Palenque Bell.

Fig. 2   Palenque Bell.

trip he brought the three bells (large, medium, and small) that he presented to the Palenque Chol community as a symbol of the founding of their town; the three bells carry the date 1573. During the present century, these bells began to appear in important historical documents. In an article by Augusto Molina, entitled "Palenque—The Archaeological City Today," there is a photo of the town church, taken in 1904 by an expedition of the Peabody Museum of Harvard University, in which the bells can be seen, even though the photo was not taken for this purpose (Molina 1978:2).

In 1923, Franz Blom undertook an expedition to Palenque, and in his report on this expedition he also published a photograph of the church bell tower, in which the three bells can again be seen (Blom 1923:15). In 1934, when the National Institute of Anthropology and History took charge of the ruins of Palenque, Miguel Angel Fernández, the archaeologist in charge of the explorations there, made reference in the part of his report touching on the town of Palenque to the fact that one of the bells carries the date of 1573 (García Moll 1985:116). In 1980, Jan de Vos published a photograph of the largest of the bells of Palenque in his book on Fray Pedro (de Vos 1980:89). In 1984, I took a photograph of this same bell, which was published on the cover of my

monograph *Palenque: Pasado y Presente* (Hardy 1985). In 1985, this bell was given to a community within the municipality of Palenque; it was later retrieved (although in two pieces), and today can be found newly sheltered in the town church.

Now, what is the importance of the bells? First, they are objects that require protection because of their historical significance; second, they are intimately related to the discovery of the ruins of Palenque; and third, the one bell remaining serves as indisputable testimony about the founding date of the town of Palenque.

The Origin of the Name "Palenque"

With regard to the origin and significance of the name of Palenque, various investigators have already undertaken to write about this theme. Some assert an Indian origin for the name, but the truth is, the word *palenque* is purely Spanish, and means, according to Spanish language dictionaries, "palisade or stockade of wood."

In the field reports of Miguel Angel Fernández, published by Roberto García Moll in his book *Palenque 1926–1945* (1985), Fernández referred to the word *palenque* as being of Spanish origin and meaning "palisade, that is, an area surrounded by wooden stakes"; he com-

Hardy González

mented that "the natives of the area referred to Palenque by the name of Otolum." Further along he stated that "Waldeck writes it Ototiun, 'house of stone,' derived from the native words *otote* and *tunich*" (García Moll 1985:22).

"Gho Chan" and "Na Chan" are other names for Palenque, invented by the canon Ramón Ordoñez y Aguiar in his report "Historia del Cielo y de la Tierra," as a result of his supposed discovery of the ruins (Becerra 1980:133). Later visitors, like Dupaix in 1807, Stephens in 1840, and Mahler in 1877, agree that the Spanish word *palenque* means "fortified place" (cited in Becerra 1980:243). Jan de Vos brought to light an important document from 1629, in which the word *palenque* is used in the sense of "a fenced site, a fortified place, a walled city" (de Vos 1980:81), referring to a ruin near Ocosingo.

The historian Vicente Piñeda invented a Sendal (Tzeltal) etymology for the word *palenque;* he proposed that the correct word was Japalenque, which he translates as "Is that a priest?" Furthermore, he believed that Otolum is an alteration of Jotulum, which he translates as "excavated land." The Palenque historian Domingo Lacroix interpreted *palenque* as a Chol word with the following composition: *pal,* "son"; *en,* "of" or "where"; and *quej,* "deer"; that is, "the land of the sons of the deer." We insist that the name Palenque has a Spanish origin. Where, then, can these meanings have come from?

Otulum or Otolum is the name of the most important stream that begins in the ruins of Palenque. This name is a word of Chol origin whose parts mean: *otot,* "house"; *tul,* "strong"; *lum,* "land"—that is, "strong house land" or "fortified place" (Becerra 1980:243). Given this explanation, there is clearly a very close relation between the Spanish name "Palenque" and the Chol name "Otolum" or "Otulum," since both words have the same meaning. Becerra remarked that "whoever gave the Spanish name of Palenque [to the town] penetrated the secret of the Chol name [of the ruins], and this could not have been done without the help of those same Indians" (1980:251).

In conclusion, there was only one person in the early history of Palenque who had knowledge, first, of the language of the Indians, and, second, of the ruins (because they are referred to in the name given to the town), and who was a speaker of Spanish (since the word *palenque* is of Spanish origin). The material presented here shows that it was Fray Pedro Lorenzo de la Nada, who, besides having discovered the ruins, knew the "secret" of their Chol name. Looking for a Spanish word that would have a meaning similar to that of the Chol word, he "baptized" the town he founded with the Chol Indians with the name "Palenque." The great Maya city also came to be known by this name, and it was possibly originally called by the Chol equivalent, "Otolum" or "Otulum," a name still used today to refer to the most important stream that rises in the ruins of Palenque.

The Demotion of Chac-Zutz':
Lineage Compounds and Subsidiary Lords at Palenque

LINDA SCHELE
UNIVERSITY OF TEXAS AT AUSTIN

Chac-Zutz' and the history he recorded on the Tablet of the Slaves has been the source of dispute since Peter Mathews and I presented the dynastic history of Palenque at the Primera Mesa Redonda (Mathews and Schele 1974). The initial dispute concerned the identities of Chac-Zutz' and Chaacal as separate individuals or as different names for the same person, a debate that was soon resolved by a more detailed study of the naming patterns at Palenque. However, at the Quinta Mesa Redonda, Peter Mathews (1983b) presented evidence of the capture of Kan-Xul by a king of Toniná, pointing out evidence for a major disruption of descent after this ignominious defeat of the royal lineage. Before this evidence came to light, I had taken the list of kings recorded on the Tablet of the 96 Glyphs as evidence that Chaacal was the son of Kan-Xul, explaining the difference in the name phrase of Kan-Xul and the person listed as father of Chaacal on the Temple 18 jambs as a substitution we did not yet understand. Mathews evaluated the same evidence in a different way, suggesting that Chaacal was in fact not Kan-Xul's son and that his father had not held the throne before him. I now believe that he was right in his interpretation of the evidence—that the accession of Chaacal represents a break in the expected father-son descent pattern at Palenque. This piece of Palenque's history seems to be even stranger because Chac-Zutz' does not appear to have been a high king at all.

The tri-figure composition of the Tablet of the Slaves is exactly like the Palace Tablet in depicting the protagonist seated in the center flanked by his parents. The iconography is indistinguishable from that of the high kings, but the text has several features that signal its unusual nature. The text begins with a standard phrase recording the T700 accession of Pacal on 5 Lamat 1 Mol. This accession is then linked to those of Chan Bahlum and Kan-Xul by unusual Distance Numbers first deciphered by Lounsbury (n.d.b).[1] The birth of Chac-Zutz' follows, linked not to his own accession, but to that of Chaacal. This pattern is unique at Palenque, where the

births are otherwise linked to the accession of this same person. Furthermore, Chaacal's accession is deliberately compared and contrasted to that of Chac-Zutz' in the following pattern:

accession Chaacal date—date accession Chac-Zutz'

Both accession verbs are the T60:713–757 expression (Mathews and Schele 1974), but, in the Chaacal phrase, the knot is infixed with a bright mirror, while the knot in the Chac-Zutz' verb has a smoking mirror. I do not know how to read this contrast, but its use seems deliberate. Mathews and I had also noticed the odd relationship in age between these two protagonists. Chac-Zutz', who was born on 22 January 671,[2] was seven years old when Chaacal was born (13 September 678), yet Chaacal acceded a year and a half before Chac-Zutz'. If they were equally qualified to hold the throne, then the younger brother took the throne first, a circumstance not duplicated at any other time in Palenque's history. In working with the chronology, we assumed that Chaacal had died a little over a year after his accession; however, too many buildings, including Temples 18, 18a, 21, and Temples 2 and 4 of the North Group, were commissioned and built for such a short reign. Chaacal is also responsible for a major remodeling of House E in the Palace during which the history of his accession and its linkage by contrived number (Lounsbury 1976) to the enthronement of the Mother of the Gods was painted on the eave above the Oval Palace Tablet.

Thus, while Mathews and I had identified Chac-Zutz' as a ruler, we had not accounted for much of the contradictory evidence. New information suggests that Chac-Zutz' was an important lineage head who held high office in the government of Palenque, but it now seems clear that Chaacal's reign was much longer than previously suspected and that he was the high king and overlord for whom Chac-Zutz' worked.

Following the dynastic history and accession of Chac-Zutz', the text of the Tablet of the Slaves (fig. 1) records three war events—a capture, presumably by Chac-Zutz', and two axe events of which he was the protagonist.

6

Fig. 1   Tablet of the Slaves (drawing by Linda Schele).

with the two other signs, the reading of the title has been taken to be *cahal*,[4] with a meaning something like "territorial governor." Both the reading and interpretation seem appropriate since *cah* is the term for "pueblo" or "community." Nobles who carried this title ruled subsidiary sites, such as La Pasadita, El Cayo, and Chinikija, under the control of the high kings of larger sites, such as Yaxchilán, Piedras Negras, and Palenque. Battle companions of kings also carry the title and it appears in the names of the wives of important rulers: Lady Zero Skull, the wife of Bird Jaguar, and Lady X-Ahau, the wife of Chaacal. At Lacanja and Naranjo, lords of this rank appear on stones with iconography indistinguishable from that of high kings, but their office was *cah*, rather than *ahau*. And as with the *ahau*, the *cahal* titles seem to have descended from parents to children. Presumably, however, the children of a marriage between a male *ahau* and a female *cahal* were of the rank *ahau*, as was the case with Chaacal's son, Kuk.

The identification of Chac-Zutz' as a *cahal*, rather than a king, yields new understanding of Palenque's dynastic and cultural history and, more importantly, links Group 4 architecturally to the Sepulturas Group at Copán. We may now assume that Chaacal lived until at least 9.15.0.0.0, since his is the last royal accession recorded in the Chac-Zutz' dynastic history. Further details in Chaacal's life must, however, await the discovery of additional inscriptions.

Group IV (fig. 2), where the Tablet of the Slaves was found, is a plaza group well west of the sacred precinct. Discovered by road workers in 1950 and explored by Zavala (n.d.), the group consists of four multigalleried buildings arranged around a large plaza. The tablet was found in a chamber on the second story of Building A, which is oriented slightly off a north–south axis. A fragment of a Gulf Coast–type mirror back was found cached in front of it. The lower story has two parallel galleries subdivided into chambers. The upper story was constructed behind the rear gallery of the lower building over solid fill. This upper gallery was not thoroughly cleared, so access routes to the tablet chamber are not readily readable from the plans; however, it is clear that the tablet was *not* set in a public or semipublic space. It would have been in the dark and only a few people at a time would have been able to view it. Chac-Zutz' was not addressing the public at large, nor was the tablet in a space that would have accommodated lineage rituals requiring large attendance. The final sentences of the text record rituals conducted on 9.15.0.0.0 and mark the completion of the third katun of the life of Chac-Zutz'. Perhaps it was commissioned for the family commemoration of these events.

In 1951, Robert and Barbara Rands were allowed to conduct ceramic excavations in Group IV, and in the process they discovered evidence of social structure that can only now be placed in a comparative framework. In 1951, three burials in the corner of the Group IV plaza

However, the three events violated chronological order, placing the earlier capture between the two axe events in the following pattern:

1.	9.14.13.11.2	7 Ik	5 Tzec	725 May 3	
	axe-war Chac-Zutz'		V near retro		
2.	9.14.11.17.6	9 Cimi	19 Zac	723 Sep 15	
	capture of Ah Manik				
3.	9.14.17.12.19	2 Cauac	2 Xul	729 May 19	
	axe-war Chac-Zutz'		V -6.48 disap		

The same axe-event occurs at Quiriguá and Dos Pilas/ Aguateca to record captures of foreign rulers.[3] The presence of two such events with a capture statement suggests that Chac-Zutz' was a war chief of some accomplishment.

The next sentence contains an unusual verbal phrase we do not yet understand, but Chac-Zutz' is named as the actor and he carries a title that identifies his rank and position at Palenque. In studying the imagery of sites along the Usumacinta, several epigraphers (Stuart 1984c, 1986a; Mathews and Justeson 1984) noticed that a particular title frequently occurred with subsidiary figures. Composed of T246 and its substitute 1004a, T181 *ah*, and an optional T178 *la*, this title was first identified by Proskouriakoff (1963, 1964), who tentatively interpreted it as the "moon family name." Lounsbury (n.d.a) demonstrated the substitution between T246 and its head variant T1104a, showing a second pattern in which T246 replaced T25 *ca* and T205 *ca* in Initial Series Introductory Glyphs at Copán. Combining this reading

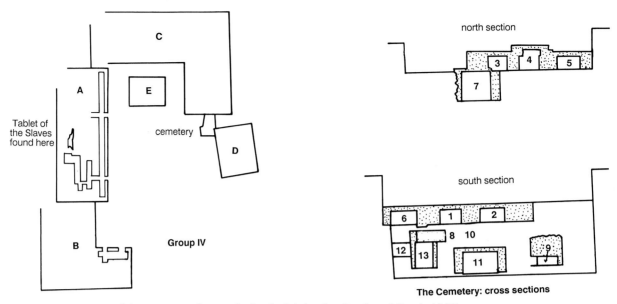

Fig. 2   Group IV and the cemetery (drawing by Linda Schele after Rands and Rands 1961).

were found; in 1959, Barbara Rands excavated ten more. Rands and Rands (1961) reported the cemetery in detail; recent conversations with Robert Rands (personal communication, 1986) confirm that the tombs were superimposed with poor furnishings including ceramics dating from Motiepa and Cascadas,[5] through Murcielagos or A.D. 450–750. The excavated cemetery (fig. 2) lies between Buildings C and D, across the plaza from the Tablet of the Slaves building. The extent of the burial area was not determined; thus, we have information from what may be only a small portion of it. Many burials were in a stone-lined tomb associated with a stucco floor about 50 cm below the plaza floor. One burial cut through the lower floor and intruded on an even earlier architectural feature that was not excavated. In the southern area of the cemetery, the Rands documented at least three levels of superimposition. The skeletal material was badly preserved, but the Rands identified adults and at least two children—one about six years of age. Some crypts contained multiple bodies; interment forms included "simple extended; primary extended in direct association with additional bones and skulls; flexed; decapitated" (Rands and Rands 1961:104).

Although unpublished, Rands (personal communication, 1975) also found a chambered tomb in the lower pyramid at the center of the plaza. The chamber was vaulted and contained only a few sherds, but its form is like dozens of small burial chambers located throughout the archaeological zone, most of them opened by Maudslay (1889–1902), Thompson (1895), Holmes (1895–1897), or Blom (Blom and La Farge 1926). The more elaborate architectural housing of this central tomb suggests its occupant was of a higher rank. The time span and superimposition of these burials identify Group IV as a long-term residential locus with burials in the plaza area spanning a period of at least 350 years.

At Copán, a residential group of remarkable similarity and even longer duration was excavated by the Proyecto Arqueología de Copán (Fash 1982, in press; Webster and Abrams 1983). This compound is one of many, both larger and smaller, that compose the Sepulturas Group to the east of the Main Acropolis at Copán. Multiple buildings are arranged around a central plaza in which Fash found a cemetery characterized by the same kind of superimposed burials spanning a much longer period of time—from 900 B.C. to the end of the Late Classic Period with a lengthy break during the Late Preclassic Period (Fash, this volume). Working with the pattern of excavated material, Fash (Fash and Larios n.d.) was able to reconstruct the iconographic program of the last phrase of construction as dedicating the residential compound to the patron gods of writing, the arts, and crafts. The immediately previous level manifested the same iconography, identifying at least the last two phases of the compound as a residence for a lineage specializing in the scribal arts. Within the main building, N9–82, a magnificent bench recorded the dedication of the final building phase by the lineage head, who boasted of the attendance of the king, Yax-Pac, at the ceremony. Fash believed the central figure in the upper register of the facade to be a portrait of this lineage head.

Group IV is the equivalent kind of compound at Palenque, but the specialization of the lineage that resided there is less evident. Since the group is very near the sacred precinct, I presume that their rank was high, an assumption supported by the use of iconography indistinguishable from that of kings. However, Chac-Zutz' was a *cahal*, not an *ahau*, although he may have been a child of the same mother as Chaacal. The two flanking figures on the Slaves can be identified as the parents of Chac-Zutz' by analogy to the Palace Tablet and the Oval Palace Tablet. The male on the left has a name phrase

| name | *u cahal* | Mah K'ina Ah Naab Pacal | Palenque Ahaual |

Fig. 3 Detail of Temple 18 jambs (drawing by Linda Schele).

distinct from that of Chaacal's father, but the mother is named with a glyph that appears on the jambs and in the stucco inscription of Temple 18. Although explicit parentage statements exist only between Chaacal and his father, I believe that his mother is named following the phrase (fig. 3) that associates by contrived number his accession to that of Lady Beastie, the goddess whose birth and accession are featured on the Tablet of the Cross (Lounsbury 1976, 1980; Schele 1984b).[6] Again based on Mathews's reevaluation of the crisis following Kan-Xul's capture, I have speculated that Chaacal, like Pacal before him, inherited the throne through his mother. If Palenque's kinship system was patrilineal as posited by Hopkins (1982), then both Pacal's and his children's claim to the throne was in question, because they belonged to the lineage of their father, rather than of their mother, from whom they claimed the throne. The rationale for this change of royal lineage advanced by Pacal was that his birth was "like-in-kind" to Lady Beastie's, the mother of the gods. In the Temple of Inscriptions east panel, he named his mother with the name of the goddess, thus equating himself with the sons of the goddess—the Palenque Triad. Chan Bahlum, whose descent problem was even more problematic than his father's, featured this Mother of the Gods in the Tablet of the Cross, proclaiming her not only to be the mother of the Palenque Triad of Gods, but also to have been the first entity to become a king in this creation. The equation is that Pacal and his children were to Pacal's mother as the Triad were to Lady Beastie. Chaacal repeats the strategy by linking his accession by a contrived number to the accession of this goddess and then proclaiming his mother to have been her equivalent in the equation of legitimate descent (Schele 1984d). If this interpretation is correct, I must also assume that Chaacal and Chac-Zutz' were half brothers, because the Temple 18 woman's name also appears next to the woman on the Tablet of the Slaves. In this scenario, the younger offspring of this woman became the king, while the older became head of his father's lineage and a very high official in government—one eligible to use the iconography of kings, albeit in private lineage space.

The prestige of Chac-Zutz' is confirmed by a comparison of the representation of another *cahal* in Palenque's history. Berlin (1955) reported a stone from the nearby site of Miraflores. Using Thompson's gray cards,

David Stuart reconstructed the inscription as naming the protagonist to be a *cahal* of a Mah K'ina of Palenque (fig. 4), although the personal name of the king is missing. This *cahal* kneels wearing a simple loincloth such as those worn in bloodletting rites. Chac-Zutz' appears in the same costume on the Tablet of the Scribe, which was paired with the Orator as stairway *alfardas* on the south side of the Tower (fig. 5). The protagonist of the Orator is named "the *cahal* of Chaacal," but this *cahal* is shown to be speaking by a speech line running to a phrase naming the king Chaacal following a bloodletting verb. The stairs on the south side of the Tower, on which a large stucco scene once rested, was flanked by two *cahals* engaged in bloodletting (or perhaps by two portraits of Chac-Zutz' engaged in this rite).

Chac-Zutz', unlike the Miraflores *cahal*, held office within the metropolitan area of Palenque. In representations intended for private lineage space, he depicted himself in a composition of kings dressed like a king and holding a bag marked with the image of the Pacal bird. We do not know if this privilege of royal iconography was unusual for *cahals* at Palenque, but imagery of this rank at Yaxchilán, Lacanja, El Cayo, and Laxtunich

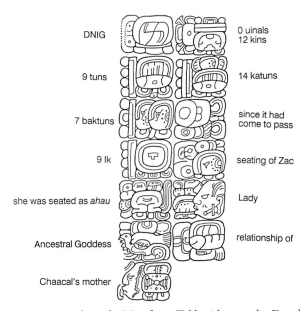

DNIG		0 uinals 12 kins
9 tuns		14 katuns
7 baktuns		since it had come to pass
9 Ik		seating of Zac
she was seated as *ahau*		Lady
Ancestral Goddess		relationship of
Chaacal's mother		

Fig. 4 Text from the Miraflores Tablet (drawing by David Stuart).

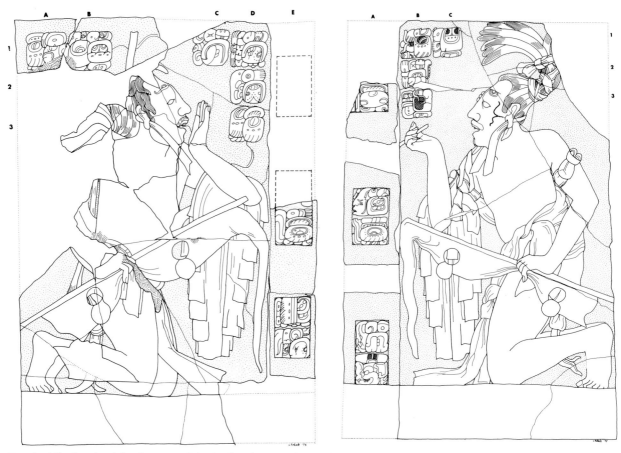

Fig. 5   The Panels of the Orator and the Scribe (drawings by Linda Schele).

(the Lamb site) is indistinguishable from the rank *ahau*, from which kings came. These people were recognized as *cahal* only through the decipherment of the glyphs and recognition of its special distribution.

The Tablet of the Slaves also hints at the special office and responsibility held by Chac-Zutz'; he sits on a pair of bound captives dressed as sacrificial victims. The text holds two references to war events and one to a capture. This association with war is consistent with the representations of Bird Jaguar's Battle Companion on Yaxchilán Lintel 8 and in other scenes; he also is consistently named as a *cahal*. I suspect that Chac-Zutz' served as Palenque's war captain, a post that must have gained importance after the ignominious capture of Kan-Xul.

These speculations as to the rank, function, and history of Chac-Zutz' may change as more is learned; however, Chac-Zutz' clearly was not the high king, but an important lineage head subordinate to the king. Group IV as the location of major records of such a subordinate and in its archaeological features, such as a subplaza cemetery, its long-term use as a residential compound, and its physical layout, is the analog of the Scribe's Compound at Copán. Group IV and the Scribe's Compound at Copán suggest that the same kind of sociopolitical organization was standard at Copán on the east-

ern frontier and Palenque on the western. In both instances, the lineages during the seventh century erected monuments using royal iconography and rivaling royal art in size and excellence. However, in both instances, the messages transferred through the art were addressed to a much smaller audience of the lineage. The larger public probably never saw them. At both sites, archaeological, epigraphic, and ethnohistorical evidence points toward a patrilineal, patrilocal pattern of social organization, with these very high lineages participating in government and holding high rank. I suspect that the close resemblance of these compounds at Palenque and Copán is not coincidental; at neither site are they unique or rare. I believe they also will be found at other sites; as more are excavated to find additional tablets, patterns of residential usage, and, most importantly, burial patterns, we will learn many more details about the responsibilities, lives, and complexities of the people who were lower than kings and higher than the campesinos.

Notes

1. Lounsbury interpreted the two notations *ox te k'al u chum tun* and *hun te k'al u chum tun* to be references to the three katun endings

between Pacal's accession and Chan-Bahlum's (9.10, 9.11, and 9.12) and the one between Chan-Bahlum's and Kan-Xul's (9.14).

2. All dates are given in the Julian calendar.

3. At Quiriguá, the event records the capture of 18 Rabbit by Cauac Sky; at Dos Pilas, the capture of Jaguar Paw of Seibal by Ruler 5. On pottery, the same event is frequently associated with decapitation scenes, suggesting both sacrifice by beheading and the use of the battle axe in battle.

4. David Stuart recently expressed doubt over the *ca* value for T246, since it also occurs in a sign he read as *tzib*, "to write." Stuart's arguments for the "scribe" glyph seem very strong, requiring either that the sign be polyvalent *tzi/ca* or that the *cahal* reading is not the correct one.

5. Rands informed me that he has subdivided Motiepa into two phases: Motiepa 400–500 and Cascadas 500–600.

6. Peter Mathews and I have long debated with Floyd Lounsbury over the meaning of this glyph on the Temple 18 jambs. Mathews and I have favored reading it as a name because of its recurrence on the Tablet of the Slaves; Lounsbury has suggested it represents the solstice points and thus a tropical year—approximately the length of Chaacal's reign in our earlier interpretation of Palenque's history. Mathews and I have never been comfortable with this interpretation, although we have never been able to muster a convincing disproof of it. The re-evaluation of the Chaacal/Chac-Zutz' relationship, however, removes the year-long reign as evidence. Time and debate will eventually decide between the interpretations or generate a new, more satisfactory one none of us has yet conceived.

The Narrative Structure of Hieroglyphic Texts at Palenque

J. KATHRYN JOSSERAND
INSTITUTE FOR CULTURAL ECOLOGY OF THE TROPICS

Each hieroglyphic inscription (or group of inscriptions) has a story to tell, and the texts of the inscriptions can be understood better if we look at them in terms of their structure as stories or narrative texts. Sometimes these stories are short and sweet and limited to a few basic facts—a pithy statement of an important event on a particular date by a titled lord or lady. Few texts at Palenque are so simple, though they are common elsewhere. An early example is found on the Leiden Plate, whose text gives an "unadorned" accession statement for an Early Classic ruler of Tikal (fig. 1). The order of elements is Date-Event-Actor, or, restated in linguistic analysis, Temporal + Verb + Subject.[1]

At other times, and particularly at Palenque, the hieroglyphic texts are quite long; besides the main event, they contain many background details and references to happenings that are outside the main storyline, but are related in specific ways to the main event. These may include the actor's parentage, even though his parents are not otherwise mentioned in the text. Very often the monuments at Palenque and elsewhere commemorate katun endings and associate the Period-Ending event with a "scattering" or bloodletting event carried out by the protagonist of the text (usually the ruler). Really long texts can give practically a full life-history of an important ruler, relating his birth or other events in his life to his accession or to some other important event (Period-Ending ceremonies, dedicatory events for monuments or buildings; ball-game and sacrificial events; war events and capture of prisoners), or connecting some of his dates to numerological and/or astronomical cycles or to anniversaries of events in the lives of important ancestors or even gods. Examples of most of these can be found in the discussion of the figures presented below.

Sometimes long hieroglyphic texts are found spread across several monuments, in a single iconographic program (for example, the Group of the Cross at Palenque), where the different sections of text might be thought of as "acts" in a play or drama, or chapters in a book. Just as in a play or book, there is a plot, sometimes even subplots, and there is some central event, or climax, which is what the play or book is about. The principal characters or actors are introduced, usually at the beginning of the story, and a time frame and setting are established. As the scene changes, to another time frame, the different episodes begin, develop, and close with an important event, then they pass away, to be replaced by the next scene. Some episodes contain flashbacks to earlier scenes and time frames, but on the whole the story progresses sequentially. Most long hieroglyphic texts relate to the legitimization of political succession by the Maya kings, and many of them are expressly dynastic in nature, emphasizing the current ruler's descent from previous rulers and the illustriousness of his parents, and sometimes even connecting the dynasty to specific deities. Again, the texts from the Group of the Cross at Palenque display this relation of mythological actors and events, and ancestral histories, to the life of the ruler, Chan Bahlum II.

In this paper, Classic Mayan hieroglyphic inscriptions are examined for their structure as literary narratives. Palenque's long texts have a discourse structure that is amazingly similar to that of modern Mayan and Mesoamerican narrative texts in general, and to Chol Mayan texts in particular (Hopkins and Josserand 1986; Cruz, Josserand, and Hopkins 1986; see also Fought 1976 and 1985 on Chortí). An ancestral form of Chol was one of the two principal languages of the Classic Maya, the other being an ancestor of Yucatec, which was spoken in the northern part of the Maya realm, while Chol once was spoken across the base of the Petén. Almost certainly the Maya who inhabited Palenque spoke an earlier form of Chol, for we have been able to identify unique features in the spoken language that match unusual features in the hieroglyphic texts of this region (Josserand, Schele, and Hopkins 1985). In both ethnohistoric and modern times, Chol has been spoken in the Indian communities surrounding Palenque.

The Structure of Narrative Texts

In order to consider Palenque's hieroglyphic texts as narrative stories not unlike modern Chol oral narrative texts, I would like to describe briefly some of the characteristics of both of these kinds of texts. A modern text and, I believe, a hieroglyphic text can be discussed in terms of three major elements: time frame, actors, and plot.

Setting the Scene

Chol narrative texts begin by setting a time frame and introducing the main actor(s). This introductory material may also include more description of the physical setting, or introduce other actors, and it often includes a little preview of what the story is about. This preview is sometimes called a *capsule* statement (Attinasi 1979:3).

In hieroglyphic texts, the first date, whether Initial Series with a Long Count or just Calendar Round (or even a Distance Number from a Period Ending or katun seating), sets the time frame and begins the time-line of the story. The equivalent of a capsule statement can often be found in the short texts that accompany the figure(s) in the principal iconographic display, or image.

Most carved stone monuments have two basic parts: an *image*, portraying a ruler or other notable, and the principal *text*, which accompanies and often surrounds the image. The space mainly occupied by the image itself may contain short stretches of hieroglyphic text; these have been called the *secondary texts*, but I prefer *caption texts* (Kubler 1973:146). These caption texts usually relate directly to the actions and/or name the actors portrayed in the image (this relation is discussed at length below, in the discussion of the caption texts from the Temple of the Cross, fig. 8). The relation of the image to the principal text is a topic for discussion in itself (see Bassie 1986), but it seems clear that in most cases the image is portraying one of the main events of the long text associated with it, that is, the iconography itself illustrates the principal actor and the central event of the entire text.

Events and the Event-line

In Mayan and Mesoamerican narrative texts in general, a plot can be considered to be composed of a series of *events* that are related to each other temporally even though they may not be presented in sequential order. These events are said to be *on the event-line;* they are crucial to the development of the story, and all lead up to the central event of the text, which is referred to as the *peak* of the entire text. This is the bare-bones structure of the simplest texts, the plot and its climax.[2]

An event, very simply, is an incident in the story: an action, a situation, the presentation and description of a character. Usually these are expressed grammatically by verbs or other predicated expressions. In the hieroglyphs these verbs include glyphic expressions for birth, capture, accession to power, acts of holding various objects (such as god manikins, staffs, bundles, and bloodletters), and the dedication of monuments and buildings. Even a date can be an event, especially if the date represented the completion of a major time cycle. A Calendar Round (CR) can function as the subject of a certain verbs, like

uht, "come to pass" (*uht* is the main sign of the Anterior and Posterior Date Indicator compounds; see Stuart 1984b). The combination of a numbered (ordinal) Period Ending and a Calendar Round also forms a predicated expression; for example, the text on Tikal Stela 22 begins with the verbal expression of a date: "The 17th katun was 13 Ahau 18 Cumku" (table 3). It is likely that the Initial Series is itself an event, separate from the actions of the ruler on that date.

Episodes and Peak Events

Usually at least some of the events in a story are elaborated into larger (i.e., longer) structures, called *episodes.* An episode is composed of more than one event, and the constituent events are tied together by a common time frame within which all the events develop sequentially. The central event of the episode, also called the *peak event* of the episode, is part of the backbone of the overall story; that is, it is *on the event-line,* and is prominently connected to the peak event of the entire text sooner or later. The subsidiary events serve as *background* to the peak event of the episode, which is stressed, or *foregrounded* in some clear way. The clear analogy here is to the use of these terms in art and theater; elements in the foreground are visually more prominent, and are set against a background, which is visually more distant. The particular techniques used in Mayan languages for emphasis or highlighting (that is, foregrounding) are discussed in more detail below; basically, they involve emphasizing the action of the event itself by placing it in a prominent position in the sentence or by repetition of the event in a second or third restatement.

It is not difficult to identify the foregrounded elements in a text, because these parts were intended by the storyteller to be more prominent, and they are very likely repeated more than once. If the same event appears in more than one episode, it can usually be shown to be important to the dramatic development of the text and to be the peak of one of the episodes, usually the first in which it appears. But when it appears in a subsequent episode, it serves as background to the peak event of that particular episode, clearly connecting the first event with the subsequent one, and tying both of them to the main event-line of the story. In glyphic texts, the ties may be between the king and his predecessors, all of whom perform the same rites, or to the gods on special anniversaries celebrated by the king during his lifetime. The exploits of the king recounted in one event may be recalled in another event by their incorporation into his prestigious titles, as in the Yaxchilán lintels of capture, and the subsequent "captor" titles carried by the ruler (Stuart 1985).

In a sense, all the nonpeak events are background to the main event, and they are directly related to that main event through a variety of techniques. In hieroglyphic texts, these techniques include temporal connections using Distance Numbers, Calendar Rounds, and anniversary expressions and personal connections via expressions of parentage and ancestry, or succession in political rule, as well as other devices.

In Chol texts, each episode is introduced by a special phrase, which indicates whether the change is temporal ("and then," "three days later," etc.) or circumstantial ("meanwhile," and other scene changers). In hieroglyphic texts the episodes are best defined as separate time frames, and temporal introducers are the most common transition markers between episodes. But it is important to distinguish between at least three or four kinds of temporal phrases: Long Counts (LC), Calendar Rounds (CR), and Distance Numbers (DN), and perhaps also phrases involving the *hel* glyph (Thompson's Glyph T573), which have been interpreted and glossed as special Distance Numbers. A Calendar Round date, stated or implied, naturally accompanies every action or event; in normal grammatical order, the CR is the first element in a hieroglyphic sentence. Distance Numbers connect one event to another event, usually within the same episode. Even though they "change the date," they normally proceed along a continuous, sequentially ordered time-line. But when the time-line itself is interrupted, by backing up in time and starting over from an earlier date, or by going forward in time with no stated connection to the last events, we can consider that the time frame has been changed, and a new episode begun. Besides the DN technique, this is often accomplished by the insertion of a new Long Count (a "backward" DN) or even a complete new Initial Series in the middle of the text.

In a multiepisode narrative, the temporal sequence of the peak events in each episode should normally proceed forward chronologically—that is, they are sequentially ordered with respect to time. The individual episodes may be quite different from each other, both in content and in structure, but there is usually considerable unity within an episode, in terms of both the events included and the grammar with which they are presented. There are also usually ties between episodes, especially adjacent ones; often this is achieved by casting back to earlier events from previous episodes (via Distance Numbers, or merely repetition of earlier events). The overall grammatical structure of the episodes can be compared to poetic stanzas, each composed of parallel sentence formations, and usually including one or more couplets. The frequent use of couplets is especially characteristic of ritual speech in Mayan languages.

In a very long story, some of the episodes are more important, and thus more emphasized, than others. The most prominent episode very likely contains the most important event of the entire story, and its grammatical markings attest to its special status. The peak episode of a long text is very often the final episode of the narrative.

Foregrounding and Focus

Peak events are usually very prominently marked, although a variety of techniques may be used to give a peak event prominence. In general, these techniques are referred to as *foregrounding;* they include repetition, elaboration, couplets and other parallel structures, and special grammatical constructions, particularly when the emphasized element is placed at the beginning of the phrase (*fronting*). Any change in the normal, or expected, word order is an indication of focus, or increased importance of the information being transmitted. Joining two sentences, especially when they are partially similar, is very common. Parts of one of the constituent sentences may then be omitted (deleted), and one or both of the parts may be further marked with a special word or affix. These techniques are discussed in some detail below (see also Lounsbury 1980; Schele 1982, 1986a:7–14, 39–41, 52–56).

In modern Chol narrative texts, the chronological sequence of events that are on the event-line is signaled by the use of the "completed action" modal, *tza'*, before the main verb. This word is the marker for preterit or, less technically, past tense, and its presence indicates that the event of the main verb is "on the event-line." The peak event of an episode is further emphasized by a variety of linguistic strategies. When it occurs within an episode, preceded by other, background events, a peak event may be marked as the featured event by a special introducing word, whose sense is not unlike a very dramatic "and then . . ." This word both marks the punctuality of the event (making it a specific point on the event-line, whether a specific date is given or not) and emphasizes its chronological position with respect to the backgrounded events. It is a focus marker for the verbal action, the event itself (as opposed to the actor/subject or any other noun phrase).

In hieroglyphic texts, the Posterior Event Indicator (PEI; Thompson's Glyph T679) often marks the peak event of an episode, or sometimes only the peak of the entire text. It immediately precedes the main verb of the peak event, thus fulfilling the role of verbal focus marker. Of the various readings that have been suggested for the PEI, I favor its interpretation as a conjunction with the value *i* (see Thompson 1962:281) for two reasons. First, it resembles the sign recorded in Landa's alphabet with that value, and, second, there is a conjunction in modern Chol (and in other Maya languages) with a similar function and the same form. Modern texts have *i* as a conjunction that sometimes precedes episode introducers and sometimes precedes the peak event verb phrase, but it has always been assumed to be from Spanish *y*. However, in contrast to Spanish *y*, Chol *i* is never used for concatenation of noun phrases, where only Chol *yik'ot* appears. Given both the function of the PEI and its suggested reading as *i*, perhaps we should reconsider the supposedly Spanish origin of the Chol focus marker *i*.

Whatever its reading,[3] when the PEI occurs as part of a posterior date indicator, it precedes the verb *uht*, which is then followed by a Calendar Round. This converts the temporal phrase into a separate sentence and has the effect of "fronting" the main verb of the peak event to initial position in the next sentence, which is the most prominent position in a sentence. This is exemplified in figure 6 (see the discussion of fronting and promotion, below).

Background

Just as each episode has a key or peak event, which is on the event-line, the episode may also include references to other events, either as a back-reference to an earlier event that was also on the event-line, to emphasize its importance and to relate it more directly to the peak event of the current episode, or as a reference to an event completely outside the storyline, but somehow related to the main actor. These events may not ever appear as peak events of individual episodes, and may not even be on the event-line of the main story, but they are tied to the main story, through some concrete temporal link to the event-line, and usually to some action of the main actor, the protagonist of the text.

An example of the first kind of back-reference can be seen in a section of text from the Cross Tablet (the main panel from the Temple of the Cross), where the accession of Lady Beastie is given as the peak of the episode (fig. 4), but it is set against the background of her birth, an event that was itself the peak of the episode associated with the Initial Series date of the Cross Tablet. The 819 day count is a good example of the second kind of background information; it is almost always earlier than the Initial Series and is always linked to the IS (and seldom linked to anything else); it is not a peak event itself, and often "interrupts" the first sentence of the text, separating the Initial Series and Calendar Round date from the event that takes place on that date.

Both of the above cases are examples of backgrounded or "old" information, and they should be clearly (and usually repeatedly) marked as such in the text. In modern Chol narrative texts, the characteristic "background" marker is the syllable -ix, which is attached at the ends of verbs and temporal adverbs or longer temporal phrases. This corresponds structurally to the Anterior Event Indicator (AEI; Thompson's Glyph T126) in the hieroglyphs, and I have previously suggested (Josserand 1984; Josserand and Schele 1984) that the -ix value is, in fact, appropriate for the AEI reading as well.[4]

When an episode has several events, those that are subsidiary to the peak event of the episode are likely to be marked with the backgrounding particle -ix (both in modern Chol texts and in hieroglyphic texts). The subsidiary events are also likely to *precede* the main event of the episode in two ways: they are temporally earlier, and they occur first in the phrase. That is, the last thing in the episode is usually the peak event, just as the last episode in a text usually contains the peak of the entire text.

Discourse Features of Hieroglyphic Inscriptions

The application of discourse analysis models to the Mayan hieroglyphic inscriptions contributes both to the overall understanding of the content of particular inscriptions and to the decipherment of specific elements and constructions in the inscriptions. It also supports the assertions that these inscriptions are written in real language, not simple schematic representations of important dates and events.[5] The discourse model gives us greater insight into the strategies behind the selection and presentation of information in a hieroglyphic text. The order of elements in a hieroglyphic text is directly comparable to the order of words in a sentence, and changes in word order are among the most common indicators of informational importance. Normal, expected word order (*unmarked* order) does not stress any part of the sentence over any other. Unexpected, or *marked* word order focuses attention on a particular element within the sentence and thus indicates its increased importance in the development of the narrative. New information is often presented in marked constructions; old information is downplayed and may even be omitted from a sentence in order to highlight what remains. Important new information may be repeated several times, or elaborated by adding extra bits of new information in each restatement.

Hieroglyphic texts are very poetic in their structure, as are traditional Mayan texts, whether they be prayers and rituals or tales of gods and heroes. The grammatical structures that characterize these language styles are formal and constrained. Where our poetry is governed by patterns of meter and rhyme, theirs is revealed in patterns of repetition and coupleting (Bricker 1974; Lounsbury 1980:107–108; Norman 1980; Townsend 1980); in stanza structures and parallel constructions (Townsend, Cham, and Ich' 1980; Cruz, Josserand, and Hopkins 1986; Hopkins and Josserand 1986); and in word plays of many kinds. The rules of poetic structure are revealed in the discourse strategies used in the texts. The particular grammatical elements or processes used to signal discourse functions (such as highlighting or backgrounding) may vary regionally and through time, but the basic strategies are always there and can be seen to persist in traditional narrative genres throughout the modern Mayan languages.

It is difficult to illustrate a single discourse feature, because the whole point of discourse analysis is to see things in context; to do that, the reader/hearer must keep in mind what has already been said or understood (the "old" information) when each new phrase begins. But as soon as more text is included in an example, to show the context, the presence of other discourse features invariably makes the picture more complex. In the following examples, individual discourse strategies are discussed, and references are made to pieces of hieroglyphic text that illustrate each point. But the glyphic text segments cannot be adequately described in terms of single discourse features; so, after the brief overview of glyphic discourse features, each hieroglyphic text is separately discussed, to show all the different discourse strategies it employs, and to place it in the context of the larger text in which it occurs. The last three figures and accompanying tables treat discourse features that relate to overall text structure, so they are illustrated by complete hieroglyphic texts.

In the hieroglyphic inscriptions, normal (expected, unmarked) word order is the same as in modern Chol (and most other Mayan languages); this is usually stated as being "verb initial," meaning that in a simple sentence with only three elements—actor (= Subject), action (= Verb), and recipient of the action (= Object)—the order of these elements is Verb followed by Object followed by Subject, or VOS. Any other order is nonnormal, or marked. Sometimes the Subject is repeated as a pronoun preceding the verb; this is not a change in order, but a special situation governed by Maya grammar. The third-person pronoun *u*, "he/she" (T1) was one of the earliest grammatical elements to be deciphered in Mayan hieroglyphs. Sentences with intransitive verbs have only two elements, the Verb and its Subject. Other kinds of sentences can be formed with two elements, neither of which is a Verb, properly speaking, but in these cases one of them acts as a Predicate, an equivalent to a Verb, and the other as its Subject. All of these sentence types are Verb-initial in Chol and most other Mayan languages, and normal order in the hieroglyphic inscriptions seems to be Verb-initial as well.

If another element is added to the basic three (Verb, Object, and Subject), it very likely contains special information; because of that, the element may well occur at the beginning of the sentence. Thus, when a sentence contains a specific time reference, the temporal word or phrase generally *precedes* even the verb. So "normal" word order for temporally marked phrases becomes Temporal + Verb + Object + Subject. If other elements are added, the order is likely to change (the new element occurs first), or some of the previous elements are dropped; this seems to be related to a restriction on the number and length of noun phrases following the verb. Thus, if both Object and Indirect Object (the recipient of an action) are specified (or Object and Instrument, or Object and Location), the Subject may be omitted (presumably the Subject is already known, that is, it is "old information"). So any change in word order can be taken as an indication of special importance, or foregrounding. In hieroglyphic texts, the grammatical techniques for foregrounding can be grouped under three broad headings: elaboration; fronting or promotion; and "marked" syntax or unusual grammar.

Elaboration and Coupleting

Elaboration is an especially common technique for highlighting the Subject/actor. It usually involves long name or title phrases (figs. 1, 2), and often includes parentage clauses (figs. 3, 6, 9). Special poetic or metaphoric phrasing may be employed (the parentage statement for GI in fig. 5; the special Distance Number introductory verbs in the Tablet of the 96 Glyphs, figs. 6 and 9; or Chaacal's accession restatement in the 96 Glyphs text, fig. 9). Elaborated verbs and verb phrases are also found; these

may include complex expressions for the verb itself (the verb at F5 in the Tablet of the Slaves, fig. 10), or lengthy complements to the verbal action (the accession phrases found in figs. 4, 6, 7, 8, and 10).

Another form of elaboration is repetition or restatement, usually by means of the ubiquitous couplet. Coupleted expressions occur at all levels of linguistic structure, from paired words to paired sentences. A very subtle couplet can be seen on the Leiden Plate (fig. 1, table 1) in the use of parallel "seating" expressions for both the date (the seating of Yaxkin) and the event (the seating of the Tikal ruler).

Given that an event consists of a statement about an action (Verb) done by a specific actor (Subject) on a specific date (Temporal), a couplet to that statement can consist of a simple restatement of the same event (by the same actor, on the same date, just said differently), or one or more of the three basic elements can be changed, while holding the rest the same. Thus, the same event can be done on the same day by another actor, as on Lintel 2 from La Pasadita (fig. 2, table 2), or the actor and date can be unchanged, but another event is performed, as a couplet to the first event, as on Stela 22 from Tikal (fig. 3, table 3), or the date can stay constant but both event and actor change, and so forth.

If the intent is to emphasize the equivalence of two events, rather than focus on one and background the other, the events can be given the same prominence in the discourse structure. La Pasadita Lintel 2 illustrates this kind of text (fig. 2, table 2). On the same date (and portrayed together in the central image), Bird Jaguar of Yaxchilán and a subordinate perform equivalent acts. BJ is shown "scattering" (part of the bloodletting rite; see Stuart 1984a), while his *cahal* holds an object that is probably a bloodletter. This is a "single episode" text with two "events," supposedly the same or equivalent, though performed by two different actors. This pairing of dominant and subordinate actors in a single image raises interesting questions about who erected the monument. The subordinate is given somewhat less prominence on the La Pasadita lintel: there is no Calendar Round asso-

Table 1. Text Structure from the Leiden Plate: Accession of an Early Classic Ruler of Tikal

Location	Structure		Content
A1–A9	Temporal Introducer	=	ISIG + LC + 1 Eb + G5 (Lord of Night), + seating of Yaxkin
B9–A10	Verb + Complement	=	seating verb + office ("seated as *ahau*")
B10–B11	Subject Phrase	=	personal name of Early Classic Ruler, + Early Classic Tikal Emblem Glyph (EG)

"On 1 Eb . . . Balam Ahau Chan of Tikal was enthroned as lord."

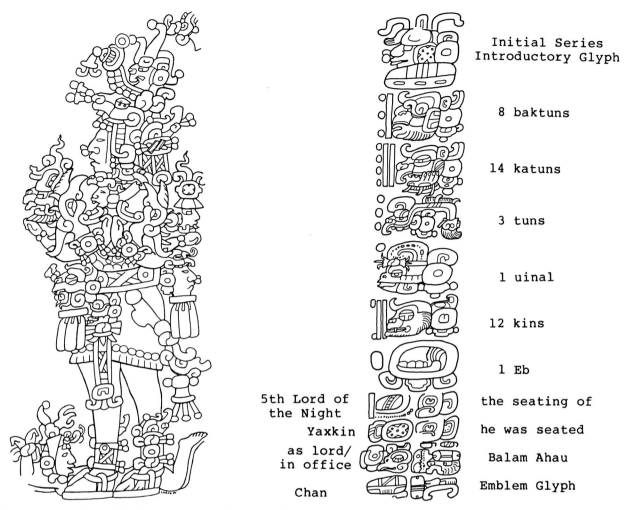

Initial Series
Introductory Glyph

8 baktuns

14 katuns

3 tuns

1 uinal

12 kins

1 Eb

5th Lord of
the Night   the seating of

Yaxkin   he was seated

as lord/
in office   Balam Ahau

Chan   Emblem Glyph

Fig. 1   Leiden Plate (Tikal). Accession to office or to rule (drawing by Linda Schele).

ciated with his text, and his name-and-title phrase is quite short, compared to Bird Jaguar's Subject phrase. Costume and ritual dominance are also given to Bird Jaguar. But visual backgrounding is minimal; in fact, the subordinate's right thumb very subtly overlaps Bird Jaguar's name phrase. This problem is addressed again in the discussion of the Tablet of the Slaves (fig. 10).

Focus, Foregrounding, and Backgrounding

Even simple hieroglyphic texts can have peak event, focus, and background. The text on Tikal Stela 22 (fig. 3, table 3) commemorates a katun ending and focuses on the bloodletting rite performed by the ruler on that occasion. The associated image is the scattering event, which is emphasized in the text by its text-final position, and by its coupleting with the main verb of the first sentence, which was the erection of the tun monument. This is a three-sentence monument:

1. The Temporal clause is an independent sentence.
2. The main clause is Verb-initial and has a very elaborated Subject phrase (perhaps involving subordinated clauses).

3. The third sentence recapitulates the event through conjoined clauses, with the event-line focus marker (PEI) on the final clause.

Note that there is a focus marker on the last Verb (at B12), which is a temporal "couplet" of the first Verb (at B2), that is, it is another action of Ruler C on the Period-Ending date. The Subject is deleted from this final sentence as well as from the background clause, but it is readily identified as the only actor in the text. The background event is the ruler's seating in an office that has been read as Batab (chief, from Yucatec Maya *baat*, "axe").

The text fragment from the main tablet of the Temple of the Cross at Palenque (fig. 4) also illustrates simple backgrounding and focus. The backgrounded event, marked by the *-ix* (T126) suffixes on both the distance numbers and on the birth verb (table 4), is Lady Beastie's birth, the event of the Initial Series date on the Cross Tablet. The Distance Number restarts us in time, in a new episode, which sets the pattern for all the remaining episodes in the text. These episodes give (or imply via Distance Numbers) the birthdates and accession dates of

Narrative Structure of Hieroglypyhic Texts at Palenque

Table 2. La Pasadita, Lintel 2: Scattering Rite by Bird Jaguar of Yaxchilán, and Paired (Coupleted) Event by His Subordinate

Location	Structure	Content
B1–9, A1–6	Temp + Pron-Vb-Obj + S	"On 7 Ahau 18 Pop BJ let blood."
C1–5	Pron-Vb Prep-Comp + S	"X, *cahal*, follows in the rite."

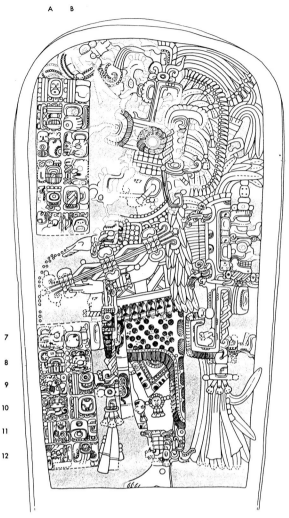

Fig. 3   Tikal, Stela 22. Period Ending and scattering rite (drawing by William R. Coe, courtesy of The University Museum, University of Pennsylvania).

Fig. 2   La Pasadita, Lintel 2. Coupleted event by two actors (drawing by Linda Schele).

Table 3. Tikal, Stela 22: Period Ending (17 katuns) and Scattering Rite

Location	Structure	Content
A1–2	Predicate + Subject (= V + S)	CR = 17th katun (equative sentence) "The 17th katun was 13 Ahau 18 Cumku." (9.17.0.0.0)
B2–A9	V-O S	V-O = "he ended the tun"/ "placed the stone" S = Ruler C + Tikal EG + Title + 28th successor + title + Child of Father, Ruler B-long title "Ruler C . . . , child of Ruler B . . . , placed the katun monument."
B9–A12	DN-*ix* Temp V-*ix* Comp	"16 kins, 1 uinal, 2 tuns ago, on 11 Kan 12 Kayab," "he was seated as *batab le,*"
B12	PEI + V-O	"and so he scattered blood." (on the Calendar Round of the Period Ending)

Table 4. Palenque, Cross Tablet, Left Side Text, E5–F9:
Simple Focus and Background, from Birth to Seating of Lady Beastie, on Calendar Round

Location	Structure	Content
E5–7	DN-*ix* V-*ix*	"It was 2 days, 11 uinals, 7 tuns, 1 katun, and 2 baktuns since (her) birth,"
F7–9	PEI-Vb-Obj Prep-Comp S Temp	"until Lady Beastie held the white bundle (became *zac uinic*) of the succession on 9 Ik seating of Zac."

the earliest recorded rulers of Palenque. The foregrounded or focused event in all cases is the "holding of the white bundle in the succession." This event has been glossed as "to become *zac uinic* ('great man') of the succession" (Schele 1983:29) and is understood as accession to rule.[6]

Tripleting

Another piece of text from the main tablet of the Temple of the Cross, Palenque, shows the use of repetition for highlighting important new information (fig. 5). The birth of GI' (or GI the son, the firstborn of the Palenque Triad) is given great emphasis by its triple presentation, in a three-sentence episode (table 5). The birth is first shown against a background of sky acts performed by the first GI (his father?), then it is restated in a short, verb-initial sentence of Verb + Object + Subject, giving no new information. (To "touch the earth" is similar to other Chol metaphors for birth: *k'el panumil*, "to see or experience the earth/world," and dialect variant *il panumil*, "to see the world.") The last sentence relates his birth to his supposed mother, Lady Beastie. Note that the subject of the last sentence is deleted; it is not Lady Beastie but GI' who is the subject, but he is related to Lady Beastie through this "parentage" phrase, as well as being related to GI the father through the backgrounded clause at the beginning of this episode.

The importance of the birth of GI the son is emphasized by the combination of several different focus techniques: (1) the use of the PEI (T679) before the birth verb (the first time it occurs); (2) the "initial" position of that verb in its clause, with the CR demoted to clause-final position, as is the pattern with such conjoined clauses, and (3) the triple expression of the event, where the first restatement again names the actor, GI, and the couplet to that restatement gives his parentage, in an elaborate and somewhat unusual phrasing. This episode is, however, the only time that GI the son is mentioned in this entire text (Tablet of the Cross), even though the Temple of the Cross has been considered to be "dedicated" to GI the son, in a manner analogous to the association of the Temple of the Sun with GIII, the second-born of the Triad, and of the Temple of the Foliated Cross with GII, the last-born of the Triad.[7] Here GI the son has been displaced from the IS date of the Cross panel by his even more important mother, Lady Beastie. Still, his birth is the first event *by an actor* given syntactic prominence (via the PEI focus marker) in the entire

Cross Group text. The only earlier PEI precedes the completion of the *mai* event on 4 Ahau 8 Cumku, when the cycle of time began anew. The events of GI the father following that date were given prominence through multiple restatements, but even though they were introduced via a Distance Number, they were not preceded by a PEI focus marker.

Fronting and Promotion

Fronting and promotion are linguistic terms for changes in word order that move an element to the beginning of the sentence (fronting), or change it to a "higher" syn-

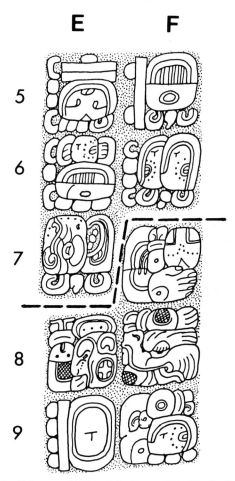

Fig. 4 *Palenque, Tablet of the Cross, E5–F9. Background and focus (drawing by Linda Schele).*

tactic category (from Temporal phrase in one sentence to Subject phrase of an independent sentence is the most common promotion in the hieroglyphs). The use of the Posterior Event Indicator results in the *fronting* of the verb, because it requires that the verb immediately follow it, and the Calendar Round date (the Temporal phrase) is displaced, and either occurs at the end of the sentence or is removed completely from the sentence. In the first case, the order of elements is PEI + Verb + Object + Subject + Temporal (see fig. 4 and table 4). In the second case, the Calendar Round can either be omitted from the text (especially if it is old information, as in fig. 3 and table 3) or be *promoted* to an independent sentence, where the CR serves as the Subject of one of a limited number of verbal expressions having to do with time.

Another sequence of accession episodes, more elaborately stated, is found in the text of the Tablet of the 96 Glyphs, from Palenque. A typical episode from this text is presented in detail in figure 6 and table 6. This is another three-sentence episode, which illustrates highlighting both by promotion of the Distance Number and Calendar Round to a separate sentence and by repetition or coupleting of the featured event. In a construction typical of Palenque texts, the Calendar Round date is removed completely from the highlighted event, by making it the grammatical subject of a separate verb. The Distance Number leads from the previous event, a Palace dedication by Pacal the Great, to the Calendar Round date of the seating of Kan-Xul (II). But neither event is given in the same sentence as the Calendar

Round. The earlier event was in a previous sentence, and the featured seating verb (for Kan-Xul) is the first element in the next sentence, thus giving it more grammatical prominence. (Note that the Distance Number leads from an event in the life of Kan-Xul's father, Pacal the Great, not from the seating of the previous ruler, Kan-Xul's older brother Chan Bahlum II.)

The noun phrases following the verb are both very elaborate. The first is the verbal complement, *ta ah po le*, "as lord of the succession" (dynasty or lineage?). Then the long subject phrase, which begins with a conflated title, continues with Kan-Xul's kingly title and name, *ma kin ah Kan Xul*, "Great Sun Lord Kan-Xul," and concludes with the Palenque "bone" emblem glyph. The normal placement of the corresponding CR would be following the subject, but this would lead to too many elaborate independent phrases following the verb. Thus, there is ample justification for the stylistic extraction of the CR phrase to a separate sentence. The final coupleted phrase restates the event, giving more information, this time in two Locative phrases, naming specific places: the "White Stone House" (their name for House E of the Palace, which was once painted white), and the "Jaguar Throne" (found inside House E).

Deletion and Unusual Syntax

When two sentences are joined, the purpose is usually to show a special relation between the event of the first sentence and that of the second. The similarity between the two sentences can result from the identity of any of the basic elements, but especially of the subjects of the

Table 5. Palenque, Cross Tablet, Left Side Text, D13–F4:
Elaboration and Focus via the Tripleted Expression of the Birth of GI′ of the Triad

Location	Structure	Content
D13–16	DN-*ix* V-*ix* Loc S	"It was 0 days, 12 uinals, 3 tuns, 13 katuns, and 1 baktun ago that Hun Ah Po GI ordered the sky,"
C17–F1	PEI + Vb + S + Temp	"and then the Triad God (GI′ the son) was born on 4 Ik 15 Ceh."
E2–F2	Pron-Vb-Obj + S	"GI′ touched the earth";
E3–F4	Pron-Vb Poss-Obj-Possr	"he continues the line of Lady Beastie, X-Kan-le-ox (title), Lady Ahau."

Table 6. Palenque, Tablet of the 96 Glyphs, C2–8: Promotion of the Temporal Phrase to an Independent Sentence, and Focus on the Event, by Fronting the Main Verb and Coupleting the Event

Location	Structure	Content
C2–D3	Pron-Vb DN-*ix*	"Night and Day cycled for 17 days, 4 uinals, 8 tuns, and 2 katuns,"
C4–5	PEI-Vb S	"until 5 Lamat 6 Xul came to pass."
D5–C7	Vb Prep-Comp S	"The many-titled, Great Sun Lord Kan-Xul, Blood Lord of Palenque, was seated as Lord of the succession."
D7–C8	Pron-Vb Loc / Prep Loc	"He sat on the Jaguar Throne, in the White Palace."

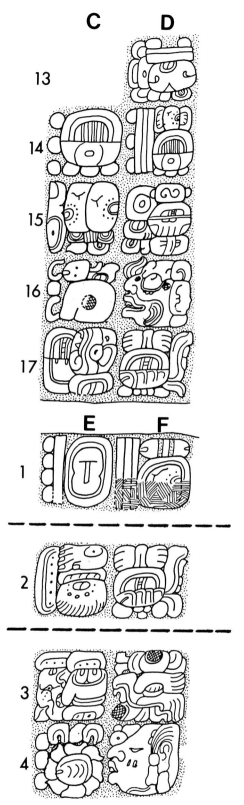

Fig. 5 Palenque, Tablet of the Cross, D13–F4. Focus and tripleting (drawing by Linda Schele).

Fig. 6 Palenque, Tablet of the 96 Glyphs, C2–C8. Fronting and promotion (drawing by Linda Schele).

two sentences, or of the verbs, that is, the action of the two sentences. In these cases, rather than repeating the common elements, one of the duplicated subjects or verbs can be omitted, or *deleted.* The text fragment from the Cross shown in table 4 illustrates the deletion of the common subject, Lady Beastie, from the first of the conjoined sentences. Note that the Calendar Round of the first sentence has also been deleted, not because it is the same as that of the second sentence, but because it is retrievable through the Distance Number (and also because it is old information, and was previously given at the beginning of the text). Subject deletion is very common in hieroglyphic texts; it can be seen in the text examples in figures (and tables) 3, 4, 5, 6, 7, 8, 9, and 10. There are several examples of verb deletion on the Tablet of the Cross, although these are not illustrated here (see also Schele 1982:36–42). A handy rule of thumb about deletion is: the more that is deleted, the more important what remains is likely to be. This is a generalization about the use of deletion to focus attention on the remaining elements. Just as prominence is given to a verb by fronting it to clause-initial position, so also stripping it of its argument (its Subject) leaves it in an even more highlighted form.

Another technique for highlighting verbal action is to isolate the verb word from any distracting elements, such as subject pronouns or tense-aspect suffixes. This is achieved by a special construction that uses an auxiliary verb, which carries the pronoun and other verbal markings, followed by the particle *ti* and the unadorned verb stem, sometimes referred to as the noun form of the verb (Josserand, Schele, and Hopkins 1985). This construction is not unlike English verb phrases with infinitives, and it is particularly suited to hieroglyphic texts, because it allows the verb to occupy an entire glyph block, without extraneous affixes to detract from its importance. Such constructions are typical of the Palenque texts, but are also found elsewhere, especially in the Southern Maya Lowlands; they are also typical of modern Chol, as opposed to other Mayan languages, although they appear sporadically in Yucatecan languages and other Mayan neighbors of Chol.

Disturbed Syntax Around the Peak

It has long been noted by epigraphers that, just when it appears that the most important events are being presented, the text suddenly gets harder to read. This is a reflection of the phenomenon of *disturbed syntax* around the peak event of the text. An example of this phenomenon is found in the last clause of the main tablet from the Temple of the Cross, Palenque (fig. 7, table 7).

The episode begins by focusing on the birth of Chan Bahlum I (an ancestor of the protagonist of these texts, Chan Bahlum II), set against a background of the birth of his older brother, Chaacal II. It then continues with two backgrounded phrases introduced by Distance Numbers, only one of which leads to the focal event of the episode, which is also the peak event of the entire text on the Cross Tablet. The episode as a whole is the peak episode, and even the first sentence has distorted or disturbed syntax. The Calendar Round that is proper to the backgrounded clause, the birth of Chaacal II, is not found within that clause, but rather at the end of the following, foregrounded clause, the birth of CB I (table 7). But the real problems begin with the following two constructions. First a Distance Number of more than forty-five years begins counting from the birth of CB I, given with its correct CR following CB I's name; this DN leads correctly to the final, focused event of the text, the accession as *zac uinic* of CB I (stated only as PEI + Verb + Complement, with both the subject and the CR deleted). But before this focused clause begins, still another DN clause is inserted, in a parenthetical construction. This second DN also leads from CB I's birth as the background event, but no corresponding foregrounded event follows; since the DN itself is somewhat eroded in the tun coefficient, we can only guess that it leads to some unspecified event, presumably in the life of CB I, between fifteen and nineteen tuns after his birth. The peak event of the Cross Tablet, then, is the accession of Chan Bahlum I; though its importance in the narrative flow is signaled through the use of the PEI, only the context provides the information necessary to identify the actor and the date of this important event. The very lack of the other grammatical elements adds to the highlighted importance of the peak event.

Discourse Analysis of Long Narrative Texts

In long narrative texts, episodes are linked together to form a discourse unit that should be studied as a whole, not as isolated parts. This discourse unit may span several inscriptions, just as iconographic programs may occur across a series of monuments or even structures, forming an integrated statement. Though the Cross Group at Palenque is the first of the long connected texts to be studied as a single narrative via the discourse model

Table 7. Palenque, Cross Tablet, Right Side Text, U6–U17: Disturbed Syntax around the Peak Event of an Inscription

Location	Structure	Content
U6–T9	DN-*ix* V-*ix* S	"It was 1 day, 1 uinal, and 1 tun, from when Chaacal (II) was born"
U9–T11	PEI-V S Temp$_1$	"until Chan Bahlum (I) was born; (since) 7 Kan 17 Mol."
U11–14	DN-*ix* Vb-*ix* S Temp	"It was 7 days, 4 uinals, 8 tuns, 2 katuns, since Chan Bahlum (I) was born on 11 Chicchan 13 Ch'en" . . .
T15–U16	DN-*ix* VB-*ix* S	["It was 2 days, 8 uinals, 15+ tuns since Chan Bahlum (I) was born" . . .]
T17–U17	PEI-Vb-Obj Prep-Comp	"until he held the sacred bundle of the succession."

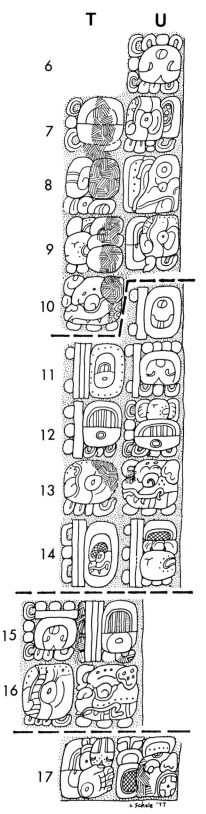

T   U

6

7

8

9

10

11

12

13

14

15

16

17

L Schele '77

Fig. 7   Palenque, Tablet of the Cross, U6–U17. Disturbed syntax around the peak event (drawing by Linda Schele).

(Josserand and Schele 1984, in press) it is clear that other texts at Palenque and elsewhere work similarly (Bassie 1986). Here I use the Cross Group to illustrate the relation of captions to the whole text, the Tablet of the 96 Glyphs to illustrate the event-line, and the Tablet of the Slaves to illustrate the structural division of a long text into episodes.

Setting the Scene: The Caption Texts

In the Cross Group, the caption texts (or secondary texts) are found around figures in central iconographic displays.[8] Karen Bassie is carrying out a detailed study (1986 and in preparation) of the relationship of these short texts to both the images that are their matrices and the long hieroglyphic texts that surround them, in effect testing hypotheses generated by the discourse analysis of the Cross Group texts (Josserand and Schele 1984, in press). The caption texts on the three main panels of the Cross Group introduce the contemporary ruler of Palenque, Chan Bahlum II, who erected these temples and almost certainly commissioned their inscriptions, which deal with the major events of his life and relate him to history, both mythological and recent.

In terms of the overall content of the long hieroglyphic texts from the Cross Group, the three tablets themselves can be characterized as follows: the Cross Tablet sets the stage for the events in the life of Chan Bahlum II by giving both mythological and dynastic history as "background" for the next two tablets (the Sun and the Foliated Cross). The mythological events constitute a second storyline concerning the births of the Triad gods, and these events are previewed in the images and caption texts from the *alfardas* that flank the stairs on each of the three temples. But this mythological tale is itself a kind of backdrop for the life of Chan Bahlum II. The mythological event-line continues as the first half of both of the next two tablets, but it is clear from the associated images that the more important storyline is that concerning Chan Bahlum II. The second tablet in the series is from the Temple of the Sun, whose texts (both caption and long texts) emphasize events in the early life of Chan Bahlum II, especially what Bassie calls his "first lineage event." The third and last tablet is that of the Foliated Cross, and its texts highlight the events in the life of the mature Chan Bahlum II, particularly those on and following 2 Cib 14 Mol (an astronomical event;[9] and perhaps also the dedication of one or more of the Cross Group temples themselves).

The caption texts on all three tablets can be considered to be in pairs: each tablet has two sets of short texts, one set associated with the smaller figure and the other with the larger figure shown on each tablet. In fact, the content of the texts is much the same on all three tablets, and the relationship between the large or small figure and the content of the set of caption texts surrounding them also remains constant. The caption texts surrounding the larger figure in all three panels contain references to

Chan Bahlum II's accession (as *zac uinic* of the succession), while the caption texts surrounding the smaller figure in the three panels all contain references to a ceremony in which Chan Bahlum II participated when he was about six years old (on Gregorian date 17 June 641 A.D.). This is Chan Bahlum's "heir apparency" event (Schele 1984a:77, 95, 114–115, 1984b) or "first lineage event" (Bassie 1986), effectively the beginning of his public life. These two events, Chan Bahlum II's first lineage event and his accession as lord of the succession, are the events being depicted in the images of the three tablets (Bassie 1986; Schele 1976:12–14 treats the smaller figure as the deceased Pacal, not Chan Bahlum).

A comparison of the caption texts from the three tablets reveals that only the Cross Tablet caption texts carry PEI, or event-line focus markers; that is, they are the only caption texts that prominently display temporal movement, from one event to another, in sequential/chronological order. This reflects the function of the caption texts as well as the main text of this temple, which is to "set the stage" for the main events in the life of CB II. In this respect, the Cross caption texts (fig. 8 and table 8) give an overview or preview of what is to come in the other two tablets.

The caption texts associated with the smaller figure (on the left in the Cross Tablet, fig. 8) begin with the Calendar Round of Chan Bahlum II's first lineage event (G–K3), identifying him as the son of Pacal and Lady

Ah Po Hel (K4–K6), and then move, via a DN, to the CR of the 9.10.10.0.0 lahuntun Period Ending, which CB II must have celebrated in his new capacity (K7–K10). Note the unusual syntax: the CR that follows the DN corresponds to the date of the Period Ending; it should normally *follow* the Verb in clauses introduced by the PEI, but here it precedes the PEI. This order would usually indicate that the CR corresponds to the earlier event, from which the DN counts. But since the CR for that event was given in the first sentence, there is no real confusion generated by this order; instead, it functions to highlight the later event, which now is the only element following the PEI.

The caption texts associated with the larger figure (on the right in the Cross Tablet) begin a new episode, with the CR of Chan Bahlum II's accession as *zac uinic* of the succession (L1–O1). The text then moves via a Distance Number of slightly over six years to the 2 Cib event by the Palenque Triad (O2–O6), and from there to the rites three days later,[10] which are associated with the 2 Cib ceremonies (O7–O15). These last rites, performed by Chan Bahlum II, are given further prominence by their double presentation, in couplet form: Chan Bahlum "lets blood" and "holds the bundle (of the bloodletter)." The first statement of this bloodletting seems to have a long noun phrase as its final element (at O10–O11), but it is unclear whether it is functioning as a subject (= CB), or as an indirect object (the recipi-

Table 8. Palenque, Cross Tablet, Central Panel: Image and Caption Texts

Location	Structure	Content
Left Text		
	Temp + Vb + S-Parentage	"On 9 Akbal 6 Xul, the many titled Lord
	G, H I J, K1–K6	(but as yet unnamed as Chan Bahlum),
		the Jaguar Lord of Palenque,
		the child of Great Pacal,
		and child of Lady Ah Po Hel,
		was displayed on the pyramid."
	DN + Temp	"17 kins, 8 uinals, and 1 tun later
	K7–8 K9	was 13 Ahau 18 Kankin,
	PEI-Vb	when the (10th katun) cycle was completed."
	K10	(i.e., the 9.10.10.0.0 Period Ending)
Right Text		
	Temp + Vb-Obj + Comp + S	"On 8 Oc 3 Kayab (9.12.11.12.10)
	L1–2 L3 M N–O1	the Great Sun Lord Chan Bahlum (II)
		held the sacred bundle of the succession."
	DN + Vb-Obj	"6 kins, 11 uinals, and 6 tuns passed
	O2–3 O4	from when he held the bundle"
	PEI-Vb$_1$	"until the sky event (on 2 Cib)."
	O5	
	Vb$_2$ + Comp + S	"The Triad (just GI?) did an event?"
	O6 O7	
	DN + Pron-Vb$_1$-Obj + Comp + S?	"On the third day he let blood . . ."
	O8 O9 O10 O11	
	Pron-Vb$_2$-Obj + S	"The Great Sun Lord Chan Bahlum (II),
	O12 O13–15	Palenque Jaguar Lord,
		Ah Po of Palenque,
		held the bundle (of the bloodletter)."

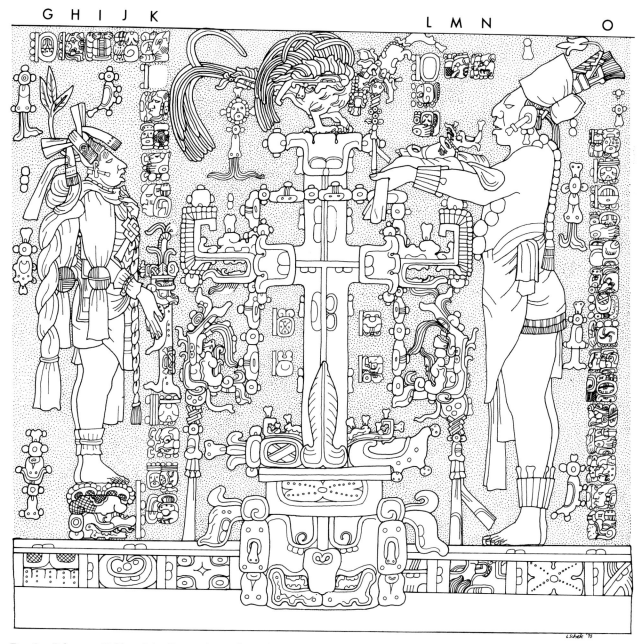

Fig. 8   Palenque, Tablet of the Cross, Central Panel. Image and caption texts (drawing by Linda Schele).

ent/beneficiary of the actions?), or as some other kind of verbal complement.

The Event-Line: Development of the Story

The event-line can be simple, as on Tikal Stela 22 (table 3), or very complex, as in the Group of the Cross inscriptions. A good example, easy to follow, is the event-line of the inscription on the Tablet of the 96 Glyphs from Palenque (fig. 9). This text is a two-episode narrative; that is, it has two sections that correspond to distinct time frames (table 9). The first episode opens

with the Calendar Round at the beginning of the text, which is not an Initial Series date, but is like IS Period Ending expressions: "On 12 Ahau 8 Ceh the 11th katun rested, under the auspices of the great Pacal of the Five Pyramids, Blood Lord of Palenque" (A1–B4). This statement sets the time frame and begins the event-line. The second sentence (A5–D1) sets the grammatical pattern for the presentation of all the events that follow, most of which involve a ruler of Palenque being seated as lord and/or doing a special rite in the White Stone House (i.e., House E of the Palace, which was once painted white, and which also housed the throne referred to in later sentences). These subsequent events are all presented using the following set phrasing as the constant pattern of development for the event-line:

1. Verb + DN=*ix* + PEI + Verb + CR
2. Verb + Complement + Subject
3. Coupleted expression.

Each new event on the event-line is introduced by a unique substitute for the verb normally used to indicate the passing of time (the Distance Number introductory verb), here replaced by poetic renderings utilizing typically Mayan couplets of paired oppositions (Day and Night cycled; Life and Death; Venus and the Moon;

Wind and Water). Then a Distance Number leads from the event in the preceding sentence to the Calendar Round date of the new event on the event-line. The CR is actually functioning grammatically as the subject of a special past-tense verb, *uhti*, "it came to pass" or "it occurred" (Stuart 1984b).

The event that took place on this date is actually the focused event, not the date itself, even though the verb preceding the CR carries the Posterior Event Indicator focus marker. In this text, the PEI serves chiefly as an indicator of temporal movement through the text, placing events on a sequential event-line. The verb of the new event is given special prominence by appearing first in its own sentence (the expected initial element, the

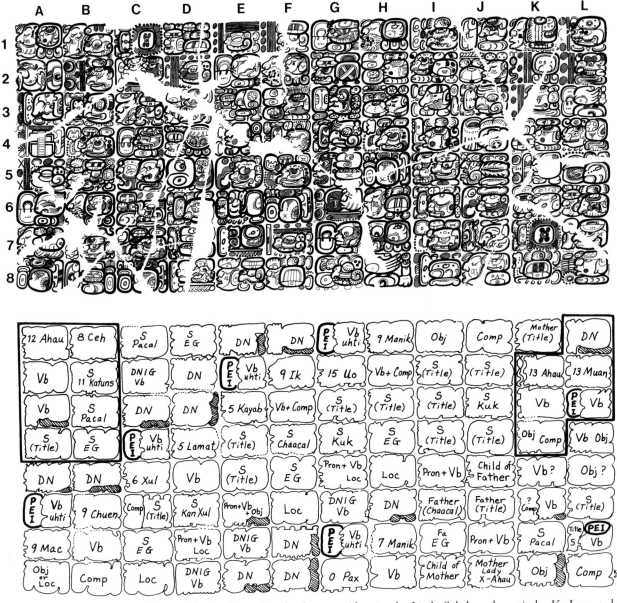

Fig. 9   Palenque, Tablet of the 96 Glyphs. Event-line development (drawing by Linda Schele; schematic by K. Josserand; shaded affixes are Anterior Event Indicators).

Table 9. Palenque, Tablet of the 96 Glyphs: Event-line Development in a Long Hieroglyphic Text

Episode I

(1)	9.11.0.0.0	On 12 Ahau 8 Ceh the 11th katun rested, under the auspices of Pacal.
(2)	9.11.2.1.11	2+ years later, it was 9 Chuen 9 Mac. Pacal dedicated his great Palace.
(3)	9.13.10.6.8	2+ years later, it was 5 Lamat 6 Xul. Kan-Xul was seated as Ah Po; he sat on the jaguar throne in the Palace.
(4)	9.14.10.4.2	19+ years later, it was 9 Ik 5 Kayab. Chaacal III was seated as *ahau;* he sacrificed with the bloodletter in the Palace.
(5)	9.16.13.0.7	2+ katuns later, it was 9 Manik 15 Uo. Kuk II was seated as *ahau;* he sat on the jaguar throne in the Palace.
(6)	9.17.13.0.7	1 katun later, it was 7 Manik, the seating of Pax. The great and many titled Kuk completed his first katun as *ahau,* he who is of royal descent, of the blood of the Great Chaacal, Lord of Palenque; and who is the child of the royal lady, the Lady Cahal.

Episode II

(1)	9.17.13.0.0	7 days earlier, 13 Ahau 13 Muan was the 13th tun,
(2)	9.17.13.0.7	and then he completed his first katun as *ahau;* he erected a monument (this stone?); he sacrificed(?), under the auspices of Pacal and then he finished his first katun as *ahau.*

CR date, having been removed to a separate sentence, as explained above). The event is usually given further emphasis by a second, parallel sentence that serves as a "couplet" to the first statement of the event (the order of the events is shown in table 9).

Notice that the second episode begins a new time frame (L1–K4); that is, it restarts the event-line by going back in time to an earlier date, the oxlahuntun Period Ending (9.17.13.0.0). The short Distance Number (of 7 days) connects this Period Ending with Kuk's anniversary event, which was the peak of the first episode. This second episode recaps the action of the first episode in a poetic manner, by beginning with a Period Ending (like the first episode) and closing with the 1 katun anniversary event, which is here given even more prominence by the addition of other events presumably carried out on the same date. The formal structure of this last sentence is chiasmic, producing a "mirror image" of parallel constructions, of the A-B-B'-A' pattern (De Long 1986).

The visual layout of the event-line is very striking on this monument; the Posterior Event Indicators or event-line markers are displayed across the text in an ascending pattern, which leads from the date of Pascal's "fire" event (the House E dedication rite?) on the lower left at A6, diagonally up, via the intermediate seating events of Kuk's direct lineal ancestors marked by the PEIs at C4 and E2, to the date of Kuk's accession, at the top middle of the panel at G1. Most of the rest of this double column is given over to Kuk's titles, a dead giveaway of who

this monument is about. The event-line continues with another date associated with Kuk, 7 Manik 0 Pax (G7–G8), when Kuk celebrated his 1 katun anniversary as Lord of Palenque; this may also be the dedicatory date for this tablet. Kuk is again given great prominence by the very elaborate name phrase for the anniversary verb; Kuk's name and many titles, plus his parentage statements, take up an entire double column on the right of the tablet. The final double column (beginning at L1) contains the second episode, or closing statement, which opens with the 9.17.13 Period Ending (not as good as a full katun ending, but 13 tuns is still a good number to celebrate, especially given the 13 Ahau 13 Muan Calendar Round). Then the 1 katun anniversary event is emphasized again by stating it twice, both times with the PEI focus marker (at L3 and L7). These are the only two times in this text that the PEI appears directly on the *event* verb rather than on the *uhti* verb that precedes the other Calendar Rounds. In addition, there are two more statements, about other events associated with Kuk's 1 katun anniversary.

The Episodes of a Narrative Text: The Tablet of the Slaves

The discourse analysis approach can lead to new insights in a difficult text by "chunking" the text into significant sections, based on the formal characteristics of event-line, peak, and temporal introducers. Schele (this volume) gives a different kind of reinterpretation of the Tablet of the Slaves, recognizing that Chac-Zutz' was not a king of Palenque, but a subordinate lord carrying a title that has been read as *cahal,* a regional governor.[11]

In the Tablet of the Slaves text, each episode is formally marked as a new time frame, and there is both unity within the episodes and contrast between them, in terms of their grammatical structure as well as their content (fig. 10 and table 10). Each new episode backs up in time slightly, to restart the time-line, except for the last episode, which starts ahead but then backs up via an unusual grammatical construction. The first episode is characterized in content by the seating events of earlier rulers, in grammatical structure by the use of the same "seating" verb in all three sentences, and by "katun endings" as approximate Distance Numbers. The second episode, which introduces the main actor, Chac-Zutz', begins with a completely different grammatical pattern as well as a different verbal expression for accession to power. The third episode concerns war, capture, and perhaps sacrifice events performed by Chac-Zutz', and the fourth and last episode connects him to a major Period Ending and celebrates his "60th" birthday (three katuns).

Episode I: This text gives a series of consecutive dates and background events, and sets the time frame with the seating of Palenque's most illustrious ruler, rather than with a more standard seating event, the seating of a katun (Period-Ending expression). Note the use of "ap-proximate" Distance Numbers in this episode, that is, katun seatings between rulers. Actual Long Counts are implied, by consecutive Calendar Round dates, and are confirmed by readers on the grounds of "shared knowledge" about who was ruler of Palenque during katun endings named by the Calendar Rounds. The dated events run consecutively from Pacal's accession through Chan Bahlum II's accession and on to that of Kan-Xul II.

Episode II: This section of text establishes a new time frame; it backs up in time. This episode contains the only Posterior Event Indicator of the whole text (and the only real Distance Number in the first three episodes). It is not the only peak event in the text, but the highlighting or focus on the other peak events is differently expressed. Note that it is *Chaacal's* accession that is emphasized, but it should be understood that this episode is only giving additional background to the main events of this text, which deal with the life of *Chac-Zutz'* (CZ), the protagonist of the text, who is also portrayed as the central figure in the image of the tablet. Note also that the text opened (in the first episode) with the seating of Pacal the Great, during whose reign Chac-Zutz' was born.

A very unusual aspect of this text is the presentation of the main character, Chac-Zutz', in a phrase that is marked as background, or previously given information,

Table 10. Palenque, Tablet of the Slaves: Episodic Analysis

Episode I: Opening/Background (No Initial Series)
(1) On 5 Lamat 1 Mol Pacal was seated as Ah Po.	9.9.2.4.8
(2) 3 katun endings later, Chan Bahlum was seated.	9.12.11.12.10
(3) 1 katun ending later, Kan-Xul was seated.	9.13.10.6.8

Episode II: The setting for Chac-Zutz's life
(1) 11 tuns and 2 katuns had passed,	9.11.18.9.17
since Ma-Zutz's birth on 7 Caban 15 Kayab,	
and then Chaacal held the shining bundle	
of the succession on 9 Ik 5 Kayab.	9.14.10.4.2
(2) On 8 Imix 7 Yaxkin, Chac-Zutz', lineage lord,	9.14.11.12.14
held the smoking bundle of the succession.	
(3) On 7 Ik 5 Zec, there was a war event.	9.14.13.11.2
(4) It was in the territory of Lord Chac-Zutz'.	

Episode III: Great moments in the life of Chac-Zutz'
(1) On 9 Cimi 19 Zac, he captured Ah Manik,	9.14.11.17.6
Ah Ahual, and Ah Chan(?).	
(2) On 2 Cauac 2 Xul, there was a war event.	9.14.17.12.19
(3) It was in the territory of Chac-Zutz'.	
(4) On 7 Imix 4 Ceh, many titled Chac-Zutz', *cahal,*	9.14.18.1.1
performs an event (sacrifice?).	

Episode IV: Dedication of the commemorative stone
(1) It is 8 uinals and 1 tun	
before the period ending on 4 Ahau 13 Yax,	9.15.0.0.0
which is the seating of the (15th) katun.	
(2) On 5 Lamat 6 Uo was the lineage event.	9.14.18.9.8
(3) He held the *ahau* bundle.	
(4) Nine days later he completed 3 katuns,	
on 1 Caban 15 Uo, since his birth.	9.14.18.9.17

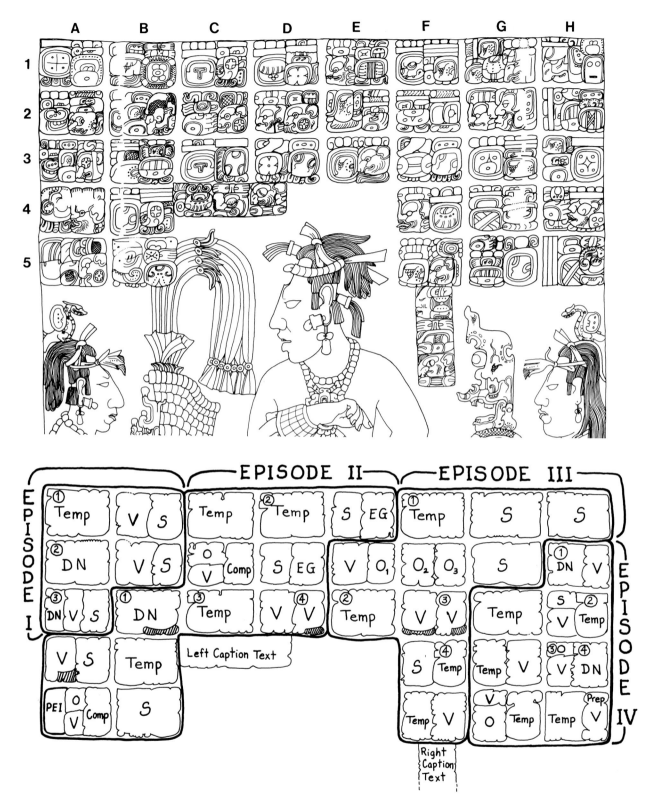

Fig. 10 Palenque, Tablet of the Slaves. Episodic analysis (drawing by Linda Schele; schematic by K. Josserand; shaded affixes are Anterior Event Indicators).

even though this is the very first time CZ is mentioned on this stone. Why is the relation between CZ and Chaacal presented in this seemingly aberrant manner? Compare this text to our own monuments erected by lower officials, which nonetheless prominently name presiding higher officials (mayor, state governor, or U.S. president). Chaacal, the presiding lord, must be mentioned, and even given the most prominence of all the actors in the text, but we should not forget who the text is about, so we must understand the subtle techniques being employed to balance conflicting pressures for prominence. Yes, Chaacal's accession is the "most important event" in some senses, since he is the ruler of Palenque in power during the period of these events. But in the text, Chaacal's accession is framed by two events in the life of Chac-Zutz': his birth, which is the first background statement of this episode, and his "lineage event," which is like in kind to Chaacal's accession in some way that is still unclear to the modern reader. This second episode ends with a "war event," which seems to carry background marking. The "land of" phrase carries the -ix suffix (T126) which marks backgrounded material, and it is possible that the verb for the war event also has the -ix suffix.

Episode III: The great moments in the life of Chac-Zutz' all seem to be concerned with war, capture, and perhaps sacrifice (CZ's greatest hits?). Once again, the time frame backs up, to restart the action with CZ's capture of Ah Manik, Ah Ahaual, and another named lord. This event followed CZ's lineage event by some five uinals (a third of a year), and preceded the war event in the previous episode by some two years. The next event in Episode III is another war event in the land of CZ. The dates indicate that the "war event" in this episode is not the same one referred to at the end of the last episode (in fact, it was some four years later than the first war event).

Notice also in this episode the use of implied Distance Numbers; none are given overtly until the last episode. Again, the sequential Calendar Rounds indicate chronological development. All three events seem to be on the event-line, without any particular emphasis on one of them (no apparent foregrounding). It is possible that the war event again carries some kind of background marking (the -ix suffix on the "land of" phrase). On positional and elaborative grounds it would appear that the last event is the peak of this episode, but its exact nature is unclear: perhaps it is sacrifice. Whatever it is, the event glyph is covered with blood signs. Note also the very long title phrase before Chac-Zutz's name. The date itself has no special significance; it follows the preceding event, the second war event, by about six uinals.

Episode IV: This is the most unusual episode in terms of time frames, for it does not back up in time and restart the time-line like the other three episodes do. Rather it starts from the other end, from the latest date on the entire tablet, and backs up from there, so a new start is

implied. Even though the event-line might be considered to be continuous, there are other fairly clear indications that these last events form a separate episode—in particular, the use of genuine Distance Numbers to connect the events within the episode. Note especially the Distance Number at the beginning of the episode, which connects Chac-Zutz' to a major Period Ending at 9.15.0.0.0. The grammar of this construction is unusual, for the backgrounded event, the PE, is actually later in time than the focused events, CZ's second lineage event and his 60th birthday nine days later.

Perhaps the lineage event is the peak event of this episode, since it is expressed in a couplet ("On 5 Lamat 6 Uo he did the lineage event; he held the *ahau* bundle"; note that the lineage event in this episode is not the same as the earlier lineage event). But the completion (on 1 Caban 15 Uo) of 3 katuns since birth seems to be more prominent, if only because of its text-final position on the tablet. Another marker of prominence for both of these events is the striking absence of the grammatical subject for both main verbs. Chac-Zutz', the agent or actor, is not mentioned, though he is clearly the person being referred to (the date is 3 katuns since his birthdate, which was given in Episode II). Note also how this last sentence restates the theme of the text, the life of Chac-Zutz', by framing the actions of the text as occurring between his birth (during Pacal's reign) and his sixtieth birthday (presumably during Chaacal's reign). This recap of the action at the end of the tale is another characteristic of both modern Chol texts and Mayan hieroglyphic texts.

Notes

1. The spelling conventions followed here use established linguistic orthographies for citations of Mayan words, except that the proper names of rulers of Palenque follow the model set forth in the *Proceedings* of the First Palenque Round Table. Abbreviations are of two kinds, those dealing with hieroglyphic terms, and those dealing with linguistic terms. Hieroglyphic abbreviations include: AEI (Anterior Date Indicator), BJ (Bird Jaguar of Yaxchilán), CB (Chan Bahlum), CR (Calendar Round), CZ (Chac-Zutz'), DN (Distance Number), DNIG (Distance Number Introductory Glyph), EG (Emblem Glyph), IS (Initial Series), ISIG (Initial Series Introductory Glyph), LC (Long Count), PE (Period Ending), and PEI (Posterior Event Indicator). Linguistic abbreviations include Comp (Complement of a Verb), Loc (Locative Phrase), O or Obj (Object of a Verb), Poss (Possessive Pronoun), Possr (Possessor of a Noun), Prep (Preposition), Pron (Pronoun Subject of a Verb), S (Subject), Temp (Temporal Phrase), and V or Vb (Verb).

2. Some basic discourse analysis references that treat the concepts presented here at greater length, with respect to Mesoamerican languages, are Jones (1979), Longacre (1979), and Jones and Jones (1984).

3. A reading of *i wal* has also been suggested for the PEI (Justeson 1984a: 350), which indicates its interpretation as a modal verb (Pronoun *i* plus modal verb *wal*, cf. Chol *woli*, the progressive tense/aspect marker). Evidence cited for this reading is the use of such a construction in colonial Chontal documents (Smailus 1975). I believe that this interpretation of the PEI as a modal verb is one possibility: it reflects the relation of the PEI to punctual time. Even interpretations of the

PEI as a third-person pronoun (Lounsbury 1974:17; Bricker 1985:68) also seem to have temporal correlates, since use of the alternate pronouns is governed by verbal tense/aspect and voice; the "split ergativity" characteristic of Cholan and Yucatec reflect the overriding influence of tense/aspect on pronominal use. But functionally the PEI acts more like a subordinating conjunction, and its interpretation as a preverbal third-person pronoun does not seem well founded (MacLeod 1984:258–260).

4. This reading for the Anterior Event Indicator was independently suggested by Will Norman (cited in Fox and Justeson 1984b: 60); Fox and Justeson also reviewed other proposals for reading T126 (1984b:54–62).

5. This is in contrast to views held by Thompson (1960:50–51) and Kubler (1973:146).

6. Note that on the Temple of the Inscriptions, Chan Bahlum I's accession is given (implied) as 9.6.18.5.12 (8 kins, 12 uinals, 1 tun since he was seated as ahau of Palenque until the Period Ending 9.7.0.0.0), and this is the same Long Count date as is given on the Temple of the Cross for his becoming zac uinic.

7. In the accompanying iconographic program, GI' the son does appear on the Temple of the Cross doorjambs and on the exterior alfardas.

8. In the following discussion I am deeply indebted to Karen Bassie for her perceptive insights on the content of the iconography and the relationship between the images and the caption texts of the Cross Group panels.

9. Lounsbury has proposed that the 2 Cib date records a Jupiter hierophany (cited in Schele 1984b:100).

10. David Stuart (personal communication) argues that the last DN construction is not "the third day," but just an ordinal, "the third (time?)." See also Riese (1984a) on hel hieroglyphs.

11. David Stuart (personal communication and 1986a) considers that the title is not read as cahal, although the sense of "regional governor" is still valid.

Acknowledgments

This material is based upon work supported in part by the National Science Foundation under Grant BNS-8305806, administered by the Institute for Cultural Ecology of the Tropics. Any opinions, findings, and conclusions or recommendations expressed in this publication are those of the author and do not necessarily reflect the views of the National Science Foundation or of ICET. The figures are reproduced by permission of the University Museum of the University of Pennsylvania (fig. 3) and Linda Schele (figs. 1, 2, and 4–10).

I would also like to thank Karen Bassie and David Stuart for their very helpful discussions of this material, and Linda Schele, for her generous sharing of hieroglyphic materials over the past three years and for the opportunities of working with her in the Advanced Seminar on Hieroglyphic Writing, where some of these ideas were first presented (in 1984 and 1985). Most especially, I thank Nicholas A. Hopkins for his very careful readings of many versions of this manuscript.

The idea of dividing long hieroglyphic texts into "chunks" and interpreting them in terms of discourse structures was anticipated by Lounsbury (1980:115) and by Kubler (1973, 1974). Clause structure has been presented at length by Schele (1982 and elsewhere), and temporal structuring of long narratives has been independently suggested by Fought (1985).

Cycles of Time: Caracol in the Maya Realm
with an Appendix on Caracol Altar 21
by Stephen D. Houston, Vanderbilt University

ARLEN F. CHASE
UNIVERSITY OF CENTRAL FLORIDA

The Maya were firm believers in cyclical time. Time repeated itself every so often, in the Maya case particularly after the passage of 13 katuns or, in westernized terms, every 256 years. Events could reoccur and good or evil things could be presaged. These events are to some degree recorded in the katun prophecies and rounds that survived into the Historic era (Roys 1933:144–163; A. Chase 1986:124–137). The passage of time and the concomitant events were inevitable. Rather than fight such cyclical time, the Maya worked around it. If something was inevitable, then why not succumb to it on your own terms?

The impact of cyclical time upon the Postclassic Maya is clearly seen in the final moments of the independent Itzá Maya of Tayasal (A. Chase 1976:159). The Itzá resisted all attempts by the Spanish at conquest and conversion, assiduously waiting until the upcoming "Katun of Change," Katun 8 Ahau. As this all-important shift began to approach, the Itzá sent an emissary, Martin Can, to Mérida circa A.D. 1695 to offer their submission (on their own terms) to the Spanish crown (A. Chase 1985c:202). Although the Itzá had successfully resisted Spanish conquest for over 180 years, their time counts dictated that, to put it colloquially, "their time was up." The successful assault on the Itzá by Ursua in fact occurred only some 136 days before the seating of Katun 8 Ahau (Tozzer 1957:64). This final conquest of the Itzá by the Spaniards in A.D. 1697 was therefore foretold in the passage of time; they believed that they were helpless to prevent this event, which essentially forever changed their way of life, their society, and their culture.

Edmonson (1984:99) commented on this fatalistic view of time in Maya society, noting that the "katuns not only chronicled the wars of Yucatan but actually caused them" (see also Farriss 1987). The cyclical nature of time was not restricted to the Postclassic Maya, but was also in evidence during the Classic Period. "The Books imply with some clarity that the thirteen katun cycle—the *may*—controlled the fate of dynasties in the major cities of Classic times and continued to do so in the Postclassic down to the fall of Mayapan" (Edmonson 1984:99).

Dennis Puleston (1979) ascribed this fatalistic view of the cyclical passage of time as perhaps the main cause behind the Classic Maya "collapse." Just as the Postclassic Maya knew that change was inevitable and attempted to deal with such change before its time, Puleston argued that the Maya collapse could also be viewed in a similar frame. A Katun 8 Ahau, or Katun of Change, was due to occur in 10.6.0.0.0 (A.D. 948 in an 11.16.0.0.0 correlation). The Classic Period ceremonial complex from the Southern Lowlands, at least as recognized in archaeological terms, ends by this date. The latest monumental Long Count dates, those from Toniná in Chiapas (Morley, Brainerd, and Sharer 1983:135) and from Tzibanche in southern Quintana Roo (Harrison 1974; Morley, Brainerd, and Sharer 1983:596), are 10.4.0.0.0, some forty years before this date. Most sites of the Southern Lowlands, however, never saw 10.4.0.0.0, but instead began to fade from the Classic Period after 9.19.0.0.0 (A.D. 810), at least in terms of their inscriptional records. No matter what internal or external reasons can be mustered to explain the collapse (Culbert 1973; Sharer 1977), it is clear that this almost mythical event also coincides, at least archaeologically, with the 10.6.0.0.0 Katun of Change. Thus, Puleston's (1979) basic argument appears valid.

I would like to expand this ontological notion of time in Classic Period Maya thought by looking at earlier Katun 8 Ahaus, particularly those of 8.7.0.0.0 (A.D. 179), 9.0.0.0.0 (A.D. 435), and 9.13.0.0.0 (A.D. 692). In short, following Coggins (1979:48) and Puleston (1979:66–68), I would argue that much of Classic Period Maya prehistory can be explained by reference to the cyclical passage of time as seen in the "Short Count" or passage of 13 katun periods. In particular, recent excavations at Caracol have yielded significant data to augment this position.

Caracol

The site of Caracol, located approximately 1,600 feet above sea level in the Maya Mountains of the southern Cayo District of Belize, offers much insight into Maya prehistory—especially the transition between the Early and Late Classic periods. The site has been known since 1938 when it was reported to the Belizean archaeological commissioner by a chiclero working in the region. Because of its monumental record, Linton Satterthwaite (1951, 1954; Beetz and Satterthwaite 1981) of the University of Pennsylvania worked at the site in 1950, 1951, and 1953. Satterthwaite succeeded in recording the majority of the carved monuments and in making an accurate transit map that hinted at the extent of the site. Later excavations at Caracol in 1956 and 1958 by A. H. Anderson (1958, 1959), the first Belizean archaeological commissioner, confirmed the existence of preserved architecture and a large number of burial chambers at the site.

In an attempt to link site development, specific structures, and individual interments to the epigraphic record, a major project sponsored by the University of Central Florida and under the direction of Diane Z. Chase and myself began work at Caracol in 1985. The recovered remains are allowing the anticipated juxtaposition of data. Most significantly, painted tomb texts continued at Caracol at least through 9.13.3.15.16 (A.D. 695), some 200 years after their last appearance at most other sites. Like Palenque, stucco hieroglyphic texts also adorned buildings during this same era. The epigraphic texts also attest to Caracol's warlike nature during the transition between the Early and Late Classic periods. While Caracol's conquest of Naranjo by Lord Kan II in 9.9.18.16.3 (A.D. 631) is well known to epigraphers, a new text on Altar 21 of Caracol (fig. 2) notes the apparent defeat of Tikal by his father Lord Water in 9.6.8.4.2 (A.D. 562).

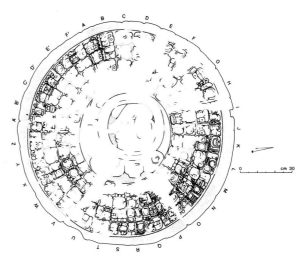

Fig. 2   Caracol Altar 21, a monument dating to 9.10.0.0.0, located in the center of the A Group Ball Court during the 1986 field season (field drawing by Stephen O. Houston, courtesy Caracol Archaeological Project, University of Central Florida).

Apart from the new epigraphic material, recent work at Caracol has revealed a vastly different site from that presented by Beetz and Satterthwaite (1981). Thus far, seven causeways are known to radiate out from what, for lack of a better term, is now referred to colloquially as "downtown Caracol" and formally as the "central precinct" or "epicenter" (see fig. 1). Four of these causeways are known to be over 3 km in length and a fifth is suspected to run at least this distance. With one exception, these causeways do not connect different sites to Caracol, but rather connect parts of Caracol to its epicenter; the areas along and between the causeways exhibit continuous settlement and areas of terracing. These intrasite causeways were used for communication, transportation, and, perhaps, ceremonial purposes.[1]

Caracol is presently estimated to cover between 28 and 50 km^2, while its overall dominion probably approximated some 314 km^2 during the Late Classic Period (A. Chase and D. Chase 1987a, 1987b:53). The epigraphic, ceramic, and settlement data all point to the prosperity of the site between 9.5.0.0.0 and 9.12.0.0.0. These data also allow for a fresh understanding of the transition between the Early and Late Classic periods and the role that the Maya concept of cyclical time may have played in this transition. Minimally, these data underscore the prime importance of Caracol in any understanding of the Classic Maya hiatus.

Models

Two models predominate in archaeological and art historical literature to account for the development and expansion of the Maya core area. One may be termed the "Teotihuacán" model, in which major growth in

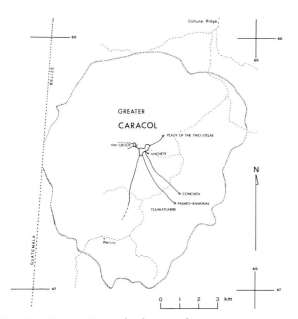

Fig. 1   Greater Caracol, showing the approximate range and location of the various known causeways relative to the central precinct of the site (map by Arlen F. Chase, courtesy Caracol Archaeological Project, University of Central Florida).

the Southern Maya Lowlands is linked via Tikal either directly or indirectly to the site of Teotihuacán (Sanders 1973:352–354, 1977:408; Coggins 1979, 1983a; Adams 1986:434–440; but see Haviland 1978:180). A second model for the Maya rise to prominence is Rathje's (1971, 1972) core/buffer zone model for the development of Maya civilization. Following Rathje, the Maya traded esoteric goods out of the Southern Lowlands in return for three needed items: salt, hard volcanic stone, and obsidian. Since trade and communication are viewed as being all-important for the rise of Maya society, the second model is not all that divorced from the first model and, in fact, the two have been conjoined (Rathje 1977:379–381). Both of these models for the evolution and expansion of Maya society, however, are clearly out-of-sync with the growing body of archaeological data. Recent archaeology in the Southern Lowlands has demonstrated that large-scale growth, represented by the development of huge Preclassic centers at El Mirador (Dahlin 1984; Matheny 1986) and smaller ones at Cerros (Freidel 1979), Lamanai (Pendergast 1981), and Tikal (Culbert 1977), preceded the advent of "Teotihuacán" related forces in the Maya area. The fact that these large sites prospered without the stela/altar cult also presents problems for Rathje's core/buffer model of Maya development, for the esoteric knowledge the Maya were supposedly trading out was only in the process of being developed by the Maya themselves. It is perhaps more appropriate to view Maya development with a less materialistic approach.

Although trade is important in any society, it is surely the simple *contact* between societies and the resulting political exigencies that lead to the development of new cultural patterns. These patterns, however, are formulated within the preexisting ideological framework. Thus, if the Maya were in fact concerned with cyclical time throughout their history, the impact of such a fatalistic belief in the repetition of events should be visible in their prehistory. Archaeologically, this does in fact seem to be the case; much of the Maya "rise and fall" appears in a cyclical fashion that is apparently tied to the passage of the Short Count, particularly as seen in Katun 8 Ahau, the Katun of Change.

8.7.0.0.0 (A.D. 179)

The earliest Katun 8 Ahau to be reviewed here is 8.7.0.0.0. Although technically before recorded Southern Lowland Maya hieroglyphic prehistory—the earliest known monument date from the Lowlands is from Tikal Stela 29 at 8.12.14.8.15 (A.D. 292)—the 8.7.0.0.0 date is significant in an ideational framework, for it does indeed effectively denote the shift in power from the primary Late Preclassic site of El Mirador to the primary Early Classic site of Tikal. Why El Mirador disappears before the Classic Period and why Tikal fully emerges can at least partially be suggested by the passage of the fitful Katun 8 Ahau.

It is clear, however, that within 100 years after 8.7.0.0.0 (i.e., by 8.12.0.0.0) Tikal had come into contact with Teotihuacán or its allies, as had Uaxactún (see Laporte and Fialko 1987). It is in fact unclear whether the development of a Maya "state" at Tikal was primary or secondary in its nature. Surely, however, the early contact between the Maya Lowland area and Teotihuacán was *not* due to the core's lack of obsidian, salt, and hard stone. Rather, politics were at play. These political forces seemed to have transformed Maya society by the end of the Early Classic Period by placing an expanded societal emphasis on lineage ancestor worship (A. Chase 1985a:38). Yet the ideological underpinnings of cyclical time continued.

9.0.0.0.0 (A.D. 435)

The next passage of a Katun 8 Ahau in 9.0.0.0.0 ushered in a major "revolution" in the Maya region: rather than having only one primary site, Tikal, several others came into existence following this Katun of Change. It is also apparent that Tikal often had a direct interest in the sites that were adopting the full core ceremonial complex following the cycle change. Sharer (Morley, Brainerd, and Sharer 1983:111–113) has pointed out that Tikal was involved in the dynastic affairs of Yaxchilán by A.D. 475 (9.2.0.0.0), some forty years before the site first exhibited an emblem glyph (on Stela 27 at 9.4.0.0.0), and was also involved in the affairs of Copán by A.D. 500, some sixty years before the appearance of an emblem glyph at this site. This therefore raises the possibility that some, if not all, of these first expansion sites had formed alliances, or minimally relationships, with Tikal to aid them in exploring and using their newly acquired status. It is indeed possible that certain of these sites' dynasties were set into motion by either colonists or direct intervention from Tikal.

While Tikal reached new heights prior to 9.0.0.0.0, perhaps through its direct or indirect connection with Teotihuacán, its initial Maya heritage caught up with the site after this date. Rather than reverting to Rathje's economic model to explain the development of the Maya area following 9.0.0.0.0, I would rather employ an ideological model. The Katun 8 Ahau that occurred in 9.0.0.0.0 was one of great significance. Even if outlying "buffer-zone" sites had previously been cowed by almighty Tikal, several took heart and followed the fortunes of the Katun of Change. Thus, what may be termed the "first expansion" of Classic Maya sites took place (see fig. 3). These sites included Copán and Quiriguá far to the southeast, which erected their initial monuments in 9.1.10.0.0 (Copán Stela 20) and 9.2.3.8.0 (Quiriguá Stela 21), respectively; Piedras Negras, Altar de Sacrificios, and Yaxchilán to the west and southwest at 9.0.0.0.0, 9.1.0.0.0, and 9.4.0.0.0, respectively; Oxkintok and Calakmul to the north at 9.2.0.0.0 and 9.4.0.0.0, respectively; and Naranjo and Caracol to the east at 9.2.0.0.0 and 9.4.0.0.0, respectively. Note,

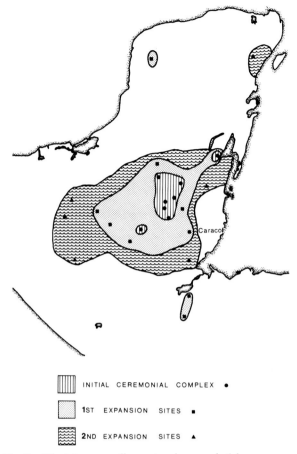

INITIAL CEREMONIAL COMPLEX •

1ST EXPANSION SITES ▪

2ND EXPANSION SITES ▲

*Fig. 3   The Maya area illustrating the spread of the core cere-
monial complex, first to primary expansion sites after 9.0.0.0.0
and then to secondary expansion sites after 9.7.0.0.0 (map
by Arlen F. Chase, courtesy Caracol Archaeological Project,
University of Central Florida).*

however, that all of these sites previously existed, but
did not exhibit the full core ceremonial complex until
after 9.0.0.0.0.

This first expansion of sites represents the initial spread
of the full Maya ceremonial complex out of the heartland sites of Tikal, Uaxactún, Yaxhá, Xultun, and perhaps Balakbal. This expansion was partially due to the
success of the Lowland Maya area and its buffer zone during the Early Classic and to the ideological climate
allowed by the Katun 8 Ahau. First expansion sites emphasized their access to the trappings of cyclical time. At
Caracol, this is clearly seen in the giant Ahau altars that
are erected to commemorate katun endings. According
to Satterthwaite (1954), the earliest of these altars was
erected to commemorate Katun 9.2.0.0.0, some forty
years earlier than the first secure hieroglyphic date at
Caracol.

As if buoyed by their success in establishing themselves at the end of the Early Classic Period, many of
the first expansion sites bridge the time between the

Early and Late Classic periods and are apparently responsible for the "Maya hiatus." The Maya hiatus, as
traditionally defined, is a period dating minimally from
9.5.0.0.0 (A.D. 534) to 9.7.10.0.0 (Mathews 1985a:31)
or 9.8.0.0.0 (A.D. 593; Proskouriakoff 1950:111; Willey
1974, 1977:397) when few stelae are known from the
Lowland Maya core. The exact dating for the end of the
hiatus is open to debate. Most authorities agree on beginning the hiatus at about 9.5.0.0.0; the end of the
hiatus, however, varies as to site and may extend at least
up until 9.11.0.0.0 (A.D. 652) in the core area (Coggins
1979:48). For Tikal, Coggins (1979:38) would start the
Middle Classic at about 9.2.10.0.0, corresponding with
a time of "political unrest" and, more importantly, the
loss of "elite goods imported from the Mexican Highlands" at the site; she would end the Middle Classic
at Tikal at 9.12.10.0.0 (see also Haviland, in press). Because of the lack of monument erection, the lack of construction activities, and the lack of rich burials in the
core during this era, the general tenet has been to view
the hiatus as a period of general decline for the Maya as a
whole. In fact, it would now appear that the reverse may
be true, for during the Maya hiatus the greatest areal
expansion of the Maya realm, at least in terms of epigraphic texts, took place. This is witnessed by the emergence of what may be termed "secondary expansion"
sites (see fig. 3) such as Toniná, Pusilha, Palenque, and
Cobá (i.e., ca. 9.8.0.0.0 to 9.9.0.0.0) at the precise
moment that what is traditionally recognized as the Late
Classic Period was coming into being.

The Maya hiatus in the core area was undoubtedly
caused by the emergence of first expansion sites after
9.0.0.0.0. At Caracol, the mechanisms for this so-called
hiatus are visible in Altar 21 (fig. 1; appendix) which
makes it abundantly clear that Caracol was either directly responsible for Tikal's "hiatus" or, minimally,
played a large part in it. Although Tikal may have a
"hiatus," the rest of the Maya area does not. Altar 21 at
Caracol notes a series of relationships and events with
Tikal going back to the 9.5.19.1.2 accession of Lord Water; an early undated relationship with Tikal is also recorded on Caracol Stela 15 (Glyph Block C13). Stephen
Houston made preliminary readings of this new monument and noted an "axe" event by Tikal against Caracol
on 9.6.2.1.11 followed by a "war" event by Caracol
against Tikal at 9.6.8.4.2 (see appendix). This dating
corresponds with the existence (or demise) of Double-
Bird at Tikal, the last known Tikal ruler prior to the so-
called hiatus. It is therefore evident, at least from Caracol's standpoint, why Tikal suffers a "setback in the
6th century" leading to tomb furnishings described as
"impoverished" (Coggins 1975; Morley, Brainerd, and
Sharer 1983:115). Once Lord Water of Caracol stripped
the Tikal core of its mystic abilities, it was possible for
the stela and altar cult to gain its greatest areal extent.

The disturbed nature of Tikal's archaeological record
during the Maya hiatus may be even more directly
related to Caracol than has been previously thought.

Caracol may, in fact, have been responsible either completely or partially for the ancient breakage of Tikal's Early Classic monuments, for what better way is there to demonstrate your disdain for a conquered city than to destroy its symbols of dominance and religion, the monuments of revered rulers? Satterthwaite (1958:75) noted that his "minimum date for the breakage" of monuments at Tikal was between 9.4.13.0.0 and 9.7.0.0.0. This correlates rather nicely with the 9.6.8.4.2 date for Caracol's war at Tikal. Shook (1957:45), in fact, had previously suggested that some of the breakage of Tikal stelae might have been due to violent action and that this action "may have been responsible for the end of the Early Classic period and perhaps for the hiatus in the known sequence of inscriptions at Tikal."

While Caracol may have been directly responsible for the core's demise and indirectly responsible for the spread of the core ceremonial cult, significant differences exited between the primary and secondary expansion sites that arose following 9.0.0.0.0. While the primary expansion sites all seem to have been at least initially influenced by Tikal, the secondary expansion sites were freed by the sudden lack of core constriction through Tikal's conquest to follow new patterns that would usher them into the Late Classic Period. The initial expansion sites, however, for the most part relied on the established formulas that had been regularized during the Early Classic Period in their attempt to persevere in dealing with their world. This is clearly seen at Caracol in the persistence of Early Classic patterns into the Late Classic Period, particularly in the retention of Early Classic traditions of painting in tombs—black-on-red and red-on-white. This would be expected in a conservative religious environment dealing with death rituals. Thus, at Caracol, it is not surprising to find Long Count tomb dates in three instances dating between 9.7.0.0.0 and 9.10.5.0.0 and a Calendar Round date of 9.13.3.15.16. However, Caracol's fortunes reversed dramatically with the next cycle of time.

9.13.0.0.0 (A.D. 692)

The 9.13.0.0.0 8 Ahau Katun of Change saw the rise again of core area sites such as Tikal. Even though Tikal explodes onto the scene immediately after the initiation of the new cycle (Coggins 1979:48; Puleston 1979:67), it operated within a drastically reduced political arena. No longer was a single site to control or, perhaps more correctly, dominate Maya politics; instead, many different sites vied for that power. Indeed, with the advent of the new Katun of Change, many different sites and rulers filled the political arena. Schele and Miller (1986: 209) noted that "after the completion of katun 8 Ahau (9.13.0.0.0, A.D. 692), both the pace of warfare and the status of the captives increased. Everywhere, kings faced kings in battle, and so, inevitably, many fell in combat and were taken captive."

Changes also occurred in other areas as well. Iconographic innovations made at such first expansion sites as Caracol were adopted by other core sites following the advent of the new cycle. Stone, Reents, and Coffman (1985:267) noted: "Artistically, many innovations introduced by the Middle Classic Caracol sculpture appear to influence other sites, notably Tikal and Naranjo, as early as 9.8.0.0.0. By 9.13.0.0.0 these influences on monumental sculpture such as the dwarf, the trifigure group, the Oliva shell girdle, and Giant Ahau Altars are in widespread use across the Maya region. But by this time during the Late Classic period, the pictorial and hieroglyphic record at Caracol appears to have sunk into relative obscurity." Proskouriakoff (1950:111), as if foreseeing the impact of Caracol on Maya prehistory, noted that "the break in the sequence and the changed artistic mode seem to be a reflection of some momentous historical event that disturbed the normal artistic development and was followed by a restoration of order and a new pulse of creative activity." It would appear that the cyclical change in 9.13.0.0.0 again had major repercussions in Maya prehistory, especially for Caracol.

Coggins (1979:46) noted that the post-9.12.0.0.0 revival of Tikal may have been through rulers who "may have come to power at Tikal through dynastic connections with a southeastern Peten site near Pusilha" after 9.9.0.0.0. I have argued elsewhere (A. Chase and D. Chase 1987b:61) that the father of Tikal Ruler A, or "Ah Cacao" (cf. Jones 1977), may have in fact come from the Caracol polity. This could be interpreted as an attempt by Caracol to manipulate Tikal's ruling dynasty prior to the onset of the next Katun 8 Ahau; this may also be linked with Caracol's conquest of Naranjo in 9.9.18.16.3, for Naranjo is one of the first sites courted by the Tikal/Dos Pilas lineage at the onset of the Late Classic Period. A woman (or women), probably from Dos Pilas, is celebrated on four stelae at Naranjo between 9.13.10.0.0 and 9.14.0.0.0 (Houston and Mathews 1985:14; Marcus 1976:165). This emphasis on, and presumably by, Dos Pilas and, indirectly, Tikal at Naranjo may be interpreted as directly reflecting Tikal's reemergence to power with the new Katun 8 Ahau as well as the eclipsing of Caracol's former sway with the advent of the new cycle. New ties with the site of Cobá far to the north (Marcus 1976:166) also may have strengthened Tikal's political base, at the same time eliminating any alliance or connection previously held by Caracol.

It may be posited that Tikal physically destroyed the symbols of power at the site of Caracol either directly or indirectly with the onset of the new cycle. If a relationship may be established between conquest and stelae destruction, as has been suggested above, then the "abnormal stelae placement" of Caracol's Stelae 3, 15, and 16 and possibly Stelae 13, 14, 21, and Altar 7—as well as other monuments—may be indicative of retaliation by Tikal against Caracol after 9.13.10.0.0, if Stela

A. Chase

21 can be used to judge the dating of such an event. This would indeed have been a capping event for Tikal's spectacular rise at the onset of the Late Classic Period and would have reaffirmed the inevitable cycle of time.

Even though time may have dictated the repetition of events and actions, the stage for these actions and events had spiraled onto a new plane between 9.0.0.0.0 and 9.13.0.0.0. Whereas Tikal had been the dominant center in the Maya area prior to 9.0.0.0.0, it could not enjoy such absolute power after 9.13.0.0.0. The Late Classic Maya were not unified politically or economically, but were rather a series of independent states. Perhaps for this reason, there are problems with attempting to apply a single cosmological model to attempt to explain the organization of the Late Classic Maya, as Marcus (1973, 1976) did. While larger "alliances" or geographically diverse gatherings may have existed, such as the one recorded on Copán Stela A for 9.15.0.0.0 involving individuals from Tikal, Copán, Palenque, and perhaps Calakmul or El Perú, no four sites represent the totality of the Maya area. Yaxchilán was clearly a military power at this time and Caracol was also very much alive again by 9.17.10.0.0. In fact, the lack of a unified Southern Lowland Maya area may account for the skewing found in the 9.15.0.0.0 text at Copán in the directions associated with each of the four emblem glyphs. The problems inherent in attempting to apply pan-Maya directionality to the spatial world of the Late Classic Maya are also evident in A. Miller's (1974) directional model, in which he associated east with rebirth and the site of Tulum while associating west with death and the site of Palenque. The purposeful and controlled organization of the Maya area, which must be assumed for such cosmological models, clearly did not exist during the Late Classic Period.

10.6.0.0.0 (A.D. 948)

The final Katun of Change in 10.6.0.0.0 saw a Lowland Maya area that had already largely turned away from many of its traditional patterns. As already noted, Puleston (1979) adequately dealt with the ideological aspects of the collapse.[2] The real question that must be raised for this katun is the relationship, if one exists, between the hiatus and the collapse. Willey (1974) once called the "Classic Maya hiatus" a "rehearsal for the Maya collapse," thus indicating that the events that caused these two recognized periods of Maya prehistory were founded in similar conditions. Willey (1974:427) felt that "the hiatus and the collapse were phenomena with a similar cause. This cause was the severance of the symbiotic relationships between Maya civilization and the other Mesoamerican civilizations that were contemporaneous with it."

Although Willey's logic followed a host of models that have all since been severely reviewed and revised, including Thompson's (1927, 1954) peasant revolt hypothesis

(Willey 1974:421, 427), Rathje's core-buffer zone model (Willey 1974:424–427), and his own models for invasion and foreign impact on Maya society (Willey 1974: 423, 427), the linkage Willey established between the hiatus and the collapse remains in the current literature. Willey (1977:397) refined his initial statement somewhat by noting that "the Classic Hiatus" was "a southern phenomenon and, especially, a Peten phenomenon." Although still tied to a model that inexorably linked the Maya to Teotihuacán, Willey (1977:406) did foresee, to some degree, the Caracol data by wondering if "Teotihuacan influence" stopped "because of a locally generated crisis within the Maya Lowlands." With the reduction of the Maya "hiatus" to core sites dealing with newly founded buffer-zone strongmen, many of the previously held models that attempt to explain this era are in need of revision, especially those that view this era as representative of a "breakdown" in the Southern Lowlands. Yet the linkage between both the hiatus and the collapse remains just as strong as when first posited by Willey (1974), but for different reasons. Relationships between these two eras can especially be seen in a consideration of politics, warfare, and cyclical time, for in essence the collapse reflects the inability of the Southern Lowlands to deal with stresses from the Northern Lowlands (D. Chase and A. Chase 1982; A. Chase 1985a; A. Chase and D. Chase, in press)—stresses that took advantage of the approaching Katun of Change. Caracol clearly recognized some of these forces and attempted either to counter them or to take control of them as the new Katun 8 Ahau began to approach (A. Chase 1985d). The events of the time, however, proved to be too much for the majority of the larger sites in the Southern Lowlands and led to their eventual abandonment, quite likely in accord with an ideological system that had already predicted such an event.

Conclusions

Cyclical time was recognized by the Classic Period Maya and in fact ordained certain aspects of their prehistory. Caracol, a first expansion site, especially illuminates the crucial era that occurred between the Katuns 8 Ahau of 9.0.0.0.0 and 9.13.0.0.0. Rather than illustrating a decline or "Maya hiatus," Caracol aptly shows that the fringe of the Maya heartland gained control of the Maya area and dedicated the beginning of the transition between the Early and Late Classic periods sometime shortly after 9.0.0.0.0. By 9.13.0.0.0, the initial core area had again begun ascendancy, probably by emphasizing this particular Katun 8 Ahau for political expediency. Perhaps because the previous Katun 8 Ahau had been so emphasized, the next led to a requisite decline of the Maya area and a major shift in patterns that ushered in the Postclassic Period. As expected, according to the tenets of cyclical time and in anticipation of the upcoming Katun 8 Ahau, Caracol began an upswing in its monumental record circa 9.18.0.0.0, but for naught: its stela record ends in 10.1.10.0.0. In closing, it is noted that the Maya preoccupation with cyclical time, when applied to the extant archaeology, can show that, in seeking matters of cause and effect in overall Maya prehistory, ideological factors must be consulted because they often contrapose materialistic interpretations.

Appendix: Caracol Altar 21

STEPHEN D. HOUSTON

On 22 February 1986, a circular stone monument was found by Arlen Chase in the central corridor of the Group A ball court (fig. 2). Subsequent excavations revealed that this monument, designated Altar 21, contained well over 160 glyphic compounds, making it the longest hieroglyphic text yet discovered in Belize. In the report that follows, this find is described and its glyphic content discussed.

Altar 21 is located on the floor of the ball court at the juncture of two axes: the transverse axis of Structures A11 and A12 and the perpendicular axis along the center line of the court. On present evidence the monument appears to be the only sculpture in the court, although another ball court carving, an evident transplant from the ball court in Group B, was found on the surface just southeast of Structure A12. It is remotely possible that further stripping of the court will uncover additional monuments.

Although carved from dense limestone, Altar 21 is now in only fair to poor condition. Natural weathering and the passage of logging trucks to the Group A aguada have conspired to break the stone into six major pieces and innumerable smaller fragments, as well as to abrade into illegibility as much as half of the hieroglyphic text. Nonetheless, it is still possible to establish the shape and dimensions of the monument. The sides of Altar 21 are convex, as is the top, which slopes gently from the center to a circumferential groove that encircles the inscription. The diameter of the altar is 127.5 cm; the maximum depth of carved relief is close to 1 cm. The absolute orientation of Altar 21 can be seen in the rendering of the monument (fig. 2).

The Inscription: General Observations

The glyphs on Altar 21 are disposed in a circular arrangement (in double columns, four rows deep) around a giant day sign with numerical coefficient. The top of this day sign points to the beginning of the text, an Initial Series, which in turn lies in the direction of the transverse axis of Structure A12.

It can be appreciated that a circular text, especially one the length of the inscription on Altar 21, presents an enormous compositional challenge to the ancient scribe: glyphic phrasing must be thought out very carefully if the text is to end where it begins. The challenge is compounded by the wedged columns, which do not permit the uniform placement of compounds of equal size. It is fair to say that the scribe(s) responsible for Altar 21 more than met these challenges. The text does not display the cramped spacing that characterizes the final clauses of a poorly planned inscription, such as Lintel 10 from Yaxchilán. The scribe also seems to have handled the problem of attenuated columns by the simple expedient of reducing to one the number of compounds in the innermost rows. This measure ensures that such compounds retain the same proportions as glyphs in the outermost rows.

The Inscription: Chronology

Table 1 summarizes the chronology of Altar 21. It can be seen from the table that many details of dating are far from understood. In general, this ambiguity stems from the eroded condition of the inscription, which at points permits little more than speculative ligatures between dates.

The first Secondary series (SS1) on Altar 21 is a useful example of both speculative reconstruction and the interpretive problems that attend an eroded text. To begin with, the Secondary Series does not appear legibly in the inscription, so its existence must be taken on faith. (The *tun* sign at G1 may form part of SS1; its subfixes, T585a:126, are appropriate for a distance number, although its prefixation and placement in the text are not.) As an alternative possibility, it may be that two Secondary Series exist in place of SS1, in which case a third date must also occur between Dates A and B. This notation has much to recommend it. For one, the great length of the Initial Series clause (fully a quarter of the inscription) suggests that the clause was once divided into at least two parts. For another, the parentage statement at J1–L1, which names Lord Kan I and his consort, signals that Lord Water figures importantly in the

A. Chase

Table 1. Summary of Chronology for Caracol Altar 21

Position	Date	Long Count	Calendar Round	Event	Transcription	Individuals	Other References
A1–?; ?	Date A 1S SS1	9. 7.14.10.*8 (1.15. 9. 6)	(3 Lamat 16 Uo)	Birth	?	*Lord Kan II *< Lord Water (Lady) (Lord Kan I)	Stela 3:A17a–A17b; NAR Panel 1: A1–B1
K2b–L2a N1b	Date B SS2	(9. 5.19. 1. 2) 16.18	9 Ik 5 Uo	Accession	T644a.181:126– T53.229:747a:24	Lord Kan I < Tikal Lord	Stela 6:A1–A3
N3–M4 O1	Date C SS3	(9. 6. 0. 0. 0) 2. 1.11	9 Ahau 3 Uayeb	Period Ending	T679a.528.116:713a	*Lord Water	Stela 6:A7–B7a; Altar 5:A1
P1 R1b–Q2a	Date D SS4	(9. 6. 2. 1.11) 6. 2.11	6 Chuen 19 Pop	Axe Event	T333.?	*Lord Water < Tikal Lord	
Q2b–R2a V3–U4	Date E SS5	(9. 6. 8. 4. 2) *9.12.18	7 Ik 0 Zip	War	T137v.510baf.137v:?	*Tikal Lord < *Lord Water < Tikal Lord	
W2b–X2a W3	Date F SS6	(9. 6.17.17. 0) 3.19	8 Ahau 13 Mac	?	?	*Lord Water	
X3–W4 Y3–Z4	Date G SS7	(9. 6.18. 2.19) 1.15. 1	9 Cauac 12 Kayab	?	?	*Lord Water	
A'1b–B'1b A'2–B'2	Date H SS8	(9. 7. 0.)0. 0 ?. 2. 3. 8.13	7 Ahau 3 Kankin	Period Ending	T1:528.116:713a	*Lord Water	Stela 6:C7; Altar 6:A1
A'1–?	Date I	?	?				
B'4–C'1a	Date J	?(9. 7.19.10. 0)	*1 Ahau 3 Pop	Ball Game	IX?:ms:23	*Lord Water	
E'1a	Date K	(9.)8. 0. 0. 0	5 Ahau 3 Ch'en	Period Ending, 8 Katun	T218:VIII.28:548:142	*Lord Water	Stela 1:A1–D1; Stela 6:C8; Altar 1:A1
G'1	Date L	?(9.10. 0. 0. 0)	*1 Ahau (8 Kayab)	Period Ending	0	*Lord Kan II	Stela 3:E7a–E7b; Altar 19:A1; NAR Panel 1:G2–H2; NAR H5

Note: The numeration of glyph blocks follows standard practice in that the alphabetic and numeric series begin with the opening date and proceed from left to right (or clockwise, as in this instance). The giant day sign at the center of the altar design is placed for chronological reasons at the end of the series, a placement that contravenes conventional reading order in Classic altar texts. Asterisks * mark unattested but reconstructible forms. < indicates a nonparental relationship; parentheses enclose parental names. Thompson numbers record the glyphic composition of the verbs.

Initial Series clause. Yet we have already seen in table 1 that the Initial Series is the birth date of Lord Kan II. Since Lord Water would probably not list his immediate ancestry were he not the principal figure in the clause, it seems likely that two clauses rather than one interpose between Dates A and B; one clause refers to Lord Kan II, the other to Lord Water and his parents.

There are other problems with the chronology of Altar 21. For example, no legible distance numbers connect Dates J, K, and L. In the case of the first two dates, this is only a minor problem: other clues allow the dates to be fixed in the Long Count. But with the third date the issue becomes crucial. To judge from the giant Ahau day sign and its final position in the inscription, Date L is likely to be a component of Altar 21's Dedicatory Date, which presumably refers to the altar's positioning in the Group A ball court, or perhaps to its date of consecration.

In the absence of a distance number, Date L must be reconstructed by other means. The coefficient of the giant Ahau day sign (here in headbanded form) is as good a place to start as any. The number of the day sign is most likely 1, as can be deduced from the space-filler. Given that all giant Ahau altars at Caracol apparently bear katun-ending dates (specified explicitly on Altars 14 and 17), it would seem that the Dedicatory Date of Altar 21 must be 9.10.0.0.0 1 Ahau 8 Kayab. This date falls squarely in the reign of Lord Kan II, whose birth date is recorded in the Initial Series of Altar 21. The references to Lord Kan II in both the beginning and end of the altar inscription suggest that the placement of 1 Ahau is correct: all other dates on the altar refer instead to his predecessors.

The Inscription: Content

Many of the events recorded on Altar 21 are attested elsewhere at Caracol (table 1). Nonetheless, several important ones are not. The first of these is an "axe" event (O2), which is associated with war and possibly with decapitation (cf. Altar 13:A21 and its image of a decapitated head; also, Adams 1971: fig. 94b; Robicsek and Hales 1981: fig. 22c; and the Madrid Codex, pp. 97–98). This event took place under the auspices of, or perhaps in the territory of, a lord from Tikal. Unfortunately, the name of the Tikal lord is almost completely obliterated.

A second event (R2b) involves war, but in the sense of major conflict rather than skirmish or ambuscade. It is the so-called shell-star event (Riese 1984b), which is now known to coincide in large part with momentous junctures in the synodic cycle of Venus (Lounsbury 1982). The form of the event at Caracol is aberrant: a full Venus sign (T510b) replaces the more usual version (T2v). Another example of a shell-star verb with full Venus glyph appears at D1a on Piedras Negras Stela 12 (Schele 1982:103) in reference to war waged by the dynasty of Piedras Negras against Pomoná, a site in Tabasco, Mexico. Regardless of its form, the shell-star on Altar 21 is the earliest yet documented in Classic inscriptions.

The shell-star event at Caracol apparently records war against Tikal, albeit in an unconventional reference. In common practice the main sign of the victimized site occurs singly, that is, without "water group" and *ahaw* titles. By contrast, the verb on Altar 21 adjoins a full Tikal emblem, indicating, perhaps, that the war affected not so much the site of Tikal as its dynasty or possibly a key member of the royal family. Presumably the effect was still profound: not a single stela at Tikal can be conclusively assigned to the period between the shell-star event and the Late Classic (Jones and Satterthwaite 1982: table 5; but note Tikal Stela 17). In addition, many Early Classic monuments at Tikal witnessed systematic violence during this period (Satterthwaite 1958:75; Christopher Jones, personal communication, 1986), a fact perhaps consistent with a successful campaign by Caracol against the Tikal dynasty (see discussion in text above).

It is worth noting in this connection that a similar gap of datable monuments characterizes the site of Naranjo after its apparent defeat by Caracol (fig. 4; Sosa and Reents 1980:10). Nonetheless, both this event and the incident recorded on Altar 21 took place (if in fact we can rely on the historical veracity of the altar text) during or just after the "hiatus," an epoch of general debilitation in monument erection. Caracol may simply have displayed opportunism rather than great strategic ability in vanquishing two prominent yet perhaps ailing centers. Possibly the martial success of Caracol contributed to its sustained activity during the hiatus.

As might be expected, the shell-star event against Tikal possesses astronomical significance. In the Julian Calendar, and according to the compelling 584285 correlation advocated by Floyd Lounsbury, this event falls on 29 April 562, or the first stationary point of Venus. Relatively few Classic dates coincide with this point (Lounsbury 1982:163), although Lounsbury suggested that 29 April 562 would have been a useful occasion to detect slight movements in Venus: from the perspective

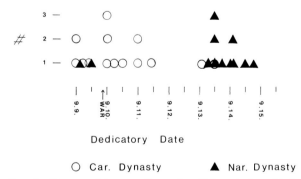

Fig. 4 Pattern of dates at Caracol and Naranjo (graphic by Stephen D. Houston, courtesy Caracol Archaeological Project, University of Central Florida).

A. Chase

of naked-eye astronomy the planet was in Taurus, midway between the Pleiades, and close to Aldebaran and Beta, all bright stars that would afford a visual framework for minute observation. The high location of epicentral Caracol may have also assisted precise astronomical measurement.

The clause that follows the shell-star event is a long one, but only a few items can be recognized: a relationship glyph (R3), probably followed by the name of Lord Water; a possible bloodletting sign (S1a, Peter Mathews, personal communication, 1985; cf. Caracol Stela 6:B12, Tikal Stela 31:C23, and perhaps Tikal Stela 12:D1); a second Tikal emblem (S2b), and a "Q-Site" emblem (U2a), erroneously identified by some as the emblem of El Perú (Schele 1984a:24).

A final event on Altar 21 bears on the nature of the monument and the question of its primary context. This verb appears at C'1b and is unquestionably a variant of the ball court glyph (cf. Schele 1982:13). As stated above, Altar 21 has been appended to the altar series at Caracol, although this may be misleading: the presence of the ball court glyph and the location of Altar 21 in the center of the Group A ball court suggest that the altar is a ball court marker, most likely in primary context. Unfortunately, a comparison of altar and marker diameters does not speak strongly for this conclusion (tables 2 and 3; quantitative information from Beetz and Satterthwaite 1981): Altar 21 is small for its class, yet considerably larger than the range of marker diameters (cf. .74 diameter for the center marker of Ball Court II-B at Copán).

Table 2. Caracol Altar Diameters through Time

Long Count Date	Number	Diameter	
9. 3. 0. 0. 0	Alt. 4	1.77	(with Stela 9)
9. 5. 0. 0. 0	Alt. 14	1.82	
9. 6. 0. 0. 0	Alt. 5	1.93	
9. 7. 0. 0. 0	Alt. 6	2.25	
9. 8. 0. 0. 0	Alt. 1	2.07	(with Stela 1)
9. 9. 0. 0. 0	Alt. 11	1.68	
9. 9. 0. 0. 0	Alt. 15	2.06	
9.10. 0. 0. 0	Alt. 19	1.81	(with Stela 11)
9.10. 0. 0. 0	Alt. 21	1.275	
9.11. 0. 0. 0	Alt. 17	1.36	
9.11. 0. 0. 0	Alt. 7	1.38	(with Stela 14)
9.17. 0. 0. 0	Alt. 2	1.17	
9.18. 0. 0. 0	Alt. 3	1.78	
9.19. 0. 0. 0	Alt. 12	1.58	
10. 0. 0. 0. 0	Alt. 13	1.60	
10. 0. 0. 0. 0	Alt. 16	1.07	
10. 0.19. 6.14	Alt. 10	1.15	(with Stela 17)
10. 1. 0. 0. 0	Alt. 18	1.60	
	Alt. 8	(not an altar, plain stone)	
	Alt. 9	(not an altar, plain stone)	
	Alt. 20	(reused stela fragment?)	
early Late Classic	BSc. 1	.69	(style date)
early Late Classic	BSc. 2	.69	(style date)

Table 3. Caracol Altar Diameters Ranked Independent of Time

Diameter	Number	Long Count Date	
1.07	Alt. 16	10. 0. 0. 0. 0	
1.15	Alt. 10	10. 0.19. 6.14	(with Stela 17)
1.17	Alt. 2	9.17. 0. 0. 0	
1.275	Alt. 21	9.10. 0. 0. 0	
1.36	Alt. 17	9.11. 0. 0. 0	
1.39	Alt. 7	9.11. 0. 0. 0	(with Stela 14)
1.58	Alt. 12	9.19. 0. 0. 0	
1.60	Alt. 13	10. 0. 0. 0. 0	
1.60	Alt. 18	10. 1. 0. 0. 0	
1.68	Alt. 11	9. 9. 0. 0. 0	
1.77	Alt. 4	9. 3. 0. 0. 0	(with Stela 9)
1.79	Alt. 3	9.18. 0. 0. 0	
1.81	Alt. 19	9.10. 0. 0. 0	(with Stela 11)
1.82	Alt. 14	9. 5. 0. 0. 0	
1.93	Alt. 5	9. 6. 0. 0. 0	
2.06	Alt. 15	9. 9. 0. 0. 0	
2.07	Alt. 1	9. 8. 0. 0. 0	(with Stela 1)
2.25	Alt. 6	9. 7. 0. 0. 0	
	Alt. 8	(not an altar, plain stone)	
	Alt. 9	(not an altar, plain stone)	
	Alt. 20	(reused stela fragment?)	
.61	BSc. 1	early Late Classic (style date)	
.69	BSc. 2	early Late Classic (style date)	

Concluding Comments

In both its content and its dates, Altar 21 is emblematic of Caracol's vitality during the hiatus. However, from the perspective of domestic affairs, the altar is intriguing rather for the apparent absence of any references to Lord Kan II's immediate predecessor, Lord Knot Ahau. The omission is systematic: in referring to the past on both this and other monuments Lord Kan II mentions only his connections with Lord Kan I and Lord Water. Indeed, Altar 21 represents little more than the glorification of Lord Water by a successor equally lucky in warfare. Further research is needed to explain why Lord Knot Ahau merited so little attention.

Notes

1. One of these causeways and its associated settlement patterns is being excavated and analyzed by Susan Jaeger of Southern Methodist University to determine the differences in interpretations garnered through a culturally defined, as opposed to an arbitrary, settlement transect. Her research has been partially supported by National Science Foundation Grant BNS-861996.

2. Other subsidiary katun cycles may have also held sway during the Classic era. Puleston (1979:68) viewed Katun 11 Ahau, occurring in 9.5.0.0.0 (A.D. 534) and 9.18.0.0.0 (A.D. 790) as being particularly significant in Tikal's history in that each ushered in a period of "impending decline" at that site. The opposite case would have been true at Caracol, where increased monument erection occurred after each Katun 11 Ahau. The fact that the Caracol monumental record reemerges in association with Katun 11 Ahau after an apparent hiatus in the middle of the Late Classic Period perhaps again exhibits the intertwined political histories that existed between Tikal and Caracol throughout the course of Classic Period Lowland Maya development.

Haviland (personal communication, 1986) sees another potential cycle at Tikal involving Katun 1 Ahau in 8.17.0.0.0 (A.D. 376), 9.10.0.0.0 (A.D. 633), and 10.3.0.0.0 (A.D. 889): "If Katun 8 Ahau was a time of establishment/re-establishment at Tikal, Katun 1 seems to have been the one of change, in the sense of 'undoing.'" No Katun 1 Ahau cycle is thus far evident in the Caracol data.

Acknowledgments

Both Diane Z. Chase, the co-director of the Caracol Project, and William A. Haviland have provided extensive comments on this paper, although not all of these have necessarily been followed; their efforts are, however, much appreciated. The excavations at Caracol during the 1985 and 1986 seasons, upon which this paper was based, were entirely funded by private donations augmented through the agencies and divisions of the University of Central Florida in Orlando. Subsequent field seasons at Caracol—undertaken during 1987 and 1988 with the support of private donations, the Institute of Maya Studies, and the Harry Frank Guggenheim Foundation—have not substantially modified the above commentary. Stephen Houston would like to thank Floyd Lounsbury for his help on astronomical matters and note that the names of Caracol rulers are taken, with some modifications, from Beetz and Satterthwaite (1981).

A. Chase

Dedication Ceremonies at Chichén Itzá: The Glyphic Evidence

RUTH KROCHOCK
SOUTHERN METHODIST UNIVERSITY

In 1982, David Kelley suggested that the pattern of dating on the inscribed hieroglyphic lintels at Chichén Itzá signaled an emphasis on the structures themselves rather than on the individual rulers mentioned in the texts. His explanation is that these are the dates of dedication ceremonies for the buildings at Chichén Itzá (Kelley 1982:2). In this paper, I present new paraphrases and commentary for parallel phrases that appear in the inscriptions of Chichén Itzá. If accepted, this new evidence will confirm Kelley's hypothesis.

The parallel phrases in question appear fourteen times (Kelley 1982:5) on eleven different lintels from Temple of the Initial Series, Temple of the Four Lintels, Las Monjas, and Temple of the Three Lintels—structures whose dates fall within a time span of three years. These phrases generally begin with a date phrase that designates the Calendar Round, a particular tun, and a day Ahau that identifies the end of a particular katun (Thompson 1937). The date on the Initial Series Lintel underside reads 10.2.9.1.9 9 Muluc 7 Zac (Thompson 1937:186). On the lintel's front, tun 10 of [katun] 1 Ahau is recorded (10.2.0.0.0 ends on 1 Ahau and the date 10.2.9.1.9 falls within the 10th tun of that katun). The dates of the Temple of the Four Lintels are 10.2.12.1.8 9 Lamat 11 Yax (on lintels 1, 3, and 4; Thompson 1937:186), and 10.2.12.2.4 12 Kan 7 Zac (on lintel 2 and possibly 4a; Thompson 1937:186; Kelley 1982:table 1). On the fronts of lintels 2 and 3 the thirteenth tun of [katun] 1 Ahau is designated. The lintels of Temple of the Three Lintels bear no Calendar Round date. On Lintel 3, however, the tenth tun of [katun] 1 Ahau is recorded, as it is on the Initial Series Lintel, so the date probably falls between 10.2.9.0.0 and 10.2.9.17.19 (Krochock 1985:6). The seven lintels of Las Monjas record only one date: 10.2.10.11.17 8 Manik 15 Uo. The dates of all four of the structures discussed above fall within three years of each other.

In each of the fourteen parallel phrases, the date phrase constitutes the first clause and a verb generally follows as the beginning of the second clause (figs. 4, 5, and 6). Kelley read this verb phonetically as *u-sotz/sutz-*

lu-na-k'al-al but did not propose a possible meaning or paraphrase (Kelley 1982:5). I would like to suggest some alternative readings based on recent work by David Stuart (1986a, 1986b) and Linda Schele (personal communication, 1986). Stuart suggested that the bat sign (T756) substitutes for the fire sign (T563a) in the Primary Standard Sequence and has suggested a phonetic value of *tz'i* for both signs. He read the compound T1.563a:585a as *u tz'ib*, "his writing" (Stuart 1986a). James Fox previously observed the same compound in the Madrid Codex, 23c and offered the reading *u tz'ib* or "his writing" (Justeson 1984a:344). Stuart (1986b) observed that the so-called "*lu*-bat" glyph replaces *u tz'ib* when the pot on which the Primary Standard Sequence appears is carved rather than painted. He suggests that its function is related to *u tz'ib* but in relationship to the act of carving. Since Stuart also suggested a value of *tz'i* for the bat glyph because of its substitution for T563, the "*lu*-bat" glyph may represent a word such as *tz'i-l(u)* or *tz'i-l(i)*. The word *tz'il* by itself does not appear in the *Diccionario Cordemex* (Barrera-Vásquez 1980) but the word *Tz'ilba* is glossed with this definition: "**Tz'ilba** [Trasladar]; ts'ilba hu'n: cosa trasladada 3: trasladar [imitar] escritura 2. ts'ilba 1: trasladar escritura o imitar 2,4: imitar 2,4,5,8" (Barrera-Vásquez 1980:885). This can be translated into English as "to transcribe or imitate writing." David Stuart's proposed meaning and phonetic value then begins to make very good sense because it may be related in form and meaning to the word *tz'ilba*.

The *u tz'il* is followed by the compound T23.683:102, which I believe reads phonetically *na-ah/ha-al* or *nahal*. T683, which Kelley read as *k'al*, is now accepted by most epigraphers as *ah* and/or *ha*. (Justeson and Campbell 1984:351). T102 has a proposed value that is generally accepted as *ki*. However, Fought's (1965) earlier value of *al* seems more appropriate here, since T178 *la* substitutes for T102 in one example of this compound (fig. 1). Most of the definitions for *nahal* translate as "salary," "earnings," "pitiable," "miserable," and "to touch inadvertently" (Barrera-Vásquez 1980:550–551) and therefore seem of little use to provide a reading for this glyph. An-

Temple of the
Four Lintels,
L.3, A2-B2

T178

Temple of the
Four Lintels,
L.4, B4-A5

T102

Fig. 1 *The Substitution of T178 la/al and T102 al. Temple of the Four Lintels, Chichén Itzá (drawing by Ruth Krochock).*

other possibility for the reading *nahal* is hidden in another definition in the *Diccionario Cordemex*: "**Nahal Sabak ti' Hu'un** 3: correr la tinta y cuando se escribe 5: correr y soltar la tinta 2: Nahal [Sabak] ti' lu'um 6: correr o soltar la tinta [por la tierra]" (Barrera-Vásquez 1980: 551). *Sabak* means "ink" and *hu'un* is a kind of tree whose name eventually evolved into the modern Yucatec word for paper. Here, the sense of the word *nahal* seems to approximate "flow" as in "flow of ink." If so, perhaps the *nahal* of the phrase *u tz'il nahal* means that the writing progressed, took place, or "flowed" in some way. Linda Schele hypothesized that the hieroglyphic inscriptions were first painted by hand with ink on the surface of the limestone before carving. Perhaps the "flow of ink" or "flow of writing" that may be implied here refers to this initial process of painting the glyphs on the stone for carving.

Another possible reading for *-nahal* was postulated by Barbara MacLeod (personal communication, 1986). She observed that two verbal endings in Yucatec, *-chahi* and *-chahal*, indicate the difference between the completive and incompletive aspect in that language. An example of the uses of these suffixes can be seen in the following sentences: *Sac-chah-i in nok'* or the completive aspect for "my clothes turned white" and *k-u sac-chah-al in nok'* or the incompletive aspect for "my clothes turn white." She believes that we may use this example as a precedent and thereby a possible explanation for the presence of the verbal ending *-nahal* in the hieroglyphs of Chichén Itzá. Further, she explained that in modern Yucatec the intransitivizing suffix *-nahi* exists in the completive aspect but the postulated ending *-nahal* has not survived for the incompletive aspect. Based on this pairing between the *-chahi* and *-chahal* endings in modern Yucatec, she believed we may assume that at one time the ending *-nahal* did exist in the incompletive aspect in Yucatec. The apparent use of *-nahal* as a verbal ending in the hieroglyphic texts of Chichén Itzá provides evidence for its existence in ancient times. If we can assume that the *-nahal* is an ancient Yucatec verbal suffix to indicate the incompletive aspect, we might read *u tz'ilnahal* as "it is

transcribed" or "it got transcribed" (MacLeod, personal communication, 1986). MacLeod's interpretation of *-nahal* makes such good sense that I favor it over the other possible meaning of *-nahal* as "flow."

If the reading of *u tz'ilnahal* as "it is transcribed" and its relationship to the word *tz'ilba*, "to transcribe or imitate writing," are accepted, I believe we can assume that the verb refers specifically to the transcription or carving of text on the lintel. In this way, the action of carving the lintel is the topic of this passage of text and, as Kelley suggested, refers to the completion of construction and thereby to the dedication of the structure.

Following the verbal phrase *u tz'ilnahal* is a compound that is spelled phonetically *u-pa-ca-ba* or *u pacab*. Kelley first read this compound as *ah pacab* or "he of the lintel or bench" since the word *pacab* is defined in the colonial Yucatec dictionaries as meaning "lintel" or "bench" (Kelley 1982:5). I believe that the pattern of phonetic substitution for the article that Kelley read *ah* warrants instead a reading of *u*. This would change Kelley's reading to "his/hers/its lintel" (see figs. 2 and 3 for a detail of the pattern of phonetic substitutions). If we can read this phrase as "his lintel," perhaps this would be one more case of the so-called name-tagging that Mathews (1979), Houston and Taube (n.d.), Justeson (1983), Stuart (1984d), and Schele have been discovering on

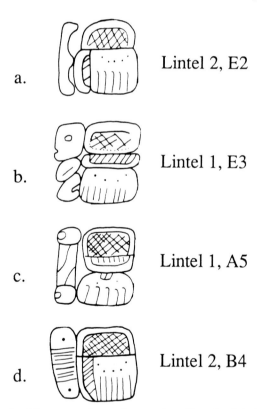

a. Lintel 2, E2

b. Lintel 1, E3

c. Lintel 1, A5

d. Lintel 2, B4

Fig. 2 *Phonetic spellings of* u pacab *on Temple of the Four Lintels, Chichén Itzá (a) L. 2, E2; (b) L. 1, E3; (c) L. 1, A5; (d) L. 2, B4 (drawing by Ruth Krochock).*

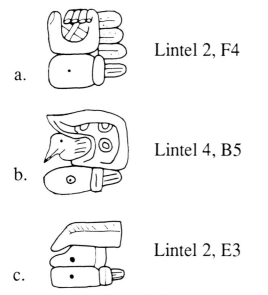

a. Lintel 2, F4

b. Lintel 4, B5

c. Lintel 2, E3

Fig. 3 Substitutions for "house" glyphs, Temple of the Four Lintels, Chichén Itzá. (a) L. 1, F4; (b) L. 4, B5; (c) L. 2, E3 (drawing by Ruth Krochock).

earplugs, inscribed bone artifacts, ceramic vessels, and now (Schele, personal communication, 1986) even on the inscribed monuments of Copán and Toniná.

Following *u pacab* in the sequence of these parallel phrases is another glyph that may also refer to name-tagging. This compound (T59.679:8) was read as *ti-i-?* by Kelley (1982:5). The readings of *ti* for T59 and *i* for T679 are generally accepted (Justeson 1984:320, 350) and I believe that the following sign, T8, is equivalent to T24 and may have a Vl (Vowel-L) value or perhaps the value *al* (Justeson 1984a:317). If one can read T8 as *al*, then a possible reading for this compound would be *ti-i-al*, perhaps equivalent to the Yucatec word *ti'a'l*, which specifies that a thing is owned by someone or pertains to a certain thing.

Definitions of the word *ti'a'l* in the *Diccionario Cordemex* read: "**Ti'a'l** 3: propio de cada uno, que es suyo, y su hacienda. 8: significa propiedad, dominio o pertenencia de algo. in ti'a'l, a ti'a'l, u ti'a'l: mío, tuyo, suyo, de aquel. . . . U **Ti'a'l** 2: suyo 8: lo suyo, su o es suyo, para, a fin de que, correspondiente" (Barrera-Vásquez 1980:788). In English, the definition for *ti'a'l* roughly translates to the phrase "that which is his" or "that which pertains to something" and the phrase *u ti'a'l* translates to "his/hers/its." Barbara MacLeod explained to me (personal communication, 1986) that, in order to be grammatically correct, the word *ti'a'l* should precede the word it modifies. If this is the case, the *ti'a'l* that follows *u pacab* probably does not refer to *u pacab* but to the following words.

In figure 4, the *ti'a'l* at A-5 precedes a verb at B-5 (T1.669b:8) that I believe can be read *u k'ahal*. Barbara MacLeod first proposed reading T204.669b:24 as *u k'ahal*

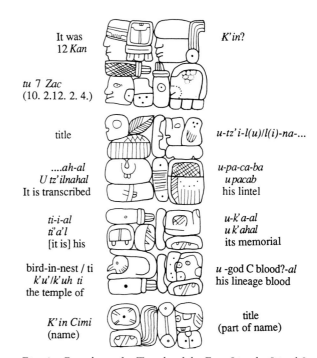

It was 12 *Kan*

tu 7 *Zac* (10. 2.12. 2. 4.)

title

....*ah-al* U *tz'ilnahal* It is transcribed

ti-i-al *ti'a'l* [it is] his

bird-in-nest / *ti* *k'u'/k'uh ti* the temple of

K'in Cimi (name)

K'in?

u-tz'i-l-l(u)/l(i)-na-...

u-pa-ca-ba *u pacab* his lintel

u-k'a-al *u k'ahal* its memorial

u -god C blood?-*al* his lineage blood

title (part of name)

Fig. 4 Paraphrase for Temple of the Four Lintels, Lintel 2, A1–B7, Chichén Itzá (drawing by Ruth Krochock).

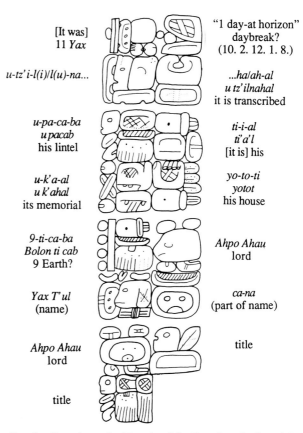

[It was] 11 *Yax*

u-tz'i-l-l(i)/l(u)-na...

u-pa-ca-ba *u pacab* his lintel

u-k'a-al *u k'ahal* its memorial

9-ti-ca-ba *Bolon ti cab* 9 Earth?

Yax T'ul (name)

Ahpo Ahau lord

title

"1 day-at horizon" daybreak? (10. 2. 12. 1. 8.)

...*ha/ah-al* *u tz'ilnahal* it is transcribed

ti-i-al *ti'a'l* [it is] his

yo-to-ti *yotot* his house

Ahpo Ahau lord

ca-na (part of name)

title

Fig. 5 Paraphrase for Temple of the Four Lintels, Lintel 1, E1–E8, Chichén Itzá (drawing by Ruth Krochock).

or "its memorial" or "its remembering" for what I believe is the same verb on the Temple of the Foliated Cross Secondary Text and the Tableritos Tablets from Palenque (MacLeod 1983:54). If this proposed *u k'ahal* compound at Chichén Itzá also carries the meaning "its memorial" or "its remembering," we might read the phrase *ti'a'l u k'ahal* as "[It is] his: its memorial . . ."

MacLeod (personal communication, 1986) noted that the word *ti'a'l* also has the meaning "in order that" or "in order to." She cited one of many examples in a collection of stories written by Alejandra Kim de Bolles (1972) in which the word *ti'a'l* clearly takes on the meaning "in order that." In the story "Chhochhlin Yetel Zinic," the following phrase appears: *Pai ten humppel chan ixim **utial** in hante* . . . (Kim de Bolles 1972:3). Roughly translated this means: "Get me a little corn **in order that** I can eat . . ."

As demonstrated above, the *ti'a'l* in most of these phrases from Chichén precedes the proposed *u k'ahal* compound. Barbara MacLeod (personal communication, 1986) suggested that perhaps the *u k'ahal* here might be read instead as *u k'a'ahal*, thus changing the verb to a passive voice. If we read the glyph *ti'a'l* as "in order that," we might then read the phrase *ti'a'l u k'a'ahal* as "in order that it was memorialized." Because the grammar of hieroglyph inscriptions sometimes seems to differ from that of modern spoken Maya, I believe that we should keep both of these possible readings in mind as

we continue with epigraphic research at Chichén Itzá.

In some cases, the *ti'a'l* does not directly follow the *u pacab*. On some of the Monjas lintels, the glyph that follows *ti'a'l* is a *tun* sign (T528) suffixed with T116 read phonetic *ne* or *ni* (Justeson 1984:324). This compound can then be read *tun-ne* or *tun*. Since the word *tun* means "stone" in several Maya Languages (Yucatecan and Cholan), this glyph may simply modify the word *pacab* and could be paraphrased as "stone lintel." The *tun* glyph is often followed by the title Ahpo Ahau, which then is followed by the glyph *ti'a'l*. The use of the title Ahpo Ahau in reference to the lintel seems a bit puzzling unless Ahpo Ahau is, in fact, the emblem glyph of Chichén Itzá. This debate over the identity of Chichén's emblem glyph, however, is a topic for a separate paper. Another possibility for the meaning of this phrase might be that the *tun* glyph followed by Ahpo Ahau is making reference to the tun-Ahau date expression. As Thompson (1937) demonstrated, the date expression usually names a specific tun in a katun ending on a specific day Ahau.

On Las Monjas Lintel 4 (fig. 6) the glyph that follows the *ti'a'l* is the hand-crossed-bands glyph (673.138:59), a compound that David Stuart (personal communication, 1986) tentatively identified as the phonetic spelling of the word *y-otot*, or the modern Chol word for "[his] house." [1] Kelley referred to this glyph as a verb for many years and I, too, was convinced that it was a verb

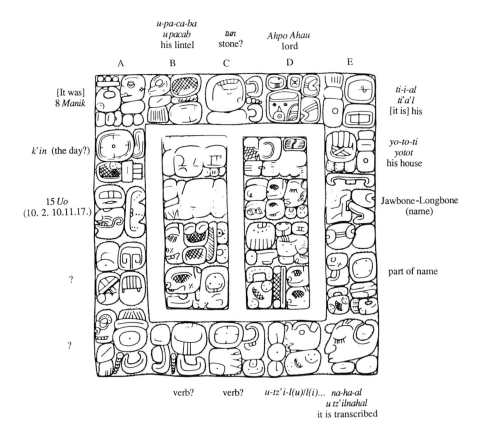

Fig. 6 Paraphrase for Las Monjas, Lintel 4, Chichén Itzá (drawing by Ian Graham, from Bolles 1977).

and went so far as to propose an elaborate argument that it was a verb for bloodletting. At the 1986 Mesa Redonda de Palenque, David Stuart demonstrated to me a pattern of substitution in which the hands-crossed-bands sign (T673) and the leaf sign (T115) freely exchange in the Piedras Negras emblem glyph. Stuart also suggested that T115 is more productive when read as *yo* in the house glyph (T115.614.515:59) than as *tu*. If this reading is correct, the hand-crossed-bands glyph compounded with T138, which I believe is equivalent to T44 read phonetically as *to*, and T59, phonetic *ti*, would read *yo-to-ti* or *y-otot*, the word for " [his] house."

I was skeptical of Stuart's reading until I considered the meaning of a puzzling glyphic substitution at Chichén Itzá. Kelley illustrated the pattern of substitution between the hand-crossed-bands glyph and a glyph of a bird in a construct of some sort (Kelley 1982: fig 2; see fig. 3). At David Stuart's suggestion, I looked up the Yucatec word for "nest" in the *Diccionario Cordemex* and found the following definitions:

K'u 1: Dios; yotoch k'u: la iglesia; u kanantech k'u: Dios te guarde; k'uben te'x a ba ti' k'u: encomendados a Dios, k'u winik: hombre de Dios, hombre divino, hombre Dios 3–9, 11: Dios 11, 13: deidad 13 abv: k'u kitbil: "señor deidad" 2. k'uil 11: deidad 3. k'u'o'b 11: pl. deidad, Dios; manes.

K'u 8: las casas o templos en que se adoraba a Dios 9: piramides antiguas 9, 11: templo 10: otero 11: piramide, elevación artifical de tierra en este forma, adoratorio 2. k'u na 11: adoratorio, templo 3ho'l lum 10: V. k'u 4. mul 10: idem.

K'u 1, 3–5, 9: nido de ave 1: u k'uu ku'uk: nido de las ardillas que son como los de los pajaros; u k'uu ubech': [nidos] de las codornices, hacenlos en el suelo; u k'uu t'u'l: cama de los conejos donde hembras paren 3. nido de algunos animales; u k'u ch'ich: nido de pajaros: u k'u tu'ul: madriquera de conejos dende paren 6, 11, 12, 13 cob: nido 6, 11: u k'u ch'o: ratonera donde está el ratón 9: cama de conejo lecho, conejera, lecho de parir 11: camada 2. k'uu 1: V. k'u 7, 8: nido 8: majada.

K'u 10. Patronimico Maya; Dios, nido de pajaros, también es elemento en varios nombres de plantas.

[Barrera-Vásquez 1980:416]

It is clear from the definitions above that the Yucatec word *k'u* not only means "bird's nest" but also "nests of other small animals, god, church, temple, ancient pyramid, and an artificial elevation of earth in this form." I therefore suggest that the bird-in-construct glyph be recognized as a bird in its nest. Although the *Diccionario Cordemex* does not make the distinction, it is actually the word *k'u'* that means "nest" and *k'uh* that means "god" and "temple" (MacLeod, personal communication, 1986). While this distinction is significant in modern speech, the difference would have been indistinguishable in the glyphs. In this way, a glyph that conveyed the idea of nest (*k'u'*) could easily be used to refer to the homophone (*k'uh*) "god" or "temple." When all the information is compiled, the following argument unfolds. The hand-crossed-bands glyph substitutes for the bird-in-nest glyph as illustrated by Beyer (1937) and Kelley (1982). If the hand-crossed-bands glyph bears the phonetic value *y-otot* and means "[his] house," as David Stuart suggested, and the bird-in-nest glyph can be read *k'u'/k'uh* meaning "nest/ancient pyramid, god, church, and temple," we have a logical substitution. "House" substitutes for "nest/temple." Another possibility for the reading of the *k'u'/k'uh* compound is that T59, which appears as a suffix to the bird-in-nest, may be acting as a phonetic complement and would signal the reader to read the glyph *yotot* rather than *k'uh*.

Still hesitant fully to accept the new readings without more proof, I remembered a glyph on Temple of the Four Lintels, Lintels 2, E3, which should be a bird-in-nest glyph because of the pattern of substitution but instead takes on another form, which I thought to be strange. Upon further inspection, the glyph resembles a house in side view with a thatched roof above and suffixed with the T59 *ti* sign below in the same way that the bird-in-nest glyph is suffixed by phonetic *ti*. We now have the third substitution—a pictographic rendering of a house in the same position as the hand-crossed-bands glyph and the bird-in-nest glyph (see fig. 3). I now believe that this provides proof that David Stuart was correct in his reading of *y-otot* for the hand-crossed-bands glyph. This also provides further evidence that the substituting glyph in the other parallel phrases, the bird-in-nest, may indeed be read *k'uh* or *k'u'* for "nest/temple."

Now we arrive at the glyph that I believe expressly mentions the dedication ceremonies for the various buildings at Chichén Itzá and thereby corroborates Kelley's hypothesis. As mentioned above, Barbara MacLeod (1983:53) proposed a reading of *u k'ah-wa* or "it was remembered" for a compound (T126.669b:130) that appears in the katun histories of Temple of the Inscriptions at Palenque. She also suggested the reading *u k'ahal* or "its memorial" or "its commemoration" for T204.669:24 as a variation of this phrase on the Tableritos Tablets and Temple of the Foliated Cross Secondary Texts from Palenque (MacLeod 1983:54). I believe that the glyph (T1.669b:8) that precedes the hand-crossed-bands glyph and the bird-in-nest glyph on Temple of the Four Lintels, Lintel 1, A6 and E4, and Lintel 2, B5, can also be read *u k'ah-Vl* or *u k'ahal* and can also be paraphrased "its memorial" or "its remembering" (MacLeod, personal communication, 1986). This proposed *u k'ahal* compound at Chichén Itzá in all cases immediately precedes either the hand-crossed-bands or the bird-in-nest glyphs. With the proposed readings of *yotot* and *k'u'/k'uh* for "house" and "nest/temple," it would seem logical to assume that the phrase *u k'ahal y-otot* could be read literally as "its memorial, the house" or perhaps as "its memorial, his house . . ."

In each parallel phrase, the names and titles of individual rulers and gods follow the phrases *u k'ahal yotot* (T4L, L. 1, A6–D1), *u k'ahal k'u* (T4L, L.2, B5–B7), and *u tz'ilnahal k'u* (T4L, L. 4, B4–B8). While these names do not seem to work well grammatically as the agents of the verbs, they do seem to be directly associated with the carving of the lintels and the dedication of the structures. Since the names and titles of individual rulers and gods follow the glyphs for "nest/temple" (*k'u*), "house" (*yotot*), and occasionally the glyph for "lintel" (*pacab*), it seems likely that the individuals are being named as the owners of the houses and lintels.

A pattern now begins to emerge. On each of the eleven lintels where these parallel phrases occur, a different individual is named at the end of the phrase as described above. With three exceptions, only one individual per lintel is mentioned in the context of these proposed "dedication ceremonies," although other individuals are also discussed in the texts. In two of these exceptions the additional individual appears on the lintel's front inscription and so, in a sense, might be considered separate from the lintel's underside inscriptions. On Temple of the Three Lintels, the third exception consists of two phrases naming different individuals directly following each other. In this way, each lintel spotlights a certain individual as the owner of the lintel or house or as the overseer of the ceremonies being performed. Because of this pattern, I believe that the *u pacab* phrases discussed above may perhaps be read specifically as "his lintel" and may be considered as more examples of the "name-tagging" previously described. This may also suggest that the *ti'i'al* glyphs that precede *u k'ahal* may name a certain individual as "the owner" or

the one in charge of the dedication ceremony. It seems more logical to assume that it is the lintels rather than the houses or buildings that are "owned" by the individuals because each structure has more than one lintel and each lintel names a different individual or pair of individuals. This evidence may suggest that at Chichén Itzá high-ranking individuals of equal status are featured on these lintels rather than a dynastic sequence of rulers as Davoust proposed (1977). Figure 7 outlines the way in which each lintel highlights certain individuals.

Since paraphrases of all fourteen parallel phrases would be too lengthy for the present paper, I have chosen three representative examples: Temple of the Four Lintels, Lintel 2, A1–B7 (fig. 4); Temple of the Four Lintels, Lintel 1, E1–E8 (fig. 5); and Las Monjas, Lintel 4, A1–Y4 (fig. 6).

Temple of the Four Lintels, Lintel 2 (fig. 4), begins with the date 12 Kan 7 Zac. The date is followed by a compound consisting of a skull and a leaf above what may be the thatching for the roof of a house (L. 2, A–3). This ends the first clause. The second clause begins with the verb *u tz'il-nahal* ("it is transcribed") followed by *u pacab* ("his? lintel"), *ti'a'l* ("that which is his"), *u k'ahal* ("its memorial"), *k'u'/k'uh* ("nest/temple"), *ti* ("of"), *u God C-blood?*, and *K'in Cimi* (a proposed ruler of Chichén Itzá: Davoust 1977). More fluently, the phrase may be read: *12 Kan 7 Zac {title?}. U tz'ilnahal u pacab. Ti'a'l u k'ahal k'uh ti u {God C blood?}, K'in Cimi*. Or "It was 12 Kan 7

Temple of the Initial Series	Entire Phrase	Name
Jawbone-Longbone	C2-C7	C6-C7
Temple of the Four Lintels		
Lintel 1 - Yax T'ul	A1-D1	A8-B8
	E1-E8	E6-E7
Lintel 2 - K'in Cimi	A1-B7	A7-B7
Lintel 3 - Double Jawbone	A1-B5?	B4?-B5?
Lintel 4 - Yax T'ul	A1-B6	A6-B6
Lintel 4a - K'in Cimi (exception 1)	A2-D2	D2
The Monjas		
Lintel 2 - Yax T'ul	A1-E5	D5-E5
Lintel 3 - Lady K'uk'	A1-E1	D1-E1
Lintel 3a - Lord Chac? (exception 2)	A1-B2	B2a?
Lintel 4 - Jawbone-Longbone	A1-E4	E3-E4
Lintel 5 - Jawbone Variant	A1-E3	E2
Lintel 6 - Yax Mul K'uk'	A1-E1	D1-E1
Temple of the Three Lintels		
Lintel 3 - Jawbone-Longbone	A1-G1	D1-E1
and K'in Cimi (exception 3)	A1-G1	F2-G1

Fig. 7 The pattern of emphasis on the individuals involved in the dedication ceremonies in the hieroglyphic inscriptions of Chichén Itzá.

Zac. His lintel is transcribed. It is his, the memorial of the house of the lineage blood of K'in Cimi." If the reading of ti'a'l as "in order that" and u k'a'ahal as "it was memorialized" is accepted, the lintel might read: U tz'ilnahal u pacab ti'a'l u k'a'ahal k'uh ti u {God C blood?}, K'in Cimi. Or "His lintel is transcribed in order that it was memorialized, the house of the lineage blood of K'in Cimi."

Temple of the Four Lintels, Lintel 1 (fig. 5), starts with the partial date of 11 Yax and most likely refers back to the date 9 Lamat 11 Yax, which is recorded at the beginning of the lintel. Following the 11 Yax is a "1 Day at Horizon" glyph that probably again makes reference to the day 11 Yax. This ends the first clause. The second clause repeats the phrase U tz'ilnahal u pacab ti'a'l u k'ahal, which would be paraphrased exactly as above. The following glyph is what Stuart read y-otot, "[his] house." The title 9 ti-ca-ba, or Bolon ti cab (9 of the Earth?; Kelley 1982:6), and Ahpo Ahau or (lord of lords) follow and in turn are succeeded by the name and titles of Yax T'ul, another presumed ruler of Chichén Itzá (Davoust 1977). In Maya, the phrase might be read: 11 Yax {1 day at horizon}. U tz'ilnahal u pacab. Ti'a'l u k'ahal yotot Bolon ti cab, Ahpo Ahau, Yax T'ul, Ahpo Ahau {title, title}. Or "[It was] 11 Yax, the beginning of the day. It is transcribed, his lintel. It is his, the dedication of his house, 9 Earth?, Lord of Lords, Yax T'ul, Lord, {titles}." Again, if we accept the alternate reading, the phrase might be read: 11 Yax {1 day at horizon}. U tz'ilnahal u pacab ti'a'l u k'ahal yotot. Bolon ti cab, Ahpo Ahau, Yax T'ul, Ahpo Ahau {title, title}. Or "[It was] 11 Yax, the beginning of the day. It is transcribed, his lintel, in order that it was memorialized, his house, 9 Earth?, Lord of Lords, Yax T'ul, Lord, {titles}."

Lintel 4 of Las Monjas (fig. 6) begins with the date 8 Manik 15 Uo, which is followed by four glyphs that have not yet been fully deciphered. The next clause begins with the familiar phrase U tz'ilnahal u pacab. The next two glyphs are a tun sign and the title Ahpo Ahau. As I discussed above, the word tun, meaning "stone," may refer to the lintel as a stone lintel. The ti'a'l follows and is in turn followed by Stuart's y-otot glyph. Here it seems likely that, instead of carrying the meaning "in order that," ti'a'l means "that which is his." We would then have a clear example of a house being called the possession of a certain person. In this case, the person named is Jawbone-Longbone, the probable father of Kakupacal (Kelley 1982:6). The phrase might read: 8 Manik, k'in tu 15 Uo . . . U Tz'ilnahal u pacab tun Ahpo Ahau. Ti'a'l yotot u {Jawbone-Longbone, titles}. Or "[It was] 8 Manik, the day 15 Uo . . . It is transcribed, his stone lintel, Lord. This is his house, Jawbone-Longbone, titles."

In this paper I have offered new paraphrases for fourteen parallel phrases in the inscriptions of Chichén Itzá. This new evidence not only provides what I believe to be a logical interpretation of these texts, but adds credence to Kelley's hypothesis that the inscriptions of Chichén Itzá record dedication ceremonies for individ-

ual structures. We have seen that each of the lintels seems to highlight a different individual and that, in this way, the lintels seem to be "owned" by those individuals. The fact that so many individuals are named in association with the dedication ceremonies makes it nearly impossible to speculate on the status or rank differences among them. The inscriptions discussed here deviate in many ways from the Southern Lowland inscriptions, such as the use of a different system of dating, the lack of birth, death, and accession dates, a greater use of phoneticism, and the performance of dedicatory ceremonies by many individuals instead of one ruler. I believe that these differences in the hieroglyphic texts of Chichén Itzá signify more than just stylistic variation. I believe that we must consider the possibility that the Maya political social structure at Chichén Itzá, before any presumed foreign invasion, differed radically from other Maya sites in the Southern Lowlands. Instead of the lintels recording the dynastic sequence of rulers as Davoust (1977) proposed, they may instead record the involvement of several high-ranking individuals of equal status in dedication ceremonies that would not only honor and memorialize the various buildings, but the individuals themselves. One very important finding, I believe, is that Kakupacal, the presumed ruler of Chichén Itzá at this time (Kelley 1982:2), is never named in direct association with the transcribing or carving of the lintels or the dedication of the temples. He does seem to be mentioned in association with the playing of the ball game on Temple of the Four Lintels, Lintel 1, and Yula, Lintel 1, and is discussed in what seem to be relationship statements that name his parents as Lady K'uk' and Jawbone-Longbone on Las Monjas lintels (see Kelley 1982). Could his exclusion from the ceremonies signal that he holds a more prestigious social rank than the others or could it suggest that Kakupacal, too, is just another high-ranking individual with a status equal to the others mentioned on the lintels? The unusual pattern of recording hieroglyphic information at Chichén Itzá not only alerts us to the possibility that the political social structure at this site may have differed completely from that at other Classic Maya sites, but may be on the verge of revealing what those differences might be.

The decipherment of the phrases offered here has resulted from the work of many epigraphers over a period of about fifty years. The hieroglyphic texts of Chichén Itzá have been among the most difficult to interpret due to the extensive use of phoneticism. With continued cooperation and pooling of resources, however, we can discover more answers to the many questions posed by the inscriptions of Chichén Itzá.

Note

1. Justeson et al. (1985:58) noted that the sound change shift from /t/ to /ch/ in Yucatec took place very late in the Classic Period. It should not be considered strange, therefore, that a word for "house" in the glyphs at Chichén Itzá, which are assumed to have been written in Yucatec, would be otot rather than otoch as it is in present-day

Yucatec. Two other glyphs for "house" appear in the texts from the Temple of the Hieroglyphic Jambs that also seem to be read *otot* rather than *otoch*.

Acknowledgments

I would especially like to thank Linda Schele, Barbara MacLeod, David Stuart, Joanne Spero, and Connie Cortez for hours of discussion, sharing of information and ideas, and valuable suggestions for the improvement of this manuscript.

All illustrations except figure 6 were drawn by the author. These drawings were produced from photographs taken by the author while participating on the Harvard University/Peabody Museum Chichén Itzá Archaeological Project, 1983, directed by Charles Lincoln. Film, film processing, and field time were provided by the project.

The Great Ball Court Stone from Chichén Itzá

LINNEA H. WREN
GUSTAVUS ADOLPHUS COLLEGE

The Great Ball Court at Chichén Itzá is located in the northwest corner of the North Terrace, the largest ceremonial plaza at the site. Four temples—the Lower Temple of the Jaguars, the Upper Temple of the Jaguars, the North Temple, and the South Temple—are associated with the Great Ball Court. The surfaces of these structures and of the benches of the Great Ball Court are lavishly decorated with sculptures and paintings that illustrate hundreds of human figures in a complex iconographic program. An additional sculptured monument from the Great Ball Court has recently been identified and warrants careful study.

In the summer of 1983, Peter Schmidt and I located a hemispherical stone (catalog number CRY 61) in the bodega of the Museo Regional de Antropología in Mérida. Although the stone was unprovenienced, Schmidt also found a reference in a museum catalog of the 1940s to a large carved stone discovered in the Great Ball Court at Chichén Itzá (personal communication). The catalog entry appears to correspond to the hemispherically shaped stone, which I call the Great Ball Court stone.

The Great Ball Court stone (fig. 1) is 52 cm in height,

99 cm in diameter, and 311 at its outer circumference. Around its base is a rim 16 cm in height and 11 cm in width. Now broken into several pieces, the stone was originally monolithic. Its surface is badly eroded. However, three panels of figural relief can be recognized on the curved surfaces of the Great Ball Court stone, and a band of twenty-four glyphs can be seen on the upper surface of the rim (fig. 2).

The Great Ball Court stone can be identified as the subject of several incomplete and substantially inaccurate reports of a sculpture discovered during the excavation and repair of the Great Ball Court conducted by the Instituto Nacional de Antropología e Historia (INAH) between 1923 and 1940. An undated memo written by Edward Thompson at Chichén Itzá has been located by Clemency Coggins in the Edward H. Thompson archives at the Peabody Museum of Archaeology and Eth-

Fig. 1   Great Ball Court Stone (photo by David Wren).

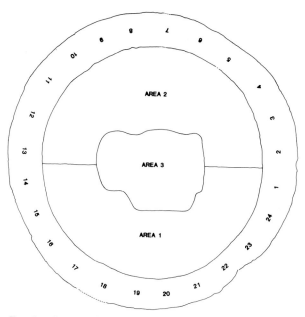

Fig. 2   Great Ball Court Stone (schematic drawing by Linnea Wren).

nology at Harvard University. In it, Thompson recounted the discovery of a "peculiarly shaped stone fragment" that resembles "a stiff round hat." Its unusual shape led Thompson to speculate that the stone was originally a fragment of a "much conventionalized stelae [sic] or a capstone to a pillar . . . or perhaps the stone cover to an urn." Thompson credited his own "systematic search" with the recovery of the missing fragments of the monument. He reported that he had photographed the stone and had made paper molds of its surfaces. Thompson's photographs and molds of the Great Ball Court stone are now lost, but Charles Lincoln has located a set of photographs of molds taken from the inscription of the Great Ball Court stone. The photographs, stored in the photographic archives of the Carnegie Institution of Washington now at the Peabody Museum at Harvard University, reveal that the inscription was badly eroded at the time of the discovery of the Great Ball Court stone and that little appreciable deterioration of the carving has occurred since then. The utility of these photographs is severely limited since the molds were divided into individual glyph blocks before the photographs were taken and no record of the original order of the glyphs was kept.

Two short accounts concerning the Great Ball Court stone were published by Cesar Lizardi Ramos (1936, 1937). According to Lizardi Ramos, the stone had been discovered in 1923 in the southern part of the Great Ball Court by Miguel Angel Fernández. Lizardi Ramos described the stone as being "shaped as a large ring for a ball to pass through" (1937:12). Although this description gave rise to later misinterpretations about the form and function of the monument, it may have been originally intended to suggest a resemblance between the shape of the stone and the appearance of a large rubber ball being struck through one of the rings that were tenoned into the eastern and western walls of the Great Ball Court.

A different location for the discovery of the Great Ball Court stone was recorded by Morley in his checklist of inscribed monuments from Chichén Itzá (1948:53). According to Morley, a "round roughly spherical altar" was found several hundred meters west of the south end of the west wall of the Great Ball Court. While Morley was undoubtedly referring to the Great Ball Court stone, his placement of the monument outside the ball court is contradicted by Lizardi Ramos's earlier statement and appears to be inaccurate.

More recently, Karl H. Mayer (1984) published a brief entry, accompanied by two photographs, describing the Great Ball Court stone. He recognized the presence of one complex scene depicting a ball game and noted that a hieroglyphic text was inscribed on the base of the stone. No provenience for the stone was listed in the labels or the then-current catalog of the Museo Regional de Antropología, but Mayer correctly identified the Maya-Toltec style of figural relief and suggested that the monument originated from a source in eastern Yucatán, presumably in the region of Chichén Itzá.

Lizardi Ramos (1937:12) briefly noted that Enrique Palacios believed an Eleventh Cycle date was inscribed on the Great Ball Court stone. A more extended discussion of this supposed date and its significance was provided by J. Eric Thompson (1937:189). Although he did not publish any illustrations of the stone, Thompson had evidently received a drawing of the inscription prepared by Fernández. This unlabeled drawing (fig. 3) has been located by Ian Graham among material deposited at the Peabody Museum by the Carnegie Institution. Accompanying the drawing when it was received by Thompson was a manuscript, now lost, by Enrique Palacios, describing the recently discovered stone. Thompson reported that Palacios had identified an Initial Series date and a Calendar Round date in the inscription. The Initial Series date was read by Palacios as 11.7.5.3.0 6 Ahau 13 Pax (GMT 1367 A.D.), with the cycle glyph and its coefficient being suppressed. The Calendar Round date was read by Palacios as 2 Ahau 3 Uayeb and was presumed to date to 11.9.16.0.0 (GMT 1417). The authenticity of these dates was apparently confirmed for Thompson by the presence of what he termed "the indubitable Mexican figures" (1937:189) also represented on the stone. In his outline of history at Chichén Itzá, Thompson, therefore, placed the stone late in the Post-Classic Period.

An alternative dating of the Great Ball Court stone was proposed by Marvin Cohodas (1978a:110). Apparently misled by the description provided by Lizardi Ramos, Cohodas identified the Great Ball Court stone as one of an earlier pair of rings used in the Great Ball Court. He acknowledged that he had been unable to locate the stone or any illustrations of its inscription or reliefs. Nonetheless, he tentatively suggested that the

Fig. 3   Great Ball Court Stone: Inscription (drawing by Miguel Angel Fernández; photo by Ian Graham).

Wren

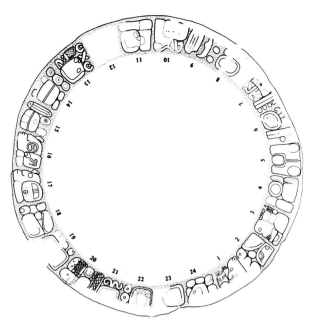

Fig. 4   Great Ball Court Stone: Inscription (drawing by Ruth Krochock).

partial Initial Series date reportedly inscribed on the Great Ball Court stone might actually record the date 9.10.5.3.0 (GMT 638) and that the Calendar Round date might correspond to 9.10.6.16.0 (GMT 639). Thus, on the basis of this and other evidence, Cohodas placed the Great Ball Court complex at Chichén Itzá in the Middle Classic Period.

My study indicates that no Initial Series date and only one Calendar Round date can be recognized in the inscription on the Great Ball Court stone. Nor is a katun-Ahau date evident. The inscription was redrawn in 1984 (fig. 4) by Ruth Krochock, who is presently undertaking an analysis of the corpus of inscriptions at Chichén Itzá. A comparison between the drawings prepared by Fernández and Krochock indicates that the earlier drawing owed much to the imagination. The single Calendar Round date inscribed on the stone in glyphs 6–7 (my numbering) appears to record the date 11 Cimi 14 Pax.

During the more than sixty years since its discovery, the Great Ball Court stone has remained poorly documented and inaccurately described. Nonetheless, this monument is of considerable importance both in understanding the significance of the ball game at Chichén Itzá and in reconstructing the history of the site.

Recent studies have stressed the secular, as well as the sacred, significance of the Mesoamerican ball game. Among its other purposes, it appears to have served as a mechanism to train soldiers and maintain elite ideology (Kowalewski et al. 1985), to unify competing warrior lineages within a polity (Fox 1985), and to mediate conflicts along interregional boundaries (Kowalewski et al. 1985; Molloy 1985; Scarborough 1985). Ball courts, or other playing fields designated for ball games, may have

functioned as dance plazas on which military encounters waged at distant places were reenacted and on which capture of prestigious prisoners by victorious rulers was celebrated before the gaze of the local populace (Molloy 1985; Schele and Miller 1986:248–253).

The ball game at Chichén Itzá evidently served a similar set of militaristic purposes, which may explain why the ball game was more important at Chichén Itzá, apparently the center of an aggressive and expansive state, than at any other site in the northern Maya Lowlands. Of the twenty-one ball courts known in this region, thirteen are located at Chichén Itzá (Robertson et al. 1985)

There is considerable evidence at Chichén Itzá to support the interpretation of the ball game as an extension of political and military activities as well as an expression of sacred ideologies. The Great Ball Court and the Tzompantli are built in close proximity to each other. Moreover, the living victors of the Great Ball Court benches and the underworld warriors on the eastern extension of the Tzompantli (Salazar 1952:40) both display the severed heads of their victims. The processional reliefs in the Lower Temple of the Jaguars, located at the southern entrance to the Great Ball Court, depict five registers of warriors converging toward the figure of a ball player (Maudslay 1889–1902:III, pl. 44–51). The jamb sculptures of the Upper Temple of the Jaguars celebrate individual warriors while the murals of the same structure depict large-scale military encounters (Coggins and Shane 1984: figs. 17–20).

The relationship between the ball game and the militaristic concerns of the polity at Chichén Itzá is further underscored by two features of the Great Ball Court stone: its function and the subjects of its figural reliefs.

The size and hemispherical shape of the Great Ball Court stone permit its identification as a sacrificial stone. At the time of the Spanish conquest, human sacrifice was a widespread practice not only in Central Mexico but also in northern Yucatán. Diego de Landa (Tozzer 1941:118–119) described the heart excision sacrifices that were practiced by the Post-Classic Maya of the region:

If the heart of the victim was to be taken out . . . , they brought him up to the round altar, which was the place of sacrifice. . . . The *Chacs* seized the poor victim, and placed him very quickly on his back upon that stone, and all four held him by the legs and arms, so that they divided him in the middle. At this came the executioner, the *Nacom*, with the knife of stone, and struck him with great skill and cruelty a blow between the ribs of his left side under the nipple, and he at once plunged his hand in there and seized the heart like a raging tiger and snatched it out alive.

At Chichén Itzá, the use of a hemispherical stone in heart excision sacrifices is clearly illustrated in a number of works of art. Two scenes from the Upper Temple of the Jaguars, one painted above the west entrance to the inner chamber (Coggins and Shane 1984: fig. 19) and the other on the south vault (Morris et al. 1931:I, 398) depict sacrificial victims splayed over hemispherical stones. A heart excision sacrifice is also illustrated on a fresco fragment found in the outer chamber of the Temple of the Warriors (Morris et al. 1931:I, pl. 145). In this example, the victim is shown stretched across the upraised coil of the body of a feathered serpent, which substitutes for the sacrificial stone. Disk H (Lothrop 1952: fig. 1) illustrates the sacrificer in an eagle headdress grasping the heart of his captive while a second victim waits his turn. Finally, a fragment of a scene, possibly representing the torso of sacrificial victim stretched over a stone with an assistant to his right, has been identified on a *tecali* vessel from the Sacred Cenote (Coggins and Shane 1984: pl. 31). The majority of these illustrations of heart excision rites occur in contexts that include battle scenes or involve warriors as the principal participants.

The association of a heart excision stone with the Great Ball Court at Chichén Itzá indicates a conver-

gence of the sacrificial rituals associated with military raids and conquests and those resulting from ball game contests. The figural reliefs incised on the Great Ball Court stone further suggest the overlay in the political and religious meanings of the ball game. On the Great Ball Court stone, two scenes depicting ball-game sacrifices, designated Area I (fig. 5) and Area II (fig. 6), are combined with a third scene, designated Area III (fig. 7), which represents elite military chiefs of Chichén Itzá. Crossed spears, similar to those that once ornamented the roof of the Upper Temple of the Jaguars, mark the divisions between Areas I and II.

The sacrificial decapitation of ball-game players is prominently displayed on the six panels of relief carved on the Great Ball Court benches, as well as on the benches of the Casa Colorada and the Monjas ball courts (Bolles 1977: figs. 221–222, 227–229). Areas I and II, carved on the lower curved surface of the Great Ball Court stone, repeat the salient characteristics of ball-

Fig. 5   *Great Ball Court Stone: Area 1 (drawing by Peggy Diggs and Ruth Krochock).*

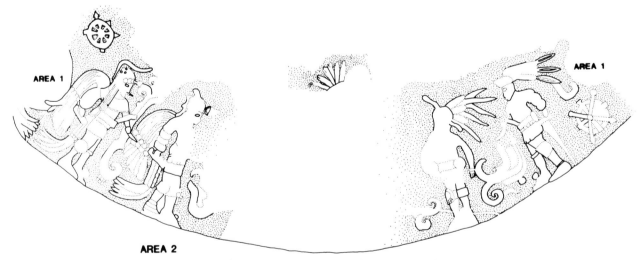

Fig. 6   *Great Ball Court Stone: Area 2 (drawing by Peggy Diggs and Ruth Krochock).*

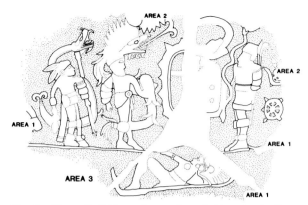

Fig. 7 Great Ball Court Stone: Area 3 (drawing by Peggy Diggs and Ruth Krochock).

game sacrificial scenes displayed elsewhere at Chichén Itzá. The relief in Area I is more fully preserved. In the center is a ball inscribed with a skull. To the left is shown a figure holding a severed head: to the right is shown the sacrificial victim, from whose neck spurt six streams of blood stylized as serpents. All six figures in the scene can be identified as ball players by their specialized ball-game paraphernalia consisting of yokes, palmas, handstones, knee pads, and slippers. The figures are divided into two teams that can be distinguished by differences in their costumes. The three players on the right wear beaded capes and back shields from which feathers sweep both upward and downward to the ground. The three figures on the left wear pectorals of roped necklaces and headdresses with large, round-ended feathers.

The range of costume attributes represented in Areas I and II is more restricted than, but nonetheless in conformity with, those depicted on the Great Ball Court bench reliefs. Tozzer (1957:I, 1939) identified members of the two teams as being Maya and Toltecs and regarded the ball-game contests as conflicts between the Maya and Toltec inhabitants of Chichén Itzá. The Great Ball Court benches were restudied by Merle Greene Robertson, who agreed that each team is characterized by a distinctive set of costume elements but argued that almost all of these attributes can be considered Maya in origin (Robertson et al. 1985).

The surface of most of the central portion of Area II has flaked away, but six serpents emerging from the neck of a decapitated victim are visible. Four ball players are also preserved. Their costumes repeat those of the two groups represented in Area I, while the identities of the teams that provide the sacrificer and the victim are reversed.

Area III covers the upper portion of the Great Ball Court stone. A reclining Bacab figure is shown in the basal zone, while above the ground line a procession of three warriors facing a fourth warrior is represented. Each of the advancing warriors is associated with serpent imagery. The figure on the left, who carries an atlatl and spears, is outlined against a cloud serpent, known in

central Mexican sources as Mixcoatl. The figure in the center is superimposed on a feathered serpent, known in central Mexico as Quetzalcoatl and in Yucatán as Kukulcan. Only the facial profile and tubular nose bead of the figure on the right are still visible, but he appears to be encircled by a precious turquoise serpent, known in central Mexican sources as Xiuhcoatl. The fourth, stationary figure holds spears and a serpent staff.

The use of serpent iconography to identify important military chiefs is also seen in the murals of the inner chamber of the Upper Temple of the Jaguars. These murals appear to represent military campaigns undertaken by the chiefs of Chichén Itzá in two distinct geographical regions (Miller 1977). Additional battles were originally represented on the walls of the outer chamber of the Upper Temple of the Jaguars (Breton 1907). Arthur Miller (1977:212–213) identified the three murals on the north end of the Upper Temple of the Jaguars (Miller 1977: figs. 4, 5, 7) as illustrations of a series of events in which a military leader from Chichén Itzá directs an attack against a settlement in southern Oaxaca, an interpretation with which David Kelley was in basic accord (1984:12–13). More recently, however, Fernando Robles and Anthony Andrews (1986:84) proposed that the "red hills" in the battle scene of mural 3 (Miller 1977: fig. 5) depict the terrain and soil of the Puuc hills. The three murals at the south end of the Upper Temple of the Jaguars (Miller 1977: figs. 8, 3, 9) appear to illustrate the conquest and subjugation of a village in the tropical Southern Lowlands, and possibly in the Petén, again by warriors from Chichén Itzá (Miller 1977:217–218; Kelley 1984:12–13).

Miller's hypothesis that foreign invasions in the Southern Maya Lowlands during the Terminal Classic Period may have originated from Chichén Itzá is supported by data from numerous sites. At Becan, the appearance of northern ceramic types and forms suggests a northern intrusion at the beginning of the ninth century (Ball 1974). At Altar de Sacrificios, a violent end to the late Boca ceramic phase seems to be indicated. It is replaced by an intrusive Fine Paste complex with Mexican and Classic Maya traits (Adams 1973). Iconographic parallels between early Tenth Cycle sculpture at Seibal and at sites in Northern Yucatán, as well as architectural similarities, suggest an intrusion from the Northern Maya Lowlands (Sabloff 1973). At Colha, the discovery of a pit containing twenty-eight human skulls, together with the occurrence of northern slate ware, argues for northern military activity (Adams n.d.). Ceramic evidence from Río Azul, as well as the stylistic similarities between Stela 4 and sculpture at Chichén Itzá, also point to an intrusion from the Northern Lowlands.

However, Miller (1977) also noted that the date of the construction of the Upper Temple of the Jaguars has been an issue of considerable debate. Samuel Lothrop (1952:69–71) argued that the Great Ball Court complex was constructed over a period of approximately 150 years. However, the architectural unity of the Great Ball

Court complex as a whole and the iconographic and thematic unity of the reliefs and murals indicate that the structures of the complex are contemporaneous. In addition, the close relationship between the plan of the Upper Temple of the Jaguars, as well as the absence of earlier layers of paint, is evidence that the paintings date to the same period as the construction of the building. Tozzer (1957:34) dated the Great Ball Court to his Chichén II phase (ca. A.D. 948–1145). Kubler (1961:63, 1976:196–197) dated the architectural complex to the twelfth century, while Parsons (1969:172–184, table 7) and Cohodas (1978a, 1978b:102–106) posited a much earlier, seventh century date for its construction. Recently Coggins (Coggins and Shane 1984) assigned the murals of the Upper Temple of the Jaguars to the Terminal Classic Period with a date of approximately A.D. 850.

The Great Ball Court stone offers evidence that the murals of the Upper Temple of the Jaguars are Terminal Classic in date. The close similarities in style, motif, and composition between the sacrificial scenes depicted on the Great Ball Court stone and the Great Ball Court benches indicate that the stone is contemporaneous with its architectural context. Although the inscription does not include an Initial Series or a katun-Ahau date, it may be possible to posit a Long Count equivalent of 10.1.15.3.6 (GMT 864) for the Calendar Round date, 11 Cimi 14 Pax, recorded in glyphs 6–7. Evidence for this date is based on several parallels between the inscription on the Great Ball Court stone and the inscriptions of the Temple of the Four Lintels, Structure 6E1, and Yula.

First, ball-game events are recorded four times in the inscriptions from the Great Ball Court stone, the Temple of the Four Lintels, and Yula. Kelley (1982:5) identified glyph C8 in Lintel 1 of the Temple of the Four Lintels as a ball-game glyph, and Michel Davoust (1986) suggested that glyph C3 of Lintel 4 of the same structure records a verb meaning "to strike the ball." Krochock (personal communication) also identified glyph D3 of Lintel 1 at Yula and glyph 5 of the Great Ball Court stone as ball-game glyphs. No other ball-game glyphs have yet been identified in the inscriptions at Chichén Itzá. The presence of a ball-game glyph in the inscription of the Great Ball Court stone clearly links the contents of its text with the subjects of its reliefs.

Second, a phrase identified by Beyer as Group 9 (Beyer 1937: figs. 43–46), also occurs only at the Temple of the Four Lintels, (Lintel 1, D1–C2, E8–F8; Lintel 3a, D1–C2), Yula (Lintel 1, H3–G4), and in the Great Ball Court stone inscription (glyphs 10–11). Glyph 11 of the Great Ball Court stone inscription may be tentatively identified as the head of God C prefixed by the blood group element, interpreted by David Stuart (1988) as a type of "blood personification." The association between the appearance of the ball-game glyph and Group 9 at Chichén Itzá suggests that the verbal compound may refer to ball-game sacrifices.

Third, the inscriptions of the Great Ball Court stone

and Structure 6E1 appear to share an identical nominal phrase. Kelley (1968) convincingly demonstrated that the name of a military captain Kakupacal is rendered phonetically fourteen times in the inscriptions of Chichén Itzá and identified this name with that of the Itzá military captain whose deeds are described in the Chilam Balam of Chumayel and other Maya historical documents (for an alternative interpretation of the significance of this compound, cf. Coggins 1986). Krochock (personal communication) pointed out that Kakupacal appears to be closely associated with ball-game events recorded in the inscriptions of Chichén Itzá. An ideographic variant of Kakupacal appears in the inscription on a column of Structure 6E1 at Chichén Itzá (Kelley 1982:10). Kelley identified the first glyphic element in the name inscribed on the column as the "fire" glyph, *kak*, and the second element as a shield glyph, *pacal*. Kelley's reading of the first glyphic element was questioned by David Stuart (personal communication), who argued for the phonetic value of *butz'a*, a value Kelley earlier considered and rejected. Kelley's reading of the second element as *pacal* is based upon the resemblance between it and the shield depicted in the Dresden Codex (Thompson 1972: Facsimile of Codex, p. 67) rather than the shields normally represented in Maya inscriptions of the Classic Period. Glyphs 21 and 22 of the Great Ball Court stone inscription may tentatively be identified as an ideographic variant of the name Kakupacal.

Two glyphs, the second of which can be read as Ah-po Ahau, frequently follow the name of Kakupacal in the inscriptions at Chichén Itzá. They are also inscribed following the name of Kakupacal on the Great Ball Court stone (glyphs 23–24). Kelley initially proposed that this glyph might represent the emblem glyph of Chichén Itzá (1976:218) but more recently read this glyph as a title such as "ruler of lords" or "king of kings" (1982:8). Fox (1984:13–18) argued that Ah-po Ahau is the second glyph in a two-glyph compound that functions as the Chichén Itzá emblem glyph.

Preceding the name of Kakupacal in the inscription of the Great Ball Court stone is a glyph (glyph 20) that is similar to a glyph recently identified by David Stuart (1986) as a verbal phrase referring to the sacrificial dedication of a monument by a patron. Although this verbal phrase is frequent at Chichén Itzá, this is the only example in which it is directly associated with the name of Kakupacal and therefore may indicate that the Great Ball Court was the only complex at Chichén Itzá actually dedicated by Kakupacal.

Virtually all the dated inscriptions at Chichén Itzá fall within a forty-year period between 10.1.17.5.13 (GMT 866), recorded on the Water Trough lintel (Thompson 1937:186; for an alternative reading, cf. Kelley 1982:13–14) and 10.3.8.14.4 (GMT 906), recorded on the Caracol Stela (Kelley 1982: table 1; for an alternative reading, cf. Thompson 1937:186). The only date, 10.8.10.11.0 (GMT 998) that falls outside this period is recorded on the High Priest's Grave, a structure that is generally accepted as late in the architectural sequence at Chichén Itzá (Tozzer 1957:43; Proskouriakoff 1970: 459). The earliest inscription containing the phonetic rendering of the name Kakupacal is in the band of the Casa Colorada that is dated to 10.2.0.1.9 (GMT 869) by Kelley (1982:14, 1983:171; for an alternative reading, cf. Thompson 1937:186) and the latest inscription is Lintel 4a of the Temple of the Four Lintels, dated 10.2.12.2.4 (GMT 881; Thompson 1937:186; Kelley 1982: table 1).

Although no date is recorded in this inscription, Proskouriakoff (1970:465) implicitly placed the text and its accompanying relief at approximately 10.1.0.0.0. She did so on the basis of similarities between the inscriptions at 6E1 and at Yula and on the basis of iconographic similarities between the figures on 6E1 and those in Puuc sites such as Oxkintok, Halal, Kabah, and Uxmal and at the site of Seibal.

It can therefore be argued that the Calendar Round date 11 Cimi 14 Pax recorded on the inscription on the Great Ball Court stone can be placed at 10.1.15.3.6 (GMT 864). This date is only two years earlier than the Water Trough lintel and less than six years earlier than the Casa Colorada band. It can further be argued that the inscription recorded the staging of a ball game, or a cycle of ball games, as part of the ceremonial rituals that were part of the dedication of the Great Ball Court complex. It can also be argued that Great Ball Court, the most important and the most prominently located ball court at Chichén Itzá, was the setting for the ball-game events recorded in the inscriptions of the Temple of the Four Lintels and Yula. Lintel 1 at Yula is dated 10.2.4.8.4 (GMT 874) and Lintels 1 and 4 of the Temple of the Four Lintels are dated 10.2.12.1.8 (GMT 881), approximately seven years later (Thompson 1937; Kelley 1982). The relationship between the Temple of the Four Lintels and Yula is underscored not only by their shared inclusion of ball-game glyphs, but also by their shared depiction of a pair of distinctive iconographic motifs, "Knife-Wing" on Lintel 1a, Yula, and Lintel 1a of the Temple of the Four Lintels (Kelley 1982: fig. 4) and "Rattlesnake" on Lintel 4a of the Temple of the Four Lintels (Beyer 1937: pl. 10) and Lintel 2a at Yula (Beyer 1937: pl. 12).

If the Great Ball Court can be dated to the Terminal Classic Period, it supports the model proposed by Peter Schmidt (personal communication) and by Charles Lincoln (1985) for the chronological overlap between buildings constructed in the two styles of architecture, Chichén-Maya and Chichén-Toltec, which are characteristic of Chichén Itzá. Chichén-Maya architecture closely resembles Pure Florescent architecture of the Puuc region in its use of decorative elements, such as Chac masks and mosaic panels of geometric design, and in its use of structural principles, such as the corbeled vault.

Chichén-Toltec architecture integrates elements typical of northern Maya Lowland architecture with non-Maya architectural features found in Central Mexico, Oaxaca, and Vera Cruz. These features include the use of feathered serpent columns and balustrades, Atlantean columns and Chacmool figures similar to those at Tula, terrace profiles similar to those at Monte Albán, and the depiction of ball game paraphernalia similar to that from El Tajín (Kubler 1961, 1962).

Nonetheless, despite the apparent eclecticism, Chichén-Toltec architecture is more than a pastiche of features drawn from contemporary Mesoamerican traditions. Rather, Chichén-Toltec architecture should be regarded as an original architectural style. Its distinctive character is evidenced by the development at Chichén Itzá of an innovative engineering technique that combined the use of wooden lintels and corbeled vaults. The architects at Chichén Itzá were the first builders in Mesoamerica to exploit a particular characteristic of wood in stone vaulted architecture—the fact that wood is strong in tension. While wooden lintels were commonly used to span openings in both Northern and Southern Lowland Maya architecture, they functioned as substitutes for stone lintels. In contrast to wood, stone is weak in tension. Such a use involved no major change in architectural forms. The builders at Chichén Itzá, however, evidently realized that, because of its tensile strength, wood could be used structurally in ways that were dramatically different from stone. Wooden beams could do what stone lintels could not—span wide spaces while still supporting heavy loads. In structures such as the Temple of the Warriors and, even more dramatically, the Northwest Colonnade, the Chichén-Toltec architects substituted rows of piers spanned by wooden beams for the solid load bearing walls that, in traditional Maya architecture, were necessary to support the heavy vaulted superstructure. They increased the distances spanned by wooden beams by two, or even three, times the distances traditionally spanned by stone lintels in the Northern and Southern Lowlands. As a result, they were able to suspend parallel rows of corbeled vaults over widely spaced supports and to create interior vaulted spaces that dwarfed the interior spaces permitted by traditional architectural techniques. Not only did this technique allow Chichén-Toltec structures to be greatly expanded in their dimensions, but it permitted them to be more varied in their plans. Thus, Chichén-Toltec architecture represents an innovative architectural style that was developed, it appears, to serve the physical requirements, expressive needs, and aesthetic desires of the distinctive polity that flourished at Chichén Itzá.

The Great Ball Court stone is inscribed with the only Maya inscription known from the North Terrace of Chichén Itzá. It is one of the few inscriptions at Chichén Itzá that is associated with figural relief. The reliefs of the North Terrace depict warrior figures who are individualized in appearance (Maudslay 1889–1902; Morris et al. 1931; Tozzer 1957). Some of these figures are associated with attributes of costume and weaponry also found in the sculpture of the Central Mexican site of Tula and are identified by pictographic signs that appear to be Central Mexican in origin. Other figures are associated with attributes found in the sculpture of the Northern Maya Lowlands, and a few are associated with attributes found in the Southern Maya Lowlands. Proskouriakoff (1970) argued that this diversity could be explained by the presence at Chichén Itzá of an alliance of groups of people drawn from several states. Thus, at Chichén Itzá, it would appear that a dynamic new society was formed by the interaction of Maya and non-Maya peoples. The result was that forms of architecture traditional to the Northern Maya Lowlands continued to be constructed to meet traditional needs, while, simultaneously, the newly emergent polity introduced different decorative motifs and developed innovative engineering techniques to serve its particular needs. This polity, it appears, was able to capitalize upon the growing weakness of the states of the Southern Maya Lowlands and to achieve stunning military successes that forever altered the Maya realm.

Symbolism of the Maya Ball Game at Copán: Synthesis and New Aspects

JEFF KARL KOWALSKI and WILLIAM L. FASH
NORTHERN ILLINOIS UNIVERSITY

> . . . the human ballgame was considered a repetition of a divine one, constituting a kind of magic by analogy, to support the victory of the light against the darkness, of the sun against the stars.
> Walter Krickeberg in *Traducciones Mesoamericanistas*

Following the successful reconstruction and study of the mosaic sculpture facade of Copán Structure 9N–82, William Fash formed the Copán Mosaics Project in 1984 with the goal of studying and preserving the thousands of fragments of mosaic facade sculptures that had originally adorned numerous eighth-century masonry structures at the site. This involves locating, cataloging (in descriptions, drawings, and photographs), and fitting the fragments together, and determining the association of individual and composite sculptures with their respective buildings. Hypothetical reconstruction of the sculpture facades and subsequent interpretive works are the principal research goals. Our ultimate scholarly objective for the CMP is the description and explanation of the notable shifts in ideological adaptations and political integration mechanisms utilized by the centralized rulership of a Maya city-state during the latter half of the eighth century A.D. These fifty years witnessed a series of dramatic changes throughout the cultural system, culminating in the political collapse of Copán, the distinguished southeast capital of the Classic Maya realm. Here we are reporting on the first mosaic facade complex studied by the CMP, with the fieldwork and methodological aspects covered by the junior author, and the comparative and interpretive section written by the senior author.[1]

Problem and Methodology

Ball Court III (Strömsvik 1952), hereafter referred to as Ball Court A III to distinguish it from the recently discovered Ball Court B, which also has three building stages (Fash and Lane 1983), was selected as the first facade complex for investigation by the CMP. Structures 10L-9 and 10L-10 were completely excavated and restored by Gustav Strömsvik of the Carnegie Institution of Washington in the 1930s. As a result, we can be certain that all of the facade pieces that were still lying about in close proximity to the two structures have in fact been recovered. This situation is in marked contrast to most of the other major architectural monuments at the site, where sections of the substructures remain unexcavated and the sculpture sample is therefore incomplete. Furthermore, during the process of clearing the two structures of Ball Court A III, Strömsvik carefully placed the fragments of facade sculpture in a series of four piles, separated from those fallen from other nearby buildings

Fig. 1   Fragments of the Ball Court A III facade in "Pile 2" (photos by William L. Fash).

(fig. 1). This left future investigators a set of virtually un-contaminated samples of tenoned mosaic sculptures that derived from Structures 10L-9 and 10L-10, which also constituted the most complete sample of any building complex from the Main Group or "site core." We selected Ball Court A III for investigation because it was constructed just prior to the commemoration of Structure 10L-26 (1st), which signals the dramatic shifts in content and format of religious and political symbolism at the site referred to above.

Early on, it became apparent that, in addition to the macaw heads and talons and serpent pieces reported by Strömsvik (1952), there was a series of other motifs associated with the Ball Court A III facade: a maize element, generally composed of four blocks, showing the chaff and kernels, with *ahau* bone motifs at the ends of the chaff; an *akbal* glyph element, also generally consisting of four blocks; a series of beaded collars with feathered fringes and dangling *ahau* head pendants; a great number of kan crosses; very large (ca. 1m-long) *ahau* bones, with plaster on all four sides; feathers with rounded ends; straight-line feathers (some with staggered ends); vegetation motifs, of two different sizes; an element with a central, rounded core shown with small circles, and miscellaneous grooved stones, most with vertical and others with diagonal grooves (fig. 2).

Over the course of the 1985 season, and particularly once it was possible to have all of the cataloged fragments in one working area, it became possible to rearticulate many of the pieces of the individual elements. Furthermore, we were able to make minimum counts for many of the elements, based on the fragments recovered, cataloged, and articulated. This methodology is borrowed from the physical anthropological study of human skeletal remains: one can make minimum counts of individuals represented in a burial population based on the presence of x number of examples of any given bone or teeth. In our case, the number of individuals was calculated on the basis of the number of examples of any given segment of a known motif (e.g., left-facing serpent eye, lower right maize element, etc.). This controlled methodological study enabled us to undertake the reconstruction of the principal (macaw) motif on a much stronger footing than if we merely set to work with no limits on the possibilities for association and number of individual elements.

Based upon the study and rearticulation (when possible) of the fragments of the individual elements, we can present a tentative listing of the minimum counts of the following elements:

Macaw heads	14
Left macaw talons	14
Right macaw talons	13
Collars	14
Left-facing serpent heads	13
Right-facing serpent heads	14
Maize elements	28
Akbal glyphs	15

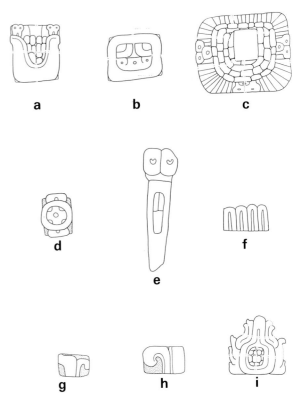

Fig. 2 Sculpture motifs from the facade of Ball Court A III rearticulated during the 1985 season: (a) maize; (b) akbal glyphs; (c) collars; (d) kan cross; (e) ahau bones; (f) feathers with rounded ends; (g) small vegetation elements; (h) large vegetation elements; (i) tails (drawings by Barbara W. Fash).

Rounded elements (tails)	13
Right side 3-tiered straight feathers	8
Left side 3-tiered straight feathers	4
Right side 4-tiered straight feathers	7
Left side 4-tiered straight feathers	11
Curved (left edge) pieces of feathers of rounded ends	29
Curved (right edge) pieces of feathers of rounded ends	23
Kan crosses	49
Large vegetation elements (combined lefts and rights)	42
Small vegetation elements	27
Long-tenoned *ahau* bones	13

Reconstruction Methodology

From the minimum counts of heads and talons, it is obvious that Proskouriakoff (1946:41) was right to reconstruct eight macaws per building (sixteen total), in that we can demonstrate the existence of at least fourteen, based on the minimum counts of heads and talons documented. The minimum count, it should be recalled, does not give us a maximum limit on the number of individuals represented. However, we believe that in the present study it does allow us to set some parameters. For example, assuming that eight principal element complexes per building is correct (and this pattern has in fact been demonstrated archaeologically thanks to good provenience data on the fragments fallen from Copán structures 9N-82 and 9M-195 in Sepulturas), we cannot reasonably interpret two macaw heads or four talons per principal element complex based on minimum counts of fourteen. We can quite reasonably posit the existence of one macaw head and two talons (one left and one right) per principal element complex, based on the minimum counts of fourteen, fourteen, and thirteen for these respective pieces.

Continuing this line of reasoning, we have tentatively concluded that each of the sixteen principal element complexes (eight for structure 10L-9 and eight for Structure 10L-10) contained the following: one macaw head; two macaw talons (one facing left, the other facing right); one collar; two maize elements; one rounded element (probably the tail); one *akbal* glyph; two serpent heads (one facing left, the other facing right); two lines

Fig. 3   Composite reconstruction of the macaw and associated motifs as reassembled in the sandbox by Barbara W. Fash, with wings in horizontal position (photos by William L. Fash).

of 3-tiered straight feathers (one left, one right); two lines of 4-tiered straight feathers (also one left, one right); four curved (edge) pieces of feathers with rounded edges, and one long-tenoned *ahau* bone. We are not certain whether the kan crosses, vegetation elements, and grooved stones were part of the principal element complexes; for this reason, we left them out of our sandbox reconstructions. The positioning of the large *ahau* bones is also unknown at present. The fitting, articulation, and assembly of the motifs in the sandbox was supervised by William Fash and accomplished by Barbara Fash, in collaboration with Linda Schele in the field.

In her reconstruction drawing, Proskouriakoff (1946) placed the macaws in the upper register, with one above each of the eight doorways on both buildings. She also placed a series of reptilian masks on each of the four corners of both buildings. Strömsvik (1952:189) stated that the serpent motifs (thought to be corner mask elements) "have eluded precise reconstruction": with good reason—the serpents were easily the most difficult motif rearticulated in the 1985 season. After an initial composite reconstruction, we realized that the serpent heads were in all likelihood the nucleus of the macaw's wings. Serpent wings are a common feature of most (indeed, virtually all) birds depicted in Classic Maya art (Maudslay 1889–1902, 5:63; Spinden 1913:60–61; Bardawil 1976). Based on this information, we placed the abovementioned number of articulated elements in the sandbox. We have come up with two basic alternatives for the presentation of the elements. One has the serpent wings in a vertical position (based on analogy with the bird shown on the east side of Copán Stela H). The other version, which we believe more likely to be correct, shows the serpent wings in a horizontal position, based on analogy with the carved wooden lintel from Tikal Temple 3. Within the two basic alternatives, there are several possibilities for the placement of certain motifs in different courses, with the variants we favor being reproduced here in figures 3 and 4.

Earlier Ball Court Sculptures Studied in the 1985 Season

A total of 1,351 fragments from piles 1–4 were cataloged, drawn, and photographed. Of these, 50 sculpture fragments were inconsistent with the rest of the Ball Court A III pieces and probably derived from other nearby buildings. One fragment of particular interest is CPN 5242, which represents the battered but recognizable bottom half of a tenoned macaw head (fig. 5). The orientation and placement of the tenon on the bottom (as opposed to the back) of the macaw head implies that it was set vertically, like the bench markers of Ball Court A III, and those found by Strömsvik in Mound 7 (Str. 10L-7), considered by him possibly to have derived from Ball Court A II (Strömsvik 1952:196). The smaller size and earlier style of CPN 5242 imply that it either pertained to the first version (IIa) of Ball Court A II with

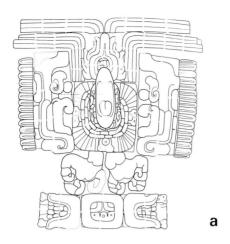

a

b

Fig. 4   Composite reconstructions of the macaw and associated motifs: (a) wings in vertical position; (b) wings in horizontal position (sandbox reconstruction and drawings by Barbara W. Fash).

Fig. 5   CPN 5242, tenon and lower part of vertically set macaw head marker from Ball Court A IIa or possibly Ball Court A I (drawings by Barbara W. Fash).

the Structure 10L-7 heads pertaining to the later, A IIb version, or possibly even to the original Copán ball court, A I. In either case, it demonstrates a continuity of macaw decoration for the ball court previously unknown at the site.

In addition to studying the fallen mosaic sculptures, the CMP set out to document and study the other sculptures associated with Ball Court A. This included the scientific illustration of the round playing alley markers found with Ball Court IIa, which had never before been drawn, by the project artist, Barbara Fash. The drawings were checked by the artist and Linda Schele using both natural and artificial light, as were the drawings of the

Ball Court IIb markers previously done by Barbara Fash. Schele also examined the inscriptions on the bench faces of Structures 10L-9 and -10 and determined that the most logical date for the commemoration of Ball Court A III was 10 Ben 16 Kayab (9.15.6.8.13), some 113 days immediately prior to the "capture" (more likely, the beheading) of the Copán King 18 Rabbit, at the hands of the Quiriguá Ruler Cauac Sky in A.D. 737. The date of commemoration of the final court is of great importance, in that the theme and elaboration of the sculpture ornamentation of this pre-"capture" building complex are in marked contrast to the more ornate and involved facades of the buildings that follow the construction of Ball Court A III (Structures 10L-26 [1st], 10L-11 [1st], 10L-22, etc.).

Copán Ball Court Sculpture in the Context of Mesoamerican Ball-Game Symbolism

As discussed above, the mosaic facade sculpture from Copán Ball Court A III includes macaws with serpent wings, *akbal* signs, long *ahau* bones, kan crosses, and maize and vegetation motifs. Although neither Stömsvik (1947, 1952) nor Proskouriakoff (1946) discussed the meaning of this sculpture, these motifs can be demonstrated to form an integral iconographic ensemble, whose symbolism correlates with that of the wider Maya and Mesoamerican ball games in general.

Virtually all investigators have pointed out the strong religious associations of the Mesoamerican rubber ball game.[2] Although details vary, two major interpretations of the sport have been proposed. Scholars such as Seler and Krickeberg concluded that the ball game was a symbolic reenactment of the battle between the forces of darkness and death and those of light and life. For Seler (1902–1923:III, 308ff., IV, 15–16) the ball in flight represented the seasonal north–south course of the sun in the firmament. Krickeberg (1966:255–256), on the other hand, preferred to interpret the game as symbolizing more obvious astral events, such as the daily death and rebirth of the sun or the sacrifice of the morning or evening star.

More recently, Knauth (1961) argued that the ball game was a sacrificial cult related to the moon and Moon Goddess, and that its ultimate objective was the promotion of agricultural fertility (see also Parsons 1969:103).

Since 1970, scholars such as Pasztory (1972, 1978), Cohodas (1975), and Gillespie (1985) have made persuasive efforts at reconciling these positions, demonstrating that Mesoamerican ball-game myths, rituals, and iconography combine both strong solar and agricultural fertility associations. A synthetic analysis of ball-game symbolism by Pasztory (1972:445) suggested:

The ball game symbolizes the disappearance of the sun into the underworld. The sun meets his death during a ball game waged by him and his brother (the planet Venus) against the gods of death and night. The underworld, a watery land of night, is the domain of the earth-moon goddess who becomes the bride

of the night sun. Subsequently the earth goddess gives birth to
the young god of maize (who is actually the sun reborn) and he
and Venus defeat the powers of darkness.

Cohodas (1975:108–110) developed a plausible
paradigm relating the dynamic play and postgame sacrifice to the seasonal death, transformation, and rebirth of
the sun-maize deity. According to this scheme, critical
ball games were played on the vernal and autumnal equi-
noxes, with the sacrificed players representing either the
dying sun (in spring) or the dismembered Moon Goddess
(in autumn).[3]

Although current interpretations favor viewing the
ball game as a metaphor for the seasonal solar and agricultural cycles, it also may be interpreted as symbolizing
the diurnal and nocturnal sojourn of the sun, whose
death, descent into the underworld, and rebirth (at
dawn) occur in both regular daily and seasonal cycles
(Pasztory 1978:131, 138; Gillespie 1985:4).

That the Maya conceived of a connection between
the ball game and the death and rebirth of the sun is evident in the account of the first fathers and the Hero
Twins in the Popol Vuh (Recinos 1950; Tedlock 1985).
As is well known, the fathers, Hun Hunahpu and Vucub
Hunahpu, are defeated in a ball game by the lords of the
underworld, after which they are sacrificed on the ball
court and Hun Hunahpu's head is hung in a calabash
tree, which is immediately covered with fruit. One day
as a young girl Xquic (blood) is passing by this tree, the
gourd-head spits in her hand, and she finds herself mi-
raculously pregnant with the Hero Twins Hunahpu and
Xbalanque. The twins again play ball with the Death
Gods, but this time win and eventually sacrifice the underworld rulers. Then Hunahpu and Xbalanque rise to
become, or to take possession of, the sun and moon.

Pasztory (1972:445) suggested that the fathers, Hun
Hunahpu and Vucub Hunahpu, represent the sun and
Venus and that Xquic equates with the young Moon
Goddess.[4] Michael Coe (1975b:90), on the other hand,
associated Hun Hunahpu (i.e., 1 Ahau) with the heliacal rising of Venus, and interprets the fathers as per-
sonifications of the morning and evening stars.

Leaving room for discussion concerning the exact
identity of Hun Hunahpu, the general content of the
Popol Vuh myth indicates a strong connection among
the ball game, the death and rebirth of astral deities including the sun, and the promotion of agricultural fertility. It is within this cosmic framework that Baudez (1984)
discussed the three sculptured alley markers of Copán
Ball Court A IIb (fig. 6). Baudez (1984:141) interpreted
the emblems (quadripartite badge minus central bloodletter) in the basal panels of the north and south markers
as the "night sun, 'dead' during its crossing the under-

a

b

c

*Fig. 6 Playing alley markers from Ball Court A IIb: (a)
north marker; (b) central marker; (c) south marker (drawings by Barbara W. Fash).*

world before the resurrection at dawn."[5] He thus argued that the action takes place in the underworld, identifying the players as mythological beings. Bones, marking the underworld context, are attached to the rope from which the ball hangs on the north marker. Mary Miller (Schele and Miller 1986:257) argued that the quatrefoil frame surrounding the scenes is another indication of the subterranean setting.[6] This same symbolism was present on the earlier markers of Ball Court A IIa (Strömsvik 1952: fig. 21; here fig. 7) and later markers of Ball Court A III, which also have quatrefoil frames and basal panels that contained symbols of the night sun (most evident on the A IIa central marker).

A stylized tree or plant appears behind each standing figure on the north and south markers. Cohodas (1975) and Pasztory (1972:446) interpreted the south plant as dead, accompanied by the number seven, referring to the night sun and death. The north plant was viewed as alive and accompanied by the number nine connoting good luck and agricultural fertility. Baudez (1984:143), however, noted that the two plants are virtually identical and related the numbers seven and nine to the depictions of long-snouted heads frequently paired with these numbers in Maya art and writing (cf. Kubler 1977). Baudez (1984:144) viewed these long-snouted heads as aspects of the earth monster, since both often sprout maize foliage from their heads. This interpretation accords reasonably well with those of Thompson (1950: 247, 276) and Kubler (1977:10). Although differing in particulars from Cohodas and Pasztory, like them he basically interpreted the numbered plants as referring to different aspects of the earth and phases of the vegetation cycle. Baudez (1984:146) identified the figure standing by the nine glyph as an anthropomorphic Jag-

uar Deity of the underworld, and the youthful figure standing beside the seven glyph as the young Maize God.[7]

The central marker, also marked by tripartite underworld sun emblems, shows the ball game in action. A human figure wearing protective gear, headband, and serpent headdress confronts a Death God whose lower jaw is formed of a human hand, like that on the head-variant for zero or completion (Thompson 1950:137).[8] His eye is shut and his bare thigh marked with black splotches of decomposing flesh (Baudez 1984:147). Like the human figure, the Death God has a plant or flower, probably to be understood as a water lily, attached to his headdress.

Because 18 Rabbit's name appears in the central inscription, Baudez (1984:147) argued that the human figure represents this ruler playing ball in the underworld. Mary Miller (Schele and Miller 1986:257), however, suggested that the anthropomorphic player is named by the glyph at A3, to be read Hun Ahau or Hunahpu, so that a deified hero rather than the human ruler is depicted. She suggests that 18 Rabbit may be shown as the ball itself.

While accepting the identification of the lefthand figure as Hunahpu of the Popol Vuh, it also seems plausible that he could be understood as the Copán ruler 18 Rabbit. Just as at their deaths Maya lords were thought to become one of the twins (Coe 1973b, 1975b:91), so during their lives they personified them during ritual reenactments of episodes from the myth. On the central marker 18 Rabbit thus "appears as the emulator of the twins of the Popol Vuh descended to the underworld to confront the lords of Xibalba in a ball game" (Baudez 1984:149) while the three markers express the cyclical rebirth of the sun and renewal of agricultural fertility.

It now remains to demonstrate the relationship between the motifs in the upper facades of Copán Ball Court A III and the basic symbolic themes of the ball game. Baudez (1984:150) briefly considered this question. His interpretation of the ball court as an underworld concourse seems correct, but his view that the benches symbolize the heavens or that the macaw personifies the "diurnal sky" seems less likely.

The macaw, which appeared from the time of Ball Court A I or A IIa to A III, is the preeminent iconographic element in the ball court sculpture at Copán. That these macaw sculptures are symbols of the sun is inferred from the name of the Yucatec deity Kinich Kakmo, "Sun-face (or eye) Fire Macaw," who was an aspect of the Sun God or a lesser solar deity. According to Lizana, Kinich Kakmo, flying like a macaw, descended at midday to burn sacrifices at his temple in Izamal (Thompson 1970:240). This deity is pictured in the Dresden and Madrid codices with fairly clear solar attributes. On Dresden 40b an anthropomorphic macaw bearing two flaming torches (Tozzer and Allen 1910:344; Villacorta and Villacorta 1930:90; here fig. 8a) is identified by a text that reads something like "his fire in the sky, the fourth macaw; drought" (Kelley 1976:174, fig.

Fig. 7 Central playing alley marker from Ball Court A IIa (drawing by Barbara W. Fash).

Kowalski and Fash

Fig. 8 Other references to the macaw in Maya art and writing: (a) Dresden page 40b; (b) Yax-Kuk-M'o, Altar Q, Copán; (c) Torch Macaw, Lintel 10, Yaxchilán (drawings by Barbara W. Fash).

64). Kelley (1976:174) suggested that the holding of torches is a reasonable symbol for drought produced by scorching solar heat.[9] A similar depiction of a macaw bearing a torch occurs on Madrid 12a (Villacorta and Villacorta 1930:248). On page 89a of the Madrid Codex a deity with Sun God characteristics wears a macaw headdress. The glyphs above read *ah kak(a) mo*, supporting his identification with the Yucatec Sun God Kinich Kakmo (Villacorta and Villacorta 1930:402; Kelley 1976:65).

In the Popol Vuh, after the defeat of the first fathers when the sun and moon are invisible, the supernatural macaw Vucub Caquix tries to convince men that it is he who illuminates the world. According to Krickeberg (1966:277), the name Vucub Caquix means "Seven Face of Fire," recalling the name of the solar deity Kinich Kakmo. Although the macaw deity in the Popol Vuh is described as an impostor of the sun, the solar association remains clear.[10]

The model for the Copán macaws was the royal macaw (*Ara macao*), a logical symbol for the sun because of its power of flight and because of its fiery, resplendent feathers. That such brilliant plumage was viewed as the sun's garb is supported by a reference in the Aztec Atamalqualiztli hymn honoring the youthful sun god hymn Pilzintecuhtli: "O Pilzintli, Pilzintli, with yellow feathers art thou passed over. On the ballcourt placest thyself, in the house of night" (Sahagún 1950–1971:III, 212–213).

The sun-macaw equation helps explain why several Classic Maya dynasts incorporated various macaw titles or epithets in their names. An important example is the name of the early Copán ruler Yax Quetzal Macaw or Yax-Kuk-M'o (fig. 8b). His name might be functionally equivalent to that of Yax-Pac, whose ideographic name "new sun-at-horizon" and phonetic name both mean

"dawn." The same idea could be expressed metaphorically by the name Yax-Kuk-M'o, "new precious (quetzal) sun (macaw)."

Another personage with a pertinent macaw name is Torch Macaw, who is named as a captive of Shield Jaguar's Descendant at Yaxchilán on Lintel 10 (A.D. 807?; fig. 8c) and Stela 7 (A.D. 771; Proskouriakoff 1964:196; Greene, Rands, and Graham 1972: pl. 52; Graham and von Euw 1977:31).[11] Torch Macaw presumably was of high status for Shield Jaguar's Descendant to have boasted of capturing him. His name recalls the macaws carrying torches in the Dresden and Madrid codices. Furthermore, the scrolls emitted from the flaming torch forming the first part of his name may simply be translated as *kak*, "fire" (Kelley 1976:148, 1982:9), indicating a relationship with the name of the Yucatec deity Kinich Kakmo. It seems probable that the Torch Macaw name is a solar epithet.[12]

Although the connection between the macaw-sun deity and the ball game is demonstrated most explicitly at Copán, this conception had a wider distribution in Mesoamerica, as is demonstrated by the parrot or macaw head that may have served as a ball court marker at Xochicalco (Easby and Scott 1970:184–185, fig. 150).

Iconographic elements such as *akbal* signs, bones, and probably kan crosses indicate that the macaw-sun deity is in the underworld. The day *akbal* is associated with night and corresponds to the Aztec day *calli* or house. Uotan, the Tzeltal-Tzotzil name for the day, also is the name of a deity and tribal ancestor associated with caves and the earth's interior. Seler (1904–1909:235) and Thompson (1950:74) considered him equivalent to Tepeyollotl, "Heart of the Mountain," eighth of the nine lords of the night and god of the day *calli*. The Maya patron of the day was the Jaguar God of the underworld (Thompson 1950:74).

In addition to having these general associations with darkness, night, and the interior of the earth, *akbal* signs, or the top part thereof, are often used to refer to underworld contexts in Maya writing or art (Thompson 1950: fig. 16, 42–43). For example, the *akbal* sign is infixed in the head of the Death God on page 28 of the Dresden Codex (Villacorta and Villacorta 1930:66).

The close connection between *akbal* and the underworld is also confirmed on numerous Classic Maya polychrome ceramics, where various anthropomorphic figures, animals, and monsters have *akbal* glyphic infixes or display the glyph in costume or accoutrements (e.g., Coe 1982:108–113). On the well-known codex-style vase illustrated by Coe (1973b:98, vase 45) a dancing underworld deity confronts the youthful GI wearing an inverted-vase pectoral marked by an *akbal* glyph. Another appears on a bag carried by the Palenque ruler Kan-Xul on Dumbarton Oaks Relief Panel 2 (Coe and Benson 1966: fig. 6). Kan-Xul, flanked by his ancestors, is represented posthumously in the underworld as GI of the Palenque Triad (Miller 1984:43)

The large *ahau* bones from the Copán Ball Court

are an obvious reference to death and the underworld (Thompson 1970:220–222, 304). God A (the Death God) sits on a throne formed of long bones on Dresden 53a (Coe 1975b: fig. 1), while crossed bones and "death eyes" appear above the infernal God L on the Vase of the Seven Gods (Coe 1973b:107). Such examples could be multiplied time and again.

The macaws, *akbal* signs, and long *ahau* bones of the facade sculpture of Court A III suggest that the entire court, including the benches and the temples, may be viewed as embodying the underworld and/or the night sky where the sun confronts his manifold adversaries. This interpretation harmonizes both with the Popol Vuh account, where the critical ball games are played in Xibalba, and with evidence from central Mexican sources. For example, in the aforementioned Atamalqualiztli hymn the ball court occupied by Pilzintecuhtli is called the "House of Night" (Youanchan). Seler (1902– 1923:II, 1096, IV, 15–16) thus argued that this ball court symbolized the earth, within which the sway of Pilzintecuhtli (interpreted as the young Maize God) begins. Krickeberg (1966:220) tended to view the ball court more as a symbol of the night sky, and thus viewed Pilzintecuhtli in this hymn as a solar deity.

In an alternate version of the Huitzilopochtli myth recorded by Tezozomoc, Huitzilopochtli (the sun) does battle with Coyolxauhqui (the moon) and the Centzon Uitznaua (the stars) in a magical ball court with a central hole known as Itzompan ("place of skulls").[13] In this version of the myth the ball court clearly corresponds to the nocturnal sky, in which the eternal war between the sun and his antagonists is fought.

Krickeberg (1966:248–249) suggested that while many ball courts (e.g., Codex Vindobonensis 7) clearly are envisioned as the night sky, some other ball courts incorporating skeletal symbols (e.g., Codex Nuttall 4; fig. 9) pertain to the underworld, supporting the "idea that the night sky and the earth, or underworld, are in their essence the same."[14]

Kan crosses with bone attachments, similar to those of Copán Ball Court A III, adorn the cornice and medial moldings of the side of the Temple of the Foliated Cross sanctuary at Palenque (Maudslay 1889–1902:IV, pl. 78). Thompson (1950:276) pointed out the frequent inclusion of the kan cross in the foreheads of long-snouted earth monsters from which maize foliage sprouts (e.g., Palenque, TFC Tablet, fig. 10; long-snouted head coupled with number seven) and suggested that "the kan (pre-

Fig. 9 Codex Nuttall 4, showing the association of a ball court and skulls (drawing by Barbara W. Fash).

Fig. 10 Central axis of the Temple of the Foliated Cross tablet, showing a kan cross in the forehead of the earth monster, and a serpent bird on top of a maize plant (drawing by Barbara W. Fash after Maudslay 1889–1902; vol. 4, pl. 78).

cious) cross is therefore a logical attribute, stressing his [the earth monster's] connection with water and the production of food."

If the Copán kan crosses were placed in a cornice band they might also have resembled the frames of piers c, d, and f of the Palenque Palace (Maudslay 1889– 1902: pls. 33, 35–37), where small roundels (probably jade jewels) alternate with glyphic signs; *yax* (pier d), completion (pier c), and an *ahau* bone element (pier f). These piers, along with pier b, also portray figures standing on water bands (cf. Coggins 1983b:26, 44–50). Since the *yax* and completion signs frequently appear in flows of liquid identified as either water (Rands 1955) or blood (Stuart 1988), it is likely that all these scenes are taking place in a liquid environment. Many of the scenes on Maya polychrome ceramics take place not simply in

Kowalski and Fash

a subterranean counterpart of the earth's surface, but in a murky "underwater world" (Schele and Miller 1986:267).[15] Since the kan cross frequently is paired with, or substitutes for, the *yax* and completion signs in liquid streams, it is probable that it was used on the Copán Ball Court facades to indicate the underworld-underwater associations of the ball game.

The final elements from the Copán Ball Court facades to be considered are the maize cobs with kernels, chaff, and attached *ahau* bones, and other foliage scrolls. Considering the general Mesoamerican ball-game symbolism discussed previously, and the specific plant iconography evident on the north and south Copán alley markers, it seems likely that the maize and vegetation motifs refer to the other great function of the ball game and its accompanying human sacrifices: the promotion of agricultural fertility and the seasonal rebirth of the sun-maize deity.

Throughout its history the Copán Ball Court conserved a basic cosmological symbolism. The alley markers, marked by emblems of the night sun and depicting players in action, picture the contest between light and darkness, life and death, and the victory of the sun (Hunahpu-18 Rabbit) over the lord of the underworld, assuring continued agricultural abundance. The bench and facade sculptures restate these fundamental themes in iconic rather than narrative form. The great solar macaws, accompanied by corn foliage, inhabit a watery underworld realm (marked by *akbal*s, bones, and kan crosses) whence they will be resurrected, like the Copán rulers Yax-Pac or Yax-Kuk-M'o, as the dawn. Like the great Teotlachtli (divine ball court) in Tenochtitlán's central temenos, where the Panquetzaliztli festival culminated in a dramatic reenactment of Huitzilopochtli's triumph, the Copán Ball Court was a place of paradigmatic cosmic conflict. Here the lords of Copán, before the eyes of their people, incarnated the Hero Twins of the Popol Vuh and relived their battles, thereby ensuring the rebirth of the sun, promoting the growth of the maize, and manifesting their sacred role as mediators between the world of the gods and that of men.

Notes

1. Funding for the 1985 season was procured by Fash from the Center for Field Research (EARTHWATCH), from the Graduate School of Northern Illinois University, and from the International and Special Programs Division of Northern Illinois University.

2. On the ball game generally, see Stern (1948), Borhegyi and Borhegyi (1963), Krickeberg (1966), and Borhegyi (1969).

3. Pasztory (1972:444, 1978:138) also viewed the sacrificial aspect of the ball game as critical, with the death of the player causing (via sympathetic magic) the cyclic death and rebirth of the sun and the rejuvenation of agricultural fertility.

4. Pasztory (1972:445) adduced correspondences between Maya and Central Mexican literary sources supporting the identity between Hun Hunahpu (1 Ahau), Xochipilli-Pilzintecuhtli (youthful incarnation of the sun, calendric name 1 Xochitl), and Centeotl (Maize God, birthdate 1 Xochitl). See also Nicholson (1971:416).

5. On the quadripartite badge, see Thompson (1950:172–173) and M. G. Robertson (1974:77–92).

6. The quatrefoil shape apparently has similar associations on the incised peccary skull from Copán (Spinden 1913: fig. 210).

7. Schele (Schele and Miller 1986:309, pl. 121) has argued that the distinctive type of downturned half-mask worn by the right-hand figure is associated with moon imagery. Perhaps it identifies this figure as the hero twin who becomes the moon in Popol Vuh.

8. Thompson (1970:378) unconvincingly identified this figure as Macuil Xochitl.

9. Thompson (1973:100) argued that the number four prefixed to the macaw glyph refers to the Sun God.

10. The macaw also possessed solar associations for the Cora and Huichol Indians of northwest Mexico (Krickeberg 1966:277).

11. On Lintel 10 the Torch Macaw name is expressed ideographically at B6b-C7b, while on Stela 7 the name appears as a torch prefixed to T582, phonetic *mo*, a substitution for the macaw head.

12. However, since it is also used to name the captive of Ruler 1 of Dos Pilas, the term "Torch Macaw" seems to be a "generic epithet of captives" rather than a personal name (Houston and Mathews 1985:10). Another macaw name is that of 12 Macaw, mother of Tikal Ruler B and probably the wife of Ruler A (Jones 1977:42; Jones and Satterthwaite 1983: fig. 8).

13. Brundage (1979;11) supplied a slightly different though not conflicting translation and interpretation. Krickeberg (1966) discussed several other ball courts with fields marked by skulls and other death symbols, which he interpreted as symbols of the sacrificed stars.

14. This concept was summarized by Brundage (1979:10).

15. Regarding the notion of an "underwater world," it is interesting that the Cora Indians of northwest Mexico believe that beneath the earth there is a dark liquid that springs from the edges of the earth and floods the sky at dusk (Krickeberg 1966:221).

Lineage Patrons and Ancestor Worship Among the Classic Maya Nobility: The Case of Copán Structure 9N-82

WILLIAM L. FASH
NORTHERN ILLINOIS UNIVERSITY

The practice of ancestor worship has been ably documented by numerous ethnographers of the twentieth-century Maya. Largely because of the ethnographic literature, ancestor worship among the Classic Maya is widely assumed, especially since the discovery of dynasties and parentage statements in the inscriptions of the Classic Period. The burial chambers and accompanying inscriptions found in the excavated pyramid temples of Tikal, Palenque, and other sites showed that kings were revered even after death. Recently, epigraphers have shown the importance of lineage perpetuation by documenting the lengths to which rulers went to ensure it by means of sacrificial rituals. Given the overwhelming evidence for ancestor worship among the ruling lineages of the Classic Maya realm, and the equally strong evidence for ancestor worship among the peasant-class twentieth-century Maya, one could predict that supernatural lineage patrons, ancestor worship, and lineage perpetuation lore would all have been pervasive among the gamut of social classes existent during the Late Classic Period. Here I present data and interpretations derived from recent excavations at Copán that support this thesis.

Copán Structure 9N-82 and Its Sculpture Facade

The present case material derives from a Late Classic residential compound of the noble class from Copán, Honduras. The site in question is the largest extended household compound in the residential sector located directly east of the Main Group or site core, known as "Las Sepulturas." Group 9N-8 has been shown to be a very elaborate and complex set of interrelated structures with its apogee in the late eighth century A.D., but with occupations stretching back to the beginning of the second millennium B.C. (Fash, Agurcia, and Abrams 1981; Webster, Fash, and Abrams 1986). Dominating the central part of the multiple-plaza Late Classic site is a raised platform, representing the accumulation of the living sites of the previous two millennia. Seated prominently at the south end of the elevated platform is Plaza A, which contained the largest and most ornate structures during the eighth century (fig. 1). In the center of the south side of Plaza A was Structure 9N-82, a sumptuous vaulted edifice ornamented with a mosaic sculpture facade and an elaborate hieroglyphic bench in the central room (Webster 1989). This particular structure was to give the archaeologists of the Proyecto Arqueológico Copán (William Sanders, director, Phase II) a unique and explicit example of lineage patrons and ancestor worship. This paper touches upon those aspects of the investigations and archaeological remains that bear directly on these questions, referring the interested reader to other writings covering these and other facets of the Plaza A and other Group 9N-8 investigations.[1]

After being cleared of vegetation, Structure 9N-82 appeared as a long, linear construction with a raised central portion. In the center of this higher central sector was a notable depression, marking the doorway and inner chamber of what turned out to be the central room of the central superstructure (9N-82 Central, or C). During the initial excavation of the building in 1980, David Webster and Elliot Abrams discovered a magnificent sculpted bench in the central room, complete with hieroglyphic inscription and complex iconography (Webster and Abrams 1983). Flanking the three-roomed central superstructure on either side were the east and west superstructures (9N-82E and 9N-82W), each with two rooms. Two other rooms were built into what had originally been a corridor between the central and west superstructures, and a tenth room was built into the east side of the substructure, directly beneath the eastern room of the east superstructure. On the front side of this array of rooms ran a continuous stairway with five risers, which united at its eastern and western extremities with the continuous frontal stairways of Structures 9N-83 and 9-81, respectively (fig. 1).

Both the superstructures and substructure of 9N-82 were built of finely dressed blocks of the local green volcanic tuff. Unfortunately, the mud mortar used in the

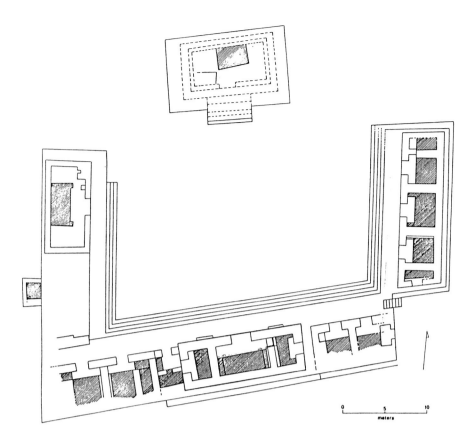

Fig. 1   Plan of Plaza A, Group 9N-8, Copán (after Larios and Fash 1985; courtesy Instituto Hondureno de Antropología e Historia).

original construction resulted in severe collapse of the upper portions of the superstructures (including all of the vaulted roofs), with the best-preserved superstructure walls standing ca. 2 m high, and most conserved only a little over a meter in height. In addition to the innumerable dressed tuff blocks, large slabs of roof plaster were found in the clearing of the superstructures and north side of Str. 9N-82, as well as many beveled, tenoned vault stones, and tenoned sculpture fragments.

The tenoned mosaic sculpture fragments discovered by Webster and Abrams in their 1980–1981 clearing of the top and front side of the structure were concentrated on the substructure terrace, steps, and adjacent plaza area in front of the central superstructure (82C). Provenience points for all of these pieces were dutifully recorded on a map, and each fragment was given a field number and subsequently fully cataloged. This methodology had already given outstanding results in Copán when applied to the 1978–1979 excavations at Ball Court B, where it was possible to make a number of behavioral inferences based on the provenience of the sculpture fragments found at that court (Fash and Lane 1983). Once the back side of the structure was excavated by the author in consultation with Rudy Larios in 1982, we had a complete excavated sample with good provenience data from which to proceed with our reconstruction of the form and content of the 9N-82C building facades.

Methodology of Facade Reconstruction

Given the fact that the all four entablatures plus the vaults had completely collapsed, our reconstruction of the upper portions of the facade of this building was based on the position of the fallen fragments and internal evidence from the sculpture pieces themselves. The excavations of the back (south) side of the building provided us with a clear pattern of fall. There three discrete clusters of tenoned sculpture fragments were discerned during the excavation, which stand out in the composite plan map (figs. 2, 3a). Upon cleaning and cataloging of the pieces from each of these three back side sculpture clusters, it became obvious that each of these three groupings contained the same basic element. These were a long-tenoned base, carved in the form of a T23 (*na*, or "house") sign, a human figure shown seated cross-legged and with its hands palms outward against the chest, a plumed headdress similar in style and layout to those of structure 10L-18 (fig. 3b), and iconic elements from the central headdress. A small feathered dais was also found with the east and west figures, which was in fact custom-fitted to line up with the bottom of the seated figures' loincloths (fig. 3c).

With regard to actually fitting the pieces together, in Copán one has the advantage that the sculpture blocks were not actually carved until the constituent blocks had been assembled on the building. This happy circum-

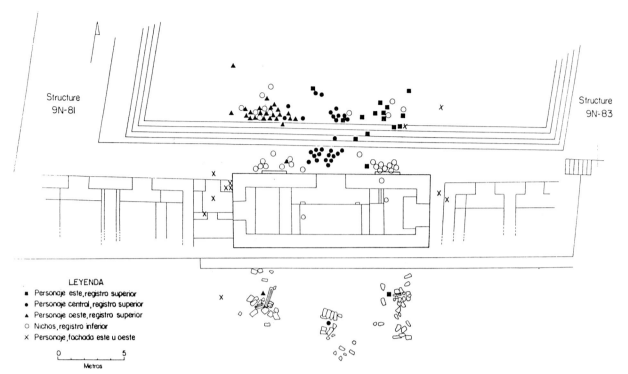

Structure
9N-81

Structure
9N-83

LEYENDA
■ Personaje este, registro superior
● Personaje central, registro superior
▲ Personaje oeste, registro superior
○ Nichos, registro inferior
✕ Personaje, fachada este u oeste

0 _____ 5
Metros

Fig. 2   Plan of Structure 9N-82, showing the distribution of the fallen fragments of tenoned mosiac facade sculpture (after Larios and Fash 1985; courtesy Instituto Hondureno de Antropología e Historia).

stance means that lines join up on adjacent blocks sharing the same motif. For example, when joining feather pieces, one lines up the edges and the central spines from one block to another, with the direction of curvature serving as a guide for which blocks are most likely to go together. In other cases, lining up of high-relief blocks can be done by vertical courses. For example, the belt pieces always fit perfectly on top of the leg pieces, and the central headdress pieces articulated with the head of the east figure (the only one found on the back side).

The fitting and rearticulation of the blocks on both the back and front sides of the building could be done with ease, once the basic patterns had been established with the south facade east figure. In fact, it was also possible to rearticulate several fragments that had been collected from the site by local representatives of the Honduran Institute of Anthropology in previous years, simply by checking the fit of lines, height of course, and tenon length in the case of feathers, and vertical alignment and proper proportion in the case of body parts. One particularly compelling case was that of the bust fragment of the south facade central figure. During the excavations in 1982, we recovered the (viewer's) left half of the bust with the hand, and the right hand, but found no traces of the right bust. In searching through the sculpture fragments stored by the IHAH, I found a right bust fragment that was missing an arm. Upon rearticulation, not only did the bust fit perfectly with the arm recovered in the excavations, but the lines of beads

corresponded perfectly with those of the companion left half of the bust. The fittings offered here are presented with complete confidence.

It remained only to determine the height at which the three figures on the south facade were tenoned into the entablature. As luck would have it, a major section of the central portion of the south facade fell intact, as a unit, apparently at the time the vault of the central room of Str. 82C collapsed. Both courses of the medial molding were preserved intact for a distance of 4.2 m (fig. 3d). Directly above the medial molding were found the still articulated pieces of the sculpted base (the T23 sign) of the central figure, indicating that the throne or seat of each figure was tenoned into the facade directly on top of the medial molding, with the figure and its headdress placed on top of the base. All of these data enabled us to produce a methodologically sound hypothetical reconstruction of the south facade (fig. 4).

For the north facade, the entablature was relatively easy to reconstruct once the south facade had been figured out. Here again there were fragments of three T23 bases, three seated figures, three sets of headdress feathers, three sets of central headdress motifs, and feathered daises for the east and west figures. The distribution map enabled us to separate the fragments of the three figures with relative ease. Of further help was the fact that the long-tenoned base fragments were very distinctive from one figure to the next. The eastern base is divided into two courses above the circular elements of the *na* sign, whereas the western base's division falls below the cir-

Fig. 3 (a) Photo of the fallen fragments comprising the east figure of the south facade of Structure 9N-82C-1st; (b) photo of the feathered headdress of the eastern figure in the interior chamber of Temple 18, Copán; (c) drawing traced from a photograph of a composite reconstruction of the fragments of the east and west figures of the north and south facades of Structure 9N-82C-1st; (d) photo of the medial molding as it fell in back of the central part of the south side of Structure 9N-82C-1st (photos after Fash 1986a:377, 378, 347, 378; courtesy Instituto Hondureno de Antropología e Historia).

cular elements, and the central base's division occurs exactly in the middle of these same rounded elements. Also, the central figure in fact turned out to be rather distinctive, having a wider base, a wider feathered headdress, a different set of central headdress elements, and a unique body posture (fig. 5). The head of the central figure was also unlike those of the south facade east figure or north facade west figure, being more distinguished in its cast and with finer treatment of the hair and adornment.

For the lower register of the facade (below the medial molding), there was a good deal of internal and excavation evidence to facilitate our reconstruction of the fallen elements, combined with the information derived from the entablatures. The resulting reconstruction is reproduced here as figure 6.

Two elements had been partially preserved on either side of the north side doorway, and these were dutifully restored by the Phase II restoration director, Carlos Rudy Larios. Study of the map of fallen sculpture demonstrated a strong concentration of pieces that were demonstrably not like the rest of the sculptures from the entablature on the terrace directly in front of the two motifs preserved in situ. In working with these fragments, Barbara Fash was able to articulate four serpent heads. Close examination of these demonstrated that one of the heads from the front of the east sculpture element had burn marks. In fact, burn marks covered the west half of the in situ eastern element, and the basal block of the burned serpent head fit exactly in the space left by Larios between two stones of the same course that were still in place when he restored the building. Furthermore, the two fragments of a bust and the left hand of a figure that, due to its lack of tenon, was obviously

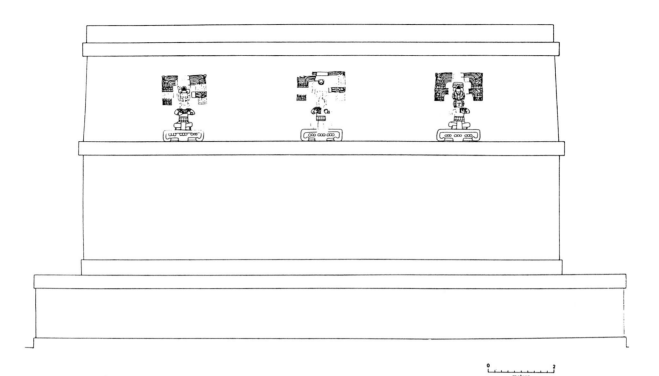

0 ⊢—————————⊣ 2
meters

Fig. 4 Hypothetical reconstruction drawing of the south facade of Structure 9N-82C-1st (after Larios and Fash 1985:125; courtesy Instituto Hondureno de Antropología e Historia).

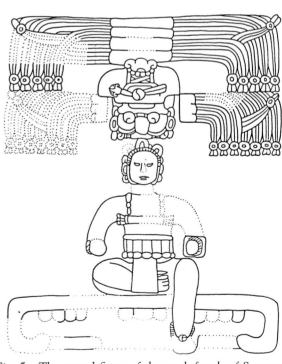

Fig. 5 The central figure of the north facade of Structure 9N-82C-1st (after Larios and Fash 1985:131; courtesy Instituto Hondureno de Antropología e Historia).

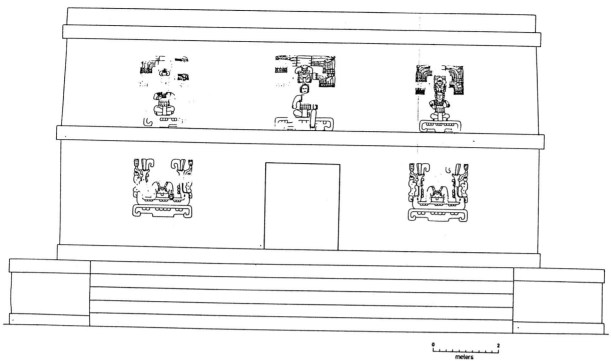

Fig. 6 Hypothetical reconstruction drawing of the north facade of Structure 9N-82C-1st (after Larios and Fash 1985:130; courtesy Instituto Hondureno de Antropología e Historia).

meant to be placed in a niche also showed burn marks that corresponded to those of both the *in situ* part of the *na* element and the fallen pieces in question. Based on the fits made by Barbara Fash, the correlations of burn marks made by William Fash, and the letter-perfect restoration done by Rudy Larios, it was possible to restore the fallen elements back onto the facade. Using the example of the restored east niche and figure (fig. 7a), it was possible to rearticulate and restore the bust and serpent heads of the west niche as well (fig. 7b).[2]

In addition to the south and north facades, the east and west entablatures were also adorned with tenoned mosaic sculptures. In the case of the west facade, many fragments were in fact found directly in front of the doorway on the west side of 82C, whereas others had fallen due north or south of the west plane of the central superstructure. For the east facade, most of the pieces recovered in the excavation were found north of the plane of the east facade of Str. 82C. The east figure was the more complete, containing (after fitting with pieces previously recovered by the IHAH staff) the seated legs, belt, and torso of a figure, at least part of both hands, and feathers from the headdress. No traces of any T23 sign base were found, in either the excavations or searches through the IHAH collections, nor was either of the two heads recovered. For the central headdress, it is possible that a large *k'in* sign formed a part of the composition (fig. 7c). One such *k'in* sign was found in the vicinity of the other fragments of the east and west facade figures, north of the building.

Structure 9N-82C-2nd and Associated Sculpture

The extensive trenching into the substructure and subsequent restoration work established that Str. 9N-82C-1st (discussed above) was originally a freestanding building. Internal structural evidence demonstrates that this central structure was built first, followed by the addition of 9N-82 West (1st), with 9N-82 East added last. Prior to the construction of the freestanding structure 9N-82C-1st, another building had existed at this locus.

Fragmentary sections of this earlier edifice—Structure 9N-82C 2nd—were found during the stabilization process, prior to the restoration of the (later) central room of Str. 9N-82C-1st (fig. 8a). The two pieces of the full-round, complete Pauah Tun sculpture were both found in the fill of Str. 9N-82C-1st, though separated by 9 m. This slightly smaller than life-size figure (fig. 8b) was decapitated and the head burned, with both pieces thrown into the fill during the construction of 9N-82C-1st. This suggests that this sculpture was originally in use in the now-destroyed earlier building and ritually killed and buried when that building was abandoned.

The figure wears a necklace whose pendant is a finely executed example of the beaded water-lily motif found on the busts in the 9N-82C-1st niches, and also found (inverted) in the headdresses of the central figures in the entablatures of the north and south facades. The figure is shown cross-legged, with a sectioned conch-shell inkpot in the left hand and a stylus in the right. The deity is phonetically identified by the netted cap (*pauah*) and

Fig. 7 (a) Drawing of the east niche of the north facade of Structure 9N-82C-1st (drawing by G. Stanley Matta); (b) photo of Structure 9N-82C-1st, after restoration by Larios (after Larios and Fash 1985:126; courtesy Instituto Hondureno de Antropología e Historia; (c) drawing of a photograph of the composite reconstruction of the figure fragments from the east and west facades of Structure 9N-82C-1st (drawing by Barbara W. Fash).

Cauac (*tun*) body markings. These same identifiers are found on the easternmost pillar under the hieroglyphic bench in the central room of Str. 9N-82C-1st, signaling that he and his colleagues are also Pauah Tuns (underworld cousins of the Bacabs). The continuity through time and space of Pauah Tun worship led us to hypothesize that this deity served as a lineage patron, or minimally the patron of the lineage or titular head of the group, through time (Webster and Abrams 1983:295, Larios and Fash 1985; Fash 1986a).[3]

Interpretation and Comparative Study of Str. 9N-82 Sculpture

The north facade of Structure 9N-82 faced onto Plaza A of Group 9N-8 and as such was the most ornate and sym-bolically explicit side of the building (fig. 6). This facade was divided into two fields, the lower one (including the doorway and decorations on either side of it) relating to the supernatural world, the upper one (the entablature) relating to the living, surface world. The serpents on either side of the doorway are characterized by fleshless, bony snouts, and by an *ahau* glyphic element capped by a *sak* ("white") sign, shown at the end of their nose-plugs. This glyph has been interpreted by Tatiana Proskouriakoff to have a meaning of "soul" or "spirit." From the split serpents' jaws emerge anthropomorphic deities: each wears a beaded, trilobed water-lily motif as a necklace pendant. The eastern deity clearly depicts a patron of scribes and artists by virtue of the conch-shell inkpot he carries in his left hand. By analogy with the earlier figure found associated with the earlier version of Struc-

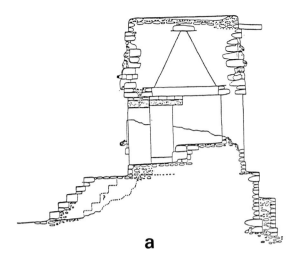

a

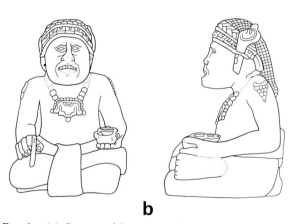

b

Fig. 8 (a) Section of Structure 9N-82C, showing reconstructed facade and conserved portions of 82C-1st, and preserved parts of 82C-2nd (after Fash 1986a:369; courtesy
Instituto Hondureno de Antropología e Historia); (b) drawing of the Pauah Tun/Scribe (by Barbara W. Fash).

the east and west figures on both sides of the building
leaves one with the impression that these individuals
were of equal stature and less important than the distinctive central figures. Their headdresses have what Linda
Schele (personal communication) refers to as the "personification head," with maize as the element in the
forehead, which is to be understood as the being or object being given life. Abundance and sustenance of life
seem to be the principal attributes of these side figures;
their identity as historical individuals can only be speculated upon at this point.

The north facade central figure is distinguished from
his two entablature companions by a number of features:
a distinctive central headdress complex, different body
position, more finely detailed facial treatment, different
clothing details, a wider base or throne, and possibly
items held in the hands (fig. 5). Of particular interest
are the central headdress elements, which should be the
diagnostic indicator of the supernatural aspects being assumed or emulated by their wearer.

I have already noted the close association between the
beaded water-lily motif and the Structure 9N-82-1st (facade) and 2nd (full-round figure) Pauah Tuns. The same
association is found on Princeton Vase 16 (Coe 1978). In
his consideration of the patrons of Maya scribes and artists, Coe illustrates figure 2 of this vessel, without including a beaded element and pendants as part of that
figure (Coe 1977b: figure 11). This element would thus
pertain to the deity pictured immediately in back of that
figure, labeled figure 1 in Coe's 1978 book and here represented as figure 9a. This individual also clearly represents a god of writing, by virtue of his "extra" ear with
T7 infix, "computer print-out" with bar and dot numerals, and conch-shell inkpot in the right hand (for a
Copán equivalent, see fig. 9b). The beaded water lily
here is shown front on, but half of it is obscured behind
the back of figure 2, as is the left hand. Even if we
were to consider the motif here as associated with figure 2 (the "Monkey Man" God of Writing: Coe 1977b,
1978:106), this would only serve to strengthen the association between this motif and the Pauah Tun of Structure 9N-82C-2nd, which has decidedly simian facial features (fig. 8b). Indeed, one is led to wonder whether the
oft-repeated association of one of the four Bacabs/Pauah
Tuns with the conch shell at Copán, Chichén Itzá (Morris, Charlot, and Morris 1931: vol. 2), and other Classic
Period sites and on painted ceramics may be in part derived from the association of this particular deity with a
conch-shell inkpot, in his guise as a patron of Maya
scribes and artists.

From the above, it may be suggested that the Pauah
Tun, tied water-lily, and beaded water-lily motifs in the
headdress of the central figure of the north facade of Str.
9N-82 are used to associate that individual with his
supernatural patron, the Pauah Tun as patron of scribes
and artists. This association finds support in the text of
the hieroglyphic bench of the central room of 82C (1st),
which according to Berthold Riese (cited in Webster and

ture 82 (2nd), in all probability it represents a Pauah
Tun/Scribe. The upper register, in contrast, contains
human figures in rich garb, whose clothing, faces, and
headdresses indicate that they are dwellers of the surface
world. Analogy with stelae, lintels, and ceramic vases of
the Classic Maya world indicates that these figures depict actual historical individuals. Given this basic framework, we can analyze the significance of the symbols and
figures depicted in the two fields represented.

For the entablatures, the east and west figures of both
the north and south facades are so similar as to be virtually identical to each other. The sharing of the (inverted) beaded water-lily motif by the central figures on
the north and south facades implies that the two facades
are two sides of the same coin, as it were: each side depicts the same three individuals. The virtual identity of

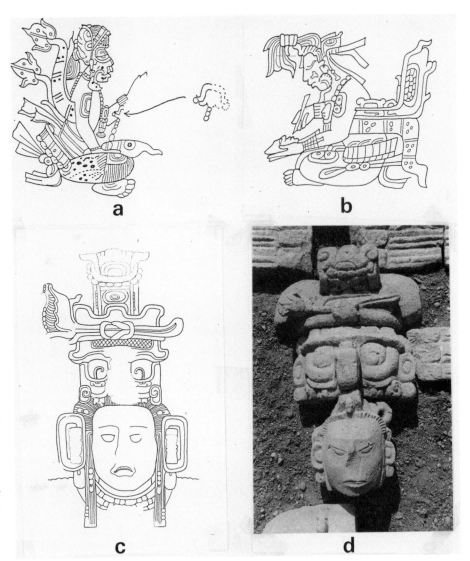

Fig. 9   (a) Princeton 16 (after Coe 1978); (b) inscribed figure on vessel from Tomb 37-2, Copán (drawing by Jose Humberto Espinoza, after Fash 1986a:373; courtesy Instituto Hondureno de Antropología e Historia); (c) detail of face and central headdress elements of north side figure of Copán Stela N (drawing by Barbara W. Fash); (d) detail of the face and central headdress elements of the central figure on the north side of Structure 9N-82C-1st (after Larios and Fash 1985:131; courtesy Instituto Hondureno de Antropología e Historia).

Abrams 1983) refers to the protagonist of the inscription (who also dedicates the temple) as "Ahau Kin," which Riese infers to mean that he was an astronomer and calendar specialist. Such an individual must, of course, have been an accomplished scribe in order to practice such an esoteric trade. It is my belief that the distinctive features and prominent placement of the central figure of the entablature signify that this figure depicts the bench protagonist. That the bench protagonist was not the ruler of Copán is itself quite clear in the inscription, which refers to Yax-Pac in a secondary clause, following the initial clause, which refers to the date of commemoration of the temple, the act of commemoration itself, and the protagonist of that action, whose name is clearly different from that of any of the Copán dynasts.

In this context it is interesting to note that the central headdress elements found on the central figure of the Str. 9N-82C-1st facade are quite similar to the most prominent central elements in the headdresses of both sides of Copán Stela N (cf. figs. 9c, d). A curved element found with the south facade central figure fragments also appears in the headdress of Stela N. Thus, the long-nosed god (personification) head, tied water lily, and inverted beaded water lily can be considered important elements in the Copán royal line's own symbolism.

The emphasis of Pauah Tun/Bacab iconography can be seen in the works of the fifteenth ruler ("Smoke-Squirrel," depicted on the south side of Stela N), but almost certainly reaches its climax in the reign of the sixteenth ruler, Yax-Pac. Examples of Pauah Tun/Bacab iconography datable to the reign of Yax-Pac include those of Temple 21 (first discovered by the author in 1984), Temple 11 (the famous "Old Man" head, and his little-remarked upon twin brother; figs. 10a, b), CV 43 Structure A (Willey, Leventhal, and Fash 1978), and the Str. 9N-82 facade and bench.

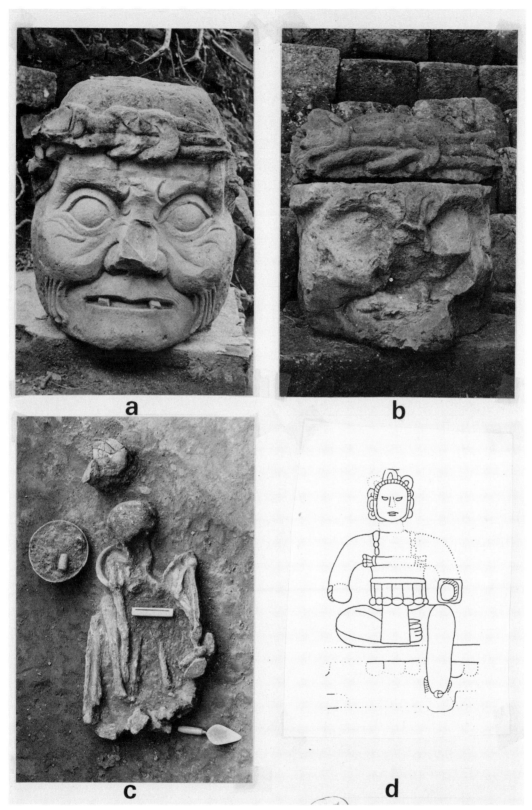

Fig. 10 (a) Photo of the "Old Man of Copán" (after Fash 1986a:382; courtesy Instituto Hondureno de Antropología e Historia; (b) photo of the "Old Man's" companion figure from the facade of Temple 11 (after Fash 1986a:382; courtesy Instituto Hondureno de Antropología e Historia); (c) photo of Burial VIII-6 (after Fash 1986a:382; courtesy Instituto Hondureno de Antropología e Historia); (d) drawing of the central figure, north facade, Str. 9N-82C-1st (after Fash 1986a:363 courtesy Instituto Hondureno de Antropología e Historia).

Two of my colleagues on the PAC resist the idea that a local lineage head would be allowed to "manifest so much pride and independence by placing his image in such imposing situation" and prefer to view the central facade figure as a portrait of Yax-Pac (Baudez in press; Riese in press). In part this may stem from their adherence to traditional models of the nature of Classic Maya art and sociopolitical organization.[4] Elsewhere, I have developed a multivariant model to explain the sudden and explosive proliferation of elite stone art during the reign of Yax-Pac (Fash 1983:258–260). The model is rooted in the demographic and environmental conditions during the reign of this last, seemingly most creative and beneficent ruler. It was argued that the requirements of the Maya socioreligious and political system had devastating effects in Copán when it developed within an ecologically maladaptive settlement system. Therein the agriculturally richest, most centralized land in the Copán Valley was given over to a series of urban wards, forcing subsistence agriculture and cash-cropping upslope. This in turn entailed deforestation, shorter fallow cycles, soil exhaustion and erosion, and eventually long-term precipitation loss. These conditions were exacerbated by factional politics among the oldest and/or most powerful lineages not only of Copán, but apparently of Quiriguá, as well. It is my contention that the whole political system would have collapsed quite abruptly without continuing tribute from the elite lineages who supported it.

This model sees Yax-Pac and his court as seeking to ensure continued tribute by bestowing the ultimate royal prerogative upon the most important lineage heads: hieroglyphic texts and relief sculptures with complex iconography. This represents a significant "sharing of information" of the highest, most sacred order, and as such is all the more interesting in theoretical terms. The consistent, overarching cosmological theme of the Yax-Pac era monuments, depicting the Bacabs/Pauah Tuns and other supernatural patrons as supporters—literally, the pillars—of the world order, makes perfect sense in this context. The fact that individuals other than the ruler Yax-Pac are cited in at least two other texts (Altar W and the frieze of Str. 9N-69) from this same residential compound indicates that local individuals also had the prerogative to dedicate inscribed and iconographically complex monuments in their own honor, within the context of their own sacred space.

Given the striking evidence for continuity of Pauah Tun/Scribe worship, the identification of the lineage head with this deity, and the broken fragments of hieroglyphic texts from previous (quite probably local) monuments in the central stairway steps of Str. 9N-82 (Webster, Fash, and Abrams 1986), it should not greatly surprise us that the local lineage head would place himself—adorned with the symbols that simultaneously signify his supernatural patron, royal patron, and lineal ancestors—in the most prominent, public position on the structure.

Riese (in press) noted that this individual was labeled "second in the sequence" of Ahau Kins in the inscribed bench text, and that the initial verb of the inscription referred to Yax ("new") Pauah Tun as well as the locative statement "in the house or temple." This indicates that both 9N-82C-1st and its predecessor, 9N-82-2nd, were houses (or "temples") of Pauah Tuns—both the supernatural deity and his flesh-and-blood followers—a conclusion bolstered by the presence of the full-round Pauah Tun/Monkey Man in association with the earlier building. Peter Mathews (personal communication) pointed out to me that this would provide a possible explanation for why the westernmost support of the bench, which structurally should show a Pauah Tun/Bacab figure, instead shows a human figure carrying the "sak ahau" (spirit or soul) glyphic element on a rope that connects him with the surface of the bench. This figure may represent the "first in the sequence"—the apotheosized ancestor of the Structure 9N-82C-1st protagonist. In this context, one is reminded of Coe's thoughts (1973b:7) on the nature of Maya residential compounds *cum* holy places:

Who, then, might have been worshipped in a Maya temple? A god or the dead ruler for whom it was raised? Here we have an example of the false use of categories derived from our own culture, for in prehispanic Mexico and Central America these might have been one and the same. The rulers were descended from the gods, and a king probably became identified with his lineage god after death. By paying homage to the man, one was also paying homage to the god. Finely-made masonry tombs lavishly equipped with grave goods have often been found underneath the floors of the palaces as well. In other words, an ancient Maya center might have been as much a necropolis for rulers as a seat for the Maya administration.

This strikes a familiar chord for the present case material. Below and in front of the northeast corner of Structure 9N-82-2nd was the grave of an adult male. Labeled Burial VIII-6, this individual had been interred in a tightly flexed position and provided with three Late Classic polychrome pots and a single, 16 cm-long, greenstone pectoral (fig. 10c). Judging from the ceramics, flexed position (generally confined to the Late Classic, in Copán), and stratigraphic context and position of this burial, it probably dates to the time of use of Structure 9N-82-2nd, and the early, full-round Pauah Tun/Scribe statue. The most compelling thing about this burial is the greenstone pectoral, which is virtually identical in size to the one depicted on the chest of the central figure of the north facade of Str. 9N-82C-1st (fig. 10d). I believe that the burial and central facade figure provide further evidence for ancestor worship and lineage perpetuation lore, with the new lineage head proudly displaying the insignia of the same supernatural patron worn by (and buried with) his scribal predecessor and ancestor. Considering the demonstrated importance of ancestor worship among the Maya and other cultures sharing a similar level of sociopolitical complexity (Sanders in press), I believe these data from Structure 9N-82 provide us with solid comparative evidence for the practice among the nonroyal elites of the Classic Period.

Regarding the status and duties of Classic Maya scribes, and the link between noble lineage and the scribal office, our best source of analogy is with sixteenth-century and Colonial Period Yucatán. In his analysis of the Titles of Ebtun, Ralph Roys wrote:

There was also the town clerk, or **escribano**, who drew up papers. Only rarely do we find his Maya title, **ah ɔib huun** or **ah ɔibul hun** (he who writes a document). In pre-Spanish times contracts were oral, and probably the only civil documents were the land maps. These may have been written by either the priests or certain nobles, to whom the knowledge of hieroglyphic writing is said to have been confined . . . .

The governors and town clerks seem to have been restricted to a small number of lineages. During the entire seventeenth and eighteenth centuries we find only seven different names in the governorship, and of the twenty governors who appear in our records during this long period fourteen were confined to three names, the Camals, Nauats, and Nohs . . . .

Although no governor of the name appears in our records, the Xuls appear to have been the second lineage of the town in number and importance. Except for the Camals, they show the most alcaldes and regidors and twice as many town clerks as any other name. [Roys 1939:45, 47, 50]

The sixteenth-century data support the idea derived from the excavations of Structures 9N-82 1st and 2nd (and the analysis of the sculptures associated with each) that the successive scribes who occupied those buildings were members of the same patriline. Indeed, the Copanecs living there seem to have deliberately belabored the continuities in lineage, office, and the supernatural patron of their profession. This is precisely what one should expect, given that important offices were passed down the male line (Landa, in Tozzer 1941:122), and that lineage was such a fundamental tenet of Maya social organization. It is ironic, in this context, that Roys could never know that genealogy was such an important, indeed primordial, concern of the Classic Period stone inscriptions. Again, from *The Titles of Ebtun*, we read:

The Maya had always considered genealogy seriously. Landa tells us: "They made much of knowing the origin of their lineages, especially if they came of one of the houses of Mayapan. The knowledge of this they obtained from their priests, which was one of their sciences; and they boast greatly of the men of their lineage who have been famous." That this pride of ancestry continued in the colonial period, is indicated by the questionnaire for the batabs in the Book of Chilam Balam of Chumayel. Here we read: "So also, these are the nobility, the lineage of the batabs, who know whence come the men and the rulers of their government." Not only de we find references to native nobility in the earlier Maya documents, but also the Ebtun papers continue to cite such nobles (**almehenob**) down to the middle of the second decade of the nineteenth century." [Roys 1939:51]

Conclusions

The excavation, documentation, and analysis of Structure 9N-82 and its associated remains have provided a solid base from which to answer some of the sociocultural questions posed by anthropologists. Aspects of religion and social organization are often among the more difficult problems on which to gain direct, irrefutable evidence. Lacking living informants, archaeologists are very much dependent upon the preservation, explicitness, and methodologically sound interpretation of the relics of belief systems. In order to be credible to our anthropologist colleagues, these analyses should be congruent or otherwise complementary to comparative materials, preferably documented sources. The inspirational aspect of the Str. 9N-82 case is that it is both congruent and complementary to emic written records of its day, and to documented sources of the colonial and modern records concerning the fundamental nature of Maya supernatural (and living) patrons, ancestor worship, and lineage perpetuation lore. More compelling yet, there is an association between those cited in the inscriptions and portrayed in the symbolism of the building and the only contemporaneously buried individual found in the thorough excavation, reconsolidation, and restoration of this multifaceted structure.

Comparative study has revealed some associations between the beaded water-lily motif, the Pauah Tun/Bacab, and other gods of writing in other works of Maya art, an association most clearly shown and conflated in the full-round Pauah Tun-Monkey Man sculpture of Str. 9N-82C-2nd. The presence of Pauah Tun/Bacab tied and beaded water-lily motifs in the headdress of the central figure on the north facade cements the association between the Room 1 hieroglyphic bench protagonist ("Ahau Kin") and the Pauah Tun in his guise as patron of Maya scribes, artists, and, apparently in this case, calendric specialists. It has been proposed here that this centralized, most public figure in the Plaza A compound of Group 9N-8 represents the protagonist of the initial, dated, locative clause of the hieroglyphic inscription.

Structure 9N-82 was constructed at a nonroyal locus and should be appreciated as a monument to the local lineage, both its contemporary head and his lineal ancestors. This conclusion is based on the good evidence for Pauah Tun/Scribe worship in successive generations (the full-round statue of 9N-82-2nd, and the facade and bench motifs on 9N-82C-1st), the fragments of earlier, probably local hieroglyphic monuments incorporated into the 9N-82C-1st stairway, the commemoration of Altar W' at this site (which does not cite the reigning dynast), and the single pectoral worn by the central figure on the facade in emulation of the one worn by and buried with the lineage head buried in association with Structure 9N-82-2nd.

It bears noting that the practice of incorporating previous monuments in the steps of later buildings was undertaken by the royal line as well. Both 18-Rabbit (in the frontal stairway of Structure 10L-2) and Smoke-Squirrel (in a reused block in the Hieroglyphic Stairway of Structure 10L-26) incorporated broken glyphic monuments that sited their predecessors into the steps of their important buildings, in honor of their ancestors. In sum, localized lineage ancestor worship was tied into worship of that lineage's supernatural patron, just as was the case for the royal line. Replication of structures and concepts in Maya social organization and cosmogony is a well-accepted fact among ethnographers and archaeologists; the present case material provides us with a unique opportunity to examine the phenomenon on a local level and scale.

The foregoing analysis has sought to draw out the interrelatedness of the supernatural world of deities and ancestors and the living world of their supplicators and descendants. From ethnohistoric and hieroglyphic data, we know that lineage ties were the ultimate determinants of Classic Maya social and political organization, and Coe (1973b) argued that only the elite lineages had any chance of escaping the underworld after death. He further surmised that scribes and calendric specialists were held in great esteem among the Classic Maya, just as they were among the later Mexica (Coe 1977), and that these occupations were restricted to elite noble lines. The facade and bench of Structure 9N-82C-1st and the burial and statue associated with Structure 9N-82C-2nd provide solid archaeological evidence for these arguments.

Notes

1. See references cited herein. The excavations at Patio or Plaza A of Group 9N-8 were financed by the Instituto Hondureño de Antropología e Historia as part of the Proyecto Arqueológico Copán, Segunda Fase, directed by William T. Sanders. Thanks are due to the institute and its representatives, to the project director, and to colleagues who helped in the excavation and study of the Structure 9N-82 sculpture: Barbara Fash, Rudy Larios, David Webster, Elliot Abrams, Stanley Matta, and Celio Villeda.

2. Although we can be sure of the horizontal positions of the various figures from the entablature, we are unable to say what the original height of the medial molding (and therefore the figures) was, since neither said molding nor the vault spring was preserved *in situ* on the structure. For this reason, Larios restored the north facade only as high as the top of the split serpent niches, as appears in figure 7b. Larios arrived at the heights of the moldings and entablature in the hypothetical reconstruction drawing on the basis of ratios of doorway width to height in other Late Classic Maya structures.

3. Unlike my colleagues, I do not consider this interpretation to be "highly speculative," perhaps owing to the fact that I was the first to suggest it.

4. The interested reader is also referred to Sanders's contribution to the 1989 monograph on Str. 9N-82 (Sanders 1989) for a thorough examination of this theoretical issue.

The Cross Pattern at Copán: Forms, Rituals, and Meanings

CENTRE NATIONAL DE LA RECHERCHE SCIENTIFIQUE, FRANCE

In Maya thought, the cyclical notion of time brought a particular importance to Period Endings, and especially to the katun, the most celebrated cycle. The end of a katun and the beginning of a new one was the occasion for reviewing the past and predicting the future, as well as for positing the coordination of the several cycles that were reckoned: solar, lunar, planetary, dynastic, and so forth. These operations were recorded on stone monuments *periodically* erected. The celebration of a Period Ending included rituals whose major purpose was to ensure a smooth transition from one cycle to the next; because the whole universe was concerned, the rites performed had a cosmic dimension.

According to colonial accounts, they included the perambulations of supernaturals (idols) and humans (priests and dignitaries) alike, in relation to a cruciform cosmic pattern. Moreover, it has been suggested recently that, at katun endings, perambulations were performed at such Classic sites as Tikal and Dzibilchaltun, using a microcosmic space oriented to the four directions.

The purpose of this paper is to demonstrate that at Copán, too, Period Endings (katun and others) were occasions for ritual perambulations performed in a cross-patterned space. Three types of cruciform stages were used for such rites: (1) a building with a cross-shaped plan (Structure 10L-11); (2) a four stairway pyramid (Structure 10L-4); and (3) a division of the city center by two axes crossing each other at a right angle.

Overlooking the Great Plaza from the south, Structure 10L-11 is one of the most imposing buildings of Copán. In 1938–1939, the Carnegie Institution excavated the superstructure, first explored by Maudslay; the pyramid was also investigated through a tunnel that branched out at several levels: sixteen different phases were then recognized, but many more are still to be identified. Hohmann and Vogrin (1982) faithfully described and mapped what the Carnegie had excavated.

The superstructure is a nearly rectangular building divided into four parts by two long, narrow rooms that cut each other at right angles (fig. 1). While the east and west halves are of equal dimensions, the northern part is twice as narrow as the one to the south. The building has four doors, each facing a cardinal direction. A pair of glyphic panels welcomes the visitor at each entrance. The main access is to the north; from the Great Plaza one first ascends the first flight of the great stairway that extends along the whole length of the north side of the Acropolis; then one walks up the central stair, 13 m wide, which leads to the superstructure. A block divides the stair into two parts; its top reaches the level of the superstructure's floor, at a height of 23 m above the Plaza. Access to the west and east doors is made possible through two small stairs that are linked to the second flight of the great stairway by two series of narrow steps. Thus, from the Plaza, one can take three independent paths: a central one to the north door of the building and two lateral ones on its east and west sides. Only to the south is there no independent access from the top of the pyramid to the temple's door.

Originally the east–west corridor was 3.5 m wide with a north wall 2 m thick and a 4 m high vault. Probably because of these proportions, the vault collapsed. Afterward, the north part of the building was reconstructed much wider, reducing the width of the corridor to less than 1.5 m.

A small chamber takes up the northern half of the southern arm of the cross. In the south, it is preceded by a T-shaped antechamber that duplicates the north entrance of the building and the east–west corridor. The room has an irregular plan with a salient to the southeast and another to the northwest, both 1 m wide. Averaging 4 m long and 2.5 m wide, the chamber is 1 m higher than the surrounding floor. From the north it is reached by three steps, while to the south one has to step directly upon the platform. Both doors were framed by sculptures that made them look like skeletal serpent mouths (fig. 2). The reconstruction following the collapse of the vault concealed the sculptures of the chamber's north door. A step carved with a bicephalic monster and twenty human figures was placed astride the two upper steps leading to the chamber. The new door was decorated with sculptures; a few were recovered by Maudslay and taken,

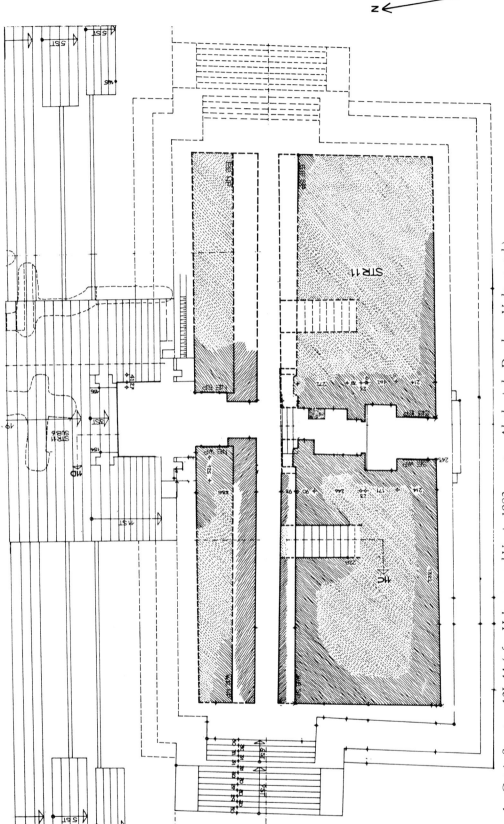

Fig. 1 *Copán Structure 10L-11 (after Hohmann and Vogrin 1982; courtesy Akademische Druck- u. Verlagsanstalt).*

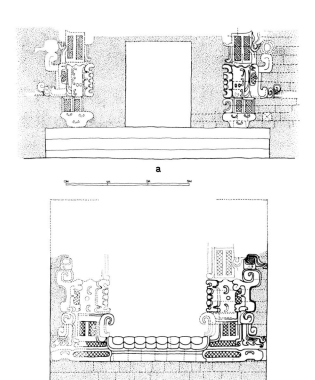

Fig. 2 North (a) and south (b) doors of the chamber of
Structure 10L-11 (after Hohmann and Vogrin 1982; courtesy Akademische Druck- u. Verlagsanstalt).

with the carved step, to London. We do not know to
what extent the reconstruction modified the meaning
and function of the structure, so this analysis is limited
to its original state.

A cache pit was built within the central chamber's fill.
It partly recovers another and much deeper pit, built
during the construction of the building platform (Hohmann and Vogrin 1982: Abb. 159). A deposit of shell
and jade was found there (Longyear 1952:19).

I suggest that the plan of the building, a cross roughly
oriented to the cardinal directions (10° east of north)
and a central chamber, reproduces a Maya and Mesoamerican cosmogram, sometimes illustrated in the manuscripts. The Tzolkin in the Madrid Codex (fig. 3a) has
the form of a Maltese cross with one loop, bordered by
footprints, between every two arms. The arms stand for
the cardinal directions and enclose deities. The center
of the cross is a large square framed by the twenty day
names; it contains two seated figures, each one in front
of the entrance of a house or cave.

The motif above them may be described as a stepped
funnel between two scrolls. It is the cleft, probably
representing a cave, often shown on the forehead of
the Earth Monster that presumably gives access to the
underworld (fig. 3b; Baudez, 1988). Thus, the central
square is an image of the underworld with one entrance
from the top (the "funnel") and two others on the sides

Fig. 3 The "stepped funnel" motif: (a) calendar from the
Madrid Codex (75–77); (b) Earth Monster from the Tablet
of the Foliated Cross, Palenque (courtesy Linda Schele).

(where the deities are seated). Elsewhere, the Dresden
Codex (29a, 30a) presents the sequence of five Gods B
or Chacs, each perched on one of the cosmic trees associated with a cardinal direction; the fifth Chac is seated
inside the earth, shown as a hollow framed by a band
containing caban signs. This example confirms that in
Maya cosmology the fifth direction is the depths or the
center of the earth.

The chamber of Structure 11, occupying a central
position and having two side entrances, is a structural
analog to the central square of the Maltese cross in the
Madrid Codex. It represents a bicephalic skeletal monster, an image of the earth as home of the dead (i.e., the
underworld). It may seem paradoxical that a raised area
actually represents a deep region; it is, however, compatible with Maya thought: a raised area is first of all a
more sacred place than its surroundings.

From the east–west corridor, certainly one and probably two stairs go southward up to a rise of ca. 3 m on a run of 4. Based on our knowledge of Maya architecture, we think that they did not lead to a roof but to a second story, totally gone today. If we are correct in assuming that the ground floor represented the earth, the second story consequently represented the sky. Several fragments of colossal sculptures, which presumably come from the facade, back up this hypothesis. These are two Bacab heads, with a wrinkled face and a water lily knotted on the forehead. One was found at the eastern foot of the building (fig. 4a); the other fell down to the Great

Fig. 4   Fragments of colossal sculptures supposedly from Structure 10L-11: (a) Bacab head; (b) serpent or crocodile head (photos by Claude Baudez).

Plaza. They were probably connected to bodies, as indicated by large pieces of hands and feet today piled up in the west court, which may come from the Structure 11 debris. I suggest that, as on the inner door of Structure 22, two Bacabs were supporting a Celestial Monster carved on the upper story; the colossal crocodile or serpent heads now lying on the floor of the west court may have been the monster's heads (fig. 4b); assuming the Bacabs were squatting, their total height would have been comparable to the ground floor's height.

If this reconstruction is correct, the whole structure is a cosmogram in which the upper story represents the heavens, and the lower, the earth and the underworld. Access from the "earth" to the "sky" was possible through two small stairs inside the building. We do not know how the Copanecs used the upper story and the stairs, but since the space of the ground floor is more suitable for passage than for occupation, I suggest that it was intended for procession rituals. In this large building (29 × 13 m in ground plan), the "living" space is limited to a chamber of irregular form and small dimensions (less than 10 m²); the remaining voids are no more than passageways whose ends open to the four directions. The access to the doors from the outside is easy, except to the south, where there are no stairs to the building platform. To enter the building from the south, one is forced to walk from one of the side stairs up to a narrow ledge along the outer walls.

The ritual paths certainly took into account the four directions indicated by the arms of the cross and the doors, plus a fifth materialized by the chamber. They might also have used the four corners of the building. Such a roundabout is indicated by footprints on the 260-day calendar of the Madrid Codex. Graffiti, whose design combines the cross with a square or a circle, illustrate similar paths. They are found in many Maya sites: from Dzibilchaltun (fig. 5a; Andrews and Andrews 1980: fig. 106) to the Usumacinta (Maler 1901–1903: fig. 27, 34a, b, 67), as well as at Toniná (Becquelin and Baudez 1982:884–888, fig. 189) and Copán (fig. 5b). They are closed courses without beginning or end and imply a cyclic movement. It has been possible to reconstruct the path of the Dzibilchaltun graffito, whose cross has been traced with one stroke (Becquelin and Baudez 1982). It alternatively links one point to its opposite and then to the closest point counterclockwise (such as N-S-E-W-S-N-W-E-N, etc.). The path on M.49 from Toniná conversely works clockwise (Becquelin and Baudez 1982). The Copán drawing has nine loops instead of the usual four; I am unable to determine what the sequence of the linked points and the direction of the rotation would have been. Although this graffito and the plan of Structure 11 may be compared, the former gives no clue as to possible paths for the latter.

Would the glyphic panels at the doors give any information on this problem? Insofar as the text has been deciphered, most of its content is dedicated to the celebration of Rising Sun's accession and gives additional

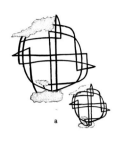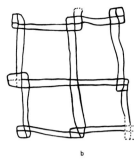

Fig. 5 Graffiti: (a) painted on floor in Structure 1-sub. Dzibilchaltun; (b) incised on floor in tunnel 2, Structure 10L-26, Copán (a: from Andrews and Andrews 1980: fig. 106; courtesy Middle American Research Institute, Tulane University; b: after a sketch drawing from the Carnegie Institution Archives).

dates in some way related to this major event. Since on the panels all texts are oriented outward, they do not indicate some doors as exits and others as entrances. If the respective length of the texts has any meaning, the north–south axis with 24 glyph blocks in both cases is favored compared to the east–west direction with only 15 to 18 blocks. According to B. Riese, for anyone passing through a doorway, the expected reading sequence would be first the left then the right panel. The sequence of doors is not demonstrated by any continuity from one panel to the other, as if we had a sentence interrupted on one panel and continued on another; assuming we begin the reading with the north door, the N-S-E-W order seems the best fit with the sequence of dates in the inscription as a whole.

The cruciform plan of Structure 10L-11 is to be compared to that of Structure 10L-4-2nd, a pyramid with four stairways oriented to the cardinal directions. Recent excavations have clearly demonstrated that it was neither a substructure for a temple nor a funerary monument (Cheek and Milla in Baudez 1983). It was also shown that the east and west stairs were a late addition with the apparent purpose of celebrating the completion of the 15th katun; the new structure was actually inaugurated together with Stela A, dated 9.15.0.0.0. I think this pyramid belongs to the structures that were specially built for the completion of a cycle. Coggins (1980, 1983b) noticed that the plan of radial structures duplicated—like the calendars in the Madrid and Fejérváry-Mayer codices, and the graffiti mentioned above—the sign for completion (T173). These "shapes of time" were probably used for three-dimensional processions, analogous to the ritual paths that, I assume, were followed in Structure 11.

Furthermore, Structure 10L-4 is located at the center (slightly shifted to the north) of a huge cross that divides the Main Group into four quadrants. The Great Plaza forms the north and south arms; to the east, it is the passage between Ball Court A and Structure 10L-3, then the sacbe that links the latter to Structure 10M-1 (fig. 6).

The western arm of the cross is first made of the passage between Structures 10L-1A, 56, and 54 on the north side, and 10L-51-52 to the south. Beyond it, there was— if I correctly interpret Gordon's (1896:25) observations— a sacbe, of which not much remains today:

From the west side of No. 54 the front of a terrace formerly faced with stone runs to the west, and continues three or four hundred yards in a straight line to another group of buildings buried in a thicket. The difference of level is about four feet, and probably corresponds to a natural slope shaped artificially.

A few yards south is the irregular edge of another terrace, also shaped artificially to some extent, but not faced with stone . . .

The building(s) at the end of the west sacbe may have been the large 10K-29 and its satellites, although it seems too close (200 m) to 10L-54 and too much to the south. If the building(s) actually was (were) 300 m distant from 10L-54, it has since been razed to the ground by the construction of a road and two landing strips in this area. A last alternative is to consider that the west arm of the cross ended 440 m from 10L-54 to 10K-16, a very large unexcavated mound, aligned with 10L-54 and 10M-1.

One may compare the cross formed at Copán by the Great Plaza and the two sacbeob with the layout recently analyzed at Dzibilchaltun by Coggins (1983b:54), which is analogous to the twin-pyramid complexes of Tikal. At Dzibilchaltun, the pyramids are Structures 1-sub. and 66, 2 km apart and linked by two sacbeob (fig. 7). They join across the Great Plaza, which is limited to the south by Structure 44, a 134 m long, 35-doorway building. It is the analog, relatively speaking, of the 9-door palace that stands on the south side of the Tikal complexes. In the north part there is an enclosure with a stela and an altar, both carved with sacrificial scenes. Coggins observed that at Dzibilchaltun the carved stelae were found on the north side of the Great Plaza; as at Tikal, this side would denote "up," with the ruler and his apotheosized ancestors in the sky. Then it may be no coincidence that at Copán most of the stelae dedicated to 18 Rabbit— precisely the ruler who built Structure 4-2nd—stand on the north side of the Great Plaza. We cannot go too far with these comparisons, however, if only because we have no information on the structures at the end of the west and east arms of the cross; the fact remains that central Copán, like Dzibilchaltun, is divided by a large cross. The Great Plaza makes up the north and south arms while the east-west axis links (radial?) pyramids through two sacbeob.

Coggins (1983) assumes that at Dzibilchaltun this axis was used as a solar observatory. I think that—as at Tikal—it could also have been used as a ritual path for processions, notably for celebrating the end of the thirteenth katun. The same function is suggested for the Copán "cross."

This division of the city into four quadrants was not

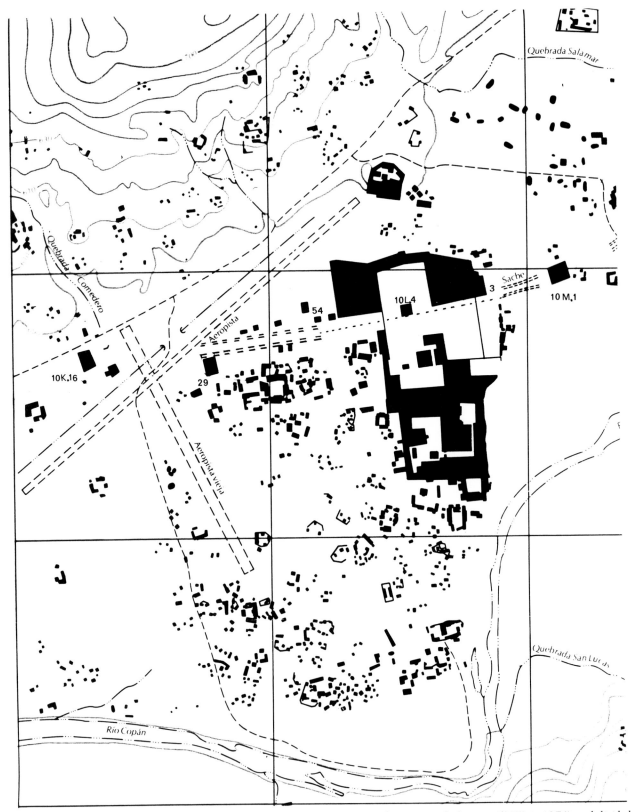

Fig. 6 The central portion of Copán. The grid is oriented to magnetic north (average declination 5°07′ in 1976) and divided into squares of 500 m on the side (drawing by Claude Baudez after Baudez 1983).

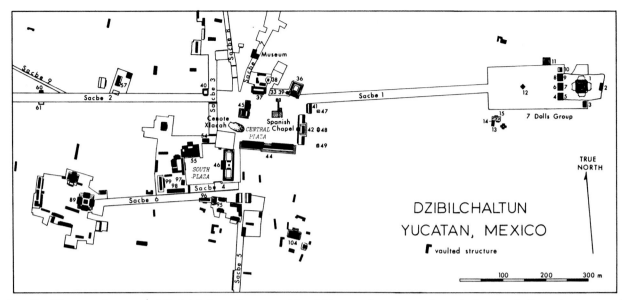

Fig. 7   The central portion of Dzibilchaltun: Structure 66 is 900 m to the west, at the end of sacbe 2 (from Andrews and Andrews 1980: fig. 2; courtesy Middle American Research Institute, Tulane University).

uncommon among the Maya and in Mesoamerica as a whole; to date, the most famous example is still Teotihuacán. In the Yucatán of the sixteenth century "every town had four ceremonial entrances at the cardinal points marked by a stone mound (a pyramid?) on either side, and a road led from each of these to the center" (Roys 1943:20). This layout was designed for the celebration of the festivals of the unlucky days, described in detail by Landa (Tozzer 1941:139ff.; Coe 1965c). These festivals look like relay races in which every year-bearer passes the torch (or rather the burden) to the next, in a counterclockwise motion. For instance, in the Uayeb days of Kan, a Kan u Uayeyab image was made and taken to the south of the town (the direction of the Kan years), where it was exposed to the image of Ek u Uayeyab, which had been there for one year, since it was set up in the Uayeb days of the preceding Cauac year. We may assume that Kan "received the burden" from Cauac. Rituals were taking place and the Kan u Uayeyab was taken to the house of a principal in the center of the town. There it stayed in the company of the god Bolon Dzacab (associated with Kan), more rites were performed, and, at the end of the Uayeb days, it was taken to the east of the town, where it stayed during the whole Muluc year. At the end of the year, it was visited by a Muluc image to which it passed the burden, and so on. Since "the New Year ceremonies for each cycle of four years were held in the *Uayeb* days of each *preceding* year, and were under the domination of the associations and auguries of that preceding year" (Coe 1965c:100), what was celebrated was the completion of the year, in the Maya way of reckoning time.

Thus, the ritual circuit, completed in four years, had the double purpose of dividing space and time into four parts (but note also the importance of the center) and ensuring the continuity of the cycle.

The Aztecs also had a ritual perambulation, called the Lordly Dance, which "was held every four years during the *Izcalli* festivals, which took place just before the onset of the dreaded unnamed and uncounted days of *nemontemi*" (Townsend 1979:46), the Aztec counterparts of the Maya Uayeb days. Moctezuma and the lords danced four times around the main ceremonial precinct of Tenochtitlán, a cardinally oriented quadrangle.

At Tikal, even if the twin-pyramid complexes were built for celebrating katun endings, it is very possible that they were also used for New Year ceremonies during the whole length of a particular katun.

At Copán, epigraphic evidence seems to link the four directions to katun-ending celebrations. On Stela A—inaugurated together with Structure 4-2nd at 9.15.0.0.0—we successively read (Maudslay 1889–1902: pl. 30, 40–48):

—The "IV chaan" expression, repeated four times.
—The four emblem glyphs (Copán, Tikal, El Perú, Palenque).
—The four directions, followed by "death" (here possibly meaning the fifth direction: the abode of the dead, the underworld).

It has been argued against the "four capitals theory" proposed by Marcus (1976) that the sequence order of the directions did not follow that of the capitals on the Stela A inscription. I think it is so because we are dealing with different matters: the capitals are given in the order of their assumed or subjective importance, beginning with Copán; the directions are also enumerated in their order of importance, beginning with east and west, as expected. But the sequence of directions is actually independent from that of capitals.

On Stela B, also inaugurated at 9.15.0.0.0, we find (Maudslay 1889–1902: pl. 37, 8–13):

O maize
  heavens

O maize
  earth

O maize
1 heavens

O maize
1 earth

"O maize" is repeated four times, coupled alternatively with "heavens" and "earth." This may mean that offerings are presented toward the four directions to the earth and to the heavens. The above sequence is followed, according to B. Riese, by the expression "forward to *tu pah*," a Period-Ending statement. I propose the following paraphrase: "for the celebration of a Period Ending (9.15.0.0.0), offerings to earth and heavens, four times (directions)."

At Copán, the cross pattern has been used in several other contexts, but always as a property of the earth. The substela caches are—with very few exceptions—shaped like a cross with the arms oriented to the four directions (fig. 8; Strömsvik 1941). This probably means that the offering is presented to the earth, as a whole. This same concern with ubiquity when one refers to the earth is evidenced in some of the Copán altars (M, F, H, N). For instance, Altar M represents the bicephalic Earth Monster with three Cauac masks carved on its body, two on the sides and one on the top. The cross pattern is found on Altar N; but this time four aspects of the underworld are shown: two jaguars, a skull and a bat, and so forth (Maudslay 1889–1902: pl. 75, 83). On the floor of the western court, a long-nosed creature is carved on three slabs. It is the same being that we can see repeated in the water friezes, an image of the fertile earth. He is seated and presents an offering toward the west. Four large double scrolls, which here mean vegetation and not smoke, radiate from his body: their arrangement follows the cross pattern (Maudslay 1889–1902: pl. 9a).

As demonstrated by its ubiquity, the cross pattern roughly oriented to the cardinal directions had a paramount importance at Copán and it is time to wonder about its meaning. Some scholars have recently argued against the conservative view that the Mayas had cardinal directions identical to ours (Coggins 1983b; Watanabe 1983). Ethnographers and linguists have observed that north and south have no native names in

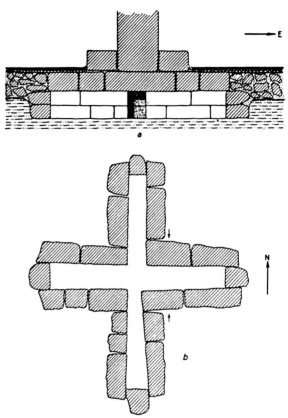

Fig. 8   Copán, cruciform chamber under Stela 6: (a) section through center of chamber; (b) plan of chamber (after Strömsvik 1941).

most Mayan languages and that what actually matters is the east–west line, which corresponds to the intersection of the diurnal path of the sun with the horizon. North and south may be no more than intermediary directions along the sun path, used to measure time; thus, in Yucatec, *nohol* and *xaman* refer more to winter and summer than to south and north. Or, as among the Mam, north may correspond to "up" and south to "down."

I think that, beyond astronomical realities, the cross pattern also functioned as a cosmological principle; applied to the earth, it meant more than four directions: it meant every possible direction on a plane. Thus, the cross expressed the whole of the earth, seen in two dimensions. When it was a frame for ritual paths, executed by the king and/or priests at Period Endings (years or katuns), it turned into a "shape of time," as Coggins put it. In these ceremonial courses, the officiants materialized the passage of time, just as the hands of a clock do.

Lifeline to the Gods: Ritual Bloodletting at Santa Rita Corozal

DIANE Z. CHASE
UNIVERSITY OF CENTRAL FLORIDA

While blood sacrifice was one of the most sacred aspects of Maya religion and is evident in Maya art almost from its onset (cf. Schele and Miller 1986) as well as in the written ethnohistoric documents of the post-Conquest era (cf. Tozzer 1941), its archaeological definition has been limited because of the difficulties involved in finding such intangible behavioral practice in the archaeological record. Archaeological deposits from Santa Rita Corozal, Belize, however, recovered during the 1984 and 1985 seasons of the Corozal Postclassic Project, contain specific evidence of ancient bloodletting that is critical in refining our understanding of who bloodlets in Maya society and in what situations. This archaeological evidence, when conjoined with ethnohistory, provides interpretations somewhat different from those derived from studies of iconography that have emphasized massive public bloodletting episodes. Rather, the archaeological evidence shows human bloodletting to be in the purview of select members of society and an aspect of ritual employed only for limited and specified occasions. This analysis also underscores the basic and largely unchanging role that blood sacrifice maintained during both Classic and Postclassic times. Despite modifications in other aspects of Maya culture between the Classic and Postclassic periods, blood sacrifice appears to have served a similar function in both eras as part of ceremonies to mark the passage of time and to ensure continued order within the universe.

While blood sacrifice was extremely significant in Maya religion, blood was not the only offering. Descriptions of religious acts in the native Maya chronicles suggest the various items that might be offered including such things as incense, candles, flowers, food, and animals (Edmonson 1984:94). Beads must have been relatively common oblations since they were noted in early contact times (Landa in Tozzer 1941:146 n. 707, 148) and are found in numerous excavated deposits at Santa Rita Corozal and other sites (Coe 1965; D. Chase 1981: 32). Well-preserved Postclassic offerings from the Cenote of Sacrifice at Chichén Itzá show that many of these kinds of items were combined into single integrated units (Coggins and Shane 1984:129–133). Archaeological examples of offerings go far beyond bloodletting; in fact, blood offerings are among the least well represented in the material record. Human burials contain numerous ritual items such as stone or pottery vessels, jadeite artifacts, and shell beads. Yet indications of blood sacrifice in burials are generally rare; when they are found, they consist primarily of indirect evidence such as a stingray spine, an obsidian lancet, or a vessel with bloodletting imagery. Caches, like burials, contain a variety of items, but these deposits more frequently have some kind of indication of blood sacrifice. Importantly, bloodletting tools themselves rarely exist in isolation, usually being part of burial or cache assemblages. Sometimes abstract representations of the bloodletting experience may be represented. In a tomb at Tikal, for example, a set of earflares with serpent iconography was found (Moholy-Nagy 1966:88); a similar set of earflares was also recovered in the tomb of a woman at Santa Rita Corozal (D. Chase and A. Chase 1986:10). Following Schele and Miller (1986:177–179), this iconography could be related to the vision serpent associated with bloodletting, as is graphically illustrated in Lintels 15 and 25 at Yaxchilán, Mexico. Thus, discussion of prehistoric ritual bloodletting must consider a wide range of archaeological contexts and patterns to get at the meaning behind the deposits and sacrifice.

We know from both ethnohistory and archaeology that the forms of blood sacrifice were many. Sometimes animals such as turkeys and dogs were acceptable for such sacrifice. These were prepared in various ways: for some ceremonies, just the hearts or heads were cut off, while in other situations the whole animal was offered; additionally, offerings of animals or parts of animals could be in either raw or cooked form (Landa in Tozzer 1941:114). At other times, however, the offerings of animals or objects were not considered to be sufficient and the sacrifice of human blood was necessary. As to who was involved in ritual blood sacrifice, Landa, in describing contact period Yucatán, noted that women did not let blood (in Tozzer 1941:114, 128); however, he at least partially contradicted himself in a description of involuntary bloodletting (Tozzer 1941:18). That women could and did let blood is apparent from Classic Period iconography, where they are distinctly associated with the act of bloodletting. This is specifically seen at Yaxchilán (Schele and Miller 1986:178, 186–190) and at Tayasal (A. Chase 1985b). We know that human blood sacrifice could take many forms (Landa in Tozzer 1941: 113–114); members of the population were known to let blood by cutting their ears with knives or blades or by piercing their tongues and cheeks with thorns or straw; men additionally practiced penis perforation; women pierced their tongues with thorns. While bloodletting was in itself an important and serious undertaking, on occasion it was necessary to do more than simply take blood; when a human life was sacrificed, certain prescribed activities also took place (Tozzer 1941:114; Schele 1984a). In most cases, however, offerings of blood, whether originating from animals or humans, were placed on or in the open mouths of idols (Tozzer 1941:114, 118).

What were the circumstances for ritual bloodletting? Much of our information from the Classic Period would suggest that it was appropriate and necessary during important times in the lives of specific individuals—most notably rulers, and particularly in association with accession and birth (A. Chase 1985:200; Schele and Miller 1986:178–180). It was suggested that blood sacrifice was key in maintaining the fertility of the natural world (see, for example, Joralemon 1974). Others (see, for example, Furst 1976 and Schele 1985b) pointed toward the role of blood loss in visions and further noted that bloodletting and vision serpents appear on stelae as part of Period-Ending rites. One popularized reconstruction of Maya ritual activity suggested that Maya bloodletting was undertaken not solely by rulers or even by a limited number of individuals, but rather by large numbers, if not most, of the population in the public plaza areas of Maya sites (Linda Schele in "Mystery of the Maya" on *National Geographic Explorer*; see also Schele and Miller 1986:178). In contrast, however, I see bloodletting as being a more private undertaking that involved a limited number of individuals and was restricted to specific occasions (see also A. Chase 1984). While ethnohistoric information is ambivalent as to the number of actual participants in any bloodletting ceremonies, these data do record that bloodletting may have fulfilled various roles—as offerings to idols (Tozzer 1941:118; Medel 1612 in Tozzer 1941:222), as sacrifices in times of misfortune or necessity (Tozzer 1941:116–118), and as parts of calendric ritual (Tozzer 1941:145, 146, 147).

Thus, while the import of blood sacrifice in Maya society is evident, there is substantial variation in its precise interpretations. While most interpretations pertaining to blood sacrifice have been derived from either iconography or ethnohistory, nonsculptural evidence from archaeological sites can also be utilized to answer such questions as: who lets blood? how? when? in what context? does this context remain unchanged throughout Maya prehistory? and how does human blood sacrifice relate to other ritual offerings? This paper attempts to answer some of these questions by using archaeologically derived examples from excavations at the site of Santa Rita Corozal in northern Belize.

Bloodletting at Santa Rita Corozal, Belize

The site of Santa Rita Corozal has been known since the end of the nineteenth century. Work there by Thomas Gann (1900, 1918) in the early twentieth century served to highlight the Late Postclassic occupation at the site. Excavations by the Corozal Postclassic Project began at Santa Rita Corozal in 1979 and were completed in the summer of 1985. While primarily initiated to answer certain questions concerning late Maya occupation at the site, the investigations at Santa Rita Corozal have ultimately yielded information on all eras of Maya prehistory from the Early Preclassic to Historic periods (D. Chase 1981, 1982; D. Chase and A. Chase 1986, 1988). Santa Rita Corozal is a singularly good site for discussion of archaeological evidence of ritual bloodletting due to the archaeological occurrence of explicit depictions of blood sacrifice in offerings recovered at the site.

Archaeological evidence for blood sacrifice is of necessity often indirect, blood itself being perishable. To interpret the act of blood sacrifice, we require either, at best, representations or remains of the event itself or, minimally, the recovery of implements associated with such an act.

Offerings of Animals

While descriptions of the blood sacrifice of animals predominate in the ethnohistory and are easily visible in Maya codices, such sacrifice is difficult to establish archaeologically. Classic Period burials at many sites, including Santa Rita Corozal, contain animal bones; one burial of a male in Santa Rita Corozal Structure 7-3rd contained the remains of both turtles and birds (for information on the nonfaunal remains associated with this individual, see D. Chase and A. Chase 1988:33). But the actual function of these remains is always in question. Were these sacrifices for blood, food offerings for the next world, symbols of some other sort, or did they serve some combination of functions? Similarly, Classic Period vessels found in special deposits at Santa Rita Corozal and elsewhere contain depictions of animals such as birds, deer, jaguar, quash, and fish or other sea creatures (see fig. 1). These representations could conceivably take the place of or serve as reminders of animal sacrifice; alternatively, they could serve any other number of functions. In the Postclassic Period, we know that sacrifice of animals for blood was common, but the archaeological evidence for these acts is likewise problematic. At Santa Rita Corozal, there is one isolated example of a turtle carapace having been buried with an individual and another case of a multitude of animal bones in a cache vessel. Animal representations are also

Fig. 1 A two-part ceramic effigy of a quash from an Early Classic burial in Santa Rita Corozal Structure 7 (S.D. P2B-1); this effigy vessel may have taken the place of an animal offering; height = 17.3 cm (photo courtesy Corozal Postclassic Project, University of Central Florida).

found at Santa Rita Corozal in the form of stone altar figures, much like those at Mayapan (Proskouriakoff 1962; see also Taube 1988). Most common during the Late Postclassic at Santa Rita, however, are ceramic figurines representing a variety of animals: jaguars, birds, quash, monkeys, snakes, dogs, deer, and other creatures (see figs. 2 and 7). These figures occur in groupings that clearly are meant to function as offerings, but are they also intended to serve as blood sacrifices? Passages from Landa (Tozzer 1941:114, 162, 163) would suggest that this may have been the case. Importantly, certain of these representations at Santa Rita Corozal also co-occur with evidence for human blood sacrifice.

Human Offerings

Evidence for human blood sacrifice is most often found in the tools of bloodletting themselves; specifically, the stingray spine, the obsidian lancet, and the "sacrificial knife." Of these three, the first two are intended as tools for self-sacrifice or personal bloodletting; the third item, the sacrificial knife, however, tends to indicate a more permanent sacrifice—the death of a sacrificial victim.

Stingray spines and obsidian lancets are found in both burials and caches at Santa Rita Corozal. A single stingray spine or obsidian blade sometimes rests in the pelvis of deceased males, but such paraphernalia are not present in most interments. In fact, only two burials at Santa Rita Corozal from among a sample of over 120 burials have stingray spines associated with them; in each case the primary individual—a male—has a single spine in the vicinity of his pelvis. Both men were important individuals at the site. Other sites show a similar pattern of only limited individuals with a spine or blade in the burial (A. Smith 1950: table 6; A. Chase 1983: table 37; Welsh 1988: appendix 1). The positioning of bloodletters in the pelvis suggests the practice of penis perforation. These may have been embedded in the penis at death; alternatively, it has been suggested that the spine's ar-

Fig. 2 Four ceramic jaguars forming part of an offering from a Late Postclassic cache in Santa Rita Corozal Structure 183; height = 9.5 cm (photo courtesy Corozal Postclassic Project, University of Central Florida).

Fig. 3 View of an Early Classic tomb in Santa Rita Corozal Structure 7. Three flint spearpoints are visible in the pelvis area of the individual; these directly covered a single stringray spine (photo courtesy Corozal Postclassic Project, University of Central Florida).

chaeological positioning could result from simply having been placed in a pouch set in the pelvis at death or attached in some way to a belt (Schele and Miller 1986: 175). Similarly, the presence of a stingray spine in the pelvis at death may not indicate a death rite associated with burial, but rather simply an implement important to the individual during life and, therefore, perhaps afterward. Landa describes stingray spines as an insignia of priests (Tozzer 1941:191). Their limited distribution in burials would favor an interpretation of these items as symbols and tools appropriate to only a designated few in Maya society. Importantly, these "limited few" included at least a few females (Welsh 1988: appendix 1), indicating that a precise one-to-one relationship did not exist between stingray spines and penis perforation.

During the Early Classic Period at Santa Rita Corozal, a particularly important man was buried in Structure 7 (fig. 3). He was clearly a ruler, as indicated by the symbols of authority within his tomb: a chert ceremonial bar, a complete *Spondylus* shell with other inlaid cut shells, three jadeite tinklers, a full-size mosaic jadeite mask (Chase, Chase, and Topsey 1988: fig. 1), a composite jadeite figure, eight ceramic vessels (D. Chase and A. Chase 1988: fig. 14) and numerous other artifacts. Along his right hip were three cinnabar-tipped spear points, undoubtedly suggesting his role as a great warrior. Resting in his pelvis was a single stingray spine.

During the Late Postclassic Period another important man was buried in Structure 216 (fig. 4). He was seated upright below an altar. He was also most likely a ruler, especially given the gold and turquoise earflares he wore in addition to a jadeite and *Spondylus* shell necklace and *Spondylus* shell bracelet (cf. D. Chase and A. Chase 1988: fig. 30). There was a single stingray spine in his pelvis. Next to him, however, a secondary individual was buried with no items of personal adornment, but ac-

Fig. 4 A flexed Late Postclassic burial from Santa Rita Corozal Structure 216 containing a high-status individual and a sacrificial victim; a single stringray spine accompanied the primary interment, while over a dozen spines riddled the body of the secondary person (photo courtesy Corozal Postclassic Project, University of Central Florida).

D. Chase

companied by numerous implements of blood sacrifice. Over a dozen stingray spines and a copper needle had once perforated the body of this individual, most likely a sacrificial victim.

The burials at Santa Rita Corozal and elsewhere in the Maya area suggest that not everyone can or does bloodlet, at least with stingray spines. It would appear to have been a limited practice in both the Classic and Postclassic periods, restricted to rulers and certain elite or selected individuals for specific ceremonies.

Other evidence for ritual bloodletting occurs in the caches of Santa Rita Corozal in the form of stingray spines, during both the Classic and Postclassic periods. One simple Late Postclassic cache consisted of a diving figure affixed to the front of a small ceramic cup found associated with Structure 37 (D. Chase and A. Chase 1988: fig. 17b). A single stingray spine was found with this vessel and the cup itself would have been a suitable container for blood. This Postclassic cache probably represents a diving god descending to receive a blood sacrifice, perhaps as described for the five unlucky days of the Uayeb in Kan years by Landa (see below) and, as such, may be a good indication of the relationship between blood sacrifice and calendric rites (see D. Chase 1985a). However, this cache varies from the majority of Late Postclassic caches encountered in recent excavations at the site in not having been placed within two larger vessels as well as in its direct association with a stingray spine; thus, it may have served a slightly altered function compared to other Postclassic caches from Santa Rita Corozal. Isolated stingray spines were also recovered in association with Postclassic Structures 189 and 218 at Santa Rita Corozal, but in no clear relationship with any ceremonial deposit.

In the Early Classic Period, six paired ceramic vessels were cached in the core of Structure 7-3rd above the tomb of the man described previously. On the lid of each of the three sets of vessels was a single hieroglyph (D. Chase and A. Chase 1986:12). Inside each set were various items including natural shells, finely painted portraits on shell or jadeite, and stingray spines—at least three spines in each of the sets of vessels. All of the spines had been burned before placement in the cache. The precise significance of this cache is not completely clear, although bloodletting may be implied. The date "7 Imix" on one of the vessel lids suggests that such a bloodletting episode would have been related either to an important event or to a specific calendar date. In both the Classic and Postclassic caches, the deposition of the spines suggests that, once used, they had to be ceremonially or ritually disposed of—in the two Santa Rita Corozal cases by their burial (and perhaps burning). The use of such bloodletters on only a single occasion has been previously noted (A. Chase 1985b:200, following Duran 1971:119–120).

Caches of chert knives or points are also found in Classic and Postclassic contexts. These are often disposed of in isolation, but frequently in important loca-

tions. It is therefore very possible that they represent used sacrificial knives. This would conform with Baudez's (1985) suggestion that lancets were for autosacrifice while sharp-edged knives were for the immolation of victims. One such cache of blades was uncovered during Corozal Postclassic Project excavations at Santa Rita Corozal in association with the Late Postclassic Structure 189. Another special deposit from Late Postclassic shrine Structure 166 consisted solely of a long-stemmed chert arrowpoint. Yet another special deposit containing a set of chert eccentrics and an arrowpoint of probable Postclassic date was recovered by Gann (1918:68) in Structure 7. Burials also sometimes contain knives or points, such as those within the Structure 7 tomb mentioned previously, but these suggest blood from war rather than from individual sacrifice.

Besides the actual implements, imagery of ritual bloodletting is also found at Santa Rita Corozal. Clay figures showing humans doing penis perforation are apparently almost unique to this site. In his early work at Santa Rita Corozal, Gann (1918:59–63) found one cache which included four warriors, four standing humans, four lizards, four alligators, four snakes, four birds, four "dragons," four jaguars, fourteen quash, three men seated on stools practicing penis perforation, and one clay penis. During the 1985 excavations at Santa Rita Corozal, a cache of clay figures was found in Structure 213 (fig. 5). There were twenty-five figurines in all, including four deer, four dogs, four quash, four monkeys, four unidentified creatures, one seated conch blower, and four penis perforators. The penis perforators formed the four external parameters for the cache grouping. Elsewhere I have identified these figurines as Bacabs (D. Chase and A. Chase 1986:16).

Bloodletting and Calendric Ritual

The ritual bloodletting occurring in the Santa Rita Corozal caches clearly forms part of a much broader spectrum of activities. I have shown previously that close similarities exist between certain Late Postclassic caches from Santa Rita and the ethnohistoric description of rituals surrounding the five unlucky days of the Uayeb, as well as the equivalent pages in the Madrid Codex (see Lee 1985); since these original papers (D. Chase 1985a, 1985b) were presented, further support for these correlations has been garnered from two additional seasons of excavation at the site. Briefly, and following Landa (Tozzer 1941:136–149), blood sacrifice is mentioned as an important part of the ritual associated with New Year's ceremonies. The activities of the Uayeb were undertaken to assure good fortune and to avoid calamity in the coming year. General blood sacrifice undertaken at this time included the sacrifice of turkeys and the offering of human blood from the ears. In certain other passages blood sacrifice is mentioned, but no specific details are given. In both the Kan and Muluc years' rites,

Fig. 5 A Late Postclassic figurine cache from Santa Rita Corozal Structure 213. The upright figures are practicing ritual bloodletting; height of bloodletters = 19.4 cm (photo courtesy Corozal Postclassic Project; University of Central Florida).

associated activities and offerings are strikingly similar to the contents of archaeological caches.

During the Kan years, additional activities to ensure prosperity could include the sacrifice of a human being or a dog. The offering of the heart of the victim was placed between two plates and accepted by an angel that descended to receive it. Diving figure caches from Santa Rita Corozal appear to fit closely the description of this angel (D. Chase 1985b:121–122). Given the general association between maize and blood (see Taube 1985), it may be significant to note that a maize god headdress occurs on one of the diving cache figures (fig. 6). Interestingly, however, these Postclassic Santa Rita figure caches tend not to contain anything resembling a sacrificial knife.

Muluc New Year rites were associated with war dances, pledges of bolts of cloth, and the offerings of dogs and/or squirrels. Evidence related to offerings and activities ascribed to Muluc years' rites are found in a number of Late Postclassic caches at Santa Rita Corozal. Two of them, mentioned above, contained figurines of men performing penis perforation. An additional Late Postclassic figurine cache that may be associated with Muluc years is seen in figure 7 and came from Santa Rita Corozal Structure 183. While Landa mentioned blood sacrifice during Muluc years, the archaeological evidence suggests that the prescribed kind of blood sacrifice was penis perforation. This association of penis perforation and Muluc year rites would appear to be confirmed in page 36 of the Madrid Codex (Lee 1985:102), the only Uayeb page on which stingray spines are illustrated (see fig. 8 and Taube 1985: fig. 8).

The penis perforators from the Structure 213 cache are particularly significant (fig. 9). That these were not mortal men is indicated by their facial features and by

Fig. 6 Late Postclassic diving-god figure from a cache in Santa Rita Corozal Structure 37; this figure may represent the "angel" described as the recipient of certain blood offerings associated with specific Uayeb ceremonies; height = 17 cm (photo courtesy Corozal Postclassic Project, University of Central Florida).

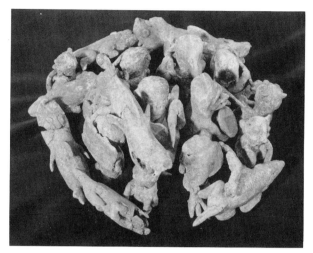

Fig. 7   Late Postclassic figurine cache from Santa Rita Corozal Structure 183; the various offerings suggest its association with calendric ritual; length of shark = 16.5 cm (photo courtesy Corozal Postclassic Project, University of Central Florida).

Fig. 9   Two of four Late Postclassic figurines of Bacabs practicing ritual bloodletting, from Santa Rita Corozal Structure 213; height = 19.4 cm (photo courtesy Corozal Archaeological Project, University of Central Florida).

Fig. 8   Drawing of a pottery vessel containing stingray spines from the Muluc ceremonies of the Uayeb rites (drawing by Diane Z. Chase after Madrid Codex, p. 36).

the superhuman act they are undertaking—bloodletting while on the back of a moving sea turtle. The four figures are most likely the Bacabs that figure prominently in each of the Uayeb rites, especially given the frequent association of Bacabs with snail and/or turtle shells (Thompson 1970). The symbolism of this cache is similar to that of a cache at Tikal containing etched obsidians, again possibly representing the Bacabs (Kidder 1947: fig. 72; Carlson 1986); both these Tikal obsidians and the hieroglyphic heads on the four sides of Río Azul Tomb 12 (Graham 1986:456) may likewise represent turtles associated with the world directions. In the case of the Santa Rita figurines, it would appear that the Bacabs are holding up the sky from the surface of the underworld by standing on the backs of turtles. This posture is in many ways similar to Classic Period imagery and, in fact, might imply that at least certain of the Classic Period portrayal of Earth Monsters or Cauac Monsters could be turtles (see, for example, the Structure 10L-18 southeast jambs at Copán, illustrated in Baudez and Dowd 1983:454–457). This also would accord well with Kurbjuhn's (1985) notion that turtles and snails, when used as bases or seats, "by definition . . . represent an image of the central, vertical axis of the world." The standing figure on a turtle is evidently common in other portions of the Maya area during the Postclassic Period, particularly in the Palenque region (Rands, Bishop, and Harbottle 1979). The blood sacrifice by the four figures in this Santa Rita Corozal Structure 213 cache implies that on certain occasions the blood of the gods was required in addition to that of human beings and animals.

Conclusions

The archaeological associations of bloodletting from Santa Rita Corozal suggest parallels and additions to what has been previously stated about ritual sacrifice and also offer insight into the relationships between the Classic and Postclassic Maya. The limited distribution of stingray spines in both Classic and Postclassic Period burials suggests most strongly that not everyone could bloodlet and that certain bloodletting paraphernalia were insignia affirming the status of certain high-ranking individuals during both eras. Virtually all male burials interpreted to be those of either Classic or Postclassic Period rulers contain a stingray spine in the pelvis. That the stingray itself comes from an underworld creature reinforces the importance of blood sacrifice and the role that such offerings played in allowing the elite to link themselves to the underworld. That blood sacrifice was necessary to celebrate certain events in an important individual's life is also seen during both times. In the Classic Period at Santa Rita Corozal, a cache, presumably naming the ruler and probably deposited sometime after his death, contains numerous stingray spines; a Late Postclassic burial contains a secondary individual who presumably bled and then died to be buried next to his ruler.

While stingray spines are evident in Classic contexts, it is Postclassic caches that confirm the importance of bloodletting in wider ceremonies beyond those of personal life. The Uayeb rites are particularly significant in this interpretation, for their whole intent is the assurance of order in the days to come. While agreeing with Schele (1985b) and others that blood sacrifices played a major role among the Maya elite, the Santa Rita Corozal examples would indicate that bloodletting was but one part of a series of activities important in binding Maya society. The clear correlations between Uayeb descriptions in Landa, pictorial accounts in the codices, and Santa Rita cache patterns establish the significance of blood ritual in the wider context of cycles of time and fertility ceremonies during the Late Postclassic Period. That this preoccupation with periods is not limited to the late Maya is clear from the associations of blood sacrifice and Period-Ending stela during the Classic Period and is also suggested in Bricker's (1981) associations of Classic Period stelae with Uayeb rites. It may be further argued that certain Classic Period caches fill a similar role as ritual markers of the passage of time. It has been argued elsewhere (D. Chase 1988) that there is substantial continuity in Classic and Postclassic caching practices, but that the abstract symbolism of offerings during the Classic Period was replaced during the Postclassic Period by more easily recognizable representations of offerings. While certain caches at Santa Rita Corozal appear to correlate very well with one or another of the Uayeb years described by Landa and indicated in the Madrid Codex, it is possible that these events also coincided with the completion of larger cycles of time (cf. A. Chase, this volume; Edmonson 1985).

Together with ethnohistory, pictorial manuscripts, and material remains from other Maya sites, the Santa Rita Corozal archaeological data confirm the significance of blood sacrifice in Maya cosmology. Archaeological contexts, however, additionally point toward a very organized system of rituals that included bloodletting in its repertoire, rather than random, spontaneous, or managed ceremonial involving mass bloodletting episodes. Certain types of blood sacrifice were clearly appropriate for specific occasions and not for others. Penis perforation must also literally not have been taken lightly; while evidently associated with Muluc years, it probably was not undertaken unless circumstances and prophecy suggested a particularly inauspicious year, since certain of the otherwise clearly Muluc-associated caches from Santa Rita Corozal do not contain bloodletting imagery.

Perhaps most importantly, however, the Santa Rita Corozal materials underscore certain basic similarities, rather than discontinuities, between Classic and Postclassic Maya ritual beliefs and activities. Thus, while art forms and architecture changed drastically between Classic and Postclassic times, the more basic aspects of Maya belief and the role of blood sacrifice in assuring the fertility and continuity of the world are shown to remain little changed through time. Blood sacrifice in both eras remained a lifeline to the gods.

Acknowledgments

This paper is based on work supported by the National Science Foundation under Grants BNS-5809304 and BNS-8318531. Thanks are due to the members of the Corozal Postclassic Project, the people of Corozal Town, the Belize Department of Archaeology, and the Division of Sponsored Research at the University of Central Florida.

D. Chase

Tlalocs at Uxmal

RUBEN MALDONADO C. and BEATRIZ REPETTO TIO
CENTRO REGIONAL DE YUCATAN, INSTITUTO NACIONAL DE ANTROPOLOGIA E HISTORIA

Several representations of the Mexica Rain God Tlaloc are found among the relief sculptures at Uxmal. Ten of these were carved on rectangular limestone building blocks (two of which were almost perfectly square) and the remains of four others are situated at the top of the facade of the North Range in the Nunnery Quadrangle (see Beyer 1969:251, 259).

Nine of the ten limestone blocks that are decorated with the faces of Tlaloc are on display at the new Uxmal museum and the other is at the Museo Regional in Mérida. For years these carvings were lying on the ground by the side of the Lower West Building of the Adivino (Temple of the Magician), where the sculptures evidently served as facade decorations above the doorways (see Ruz Lhuillier 1969).

The initial task in the preparation of this brief study was to prepare rubbings of the reliefs on rice paper (figs. 1 and 2). The reproductions were then photographed, reduced, and numbered. Measurements, together with other data derived from an analysis, were compiled in table 1.

This is the publication illustrating all of the known Tlalocs from the Adivino, although some of these reliefs have been described by earlier investigators. Our number 4 was reported by Seler (see Tozzer 1957: fig. 209); number 3 was noted by Piña Chán (1975), and number 8 was cited by Ruz Lhuillier (1969).

The Lower West Building of the Adivino is the earliest of several superimposed structures that form the highest pyramid at Uxmal, so if the ten Tlaloc carvings really did come from that edifice, they constitute part of the earliest construction phase of the most prominent architectural complex at the site. Carbon-14 analysis of a wooden lintel from the Lower West Building of the Adivino produced a date of A.D. 560 ± 50 (Andrews V 1982:4).

The four representations of Tlaloc on the North Range of the Nunnery Quadrangle, parts of which can still be seen, crown towers of four superimposed figures of the type traditionally known as "Chac masks." These Tlalocs were apparently produced at a somewhat later time than those of the Adivino. The carbon-14 estimate from a wooden lintel in this building is A.D. 885 ± 120 (Andrews V 1982:4).

The ten relief carvings listed first are all more or less rectangular and about the same size, averaging 53.5 cm long by 47.7 cm wide. All exhibit in low relief the face of a water or rain deity, for the classic round, goggle-shaped eyes of the central Mexican Tlalocs are especially prominent. The moustache and teeth also recall central Mexican iconography, although the projecting fangs usually found on Tlalocs are lacking. The figures also have open mouths and an angular, pointed chin with projections on the sides that can doubtless be interpreted as beards; these characteristics could indicate a relationship to Quetzalcoatl. The most significant symbolism, however, is the Teotihuacán year sign, repeated in triplicate—over the headdress and at the ears; for this reason Piña Chán (1981) named these reliefs "Lord of Time Tlalocs." Other elements include plumes that appear as the background for the faces and in some examples are attached in a vertical or oblique fashion to the ear ornaments, which may also be formed of feathers. Linear features, undulating at the ends, come out of the sides of the headdress, give a feeling of movement to the sculpture despite their markedly geometric character (see figs. 1 and 2).

Comparisons show the base below the faces of these representations to be similar; only in two examples do the points of beards penetrate the straight outlines of the bases (fig. 3). One case is fairly obvious (fig. 3; B6) while the other is barely noticeable (fig. 3; B1). It seems that the facial features go beyond their originally intended confines on these two blocks because of a lapse in the artist's skill.

On the basis of facial outline, the Tlalocs can be divided into two groups (fig. 3; E1 to E4 and E5 to E10). In the first group, the eyes are enclosed within the outline; in the second, the eyes form part of the facial contours. This contrast in basic design may represent more than just differences between artists. Possibly the reliefs were carved during distinct periods, but the interval be-

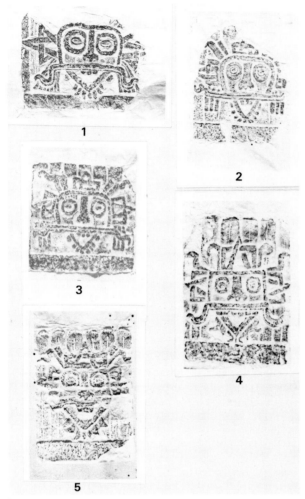

Fig. 1   Rubbings of the Tlaloc relief sculptures, the Adivino, Uxmal.

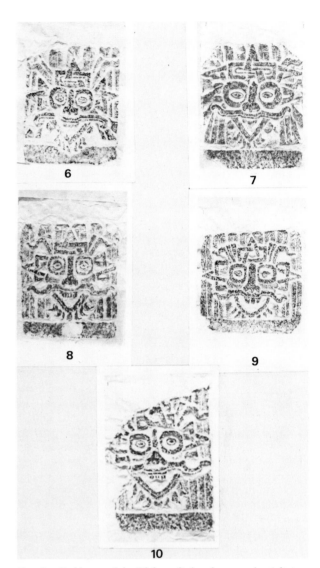

Fig. 2   Rubbings of the Tlaloc relief sculptures, the Adivino, Uxmal.

Table 1.   Measurements of Tlaloc Representations at Uxmal

No.	Length	Width	Max. thickness	Teeth	Incom- plete
1	0.60	0.52	0.29	3	X
2	0.555	0.47	0.25	3	X
3	0.55	0.54	0.33	3	
4	0.55	0.42	0.265	6	
5	0.545	0.42	0.27	3	
6	0.428	0.54	0.29	3	
7	0.54	0.44	0.34	3	
8	0.54	0.465	0.205	3	
9	0.525	0.53	0.325	3	
10	0.54	0.43	0.30	3	X

tween the making of the two groups of carvings could not have been very great.

The year signs form part of the headdress in all cases except one (fig. 3; D1), where the absence of this feature seems due to either deterioration or perhaps lack of space for this feature on the block. These symbols are also found on either side of the headdress; so, significantly, the year sign is present on all of the Tlaloc representations.

Analysis of these year signs, both those at the top of the heads and those at the sides, resulted in the conclusion that the classification on the basis of form (the type of intertwining) or combinations of form was not significant. What does seem important is the presence of these signs rather than the degree of variation between them.

The other prominent features on the face of the Tlalocs that must be examined are the moustaches and whiskers projecting from the jaws. Individual comparison of these features does not reveal any great differences, but viewing the moustache and whiskers together permits isolation of two major groupings (fig. 3; H1 to

Maldonado C. and Repetto Tio

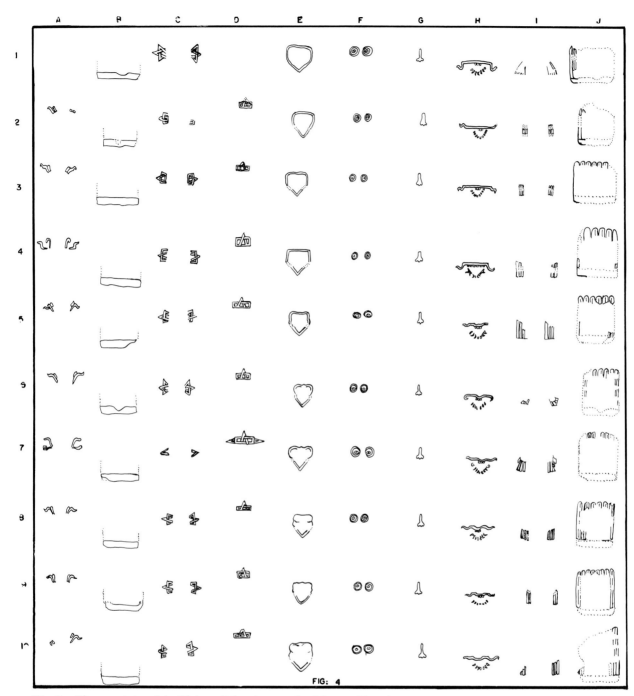

Fig. 3 *Characteristics of the Tlaloc relief sculptures, the Adivino, Uxmal.*

H3 and H5 to H10); only one of the examples (H4) appears to be transitional between the groups.

On each of the sides of the headdress coming out of the heads are pairs of wavy elements, similar on all of the figures, that indicate movement and seem to symbolize the thunderbolts and lightning that are mentioned in historical documents as being associated with this Rain God.

Significant differences were not encountered between the plumes that frame the Tlaloc figures or the earplug pendants. The eyes, the "goggles" surrounding the eyes, and the noses also seem relatively uniform.

The comparisons of the various elements that make up the Tlaloc faces result in formulation of two groups consisting of figure 1, numbers 1 to 3, on the one hand, and figure 2, numbers 6 to 10, on the other. One carving, figure 1, number 4, appears to be transitional between the two groups. Within these two groups the observed contrasts appear to be due to the work of different artisans; there is also the possibility that this variation resulted from the art of being produced at distinct times.

The vestiges of Tlalocs that crown the four towers on the facade of the North Range of the Nunnery Quadrangle have the year sign in the area of the mouth and beard as a distinctive additional characteristic. Seler (in Tozzer 1957) described one mosaic sculpture that had earplugs and a mouth exhibiting the year sign; today only the lower part of the mask and six teeth remain intact. The characteristic plumes are placed horizontally. Two other areas having fragmentary remains of masks with the characteristics of this deity are found on the west side of the North Range, and on the east side there is a Tlaloc that is still well preserved up to the level of his eyes. This representation has circular earplugs rather than the year sign; the year sign, however, is found in the mouth. All four of these Tlalocs were carved and put together with greater care and larger dimensions than the ten examples from the Lower West Range of the Adivino.

In the drawings of Waldeck one can observe the remains of one of these Tlalocs in a good state of preservation. There are differences, however, between reality and the imagination of the artist; for example, the year sign cannot be observed within a mouth that appears greatly reduced in size.

Enrique Juan Palacios (1945:447) observed that these Tlalocs that he termed "Mexican" were aesthetically out of harmony with the finely worked and formed Maya Chac masks.

The fact that these Tlaloc figures are found above four masks considered representations of Chac could be significant. According to Thompson (1960:10, 11), many of the Maya gods were in groups of four, each associated with one of the cardinal directions and a color; at the same time, however, the four Chacs were conceptualized as one. Thompson held that in these aspects, as well as many others, Maya and Mexican concepts, including their gods, were remarkably similar.

From Landa's (1959:62, 63) writings, we learn that the four Bacabs and the Chacs were similar if not homologous. Apparently the function of the four Bacabs who were celestial deities was to support the sky at each of the four cardinal points so that it does not fall. It is curious that one of the Maya names possessed by each of these four Bacabs end in *xibchac*, a term that can be translated as "the great or portentous man." Thus, the Bacab of the south was called, among other names, Kanxibchac; of the east, Chacxibchac; of the north, Zacxibchac; of the west, Ekxibchac. The corresponding colors are yellow, red, white, and black, respectively.

Fray Bernardino de Sahagún (1981:45), while preserving the traditions of the Mexicas, described Tlaloc in the following words: "This god called *Tlaloc Tlama-*

cazqui was the god of rain. They held that he brought the rains . . . , they also held that he sent hail and thunderbolts and the storms and the perils of rivers and the sea . . ." He also stated that during the festival of the first month of the year, called Atlacahualco by the Mexicans, they prepared a great feast in honor of the Rain Gods called Tlaloque and many unweaned children with two swirls (cowlicks) in their hair and born on an auspicious day were sacrificed for this occasion, all for the purpose of ensuring rain (Sahagún 1981:130).

The Mexica were fervently devoted to Tlaloc and worshiped him throughout the land. His figure was placed in one of the two highest sanctuaries, next to that of the god Huitzilopochtli, within the great Templo Mayor of Mexico City. There his statue was carved of stone, with a frightening face like that of a serpent, with very large fangs, red as the fire of lightning hurled in the tempests. He had a crown of green feathers and a collar of green stones set with an emerald; at the ears were jewels from which hung silver earrings; in the right hand was a wavy, violet colored staff resembling the lightning. The feast of this grand idol was held on 29 April at Pantitlán, where there was a large sink in the lake; there a small girl was flayed and thrown to the waters as a sacrifice while kings and nobles tossed in much jewelry (Duran 1965:135–137).

The historical sources tell us (Torquemada 1969:II, 45–46, 266–267) that Tlaloc was the oldest of the gods that existed on earth, living on a high mountain where he produced the water and rain. In both the high sierras and lower mountains, lesser deities subject to Tlaloc were charged with the formation of rain clouds. In the sixth Mexica month that began at the first of May a festival was held for the Tlalocs as a plea for the growth and protection of their fields. Two children were sacrificed at these fiestas by taking them to a whirlpool in the lake by the side of what is now the Cerro de la Estrella; there the canoe, which also held the hearts of other sacrificial victims, was sunk.

Those who drowned, were struck down by lightning, or died of dropsy, tumors, abscesses, and wounds and the children sacrificed in honor of Tlaloc went to Tlalocan, the paradise of the gods. They also believed that on one day of the year children sacrificed to Tlaloc, maintaining their invisible form, came to a certain place in the temple. Tlaloc was colored blue and green to imitate the appearance of water; in his hands he held a long, wavy rod of gold that represented lightning. In another festival to this god, four children of six or seven years of age were bought and sealed in a cave to die of hunger and fright. The first flowers were also offered to this god (Clavijero 1968:148, 154, 171, 173).

In addition to the information from the chroniclers, there exists archaeological evidence concerning Tlaloc, the Lord of Time. At Bonampak he is represented with the year sign as a headdress. More representations adorned with the year sign can be found at Copán and Yaxchilán

(Proskouriakoff 1950:101). Tlalocs without the year sign can be seen at Bilbao, Guatemala (Piña Chán 1975), and in the Tiquisate region (Hellmuth 1978:52). Two other Tlaloc figures at Sayil (Pollock 1980:123) are reminiscent of the carvings at nearby Uxmal.

Outside of the Maya area, representations similar to the ones we illustrate can be seen on Stela 2 of Xochicalco (Piña Chán 1981), where the god Quetzalcoatl is apparently transformed into Tlaloc, Lord of Time, with the year sign as a headdress, the round Tlaloc goggles, projecting fangs, earplugs, a moustache with fangs coming out, a forked tongue, and the glyph seven Quiáhuitl (water or rain).

Tlaloc symbolism is frequently found on painting and sculpture at Teotihuán, and examples of the year sign are also abundant. The people of Teotihuacán have been considered the inventors of the year sign (Beyer 1969: 262), for this element has even been encountered on the supports of pottery cylinder vases at that site (Séjourné

1966:88). If this is true, the symbol could have been an importation to the Maya area.

The presence of ceramics painted or appliquéd with abstract facial features of Tlaloc such as the goggle eyes, the moustache, and, in some cases, the fangs have also been documented for northern Yucatán. Such is the case of the incensarios of Balankanché (Andrews 1970), the slateware plates with negative painting at the bottom, or the Peto Cream plate recovered from the cenote of Dzibilchaltun.

In summary, from comparison of the ten carvings illustrated in this paper and the well-known iconography of the figures from the facade towers of the North Range of the Nunnery Quadrangle, we can state that the Adivino figures are indeed depictions of the Water God Tlaloc. Both groups of carvings include similarities and contrasts, but the differences between the Nunnery Tlalocs and those of the Adivino are most easily explained by the time that passed between their creations.

The Period-Ending Stelae of Yaxchilán

CAROLYN TATE
DALLAS MUSEUM OF ART

A word for "stela" survives in Yucatec, *manak'*, and it is glossed in the Cordemex dictionary as *rastro o senal que se parece de lejos*. A related word, *manak' chi'*, means *acordar o traer a la memoria*. These translations summon the mental image of a throng of participants gathered in a gigantic plaza, using the stelae as mnemonic devices and integrating this occurrence of the ceremony with the previous times the same ceremonies occurred. With the pyramids as backdrops, the stelae were focal points for public rituals that were enacted in the plazas. For the populace, the stelae provided a static image of the ruler engaged in self-sacrifice or as a victorious warrior and protector. The kings used the stelae as proclamations of their piety and commissioned the carving of the tall stone shafts to manifest their role as the paradigm for human behavior toward the deities and the cosmos.

At Yaxchilán, over thirty stelae once towered over the people gathered in the spacious ceremonial plazas. The subset of eleven nearly identical stelae that forms the focus of this investigation was erected in the Late Classic era (between about A.D. 636 and 800). The stelae were situated in front of Structures 39, 40, and 41 on the South Acropolis, Structure 33, at the heart of the site, and in front of Structure 20 on the southeast Plaza (see fig. 1). These buildings and one side of their stelae all faced the river, and the stelae were visible, from afar, as the word *manak'* suggests, to any riverine travelers.

Very little scholarly attention has been paid to the stelae of Yaxchilán for several reasons, the most significant of which is their state of preservation. When the stelae toppled under the lashing winds and rain of the jungle, they fell in varying directions, and different sides landed facing the ground. Up on the South Acropolis, in front of Structure 41, the stelae fell away from the temple. Sections of those stelae slid down the hill, and the river sides, face down, were preserved from the torrential rains, while the temple sides were largely eroded. On these stelae, a warrior image was preserved. The stelae in front of Structure 20 and Stela 1 in the Main Plaza were blown toward the temple and fell with the temple side downward, and a triple register image was preserved.

The problems with these stelae are, first, whether enough evidence remains of the original carving to reconstruct what the images were on the eroded sides; second, what specific dates and events were recorded on the eroded sides; and third, what the images on the stelae tell us about Maya kingship.

With some detective work, it is possible to reconstruct the imagery carved on the two broad surfaces of this group of at least eleven stelae. With the aid of a complete chronology of the site (Tate 1986:426–430), the remaining glyphs on each stela, and an analysis of the type of information presented on this group of stela, it is also possible to suggest dates and events for the eroded temple sides of Stelae 18, 19, and 20.

Sources of visual and descriptive evidence for the reconstruction of the data on the stelae are the photographs and texts published by the early explorers of the Usumacinta Valley. Teobert Maler (1903) published ex-

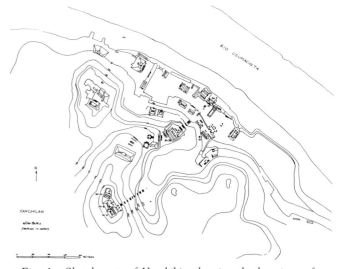

Fig. 1 Sketch map of Yaxchilán showing the locations of stelae in this article (drawing by Carolyn Tate).

cellent photographs of the stelae he and Alfred Percival Maudslay had encountered. Less discernible photographic images of stelae he and the other members of the Carnegie's Fourteenth Central American Expedition discovered were published by Sylvanus Morley in 1938. Merle Greene Robertson made rubbings of many Yaxchilán stelae, published in her book of 1972 (Greene, Rands, and Graham 1972). Ian Graham made drawings of some of the stelae. The images, Maler's careful observations about what was on the eroded sides of the stelae, and my own observations make it possible to state without equivocation that this group of stelae shared the same format, and to reconstruct much of the eroded information.

The design of the stelae is sufficiently regular to be described as having a format into which practically identical images were inserted. Hieroglyphic texts on the stelae differentiate the name, attributes, and dates of one ruler from those of another and create a specific historical-ritual document of the ruler as the actor in a cosmic paradigm.

Format: The Temple Side

On the sides facing the temples, these stelae had a three register composition (see fig. 2). Maler made the initial interpretation of the central register. He operated under the premise that the Mayas did not erect monuments to human endeavors, but made images of their gods. His comment about Stela 3 (see fig. 3) is typical:

The representation on the "deity side" shows us Ketsalcoatl as a beneficent deity, as is usual on the stelae of Yaxchilan. He holds with both hands the "string of joys," ornamented with little heads of bees and bordered with cocoa beans, which he has just taken from the "chest of good fortune" at his feet. Before him and behind him stand a man and a woman stretching out their hands to receive benefactions. [Maler 1903:122]

Since Maler's era Tatiana Proskouriakoff (1963, 1964) proved that these figures were not beneficent deities but historical individuals. She, Morley, and I have figured out the dates recorded, which are Period Endings and accession anniversaries. The activity of spilling a liquid from the hands can also be placed in the context of ancient Maya ritual activity. Because of comments made by the Spaniards who observed the Maya in the sixteenth century, it is known that the ancient Maya frequently drew blood from their bodies, using stone blades, fish spines, and plant thorns to pierce their ears, tongues, and penises. By relating the dots bordering the flowing liquid on these stelae to the dots issuing from Lady Xoc's mouth on Lintel 24 of Yaxchilán, David Stuart (1984e) realized that the "chest of good fortune" and "ropes of honey" represent the king's blood flowing into a sacrificial receptacle.

At the top of the temple side of the stelae are cartouches formed of an oval with the corners removed as if

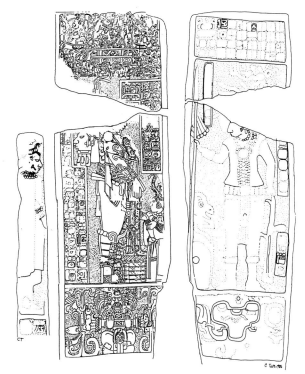

Fig. 2   Stela 1 (narrow edge drawn by the author; temple side drawing is a field drawing by Ian Graham; river side drawn by Carolyn Tate).

bitten out. From the notched corners of the cartouches project skeletal serpent fangs. These cartouches exist at several Maya sites, including Palenque and Tikal, but their identification depends on their context on these stelae from Yaxchilán (see fig. 4). On the upper register of Stela 11, in a semantic niche corresponding to the position of the oval cartouches, the parents of Bird Jaguar are named. In the other examples, the individuals in the cartouches are not named, but iconographical details suggest that they, too, are the deceased parents of the sacrificing ruler. They hold skeletal serpent bars and wear skeletal headdresses, sometimes of the Quadripartite Monster (Robertson 1974), the symbol of the sun in its journey through the underworld, the area of death, burial, and regeneration. At the upper edge of these stelae are images of the king's divine royal ancestors.

Between the cartouches is the bust of a supernatural character. It wears the crossed-bands pectoral that identifies it as one of the Hero Twins, or the related deities, GI and GIII of the Palenque Triad, who correspond mythically to the sun and Venus (see Schele and Miller 1986:48, 51–52; and Tedlock 1985:35–37; 232–237, for discussions of the Hero Twins).

Separating the ancestors and the Hero Twins from the ruler is a spatial indicator known as a sky band. It is a saurian monster infixed with symbols securely associated with the heavens, including Lamat signs for Venus, God C glyphs, and moon and sun signs. The band is terminated on each end by a monster head, whose gaping

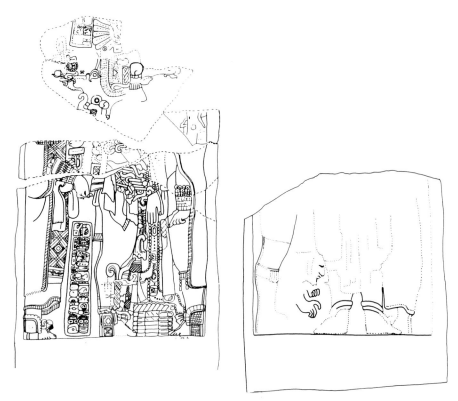

Fig. 3   Stela 3 (drawing by Carolyn Tate).

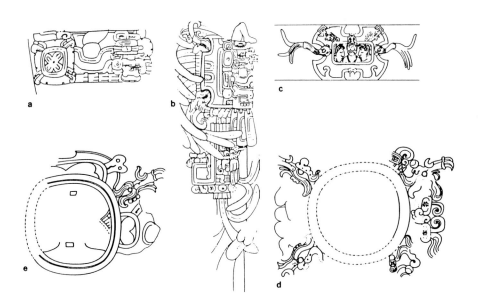

Fig. 4 Ancestor cartouches. (a) Tikal Stela 1, base, detail (drawing by W. Coe in Jones and Satterthwaite 1982, fig. 1); (b) Tikal Stela 5, detail of back-rack (drawing by W. Coe in Jones and Satterthwaite 1982, fig. 7); (c) Stucco and stone cartouche, Palenque House D (drawing by Merle Greene Robertson 1985b, fig. 358); (d) Stucco cartouche, Palenque House A, Medallion 11 (drawing by Merle Green Robertson 1985b, fig. 136a); (e) Stucco cartouche from Palenque House A, Medallion 13 (drawing by Merle Greene Robertson 1985b, fig. 138b).

mouth contains images of GI or GIII. The sky band stretches across the upper register of the stela, as the sky stretches above the heads of humans. The sky band monsters, infixed with images of the Hero Twins and sun and Venus, are representations of the processes by which the sun, moon, and planets are born, travel, die, and are renewed. Their presence on these stelae indicates that the king's bloodletting maintains these cyclic phenomena.

Below the feet of the ruler is a frontal monster. Images

in Maya art are rarely frontal and, except in the very late Classic, frontal images are of supernatural beings. These monsters are a specific reference to the supernatural owner of the locality of Yaxchilán. This is most clearly seen on Stela 4 (see fig. 5), where a frontal muan bird, the personification of "sky," has a "split sky" glyph, the emblem glyph of Yaxchilán, infixed in its forehead. On Stela 7 (see fig. 6), the lower register contains a profile monster with a "split earth" glyph, probably a reference

Tate

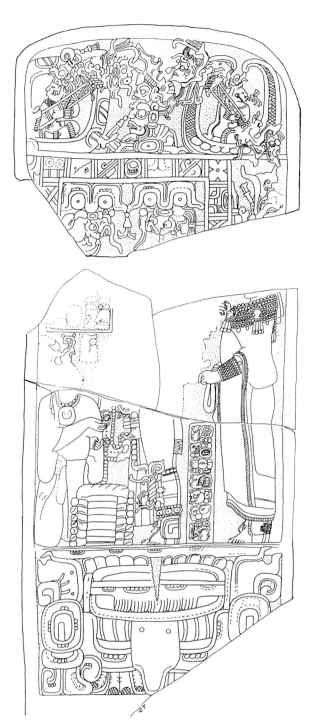

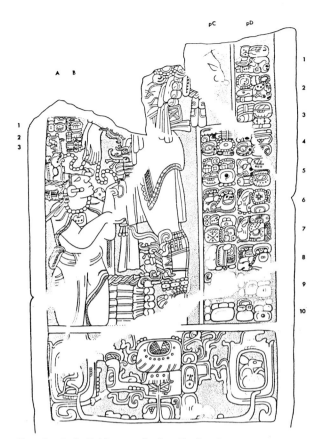

Fig. 6   Stela 7 (drawing by Ian Graham).

Fig. 5   Stela 4 (drawn by Carolyn Tate after field drawing by Ian Graham).

to "our place," "our earth." Cartouches containing a monkey, symbol of the day or sun, and a rabbit, symbol of the moon, emanate from the eye of the Split Earth Monster.

The metaphor presented on the three registers of the temple side of the stelae might be paraphrased as follows:

the ruler is responsible for uniting our place to the celestial and underworld realms. His blood nourishes the earth and the heavens, from which spring the eternal cycles of the sun, Venus, and the moon, the bodies whose travels regulate our lives and most visibly unite this earth with the cycles of the heavens. I agree with the suggestion of David Freidel, Susan Yaeger, and Maria Masucci (this volume) that this stacking of information signals a process of transformation: in this case, the transformation of blood to sustenance for place, ancestors, and supernaturals.

Format: The River Side

The river side of each stelae shows the same historical ruler who is portrayed on the temple side. On the river side, the ruler always wears the traditional Yaxchilán war outfit, composed of a spear, a long scarf, a flexible shield, and a short kilt fringed with jaguar claws. The glyphs on the surviving river sides record the date of a capture and the lengthy titles of the king.

Both sides of these stela have formal precedents at Yaxchilán. The major images, a ruler in profile, letting blood, and the ruler as warrior, appear on Yaxchilán stelae from the Middle Classic Period. Stela 27 is the earliest dated stela at Yaxchilán. It records the Period

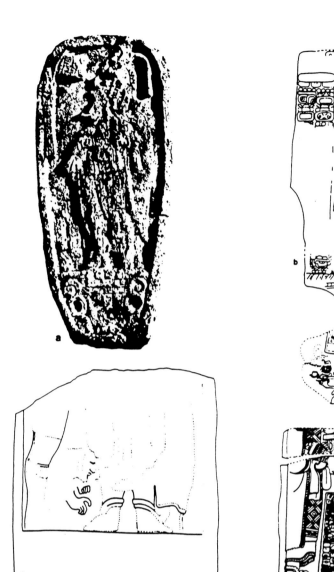

Fig. 7 (a) Stela 2 (photo from Maler 1903; reprinted with permission from the Peabody Museum of Archaeology and Ethnology); (b) Stela 27 (drawing by Carolyn Tate and Constance Cortez); (c) Stela 3 temple side (drawing by Carolyn Tate); (d) Stela 3, river side (drawn by Carolyn Tate).

Ending 9.4.0.0.0 and shows a ruler letting blood into a receptacle. Stela 2 marked the Period Ending 9.9.0.0.0 and portrays a Yaxchilán king with a spear, as a warrior. The first known stela of the Late Classic period, Stela 3, combines bloodletting iconography on the temple side and warrior imagery on the river side. This beautiful stela became the standard Period-Ending format for the remaining ten katuns of Yaxchilán history, and for all the stelae in this study (see fig. 7). Stelae 10 and 11, erected by Bird Jaguar IV, are variants on this theme. Stela 10 is the marker for the Period Ending 9.16.15.0.0, and Stela 11 is Bird Jaguar's accession monument (see Maler 1903 for illustrations of these stelae). Several other stelae of which only fragments are known were also double format Period-Ending stelae: 8, 30, and 31, and an unnumbered fragment found in the pedestal platform of Stela 3 (see fig. 12 below).

Reconstruction of the Hieroglyphic Data

The temple side of the stelae shows a ruler bloodletting in a cosmic setting, and the river side portrays the ruler as warrior. The two sides of the stelae contained different types of historical data as well. Because various examples of the temple and river sides are preserved, with the aid of a thorough chronology of the site (Tate 1986: 426–430), it is possible to reconstruct the dates and events of some of the eroded monuments.

Several texts survive on the temple sides of the stelae. A clearly preserved hieroglyphic text on the temple side of Stela 3 (see fig. 3) records a verb and the name of the ruler. The verb is the completion hand (T713b; Thompson 1971: fig. 32). "His first katun as ahau of the lineage" (noted by Proskouriakoff 1964:185) is what he completed, and Bird Jaguar, 6 Tun, Captor of Great

Fig. 8 Stela 6 (drawing by Carolyn Tate; temple side drawn after the field drawing of Ian Graham; river side drawn by Carolyn Tate).

Moon, Blood of the Throne of Yaxchilán is named as the ruler. These titles refer to Bird Jaguar 3, father of Shield Jaguar the Great (Tate 1986:469a) and prove that this is the earliest stela of this group.

On Stela 6, temple side, survives a Long Count date with head variant numerals (see fig. 8). The date can be clearly read as 9.11.16.10.13 5 Ben 1 Uayeb, and the event recorded is the completion of two katuns as *ahau* of the lineage by Bird Jaguar 3. Thus, the date of Stela 3, the completion of one katun as *ahau* of this ruler, can be easily reconstructed as 9.10.16.10.13, and his accession date as 9.9.16.10.13, although no known monument records that date.

Stelae 1 and 4 contain 819 day counts prior to Hotun Endings. The focal event on the temple sides of these stelae were Period Endings.

From this sample, it is possible to generalize that the hieroglyphic information on the temple sides of the stelae concerned accession anniversaries and Period Endings celebrated by the rulers. Some glyphic data also survive on the river sides of several stelae. The three stelae with legible glyphs on their river sides were originally on the edge of the platform of the South Acropolis. As the ancient visitor climbed the steep stairway to Structure 41, three images of Shield Jaguar as a warrior loomed at the summit.

At over 4 m tall, Stela 19 was the largest of the stelae in front of Structure 41 (see fig. 9). Maler (1903) gave a sufficient description of the temple side to prove that it

was a three-register cosmogram. The river side of this stela was one of the records of the capture of Ah Ahaual, on the date (9.12.8.14.0) 11 Ahau 3 Pop. Proskouriakoff (1963) thought, and I agree, that this stela was probably the original record of the capture of this prisoner. The nominal phrase referring to Shield Jaguar on this monument suggests he was young when this stela

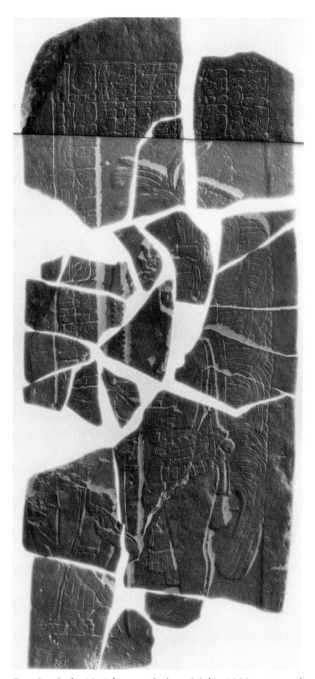

Fig. 9 Stela 19 (photograph from Maler 1903; reprinted with permission from the Peabody Museum of Archaeology and Ethnology).

Fig. 10 Stela 20 (drawing by Carolyn Tate after the field drawing by Ian Graham).

Ending 9.12.10.0.0. I think that it is most likely the record of his accession, because no known stela records this important occasion. It was also the tallest stela and located in the center of the group that faced the long ascent from the valley, making it the most prominent stela on the acropolis.

Stela 20 (see fig. 10) records the date 9.13.9.14.14 6 Ix 16 Kankin as the date of the capture of Ah Kan by Shield Jaguar, who is here named with a 3 katun title. The temple side of Stela 20 probably recorded the Period Ending 9.13.10.0.0, the only Period Ending between the capture of Ah Kan and the time Shield Jaguar attained his 4th katun.

Following a similar line of reasoning as for Stela 19 and 20, if the temple side of Stela 18 (see fig. 11) represented a Period Ending, the next Period Ending after the capture of Ah Chuen on 9.14.17.15.12 is the Katun Ending 9.15.0.0.0.

All the buildings with which Period-Ending stelae were associated faced northeast, toward the summer solstice sunrise, and the river. All of them had lintels or steps that documented accessions of rulers. The vertical format of the stela was chosen as the public document of the primary function of the rulers. What does the ver-

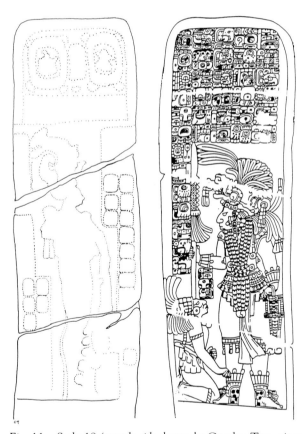

Fig. 11 Stela 18 (temple side drawn by Carolyn Tate; river side drawn by Ian Graham).

was erected. When he captured Ah Ahaual, Shield Jaguar was in his second katun of life. The Maya kings did not usually record the katuns of a ruler's life until he began his third. Shield Jaguar lived to be around ninety-five years old, and his 4 and 5 katun titles always appear in his nominal phrases. The capture statement on Stela 19 includes no katun title, and it is likely that this stela was carved before 9.12.15.0.0, when he earned his 3 Katun title.

Accepting that Stela 19 was carved to commemorate an important event shortly after 9.12.8.14.0, then there are two possible reconstructions of the date of the stela: Shield Jaguar's accession on 9.12.9.8.1, or the Hotun tical shape and the format of the stelae reveal about the ideal they were meant to convey?

The Cosmogram

The Mayas conceived of the universe as having three superimposed levels: the heavens, the underworld, and the terrestrial realm. In plan, the universe is quadrilateral or circular with four important points, which new evidence interprets as the solstitial rise and set points, rather than the European concepts of the cardinal directions (see Vogt 1985). In the center of the four directions is an axis mundi connecting the three levels of the cosmos, which reaches above to the zenith and below to the nadir of the sun's transit (Vogt 1985).

On these Yaxchilán Period-Ending stelae, images of the royal ancestors and the heavenly bodies appear above the ruler and the sacred territory appears below the ruler. The ruler and his blood are the axis that connects the ancestral heavens and the underworld. The form of the stela is a symbol of the axis mundi, and the ruler is its personification.

Many Maya monuments subtly demonstrate the concept of the axis mundi. On the Sarcophagus Lid in the Temple of the Inscriptions at Palenque, Pacal is shown falling into the underworld as he died, via the axis mundi portrayed as a tree, marked with God C signs. That it is a tree is shown by the glyph woody material, *te,* on the trunk (Schele 1976:28).

The modern Maya still contact their ancestors through trees and crosses. Evon Vogt related that the modern Tzotzil erect crosses at the sacred spots in their environment; the crosses serve as a "doorway," a "channel of communication to some deity in the cosmological system" (Vogt 1981:120, 1976: chapters 1 and 3). The concept of the tree or axis as the medium for the attain-

ment of immortality persists, as indicated by the gloss for the Spanish word *inmortal* in the de Delgaty *Vocabulario Tzotzil.* The word is *yoyal balumil, eje de la tierra,* literally, axis of the earth (Tate 1980:72).

The World Tree at Palenque was marked with the God C image. God C appears on the loincloth of rulers engaged in Period-Ending sacrifices at other sites. It symbolizes the lineage blood that has been shed. What is shown is not the act of letting blood, but the results. All Maya Period-Ending stelae had to make some reference to bloodletting; but at Yaxchilán no God C loincloth was needed to symbolize the bloodletting because it was explicitly portrayed. The ruler's progenitors are shown above him, and his blood and bloodline are organized pictorially into a vertical composition symbolizing the axis mundi.

In Classic times, I suspect that the stelae were markers of sacred place in the ceremonial center. The axis mundi was located between the temples that recorded the history of the sacred lineage and the plazas where the people convened.

During the Period-Ending and accession ceremonies, the king probably sacrificed his blood in the privacy of the temples. Outside, on the steps of the temples, the members of the royal court looked toward the Plaza. They saw the images of the kings letting blood on the ancient stelae. The populace, down in the Plaza, looked up toward the temples. On the same stelae, they saw the larger-than-life images of generations of kings as the vanquishers of enemies. Anyone traveling on the Usumacinta who looked up at the majestic ceremonial center also saw generations of warriors guarding the site. For both the priests and the populace, the stelae were carved to portray an ideal: eternal sacrifice of self and captives as the proper behavior to ensure harmony among the territory, the ancestors, and the cosmos.

The Structure 8 Tablet and Development of the Great Plaza at Yaxchilán

RAMON CARRASCO V.

CENTRO REGIONAL DE YUCATAN, INSTITUTO NACIONAL DE ANTROPOLOGIA E HISTORIA

The purpose of this paper is to recount some of the changes in the Great Plaza at Yaxchilán and to propose some ideas about relationships between epigraphic data and architectural information. These relationships can be understood only through knowledge gained by excavation; the data described here resulted from my participation (during the 1976 and 1978 through 1980 field seasons) in the Yaxchilán Project, directed by *arqueólogo* García Moll.

Much of the time our understanding of the architectural and spatial development of an archaeological zone is limited to recording physical changes that occurred in the course of history, but one line of inquiry made possible by the presence of epigraphic data is to enrich this perspective through analysis of associations between inscriptions and architecture. By comparison with sites such as Piedras Negras or Palenque, where sequences integrating both epigraphic information and architectural data have already been worked out, Yaxchilán presents a greater degree of difficulty for any attempts to establish a correlation between architecture and the inscriptions, due to topography and the pattern of construction activities carried out by the rulers of that site.

On the basis of chronological and stylistic divisions taken from Cohodas, García Moll (1975) worked out an architectural sequence for Yaxchilán. The greatest antiquity is assigned to Group IV, which was followed by the construction of the buildings associated with Shield Jaguar—Structures 23, 34, 41, and 44. Next is a period of transition represented by Altar 1, the ball court markers, and the stelae of Structures 39 and 41. According to García Moll, the basic layout of Yaxchilán was then determined during the reign of Bird Jaguar, who ordered the building of Structures 2, 13, 16, 21, 54, and 55 of Group I, Structure 33 of Group II, and Structure 42 of Group III. The final period is represented by Structure 20.

With recent advances in epigraphy, it has been possible to determine with greater precision the names of the different rulers and personages at Yaxchilán; the last three rulers were Shield Jaguar I, Bird Jaguar III, and Shield Jaguar II. Many details of the labors of Shield Jaguar I and his predecessors have not, however, been determined due to lack of archaeological data, although it is known that the urban development of Yaxchilán began in Early Classic times. Archaeological fieldwork has established the existence of substructures under Structures 7, 8, 23, 77, and Stela 3. It is probable that substructures will also be encountered in other sectors of the Great Plaza, especially below Structure 5, Structures 4 and 6, and Structures 16, 17, 18, and 19.

Originally, the landscape where the first structures were built was dominated by two steep depressions or *cañadas* that determined the distribution and form of the settlement; one of these was situated to the east and the other on the west. Thus, the Great Plaza was divided into four parts at different levels, two on elevations and two in depressions (see figs. 1 and 2a). Excavations have shown that a substructure resting on a plastered floor exists under Stela 3. This floor, encountered at a depth of 2.05 m, is situated in the east *cañada*. The feature probably represents the level of the plaza in this area before 9.16.0.0.0. The other low-lying area of construction is situated in the west *cañada* at the level of Structures 19 and 77. This area was partly covered when the terrain was leveled for the building of Structure 19 and associated architecture. A platform was laid out at the east edge of the elevated area between the two *cañadas*; this platform was later covered by Structure 8. I assume that, under the other elevated complex below Structure 4, there exists a substructure forming the edge of the buried plaza on which the substructure below Stela 3 was built (see fig. 3).

The corner of a platform that also served to support a stela was located under the platform of Stela 3. This substructure, probably quadrangular in form, had sloping walls with a cornice, both covered with a layer of stucco. The veneer stone of both the walls and the stela base was neatly dressed by contrast with that of Stela 3 (fig. 4).

Under Structure 7, a substructure with paint remaining on the stucco covering was encountered at approximately the same level as the floor of the substructure

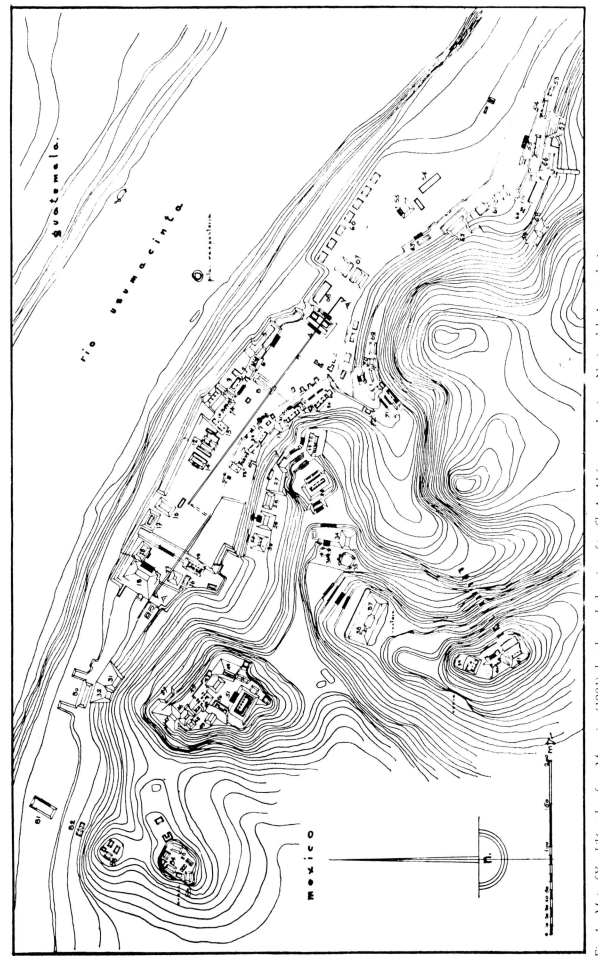

Fig. 1 Map of Yaxchilán taken from Marquina (1981) that shows the location of profile A–A' (courtesy Instituto Nacional de Antropología e Historia, Centro Regional de Yucatán).

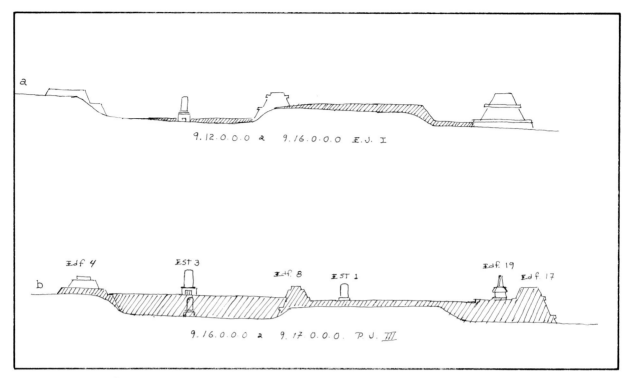

a

9.12.0.0.0 a 9.16.0.0.0 E.J. I

Edf 4   EST 3   Edf. 8   EST 1   Edf. 19   Edf 17

b

9.16.0.0.0 a 9.17.0.0.0 P.J. III

Fig. 2 Drawing of the profile A–A' showing two construction phases of the Great Plaza (drawing by Ramón Carrasco).

under Stela 3. East of Structure 7 one can observe the sealed doorways of Structure 6 that once opened toward the Great Plaza, covered to the level of the plaza by fill and the remainder closed off by later construction. This building probably rests on a platform built up from the level of the floor of the substructure of Stela 3 (fig. 5).

During the clearing of the partly collapsed north passage of the labyrinth of Structure 19, the rounded corners and sloping walls (*talud*) of the lower portions of the base of Structure 77 were located. The three superimposed terraces that supported Structure 77 were buried to a depth of 3.59 m by the building of the Structure 19 complex.

Excavation subsequent to the discovery of a stone tablet with hieroglyphs resulted in the finding of buried architecture below Structure 8. These explorations showed that the substructure also had sloping walls (*talud*) and a cornice built of neatly dressed stone that was covered with stucco (fig. 6). These similarities between the details of the substructures of Stela 3 and Structure 8 suggest that this low plaza group exhibits an architectural homogeneity that indicates similar periods of construction, which possibly correspond to the reign of Shield Jaguar I or earlier.

It is probable that around 9.16.0.0.0, Bird Jaguar II planned one of his most ambitious projects, ordering the filling of the low areas near the river shore to erect or modify various buildings (fig. 2b). To carry out this grand landfill project, an engineering technique was em-

ployed involving creation of a network of retaining walls averaging 0.75 m high that were then loaded with fill to form a base. Another network of retaining walls was then interlaced over the earlier ones. This method was continued until the desired level was reached. The technique resulted in greater structural strength as well as a uniform final surface (fig. 7).

After creating the Great Plaza, Bird Jaguar III ordered the erection of Stela 3, placing it over the walls of a platform that supported two fragments of another stela on which the name clause of Shield Jaguar I was identified (figs. 8-9). We assume that these fragments are parts of the stela that once stood on the buried substructure.

Schele (1982:213) analyzed the singular text on Stela 3, attributing it to Bird Jaguar II and interpreting the date of dedication as 9.12.5.0.0 (?). On the basis of new information from twelve small fragments belonging to the monument that were found when it was excavated in 1976, I proposed that the stela dates from the reign of Bird Jaguar III "the Great." Together the fragments form part of a cartouche with the name clause of Shield Jaguar I (fig. 10). Though the clause is incomplete, the glyphs that refer to the name of the personage having been lost, one of the titles of that ruler, "Captor of Ah-Ahaual," can be recognized in the remaining text.

Stela 3 was sculpted on two sides with two similar scenes. On the side that is best preserved, reference is made to a ceremony in which Bird Jaguar II and Shield Jaguar I, accompanied by a woman, participate. The

Carrasco V.

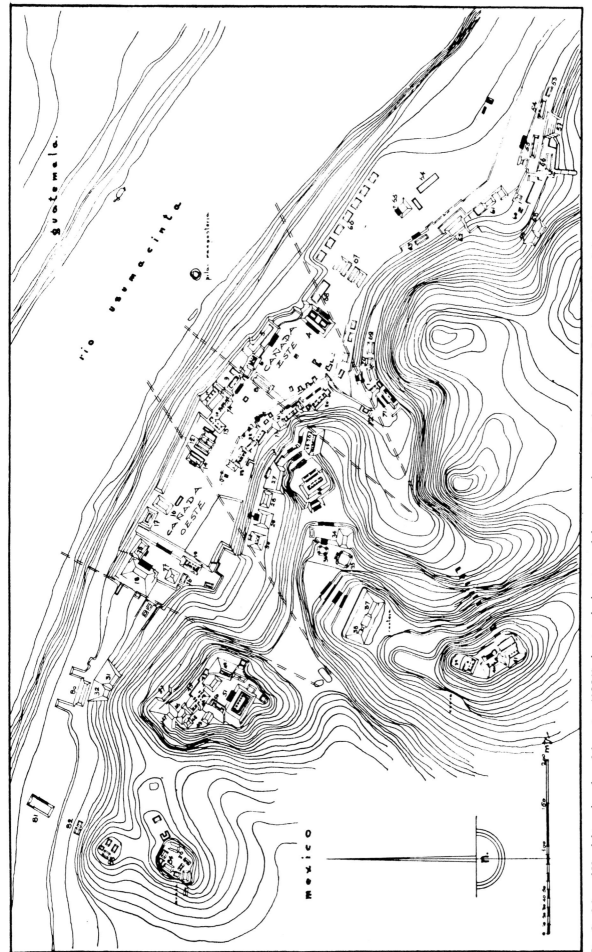

Fig. 3 Map of Yaxchilán taken from Marquina (1981) showing the locations of the east and west cañadas (courtesy Instituto Nacional de Antropología e Historia, Centro Regional de Yucatán).

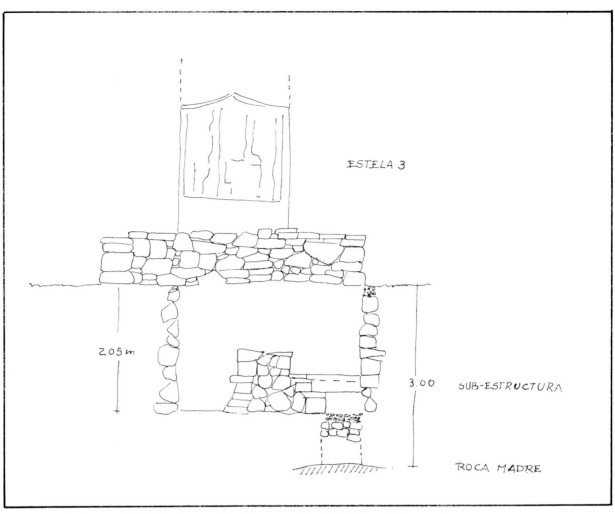

Fig. 4 Profile drawing of Stela 3, showing the substructure (drawing by Ramón Carrasco).

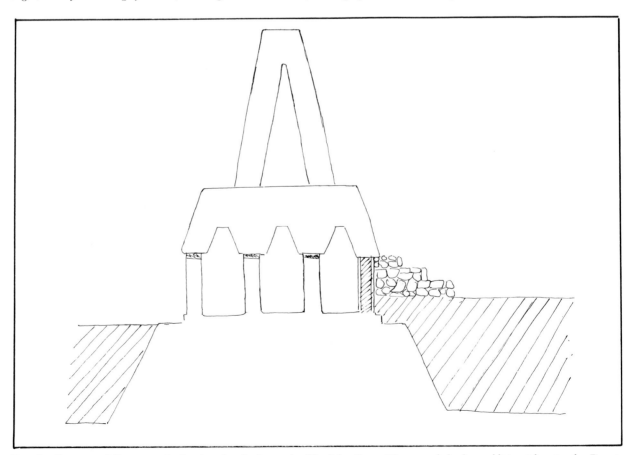

Fig. 5 Drawing of Structure 6, showing the platform, the fill of the Great Plaza, and the late addition (drawing by Ramón Carrasco).

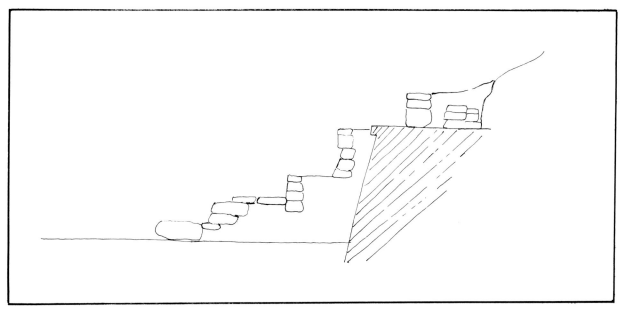

Fig. 6   Drawing of Structure 8, showing the substructure in profile (drawing by Ramón Carrasco).

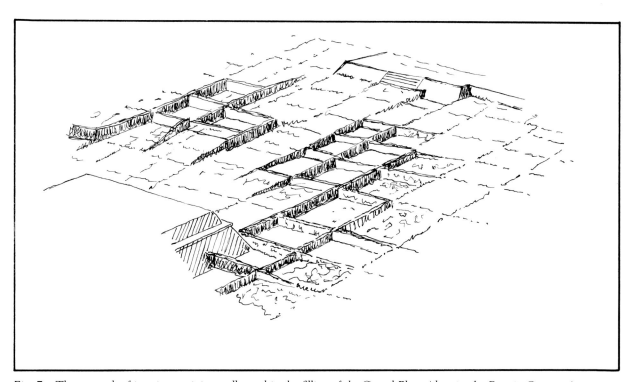

Fig. 7   The network of interior retaining walls used in the filling of the Grand Plaza (drawing by Ramón Carrasco).

Fig. 8   Fragment of Stela no. ? (front side).

Fig. 11   Tablet of Structure 8.

Fig. 9   Fragment of Stela no. ? (back side).

Captor	Ah Ahaul
T.12: 544:14	T.P.:87 103
Yaxchi- lan I	Yaxchi- lan II
Bacab	Batab

Fig. 10   Clause formed by the twelve fragments from Stela 3 (drawing by Ramón Carrasco).

other face apparently represents Bird Jaguar III in a ceremony similar to that of his predecessors.

In sum, we have two facts. First, both Bird Jaguar II and Shield Jaguar I are mentioned on the stela, represented in the scene that is best preserved. Second, within the platform that supported the stela, two frag-

ments of another stela on which Shield Jaguar I is mentioned were used as fill. These data are the evidence for the position that Stela 3 was erected at the command of Bird Jaguar III "the Great."

As part of his project modifying the Great Plaza, Bird Jaguar III ordered the erection of Stela 1, the excavation of which showed that the thickness of fill in the area was not very deep. At the same time, he commanded that the substructure under Structure 8 be covered over, thus creating a platform decorated with anthropomorphic heads for the placing of a tablet to commemorate the date of his designation as Shield Jaguar I's successor (fig. 11).

The tablet of Structure 8 was found in the northwest corner of that building. The upper portion of this monument, which should hold glyph blocks that contain calendric information together with the name and title glyphs of two of the three persons mentioned in the text, is missing (fig. 12).

I assume that the first two glyphs should be a Calendar Round date followed by the name and titles of Shield Jaguar I, ruler of Yaxchilán between 9.12.0.0.0 and 9.15.10.0.0. The second clause ought to mention Bird Jaguar III, who ruled between 9.16.0.0.0 and 9.17.0.0.0. The third and last clause refers to Lady Ik-Skull, mother of Bird Jaguar III.

Of the elements making up the first clause, those that refer to the name of the personage have been lost. Nevertheless, "Captor of Ah-Ahaual," one of the titles of Shield Jaguar I, can be recognized at 2B–3A. At A4 is a glyph, the principal sign of which is T685, repeated in D6; Schele (1982:123) proposed that this glyph makes reference to the act of designating a successor. On the tablet of Structure 8, such an event would be linked to the right of succession inherited by Bird Jaguar III because he was the son or descendant of Shield Jaguar I and Lady Ik-Skull. This first clause ends with the two emblem glyphs of Yaxchilán, the sign for west and the combination Batab-Bacab.

The second clause, like the first, is incomplete and

A B C D   A B C D

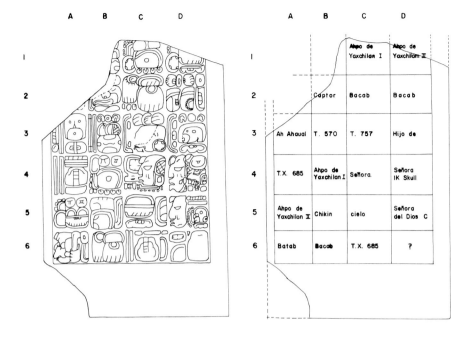

	A	B	C	D
1			Ahpo de Yaxchilan I	Ahpo de Yaxchilán II
2		Captor	Bacab	Bacab
3	Ah Ahaual	T. 570	T. 757	Hijo de
4	T.X. 685	Ahpo de Yaxchilan I	Señora	Señora IK Skull
5	Ahpo de Yaxchilan II	Chikin	cielo	Señora del Dios C
6	Batab	Bacab	T.X. 685	?

Fig. 12 Tablet of Structure 8 (drawing by Ramón Carrasco).

has only the two emblem glyphs of Yaxchilán and the compound Bacab T74:528.528.87. This last combination has been identified by David Stuart as a substitute for the title Batab (Schele 1984b:28). I believe this clause makes reference to Bird Jaguar III since the third clause specifies in D3 that the person of the second clause is the son of Lady Ik-Skull. This woman is the mother of Bird Jaguar II and is mentioned as such on Stela 11.

The name clause of "Lady Ik-Skull, Sky, Lady of God C," is followed by the glyph T685, which has been identified as "marking the designation of a successor." This glyph, which has the numeral X affixed, precedes the names of the parents of the protagonists in the text, making reference to the right of succession of Bird Jaguar III, son of both Shield Jaguar I and Lady Ik-Skull, the first being ruler of Yaxchilán and the second his wife.

Glyph T685 is found four times in the inscriptions of Palenque; in three cases the glyph appears associated with the protagonist—in one of these it is mentioned after the name of the ruler, the son of Lady Ahpo-Hel. In the fourth case T685 is associated with the name of the father of the protagonist. This clause is similar to that of the tablet of Structure 8 at Yaxchilán. The varia-

tions under which T685 occurs make us think that it is not restricted to the *designation of a successor* but specifically means *right of succession, being the son of* . . .

Finally, I should mention that the text ends with a partly eroded glyph that has the sign *kin* as an affix.

The finding of new sculpted monuments and their epigraphic analysis has, in recent years, made possible the reconstruction of the dynastic history of Yaxchilán. Nevertheless, there are still some problems that require explication. One of these relates to the first dynastic period, the rule of Shield Jaguar I, whose date of birth and life's work remain largely unknown. Any attempt to go back to times prior to Shield Jaguar I is hampered by both an absence of texts and knowledge of construction activity. It is difficult to believe that rulers before 9.11.0.0.0 were not interested in leaving testimony or evidence of their reign. Mindful of such breaks in the history of Yaxchilán, I have tried in this short presentation to give an account of architectural changes at the site that resulted from the labors of rulers, especially Bird Jaguar III. Prior to 9.16.0.0.0, the layout of the center of the site, formed by the two *cañadas* that cut across the center from north to south, was very different from the form that it acquired in later times.

Damming the Usumacinta:
The Archaeological Impact

S. JEFFREY K. WILKERSON
INSTITUTE FOR CULTURAL ECOLOGY OF THE TROPICS

In 1983, I addressed the Fifth Mesa Redonda concerning the alarming news of a massive dam project to be undertaken on the Usumacinta River. Since the meeting, much has transpired and many more details of this immense hydroelectric project have been confirmed.[1] As a result we can now more accurately examine the major factors that have an impact upon the ample archaeological patrimony of the region.

This brief presentation concentrates upon six aspects: (1) a general background of the threatened region; (2) the basic facts about the proposed dams; (3) a preliminary appraisal of the archaeological risk; (4) the current status of the dams; (5) a review of the archaeological input into the decision-making process; and (6) some suggestions of what we, as concerned scientists and individuals, can do about this situation.

Profile of a Declining Wilderness

The Usumacinta River drains a 106,000 km^2 area of northern Guatemala and southeastern Mexico. This large region represents 42 percent of Guatemala and major portions of the Mexican states of Chiapas, Tabasco, and Campeche. Following the demise of the Classic Period Maya cities, most of the broad Lowland region slowly became a true wilderness. By the time Hernán Cortés struggled across it in 1525, this great belt of rain forest was an established area of refuge for fleeing Maya groups.[2] Although towns and villages were few, Indian merchants found the shorter routes through the forest convenient until colonial rule and drastic population decline ended such commerce.

Throughout the colonial period, the Usumacinta region became a still greater void. Although a few towns, such as Palenque, were founded on its margins, and Spanish entradas encroached upon it, the European impact was minimal. This situation was to change rapidly with independence in the nineteenth century and the availability of new technologies, as well as markets, for lumber exploitation and agricultural endeavors.[3]

Throughout that century, population grew, particularly on the Tabasco Plain, and the exploitation of the resources of the isolated region upstream from the San José Canyon increased. It soon became necessary to define the extremely vague border between Guatemala and Mexico. After much dispute, the present river boundary following first the Usumacinta proper, and then its main tributary, the Chixoy or Salinas, was ratified at the very end of the century.[4]

During this same period, archaeological discoveries were constant and many of the major Maya cities we are aware of today were recorded. The more accessible riverbank sites such as Yaxchilán and Piedras Negras attracted particular attention (Charnay 1885; Maudslay 1889; Maler 1901).

The first half of the twentieth century was a time of increasing lumber exploitation and slow reduction of the rain forest. Although much of this vast rain forest persisted into the twentieth century, it is now severely threatened. On the Mexican bank the Lacandón Forest was estimated to have covered 1.3 million hectares in 1875. By 1960, it had been reduced by only 6 percent. Yet by 1982, just one year before the last Mesa Redonda, it had suffered a 42 percent reduction! It is *conservatively* estimated that by 1990 nearly 70 percent of the forest will have been cleared.[5]

Population in the region has also risen from an estimated 12,000 in 1965 to over 200,000 today. At this writing the Mexican government continues an active policy of forming new *ejidos* in the forested area. In short, the rate of environmental alteration has greatly accelerated, particularly in the period from 1970 to the present.

Other resources have also been exploited. During this same period highly organized looting of archaeological sites, especially in Guatemala's El Petén, reached incredible proportions. It has abated somewhat due to more effective government enforcement as well as the guerrilla presence in more extensive portions of the rain forest.

As the region has been opened up to settlement and mechanized lumbering, there have also been extensive studies of petroleum and hydroelectric power potential. This has led directly to exploratory drilling in the previously isolated Marqués de Comillas Zone and the formulation of a large-scale dam project.

The Dams

The origin of the dam projects on the Usumacinta goes back thirty years or more to the first efforts to estimate the hydroelectric potential of this vast region.[6] As roads and the Ferrocarril del Sureste made the area around Tenosique more accessible, attention focused on Boca del Cerro, the point where the Usumacinta breaks free of the Sierra de Chiapas. In fact, plans for this original site have been dusted off and incorporated into the new multidam project (fig. 1).

Although the Usumacinta is an international border, the early proposals and concepts were essentially Mexican. Alarm in Guatemala over the possible unilateral construction of this and other dams, with the inevitable flooding of the lower Guatemalan bank, led to preventative action. In the mid-sixties cooperative villages were established on both the Río de la Pasión and the Usumacinta proper. The presence of the settlements in the threatened areas was thought to be a significant deterrent. In point of fact they, as well as deteriorating bilateral relations, were sufficient to halt further development of the proposal. Mexico instead undertook major dams (La Angostadura, Chicoasén, Nezahualcóyotl-Malpaso) on the neighboring Grijalva system and did not return to the Usumacinta concept until the late 1970s.[7]

At that time both countries agreed to full-scale feasibility studies of the Usumacinta in preparation for a joint project of massive proportions. The studies were to be carried out under the auspices of the already existing and jointly constituted International Limits and Water Commission (CILA). This organization is considered a part of the Foreign Relations ministries of each country. Representatives of the various government agencies concerned with the dam project formed a committee, headed by the CILA commissioner in their country. These committees directed surveying and field analysis and met periodically with their counterparts.

Eleven different segments of the river between Boca del Cerro and El Chorro were analyzed for dam construction potential.[8] Twenty-six locations within these segments were measured for dams. Five segments and fourteen dam locations were rejected. The remaining possibilities were grouped into seven dam configurations at five points on the river: Boca del Cerro, La Linea, El Porvenir (next to Piedras Negras), Salvamento (just downstream from Yaxchilán), and San Fernando (near the once famous lumber center of Agua Azul or "Filadelfia"; fig. 2, 3, 4).

The bend in the river at Yaxchilán had been ruled out as a dam location by late 1982 but was revived for consideration by the Mexican delegation in the winter of 1984–1985. Its status is still pending.

As a result of the field inspection, the proposal came to be defined in terms of the construction of two to four dams that would produce between 2 and 3.7 megawatts of electricity. The inundated areas would vary according to which of the seven different dam configurations were selected. However, if the highest level studied is chosen, in excess of 1,315 km^2 will be flooded.[9] Potentially, a staggering 525-km segment of the Usumacinta River system would be directly affected by water backed up by these dams.

Although relative proportions change with the various possible dam combinations, at basin levels now being considered, 67 percent of the flooding would be in Guatemala and 33 percent in Mexico. These disproportionate figures reflect the topography of the region, for the Lacandón Forest is generally higher than the low areas west of Guatemala's Sierra del Lacandón.

The electricity to be generated greatly exceeds Guatemala's current needs and is far from major urban centers. Excess electricity is likely to be sold to Mexico or Central American countries.

Archaeological Risk

Of critical importance for assessing the archaeological impact of this project are the heights of the dams. Virtually all the dam combinations threaten known archaeological sites, but some more than others. Current studies concentrate upon the highest dam holding back water at the 105- or 120-m contour line. Both these levels have severe implications for major sites. Currently, the higher of the two levels is favored by the participating engineers since more electricity can be produced at a cheaper per unit cost (fig. 3).[10]

A second factor in any calculation is the role of the seasonal and cyclical flooding of the Lacantun, Chixoy, and Pasión tributaries of the Usumacinta. Not only do they rise dramatically during each rainy season, but there is apparently a multiyear cycle. The highest recent flood of the Pasión, without any dams to hold water back, reached the 117-m contour level at Sayaxche. What would happen if a similar, or greater, volume of water descended upon the dam basins has yet to be fully calculated. Unquestionably, there would be still more damage to archaeological sites.

A third factor in any archaeological consideration is the problem of locating affected sites. There are numerous small and medium-sized centers within short distances from the river and adjoining low-lying areas. Many, in spite of much systematic looting in recent years, have never been surveyed or mapped.[11] Basically, we do not really know at this time how many sites lie within the potentially affected area. In spite of decreasing isolation the region, particularly the threatened Guatemalan side of the river, is still an archaeological frontier.

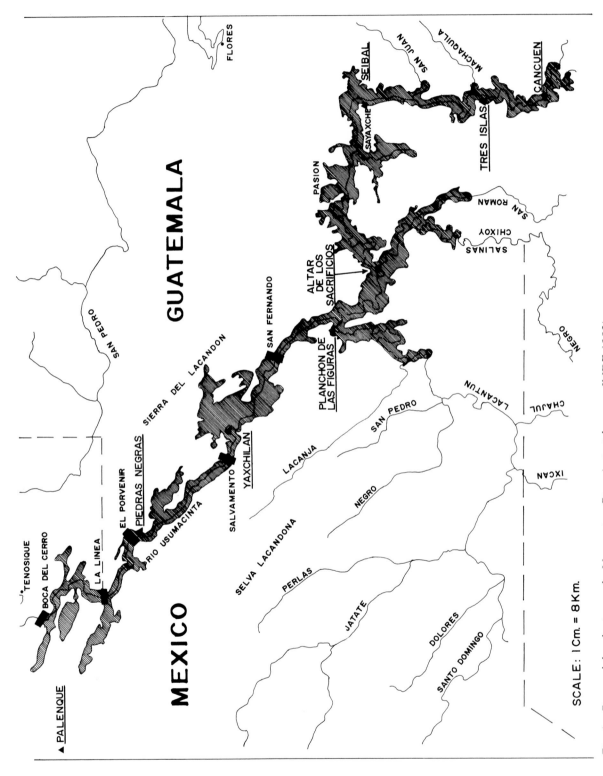

Fig. 1 *Proposed dam basins on the Usumacinta River (principle source INDE 1982).*

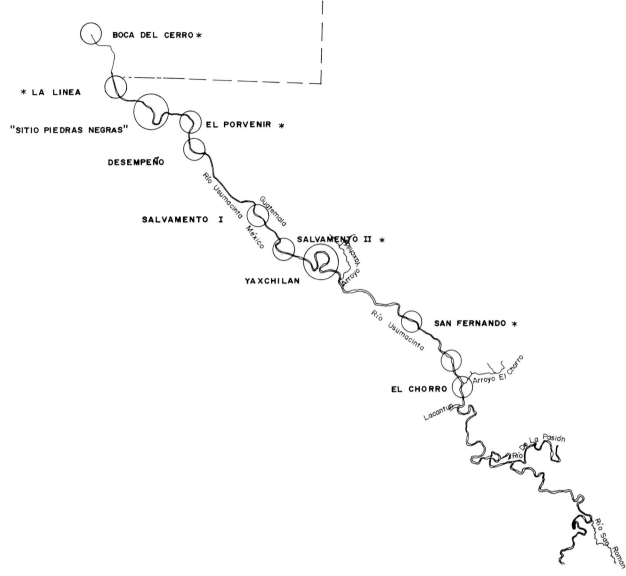

Fig. 2   Analyzed dam sites on the Usumacinta River (after INDE 1982). Asterisks (*) indicate selected sites.

Fourth, many sites outside the actual dam basins would be destroyed, or looted, in the process of establishing access roads and the inevitable land clearing that would accompany dam construction. There is no way, at the moment, of quantifying this risk except to realize that, given the considerable density of sites in many adjoining areas, the secondary damage could be nothing less than extensive.

It is important to bear in mind that the total archaeological risk is not solely a matter of which sites are to be flooded, but rather a question of all sites that would be affected by this massive project. It is in fact possible that secondary destruction might in the long run be greater than the not inconsiderable primary damage from flooding.

Let us briefly consider the implications for some of the better-known Usumacinta sites.

Piedras Negras

Moving upstream from Tenosique and the Boca del Cerro dam location, the first major riverbank site is Guatemala's Piedras Negras. Most of the city is on land over 80 m in elevation.[12] Nevertheless, virtually all of the dam configurations would flood portions of it (figs. 5 and 6). The lowest would transform the site into a series of promontories; the highest would flood practically everything beneath the level of the West Group Plaza.[13] Much of the East Group and practically all the earlier South Group buildings, which have had little exploration, would be lost.

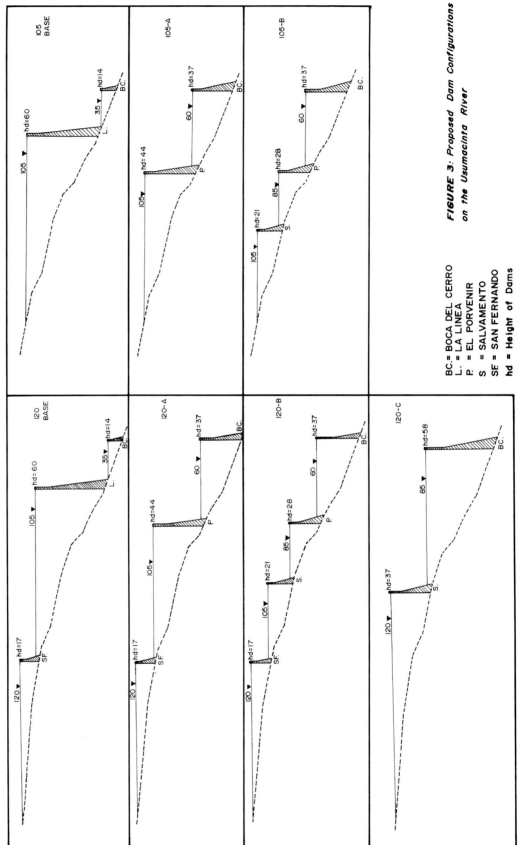

Fig. 3   Proposed dam configurations on the Usumacinta River (after INDE 1982).

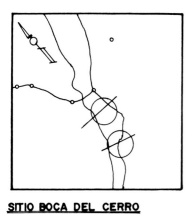

SITIO BOCA DEL CERRO

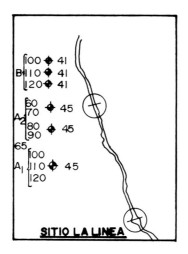

SITIO LA LINEA

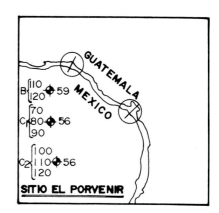

SITIO EL PORVENIR

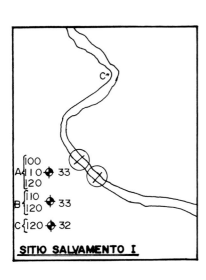

SITIO SALVAMENTO I

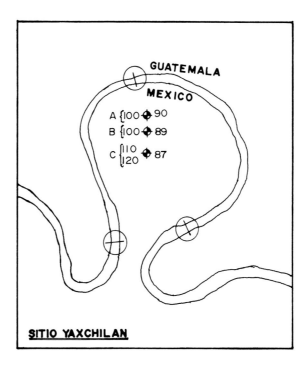

SITIO YAXCHILAN

SITIO SAN FERNANDO

Fig. 4   Dam locations under consideration on the Usumacinta (after INDE 1982).

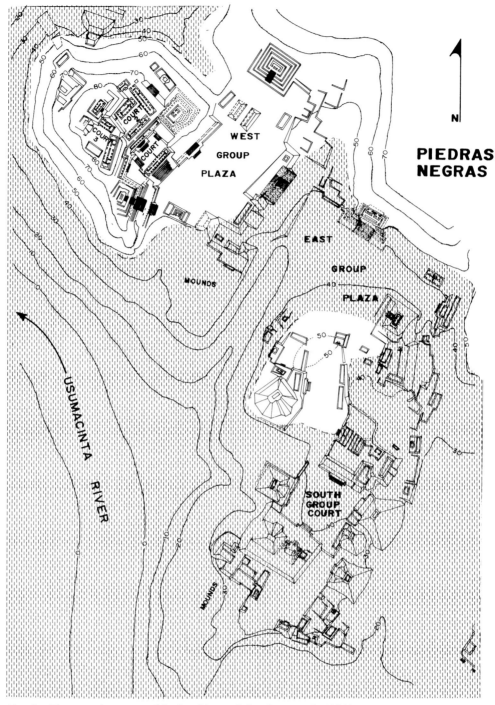

Fig. 5   Threatened portions of Piedras Negras (after Paris et al. 1939).

In addition to the site itself, portions of its original support area would also be directly threatened (Wilkerson 1983). The probable placement of the El Porvenir dam just over 1 km downstream from the city would result in the flooding of all the unsurveyed low areas that surround the site. There is no doubt that any of the dams would have a catastrophic impact on Peidras Negras, unquestionably one of the most important Maya sites known.

In the vicinity of Piedras Negras, and between it and Yaxchilán, are a series of smaller sites such as Busilja, La Mar, El Cayo, Texcoco, Chicozapote, and Anaite.[14]

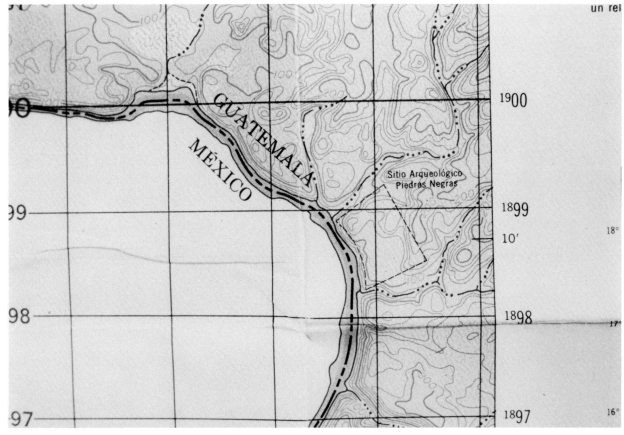

Fig. 6   Location of Piedras Negras (detail 1:50,000 sheets, Guatemala).

Any portions of these centers that lie beneath 105 m in elevation are directly in jeopardy. Texcoco, on the Guatemalan side of the river, would probably disappear completely (fig. 14 below).

Yaxchilán

Yaxchilán is another major site directly threatened by the projected basins. However, its precise status is still in doubt. It was originally disregarded in late 1982 as a construction location, but the Mexican commission reopened the question of locating a dam on the bend around the site in the winter of 1984–1985.

There are three proposed locations in the huge river bend. One is upstream from Yaxchilán near the start of the loop; another is at the corresponding downstream position. The third, incredibly, is at the site itself. The downstream location is actually the most threatening to the city: it is considered ideal for a basin height of 110 or 120 m, as opposed to a 100 m height for the other two (fig. 4).

At risk at Yaxchilán, regardless of the nearest downstream dam location, is the lower riverbank area of the city. Not only would the famous "rock pile" in the river itself be covered, but also numerous buildings in the great expanse of the lower portion of the site. Any water

level over 100 m is bound to affect it. This will be all the more true if no dam is built upstream to take the brunt of normal wet season flooding. If the Salvamento dam, several kilometers downstream, is built to its maximum height of 120 m, virtually all structures on the riverbank will be covered by the basin (fig. 7).

Archaeologist García Moll's strategy of excavating and reconstructing the riverbank buildings is to be complimented. Apart from the discovery of significant new sculpture (Wilkerson 1985:541), he demonstrated the exceptional value of the threatened riverbank structures and made it more difficult to flood them.

The problem of Yaxchilán, however, does not end with the direct impact on the Mexican riverbank. Any dam near the city, or any nearby high dam downstream, will inundate a massive adjacent area on the Guatemalan side. This region includes significant satellite sites such as La Pasadita and certainly the majority of the support area for ancient Yaxchilán (Wilkerson 1983). Although this area has been looked at, it has never been adequately surveyed or excavated (fig. 8).

Our understanding of Yaxchilán or any of the riverbank sites will never be adequate, even if they are not flooded, until we can view them in the context of their immediate support areas. The Usumacinta has only been

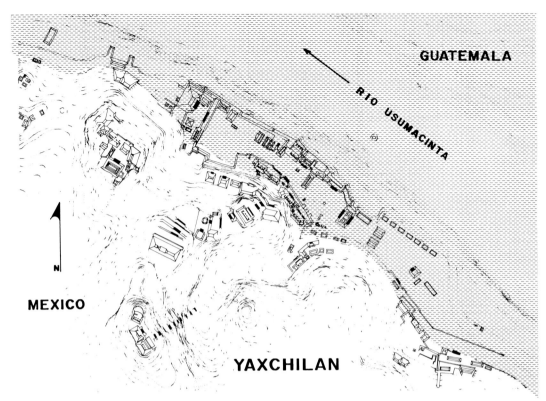

Fig. 7 Threatened portions of Yaxchilán (after Marquina 1964).

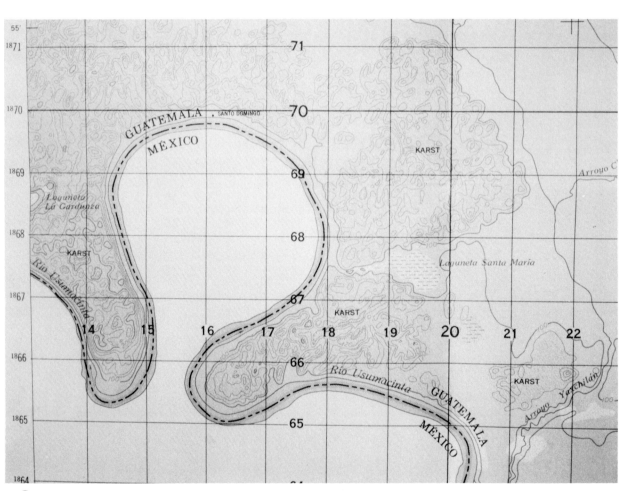

Fig. 8 The river loop around Yaxchilán and the Low Guatemalan (detail 1:50,000 sheets, Guatemala).

a political border for less than a century. It was, and still is for the inhabitants of the region, a unifying highway, not a boundary.

Río Lacantun Sites

The Río Lacantun will be affected from the vicinity of Pico de Oro to the confluence with the Usumacinta. Apparently there are no large riverbank sites in this stretch of river. However, small sites between the 105- and 120-m contour levels could be affected. These include El Palma, Yaxun, San Lorenzo, and Planchón de las Figuras (fig. 15 below).[15]

This latter site is extremely important for its dozens of formal and graffitilike depictions on an huge riverbank slab of limestone (Wilkerson 1985; Stuart and Wilkerson 1985; García Moll 1986).[16] It is already underwater nearly half of the year due to seasonal flooding; any permanent rise in water level, however, modest, will inundate it permanently. This site clearly demonstrates that more than standing architecture is threatened by the dams.

Altar de Sacrificios

This well-known site near the confluence of the Río de la Pasión and the Usumacinta is at extreme risk if the dams are built. Most of the area occupied by the site is just above the 110-m elevation. Flooding to the 120-m line will come close to inundating it completely, as well as considerably altering the confluence of the two rivers (fig. 9).

Río de la Pasión Sites

At sites upstream from Altar de Sacrificios on the Pasión and in the Laguna Petexbatun there would certainly be some damage. Most of the known sites, however, are above the 120-m elevation. However, portions of Aguas Calientes, Tres Islas, and Cancuén, as well as the low area across from El Seibal could be flooded. Further backup of seasonal flooding by the dam basins is likely to affect many of the Pasión sites adversely. It should also be pointed out that there are certainly numerous unreported small sites along the middle and upper Pasión that may be touched, by water backup (figs. 10–13).

Chixoy (Salinas) Sites

This is again a case of small and medium sites, most of which are unrecorded, being affected by the basins. There are a number on both banks in the vicinity of the Mexican *ejido* of Roberto Barrios. Most show pitting from looting and the majority are low enough to be flooded, or at least partially inundated, by the dam basins. Apparently, there is no major site on the immediate banks of the affected portions of the Chixoy.

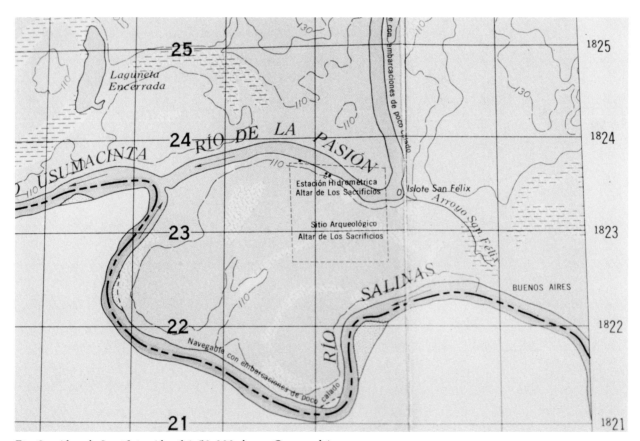

Fig. 9   Altar de Sacrificios (detail 1:50,000 sheets, Guatemala).

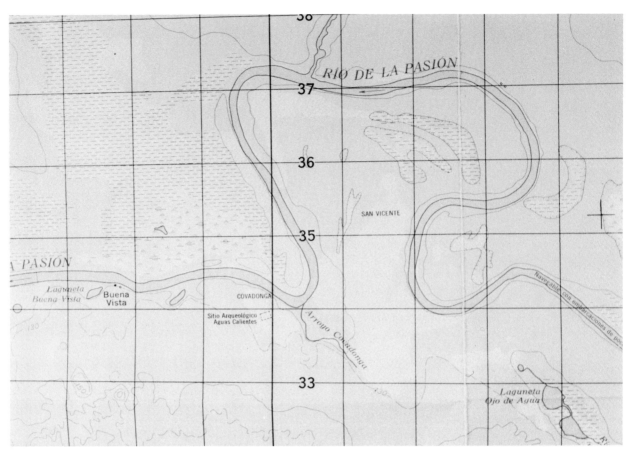

Fig. 10   Location of Aguas Calientes (detail 1:50,000 sheets, Guatemala).

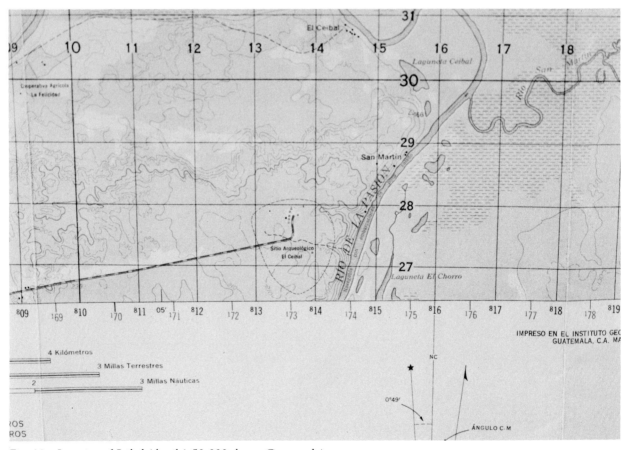

Fig. 11   Location of Seibal (detail 1:50,000 sheets, Guatemala).

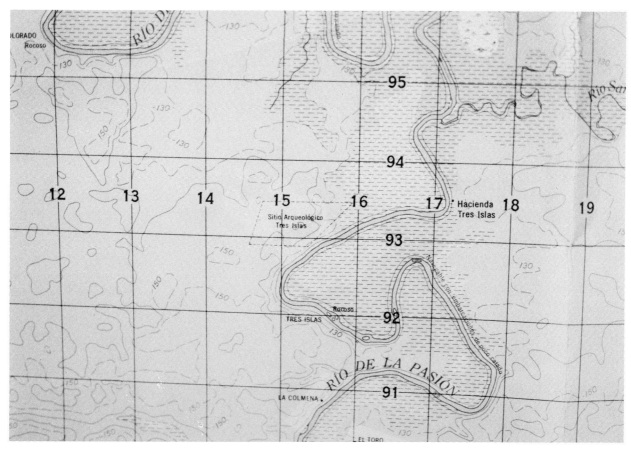

Fig. 12   Location of Tres Islas (detail 1:50,000 sheets, Guatemala).

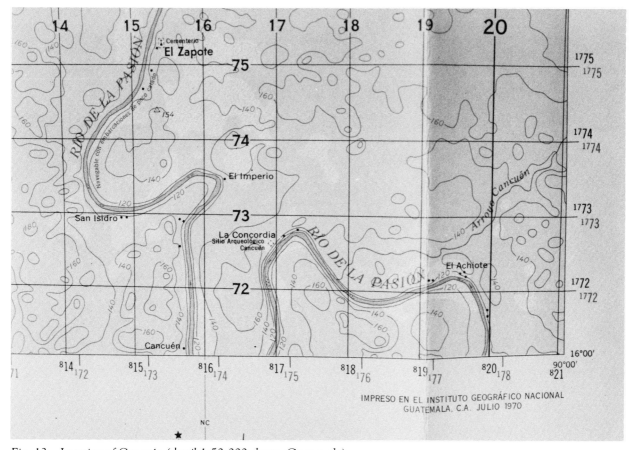

Fig. 13   Location of Cancuén (detail 1:50,000 sheets, Guatemala).

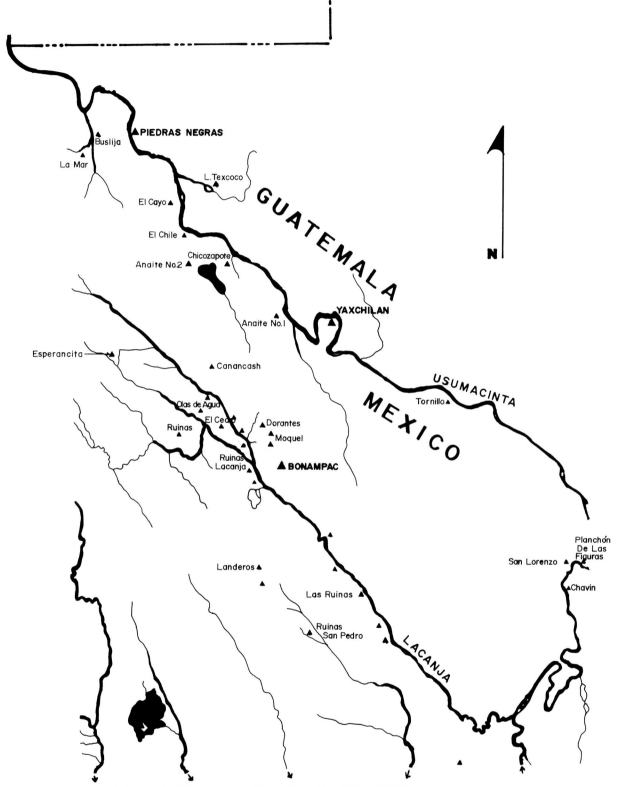

Fig. 14 *Sites recorded along the Usumacinta by Frans Blom (detail Blom 1953).*

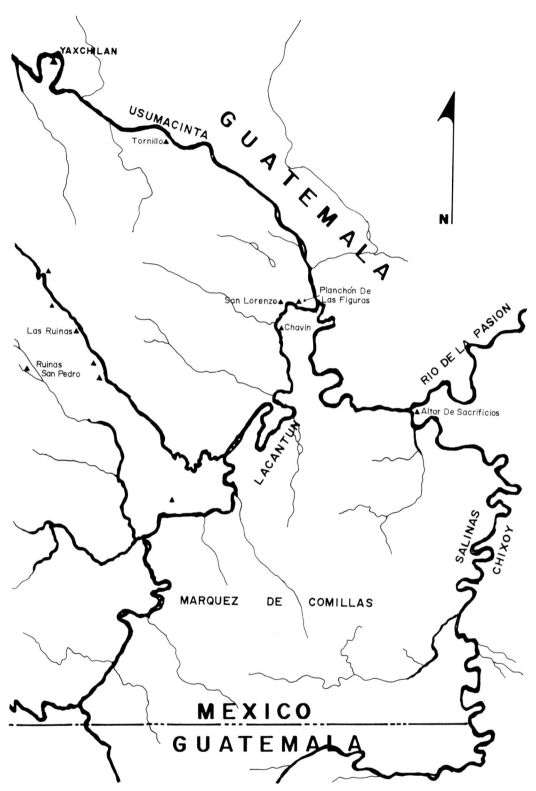

YAXCHILAN

USUMACINTA

G U A T E M A L A

Tornillo

N

Planchón De
Las Figuras

San Lorenzo

Chavin

RIO DE LA PASION

Las Ruinas

Ruinas
San Pedro

LACANTUN

Altar De Sacrificios

SALINAS

CHIXOY

MARQUEZ   DE   COMILLAS

M E X I C O

G U A T E M A L A

Fig. 15   Sites along the Lacantun recorded by Frans Blom (detail Blom 1953).

Present Status of the Dam Project

The present dam project was proposed during the heady years of petroleum affluence in Mexico. By late 1982, when the peso crashed and a severe economic depression set in, field activities by Mexican personnel had been greatly reduced. Guatemalan surveyors and engineers, working from the onset with more modest budgets, continued their field activities until guerrilla activity by the FAR (Fuerzas Armadas Rebeldes) picked up in the second half of 1983. During 1984, their major camps at Salvamento, Porvenir (near Piedras Negras), and La Linea were occupied and/or destroyed by the FAR. Since that time, the economic situation in Guatemala has worsened and little field activity has taken place.

Nevertheless, the scope, basic costs, and possible dam locations had all been determined by late 1982. There still remains some surveying to be done, as well as the selection of the final dam configurations.[17] Because deliberations of the joint commission and its recommendations to the two governments are kept secret, it is not publicly known if such a momentous decision has already been reached. Mexico particularly has strictly avoided any publicity about the proposed dams or even the nature of the preliminary research.[18]

In spite of the delays due to financial problems and intensified guerrilla activity, this international hydroelectric project has not been canceled. Both the Mexican and Guatemalan commissioners, as well as other project participants, have made it clear that the project retains the highest priority in their respective countries and will be resumed as soon as conditions permit. Essentially, the project has been delayed. Although most field crews have been withdrawn, the commissions continue to function and the already established core plans are being refined.

It is also pertinent to note that the guerrilla opposition to the dams is not based upon espousal of ecological or archaeological factors. Interviews (Wilkerson 1985, 1986) have shown that the opposition has been to the project being undertaken by either the previous military (Victor Mejias) or the current civilian (Cerezo) governments. In other words, once in power the FAR would consider damming the Usumacinta appropriate.

In summation, both Mexico and Guatemala continue to favor the construction of the dams and both will press ahead in the near future. Also, the guerrillas oppose the construction by any Guatemalan government of which they are not a part, but not the concept of the dam project itself. The current delay is, however, an unusual opportunity to make the magnitude of the archaeological impact clear to those who participate in the dam decisions.

Archaeological Input into the Decision-making Process

As originally constituted six years ago, the commissions in Mexico and Guatemala did not have any member who represented either archaeological or environmental concerns. Their purpose was, and is, to determine if the dams could be undertaken and how. Collateral damage to archaeological sites or the rain forest environment was not quantified or, for that matter, appraised as a determinant factor. Input from these quarters was initially nonexistent.

Following the 1983 discussion of the dam project in the forum of this Mesa Redonda, interest among personnel of the Instituto Nacional de Antropología e Historia in both Guatemala and Mexico increased. In 1985, the director of Guatemala's INAH (Lic. Edna Nuñez) was included in the commission. This is an important precedent that, year and a half later, still had not resulted in a corresponding Mexican appointment.

While the effectiveness in Guatemala of INAH's participation in the commission will have to be judged by the future, INAH put forth a significant initial proposal to examine the threatened region (INAH 1985). Due to lack of funding, both within Guatemala and abroad, this has not yet been implemented.

On the international level, interest has been growing and has been manifest in several ways. There has been some discussion in various newsletters. Also, there was a well thought out resolution formulated by the German Ethnological Society in late 1983 and forwarded to the Mexican and Guatemalan governments through the West German Foreign Ministry.[19] Neither government publicly acknowledged receipt of the resolution. However, once it was published by a German news agency, the Guatemalan vice-minister of foreign relations held a press conference and acknowledged not only the resolution but also the dam project itself (*Prensa Libre*, 9 November 1983). This is a clear demonstration that rational and well-reasoned concern on the part of the international scientific community can effectively aid efforts by colleagues in the affected countries.

In general, input into the decision-making process by individuals and institutions concerned with the archaeological impact of the dam projects has grown from nothing in 1980 to a very hesitant first step over the last few years. Much more will certainly be needed if a totally adverse impact is to be avoided in the immediate years ahead.

Avenues of Reaction

Electricity is a modern necessity. Hydroelectric dams are a major option available to countries with the appropriate rivers. Major dam projects have never been canceled on solely archaeological grounds, not even in the exceptional case of the Nile. Such are the basic facts of policy making that we must deal with in realistically assessing the available avenues of reaction.

Certainly, it is pertinent to question whether the Usumacinta dams are really needed in both countries at this time; if they will be situated too far from the primary metropolitan use-areas to be cost efficient; if the gigantic expense of large-scale dams is consistent with long-term debt reduction policies; and if the loss to national and international patrimonies implicit in flooding the drainage is outweighed by short-term energy benefits. Nevertheless, short of a clear and loud statement of engineering infeasibility, the joint international commission is bound to announce its recommendation to proceed. Indeed, it may already have done so.

Public debate and consultation with the scientific community has not characterized the process of formulating the dam project to date, so there is no reason to believe that such procedures will suddenly and automatically be given pivotal roles in the final decision. If concerned individuals and institutions wish to have the archaeological and artistic issues heard, there must be a concerted effort to place them before interested segments of the public and the officials who must act on the commission's recommendations. Let us not forget that the dam project requires the consent and participation of the governments of two countries. Should one decide that proceeding would not be in its best interest, then the project will not be undertaken.

A first step in this direction is to make sure that all who study the archaeology and art of the Usumacinta region are aware that it is threatened. Another is to support our Guatemalan and Mexican colleagues in any effort to participate in the decision-making process in their countries. Still another is to increase research in the region and demonstrate the singular importance of these ancient resources in all available forums.

A different avenue, bearing in mind that archaeologists and art historians alone have never stopped a large dam, is to make other colleagues in the environmental sciences aware of the situation. There are many cases where combined proposals have more weight and are likely to attract a broader audience. There is certainly no reason why carefully crafted proposals of large natural parks around major sites could not be put forth.[20]

Of critical importance to the implementation of the dam project is international funding. The dam costs were estimated to total between 2.1 and 3.7 billion 1982 dollars depending on the final dam configuration. Most if not all of this funding must be sought abroad through banks and international lending organizations. Much international concern can be concentrated on these institutions. It would not be inappropriate or out of proportion, given the unique cultural attributes of the affected Maya cities, to propose that 1.5 percent of the total expenditure be devoted to the support of proper investigation and salvage in the threatened region. That could generate between 32 and 56 million dollars for emergency research. Even so, these amounts alone could never cover all the needed salvage operations.

The proposed damming of the Usumacinta should be a matter of grave concern to all Precolumbianists.[21] By virtue of unforeseen delays, the pace of the dam proposal has momentarily slowed. We have been given time carefully to consider our arguments and to propose appropriate action. Do we forfeit the very heart of Mesoamerican art and architecture without fully knowing its extent and value? If we do, perhaps we can be likened to the mindless people whom the heart of Heaven destroyed by a deluge in the First Creation of the Popul Vuh (Edmonson 1971:25, 26):

Then their flood was invented by the heart of Heaven
A great flood was made, and descended on the heads
of those who were dolls
who were carved of wood.

If the dams are to be built, and the delicate creations of the Maya inundated, it behooves those of us who cherish knowledge of the past to demonstrate the value of salvaging this great patrimony of all humankind.

Appendix A

RESOLUTION OF THE DEUTSCHE GESELLSCHAFT FÜR VÖLKERKUNDE
11 OCTOBER 1983
(Sent to the governments of Mexico and Guatemala, October 1983)

El motivo de la presente carta es elevarle la Resolución emitida el día 11 de octubre de 1983 por la Sociedad Alemana de Etnología en el curso de su reunión bianual. Lleva el texto siguiente:

La 'Deutsche Gesellschaft für Völkerkunde' (Sociedad Alemana de Etnología) expresa profunda preocupación acerca del projecto de represas en el Río Usumacinta, las que constituyen una amenaza grave, tanto para la población del area afectada, como para testimonios únicos e irrepetibles de la Cultura Clásica Maya.

Se ruega a las instituciones responsables en México y Guatemala de evaluar otra vez cuidadosamente las ventajas y los inconvenientes de este projecto. Acaso que el plan siga vigente, se deberían realizar por lo menos todos los esfuerzos, no sólo para la indemnización de la población afectada, sino también para la protección de los sitios arqueológicos de fama mundial.

Deutsche Gesellschaft für Völkerkunde,
Anthropologische Gesellschaft in Wien,
Österreichische Ethnologische Gesellschaft,
Tagung vom 10.–14 Oktober 1983 in Freiburg.

Notes

1. Background research on the region has been carried out since 1980 with the aid of the Institute for Cultural Ecology of the Tropics (1980–present), National Geographic Society (1984–1985), and Yale University (1983). Portions of the data have been presented in Wilkerson (1983, 1985, 1986).

2. The best approximation of Cortés's route through the lower Usumacinta region is by Scholes and Roys (1968). Although their analysis of the route is thorough, it is not totally convincing with respect to the area of the San Pedro tributary.

3. An excellent example of a nineteenth-century descriptive appraisal of a major portion of the Usumacinta for potential use is the study of Marciano Barrera (1965). Originally published in 1865 in numerous newspaper segments during the time of the Emperor Maximilian, it reflects the predominant view of tropical resources at the time. To facilitate its use by modern scholars, the Institute for Cultural Ecology of the Tropics is preparing an edition of this useful but little-known work.

4. Much of the history of the wildly fluctuating border between the two countries is contained in the annotated 1895 map of Miles Rock. The crucial role of this American engineer, employed by the Guatemalan government to represent it in the often emotionally charged negotiations with Mexico, is another little-known aspect of Usumacinta history.

5. These figures are extracted from detailed studies undertaken by personnel of Mexico's Secretaría de Agricultura y Recursos Hidráulicos (SARH 1983:10–11, 1984:3). It should not be assumed that remaining portions of the forest are untouched: the figures include a rapidly growing portion of "disturbed forest." For example, in 1982, 18.3 percent of the still forested area was considered disturbed.

6. Apart from the locations on the Usumacinta, up to sixteen separate projects have been proposed on its Mexican affluents (SARH 1983:6; SARH 1976a: map 20) and two on the Guatemalan tributaries (Renato Fernández, Instituto Nacional de Electrificación Guatemala, personal communication). The Mexican potential in the Lacandón Forest area is thought to total at least 3,740 MW annually (SARH 1983:13). The Grijalva dams are described in detail in Secretaría de Recursos Hidráulicos (1976b).

7. Guatemala also undertook a major hydroelectric dam project of its own on the upper Chixoy, the principal tributary of the Usumacinta.

8. In ascending order these are Boca del Cerro, La Linea, "sitio Piedras Negras" (actually Busilja), Porvenir, Desempeño, Salvamento, Yaxchilán, San Fernando, and El Chorro.

9. These data are abstracted from the study prepared by the Instituto Nacional de Electrificación in 1982. At this time these projections are still considered valid by Guatemalan and Mexican engineers.

10. This was confirmed in interviews with participating engineers from both countries in 1985.

11. Many of these uncharted sites have sculpture. A 1984 trip by muleback toward the Sierra del Lacandón from the Guatemala cooperative of Bethel showed there are many such sites yet to be examined (Wilkerson 1985:533–536).

12. It should be noted that in the University of Pennsylvania site map (Paris et al. 1939), the 1:50,000 sheet for the area and the new survey for the dams do not necessarily match because different base data are utilized.

13. In late 1982–early 1983, a major base mark was placed directly in front of the stucco mask on building K-5. Another was situated in the old Fordson tractor abandoned nearby by the University of Pennsylvania excavation team in the 1930s. Both carved stones and stucco in the vicinity were also defaced.

14. Most of these sites were visited by Maler (1901–1903) and are listed on Blom's map of the Lacandón Forest (1953).

15. There are also small riverbank sites on the Usumacinta upstream from Yaxchilán. Those that are in whole or part beneath the 105 and/or 120 contour lines are threatened. These include El Tornillo on the Mexican bank and Ixcoche on the Guatemalan side.

16. Planchón was first recorded by Maler (1901–1903) in 1900, then by Mulleried in 1927, and third by Bullard in 1965.

17. Surveying the basin contours on the Guatemalan bank is critical to the overall project because of the large areas to be inundated. However, it is made extremely difficult by the complicated karst topography. Undetected "saddles" between forested hills, or porous spongelike limestone, could allow massive flooding of portions of the region between the Usumacinta proper and the San Pedro.

18. So effective has the publicity blackout been that Lacandóns, from Naja, attending the 1983 Mesa Redonda, indicated that they had been unaware of the purpose of the large crews that had been operating in their traditional region for over three years. Also, during extensive travels in the affected area (1983–1985), outlined in Wilkerson (1985), we encountered villages on the Guatemalan bank with some awareness of the dam survey but practically no knowledge of the project among their Mexican counterparts.

19. A copy of that resolution is appended to this article.

20. Guatemala's Tikal Park is a most important precedent in this respect. It is sufficiently large enough not only to protect, and enhance, the archaeological remains, but also to shelter the endangered flora and fauna of the rain forest environment. Parks of similar, and even larger, extent could still be established at Yaxchilán and Piedras Negras. It would also be possible to propose international parameters for such parks. The Guatemalan area in front of Yaxchilán, including the artistically significant site of La Pasadita, might also be set aside to complement the archaeological site on the Mexican side. The same could be done in the Mexican area in front of Piedras Negras.

21. Subsequent to the Sexta Mesa Redonda de Palenque, and intensive discussion by participants from numerous countries, a resolution was passed by the Mesa Redonda. Copies of the resolution in Spanish, English, German, and French were forwarded to the foreign ministers of Mexico and Guatemala a week later.

The Teotihuacán-Kaminaljuyu-Tikal Connection:
A View from the South Coast of Guatemala

FREDERICK J. BOVE
SOCIAL PROCESS RESEARCH INSTITUTE, UNIVERSITY OF CALIFORNIA, SANTA BARBARA

The transition between the Terminal Formative and Early Classic Periods in Mesoamerica (ca. 200 B.C.–A.D. 300/400) is marked by widespread social, political, demographic, and economic dislocations and restructuring. The importance of this period cannot be overstressed. There is evidence of large-scale population dislocations and cultural disruptions during the Formative-Classic juncture, which some believe may ultimately be related to the emergence of Teotihuacán as a power center of pan-Mesoamerican significance. It was perhaps the most critical transformation in Mesoamerican cultural development (e.g., J. A. Parsons 1971: 237–238). In Guatemala "many flourishing and important Preclassic sites . . . in the Department of Guatemala were permanently abandoned by the beginning of the Early Classic Period" (Borhegyi 1965:12–20). On the Guatemalan coast "all the Preclassic sites examined in the Mexico-Guatemala border seemingly were abandoned at some time at the end of the Preclassic Period" (Shook 1965:185–186). At the impressive Chiapas coastal site of Izapa near the Guatemalan border the "Protoclassic" Period is divided into two distinctive style horizons, a division due to "both local and foreign events of unusual historical impact"; the investigators suggested, surprisingly, that these abrupt changes were "due to conquest from an area to the east of the Soconusco" (Lowe, Lee, and Martinez 1982:135–139). These events have led some observers to suggest a near abandonment by coastal populations until the Late Classic (e.g., Sanders 1972:101–153). Others, however, theorize that "this important temporary abandonment, or shift, in occupational pattern on the Guatemalan Pacific Coast is mainly deceptive due to a failure to recognize Early Classic materials which are non-Maya" (Norman 1976: part 2, 2–3; Lowe, Lee, and Martinez 1982).

Elsewhere in southern Mesoamerica, El Mirador, apparently the largest Lowland Maya center in the Late to Terminal Formative Period, was abandoned largely by the Early Classic in favor of Tikal and other emerging Maya centers (Matheny 1980; Demarest 1984). At Tikal itself "the ceramic transition between the Preclassic and Early Classic complexes . . . is striking," arising from a cultural change of great magnitude (Culbert 1977:37). The stability at Chiapa de Corzo in the Grijalva Depression of Chiapas is disrupted with the appearance of a completely different artifact assemblage during the "Late Protoclassic" Istmo Phase. This action is seen as a violent overthrow of the existing order with the principal external influence from the Soconusco region (Lee 1969: 196). In Yucatán "one of the most intriguing questions in northern Maya archaeology concerns the collapse of Formative social and political organization in the Dzibilchaltun area by about A.D. 250. The collapse of Komchen coincided roughly with the rise of Teotihuacan, but no hard evidence links these events" (Andrews V 1981: 324). A shock occurs at Edzna in Campeche, Mexico, in the "Protoclassic" Period after a time of dynamic growth during the Late to Terminal Formative Baluarte Phase. Here during the same period a moated fortress was constructed with a raised causeway providing restricted access. Transitional phase pottery (Cepas and Poderes) is found mainly in the fortress complex together with a drastically reduced occupation limited to the site's peripheral areas (Matheny et al. 1983). Evidence of fortifications evidently built during the same period also appear at Becan with a moat (or fortified ditch) having a total vertical height of 11 m; El Mirador with a high wall; and Tikal-Uaxactún with a fortified ditch separating the two centers.

Are these events due primarily to the priority of local evolutionary demographic and economic changes, or are they politically motivated, perhaps as a local response to the regional expansion of Teotihuacán? Do these processes culminate in increasing warfare leading to related sociopolitical restructuring and agglomeration—the warfare hypothesis (e.g., Webster 1977:335–374)? Are the events triggered in part by violent physical episodes such as the Ilopango eruptions in El Salvador or drastic climatic shifts—the drying trend hypotheses, with their postulated far-ranging cultural effects (Sheets 1976, 1979:525–564; Dahlin 1983:245–263)? Or are they part of a wider Mesoamerican structural transformation involving the shift from ranked societies (chiefdoms) to the development of the state and Maya civilization itself? Are they the result of secondary state formation processes triggered by the Teotihuacán primary state? Are they a result of Teotihuacán domination to secure monopolistic control of key commodities or exotics such as cacao, obsidian, cotton, salt, and jade?

The exploratory research discussed here focused on this critical period on the South Coast of Guatemala, believed to be a "key connecting link between the greater Mexican highlands and the Maya lowlands via which both cultural and stylistic relationships were maintained . . ." (L. A. Parsons 1986:108). The project is an important stage in an active regional program emphasizing changes in social, political, and economic processes in a particularly strategic but poorly known area of Meso-america. My own research, centered in the Department of Escuintla, has revealed a surprising number of large Middle to Terminal Formative centers uniformly distributed on the Pacific Coastal Plain, evidencing the evolution of either complex chiefdom organizations or protostates (Bove 1981, 1989a). All of these centers either were abandoned or experienced a strong disruption during the transition into the Early Classic. The preliminary field season completed recently (1986), however, fully revealed and helped clarify the key role of Balberta, a major regional, possibly fortified, Early Classic center located 19 km from the Pacific Coast and 90 km southwest of Kaminaljuyu. Shook (personal communication, 1983, and 1969 field notes) commented that "the site is most unusual in that the principal (or lower) platform of some 500 × 400 m supports the most formal arrangement of steep-sided mounds that I can recall outside of Teotihuacan." Balberta is key in this research effort because no exposed Early Classic sites are known on the South Coast. With the exception of a few solitary mounds, all known are deeply buried under Late Classic reconstructions. In short, I believe that we could have a microcosm of the transitional period since the linkage between the abandonment (or nearly so) of the numerous and nearby hierarchically distributed Formative centers and the development of Early Classic Balberta is what we are trying to document (fig. 1). I emphasize that the project has just begun its effort in this rich but poorly known area, and the results to be discussed are incomplete.

The recent fieldwork at Balberta shows a unique change in site morphology (architecture) and agglomeration (centralization) from the preceding Formative Period. Balberta departs dramatically from the typical Formative pattern of structures formally aligned into parallel plazas into a compact, almost rigid urbanlike pattern. The 20 ha central zone is built on a low platform supporting 26 structures ranging from an impressive two-level platform of 160 × 180 m to 14 m high pyramids. Most structures are formally arrayed in rows surrounding the central pyramid in the immense 380 × 240 m central plaza (figs. 2, 3). The entire central complex is protected by a wall and a ditch that is an extension of a drainage deliberately diverted to protect the northeastern and eastern zones with the wall(s) protecting, or at least delineating, the remaining perimeter. Surrounding the center are irregularly distributed residential and probably other special function structures.

Some evidence exists for increasing agglomeration at this time instead of the more dispersed population distributions in earlier periods. This is based on a "brecha" survey and excavation program north of the main site. Here we took advantage of a natural "brecha" during the cane-cutting season in 1986. The surveyed area was roughly 3 km long by 500 m wide, or approximately 1.5 km^2, and all house mounds were test pitted. While they were all occupied in the Terminal Formative, a lesser number have evidence of Early Classic occupation. Although the initial results suggest a reduced population based on a lower house mound count occupied during the Early Classic, there is evidence of increasing agglomeration instead of the more dispersed population distributions in earlier periods. Of great importance is the fact that this apparent residential transition is mirrored in the abrupt stratigraphic change clearly linked with the construction of Early Classic Balberta. Further evidence for settlement pattern changes was tested in the dry season (1986–1987) through intensive controlled surveys and related test pitting in other zones surrounding the center.

In 1986, in addition to the "brecha" excavations, teams led by Guatemalan graduate archaeology students from the University of San Carlos (the national university) opened up 43 separate suboperations in central Balberta and nearby into a probable *sacbe* and related structures. These ranged from 2 × 2 m test pits to long trenches and extensive excavations totaling 126 m^2 of excavated surface in one instance. The sampling programs included random and purposeful strategies; we were guided in part by the results of limited test excavations and surface collections made in a much abbreviated 1984 season, as well as seven deep trenches cut by a back-hoe early in the 1986 season, primarily into the platform and walls.

The preliminary findings indicate that Balberta was originally an important Late Terminal Formative center possibly affiliated with San Antonio, a Late Terminal Formative center with sculpture 6 km west. About A.D. 250–300, the main complex of Early Classic Balberta was constructed, a process that destroyed, or at least radically modified, all Late Terminal Formative structures and activity areas. Pure Formative constructions, debris, and trash pits were uncovered under mixed Early Classic and Formative fill in several places, helping to delineate roughly the approximate dimensions of Formative Balberta. Two uncorrected radiocarbon dates from these pure Terminal Formative levels are 1650 +/− 95 (A.D. 205–395); and 1780 +/−80 (A.D. 90–250). Where no Late Terminal Formative constructions were present, however, the Early Classic structures rest on virtually sterile soil.

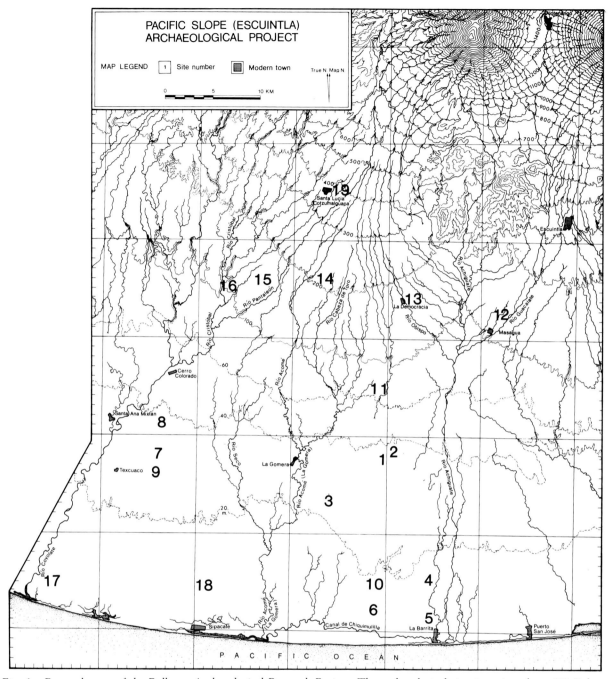

Fig. 1   Research area of the Balberta Archaeological Research Project. The archaeological sites investigated are (1) Balberta, (2) Pilar, (3) San Antonio, (4) Giralda, (5) La Rubia, (6) Vista Hermosa de los Cerritos, (7) Anna, (8) Bonampak, (9) Bonanza, (10) Tzuy-Lopez, (11) Reynosa. Other sites of interest include (12) Los Cerritos-Sur, (13) Monte Alto, (14) El Balsamo, (15) La Morena, (16) Cristobal, (17) La Selva, (18) Site No. 450201, and (19) Bilbao.

We have proven that the platform itself, which was built and occupied during several stages, was an extensive residential zone, probably elite. In the later stages the upper platform seems to have been principally used as a residential area, while the lower platform may have been an area of specialized activity, possibly including ceramic production and cacao processing. The latter idea derives from the discovery of four separate caches consisting of large urns and flaring rim jars deposited in the upper levels of a small structure atop the huge two-level platform (figs. 4–8). Each of the vessels contained varying amounts of cacao beans that I first believed

Fig. 2 *Oblique aerial view of Balberta to the south with the giant platform in foreground.*

Fig. 3 *Aerial view to northwest of Balberta central plaza.*

Fig. 4 *Cache no 1; each vessel contains mock cacao.*

Fig. 5 *Close-up of Cache no 1.*

Fig. 6 *Uncovering Cache nos. 2, 3, 4.*

might have been petrified, which a Guatemalan government agricultural expert in cacao identified as *criollo*, a native species found from Mexico to Panama (figs. 9, 10). It is believed to be antecedent to modern varieties when it was crossed by the Spanish during the colonial period with a disease-resistant South American variety called *forestero* to yield *trinitario*, the predecessor to

Bove

Fig. 7   Cache nos. 2, 3, 4.

Fig. 9   Cacao effigy beans in situ on sherd fragments.

Fig. 8   A portion of suboperation 27 showing platform area after cache vessel removal.

Fig. 10   Ancient effigy cacao on left compared to modern hybrid variety purchased locally on right.

modern varieties including *Theobroma cacao* (e.g., Bergman 1959). The vessels themselves are Early Classic, of a type believed to be a local evolutionary product derived from an earlier antecedent-Monte Alto Brown Ware (Marion Hatch, personal communication, 1986).

Testing of the cacao "beans" by Dr. C. Earle Smith of the University of Alabama and the Smithsonian Institution (R. L. Bishop and H. Neff, personal communication, 1987) has shown them to be ceramic, made of local clay derived from the weathering of volcanic materials including kaolinite, mica, and quartz with no organic material present. They were either not fired or fired to a very low temperature of approximately 500°. "The beans are cleverly made and the modelers had a very good eye for the variation which is normal among seeds borne in large numbers in a single fruit. They also reproduce a normal range of variation visible in modern *criollo* today" (C. E. Smith, personal communication, 1987).

The find is important, not only because there is no

hard evidence (to my knowledge) for Early Classic cacao use, but especially when combined with the discovery at Balberta (at this writing) of over 120 green obsidian artifacts, doubtless from the Pachuca source. These include mostly blades, many used and retouched, flakes including platform trimming flakes, and stemmed projectile points identified as probably having been manufactured in Teotihuacán (Michael Spence, personal communication, 1986). On top of the small platform structure in association with the cacao offerings alone we discovered 80 green obsidians (or 65 percent of the site total), almost all near the surface (the upper 40–60 cm). The other green obsidians found at Balberta are from a variety of household and presumed ceremonial contexts and all seem associated with the Early Classic occupation. Only two have been found outside the central complex and these were both projectile points. The spatial distribution of green obsidian in the Maya area to the north is spotty, ranging from a handful at Kaminaljuyu to over 500 at Tikal, with the highest frequency there in the

Early Classic Manik Phase (e.g., Moholy-Nagy et al. 1984:104–117). At Teotihuacán there is a significant increase of green obsidian in local workshops during the late Tlamimilolpa and early part of the Xololpan phases, reflecting in part the increased Maya market demand (e.g., Spence 1981:769–788; Santley 1983:69–124). The earliest green obsidian found in the Maya Lowlands (and Kaminaljuyu) dates to about A.D. 250, although the Altun Ha offering could be earlier (Pendergast 1971: 455–460; Pring 1977:626–628). The number so far discovered at Balberta is among the highest in southern Mesoamerica.

Although no textiles have even been recovered in the excavations, the recovery of spindle whorls in Late Terminal Formative and Early Classic contexts at Balberta, and in a Late Terminal Formative to Early Classic mound at Giralda, is indirect evidence of textile production. These are the earliest ceramic spindle whorls encountered in the region and appear to be hand-crafted rather than mold-made as they were in later periods. Mold-made spindle whorls are widely distributed in the Late Classic on the South Coast. Among the sixteen Terminal Formative burials found in house mounds in the "brecha" survey during the 1986 season were a number of females, many with spindle whorls as part of the grave goods along with comal-like plates or shallow bowls and ground stone. The Balberta zone could offer the earliest evidence for specialization in cotton production and spinning/weaving on the South Coast during the Late Terminal Formative to Early Classic Period.

A puzzling phenomenon is the relative absence of figurines from Balberta, Giralda, and even Late to Terminal Formative La Bonanza. From all surface collections at Balberta, which were intensive, and from 177 m³ of excavations in 1984, only 3 figurine fragments were found, or 0.0494 for every 1,000 sherds—a figure far below the 4/1,000 sherds (0.004) from Early Ajalpan deposits in the Tehuacan Valley of Mexico (i.e., Tehuacan had 25 times more). Our 1986 ratio substantiates the trend that is evidently well established by the Terminal Formative. Figurines are so plentiful in Early and Middle Formative sites that a figurine cult probably existed. The sudden decline at Balberta is another portent of the deep changes occurring in the ritual/ceremonial area and shows that by the beginning of the Early Classic there was a shift away from ritual household activity to large-scale state religion—witness the giant plazas and huge temples formally aligned in rows at Balberta.

Since we are actively engaged in the research project at this writing, I now present a brief review of some of the interesting current research questions.

1. What are the local chronological sequences at Balberta and the surrounding Formative centers?

Because area chronology for the transition period is not well documented, the existing regional ceramic chronology must be refined. Given the same relative size and regular spacing of the nine Late Terminal Formative

major centers I viewed them previously as being contemporaneous and politically competitive (Bove 1981, in press, a). I am reexamining this position: most ethnographically and ethnohistorically known chiefdoms were probably subject to marked status and political competitiveness among elites with short bursts of construction activity combined with rapidly changing cycles of political hegemony and instability (Sahlins 1958; Goldman 1970; Earle 1978; Helms 1979). This is being evaluated via an intensive controlled surface collection program at all nine sites combined with extensive excavations at Balberta and supplemented by data from the previous regional surveys.

2. Is there a significant artifactual and architectural break between the Late Terminal Formative and Early Classic? Does the distinctive architecture present at Balberta in the Early Classic correlate temporally with a distinctive ceramic or other artifactual complex, or both? Does the Early Classic evidence document an intrusive move by a nonlocal group, and if so from where? Were actual Teotihuacanos attracted to the region? If so, was the interaction initially reciprocal—some type of exchange between "equals"? Was the interaction direct, or was it mediated by some other center such as Kaminaljuyu? Were these Pacific Coast Guatemalans incorporated into some type of Teotihuacán "realm"? Were they actually conquered, or just economically linked (Joyce Marcus, personal communication, 1986)?

For example, Sanders and Price (1968) suggested that the introduction of large-scale ceremonial architecture of a foreign style in a local sequence is evidence that the foreign power has secured control over the surplus labor of a local population. The question to be answered, of course, is whether this is a foreign style or a local development.

3. Do local polities during the Terminal Formative become more centralized or more fragmented before their transformation/abandonment?

The goal is to evaluate if political change was instigated primarily by economic and demographic factors (Sanders and Webster 1978; Sanders, Parsons, and Santley 1979), or by political factors (e.g., Earle 1978). This will be approached by measuring changes in site size, public architecture, and site relations at the key sites before and after the development at Balberta to see if local centralization increased like a "secondary" state because of increasing pressure of a more powerful neighbor such as Kaminaljuyu in the Highlands or perhaps as a local response to Teotihuacán's expansion. This question is linked to question 1 since two effects of increasing status rivalry and accompanying political instability are population relocation and the limited duration of centers. In turn, these events are tied to the lack of boundary maintenance.

4. Is there increasing warfare between the Terminal Formative and Early Classic?

To the north in the Lowland Maya region, growing

evidence exists for defensive fortifications during the transitional period at Becan, Tikal, El Mirador, and Edzna, for example. It has been suggested that the evolutionary significance of warfare lies in its ability to institutionalize preexisting ranking and economic stratification and that a frequent adaptive response to the stress of warfare is population nucleation (e.g., Webster 1977:335–372). On the South Coast of Guatemala during the Terminal Formative, increasing social economic competition could have caused a significant increase in warfare. We will approach this by examining the changing relations between centers before and after the transition. At Balberta, data from our recent excavations are currently being analyzed to help resolve the function of the wall and moat/ditch. Are they defensive in character, or do they act to delimit a special zone within Balberta accessible only to special persons as elites and priests? The presence of black and green obsidian stemmed projectile points and the wall are certainly suggestive of militancy.

I now briefly review other evidence for what appears to be a decisive social, political, and economic restructuring—a cultural disruption—at this time.

1. The potbelly sculptural style, which is widespread during the Late Formative (ca. 500–200 B.C.), ceases abruptly by the Terminal Formative (Parsons 1981, 1986; Demarest 1984; Bove, 1989b; Marion Hatch, personal communication, 1986).

2. The manufacture and distribution of Usulutan decorated pottery all but ceases on the South Coast of Guatemala. In fact, there seems to be a correlation between the spatial and temporal distribution of Usulutan with the potbelly style.

3. The earliest Long Count dated monuments that initially appear in the coastal peripheral belt at Tres Zapotes, Chiapa de Corzo, Abaj Takalik, and El Baul are no longer found, the latest probable date being A.D. 37 at El Baul and between A.D. 83 and 126 at Abaj Takalik. In other words, these are found in Terminal Formative contexts (usually Late Terminal Formative) with Terminal Formative dates and are not contemporary with the potbelly style. The Long Count dated monuments are transitory on the South Coast and may well be intrusive themselves.

4. The initial appearance of green obsidian in southern Mesoamerica from the source in Pachuca, Hidalgo, Mexico.

5. The abandonment, or drastic reduction in size, of many Guatemalan Highland and South Coast sites. Elsewhere the list includes Chiapa de Corzo, Izapa, Komchen, El Mirador, and Edzna. At Kaminaljuyu the very Early Classic Aurora Phase is extremely limited in its spatial distribution.

6. The earliest fortifications appear at Edzna, Becan, and Tikal-Uaxactún, others in Yucatán and, of course, Balberta.

The nature and precise duration of Teotihuacán's in-

teraction in southern Mesoamerica still remain an enigma, especially given the fragmentary archaeological research completed in key zones and the complexity of the mechanisms involved. Although Adams (1984) for one suggested that "the Early Classic period in the Lowlands begins with military intervention by Teotihuacan and its subsequent domination of Tikal through a series of collaborationist rulers," I am not convinced that Teotihuacán sent *large* numbers of emissaries, or merchant warriors, to Kaminaljuyu, Tikal, or the South Coast of Guatemala, believing instead that essentially all development was local. And even though the Teotihuacán primary state could have "influenced" the rise of secondary states in southern Mesoamerica, it smacks too much of outmoded prime mover theories. In a seminal article Sanders (1974) argued that, by the Terminal Formative, Kaminaljuyu was a highly developed chiefdom and then shifted rapidly from ceremonialism toward temple construction, a focus on high gods, with an increase in centralization. He believes this occurred between the Arenal and Aurora phases and was completed by Amatle I. "The fact that this apparent centralization takes place during the Early Classic period prior to the direct Teotihuacan takeover is interesting" (Sanders 1974:112).

We could have a parallel development on the South Coast, but where are the Teotihuacanos? Willey (1977), referring to the Maya Lowlands, believed that while Teotihuacán emissaries made direct contacts that were heaviest in the Early Classic, they started contacts in the "Protoclassic," whether direct or indirect. An argument bearing on this is presented where Sanders described two sequent "waves" of Teotihuacán influence at Kaminaljuyu (1974:405–406). The first left its imprint in architecture; Sanders related this to the presence and power of important Teotihuacán nobles or emissaries at Kaminaljuyu. The second is documented in ceramics and manufactures and perhaps represents the descendants of the Teotihuacán visitors in a more settled, or acculturated, situation in the Highland Maya context. It is possible these two waves are in the Tikal record as well: the first in stela inscriptions and portraiture dating to the late eighth and early ninth Baktun and subsequently around A.D. 400–550 in ceramics. Thus, while the strongest "wave" of Teotihuacán influence is about A.D. 400–550, there are stelae and other indications of a Teotihuacán presence a century or two earlier, A.D. 200–300 or so. Moreover, as suggested (Janet Berlo, personal communication, 1986), because the same general patterns were probably *not* in operation on the South Coast, given a different cultural trajectory and social organization and especially the early dates for Early Classic Balberta, I would *not* expect to find the typical Teotihuacán "Middle Classic" diagnostic package such as Teotihuacán-style incensarios, tripod cylinder vases, candeleros, floreros, and others, but "influence" perhaps only in the architecture and the initial presence of green obsidian. According to Berlo, Teotihuacán contacts could have taken different forms with different results: for example, in Escuintla ceramics; in Kaminaljuyu architecture; and in Petén incorporation into the historical and dynastic records without much direct ceramic or architectural mimicry.

Another point is that the regional transformation in the transitional period is traumatic. The settlement pattern and related regional sociopolitical organization, as we currently understand it, depart radically from the numerous and probably weakly organized chiefdoms by the Terminal Formative to a statelike organization centered at Balberta. Warfare is possibly one of the key variables that triggers the evolutionary mechanisms toward state establishment in this case. The institutionalization of warfare could be a response to other socioeconomic pressures, including a possible Teotihuacán or surrogate threat (Flannery 1972; Webster 1977; Wright 1977:379–397; Redmond 1983). Another related possibility is not unlike the situation in Hawaii, where one purpose of warfare was to capture populations in order to increase the subsistence base and channel part into the political economy (Earle 1978). It could also help to explain the massive desanctification of the potbelly and stela cults at the end of the Formative on the South Coast.

While these speculations are interesting, the South Coast must be understood in terms of itself and not in terms of Teotihuacán, Izapa, Kaminaljuyu, or Tikal (Joyce Marcus, personal communication, 1986). To evaluate properly the contributions of developments on the South Coast, we must collect data and elaborate arguments based on local developments before integrating them, or comparing them, with other regional sequences because we can now see that the region has its own integrity. We need to understand it in its own terms rather than simply as a reflection of its neighbors.

Acknowledgments

The research on which this paper is based was supported by grants from the National Science Foundation (BNS-8520055) and National Geographic Society (2801-84, 3243-85) with the assistance of the Instituto de Antropología e Historia, Guatemala, and the Social Process Research Institute, University of California, Santa Barbara. I am particularly thankful to the excellent group of University of San Carlos archaeology students who played so important a role in the project. They are Barbara Arroyo, Edgar Carpio, Ramiro Figuero, Carlos Herman, Brenda Lou, Sonia Medrano, and Sergio Rodas. Special thanks to Enrique Linares and the people of the Parcelamiento Pilar. I also wish to thank the management and personnel of Pantaleon S.A., especially Julio Herrera, Miguel Fernández, and Leonel Borja; and Don Roberto Alejos of El Salto S.A.

Olmec Bloodletting: An Iconographic Study

ROSEMARY A. JOYCE
PEABODY MUSEUM, HARVARD UNIVERSITY

RICHARD EDGING and KARL LORENZ
UNIVERSITY OF ILLINOIS, URBANA

SUSAN D. GILLESPIE
ILLINOIS STATE UNIVERSITY

One of the most important of all Maya rituals was ceremonial bloodletting, either by drawing a cord through a hole in the tongue or by passing a sting-ray spine, pointed bone, or maguey thorn through the penis. Stingray spines used in the rite have often been found in Maya caches; in fact, so signifi-cant was this act among the Classic Maya that the perforator itself was worshipped as a god. This ritual must also have been frequently practiced among the earlier Olmec . . .

Michael D. Coe
in *The Origins of Maya Civilization*

The iconography of bloodletting in the Early and Middle Formative (ca. 1200–500 B.C.) Olmec symbol system is the focus of the present study.[1] We have identified a series of symbols in large- and small-scale stone objects and ceramics representing per-forators and a zoomorphic supernatural associated with bloodletting. While aspects of this iconography are com-parable to later Classic Lowland Maya iconography of bloodletting, its deployment in public and private con-texts differs, suggesting fundamental variation in the way bloodletting was related to political legitimation in the Formative Olmec and Classic Maya cases. Our point of departure is the relatively well-documented iconography of autosacrifice among the Lowland Maya.

Maya Bloodletting

The nature and iconography of bloodletting among the Lowland Classic Maya have been elucidated in a series of studies (Joralemon 1974; Schele 1984a; Stuart 1984e). Maya autosacrifice imagery includes scenes related to bloodletting, iconographic elements indicating autosac-rifice, and glyphs referring to bloodletting. Most scenes shown take place after the act of bloodletting and in-clude holding paraphernalia of autosacrifice, visions of blood serpents enclosing ancestors, and scattering blood in a ritual gesture. The paraphernalia of bloodletting may also be held, not simply as indications that an act of autosacrifice has taken place, but as royal regalia. Two elements are common both in scenes of bloodletting and

as royal regalia: the personified bloodletter, which Coe (1977a:188) referred to as a god, and bands tied in three knots. Three-knotted bands mark the wrists and ankles of participants in autosacrifice, mark staffs held in blood-letting rituals, and form part of the personified bloodletter.

The personified bloodletter (Joralemon 1974) has a profile, long-nosed face above the long shaft of the per-forator that forms a central prominent tooth. Three knotted bands and a three-lobed or three-tufted element form a headdress for the personified bloodletter. Natu-ralistic perforators are also depicted in Maya art. These include stingray spines, pointed awl-shaped objects (per-haps bones), maguey thorns, and a lobed stone per-forator. The single-lobed stone perforator is also the main sign of a glyph for the act of letting blood (T712; Schele 1982:64–69). An alternative expression for the same act shows a hand grasping a fish (Proskouriakoff 1973).

Bloodletting among the Maya has been associated with varied supernaturals. Prominent among these are the Palenque Triad of deities (Berlin 1963), the Paddlers or floaters (Schele 1984b:31–32; Stuart 1984e:10–15), and God K (Robicsek 1979; Schele and Miller 1983:3–20; Stuart 1984e:13). All have associations with dynastic genealogy and royal legitimation. The Pal-enque Triad includes a saurian or fishlike supernatural (GI) whose face is marked with small fins. In a jade mask probably from Río Azul, Guatemala, this supernatural has a central tooth in the form of a stingray spine of shell rubbed with cinnabar (Adams 1986: cover photo). The stingray spine, or alternatively an awl-shaped perforator, forms the distinctive nose ornament for one of the floaters, referred to as the "Fish" God (Stuart 1984e:11).

Maya autosacrifice, using any of the kinds of perforators noted, produced blood that was spattered on paper or scattered in a ritual gesture. Blood-spattered paper in bowls or baskets is displayed, and apparently burnt, during rituals that produce visions of serpents with ancestors in their jaws. Two of the Palenque Triad have been identified with the Hero Twins of the Popul Vuh (Freidel and Schele 1988), divine mythical ancestors of Maya rulers. The floaters, suspended above Maya rulers in S-shaped blood scrolls, also appear to represent divine ancestors (Stuart 1984:11).

Through blood sacrifice, Maya rulers stated that they gave birth to and nurtured the gods who had been their ancestors, a claim that formed an important basis of elite legitimation and justification (Freidel and Schele 1988; Stuart 1984e). The processes of elite legitimation and justification were equally important to the Early and Middle Formative rulers whose dynastic monuments form a major part of Olmec art. An examination of the Formative Period record suggests that autosacrifice formed a major theme of the Olmec symbol system.

Iconography of Olmec Bloodletting

Bloodletting is attested in the archaeological record from Early and Middle Formative sites such as La Venta, Chalcatzingo, and San José Mogote in the presence of shark's teeth, stingray spines, and obsidian blades that probably functioned as perforators (Flannery 1976:341–344; Coe 1977a:188; Grove 1984:108). In addition, perforators and iconography suggestive of bloodletting are found in the widespread Early and Middle Formative Olmec symbol system.

The Olmec symbol system, developed in sites of the Olmec archaeological culture of the Mexican Gulf Coast such as San Lorenzo and La Venta, was expressed in a variety of media. These included large-scale cave paintings and stone sculpture and small-scale ceramics and portable stone carvings, especially jadeite and other greenstone. The Olmec symbol system is found, outside of the heart of the Olmec culture, from Guerrero to Honduras and El Salvador. A number of studies of the iconography of the Olmec symbol system (e.g., Coe 1965b, 1968; Grove 1973, 1981, 1984; Joralemon 1971, 1976) have established the range of motifs and their combinations in this widespread art style.

Much large-scale Olmec art consists of portraits of rulers and monuments recording the legitimacy of and justification for elite rule (e.g., Coe 1972; Grove 1973, 1981). Portable art may also relate to individual rulers, as has been suggested for certain figurines from Chalcatzingo (Grove and Gillespie 1984). Included among small-scale objects are a number of depictions of bloodletting instruments that provide a starting point to establish the iconography of Olmec autosacrifice.

Images of Bloodletters

Coe (1977a:188) noted that a jade effigy stingray spine was found at La Venta in a tomb in Mound A-2. The jade effigy accompanied several actual stingray spines, a shark's tooth, and a jade "ice-pick" perforator (Drucker 1953:23–26; Drucker et al. 1959:272). Other jade perforators of this kind were found in two other probable La Venta burials (Drucker et al. 1959:273–274). One was at waist level (Drucker 1952: fig. 22). "Ice-pick" shaped perforators are part of a group of portable stone bloodletting instruments that may have been functional (fig. 1a). One such bloodletter was included in an Olmec style cache in Real Xe phase Seibal (Willey et al. 1975: 44). Griffin (1981:219–220) noted a number of examples without provenience from Guerrero. Another form of probable stone bloodletter is represented by a depiction of a hafted knife, with three knotted bands around the handle (fig. 1b), from Ejido Ojoshal, Tabasco (Joralemon 1971: fig. 65). A second fragment, from Paso del Toro, Vera Cruz, may derive from an identical form (Joralemon 1976: fig. 10e1). As in the Maya case, Olmec iconography marks instruments and participants in bloodletting with bands and other elements in sets of three.

Fig. 1 Olmec bloodletters: (a) "ice-pick" style (redrawn by Rosemary Joyce after Joralemon 1971, fig. 124); (b) three-knotted hafted point (redrawn by Rosemary Joyce after Joralemon 1971, fig. 183).

Fig. 2 Design from an incised grayware vessel reportedly from the vicinity of Chalcatzingo, Morelos (drawing by Richard Edging, based on photographs).

A complex composition employing the motif of three knotted bands is a Middle Formative ceramic vessel from near Chalcatzingo, Morelos (Gay 1971: pl. 23), which we believe represents a personified bloodletter (fig. 2).[2] The unique form of this vessel (an in-tapering cylinder) is reinforced by the use of incised iconography otherwise limited in the Middle Formative to stone objects. The vessel has a central panel with a profile head flanked by a pair of hands holding torch and knuckleduster motifs (Joralemon 1971:12, 16). The central panel includes a profile head that incorporates elements of two profiles incised on the limbs of the seated Las Limas figure (Coe 1968; cf. Joralemon 1971, 1976: fig. 3b, 3f). This central face also has a forehead ornament that is duplicated on jade celts (Joralemon 1971: fig. 33, 1976: fig. 10g). This unique vessel represents the application of contemporary iconography of stone incising to a container, which because of its unique shape must be of nonordinary function.

The precise nature of this function is suggested by the secondary iconography of the vessel. Four "shark's tooth" motifs are spaced around a central panel. The central panel framework is composed of three horizontal elements, a basal motif, and upper motifs. The base of the frame appears to be a mouth with incurved fangs, identical to a basal motif on Monument 21 from Chalcatzingo (David Grove, personal communication; cf. Grove 1984: fig. 12). The top element has a motif found on the torch in the right hand, above a crossed band with three tabs on either side. We identify the three main horizontal elements as three knotted bands, with a loop to the right and two ends to the left. The knot on the center loop is obscured by the central profile head. Together, the three knots and profile face with central prominent tooth re-

produce the essential features of the Classic Lowland Maya personified bloodletter (Joralemon 1974).

The facial features of the proposed Formative personified bloodletter, as noted, combine the eye and mouth of Las Limas profile D with the stripe through the eye of Las Limas profile E, respectively the lower and upper heads on the right hand side of the Las Limas figure (fig. 3). We suggest the identification of the face with empty crescent eye and central tooth with a supernatural with fish features and bloodletting associations. Depictions of these facial features on a profile, finned, legless zoomorph are present in large and small-scale Olmec art from both the Gulf Coast and Highlands (fig. 4).

The Fish Zoomorph

A number of examples of the fish zoomorph were subsumed by Joralemon (1976) under his "Olmec Dragon." The body of this fish may be marked by a single large crossed-band motif—for example, San Lorenzo bas-

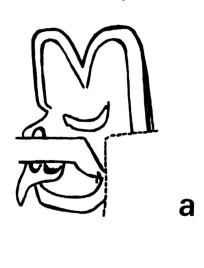

a

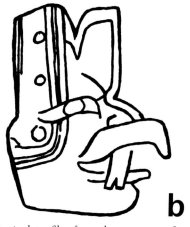

b

Fig. 3 Incised profiles from the greenstone Las Limas figure: (a) God VIII, Profile D (the fish zoomorph) (redrawn by Richard Edging after Joralemon 1971, fig. 253); (b) God VI, Profile A (redrawn by Richard Edging after Joralemon 1971, fig. 232).

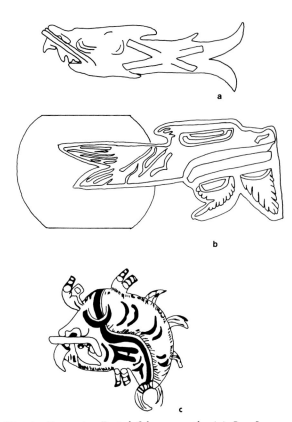

Fig. 4 *Formative Period fish zoomorph: (a) San Lorenzo Monument 58 (redrawn by Rosemary Joyce after Joralemon 1976, fig. 5d); (b) tecomate from Las Bocas (redrawn by Rosemary Joyce after Joralemon 1971, fig. 100); (c) design from a ceramic plaque from Tlapacoya (redrawn by Rosemary Joyce after Joralemon 1976, fig. 4f). Note U-shaped markings at gums (b, c) and crescent eye.*

relief Monument 58 (Joralemon 1976: fig. 5; fig. 4a). The same zoomorph is depicted on ceramics from the Highlands of Central Mexico. Ceramic representations have more variable body markings, including, but not limited to, the crossed-band motif. They all share the crescent eye and prominent tooth, usually with U-shaped markings at the gum line. On the Morelos vessel (fig. 2) these gum markings are inverted and form a trilobal motif, which in later Mesoamerican iconography was a prominent sign of liquid (water and/or blood; Stocker and Spence 1973). On a tecomate from Las Bocas (fig. 4b), the teeth are serrated (Joralemon 1971: fig. 100). A plaque from Tlapacoya (fig. 4c) has the band through the eye also noted on the Morelos vessel, typical of Las Limas profile A (Joralemon 1976: fig. 4f).

A number of Highland Mexican Formative monuments may represent a version of this zoomorph with somewhat more serpentine characteristics (fig. 5a, b). These include the zoomorph of Chalcatzingo Relief V, whose body is marked with crossed bands, which floats over a series of S-shaped scrolls (Grove 1984), and Oxtotitlán cave painting I-C (Grove 1970). These serpen-

tine zoomorphs share the crossed-bands body markings and a series of fins, often referred to as feathers or wings, with the fish zoomorph. In addition, they may have the essential crescent-shaped eye and teeth of the fish zoomorph.

The central tooth motif is also found on a series of frontal heads in which the eyes are marked with an asymmetric motif: a crossed band on one side, and a dotted **U** bracket on the other—for example, Laguna de los Cerros Monument 1 (fig. 5c). Two circumstances suggest that this pair of motifs is also related to the bloodletting fish zoomorph. A jade perforator (fig. 1a) has the same pair of elements incised on the head. Fragmentary bas-relief San Lorenzo Monument 30 (Joralemon 1971: fig. 8) depicts the profile of a zoomorph, whose anthropomorphic face has the eye replaced by the crossed-band motif and in whose mouth is a prominent central tooth (fig. 5d).

In addition to these representational depictions, certain associated abstract elements of the fish zoomorph can be identified. Prominent among these is a serrated outline oval, with interior cross-hatching or other tex-

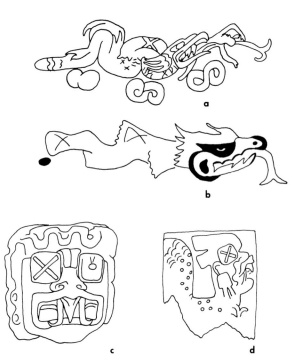

Fig. 5 *Depictions related to the fish zoomorph. Reptilian Highland Mexican zoomorphs: (a) Chalcatzingo Relief V (redrawn by Rosemary Joyce after Joralemon 1971, fig. 244); (b) Oxtotitlán Cave painting I-C (redrawn by Rosemary Joyce after Joralemon 1971, fig. 243). Note crossed-bands body markings (a, b), prominent upper tooth row (a), and crescent eye (b). Anthropomorphic face with asymmetric eyes: (c) Laguna de los Cerros Monument 1 (redrawn by Rosemary Joyce after Joralemon 1971, fig. 125); (d) San Lorenzo Monument 30 (redrawn by Rosemary Joyce after Joralemon 1971, fig. 8). Note prominent central tooth.*

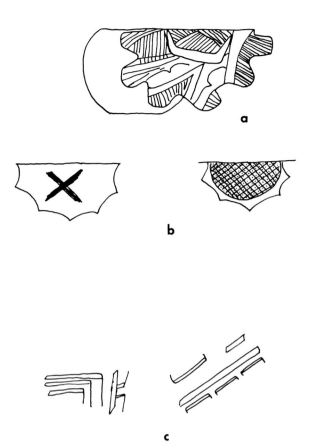

a

b

c

Fig. 6   Incised abstract motifs form Formative Period ceramics: (a) tecomate from Las Bocas; note crescent eye motif (redrawn by Rosemary Joyce after Joralemon 1971, fig. 45); (b) fish zoomorph motifs (drawing by Rosemary Joyce; compare Coe and Diehl 1980, figs. 140b, e); (c) crocodilian motifs (drawing by Rosemary Joyce; compare Coe and Diehl 1980, figs. 138a, 143i).

tured patterning (fig. 6a, b). On an unpublished incised stone figure from the Pacific Slope of Guatemala, a profile full-body figure of the fish zoomorph is placed in a position opposite, and complementary to, a representation of a crocodilian (personal observation based on drawing by Linda Schele). Along with the diagnostic crossed bands, the body of the fish zoomorph is marked with oval motifs. These are shown three additional times as the interior of a serrated motif, incised below the belly, within the spread jaws, and above the head of the fish. Two of these serrated motifs have attached brushlike fin motifs, comparable to the tail fin of the zoomorph. The example in the jaws of the zoomorph is attached to a series of dots reminiscent of the Lowland Maya conventionalization of blood (cf. Schele 1984a; Stuart 1984e). The suggestion that the serrated motif, with or without the tailfin, stands for the fish zoomorph is reinforced in this composition by the complementary presence of a shorthand profile of the crocodilian, Joralemon's (1976) Olmec Dragon, above the head opposite the fish zoomorph.

Crocodilian and Fish in Ceramic Iconography

The abstract version of the crocodilian is widely recognized as a major incised motif on Early Formative Gulf Coast Olmec ceramics. An evaluation of the ceramics of San Lorenzo (Coe and Diehl 1980) suggests that it occurs in complementary distribution with the newly identified abstract motif of the fish zoomorph. Incised ceramics of the types Calzadas Carved and Limón Incised are hallmarks of the San Lorenzo phase of the Early Formative. Calzadas Carved and Limón Incised are, respectively, polished gray to black and differentially fired types. They share two dominant flat-bottom, flaring wall open-bowl forms, with simple direct rims or complex bolstered and down-turned rims. In addition, rarer examples of incurved rim vessels (tecomates) and jars are found in Calzadas Carved, but in numbers too small to permit real assessment of their characteristics.

The illustrations provided in Coe and Diehl (1980, vol. 1, figs. 138–145) were used as a basis to tabulate motifs and their associations with the direct and complex rim bowl forms. There is no way to tell how representative these illustrations are of the proportions of different motifs and motif-form combinations in the type, but unless some kind of deliberate selection is operative, the two forms should have frequency roughly equivalent to the motifs of the crocodilian Olmec Dragon and the fish zoomorph. This is not the case: in Calzadas Carved, with roughly equal numbers of illustrations of direct and complex rims (19 bolstered, 22 direct rims), all the explicit crocodilian profiles (2) are on bolstered rim bowls, and all the serrated outline oval motifs (3) are on direct rim bowls (cf. fig. 6b and 6c). The majority of the bolstered rim bowls carried horizontal brackets (10), or K-shaped motifs (4), parts of crocodilian jaw row and hand-paw-wing motifs. The majority of direct rim vessels carried unique panels of design (9) or crossed-band motifs (4), the body marking associated with the fish zoomorph. Limón Carved Incised had no crocodilian iconography (brackets, K motifs, hand-paw-wing motifs). No serrated outlines or crossed-band motifs, typical of the bloodletter zoomorph, were found. Most depictions were a double scroll alternating with a dotted or cross-hatched circle in a few cases.

A survey of published illustrations of Highland Mexican ceramics with incised Olmec style iconography (Coe 1965a, 1968; Joralemon 1971) provided confirmation for the distinctiveness of these three sets of iconography, for their complementary distribution, and for their identification with zoomorphs more explicitly depicted in Olmec frontier art.[3] The incised iconography is found on a wider range of vessel forms, including bottles, flaring wall bowls, and cylinders, in the Highland sites. Double scrolls, as in the Gulf Coast, are found separately from the other motifs. They are common on bottles with incised birds, or in the shape of birds, where they form a base panel. Crocodilian motifs including explicit profiles, hand-paw-wing, and K motifs are common on flat-bottom, flaring wall bowls and cylinder forms. The crossed-band motif is found on several vessels in the Highlands with apparent crocodilian depictions—for example, marking the mouth.

The serrated motif identified with the fish zoomorph is commonly found only on bottles or tecomates in the Highland sample. A pair of tecomates from Las Bocas—almost identical in form, size, and surface treatment (Coe 1968: figs. 23, 24)—includes one with a full-figure version of the fish zoomorph (fig. 4b). The second teco-mate (fig. 6a) has a serrated cogwheel with intricate internal design, including a crescent U-shape identical to the eye motif of the fish zoomorph. In other Highland Mexican ceramics, the abstracted body marking is generally insufficient to specify the fish zoomorph, and the representations of the mouth and teeth are given greater prominence.

The contrast between the crocodilian and fish zoomorph motifs is maintained on the Gulf Coast by their use on bowl forms with different rim treatment. In the Highlands, the contrast becomes one between open bowls, decorated with crocodilian motifs, and restricted vessels (tecomates and bottles) with fish zoomorph motifs. This association of form and motif appears to hold even in incised ceramics from Izapa on the Mexican border in coastal Chiapas (Ekholm 1969) and from Copán, Honduras (personal observation; unpublished data of William Fash). The serrated outline of the abstract motif associated with the fish zoomorph also marks the edge of a number of depictions of knuckledusters, suggesting that these enigmatic objects are also related to autosacrifice.

The Knuckleduster Motif and the Bloodletting Zoomorph

The serrated edge of many examples of knuckledusters may mark these as symbolic bloodletters. A small stone sculpture of an elaborately dressed seated ruler in the Dumbarton Oaks collection (Benson 1971) has three knotted bands at each wrist and ankle, a detail of costume that in later Maya iconography marks participants in bloodletting. The main element of the headdress that this figure wears has a pair of hands holding knuckledusters with an incised serrated edge (fig. 7a).

The knuckleduster (Coe 1965b: 764–765) is a common motif, both in the headdress (fig. 7a, 7d) and held in the hands (fig. 7b, 7c, 7e, 7f). When held in the hands, it is generally paired either with a second knuckleduster (fig. 7b, 7e) or with a torch motif (fig. 7c, 7f). Serrated (fig. 7a–c) and unserrated (fig. 7d–f) knuckleduster forms occur in all of these contexts. The incised Middle Formative vessel from Morelos, in addition to the central profile that we believe is a personified bloodletter, has a pair of hands holding a serrated knuckleduster and torch (fig. 2).

The referent of the knuckleduster is problematic. Various suggestions (weapon, ball-game implement, or ritual object) have been made (Coe 1965b: 762–765; Benson 1971: 19–23; Cervantes 1969), but no archaeo-

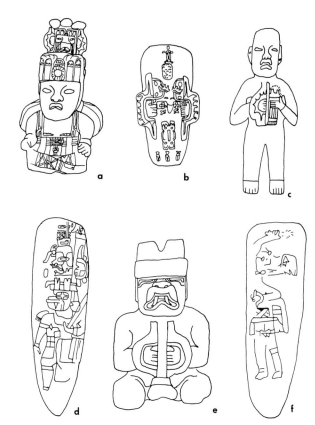

Fig. 7 "Knuckledusters": (a) Serrated pair in headdress of seated greenstone figure (note three knotted bands at ankles; similar bands are present at wrists) (redrawn by Rosemary Joyce after Joralemon 1976, fig. 4c); (b) serrated pair held by hands of stylized figure incised on celt (redrawn by Rosemary Joyce after Joralemon 1976, fig. 19i); (c) serrated, held with torch by standing greenstone figure from Puebla (redrawn by Rosemary Joyce after Joralemon 1971, fig. 20); (d) plain, in headdress of stylized figure on incised celt (redrawn by Rosemary Joyce after Joralemon 1971, fig. 33); (e) plain pair, San Lorenzo Monument 10, held by seated figure (redrawn by Rosemary Joyce after Joralemon 1971, fig. 222); (f) plain, held with torch by flying figure incised on celt (redrawn by Rosemary Joyce after Joralemon 1971, fig. 36).

logical example of the object represented by knuckledusters is known. This implies that the material must have been, in whole or part, perishable or that the depiction is wholly symbolic, standing for something else that is found, such as the natural stingray spine bloodletters that came from the sea. The interpretation of knuckledusters as symbolic perforators greatly expands the number of Olmec depictions related to bloodletting by rulers.

Bloodletting and Olmec Rulers

The knuckleduster is held as an item of royal regalia, as well as being depicted on celts (such as the split celt from La Venta Offering 4; Drucker et al. 1959: fig. 40),

Joyce et al.

carried by the flying figures that Cervantes (1969) suggested were actively involved in ritual. Grove (1984) demonstrated that the similar flying figure in Chalcatzingo Relief XII was literally in the air, accompanied by birds. The flying Olmecs strongly recall the floaters of Classic Lowland Maya iconography, divine ancestors who appear among blood scrolls in dynastic monuments (Stuart 1984e:10–15). Similar subsidiary floating figures are noted in La Venta Stelae 2 and 3, depicting Olmec rulers amid symbols of their legitimacy. These floaters are suspended, like the flying Olmecs, in midair. If the consistent association in ceramic iconography between S-shaped scrolls and birds indicates that the abstract motif stands for the zoomorph in the same way that other motifs stand for the crocodilian and fish zoomorphs, in addition to marking the place as the sky, the birds in Chalcatzingo Relief XII may also be a reference to S-shaped (blood?) scrolls like those below the fishlike reptilian zoomorph of Chalcatzingo Relief V.

Implicit references to bloodletting may also be present in historical monuments in regalia worn by the main figures. Grove (1973, 1981, 1984) suggested that the headdresses of human figures in Olmec art include both personal identification and signs identifying previous rulers. The headdress of one figure on La Venta Stela 2 consists of a fish, possibly relating to divine ancestors identified with the fish zoomorph. The presence of three knotted

Fig. 8 Humboldt Celt; note lower motifs, "shark's tooth," and cross-sectioned bowl (redrawn by Rosemary Joyce after Joralemon 1971, fig. 32).

bands on the arms and legs of a seated portrait figure (Benson 1971), in whose headdress were a pair of knuckle-dusters, has been mentioned.

The use of bloodletting paraphernalia as regalia of rule is in somewhat marked contrast with the apparent absence of bloodletting related scenes in Olmec dynastic art. Absent from Olmec imagery are the representation of the act of bloodletting, holding the bowl with the paraphernalia of bloodletting, and the subsequent visions of blood serpents framing ancestors. La Venta Monument 19, in which a human figure reclines above a crested rattlesnake while holding a bag in one hand and an indistinct object in the other, could be an example of the latter type of scene. Sheptak (personal communication, 1986) noted that similar bags are strongly associated with events that feature bloodletting acts in Classic Lowland Maya art. The serrated outline abstract motif of the fish zoomorph is common on the interior base of Middle Formative bowls (Grove, personal communication) where it may mark these as appropriate receptacles for bloodletting paraphernalia. While no reliefs depict Olmec rulers holding a bowl containing a bloodletting instrument, the highly abstract Humboldt Celt (Joralemon 1971: fig. 32) shows a motif found on the Morelos vessel, which we interpret as a shark's tooth perforator, above a cross-sectioned open bowl (fig. 8). This may be an early textual reference to bloodletting.

Conclusions

In the preceding pages, we have discussed a series of images in Early and Middle Formative Olmec art that we feel are related to the practice of bloodletting. Primary among these images is a fish supernatural, which we feel is identified with the personified bloodletter. For the Olmec, the archetypal perforator had a marine source, particularly in the stingray spine (imitated in jade at La Venta) and shark's tooth (which may have iconic significance on the Humboldt Celt). The marine zoomorph identified with the perforator was limbless, provided with fins, and identified by a prominent central tooth and crescent-shaped eye.

The marine zoomorph, which in some Highland Mexican sites may have more serpentine features, was in distinct, complementary distribution to the crocodilian Earth Monster that has been called the Olmec Dragon, with which it has sometimes been merged. This complementary distribution is found both in versions of these zoomorphs incised on stone human figures and in incised ceramic iconography. It is maintained equally for full-body depictions of the zoomorph, for profile heads, and for abstract symbols that stand as badges for the whole zoomorph.

The prime abstract motifs that stand for the fishlike zoomorph are body markings, especially the crossed-bands motif and a serrated outline oval motif. Crossed bands infixed in or above one eye mark frontal anthropomorphic masks with a prominent central tooth, suggesting the identification with the fish zoomorph. The same asymmetric pair of motifs marks the head of an "ice-pick" style perforator, tying the central tooth directly to the point of the bloodletter.

The serrated motif is common in abstract incised ceramics of the Early Formative. Pairing of this motif with full-body depictions of the marine zoomorph in Highland ceramics reinforces the identification of the motif as symbol of the zoomorph. The same serrated form marks many examples of the enigmatic knuckleduster. This hints at the identification of the knuckleduster as a symbolic perforator, a suggestion that finds support in a number of areas.

Knuckledusters occur as symbols of power, held in pairs or with a torch motif, and as an element in the headdress of anthropomorphic figures. An elaborate stone figure with paired knuckledusters in the headdress has three knotted bands at wrists and ankles, an element of dress that in Maya imagery marks bloodletting participants. Three knotted bands, a rare motif in Olmec iconography, are incised around a personified bloodletter head on an unusual ceramic vessel, along with paired torch and knuckleduster, and four shark's teeth motifs. From the top of the three-knotted panel, and from the top of the torch in this depiction, protrude single pointed spines. Three knotted bands are also carved around an object that appears to represent a celt hafted in a torch-like bundle of reeds, with a profile crocodilian handle.

The imagery of bloodletting in the Formative Period has suggestive parallels to established Classic Lowland Maya autosacrifice iconography. Perhaps most intriguing of these is the possible relationship between the fish zoomorph of the Formative and the Maya Fish God floater and GI of the Palenque Triad. Both of the latter anthropomorphic supernaturals have a series of features associating them with the marine environment, including the presence of small fins on the face of GI and the use of a stingray spine nose ornament by the Fish God floater. A portrait mask of GI shows the central tooth of the supernatural as a stingray spine. An underlying Mesoamerican conception of the stingray spine as archetypal perforator may be indicated.

Minimal suggestions of the continued relationship of a similar fish supernatural with bloodletting during the Lowland Maya Classic Period may be found in glyphic expressions for bloodletting, T714 and T712. The fish in expression T714 ("hand grasping fish") may stand for the fish supernatural as personified bloodletter. In two early inscriptions (Schele 1982:86, 235), the T712 perforator has a serrated prefix comparable to the abstract motif of the Formative Period fish supernatural. No interpretation has been suggested for this affix on the bloodletter glyph. On one example, the Hauberg stela (Greene, Rands, and Graham 1972:252–253), a Maya ruler with a prominent central tooth in his mouth carries the blood-generated ancestral serpent on which floating ancestor figures climb (Schele 1982:86–87). It is pos-

sible that the serrated prefix in these two cases specifies a bloodletter of marine origin rather than any of a number of other types of perforators.

The practice of bloodletting and its association with supernaturals with marine characteristics in the Formative Period and among the Classic Lowland Maya are presumably reflections of a shared Mesoamerican belief system of some antiquity. Bloodletting validated the lineal connection with ancestors in both Olmec and Maya iconography through the manifestation of ancestral figures (the floaters). The Formative Period practices of holding bloodletters as royal regalia and inserting them (in the form of knuckledusters) in the headdress probably are related primarily to the idea of legitimate lineal descent.

Differences in the deployment of symbols of autosacrifice are as obvious as points of comparison. Maya bloodletting imagery forms a major part of public art and is essential to the process of elite legitimation. The Classic Maya "scattering" gesture is a public act without apparent parallel in the Formative Period. Large-scale public art of the Formative Period emphasizes the connection of elite with the supernatural more directly through the emergence of rulers from the cave mouths of the underworld with personified power.

Unlike the Classic Lowland Maya, Formative Period rulers did not make their own bloodletting central to continuation of the natural world. Rather than representing the ruler as a manifestation of divine personality in the natural world, Formative Period iconography presents the ruler as specially capable of passage to and from the supernatural world. While the separation between rulers and commoners was in both cases clearly dependent on the unique relationship of rulers to the supernatural, it was a Maya innovation that placed the ruler in the lineage of the gods. In the process autosacrifice, in which lines of descent were recreated, became a central focus of public elite legitimation.

Notes

1. This essay is based in large part on discussion and papers produced for a seminar in Mesoamerican Iconography at the University of Illinois in 1985. The authors would like to acknowledge the contribution of David Grove, both in providing the context in which the issues discussed were raised and in encouraging us in our development of these ideas. Joyce produced the final draft; any errors or infelicities of expression are entirely her responsibility.

2. David Grove originally suggested that this unique vessel was not authentic. Subsequently, based on the agreement between the baseline design and that on a newly discovered monument from Chalcatzingo, he reevaluated this vessel and concluded that it is certainly authentic, although still unique.

3. "Frontier art" is a concept developed by Grove (1984), to describe the greater explicitness in Formative Period art outside the Gulf Coast heartland. In his view, frontier art is more explicit because the audience to which it is addressed is not yet fully conversant with the conventions of Olmec art as developed and expressed in the heartland. Hence, Highland Mexican ceramics depict full-body zoomorphs, while Gulf Coast ceramics feature largely abstract motifs.

Olmec Iconographic Influences on the Symbols of Maya Rulership: An Examination of Possible Sources

F. KENT REILLY, III
INSTITUTE OF LATIN AMERICAN STUDIES, UNIVERSITY OF TEXAS AT AUSTIN

Ever since the 1926 discovery of the quintessential Olmec site of La Venta, there has been considerable academic speculation as to the relationship between Middle Formative Period Olmec art and iconography and the art and iconography of the Classic Period Maya. The opinions expressed within that often heated debate have varied from a hesitant identification of the La Venta monuments as products of Maya culture (Blom and La Farge 1926:85) to the conclusion that "no linear scheme of stylistic development originating in the Olmec culture can fit the varieties of sculpture that we can now observe in the two Maya areas" (Proskouriakoff 1968b:128). However, with the advent of new and intensive archaeological and iconographic research methods and the shrinking of the temporal distance between the Olmec and Maya, it has become obvious that strong iconographic analogies *do* exist between the two cultures and that these analogies reflect the survival of certain Olmec beliefs and their incorporation into the political and religious systems of the later Maya.

The Function of Olmec Iconography

To isolate Olmec holdovers within the complex iconography of the Maya, it is important first to determine exactly what we mean by "Olmec." For the purpose of this paper, Olmec refers not only to the first inter-Mesoamerican art style, but also the belief system that is reflected in the iconography associated with that style. Between 1200 B.C. and 500 B.C. portable objects rendered in the Olmec style and bearing a complex iconography spread throughout Mesoamerica (Coe 1965b). The actual mechanism by which these objects spread is not known, but current anthropological theory favors some form of trade network. Within such a network works of art, enhanced with symbols derived from the natural environment (Reilly 1987), functioned as valuables exchanged for services and commodities (Flannery 1968:105–108). Such art objects, with their accompanying iconography, could be displayed and manipulated for political purposes by emerging power elites outside the Olmec "heartland" in imitation of Olmec rulers who used the iconography as a pictorial "royal" charter. This charter functioned as a public justification for the hereditary and perhaps divine status with which Olmec rulers were vested in their "heartland" polities.

Facade Masks and Paired Oppositions

The identification of elements of the Olmec iconographic system within later Maya art should be predicated on the testable hypothesis that certain elements of the Maya system can be visually identified in the Olmec system and that these elements perform similar functions in both systems. One obvious link between these two systems is the use of large stone and/or plaster masks as billboards for the display of symbolic information. The Maya were constructing architectural facades that displayed such masks between 150 B.C. and 50 B.C. at the Late Formative Period sites of Mirador, Uaxactún, and Cerros. On the Pacific Coast at Tzutzuculi, a Middle Formative site with strong iconographic links to the Olmec "heartland," similar facade masks, executed in the Olmec style, were erected by 650 B.C. (McDonald 1983:37). At the above-mentioned Maya sites large, multitiered buildings were constructed with elaborate zoomorphic masks placed on either side of a central staircase. At the site of Cerros, in particular, four zoomorphic masks, two of which are blunt-snouted and two long-snouted, are so positioned on Structure 5c-2nd that they symbolically replicate the daily course of the sun (fig. 1a). Linda Schele and Mary Miller have demonstrated (1986:106) that this pyramid with its facade masks served as a stage for the public demonstration of the supernatural power of the Cerros ruler.

The two facade masks at Tzutzuculi (Mons. 1 and 2) depict zoomorphic heads incised on stone slabs measuring approximately 1.5 m high by 1 m wide. Like the masks at Cerros, those at Tzutzuculi flank a wide staircase (fig. 1b). Also, as at Cerros, the Tzutzuculi masks

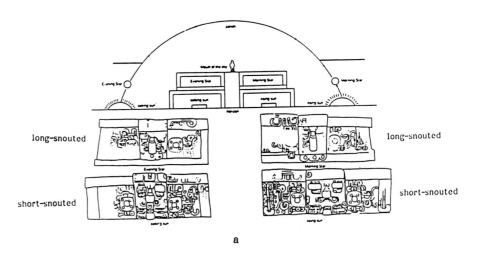

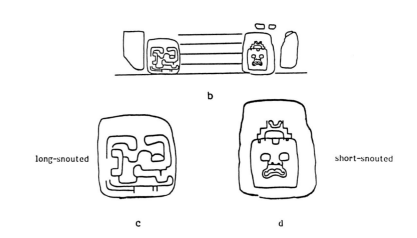

Fig. 1 Facade masks from Cerros and Tzutzuculi: (a) Facade of Structure 5c-2nd at Cerros with a pair of short-snouted and long-snouted zoomorphic masks placed on either side of the central staircase (drawing from Schele and Miller 1986: fig. 11.1); (b) facade of Mound 4 at Tzutzuculi with a long-snouted mask placed on the right of the staircase and a blunt-snouted mask placed on the left (redrawn by Kent Reilly from McDonald 1983: fig. 12); (c) Monument 2, Tzutzuculi (redrawn by Kent Reilly from McDonald 1983: fig. 31); (d) Monument 1, Tzutzuculi (redrawn by Kent Reilly from McDonald 1983: fig. 29).

are rendered as a paired set of short-snouted and long-snouted oppositions. The only difference, besides that of style, is that at Cerros a long and a short-snouted mask are paired and placed on either side of the staircase and at Tzutzuculi the long-snouted mask (fig. 1c) is placed on the right and the short-snouted mask (fig. 1d) on the left side of the staircase.

The Late Formative Period Maya were manipulating long-snouted and blunt-snouted architectural masks for religious and political purposes. The erection of such masks on a similar structure 550 years earlier at Tzutzuculi implies that the origins of such paired oppositions and the artistic canon by which they were manipulated is found in the art styles of the Middle Formative Period. In order to test this hypothesis, other examples of Olmec and Middle Formative Period art depicting paired oppositional iconography should be scrutinized for their political implications. Information gained from such an analysis will shed light not only on Olmec iconographic usage and political structure but on the specifics of the iconography and political structure of the Classic Maya as well.

"Slim": A Middle Formative Period Sculpture Executed in the Olmec Style

Within the corpus of Olmec-style art, no single piece of sculpture is more relevant to the above hypothesis than "Slim," a green stone statue from the Pacific Coast of Guatemala (Reilly 1987). Standing 65.5 cm tall and measuring 11 cm at its widest, "Slim" is a depiction of a thin, and probably adolescent, Middle Formative elite personage (fig. 2a). Dressed only in a fringed belt and apron or penis sheath, the statue cannot be called a portrait in the strictest "western" sense, because the head and facial features are hidden behind a mask and under a bell-shaped hat. Clues to the function and ritual use of the statue are offered in the symbols (fig. 2b) incised on the body and on the two scepters held in the crook of either arm (it has been reported that a looted burial, on the Mexican Gulf Coast, contained scepters identical to those held by "Slim"). Many of these "secondary" symbols can be interpreted outside this specific sculptural context but they were intended by the artist to be viewed (and read) as a compositional whole. In the case of

152

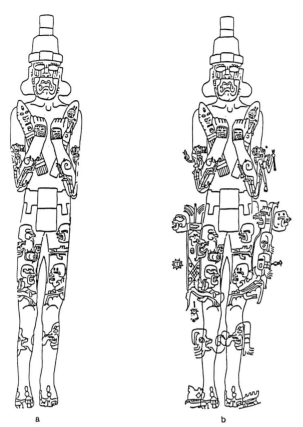

Fig. 2 (a) "Slim": a greenstone statue, executed in the "Olmec Style" from the Pacific Coast of Guatemala (drawing by Gillett G. Griffin, 1985); (b) "Slim": with the incised, secondary iconography "rolled out" (drawing by Gillett G. Griffin, 1985).

"Slim," the totality of the iconographic information is best recovered by dividing the statue into three units—the head, torso, and lower limbs. Within these three divisions the symbols that make up the iconographic units are examined here for a natural origin and/or a specific ritual action. The interpretations from each division are viewed together to understand the totality of "Slim."

"Slim": The Headdress

As previously stated, the facial features of "Slim" are hidden from view by an elaborate mask and under a bell-shaped hat or headdress (fig. 3a). This headdress, with its blocklike projection, resembling nothing so much as the business-end of a "plumber's helper," is surprisingly unadorned for an article of apparel that most probably functioned as an important piece of ritual attire. Like the later Maya, the Olmec used headdresses as billboards for the display of names, titles, and ritual information. Since there are no incised symbols on this headpiece, we must assume that the information it was designed to convey is displayed in its shape. There are several depictions of Olmec headdresses with projections extending above their crowns. The three that most closely resemble "Slim's" hat are the two on the left side of San Lorenzo Mon. 14 (fig. 3b), the right side of La Venta Altar 5 (fig. 3c), and a third carved on the summit of the Cerro Chalcatzingo Mon. 10 (fig. 3d). The exact meaning of "Slim's" hat is not easily discernible, but one may hypothesize that its function may be unique to the ritual in which "Slim" is participating.

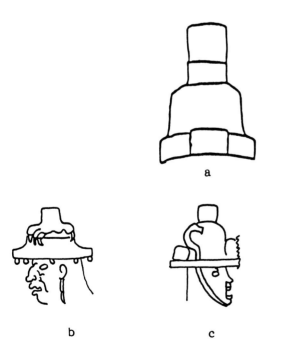

Fig. 3 (a) "Slim": the hat or headdress (drawing by Gillett G. Griffin, 1985); (b) head of relief figure on the left end of San Lorenzo, Mon. 14 (redrawn by Kent Reilly from Coe and Diehl 1980: vol. 1, fig. 438); (c) head of relief figure on right side of La Venta Altar 5 (drawing by Kent Reilly 1986); (d) head of Chalcatzingo Mon. 10 (redrawn by Kent Reilly from Gay 1972: fig. 34).

"Slim": The Mask

Positioned below the front brim of "Slim's" headdress and flanked by large, unadorned earflares is an elaborate face mask (fig. 4a). The mask is secured to the head by tie-ribbons located on either side of its mouth. The mouth itself is drooping and contains two fangs that descend from an otherwise toothless upper gum. The upper lip, topped by a pug nose, extends beyond the mouth in a triangular overhang. From each ovoid eye (perhaps once inlaid with obsidian or magnetite) descend three stripes, each of which ends at the top of the U-shaped mouth bracket. The crenellated elements, above the eyes, are commonly referred to as flame eyebrows. The different elements that make up this elaborate mask appear to be a fusion of the traits that define the two raptorial-beaked, avian-zoomorphic images incised on the shoulders of the Las Limas Figure (fig. 4b). These Las Limas Figure shoulder images were interpreted by Joralemon as a symbolic depiction of the celestial realm of a trilevel cosmos (personal communication, 1983).

The supernatural status of these avian-zoomorphs is emphasized by their cleft-heads and the split-ended serpent's fangs that descend from their beaks. The avian-supernatural on the left shoulder (fig. 4c), may derive from the harpy eagle (*Harpia harpyja*). The harpy eagle's most prominent feature, a distinctive erectile crest, can be seen as the flame eyebrow of the zoomorph on the left shoulder of the Las Limas Figure and correspondingly on "Slim's" mask. Both the mask and the left shoulder image also have a mouth bracket. The avian-zoomorph on the right shoulder (fig. 4d) is distinguished from its counterpart on the left by three stripes running through the eye and by three dots, which I believe function as a water symbol, positioned behind those stripes. Similar striping can be seen below the eyes of "Slim's" mask. I believe that this right shoulder zoomorph, like its counterpart on the left shoulder, is also derived from a bird of prey. Candidates would be either the osprey (*Pandion haliaetus;* Reilly 1987:71) or a member of the falcon family (*Falco*). It is a bit difficult to turn the overhanging upper lip of "Slim's" mask into the cruelly hooked beak

Fig. 4 "Slim": the mask with accompanying illustrations showing the natural sources of the incised elements. (a) "Slim": the mask (drawing by Gillett G. Griffin, 1985); (b) the Las Limas Figure (drawing from Wicke 1971: title page [1]); (c) the left shoulder image from the Las Limas Figure (drawing from Joralemon 1976: fig. 3c); the harpy eagle (drawing by Kent Reilly, 1988); (d) the right shoulder image from the Las Limas Figure (drawing from Joralemon 1976: fig. 3b); the osprey (drawing by Kent Reilly, 1988).

osprey

harpy eagle

a

d

b

c

of a raptorial bird. However, when one takes into consideration that the other motifs on the mask are a conflation of avian imagery, then the argument can be made that the mask depicts an avian supernatural and, as Joralemon proposed, the celestial level of the trilevel Mesoamerican cosmos.

"Slim": The Torso

If the iconography on "Slim's" head and mask relates that part of his body to avians and the celestial realm, the incised iconography on the two scepters and bent arms associates the torso of the statue with the rituals of rulership that are performed in the earthly realm (fig. 5). Examining the incised imagery on the right arm, we find, on the back of the right hand, a cartouche containing the frontal view of a noseless face (fig. 6a). Three dots are positioned above the almond-shaped eyes of this face and the outlined mouth contains what, at first sight, seems to be a single descending fang. Once again the three dots motif leads me to associate this image with a watery liquid (in this case blood). Below this right hand image can be seen the feet of the human figure that arcs around the bent arm (fig. 6b). Between the soles of the feet and the back of the hand is an elegantly

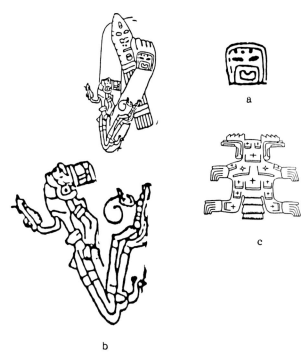

Fig. 6 *"Slim": the incised iconography on the right arm. (a) The frontal-facing zoomorph incised on the back of the right hand (drawing by Gillett G. Griffin, 1985). (b) The arcing, bound, and sacrificed captive figure incised on the right arm (drawing by Gillett G. Griffin, 1985). Note the head drawn with a "whip-lash" line above the feet and the element that resembles a tail emerging from the feet. (c) The pelt worn by the "Blind Shaman Of Atlihuayan" (drawing from Joralemon 1976: fig. 4a). Note the resemblance of the layered tail of this pelt to the tail emerging from the feet of the bound captive that arcs along "Slim's" right arm.*

incised head whose occipital region has been depicted with a single whip-lash line. From the feet themselves projects an element, difficult to decipher, that bears some resemblance to a profile view of the layered tail of the zoomorphic pelt worn by the Atlihuayan "Blind Shaman" (fig. 6c). The figure to whom these feet belong is equipped with earflares and wears a bowler-shaped hat with either a knot or a bone tied to the crown. His forearms are tied together behind his back (an act not only painful for the captive but with the advantage for the captor of thrusting the victim's chest forward), and his legs are tied below the knees. He is most likely a depiction of a bound sacrificial victim.

This tragic captive has his eyes closed in death and his belt and loincloth wrenched aside in order to reveal the cause of death—a large cavity in his abdominal area. That the death wound was inflicted in a ritual is implied by the long-necked, flame eyebrowed zoomorph emerging or released or torn from the thoracic cavity of the captive. In Mesoamerica the ritual of human sacrifice was practiced in order to sustain the gods who had shed

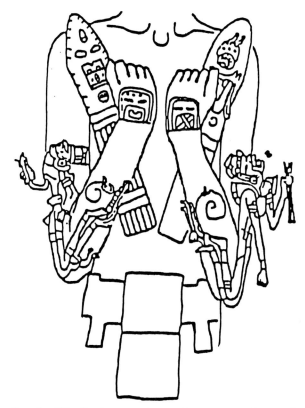

Fig. 5 *"Slim": the incised secondary iconography on the torso (drawing by Gillett G. Griffin, 1985).*

their own blood and mixed it with maize to create humankind. The gods created man and sustained him with the fruits of the soil; Mesoamerican rulers, as Oscar Wilde said, returned the favor, and in turn nourished the gods with human blood. If sacrificial acts were not performed, then the gods, and in turn the world, would die. Sustaining the gods was one of the primary functions of Maya rulers. The presence of a slaughtered captive, and, as we will see, other bloodletting iconography on a Middle Formative Period statue implies that, early in Mesoamerican history, *capture and sacrifice* (Schele and Miller 1986:209–226) was one of the two great ritual acts on which rulership was visually chartered.

The ritual instrument that has dispatched the bound captive may very well be the scepter held in the crook of the right arm (fig. 7a). I have previously identified this scepter (1987) as belonging either to a group of objects identified by Coe as "torches" (1965b:762) or to a vegetative symbol set where it functions as a bundle of bound maize stalks (V. Fields, this vol.). I am currently convinced by arguments presented by Joyce et al. (this vol-

Fig. 7 "Slim": the scepter carried in the right arm. (a) The right arm scepter/bloodletter (redrawn by Kent Reilly after Griffin 1985). Note the face on the blade, which identifies this ritual instrument as a personified supernatural and the dotted lines that indicate where the third set of bindings should be located. (b) Four examples of elements that function as "double merlons" (drawing by Kent Reilly, 1988). (c) The Classic Maya personified bloodletter (redrawn by Kent Reilly from Schele and Miller 1986: fig. IV.1).

ume), David Grove (1987b), and Brian Stross (1986) that many of the objects previously identified as "torches" are in fact bloodletters. An examination of the edges of the "business-end" of the scepter/bloodletter reveals the incised lines that indicate the fractures caused by pressure flaking along a flint or obsidian blade. Among the Classic Period Maya, ritual objects, such as bloodletters, were considered to embody the supernatural power of the ritual in which they were used (Schele and Miller 1986:176). That a concurrent belief was held in the Middle Formative Period is indicated by the engraved face on the surface of the blade (see fig. 7a). The face, consisting of two almond-shaped eyes surmounted by a "pendant dot" (Joralemon 1971: motif 128), has a squared open mouth with a single descending fang. Positioned within the mouth is a double merlon symbol (fig. 7b; Benson 1971:10) and a motif consisting of an oblong element flanked by two circles. Below the mouth and just above the top double-band, which secures the handle at the base of the blade, is an incised circle that also contains a double merlon. The handle of the bloodletting knife consists of a bundle of short sticks secured around the shaft of the blade. Two of the double bindings that hold these sticks in place (the knots that secure these bindings must be located on the other side of the handle) are visible above and below the cradling arm. I suggest that besides the two explicit bindings a third implicit binding is to be understood as in place behind the arm of stone. Three knotted bands were identified by Joralemon (1974:63) as a crucial motif within the Maya bloodletting symbol set. A prominent Maya bloodletting symbol was the personified bloodletter (fig. 7c). The three knotted bands form the headdress of that deity. This motif of three knotted bands has been shown to have its origin as an Olmec bloodletting symbol set by Joyce et al. (this volume) and D. Grove (1987b). Now it can be demonstrated that a precursor to the Maya personified bloodletter also existed within the Olmec bloodletting symbol set.

The iconography incised on "Slim's" left torso (see fig. 5) appears, at first glance, to mirror the themes of capture and bloody sacrifice we have seen depicted on the right side. This, however, is not the case: the placement of the engraved symbols may be the same, but the thematic message has taken a different direction. On the back of the left hand (fig. 8a) is once again incised a cartouche containing a noseless face. The features of this face include trough-shaped eyes (Joralemon 1971: motif 6b) and a wide-open mouth containing a crossed-bands motif. Below the right-hand face, and in contrast to the slaughtered victim on the right arm, we see a living unbound arcing figure (fig. 8b). As we saw on the bound captive, a profile head consisting of a single spiral line is also attached to the feet of this left arcing figure. From under these feet emerges a jawless and zoomorphic head with a fish-fin element behind its upper jaw. The arcing figure is positioned so that his right arm extends downward and his left arm is bent upward at the elbow. In his

Fig. 8 "Slim": the incised figures on the left arm. (a) The frontal-facing zoomorph incised on the back of the left hand (drawing by Gillett G. Griffin, 1985). (b) The arcing "flying torchbearer" incised on the left arm (drawing by Gillett G. Griffin, 1985). Note the double merlon above the chin. (c) El Volador, the "Flying Olmec," Chalcatzingo, Mon. 12 (drawing by Kent Reilly, 1988). (d) An Olmec "Flying Figure" incised on a jade celt of unknown provenience (redrawn by Kent Reilly after Grove 1984: fig. 33).

left hand the figure holds either a "torch" or some other ritual object. On the chest hangs a pectoral, and his limbs bear wrappings or jewelry. The waist is covered by a short skirt and around his shoulders hangs a short fringed cape. The fringed edges of this cape seem to move, as if the wearer is facing a strong breeze. On his thrown-back head this "torchbearer" wears a cap equipped with flaps that hang down to the level of his earflares. The crown of this cap is cleft and surmounted by an element that can best be described as a pitched roof. Around his forehead the "torchbearer" wears a headband; the individual parts consist of an oval center element flanked by four rectangular elements (only two of these flanking elements can be seen since the head is rendered in profile). Virginia Fields (this vol.) demonstrated that similar Middle Formative Period headbands carrying vegetative symbols are ancestral to the Jester God headband worn by Maya rulers. This Jester God headband was functioning as the "royal" crown for the Maya rulers as early as the Late Formative Period (Schele and Miller 1986:53). There is no known reason to doubt that an identical headdress was performing a similar function in the Middle Formative Period (Fields, this vol.). By wearing such a headdress the "torchbearer" on "Slim" is identified as a ruler.

If the costuming and posture identify the figure on "Slim's" right arm as a captured sacrificial victim, then one might assume that the "torchbearer" on the left arm is doing the capture and sacrificing. This may very well be the case. But the question then arises as to the identity of the ceremony involving the capture and the sacrificial blood. Our only hope for making that identification is by linking the "torchbearer" to a symbol set having a clear ritual association. In this case, the comparable symbol set would be the one containing the Olmec Flying Figure (fig. 8c). The individual sculptural composition, within the Flying Figure symbol set, that most resembles "Slim's torchbearer" is Chalcatzingo Mon. 12 (fig. 8d).

Olmec Flying Figures, "Double Merlons," and Ancestor Communication

The elaborately costumed figure on Chalcatzingo Mon. 12 is commonly known as El Volador, the Flying Olmec. Several symbolic devices, within the overall composition of Mon. 12, identify him as both "flyer" and ritual participant. The Quetzal and parrot, carved above and below the flyer, serve as symbolic locatives, identifying the location as air and the action as flight. The ritual nature of that flight is indicated by both costume elements (Angulo V. 1987:148) and the shaft held in the right hand. This shaft is badly eroded and could be one of several symbolic objects—torch, bloodletter, or scepter—that are standardly held by Olmec flyers. Several motifs and the thrown-back head posture of "Slim's torch bearer" indicate that he is also a flyer. These motifs are the outheld torch, which if functioning as a bloodletting symbol indicates that the act of flight was initiated with bloodletting, the fringed cape blown back from his shoulders by the rush of fast flowing air, and the double merlon or cleft symbol incised slightly in front of his head. The meaning of this last iconic element has long been an open question.

I now feel certain that both the double merlon and the cleft element function as symbolic entrances to the Olmec sacred mountain and the underworld that the mountain contains (Reilly 1988). The cleft motif has long been recognized as functioning in some such fashion because of the many depictions of vegetative motifs sprouting from clefts. Grove reasoned that the importance of the Highland site of Chalcatzingo derived from the cleft (underworld entrance) between its two guardian mountains (Grove 1987a:431). The difference in the shapes of the cleft element and the double merlon (fig. 8d) is simply a variation of the same function. I propose that the puzzling geometric shape of the double merlon is in fact a cross-sectional rendering of one of the walled and enclosed courts or sunken patios that form important architectural units at Middle Formative Period sites. Such cross-sectional renderings are present in Maya art in the depiction of architectural units, ball courts, and pyramidal fronts. They also can be seen in Mixtec codices, where they represent valleys and riverbeds. The shape, then, of the double merlon is determined by the enclosing wall and the flat surface of the court itself. The function of the double merlon was symbolically to represent the ritual function of the enclosed court. In my opinion, the plazas within such delimited spaces were intended as a focus for ancestor communication and lineage ritual activity (Reilly 1988). This premise is supported by the presence within these courts (Drucker 1952) and patios (Fash 1987) of elaborate burials equipped with elite-status grave goods. Today's elite are tomorrow's ancestors; since the dwelling place of the ancestors is the underworld, the site of any elite interment becomes an important locus for access to underworld power and the Middle Formative Period location for the second great ritual that chartered Mesoamerican rulership, *ancestor communication* (Schele and Miller 1986:175–196).

The exact sequence of the ritual performances enacted in these enclosed courts and sunken patios may never be known. One can postulate that they revolved around bloodletting. Among the Classic Period Maya, the moment that was chosen to symbolize the entire ritual of ancestor communication artistically (in much the same way that a Renaissance artist would represent the entire Mass with a depiction of the elevation of the Host) was the act of "royal" autosacrifice. It was this act of royal bloodletting that opened the portal to the supernatural (Schele, personal communication, 1988) in the same way that, at the moment the Host is consecrated in the Mass, the veil between heaven and earth parts and the divine is made manifest here on earth. Because the Middle Formative Period is lacking in depictions of autosacrifice (though not in depictions of sacrificial ritual), I believe the ritual event chosen to represent ancestor communication artistically was the flight across the open supernatural portal by the central agent (the ruler) of the ritual. This hypothesis is supported by the many Middle Formative Period depictions of human figures holding torches and positioned in the human-flight posture. While for the Maya ancestor communication was achieved by bloodletting and earthly manifestation (Schele and Miller 1986:175), for the Olmec bloodletting also opened the supernatural portal, but it was the living ruler who was perceived to journey to the ancestors.

Crossing into the underworld was an action fraught with danger. The numerous depictions of transformation figures within the Middle Formative Period sculptural record tell us that overcoming those dangers rested on the ruler's ability to transform himself into magical animals, such as the werejaguar. Because of the widespread presence of shamanic activity in both North and South America (Hoppal 1987:85–86), I suggest that actions such as transformation and underworld travel had, in an earlier period, been the province of charismatic shamans. The survivals of shamanistic paths to power in Olmec rulership rituals indicate, that, by the Middle Formative Period, such powers were also being exercised by political rulers in much the same way they were exercised by the Late Formative Maya (Freidel and Schele 1988:547–

567). The personal charisma that was so important in shamanistic ritual would still perform an important role in the functions of rulership. However, the source of that charisma would now derive as much from the office of ruler as from the personality of the individual who held that office. The enactment of similar ancestor communication rituals, for similar purposes, by both Olmec and Maya rulers indicates that the Olmec ruler, like the kings of the Classic Maya, gained his office through a blood relationship to those lineage ancestors with whom he communicated in order to rule.

In these ancestor and underworld rituals what, if any, would be the function of the left arm scepter (fig. 9)? Certainly such an object would relate to the "flying torch bearer" in the same way that the right hand scepter/ bloodletter relates to the arcing disemboweled captive. The left scepter has the same size and shape as its right arm counterpart, but it lacks the pressure flaking marks that would identify its "business-end" as a cutting edge. The left scepter like its right counterpart is also personified, but with a profile face rather than a frontal presentation. Unfortunately, this profile is difficult to describe because a great deal of it is hidden by the unbreakable grasp of a stone hand. We can discern that this profile face has a cross-banded, flame-fringed eye that is almost identical to that of the eye of the personified cave depicted in Relief 1 at Chalcatzingo (fig. 9a). Since the

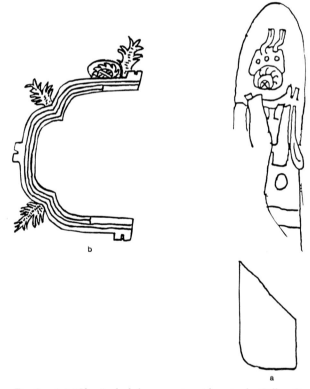

Fig. 9 (a) "Slim": the left arm scepter (drawing by Gillett G. Griffin, 1985). Note the profile face with the cross bands in the eye. (b) The personified cave from Chalcatzingo, Mon. 1 (drawing by Kent Reilly, 1988).

Chalcatzingo cave supernatural is an underworld entrance, one can assume that if the rest of the face on the left scepter were visible it would function similarly. I believe the personified right arm scepter must have functioned symbolically like a shaman's baton and served as a key to the door of the underworld. If so, the function of some of the ritual objects held by Olmec flyers is explained.

"Slim": The Double Merlon Belt

As noted, the iconography incised on "Slim's" torso represents the two great ritual acts of the Mesoamerican "royal charter": *capture and sacrifice* and *ancestor communication*. Such rituals were of course performed within the second and earthly level of the cosmos. In this Mesoamerican cosmic view, the surface of the earth was seen as a thin membrane, punctured with supernatural portals, separating the terrestrial realm from the underworld. The belt worn by "Slim" (fig. 10a), symbolically performs the same function as the surface of the earth. Tied with an elaborate knot, above bare buttocks (fig.

Fig. 11 "Slim": the incised secondary iconography located on the left and right thighs (drawing by Gillett G. Griffin, 1985).

10b), this scanty but important item of ritual costume divides the iconography of the torso (the earth) from that of the lower body (underworld). The lower border of the belt is cut to form double merlons and thus replicates the underworld portals, both natural and constructed, that are to be found on the surface of the earth.

"Slim": The Lower Body Iconography

Beneath "Slim's" belt, as beneath the surface of the earth, lies the underworld. As we shall see, the two bicephalic zoomorphs (fig. 11) incised on the left and right thigh are symbols of the underworld power—water and vegetative fertility—that the earthly ruler ritually ensures in order to sustain the life of his people. Both of these creatures are postured with their long-snouted heads pointed downward, while on their tails they carry blunt-snouted heads or masks. The zoomorph on the right thigh (fig. 12a) is open-mouthed. Within that mouth can be seen a bifurcated tongue and a split-end, backward-turning fang. The three dots and bryozoan-covered *Spondylus* shell (Spondylidae) that emanate from the mouth function as symbolic locatives placing this supernatural in the waters of the underworld. Similar images of the *Spondylus* shell (without the algaelike bryozoans) can be seen below the zoomorph and above the mask he carries on the upper end of his barlike body. The *Spondylus* shell, above the back, is attached to a banded snakelike creature. Functioning as an abbreviated symbol for the full-figured zoomorph below it, the

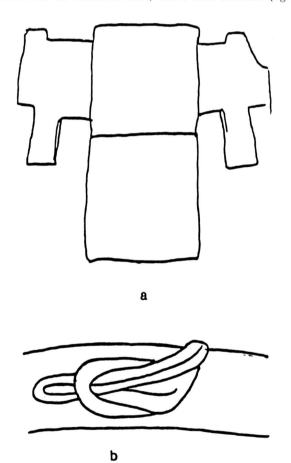

a

b

Fig. 10 (a) "Slim": the belt and apron (drawing by Kent Reilly, 1988). Note the double merlon pattern cut in the bottom of the belt. (b) "Slim": the elaborate knot, at the small of the back, with which the belt is tied (drawing by Kent Reilly, 1988).

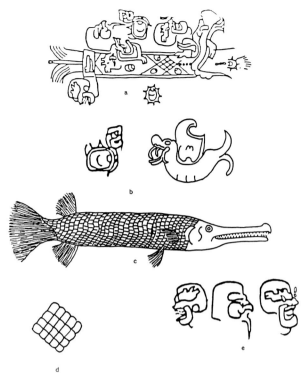

Fig. 12 (a) "Slim": the piscine-zoomorph and accompanying motifs incised on the right thigh (drawing by Gillett G. Griffin, 1985); (b) "Slim": the snake-shell motif positioned above the mask on the back of the right-thigh piscine-zoomorph and the Classic Maya Shell Wing Dragon (drawings by Kent Reilly, 1988); (c) the tropical alligator gar (drawing by Kent Reilly, 1988); (d) the cross-hatched pattern formed by a gar fish's ganoid scales (drawing by Kent Reilly, 1988); (e) "Slim": the three profile heads located above and below the body of the piscine-zoomorph (drawing by Gillett G. Griffin, 1985).

drooping corner" (Joralemon 1971: motif 6). Above this frame is a configuration consisting of a bifurcated fish tail supported by a central shaft. Since symbolic locatives function as both locaters and definers of action, the motif of the fish tail functions as a symbolic locative, placing this zoomorph in a watery habitat and identifying the action as swimming.

The actual creature from which this supernatural zoomorph derives is difficult but not impossible to discern. I once believed it to be a shark (Reilly 1987:96) but following a suggestion by Linda Schele I am now convinced it is the giant tropical alligator gar (*Lepisosteus tristoechus*). The tropical alligator gar (fig. 12c), often seen for sale in the fish markets of Tampico and Vera Cruz, has been known to reach lengths of up to twenty feet (Norman and Greenwood 1963:96) and, like the famous bull shark, can pass from fresh to salt water (Herald 1964:58). I have noticed the featherlike construction of the gar's fins and tail. The length of the jaws is noticeable in even the most casual of examinations. Certainly the bulbous projection on the end of the upper jaw of this piscine zoomorph is so configured as to resemble the bulbous beak on the end of the upper jaw of the tropical gar. Another feature of the tropical gar that might be depicted on the zoomorph is the ganoid or diamond-shaped scales (fig. 12d). These ganoid form patterns are suggestive of the cross-hatching seen at the transepts of the crossed bands so prominently displayed on the body of the right thigh zoomorph. Interestingly enough, the gar's vertebrae are reptilian in construction (Herald 1964:58), each vertebra having a ball and socket joint at either end. Such a feature allows the gar to float up on prey, looking like a log. Then the gar's body coils into a S-shaped spring from which he launches himself, in a snakelike motion, at unsuspecting prey.

Three profile heads are positioned around the gar-zoomorph (fig. 12e), one under the tail, one lacking a flame eyebrow but equipped with a beard, and one above the mask carried on the gar-zoomorph's back. All three of these heads have humanlike qualities, but they have enough compositional variation not to be considered identical. Taking into consideration their placement in the underworld and the fact that two of them have flame eyebrows, I suggest that these three profile heads, and the three on the left thigh, function as ancestor images.

Below the right knee, an incised blunt-snouted supernatural face (fig. 13a) displays elements that link it iconographically with the symbolism displayed on the right torso and thigh. Issuing from the open mouth, a speech scroll terminates in a human head with crossed bands in its mouth. Projecting from the head is what appears to be a perforator blade, an association with the capture and sacrifice themes of the right arm and scepter. The eye is prominently marked with a diamond/star-shaped iris. From behind the mouth a fish fin emanates, thus linking the profile head to the gar-zoomorph immediately above him. My feeling is that we are seeing another depiction of a personified perforator—an identi-

snaky *Spondylus* resembles the shell-wing dragon of the later Maya (fig. 12b) too strikingly to be accidental.

The upper jaw of this underwater supernatural ends in a distinctive bulbous projection. The nose atop the jaw appears humanoid, while the eye behind the nose is topped by a flame eyebrow very different in shape from those seen on "Slim's" mask. Besides carrying a mask, the elongated body of this zoomorph is marked with a large crossed-bands motif. The arms of the crossed bands are marked with small ovals that resemble nothing so much as a seed or acorn. The diamond-shaped cartouche formed by the crossing bands is incised with cross-hatching. The eye of the head or mask, positioned behind the cross bands, is indicated by a wavy cross band and is surmounted by a distinctive flame eyebrow. The mouth of the mask is bordered by a framing device. At least two fangs descend from the upper jaw and an elongated upper lip.

The zoomorph's tail assemblage begins in a rectangular frame that contains an "L-shaped element with a square

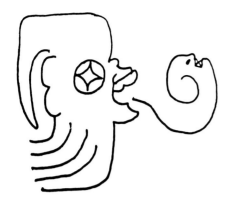

a

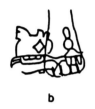

b

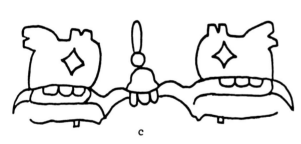

c

Fig. 13 (a) "Slim": the profile incised below the right knee (drawing by Kent Reilly, 1988). (b) "Slim": the incised image on the right foot (drawing by Gillett G. Griffin, 1985). The spaghettilike appearance of this image is caused by lines cut into the foot to represent the toes. (c) "Slim": the reconstructed right foot image (drawing by Kent Reilly, 1988).

fication that makes sense when one remembers that needle-sharp gar teeth make excellent bloodletters.

The far from clear incising on the right foot (fig. 13b) leads me to deduce that we are dealing with an image similar in function to the profile head directly above. In this case we see the frontal view of a supernatural head. The image has been so constructed that it wraps around the foot. Since the space between the feet is too narrow

to complete the incising, we must visualize the missing half as a mirror image to the completed half (fig. 13c). What is depicted is an abstract rendering of a zoomorphic head with diamond-shaped eyes and flame eyebrows. Either a perforator blade or a claw or beak curls out from under each eye. The mouth appears open and a trilobed element supports a pendant dot at the forehead.

Moving from the right to the left thigh, we are presented with another supernatural creature (fig. 14a) whose gaping toothy jaw, squared projecting nose, heavy eye ridges (flame eyebrows), and saurian tail identify him as a crocodilian-derived zoomorph (fig. 14b; Reilly 1987:101). The legs of this zoomorphic crocodilian also function as a symbolic locative, identifying the locomotive action as walking. In the water a crocodilian moves only with his tail. His legs are stretched back along his body. I might add that this legged zoomorph paired against the legless zoomorph on the right thigh sets up a legged and legless iconographic opposition first proposed by David Grove (personal communication, 1987). Fastened on the tail of this "Olmec dragon" (Joralemon 1976) is a mask

Fig. 14 (a) "Slim": the crocodilian-zoomorph and accompanying motifs incised on the left thigh (drawing by Gillett G. Griffin, 1985). (b) The real-life crocodilian from which the crocodilian-zoomorph on "Slim" is constructed (drawing by Kent Reilly, 1986). Three species of crocodile—Crocodylus moreletti, Crocodylus actus, and Caiman crocodylus fucus—are indigenous to the Olmec climax zone. (c) "Slim": the mask on the back of the crocodilian-zoomorph's tail (drawing by Gillett G. Griffin, 1985). Note the similarities—flame eyebrow, striping under the eye, overhanging upper lip, and the tie-ribbons that hold the mask in place.

Fig. 15 (a) "Slim": the three profile heads located above and below the body of the crocodilian zoomorph (drawing by Gillett G. Griffin, 1985). (b) "Slim": the "glyphic" element incised above the back of the crocodilian-zoomorph (drawing by Kent Reilly). This "glyphic" element is a head variant of the zoomorphic image carved below it. (c) La Venta, Mon. 6 (drawing from Joralemon 1976: fig. 9c). This large sarcophagus is carved in the likeness of a crocodilian-zoomorph. This supernatural hangs unmoving on the surface of the water; from his back sprout vegetative elements whose shape is reminiscent of the squash plants depicted at Chalcatzingo. (d) A crocodilian posed for water dancing (drawing by Kent Reilly, 1988).

equipped with a blunt snout placed over the curving beak of a raptor bird (fig. 14c). This mask resembles in every way the raptor bird mask worn by "Slim." An abbreviated rendering of the head of the saurian supernatural on the left thigh (fig. 15b) mirrors the positioning of the abbreviated snake-shell, gar supernatural motif on the right thigh. As with the gar supernatural, the saurian supernatural is bracketed by three ancestor profiles (fig. 15a). A vegetative element emerges from beneath the saurian-zoomorph's belly plate, serving as the symbolic locative that identifies this supernatural as a representation of the earth itself, a common Meso-american belief. An examination of La Venta Mon. 6 (fig. 15c), a large stone sarcophagus, amply demonstrates that the Olmec shared that belief. Wrapped around the sides of the sarcophagus, a supernatural animal with many of the above described saurian attributes floats in the water (Muse and Stocker 1974). Split-stemmed plants emerging from the back plates (scutes) of the sarcophagus image demonstrate that his back was the surface of the earth and that he had strong connections with vegetation and fertility. Why a supernatural derived from a crocodilian should be vested with such an

attribute can only be determined by investigating the natural history of crocodilians.

Crocodilians, Vegetation, and Water Dancing

Among the most bizarre abilities of crocodilians is *water dancing*. It is common knowledge that the bellowing of male crocodilians is often mistaken for thunder. In fact, thunder can trigger the bellowing of crocodilians. They have even been known to bellow in response to the sonic boom of the space shuttle (Ackerman 1988:64). Such an action in itself could associate crocodilians with rain and thus vegetative fertility. But the act of water dancing is even more astonishing. The male crocodilian will belly down in shallow water, lift his head and tail high out of the water (sometimes wagging the heavy tail like a dog), and with his mouth clamped shut puff up his throat (fig. 15d). Then, as Ackerman described it, "the water suddenly dances high all around his body in an effervescent fountain full of sparkle in the sunlight, and a thundering bellow fills the air like distant war games" (1988:65). Another researcher described the same effect, less poetically but just as accurately, as looking like a struck tuning fork placed into a pan of water (Toops 1979:28). So the reason for associating crocodilians with vegetative fertility is based on sympathetic magic: they can call the thunder and bring down the rain!

Below the left knee, as below the right, is incised a profile head (fig. 16a). But this time it contains thematic elements of the left torso and thigh. In front of the image's blunt snout is positioned an incised tear-shaped element. From the open mouth a speech scroll emanates. Around the forehead is tied a headband similar to that worn by the arcing "torchbearer" on the left arm. Attached to the back of the head is a crocodilian paw identical to the ones that can be seen on the saurian supernatural above. Wrapped above this paw is some form of bracelet incised with either a double merlon or a cleft device, perhaps symbolizing the supernatural-saurian's ability to create an underworld portal in the same way that his natural counterpart can dig a nest.

Wrapped around the left foot is another incised frontal-facing image similar to the one on the right foot (fig. 16b). The individual elements of this supernatural head are not clear, but appear to duplicate at least the eye shape and flame eyebrow of the mask tied to the tail of the saurian supernatural. Nostrils are indicated and once again a pendant dot can be seen in the forehead (fig. 16c).

"Slim": The Iconographic Message

As with many compositions executed in the Olmec style, we have seen that "Slim" is divided into primary and secondary information. The primary information is that "Slim" is the portrait of a ruler, costumed for what I believe is a bloodletting ritual. The secondary information is carried by incised symbols and long-snouted and

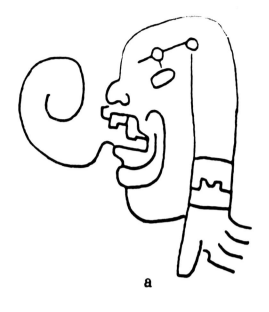

a

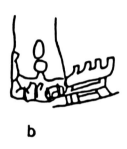

b

c

Fig. 16 (a) "Slim": the profile head incised below the left knee (drawing by Kent Reilly, 1988). (b) "Slim": the incised image on the left foot (drawing by Gillett G. Griffin, 1985). The spaghettilike appearance of this incised image is caused by lines cut into the foot to represent the toes. (c) "Slim": the reconstructed left foot image (drawing by Kent Reilly, 1988).

blunt-snouted zoomorphic oppositions. What these secondary symbols describe is the ruler's axial position within the trilevel cosmos and the nature of the public ritual that charters his rule. All this information taken together tells us that by the Middle Formative Period the charter of "royal" power proclaimed the ruler to be the axis mundi and the cosmic fulcrum, which held the opposing forces of nature in balance. Certainly the Classic Period Maya defined the charter of their rulers in a similar way (Schele and Miller 1986). "Slim," however, is not the only iconographic depiction of the charter of Middle Formative rulership. Certainly the bas-reliefs at Chalcatzingo proclaim the same "royal" charter but in a much larger and thus more public way.

Chalcatzingo

The sculptures at Chalcatzingo have been classified by David Grove (1987b) as either mythico-religious or public. The mythico-religious monuments are carved on the talus slopes of the largest of the two volcanic cores that mark the archaeological site of Chalcatzingo. Marie Elena Bernal and I suggested to Grove that Chalcatzingo should be laid out in relation to the Cerro Chalcatzingo in the same way that La Venta Group A is laid out to its volcano-shaped pyramid. Grove, after checking his maps, concurred with our view and determined that a north–south axis did exist. The axis determined by Grove extends from approximately the highest point on the summit of the Cerro Chalcatzingo down through the middle of the archaeological site at its base (Grove, personal communication, 1988). When I ran Grove's axis line across the mountain's talus slope, I saw that it divided the mythico-religious monuments into two complementary groups, each of which reflects one half of the secondary iconography on "Slim."

Dividing the mythico-religious bas-reliefs into three groups or stations was first proposed by Carlo Gay (1971: 37). Since Gay's proposal, several more of the "boulder sculptures" have come to light, expanding the total number of reliefs. On the summit of the Cerro Chalcatzingo is the single carving Mon. 10, which in the Gay system is labeled Station C. Mon. 10 (discovered by Gillett Griffin in 1969), is a boulder carved with the image of a frontal-faced, goggle-eyed head and a raised and braceleted left arm with outward-facing palm. The similarity of the hat worn by this figure to the headdress worn by "Slim" has been noted earlier (see fig. 3d). The headdress similarities and the location of this single goggle-eyed human head on top of the Cerro suggest that, like the masked head of "Slim," Mon. 10 functions as a celestial metaphor.

The Iconographic Relationship of "Slim" and the Chalcatzingo Bas-Reliefs

The bas-reliefs on the talus slopes to the right (Station A) and left (Station B) of Grove's axis line (fig. 17) also

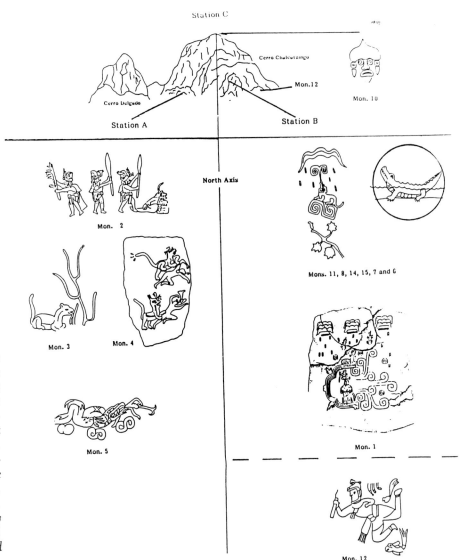

Fig. 17 Chalcatzingo: the Cerro Chalcatzingo and the arrangement of the bas-reliefs into three groupings or stations (drawings of the Cerros Delgado and Chalcatzingo by Kent Reilly, 1988; Station C: Mon. 10 by Kent Reilly, 1988; Station A: Mons. 2-4 from Grove 1968: figs. 3 and 4, and Mon. 5 from Joralemon 1971: fig. 244; Station B: Mon. 14 by Kent Reilly, 1988, Mon. 1 from Coe 1965b: fig. 10, and Mon. 12 by Kent Reilly, 1986).

have their counterparts in symbols incised on the right and left sides of "Slim." The right body themes of bloodletting and capture and sacrifice are certainly reflected in the several bas-reliefs of Station A. Within Station A, Mon. 2 (fig. 18a), with its obvious depiction of a human sacrificial ritual, is certainly a counterpart to the bound and sacrificed captive and the personified sacrificial knife on "Slim's" right arm (fig. 18b). Mon. 5 (Angulo 1987:147–148) is a depiction of a supernatural "peje lagarto/alligator gar" who is furiously biting the left leg off a supine human (fig. 18c). Mon. 5 is certainly the pictorial counterpart of the gar-supernatural incised on "Slim's" right thigh (fig. 18d). Figure-eight water scrolls positioned below the supernatural "peje lagarto" perform the same symbolic locative function on Mon. 5 that the *Spondylus* shell and water dots did on "Slim." The subject matter of Mons. 3 and 4 (fig. 18e) is more difficult to

equate with the iconography on "Slim's" right side. Yet these two monuments, with their depictions of attacking supernatural felines dominating supine humans, continue the overall right-of-axis theme of bloodletting and may very well be transformation (werejaguar) images associated with the ritual journey into the underworld.

The monuments of Station B, Mon. 1 and Mons. 11, 8, 14, 15, 7, and 6, are positioned to the left of the axis line. Mon. 1 (fig. 18f) is a depiction of an elaborately costumed personage, seated in the mouth of a personified cave. Commonly identified as "El Rey," Mon. 1 is the best known of all the Chalcatzingo reliefs. Given that "El Rey" is seated on a bench and carries a ceremonial bar, both of which are marked with figure-eight water scrolls, and that water or cloud scrolls issue from the personified cave/underworld entrance in which he is seated, a ritual can be assumed to be taking place. The

Reilly

function of that ritual is reflected in the symbols carved around the personified cave. Consisting of rain-clouds, !-shaped raindrops, and maize vegetation, these symbols bespeak water and agricultural fertility. The symbolic locative that tells us that the ritual takes place in an underworld entrance is the personified cave itself. Being able to identify this symbolic locative also allows us to identify "El Rey" as a portrait of either a Chalcatzingo ruler who has obtained the rain through ancestor contact or the ancestor (perhaps the progenitor of the Chalcatzingo ruling lineage), who is contacted in order to ensure the rain. One way or the other, by rendering this ceremony in stone, the Middle Formative rulers at Chalcatzingo have frozen the ritual in time and space. Ancestor contact is a theme we have seen on "Slim's" left arm. The placement of Chalcatzingo Mon. 12 (fig. 18g) on the left of the site axis further emphasizes that within

the Middle Formative Period artistic canon the portrayal of underworld flight and ancestor communication was on the left side of sculptural compositions (fig. 18h).

I am convinced that Mons. 11, 8, 14, 15, 7, and 6 were meant to be understood as a unified composition (fig. 18i). Taken together, they are the earliest depiction of a natural phenomenon (crocodilian water dancing) in Mesoamerican art. Located across a drainage gully from Mon. 1, this monument group consists of a series of squash plants in various stages of development. Atop the squash plants are a series of figure-eight water scrolls. Atop the water scrolls perch saurian zoomorphs. Over these saurian zoomorphs float rain clouds from which !-shaped raindrops fall.

Many of the elements that make up this composition are badly eroded, but at least three of the saurians (Mons. 14, 15, and 8) are depicted in the crocodilian water

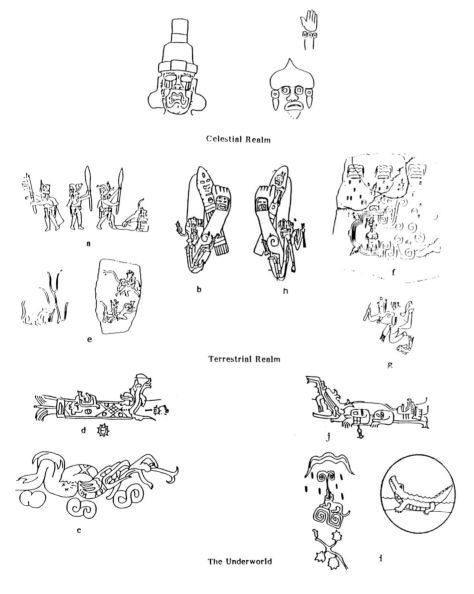

Celestial Realm

Terrestrial Realm

The Underworld

Fig. 18 "Slim" and Chalcatzingo: a comparison of the thematic content of the iconography. Celestial Realm: the head of "Slim" (drawing by Gillett G. Griffin, 1985); Chalcatzingo, Mon. 10 (redrawn by Kent Reilly after Gay 1972: fig. 34). (a) Chalcatzingo, Mon. 2 (drawing from Grove 1968: fig. 3). (b) "Slim," the right torso iconography (drawing by Gillett G. Griffin, 1985). (c) Chalcatzingo, Mon. 5 (drawing from Joralemon 1971: fig. 244). (d) "Slim," the piscine-zoomorph (drawing by Gillett G. Griffin, 1985). (e) Chalcatzingo, Mons. 3 and 4 (drawing from Grove 1968: figs. 4 and 5). (f) Chalcatzingo, Mon. 1 (drawing from Coe 1965b: fig. 10). (g) Chalcatzingo, Mon. 12 (drawing by Kent Reilly, 1988). (h) "Slim," the left torso iconography (drawing by Gillett G. Griffin, 1985). (i) Chalcatzingo, Mon. 14, compared to the crocodilian water dancing posture (drawing by Kent Reilly, 1988). (j) "Slim," the crocodilian-zoomorph (drawing by Gillett G. Griffin, 1985).

dancing posture. As they sit upon water scrolls with their heads and tails arcing high out of the water, bifurcating scrolls of liquid eject from their closed snouts in a stylized representation of the upside-down rain that forms around their bodies when they water dance. From overhead, in answer to their stony bellowing, clouds form and rain falls. Depicted in water dancing posture, this grouping of Station B monuments performs the identical symbolic function as the saurian-supernatural on the left thigh of "Slim" (fig. 18j).

Not only is the placement of the mythico-religious monuments at Chalcatzingo similar to the placement of the secondary information on "Slim," but the axial position of the Middle Formative ruler is also indicated. Just as the primary information on "Slim" was the portrait of a young ruler who is the axis mundi within a trilevel cosmos, the primary information proclaimed at Chalcatzingo is, as Townsend observed in his study of the pyramid and sacred mountain, that "the mountain monuments were places where the integration of polity and physical environment was ritually established, where the memory of kings was consecrated. . ." (1982:61). With the carved portrait on the summit and the charter of rulership carved on its flanks, Cerro Chalcatzingo became the axis mundi and the ruler of Middle Formative Chalcatzingo metaphorically became the mountain.

As we have seen, in the Middle Formative Period, the two great ritual functions of Mesoamerican rulership—*capture and sacrifice* and *ancestor communication*—were symbolically depicted in an artistic canon that required their placement on the right and left side of a compositional axis. The symbol sets used to represent these charter rituals contained, among other elements, zoomorphic images that functioned as paired oppositions. Such paired opposition could be expressed as long snoutedness/blunt snoutedness or legged/legless. It is also apparent that these oppositions can be characterized as the elements of the religious equation blood sacrifice enacted by the ruler = ancestor communication and vegetative fertility, which was seen to charter Middle Formative Period rulership ritually and thus visually.

The Survival of the Middle Formative Artistic Canon

As the symbolic expression of Olmec "royal" power, the placement of similar symbols in the same compositional form had lost little of its graphic meaning by Classic Maya times. On the sarcophagus lid in the Temple of the Inscriptions at Palenque (fig. 19a), Pacal falls down an axis mundi tree into the geometrically shaped jaws of the underworld maw. In the branches of the axis mundi tree is hung a bicephalic celestial serpent. From the serpent's open mouth on the right of the compositional axis emerges the torch-pierced head of God K, deity of royal office and royal bloodletting; from the serpent's open mouth on the left of the compositional axis emerges the vegetatively-derived Jester God. The compositional placement of

these gods echoes the positioning of their precursors on "Slim" and on the Cerro Chalcatzingo.

The Dumbarton Oaks panel (fig. 19b) displays the same imagery and positioning as the sarcophagus lid. As Kan-Xul, the son of Pacal, emerges from Xibalba, his progenitors offer him the symbols of charter and power. On Kan-Xul's right the Lady Ahpo-Hel offers up the image of God K. On his left Pacal holds the image of a vegetative-headed personified world tree.

It seems certain that the Maya rulers at Palenque were manipulating these symbolic power complexes very much to the same purpose and within a similar artistic canon as their Middle Formative predecessors. Thus, it can be said that both Olmec and Maya rulers chartered their rule by symbolically manipulating the power of nature within a similar cosmic view.

If my assessment is correct, emerging elites in the Mesoamerican Middle Formative Period were encoding and manipulating the rhythms of nature in their ritual and art to breathtaking effect. In other words, derived from a Middle Formative Period matrix, the power of later Maya rulers was the power of the oppositions perceived within the cosmos itself. What balanced and controlled these oppositions was, for both the Olmec and the Maya, "the Blood of Kings."

Fig. 19 (a) Palenque: the sarcophagus lid from the Temple of the Inscriptions (drawing from Merle Greene Robertson 1983: fig. 99); (b) Palenque: the Dumbarton Oaks Panel (drawing from Schele and Miller 1986: fig. VII.3).

Reilly

The Iconographic Heritage of the Maya Jester God

VIRGINIA M. FIELDS
LOS ANGELES COUNTY MUSEUM OF ART

The Jester God, a primary icon of power in Classic Period Maya art, was first defined by Schele (1974:49) in her analysis of the accession iconography of the Group of the Cross at Palenque. The Jester God, named for the resemblance of his tri-pointed forehead to the cap of medieval court jesters (Schele and Miller 1986:53), is one of the earliest symbols associated with Maya rulership and is primarily found attached to the ruler's headband or, in its full-bodied form, held as a scepter.

Freidel and Schele (1988) discussed the appearance of the Jester God's prototype during the Late Preclassic, where it developed as the personification of a three-pointed shape worn on a headband. Throughout Maya history the Jester God is closely associated with royal portraiture, especially on those monuments commemorating a ruler's accession to office.

The Oval Palace Tablet at Palenque (fig. 1), for example, features the accession of Pacal, a prominent seventh-century ruler at that site. In this scene, Pacal's mother, Lady Zac-Kuk, offers her son a symbol of his newly acquired authority, the drum major headdress. Lady Zac-Kuk wears a version of the Jester God headband more characteristic of the Early Classic Period, where the deity is depicted in an anthropomorphic form. Pacal, who is seated on a double-headed jaguar throne, wears a typical Late Classic form of the headband in which the Jester God is shown as a zoomorph with serrated, xoc-like teeth.

An accession monument from Bonampak, Sculptured Stone 1 (Mathews 1980: fig. 9), shows a ruler in a posture identical to Pacal's on the Oval Palace Tablet. A seated nobleman presents the ruler with a Jester God headband, and the seating glyph at A2 records the ruler's accession to power at the site (Mathews 1980:72).

A complex of maize iconography that originated among the Olmec appears to have given birth to the Maya Jester God. The central maize stalk, the maize ear, and flanking leaves are represented in a variety of forms on Olmec-style portable objects and monumental sculpture. In Olmec sculpture, maize imagery is consistently found on the foreheads of, or emerging from the cleft heads of, supernatural beings, identified as such by the presence of various nonhuman features such as snarling downturned mouths and flame eyebrows. When the stela format became the predominant mode for royal portraiture, maize imagery was adopted and featured in the headdresses of human rulers, signifying both the power of the icon and the ruler's own powers to ensure continued agricultural fertility. The icon was of such importance to the Lowland Maya that it became the semantic equivalent of the highest royal title, *ahaw* (Fields 1989).

Fig. 1   The Oval Palace Tablet (from Robertson 1985: fig. 91).

167

Various renditions of the maize iconographic complex are manifested throughout a widespread area of Formative Period Mesoamerica, from Guerrero to El Salvador. Although this area is culturally diverse, features characteristic of the art style ascribed to the Olmec are common. The presence of Olmec-style ceramic vessels and figurines, finely carved jades, and monumental stone carving in the far-flung reaches of Mesoamerica, however, does not necessarily imply an actual Olmec presence at these sites, according to Grove (1984:17). Grove suggested that Olmec-style art outside the Gulf Coast heartland may represent a symbolic repertory shared by a number of contemporary societies in southern Mesoamerica around 1000 B.C.

The presence of such exotics as pyrite mirrors and obsidian at Gulf Coast sites indicates that trade was a factor in spreading the concepts and artifacts of elite behavior. In terms of the maize complex, archaeological, botanical, and iconographic evidence can be drawn upon to illustrate how a powerful symbol was adopted by rulers throughout Mesoamerica who wished to demonstrate their role as intermediaries between their people and the forces of nature.

The most realistic depiction of maize, whose form gave rise to the Maya Jester God, is found on a jadeite hacha (fig. 2) discovered near El Sitio, Guatemala, by a farmer while clearing his *milpa* (Navarette 1971). The cob is oval and clearly marked with kernels and is flanked by leaves. The presence of hieroglyphs implies a late or

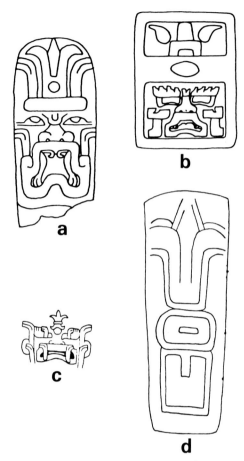

Fig. 3   (a) celt of unknown provenience (after Covarrubias 1957: fig. 34); (b) lower portion of Monument 15 from La Venta (after Covarrubias 1957: fig. 19); (c) celt of unknown provenience (from Joralemon 1971: fig. 171); (d) celt of unknown provenience (from Joralemon 1971: fig. 173).

"epi-Olmec" date for the object, although Ekholm-Miller (1973) has cautioned that the image on the front and the inscription may not be contemporaneous. Joralemon's (1971:13) cleft-ended vegetation appears around the figure's mouth.

Figures 3a–d illustrate more geometricized forms of the maize cob motif. All four images depict the cob as a tripartite element: a central pointed or rounded cone, flanked by "leaves" and situated above a circular element known as a "seed corn dot" (Joralemon 1971). Cleft-ended vegetation frames the faces in figures 3a and c. Two celts from La Venta Offering 1942-c (fig. 4a–b) show the maize motif sprouting from and above a cleft in the figures' foreheads, flanked by "leaves" as well as by cleft-ended vegetation in figure 4a.

The maize icon in figures 5a–d is banded, as in figure 3c. The image emerges from a forehead cleft in figures 5a, c, and d, and is the central icon of the headband in figure 5b. Joralemon's (1971) "feathered corn dot" appears on figure 5a, while the banded maize element in

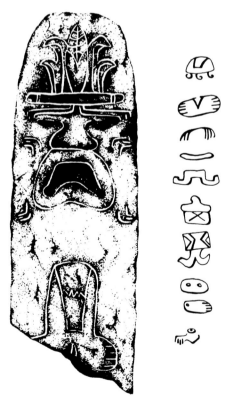

Fig. 2   The El Sitio hacha (after Navarrete 1971: fig. 5).

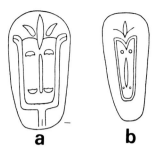

Fig. 4 (a) and (b) celts from La Venta Offering 1942-c (after Drucker 1952: fig. 47b and c).

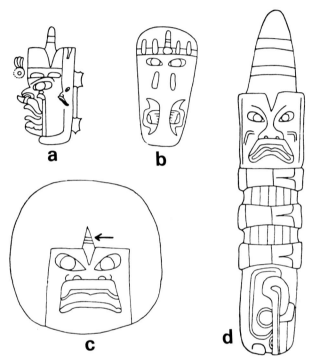

Fig. 5 (a) celt from La Venta Offering 2 (after Drucker, Heizer, and Squier 1959: pl. 25); (b) celt from La Venta Offering 1942-c (after Drucker 1952: fig. 47a); (c) a round plaque from Guerrero (from Joralemon 1971: fig. 185); (d) celt from Ejido Ojoshal, Tabasco (after Nicholson 1967:70).

figure 5b sits atop a seed corn dot. Headbands featuring a central image flanked by pairs of clefted elements are found on a variety of objects from Vera Cruz to Oaxaca (fig. 6). These clefted elements most likely represent vegetation, as Joralemon (1971:13) suggested: in figure 7, the cleft elements appear to substitute for leaves.

Maize imagery appears in both supernatural and human contexts on monumental sculpture. A relief carved on a rock near Xoc in east-central Chiapas (Ekholm-Miller 1973) depicts a striding figure, probably a human in costume. Grove (1984:57–58), who discussed this figure and the San Miguel Amuco stela in the context of frontier Olmec-style carving, described the distinctive face coverings on these figures as bird-serpent masks.

The Xoc figure's headdress is topped by a banded cone maize motif, as seen in figure 5, and he clutches a tablet, which Ekholm-Miller (1973:17) suggested is a stone celt with vegetal motifs.

A similarly posed figure can be seen on the San Miguel Amuco stela, a carved sandstone slab found near the Guerrero-Michoacan border (Grove and Paradis 1971). A tripartite element is attached to the top of his headdress, and a vertical cleft-ended element appears at the back of his head. In his left arm he clutches a bundle, generally identified as a torch, which Joyce et al. (this volume) found occasionally depicted in association with Olmec bloodletting paraphernalia. Bloodletting has been identified as a primary responsibility of Mesoamerican rulers (Joralemon 1974; Schele 1984a; Stuart 1984e), and the association of maize iconography and bloodletting is also found on such Late Classic monu-

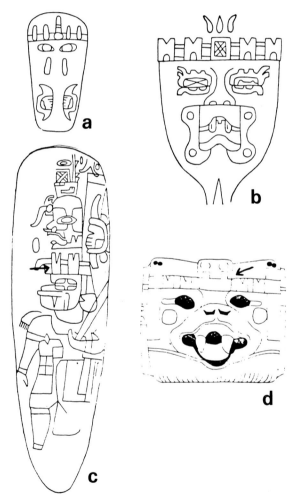

Fig. 6 (a) celt from La Venta Offering 1942-c (after Drucker 1952: fig. 47a); (b) celt from Los Tuxtlas, Vera Cruz (after Pina Chan and Covarrubias 1964: fig. 1); (c) celt of unknown provenience (from Joralemon 1971: fig. 33); (d) jade object from Oaxaca (from Joralemon 1971: fig. 254).

Fig. 7 (a) celt of unknown provenience (after Covarrubias 1957: fig. 33); (b) celt from Arroyo Pesquero (from Nicholson 1976: fig. 20).

Fig. 8 La Venta Stela 2 (after Drucker 1952: fig. 49).

ments as Palenque's Temple of the Foliated Cross wall panel.

The clearly human central figure on La Venta Stela 2 (fig. 8) wears a complex headdress whose lower portion features the cone and flanking leaves of the maize icon. The maize shape emerges from a cleft in an element that resembles the bar and dot arrangement found on the celts from La Venta Offering 1942-c (see fig. 4).

The widespread occurrence of the maize icon is illustrated by its appearance in the headdress of a Monte Alban I figurine (Bernal 1969: fig. 27), described as a deity with a serpent mask. The headdress is similar to the one worn by the ruler on La Venta St. 2 (fig. 8).

On a low relief panel from the South Coast of Guatemala (fig. 9), described by Parsons (1986:121) as Late Olmec (900 to 700 B.C.), the cone flanked by leaves motif has acquired a zoomorphic representation. Both zoomorphic and anthropomorphic forms appear in the Maya Highlands and Lowlands. On the lower right side of the Late Formative Stela 5 from Izapa (Schele and Miller 1986: fig. III.6), a seated figure wears a headdress whose central element is an anthropomorphic head wearing a tripartite cap. Schele and Miller (1986:140) described the seated figure as a spangle-turbaned scribe, who is in the process of shaping a human body at the time of creation, but that appears to be the task of the smaller figure adjacent to the armless human form. The presence of the Jester God on the front of the larger figure's headdress, as well as the jaguar-eared zoomorph atop the parasol held by a retainer, suggest that the larger figure may well represent a ruler. The implement in his hand may be a bloodletter rather than a scribal tool, since the act of bloodletting was crucial to the generation of life.

The Dumbarton Oaks jade pectoral (Coe 1966; see also Schele and Miller 1986:119–120), carved on one side with the image of an Olmec supernatural, is incised on the reverse with the portrait of a Late Preclassic Maya ruler. The seated ruler's headdress features the zoomorphic Jester God as the central element on a headband, whose paired flanking elements resemble the cleft-ended vegetation seen in figure 6b–d. The accompanying glyphic inscription was described by Schele and Miller (1986:120) as the earliest historical text and the first royal accession record to have been deciphered in Maya inscriptions.

The ruler portrayed on a greenstone pectoral found in Tikal Burial 85, which dates to ca. A.D. 1 (W. Coe 1967:43), wears a similar headband, as pointed out by M. Coe (1966:14). The central element is tri-pointed and situated above what has been described here as a seed corn dot. The paired flanking elements are again cleft-ended.

The rulers depicted on Tikal Stela 2 (Jones and Satterthwaite 1982: fig. 2) and on the Leiden Plaque (fig. 10), ascribed to the site of Tikal, wear the anthropomorphic version of the Jester God, that is, a little head wearing the tri-pointed cap. A similar image ap-

Fig. 10   The Leiden Plaque (from Schele and Miller 1986: fig. 12).

Fig. 9   Low-relief panel from the South Coast of Guatemala (from Shook and Heizer 1976).

pears on a huge Early Classic cache vessel in the Duke University Museum collection (Dorie Reents-Budet, personal communication).

Later Early Classic monuments from Cerro de las Mesas and San Miguel Chapultepec (Stirling 1943) depict the tripartite motif above an *ahaw*-like image, af-

fixed to the front of the ruler's headdress. The Jester God motif on Cerro de las Mesas St. 8 is identical to the tripointed element on the Tikal greenstone pectoral.

The Maya Jester God clearly arose from an Olmec iconographic complex, identified here with maize vegetation. To explain how such a phenomenon occurred, it is necessary to explain briefly the role maize played in Mesoamerica and to describe the process whereby natural symbols are adopted by those in authority and used to enhance their personal power, as well as to describe how such powerful symbols may be adopted and utilized in contexts similar to but divorced from their original contexts.

As Michael Coe (1968:26) stated, "The key . . . to the understanding of Mesoamerican civilization is corn. Where it flourished, so also did high culture"; this statement is supported by both archaeological and botanical evidence. The Olmec heartland is generally recognized as occupying the rich riverine lowlands of southern Vera Cruz and western Tabasco, and such sites as San Lorenzo Tenochtitlán, La Venta, Laguna de los Cerros, and Tres Zapotes flourished between 1500 and 500 B.C. Rivers appear to have played a key role in the development and maintenance of Olmec society, serving as the principal routes of communication and commerce, and the annual floods left rich levee deposits where a variety of crops could be planted (Grove 1984:14). The archaeological record indicates that the Olmec had advanced social and economic systems with commercial networks extending throughout Mesoamerica.

Rich alluvial soils as well as a temperate climate well-suited to maize agriculture also characterize the broad mountain valleys of Central Mexico, where the important Formative Period site, Chalcatzingo, is located on the terraced hillside of the base of two peaks adjacent to the Amatzinac River in Morelos (Grove 1984:19–21). By 700 B.C., monumental architecture and bas-relief carvings are found at Chalcatzingo, as well as throughout the "Olmec frontier," extending to the south and east as far as western Honduras and El Salvador (Bernal 1969:186–187).

The origins and subsequent development of Olmec civilization were a source of debate among archaeologists and art historians until excavations at San Lorenzo on the Gulf Coast established a long, continuous stratigraphic sequence (Grove 1984:136). The origins of domesticated corn in the New World have been a similar source of debate among botanists, who have proposed a number of theories to explain the phenomenon. One prominent theory, espoused by Beadle (1977, 1978), has long held that the grass, teosinte, which is of the same species as corn (Zea mays), was ancestral to domesticated corn. Beadle's extensive cytological and genetic studies have reportedly demonstrated this relationship.

Beadle's primary adversary is Paul Manglesdorf (1974, 1986), who, in his most recent publication, proposed that both modern corn and annual teosinte are descended from the hybridization of perennial teosinte with a primitive podcorn. Paleobotanical studies have demonstrated that Formative Period corn is not standardized and is genetically diverse with a wide range of phenotypes. A recent explanation for corn's origin, proposed by Iltis (1983a, 1983b), does much to explain the appearance of corn in the archaeological record, which apparently led to the establishment of permanent villages in Mesoamerica by 2000 B.C.

In the taxonomic classification proposed by Doebley and Iltis (1980), the annual teosintes, still locally prevalent in Central Mexico valleys, gave rise to maize. Teosinte is a weedy pioneer that colonizes natural scars in the landscape, such as the temporary living sites of hunting and gathering peoples (Flannery 1973:291). As Flannery has noted, teosinte grows in stands up to 2 m in height and is also associated with naturally occurring wild runner beans and wild squash, giving rise to the Mesoamerican dietary triumvirate. Although corn and teosinte hybridize and there are no apparent chromosomal disparities or gene differences between them, there is a structural difference (Gould 1984:14). As explained by Gould, teosinte has a central stem and many long lateral branches of comparable length and strength, each branch ending in a male tassel. The female ears grow laterally; the kernels are encased in a stony outer covering and can be used as food only if popped. Teosinte kernels are self-dispersing, unlike modern ears of corn, which are totally dependent on human intervention for their propagation.

According to Gould (1984), corn has a central stem

with a male tassel, and the female cob occurs at the terminal end of stout branches—that is, the teosinte ear, sprouting laterally, and the corn ear, sprouting terminally, are not homologous structures. The corn ear's structural equivalent is the teosinte male tassel, and what Iltis (1983a, 1983b) proposed is that a catastrophic sexual transmutation occurred, whereby the male tassel spikes were abruptly transformed to small and primitive versions of the modern ear of corn, which proved a useful food. As larger kernels were continuously selected by horticulturalists to propagate, ordinary selection built a bigger and fuller ear from the "initial runty but useful condition" (Gould 1984:18).

An association between teosinte and the origin of corn is also found in the oral tradition of the Pocomam-speaking village of San Luis Jilotepeque, Department of Jalapa, Guatemala (Smith-Stark 1978). Smith-Stark (1978:57) suggested that the story is traditional and not recently introduced, because there is no Spanish translation for sila:k', the Pocomam word used to describe teosinte, and confirmed by Smith-Stark to be that plant.

Smith-Stark (1978:59–60) provided a free translation of the discussion between two Pocomam men, in which one man recalls that his grandfather said "corn appeared on teosinte." The second man confirms that after seven years, teosinte plants "become" corn, ". . . corn appears after seven years . . . Until we complete the seven years, we plant it [i.e., teosinte], and then it yields corn." Coe and Diehl (1980 [v.2]:43) discovered in the course of their ethnological investigations at Tenochtitlán that native and domesticated corn is sown deliberately by local farmers, a practice that strengthens native breeds. Iltis has also stated (1983a) that Mexican farmers still cope with invading teosinte plants, which interbreed with their corn plants, producing an incredible array of maize varieties.

Maize and the Mesoamerican Lifestyle

In 1973, a productivity experiment among Zapotec farmers by Anne Kirkby yielded information that the cultivation and clearance of land was not considered worthwhile unless yields of at least 200 to 250 kilograms of shelled maize per hectare were produced (Flannery 1973:298). Flannery related that Kirkby discovered a linear regression relationship between mean corn cob length and yield in kilograms per hectare for fields in the Valley of Oaxaca and used this relationship, as well as figures on mean length of corn cobs from archaeological excavations, to calculate estimated yields for various periods in prehistory. She discovered that maize did not cross the critical threshold of 200 to 250 kilograms until sometime between 2000 and 1500 B.C., and it is at this time, according to Flannery (1973:299), that "permanent villages on good alluvial agricultural land became the dominant type of settlement in Mesoamerica."

This date coincides with the "pre-Ojochi" phase at San Lorenzo, which is characterized by semi-sedentary villages and the possible use of river levees for some agricultural activity (Coe and Diehl 1980 [v. 2]:139). Although Coe and Diehl (1980 [v. 2]:150) suggested that the ceramic inventory of the first fully Olmec component at the site, the San Lorenzo phase (1150–900 B.C.), implies the arrival of an immigrant group, Grove (1984:154) disagrees. He suggested that the traits identifying the appearance of Olmec civilization (monumental architecture, carved monuments, characteristic ceramics and ceramic motifs, and the use of jade) do not appear as a full-blown complex but rather appear individually as aspects of a gradual *in situ* development. Regardless of the nature and timing of the processes that resulted in Olmec civilization, the important points for this discussion are that San Lorenzo is located at the optimum point in the river system for the maximum agricultural exploitation of the rich levee soils (Coe and Diehl 1980 [v. 2]:147), and that San Lorenzo appears to be the site where monumental sculpture first appeared (no later than 1150 B.C., according to Coe and Diehl 1980 [v. 1]:294).

The maize plant proved to be a potent symbol of the social order that developed around the production and management of the crop. Initially depicted on portable objects and monuments with supernatural associations, the symbol was adopted by rulers who identified themselves as crucial to the process that resulted in such abundance.

The widespread occurrence of the maize iconographic complex most likely is a byproduct of extensive Formative Period interregional exchange networks, in which trade in obsidian, shell, and iron ore was documented by Cobean et al. (1971) and Pires-Ferreira (1976). Jade has also been commonly cited as the primary motive for trade among the Olmec (Paradis 1981:206).

Henderson (1979:87) suggested that a major jade source for the Olmec was probably located in the highlands of Guerrero, in the Middle Balsas region, and he stated that more Olmec jade objects have been found in Guerrero than in all the rest of Mexico. It may also prove significant that monumental sculpture from Guerrero depicts both the "maize headband," found on a cleft-headed supernatural from the site of Teopantecuanitlan (Martinez Donjuan 1982), and the tripartite maize motif on a human figure (the San Miguel Amuco stela).

The sudden biological transformation of the corn plant and its revolutionary impact on the early Mesoamerican lifestyle lent potency to maize as a symbol representing the powers of nature. Initially depicted on portable objects and monuments with ritual or ceremonial associations, the symbol was adopted by human rulers, who recognized that by identifying themselves as in control of such powers of the universe, their own power to rule would be validated. The widespread occurrence of the maize iconographic complex most likely reflects the extensive Olmec economic network. It is possible that, as Henderson (1979:85) suggested, either the elite at re-

gional centers were Olmecs from the Gulf Coast, or local elites adopted the symbols and status trappings of the more prestigious group with which they had economic ties, an idea first proposed by Flannery (1968). The power of the symbol was such that, from its origins on ritual and ceremonial paraphernalia, it was adopted as a secular symbol over a widespread area of Mesoamerica.

The processes whereby symbols are transformed and manipulated have been defined by political anthropologists, who normally work with ethnographic populations but whose theories have applications for archaeological cultures. As stated above, the emergence of monumental sculpture in Mesoamerica is generally credited to the Olmec, who were also the first to depict political themes on their monuments. The continued primacy of political themes in later Mesoamerican monumental art suggests a parallel continuity in the way symbols were manipulated.

In describing the derivation and manipulation of political symbols, Cohen stated that symbols, while they can be said to be "phenomena *sui generis* existing in their own right and observed for their own intrinsic values . . . are nearly always manipulated, consciously or unconsciously, in the struggle for and maintenance of, power between individuals and groups" (1974:xi). He suggested that most symbols that are politically significant are overtly nonpolitical, and that these symbols are most efficacious since their potency is derived from their ambiguity. In Cohen's interpretation, the ambiguity of symbols may derive from the fact that symbolic forms and patterns of symbolic action that serve to develop, maintain, and express power relations are frequently adapted from the symbolism associated with ritual. Freidel (1981) has also pointed out that in hierarchical societies, the symbols of cosmic order that form the basis for religion and ideology are often the same as those that signify power relationships.

When the Maya underwent their significant cultural transformation during the Late Preclassic period, they found it necessary to develop symbols to express their new hierarchical social and political order. As detailed by Freidel and Schele (1988), the new social order found its expression in enormous pyramidal structures adorned with huge sculpted masks, found at the sites throughout the Maya Lowlands. The Maya were able to draw from a symbol system that had existed for many generations and that expressed the elite concepts that now applied to them. An important component of that symbol system was the "maize headband," a central tripartite motif flanked by cleft elements, found on the upper masks on Cerros Str. 5C-2nd, and recognized by Freidel and Schele (1988) as the prototype of the Jester God headband.

According to Thompson (1960:8), Maya civilization was based primarily on maize, and subsequent investigations have reiterated not only the important role of maize in Maya subsistence but also the sophisticated intensive agricultural techniques practiced in the Maya region as early as 600 B.C. (Matheny 1978). Maize also carried enormous cosmological significance for the Maya. Humans were created from maize by the gods, who wished to be honored and sustained by their creations (Tedlock 1985:77–80), acts that were accomplished by ritual bloodletting.

Taube (1985, 1989) supplied further evidence of the significance of maize by documenting the prominence of the maize god in Classic Maya vessel scenes and by providing glyphic and linguistic evidence of the importance of the tamale as the principal maize product of the Classic Maya. Taube (1989) identified an association of the tamale with various Maya deities, and possibly with a particular supernatural region as well.

The relationship between humans and maize, the source of their existence and sustenance, accounts for the significance of maize as a royal symbol. The quintessential Classic Maya expression of the intimate relationship between kingship, maize, and the ritual act of bloodletting is found on the tablet from the Temple of the Foliated Cross at Palenque. The tablet, one of three documenting the royal accession of Chan Bahlum, also celebrates the birth of God K/GII, who is primarily associated with royal lineages and bloodletting as well as with maize (Taube 1989:46). The iconography of the tablet appears to represent the birth of humans from maize (Schele 1976:24). Schele (1976:23) also notes that the iconography on the Foliated Cross tablet links the life cycles of humans and maize, and that blood sacrifice is involved with the perpetuation of these life cycles.

The various representations of maize as a tripartite motif, which originated among the Olmec, crossed cultural and chronological boundaries and eventually assumed the identity of the primary icon of Maya rulership, the Jester God. The importance of the symbol lies both in its meaning as related to maize and in its power as an object to express royal authority.

The Bearer, the Burden, and the Burnt: The Stacking Principle in the Iconography of the Late Preclassic Maya Lowlands

DAVID A. FREIDEL, MARIA MASUCCI, SUSAN JAEGER, and ROBIN A. ROBERTSON
SOUTHERN METHODIST UNIVERSITY

The Lowland Maya read their art much as they read their hieroglyphic texts. Just as there is order and direction in the reading of texts, so there is order and direction in the apprehension of symbolic compositions such as stelae, wall panels, and buildings. In general, the Maya worked with a threefold syntax: concentric, horizontal, and vertical.

The vertical format is defined as stacking and is readily illustrated in the arrangement of offerings, objects, and performers in ritual settings. Iconographically, stacking is associated with formal and sequential transformations of one substance or entity into another. This principle is dynamically illustrated on a vase from the American Museum of Natural History collection (fig. 1) where the Great Blood Vision Serpent emerges from an architectonic Cauac. Note that the World Tree also emerges from this Cauac.

Another example of stacking is found on a bone haft (fig. 2), again from the American Museum of Natural History, which displays a "wood"-marked Vision Serpent emerging from the base of a pyramid. Bruce Love (1984a) pointed out the stacking of offerings in the Chilam Balam ritual and their correspondence to depictions in the Tro-Cortesianus Codex. In these depictions, offerings have been placed before trees carrying snakes, the magical Acante, which, together with their stone counterparts, the Acantun, marked the four corners of space within which ritual specialists communed with the supernatural powers (Roys 1965).

The Acantun/Acante relationship illustrates the iconological feature of stacking for the Maya: lining up the vertical of main objects or agents upon or below specifying icons and concepts. In this case, an Acante, a snake tree, becomes an Acantun, a stone-snake tree, by placing it upon a Cauac glyph. Linda Schele (personal communication, 1986) pointed out to us that the word intended here is acan, meaning "to establish, to place upright," and that the snake icon, can, is primarily aimed at that phonetic reading. Certainly this is commensurate with the function of these posts.

There are, of course, other implications of the stack described above, but the simplest one is that the stacking qualifies the meaning of objects placed one on top of the other. The seating of King Curl Snout upon his name glyph on Stela 4 at Tikal (fig. 3) is an Early Classic monumental example of this principle. A Late Classic

Fig. 1 *Line drawing of the Blood Vision Serpent rising out of the architectonic Cauac from the American Museum of Natural History vase (drawing by Linda Schele).*

175

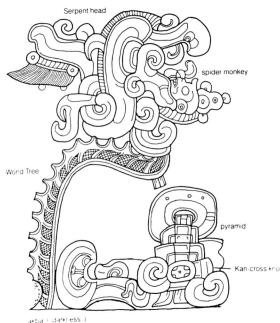

Fig. 2   Line drawing of the incised decoration on a Proto-classic Period bone haft from the Maya Lowlands (drawing by Linda Schele).

example is found on the sides of Pacal's sarcophagus at Palenque (fig. 4), where the ancestors of the lineage wear icons of their names as helmets.

Less literal are the qualifying icons placed under the Late Classic images of Pacal and Chan Bahlum in the Temple of the Foliated Cross (fig. 5). On the right side, Pacal is standing upon a corn plant, which is being drawn into a conch shell. The glyphic text (Stuart 1978)

suggests his passage into the realm of the dead. Chan Bahlum, on the left side, is emerging from the cleft head of the Cauac monster. Here the glyphic texts in the eyes of the monster suggest the "greening of the corn seed" (Freidel and Schele 1985). That this is a direct metaphor for birth or rebirth is shown by its use in the birthing text of GII of the Triad Gods flanking it (Freidel and Schele 1985). More generic use of this principle is seen in the pervasive designation of rulers as captors by placing them upon the bodies of their victims (cf. Schele and Miller 1986:213).

More complex readings of vertical stacks involve not merely qualifications of the status of some central image, but also the notion of sequential order and transformation linking such stacked images. Perhaps the single most spectacular example of this reading is seen on a Late Classic tripod plate (fig. 6; Schele and Miller 1986:

Fig. 3   Line drawing of Tikal Stela 4, showing Curl Snout sitting upon his name glyph (drawing by William R. Coe, University of Pennsylvania Tikal Project).

Freidel et al.

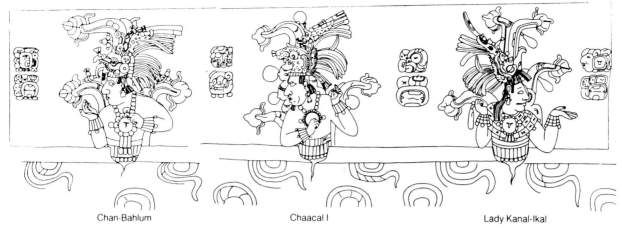

Chan-Bahlum   Chaacal I   Lady Kanal-Ikal

Fig. 4 Line drawing of one side of Pacal's sarcophagus at Palenque, showing ancestors with variable denotative helmets (drawing by Merle Greene Robertson).

Fig. 5 Line drawing of the Tablet of the Foliated Cross at Palenque (drawing by Linda Schele).

pl. 122) painted in the codex style. Schele and Miller (1986:310–311) interpreted the scene on the plate as Chac Xib Chac, the executioner, becoming his twin, the Water-lily Jaguar. He is also the World Tree becoming the Blood Vision Serpent. The dynamism of the scene (i.e., the fact that the transformations are sequential) is indicated by the Celestial Bird Deity at the top, which is flying upward bearing the wound of the Water-

lily Jaguar's claws. The Jaguar is, in turn, emerging from the Trees. The transformational principle is the more important of the reading strategies involving stacked images and is also more frequently encountered in the corpus. It is not contradictory to the principle of qualification, because it is possible to read the icons that are names or qualifications as transformational states of the principal image. This hypothesis has clear implications

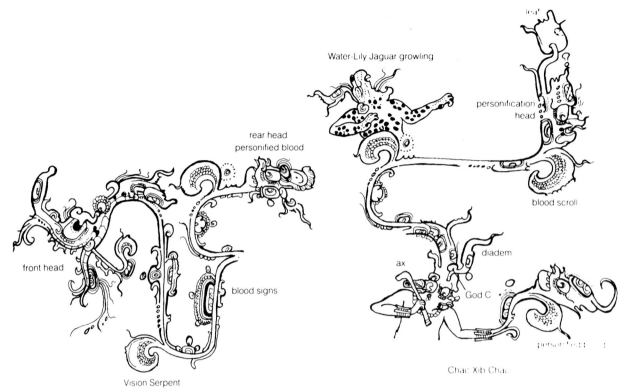

Water-Lily Jaguar growling

personification
head

rear head
personified blood

blood scroll

front head

diadem

ax

blood signs

God C

Vision Serpent

Chac Xib Chac

Fig. 6   Line drawing of detail from the Cosmic Pot, showing Chac Xib Chac becoming the World Tree and his brother, the Water-lily Jaguar (drawing by Linda Schele).

for the relationship between such stacked entities as rulers and their captives on Classic Period monuments.

Stacked Offerings and Transformation

The stacking principle is found in virtually every medium of the Maya corpus, but one of its most striking expressions is the ceramic censer stand of the Classic Period. The Palenque stands (fig. 7) are especially intricate and show the dynamic movement of the central image into and out of those above and below. For the most part, these Palenque censer stands represent GIII of the Triad, but human portraits and representations of other deities also occur. The effigy drum censer stand is a very ancient tradition among the Lowland Maya. It is clearly present by the Late Preclassic Period at such sites as Cerros in northern Belize, and then is found almost continuously right through to the fabulous Late Classic "idols."

In principle, these Late Preclassic unslipped stands elaborately decorated with modeled, appliqué, and punctate elements function as components in "assemble-it-yourself" stacks of vessels used in rituals involving burnt offerings (fig. 8; Borhegyi 1959). The following discussion shows that compositional and iconographic connections can be established beween the corpus of effigy censer stands and other Late Preclassic examples of the stacking principle, including the monumental architectural facades such as those found at the site of Cerros.

Insofar as the iconological arguments above hold, we suggest that the dynamics of transforming offerings from the status of unburnt or spiritually unconsumed to burnt or consumed are directly analogous to the transformations celebrated on architectural facades. More importantly, they are analogous to the transformations royal individuals undergo in monumental depictions of ritual when they are part of, or witness to, stacks of icons.

The focus on architecture and the focus on carved stone monuments showing royal people do not come together in time, but rather follow one after the other from the late Preclassic to the Proto-Classic (Schele 1985b). In terms of the stacking principle, the developmental pattern evinced in these media expresses a sequential working out of the definitions of rulership and nobility as these pertain to transformational states. In this respect, it is important that the correspondence between the stacking of implements in ritual offerings and the stacking of decoration on the architectural theaters for such ritual is worked out in the Late Preclassic Period.

Late Preclassic Stacking

At the site of Cerros in northern Belize (Robertson and Freidel 1986), the project ceramicist Robin Robertson noted (Robertson, in press) the remains of Late Preclassic modeled, unslipped, effigy censers of a kind comparable to those found elsewhere in the Maya Lowlands

Freidel et al.

Fig. 7 Photograph of a cylinder effigy censer from and offering in the Foliated Cross Structure at Palenque (from Rands and Rands 1959).

Fig. 8 Photograph of Stela 11, Kaminaljuyu (photograph by Stuart Rome).

during the Classic Period. These pieces came from the nucleated community, which preceded and was partially contemporaneous with the ceremonial center. It must be noted here that the censer assemblage from this context at Cerros is highly fragmented—not a single example of a Late Preclassic effigy censer stand was found unbroken, nor is a fully reconstructible example available. However, the predominance of certain elements in the assemblage provides the basis for the following discussion.

Maria Masucci and Robin Robertson conducted an analysis of possible censer forms and found that the most common one was the cylinder or drum-shaped censer, which would have constituted the basal portion of a stack of vessels used in offerings (other forms represented in the censerware from Cerros include dishes smudged on the interior from burning). A clear Late Preclassic depiction of stacked censerware is found on Kaminaljuyu Stela 11 (Fig. 8), employing drum cylinders with "keyhole" cutouts. Fragments of such keyhole elements are also found in the Cerros assemblage.

Archaeological evidence for such a censer assemblage in the Maya Lowlands, and in the vicinity of Cerros, is available from the site of Santa Rita Corozal, located across Corozal Bay from Cerros. Figure 9 shows two Early Classic effigy stands, similar to those from Uaxactún (fig. 10), placed in a niche within Structure 7-3rd. These two unburnt effigy stands display modeling and cutout elements. The vessel on the right side has a long loop nose or snout, as found on the Uaxactún examples and the reconstructed form from Late Preclassic contexts at Cerros. Flanking this snout, there are large cutout mouth

Fig. 9 *Stacked censer vessels from an Early Classic termination ritual in Structure 7-3rd, Santa Rita Corozal (photograph courtesy of Arlen and Diane Chase, Santa Rita Archaeological Project, University of Central Florida).*

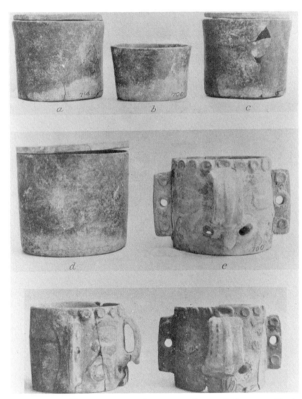

Fig. 10 *Effigy censers and associated vessels from an Early Classic offering in E-VII-platform, Uaxactún (photograph from Ricketson and Ricketson 1937, pl. 85; reprinted courtesy of the Peabody Museum of Archaeology and Ethnology, Harvard University).*

panels. Smaller versions of these mouth panels are found on the Uaxactún examples and also on Early Classic examples from a ritual deposit on Structure 4B at Cerros (Walker 1986). The left-hand vessel in the niche in Structure 7-3rd has two rectangular cutout elements. Given the stack of plates on top of this vessel, it is logical to interpret this vessel as being in the correct position for assembly; the rectangular elements are the eyes of the total mask depicted on the two vessels when conjoined. This principle of stacking an inverted effigy vessel on top of a lower one to form a single image is well attested in Early Classic Lowland Maya ceramics (e.g., Gallenkamp and Johnson 1985: pls. 48 and 49). The rectangular eye elements correspond directly to the independently arrived at reconstruction of the Late Preclassic effigy stand at Cerros. The interment of the effigy stands with three plain plates, also stacked with an inverted one on top of another upright one, formed part of a termination ritual (cf. Robertson-Freidel 1980; Garber 1983) for Structure 7-3rd before it was buried inside the core of a new construction at Santa Rita. The platters would have surmounted the effigy stands in ritual activity as they do in the deposit (Chase and Chase 1986:11).

A hypothetical composite effigy censer for Cerros (fig. 11) has been assembled by Robertson and Masucci to accommodate all of the fragments recovered to date. The reconstruction is in part based on an Early Classic drum censer (accompanied by three small plain plates with smudged interiors) that was recovered from the altar of Structure 4B. Although this censer is more anthropomorphic and its cutouts more geometric than the reconstructed Late Preclassic censer, it possessed the same

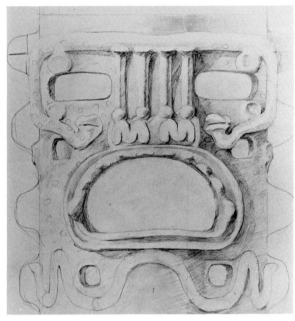

Fig. 11 *Composite effigy censer stand from Late Preclassic contexts at Cerros, Belize (interpretation by Robin Robertson and Maria Masucci; drawing by Karim Sadr).*

Freidel et al.

Fig. 12   Restoration drawing of the Late Preclassic facade on Structure 5C-2nd at Cerros (interpretation and preliminary drawing by David Freidel; inked final drawing by Karim Sadr).

flanges and the loop nose surmounted by four vertical, triangular appliqués terminating in appliquéd bosses.

A number of diagnostic elements in the composite effigy can be found on monumental architectural decoration and on later forms of the censer stand. For example, the mouth on the composite is filled with triangular teeth, diagnostic of the shark (Jones 1985). In Early Classic examples of the effigy stand found in a wing of Structure E-VII-1st at Uaxactún (fig. 10), the triangular teeth have been reduced to the singular "bloodletter" in the upper gum. This shark's tooth is characteristic of depictions of the Ancestral Heroes, GI and GIII of the Triad, in the Classic Maya corpus.

Referring again to the Uaxactún cylinders, the loop-nose variant of the long-lip of Venus as the Celestial Monster is combined with the fish barbel of Venus as GI or Chac Xib Chac (Freidel and Schele, 1988). The Cerros censer assemblage includes a loop-nose fragment that, on the composite, is decorated with lines and dots (fragments of which are represented in the assemblage). The line and dot motif is found on the long-lipped snouts of the Venus upper masks on Structure 5C-2nd at Cerros (fig. 12) and these have been interpreted by Freidel (1983) as representing sacred liquids.

We observe a stacking of elements on the Cerros composite effigy beginning with a crullerlike appliqué on the bottom. The cruller is a consistent diagnostic of GIII or the JGU Sun. Another element in the censer assemblage, which was not included in this composite, is a rectangular appliqué fragment with four parallel incisions that create the impression of felinelike digits. This again suggests a jaguar image.

Above the cruller is the shark's mouth element that,

in turn, is surmounted by the loop-nose element, decorated with snakelike squiggles. These occur as eyes in the Early Classic cylinder corpus and they appear to be Lamat minus the dots. There are four large appliqué dots at the sides of the eyes. This four-part arrangement recalls the quincunx design of the earflares of the monumental images on Structure 5C-2nd, which also carry bosses painted as dots. Framing the eyeholes of the composite effigy is a double-headed serpent in appliqué. This serpent is decorated with punctuated dots. While the double-headed serpent does not exist as such in censer assemblage generally, the motif is suggested by the monumental iconography of Structure 5C-2nd. On the composite, it serves as an expression of the Late Preclassic *caan-ca'an* sky frame of the monumental panels.

The cylinder carries flanges in the earplug position, in this case with four distinct tabs on each side. The use of such flanges is standard in the censer corpus throughout its development and shows a sustained correspondence with panels flanking main masks on architecture. Finally, the whole is decorated with reed punctuation—dots representing the sacred substances: blood, fire, smoke, and water (Freidel 1983). These are the elements of which ritual offerings are composed.

The predominance in the Cerros censer assemblage of the elements comprising the composite effigy strongly suggests that the stack of Venus above sun found on the monumental panels of Structure 5C-2nd (fig. 12; Freidel and Schele, 1988) is represented in the stacked images described above. The monumental panels are a contemporary or slightly later iconographic expression than the composite censer found in the nucleated village at Cerros. Certainly, the cruller is a GIII diagnostic, and this is

Fig. 13 Line drawing of Blood Vision Serpents from the Early Classic Period Hauberg Stela and Late Classic lintels at Yaxchilán (drawing by Linda Schele). The Early Classic serpent is cradled as an object; the Late Classic versions are rising out of the bloodletting bowl.

found on the lower of the two images. Further, as stated above, the use of the sky frame on the composite effigy is suggested by analogy with the monumental frames.

Both the censer and monumental stacks register the iconological principles of transformation. In the case of the facade on Structure 5C-2nd, Freidel and Schele (1988) maintained that the images show the Heroes not only as Venus and the sun, but also as elder brother and younger brother who, through sacrifice, become progenitor and descendant. This transformation perforce envisions the one becoming the other: parent becomes child, and child becomes parent. In the case of the censer assemblage, the transformations that take place are real and material: in the course of the ritual, paper and other material become spattered with sacrificial blood. The bloodied offering is burnt and becomes residue and smoke. The Classic Period depictions of such material transformations were well described by David Stuart (1988), Linda Schele (1976), and others. In these cases (fig. 13), the iconographic expression of the transformation and the ensuing connection with the supernatural world are given in the Blood Vision Serpent (Freidel 1983).

On the Late Preclassic Stela 11, the contents of the burning and smoking offering have been misidentified as interior loops of clay. While this might be one material referent, the icon within the bowl is, in fact, an upended J-scroll-and-bracket motif. This motif represents the orifice of the divine, as identified by Garth Norman (1976) and Jacinto Quirarte (1974). It also represents the sacred blood, fire, smoke, and water as identified by Freidel (1983) on the panels of Structure 5C-2nd. Like the bifurcate and trifurcate variants of the J-scroll-and-bracket motif in the mouths of polymorphs on those panels, the Classic Period depictions of the Blood Vision Serpent are decorated with circles and dots, which Freidel (1986) associated with these sacred liquids.

The direct connection between the cylinders at Cerros and burnt offerings can be seen in the fact that the cutouts of the effigy fragments are smudged by smoke emanating from smoldering fire within them. Finally, a circular blackened smudge was discovered on the threshold of the superstructure on top of Structure 5C-2nd of the same general diameter as the cylinders.

There is a prospect that a "burden" was placed in the stack between the effigy censer bearer and the burnt offering in an open bloodletting bowl above. One clue to this component is seen in the preserved stack in Structure 7-3rd at Santa Rita: the uppermost vessels are a pair of plates inverted lip-to-lip. This pattern is in fact typi-

Freidel et al.

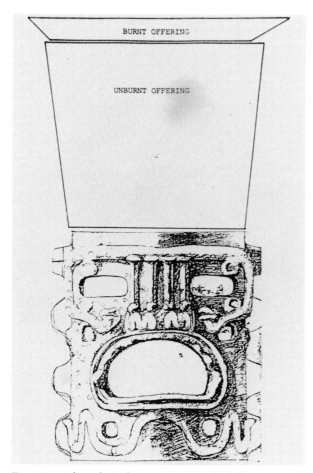

BURNT OFFERING

UNBURNT OFFERING

Fig. 14   A hypothetical reconstruction of a full censer stack at Cerros, based upon in situ *Early Classic Period assemblages found in Structure 4B at Cerros, and Structure 7-3rd at Santa Rita Corozal (drawing by Karim Sadr).*

cal of buried dedicatory offerings in the Maya Lowlands, as, for example, in the case of Late Preclassic cached offerings on the central axis of Structure 5C-1st at Cerros (Freidel 1986). The Early Classic censer stacks found crushed *in situ* on the summit of Structure 4B at Cerros (Freidel 1979) included straight-rimmed buckets with lids. The dedicatory lip-to-lip vessels at Cerros showed no smudging on the interior and presumably contained perishable offerings that either had been previously burnt or were unburnt. One of these caches, at the summit of Structure 5C-1st, contained a single tubular jade bead and flecks of volcanic hematite. It is possible, then, that the most complete stacks of vessels used in ritual contained both offerings to be consumed in fire and offerings to be buried in dedicatory locations within structures (fig. 14).

Conclusion

In the iconology of the ancient Maya, stacking primarily represented transformation of beings and materials from one state to another. It seems likely that the literal transformation of sacrificial offerings from an unburnt, falling (scattered) state to a burnt, rising state was a sign for such symbolic mysteries as the transformation of material things into the divine spirit represented by the Blood Vision Serpent long before the advent of Late Preclassic decorated architecture. It may well have been this sign and this transformational logic that served as the theological armature for the fashioning of a concept of descent and dynasty out of the egalitarian mythos of the Ancestral Heroes.

Beyond Rainstorms: The Kawak as an Ancestor, Warrior, and Patron of Witchcraft

JOANNE M. SPERO
UNIVERSITY OF TEXAS AT AUSTIN

In Classic and Post-Classic Maya iconography, the representation of the Earth Lord, who is also the God of Storms and Lightning in Maya cosmology, is a zoomorph known in contemporary literature as the "Cauac Monster." Its name is derived from its diagnostic markings, which consist of what resemble clustered grapes and the half-circlets or swirls framed by a line of "water" dots that characterize the glyph for Cauac (fig. 1), glyph T528 in J. E. S. Thompson's *A Catalog of Maya Hieroglyphs* (1962:452). Kawak (Cauac) is the nineteenth day name in the sacred round of days in the Tzolkin of Mayan calendrics, and is related to thunderstorms and rain (Thompson 1971:87).

Cognates of the Yucatec word *kawak* as "lightning, thunder" and/or "19th day name" are found in at least twenty-one of the extant Mayan languages. According to Kaufman and Norman (1984:117) the Proto-Mayan word for "lightning" and "thunder" can be reconstructed as *kahoq*. Mayan speakers in the Highlands of Guatemala use the forms *kahoq* (Cakchiquel, Pokomchi), *kawoq* (Ixil, Quiché), *kʸooq* (Mam), or *kaaq* (Kekchi). Among the Cholan and Tzeltalan languages, where Proto-Mayan initial /k/ evolved into an initial /ch/, we find the Tzeltal form *chahwuk* [*chaʔuk*] for "thunder, lightning"; *chauk* in Tzotzil; *chawuk* in Tojolabal and Chuj; *chahk* in Chol; *cháwAk* in Chontal; and *chaak* in Yucatec, Mopan, and Itzá. Yucatec also retains the archaic pronunciation *kawak* for the nineteenth day name, in addition to the borrowed form *chaak*, the Yucatec word for "rain," and the name of their Rain God.

The "Cauac Monster" as a Locale

In 1978, at the Tercera Mesa Redonda de Palenque, Dicey Taylor identified the Cauac Monster as an indicator of a "supernatural locale, such as a cave on the surface of the earth" (Taylor 1978:83), thus dispelling J. Eric Thompson's notion that the Kawak was a celestial dragon associated with the Itzamnas, gods of rain (Thompson 1971:87). Taylor observed that in Classic Maya art, the Kawak zoomorph often functioned as a

Fig. 1 Glyph for Kawak—T528 and variants (redrawn by Joanne Spero from Thompson 1962:452).

Fig. 2 Bonampak Stela 1, detail of the Kawak zoomorph at the base of the stela (drawing by Linda Schele; Schele and Miller 1986:45).

Fig. 3 Palenque, Temple of the Foliated Cross, detail of the Kawak zoomorph on which Chan Bahlum stands (drawing by Linda Schele 1974:54).

pedestal or bench that formed a platform on which rulers or deities stood or sat, and that these creatures or personified bases were always found at ground level, indicating the connection of the Kawak zoomorph with the earth (1978:80).

Some beautifully executed examples of Kawak zoomorphs on which Classic Maya rulers are standing are found at Bonampak on Stela 1 (fig. 2), and on the Temple of the Foliated Cross at Palenque (fig. 3). On codex-style pottery from the Late Classic, deities and rulers sit on Kawak-marked thrones or benches (Taylor 1978: figs. 3, 4, and 5; Robicsek and Hales 1981: fig. 28a). In the Post-Classic Maya codices, God B is occasionally found sitting on Kawak heads (Codex Dresden 34c, 41a, and 66b); and various deities—Gods A, B, C, and E—sit on benches or slabs with Kawak markings

Fig. 4 Rollout photograph of Vase 1377 (photograph copyright Justin Kerr 1980).

Fig. 5 Vase of the Seven Gods (drawing by Michael D. Coe; Coe 1973:107–109).

(Codex Dresden 29b; Codex Madrid 58a, 59a, 99a, and 100a). Temples in the codices sometimes bear the T528 Kawak markings (Codex Dresen 38c; Codex Madrid 11c, 84c, and 96a).

Another context in which Kawak creatures were employed by Classic Maya artisans (Taylor 1978:80–81) was their portrayal as enclosures or niches that framed rulers, seemingly indicating that the scene takes place in a cave, as at Seibal Stela 3, and Piedras Negras Throne 1. On the vase in figure 4, two royal personages sit inside niches or thrones marked with Kawak, as they watch a ritual sacrifice taking place on a Kawak altar. On the Vase of the Seven Gods (fig. 5), God L, a deity associated with the underworld, sits on a jaguar throne inside a frame of multiple Kawak heads (Coe 1973b:107–109). The message conveyed in these contexts is that the protagonists are linked to the powers that lurk in the bowels of the earth.

The Evolution of the Kawak Zoomorph

Carolyn Tate (1980) examined the evolution of the Kawak zoomorph in Mayan art and its connection to vegetation, the earth, God K, and the ancestors and concluded that the Kawak "was a place, the earth or ancestral abode, for the transformation of matter into energy" (Tate 1980:111).

The history of the use of the Kawak as a symbol of the earth, or the Earth Lord, can be traced back to the

Fig. 6 *Chalcatzingo Relief I. The Olmec Earth Lord/Rain God is shown sitting inside of a cave (redrawn by Joanne Spero after Joralemon 1971: fig. 142; original drawing by Michael D. Coe).*

Olmecs (Taylor 1978:81–83; Tate 1980:21–23). Relief I at Chalcatzingo (fig. 6) shows a figure sitting inside a cave or niche. There are clouds dripping rain above the cave, and volutes that symbolize wind, clouds, or mist issue from the mouth of the cave. The cave itself is marked by foliation and crowned by a crossed-bands motif. Of particular importance to this study is the quatrefoil shape of the enclosure or cave, interpreted by Joralemon (1971:49) as the mouth of a jaguar. When compared to Chalcatzingo Relief IX (Joralemon 1971: fig. 141), which shows the open mouth of a beast with a jaguar nose and fangs, it can be seen that the cave is personified as God I of the Olmec pantheon, a jaguar Lord of the Fiery Earth (Joralemon 1971:49, 90).

Classic Maya artisans, like their Olmec forebears, used the quatrefoil niche to represent "an opening between cosmic realms," a yawning chasm in the earth's crust that leads to the underworld (Tate 1980:47). In Maya iconography, one of the earliest appearances of a quatrefoil niche in combination with a Kawak head is found on a peccary skull, dated 8.17.0.0.0, from a Copán tomb (Robicsek and Hales 1981:190). At the top of the skull, two rulers sit on jaguar thrones inside of a quatrefoil cartouche (fig. 7). At their feet is a very early representation of a Kawak head out of which rises the symbol for *pop,* a word meaning "woven mat" in the Mayan languages, and a connotation of royalty. Inside the *pop* symbol and on the Kawak head are T528 clustered circlets. The figures surrounding the cartouche are frequently found in underworld scenes on pottery vessels: a jaguar, a long-lipped humanoid holding a scepter, a monkey, a bird, a skeletal figure, a deer, and a pack of peccaries.

Both Carolyn Tate and Walter F. Morris, Jr., note that in Classic Maya weaving, as in iconography, the quatrefoil shape represents the maw of the Earth Lord. Combined with the *pop* motif, it symbolizes the emergence of ancestors from the underworld. In Classic Maya scenes that accompany accession rites, as on Lintel 25 at Yaxchilán, clothing woven with the "quatrefoil-*pop*" motif was worn to show that the royal ancestors were symbolically present to legitimize the new ruler's ascent to the throne (Morris 1985:75, citing Tate 1980). The association of Kawak with the ancestors was particularly strong, as the "Cauac Monsters regularly occurred in the accession scenes of rulers, especially when mention was made of the parentage of the ruler" (Tate 1980:109).

The Kawak zoomorph achieved Early Classic sophistication on the Tzakol tripod (fig. 8), ca. 9.2.0.0.0 (Tate 1980:36). The top of its head is composed of a partial quatrefoil depression that contains the crossed-bands motif and vegetation, all symbols used by the Olmec to depict the Earth Lord of their era. To this, the Maya added their own visual information, constructing a zoomorphic face whose forehead, nose, and teeth are clearly marked with the T528 (Kawak) clustered grapes and dotted swirls.

The theme of Kawak as Earth Lord was perpetuated at

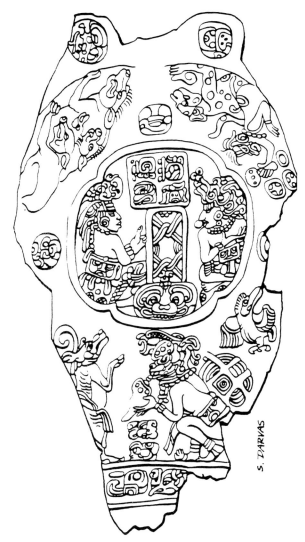

Tikal. On the periphery of Tikal's Altar 4, ca. 9.4.0.0.0, an old god or ancestor reaches out from the underworld through a quatrefoil niche with a bowl of offerings or bloodletting implements in his outstretched hand. The niches alternate with long-nosed zoomorphs marked with the Kawak circlets (Tate 1980:40).

According to Carolyn Tate's investigation, throughout the Early and Middle Classic the Maya portrayed the Cauac Monster with variations from site to site, but in each case its function was the same: "it indicated a place below the acceding ruler where his ancestors dwelt and from where they conferred their power and legitimacy" (Tate 1980:52). The use of the Kawak zoomorph on Mayan monuments underwent a hiatus from ca. 9.8.0.0.0 to 9.13.0.0.0, when Chan Bahlum began commemorating his ancestral bloodline in stone on the monuments of the Cross Group at Palenque (Tate 1980: 52–55). At the same time (9.13.0.0.0), Stela 1 was erected at Bonampak (Tate 1980:57). The Kawak head on which the ruler stands (cf. fig. 2) has an ancestral figure, or perhaps the Maize God (Schele and Miller 1986:45), looking up from the cleft in its forehead, and two similar profiles emanating from the upper corners of its ear assemblages.

Other depictions of the Kawak zoomorph on monumental art in the Late Classic include Machaquilá Stela 13, 9.14.0.0.0, Copán Stela B, 9.15.0.0.0, and Altar M at Copán. From the terminal Classic is Seibal Stela 3, 9.19.0.0.0. (For a comprehensive chronology of the Cauac Monster in Maya iconography, see Tate 1980.)

Possibly the last use of the Kawak visual complex carved in stone at Palenque, dated 9.16.0.0.0, according to Tate (1980:67) was the Creation Tablet (fig. 9). The figure on the left side, probably a ruler, is marked with *ahaw* on his belt and pectoral, with Venus on his cheek, and is holding a serpent-hafted axe. The figure on the right wears a GI headdress (the shell diadem with crossed bands) and is marked with half-quatrefoils. Both sit on glyphoid Kawak heads inside quatrefoil cartouches. The figure with the GI headdress seated within a quatrefoil, with volutes curling outward from his mouth, is visually reminiscent of the Olmec depiction of the Earth Lord/Rain God on Chalcatzingo Relief I (cf. fig. 6).

The Modern Kawak: Cave Dweller, Ancestor, Patron of Warfare and Witchcraft

Far from being an idea of the past, the Kawak still has a place in contemporary Maya cosmology. Known as *chauk* [*?anhel*] among the Tzotzil, he is the Earth Lord and Lord of Lightning. In some communities, *chauk*, as Lord of Lightning, is subservient to *yahval balamil*, the Earth Lord, while in others no distinction is made between the two deities, and their names are interchangeable (Laughlin 1969:177). As Earth Lord, the *chauk* lives in mountain caves, from which he controls the rain clouds and discharges thunder and lightning bolts. His underworld quarters can be approached through openings in the

Fig. 7 Carved peccary skull from Copán Tomb 1 (reprinted with permission from Robicsek 1972:143; copyright Francis Robicsek 1972).

Fig. 8 Tzakol Tripod (drawing courtesy Carolyn Tate, 1980:36).

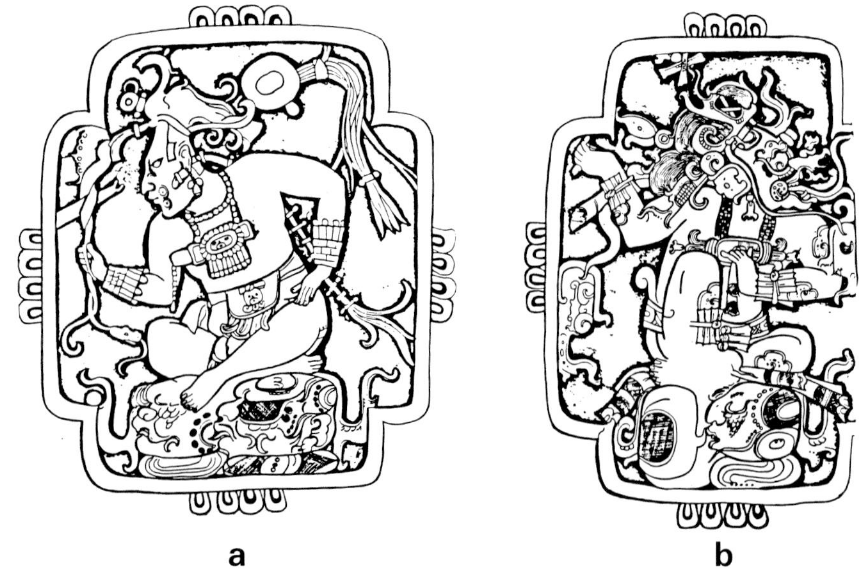

Fig. 9 (a) Palenque Creation Tablet (left side), portrait of a ruler; (b) Palenque Creation Tablet (right side), GI of the Palenque Triad (drawings by Linda Schele).

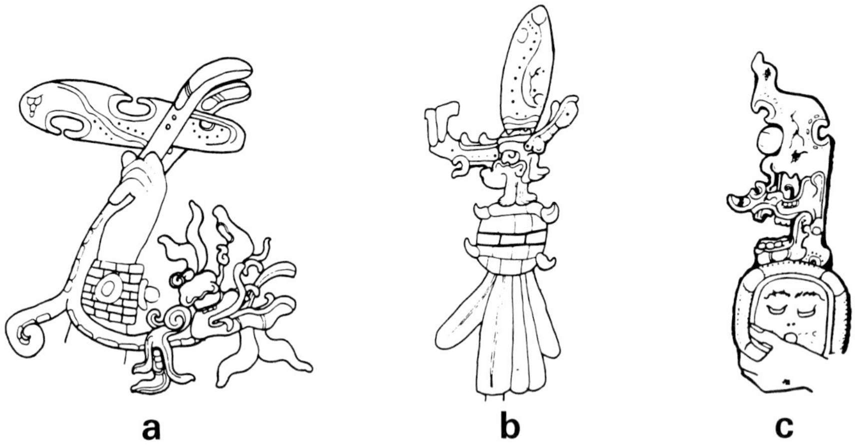

a   b

Fig. 10 Classic Maya weapons with Kawak markings at Palenque: (a) Tablet from Dumbarton Oaks, detail, Kawak axe (after Schele 1974:52, fig. 13b); (b) Temple of the Cross, detail, Kawak spear (after Schele 1974:52, fig. 13a); (c) Tablet of the Slaves, detail, shield and eccentric flint personified with Kawak markings (after Schele 1974:52, fig. 12b; drawings courtesy Linda Schele).

a   b   c

earth's crust called *ch'enetik*—caves, waterholes, and limestone sinks—which are considered to be both sacred and dangerous (Vogt 1969:302, 387). He is the guardian of the animal spirits of the people, called *naguales* in Spanish, and *chanul* or *wayhel* in Tzotzil. These animal spirits are kept by the Earth Lord *chauk* in innermountain corrals, and among them the jaguar is the most powerful. The ancestors (*totilme?iletik*) are another faction that lives in caves inside the mountains (Walter F. Morris, Jr., personal communication, 1986).

Accordingly, in contemporary Tzeltal cosmology, the ancestors (*me?tik tatik*), the naguales, and the *tatik cha?uk* (the Lord of Lightning, or *rayo*) live together in sacred caves that overlook the communities. The *rayo* lives in the deepest parts of these caves, in places where common men dare not approach because they would run the risk of having their soul captured and of losing their life (Hermitte 1970:34, 38–39).

In contemporary Mayan languages, the Kawak is referred to as the collective father or grandfather. For example, in Chol, the *chahk* is called *lak mam*, "our grand-

father" (Hopkins and Josserand 1985). The Tzeltal of Amatenango (Tzo?ontahal) call him *tatik cha?uk*, "our father lightning" (Nash 1970:141). In Jacaltec he is *komam k'uh*, "our grandfather lightning" (Day 1971).

These current beliefs reflect what studies of Classic Maya iconography (Taylor 1978; Tate 1980) tell us of the Precolumbian Kawak: it lived in caves in the underworld that could be approached through openings in the earth's crust (the quatrefoil niche) and it was associated with the ancestral bloodline and with the ancestors (who also lived in the underworld).

Iconography, linguistics, and folklore show that there is a historical connection between the Kawak and warfare. On Classic Maya monuments, axes, spears, and eccentric flints are sometimes marked with T528 at Palenque, as shown in figure 10, and at Naranjo (Stela 30) and Yaxchilán (Lintel 45). Axes and spears marked with Kawak are also found on pottery vessels (cf. Robicsek and Hales 1981:116 and Coe 1978:67–68).

Among the Mayan languages having linguistic associations between Kawak and weapons, we find that in

Yucatec the term for "flint" is *bat chaak*, the axe of the Rain God *chaak* (Barrera Vásquez 1980:39). In Lacandón, *u ya?ax baat hahanak'uh* is "lightning, the axe of the Rain God" (Bruce 1979:334). Quiché has the word *ch'ab*, which means "thunderbolt, ray, shaft, arrow, blade, glass, and lance" (Edmonson 1965:19). The Kekchi have *xmaal kaaq*, meaning "the axe of the ancestors" (Sedat 1955:104). These are the axe-shaped celts believed to be thrown to the earth by lightning (Robicsek 1978:61, citing Sedat, personal communication). In Chol, "obsidian" is called *hacha lak mam*, "axe of our grandfather," since it is thought to be produced by lightning (Aulie and Aulie 1978:61).

The belief that lightning is the protector of the community and the crops is found among the Tzeltal (Hermitte 1970:90–91), the Tzotzil (Guiteras-Holmes 1961: 290–291), the Chol (Aulie and Aulie 1978:46), the Tojolabal (Ruz 1982:196–197), and the Jacaltec (Montejo 1984). In historical records, accounts of lightning used in battle date back to the colonial documents, the *Annals of the Cakchiquels* (Recinos and Goetz 1953: 102), and the *Título de Totonicapán* (Carmack and Mondloch 1983:222, 253).

In modern folklore, there are many tales that narrate the use of lightning in battle. One story that names lightning as the patron of warfare is the epic Jacaltec folktale entitled *El Kanil, Man of Lightning*, published in 1984 by Victor Montejo, a native Jacaltecan (brief versions of this story are also published in La Farge and Beyers 1931). According to legend, Kanil was one of the "first fathers" of Jacaltecans, the chief of the four year-bearers, and the patron of the *k'uh winaj*, or "lightning men." When the Jacaltecans were pressed into battle to fight a foreign enemy, the sorcerers of the town volunteered to be the army, because they were *naguales* who could become serpents, jaguars, biting toads, poisonous flies, shrewd foxes, and rabid dogs. They chose two young boys as their porters. One of the porters, a lad named Xuwan, had little confidence in the effectiveness of sorcerers and feared for their lives. So one night, he went to the mountain homes of the various *k'uhs*, the "lightning man/gods" who were the guardians of Xajla? (Jacaltenango). Finally, the *k'uh* Kanil agreed to give Xuwan the power of lightning, and made him a *k'uh winaj*. In turn, Xuwan converted the other porter, Juan, into a lightning man. When the band of sorcerers met the enemy, it was Xuwan, Juan, and a third lightning man from Chiapas who won the battle by striking at the enemy with their lightning (Montejo 1984:23–61).

Beliefs concerning *naguales* have some antiquity in the Maya region. In the Popol Vuh of the Quiché Maya (Edmonson 1971:233), the cacique Q'uq' Kumatz was a *nawal ahaw* (*naval ahav*, a "nagual lord"), who traveled between the sky and the underworld and transformed himself into a serpent, a jaguar, an eagle, and a pool of blood. He used his sorcery to fight his enemies. Another Quiché document, the *Título de Totonicapán* (ca. 1554), records the magical powers (or *naguales*) used in pre-

Conquest battles by the Quichés. The supernatural powers they summoned were *ch'abi q'aq'*, "flaming arrow or fireball"; *kaq tikax*, "red flint"; *kaq'ulja*, "lightning"; *uk'ux kaj*, "heart of heaven"; and *kaj eqam*, "the four year-bearers" (Carmack and Mondloch 1983:12, 149, 253). In the Chiapas area, the existence of *naguales* was mentioned by Fray Núñez de la Vega, bishop of Chiapas at the turn of the eighteenth century, who wrote of the "poder de ciertos individuos de transformarse en tigres, leones, bolas de fuego, y rayos" (Hermitte 1970:87).

In the Tzeltal community of Pinola (Villa las Rosas), everyone has at least three *naguales*, but the most powerful members of the community, the *me?iltatil* (mothers-fathers) may have up to thirteen. Common people have *naguales* that are not very strong, such as hens, coyotes, or hawks. *Brujos* (*ak'chameletik*) might be jaguars, monkeys, deer, or bulls. But the most powerful of all *naguales*, those of the *me?iltatil*, are lightning, meteors (balls of fire or comets), and whirlwinds (Hermitte 1970:7, 45–49).

Today in Pinola, individuals whose top *nagual* is lightning are called *hombres rayos*. They are warriors extraordinaire because they can fly so high that they are practically immune from harm. It is their job to protect the community and the crops from the attacks of evil winds or malicious *brujos* (*ak'chameletik*), and to punish those who deviate from the norms of society (Hermitte 1970: 140). Their power is derived from the *chahwuk*, who among the Tzeltal of Tzo?ontahal (Amatenango del Valle) is called *tatik cha?uk* (our father lightning), and is the patron of curing and witchcraft (Hermitte 1970:90–91; Nash 1970:141).

Ethnographic evidence shows that among the Maya today there is a strong relationship among curing, witchcraft, and the Kawak cult of the caves. Traditionally, *tatik cha?uk* was the prototype of the old curers in Tzo?ontahal. From his caves he controlled the rains and sent destructive lightning bolts. The curers were his intermediaries. Today the syncretic counterpart of *tatik cha?uk* is a saint called Tatik Martil, whose symbol is a cross. It is said that only those who know how to cast spells can speak with him. He is the one people go to when they want to make illness. (The Tzeltal word for *brujo*, "evil sorcerer," is *ak'chamel*; *ak'*, "to cast," and *chamel*, "illness or death.") Conversely, Tatik Martil is also petitioned for protection from evil (Nash 1970:13, 16, 141, 205).

Among the Tzotzil of Zinacantan, the *h?iloletik*, "seers," and the *totilme?iletik*, "mothers-fathers" (the political-religious leaders of the community), pray to the *chauk/* Earth Lord at shrines marked with crosses at the entrances to caves or at waterholes. The *chauk* and the ancestors are asked to send rain and to protect the crops and the community. If a person should become ill, the cause is thought to be supernatural. Perhaps his animal spirit has been let out of the corral as a type of punishment, or lightning could have knocked out a part of his soul. Possibly the person has fallen and lost his soul. If this has happened, it is thought that the soul has stayed in the earth, in the custody of the *chauk*; if it is not released, the victim will die. The *h?iloletik* go to the special caves or other sacred openings in the earth's crust where they can petition the *chauk*/Earth Lord to release the soul (Vogt 1966:360, 365, 1969:301).

Similar beliefs exist among the Chol, except that their Lord of Earth and Water is the *ahaw* who lives in caves. During curing ceremonies, the spirit of a *xwuht* (*curandero*) enters a cave to talk to the *ahaw* in order to convince him to release the victim's soul (Whittaker and Warkentin 1965:135–138). The *ahaw* is said to be the companion of the devil, whose name is *xiba*. *Xiba* is also a Chol word for the type of *brujo* that casts evil spells (Aulie and Aulie 1978:28–92, 136).

According to Mexican anthropologist Mario Ruz, Tojolabal *hombres rayos*, "lightning men," receive their power from the *chawuk* of the caves, as do the *hombres rayo* of the Tzeltal. However, among the Tojolabal, there are two types of lightning men: the *yaxal chawuk*, "green lightning," who guards the community and the crops, practices curing, and converts himself into lightning to attract rain; and the *takin chawuk*, "dry lightning," who is an evil sorcerer or *pukuh*, *brujo*, in league with the *niwan pukuh*, "great *brujo* or devil," the lord of the underworld, who is also a cave dweller (Ruz 1982:56, 63–65).

There are several codex-style vessels photographed by Justin Kerr and published in *The Maya Book of the Dead* (Robicsek and Hales 1981:22–24) that show an underworld scene in which it appears that a jaguar/child is being sacrificed by GI. The scene in the Metropolitan Museum Pot (fig. 11) has been interpreted as an illustration of the passage in the Popol Vuh in which the Hero Twins sacrifice one another in front of the Lords of Xibalba (Edmonson 1971:137). GI, who is said to be Hunahpu of the Popol Vuh in the act of sacrificing his brother Xbalanque, is shown holding a disk marked with God C, and wielding an axe. The "baby jaguar" has

been identified as GIII of the Palenque Triad, or Xbalanque of the Popol Vuh. The Kawak zoomorph is the sacrificial altar (Robicsek and Hales 1981:40–41; Schele and Miller 1986:271, 274).

In the light of ethnohistoric data and contemporary ethnography, I propose a somewhat different interpretation of the scenes in this series of pots. Clearly, the scene takes place in the underworld, or Xibalba, as indicated by the presence of the Kawak zoomorph altar. GI and the Death Lord face each other from opposite sides of the Kawak, and appear to be fighting for possession of the baby jaguar. The baby jaguar is portrayed as either falling onto or entrapped in the curved appendages of the Kawak, and he is in a state of transformation between a human and a jaguar. This recalls another passage in the Popol Vuh, when Q'uq' Kumatz, the *nawal ahaw*, transformed himself into a jaguar (among other forms) and, in so doing, stayed for a week in Xibalba (Edmonson 1971:233).

The scenes in the vessels shown in figures 11–16 are suggestive of sorcery. It may be that the baby jaguar is the animal soul of the ruler for whom the pot was commissioned. In life, the ruler may have been the embodiment of GIII, so in death his soul appears as an aspect of GIII, the baby jaguar, which has fallen into the underworld and is now at the mercy of GI and the Death Lord, who are the sorcerers. These scenes may depict an afterdeath ritual in which the outcome of the battle between GI and the Death Lord determines the fate of the soul.

GI, who holds weapons marked with Kawak and takes the pose of a warrior, seems to be affiliated with the Kawak. The personified flint disk-blade that he carries is the God C head that is part of the muzzle of the Kawak zoomorph. Often the disk is marked with the T528 Kawak markings, as though it might be a conflation of God C and the Kawak. Since God C is found in other contexts on the "world tree" (cf. Palenque TFC) and on the loincloths of rulers (Naranjo Stela 28 is one example) and is associated with blood sacrifice, the God C disk

Fig. 11   The Metropolitan Museum Pot. Rollout photograph, #521 (copyright Justin Kerr 1979).

Fig. 12   Vase #1003. Rollout photograph (copyright Justin Kerr 1979).

Fig. 13   Vase #1152. Rollout photograph (copyright Justin Kerr 1980).

Fig. 14   Vase #1370. Rollout photograph (copyright Justin Kerr 1984).

would appear to be a symbol of the sacred essence of life, the regenerative fluid of the universe, the "cosmic sap"— blood, water, semen, and the sap of vegetation. It is also a sacrificial blade; the blood of sacrifice is a regenerative liquid. GI, by virtue of his stance as an opponent of the Death Lord, and by the emblems that he carries, fulfills the dual office of sacrificer and regenerator.

His glyphic name in three of these scenes is T16:556, or *yax naab* (figs. 13, 17, 18). This reading is derived from the combination of T16, *yax,* and the T556, an

Fig. 15   Vase #1644. Rollout photograph (copyright Justin Kerr 1984).

Fig. 16   Vase #1815. Rollout photograph (copyright Justin Kerr 1980).

imix with a darkened circle that represents a water lily, and is read as *naab. Naab* (or *nahg*) also means "lake or ocean" in the Tzeltalan languages, and "rain" in Jacaltec, Chuj, and Kanjobal (Schele 1979:14, 16). Twice (figs. 17–18), the *yax naab* epithet is followed by the head variant for GI of the Palenque Triad, which, because it is sometimes appended with the glyph for the phoneme /ki/ (T102), is read as *chak* (Linda Schele, personal communication, 1986), giving GI the title of Yax Naab Chak: "Green Water Chak," or "Green Rain Chak."

In the present era, there are lightning men or *naguales* of *rayos* in the Tzeltal area who are called *yaxal chahwuk* (Basauri 1931:115; Slocum and Gerdel 1976:93). As mentioned earlier, the Tojolabal *yaxal chahwuk* is a lightning man whose office is to protect the community by fighting the forces of evil. In the Chilam Balam of Chumayel, a "Yaxal Chak" is mentioned three times (Roys 1967:77, 133, 151). His name is written both as Yaxal Chak and as Yax Haal Chak, which translates as "Green Rain Chak." The word *yaxal* may be an ellipsis of the two words *yax* and *haal.* The word for "water" in most Mayan languages is *ha?.* In the Yucatecan and Greater Tzeltalan languages, the word for "rain" is usually *ha?* or *ha?al.* In the Mayan languages of Guatemala, the word for "rain" is *nab', hab'al,* or *hab'* (Schele 1979:14).

Because the word for "rain" is *ha?al* in some Mayan languages, and *nahb'* in others, it may be that the Yax Naab Chak title for GI found particularly on these Classic Maya vases is essentially the same epithet that is

Fig. 17   Vase #1815, detail of the Yax Naab Chak title for GI, T16:556, 1011 (copyright Justin Kerr 1986).

Fig. 18   Vase #1644, detail of the Yax Naab Chak title for GI, T16:556, 1011:102 (copyright Justin Kerr 1986).

given to the *yaxal chahwuk* of the contemporary Maya, and that GI in this guise is the prototype of the *hombre rayo*, the lightning man still found today among the Maya of Chiapas and Guatemala.

In figures 11–16, Yax Naab Chak (GI) is shown in cosmic battle with the Death Lord. It is my opinion that these scenes depict a ritual that is repeated in current practices: when a person becomes ill, it is because his animal soul or *nagual* has become separated from him and has fallen (or has been sent by sorcery) to the underworld, where it is kept in the custody of the Kawak who lives in caves. The family of the victim petitions a *curandero* who is capable of magically entering the cave and fighting the evil *brujo* who has cast a curse on the victim. Unless the soul is released, the one whose soul is trapped in the underworld will die. In these scenes, Yax Naab Chak (GI) is the prototype of the Tojolabal and Tzeltal *yaxal chahwuk* and the Chol *xwuht*. The Death Lord is the prototype of the evil sorcerers: the Tojolabal *takin chawuk*, or *pukuh*, the Tzeltal *ak'chamel*, and the Chol *xiba*. The baby jaguar represent the ruler whose soul has gone to the underworld. In life the ruler may have been a *nagual* jaguar and the embodiment of GIII; in death his soul has become the Jaguar Sun of the underworld.

Conclusion

It can be seen that the Kawak was a multidimensional concept. Kawak was (and still is) conceived of as a spirit of underworld caverns, the Lord of Earth and Water, and the guardian of the ancestors. He is considered to be an ancestor himself, since he is called *lak mam* (Chol), "our grandfather," *tatik chawuk* (Tzeltal), "our father lightning," and *komam k'uh* (Jacaltec), "our grandfather lightning." Because men petition for his powers in battle, and Kawak symbols adorn their weapons, he is the patron of warriors. Lightning men, whose prototype was the axe-wielding GI (Yax Naab Chak) on codex-style pottery, derive their supernatural powers of good and evil from the kawak; as such he is the patron of witchcraft and curing.

Aspects of Impersonation in Classic Maya Art

ANDREA STONE
UNIVERSITY OF WISCONSIN–MILWAUKEE

The importance of impersonation—in which ritualists disguise themselves as supernatural, animal, or human characters—cannot be overstated as a contributing factor in the evolution of Mesoamerica. It was an adaptive strategy for the consolidation of power in the political arena and at the same time held a profound philosophical meaning for those who practiced and watched these performances. Impersonation signaled the presence of the sacred to such an extent that as an act, by itself, it held sacred meaning. Townsend (1979:28) found that the Nahuatl expression for impersonator, *teixiptla*, encompasses a broader range of objects, such as effigies and ritual costume, whose common denominator is that they all manifest the divine. This high esteem in which the Aztecs held the living impersonator comes to life in a handsome portrayal of Ehecatl-Quetzalcoatl (fig. 1). The naturalistic zoomorphic body of a writhing serpent seems to portray the "real" Quetzalcoatl incarnate; yet no attempt is made to hide the fact that the head is that of an impersonator of Ehecatl, Quetzalcoatl's Wind God avatar. On the contrary, this point is emphasized. A clear signal is sent that the act of impersonating the god was esoterically as meaningful as the god's holy presence. In addition, by impersonating gods, human beings could interject their presence in supernatural affairs. Thus, impersonation provided a powerful interface with the sacred.

Since impersonation allows humans to assume the attributes and sacred powers of the gods, it has a central role in the formation of stratified societies whose political power rests on the divine nature of their leaders. From a political standpoint, impersonation provides a strategy for supporting claims of divinity and wielding supernatural powers—claims that cannot be substantiated through mundane logic and discourse. Such claims rest on a metalanguage of ritual and symbol, which by its sanctity circumvents tests of rational proof (Rappaport 1971:30). Within an ideological system of the divine, impersonation, by its concrete nature of being sensible to sight, gives an illusion of empirical reality, making it

Fig. 1 *Ehecatl-Quetzalcoatl impersonator (The Cleveland Museum of Art, purchase from the J. H. Wade Fund).*

particularly useful in manufacturing the sacred context in which political leaders want to place themselves.

In fact, the rise of complex societies in Mesoamerica can be directly linked to the development of impersonation cults and the rise of divine right political systems. There also seems to be a correspondence between the level of social complexity and the complexity of the impersonation tradition. Complexity (e.g., the number of beings impersonated, the richness of the iconographic system used to accomplish this end, and the complexity of referential levels) contributes to the persuasive powers of an impersonation tradition, weaving a thick symbolic web that renders it invulnerable to logical attack.

The artistic evidence suggests that pre-Olmec art is poorly represented in terms of humans dressing as supernaturals or animal-deities. Indeed, the art of Xochipala, which may be the first developed pre-Olmec artistic tradition, consists largely of naturalistic portraits with little concern for symbolic costume (Gay 1972:21). It can be surmised that the Olmec impersonation cult, seen in the wearing of elaborate masks and donning of supernatural attributes, reflects the consolidation of rulership based on associating the elites with cosmic powers. In Mesoamerica impersonation was an important component in the rise of complex societies, and its consequent unprecedented elaboration shows the continuing support it provided as a basis of ritual and power. I might go so far to say that the success or failure of a political system in Mesoamerica was closely tied to the sophistication of its impersonation tradition.

Impersonation in the Maya Area

In the past, as today, impersonation flourished in the Maya area and seems to have held the prestige that we see in Aztec society. An important component of impersonation paraphernalia, masks were held in high regard by the Maya. Figures wearing masks and costumes "X-ray" fashion on Maya vases and on stelae convey a sense of great power (see Robicsek and Hales 1982: no. 3 and Yaxchilán Stela 11). As pointed out to me by Matthias Strecker (personal communication, 1986), Maya caves have yielded both a wooden mask (Strecker, in press) and several carved in stone (Navarette and Martínez 1977: figs. 6 and 7). In light of the sacred nature of caves for the Maya, these masks must have been held in high esteem. Colonial Maya literature reveals that the gods frequently donned masks (Thompson 1970:277; Edmonson 1985:262). In the Madrid Codex and on Maya polychrome vessels the gods are shown carving masks, as well.

The best candidate for a word expressing the idea of impersonator in Maya languages is also the word that means mask, *k'oh*. This word (or a cognate) is recorded in numerous Maya dictionaries.

Yucatec: *koh (k'oh): carátula o máscara; el que está en lugar de otro, que es su teniente y represente su persona.* [Martinez Hernandez 1929:519]

Mopan: *c'ooj (k'ooh): máscara.* [Ulrich and Ulrich 1976:62]

Cholti: *choh: máscara.* [Moran 1935:43]

Tzotzil: *c'oj or c'ojil (k'oh or k'ohil): máscara.* [Hurley and Ruíz 1978:32]

Tzeltal: *c'oj (k'oh): máscara.* [Slocum and Gerdel 1976:73]

Mocho: *k'oh: máscara.* [Kaufman 1967:78]

Quiché: *qoh (q'oh): máscara de teatro.* [Brasseur de Bourbourg 1862:211]

In colonial Yucatec dictionaries *k'oh* is defined in the most complete terms and means representative, substitute, an image or figure that stands in for something else (Barrera Vásquez 1980:27), which seems close to the idea of impersonator. In Quiché the word *q'oh* is incorporated into the word for "custom" as *q'ohlem* (Brasseur de Bourbourg 1862:211).

For the Maya, impersonation could be viewed as an act of literal transformation, an event of supernatural significance. An observation by Thomas Gage (Thompson 1958:247) bears witness to this fact. Upon hearing confession from Highland Guatemalan Indians just prior to their impersonation in a religious dance drama, he commented: "When I lived among them, it was an ordinary thing for the one who in the dance was to act St. Peter or John the Baptist to come first to confession, saying they must be holy and pure like that saint, whom they represent, and prepare themselves to die."

Switching Gender and Status Roles

The Classic Maya elite engaged in one form of impersonation that involved switching gender and status roles. This tradition of what might be termed "social impersonation" is well attested in Maya culture. Characters portrayed in colonial and modern festival dramas quite often fall into such a category. Bricker (1973:215) reported that masquerading as women is one of the major themes of ritual humor in the Maya area. According to Cogolludo (1867–1868:I, 300), in the early colonial period actors dressed up in the white robes of priests, suggesting a form of social parody.

Recognizing social impersonation in Classic Maya art may be difficult, because it is less obvious than donning the grotesque attributes of the gods. Hieroglyphic texts and analysis of complex iconography often provide the necessary clues. One case, demonstrated by Linda Schele (1984a), showed that the Orator and Scribe Tablets from Palenque portray elite Palencano males impersonating captives. They are "bound" with loosely hanging strips of cloth and seem to be engaged in autosacrifice.

Another case of role switching is seen in the Maya ruler taking on the persona of women, the subject on which I wish to focus. This is an extremely important aspect of the Maya impersonation cult: it draws attention to the significant role of fertility in Maya kingship. It is my view that in Maya kingship the traditional fertility role of women was appropriated and relexified through the symbol system, especially the bloodletting complex, so that it appeared to belong "naturally" to the male ruler. Social impersonation was a primary means of accomplishing this transferal.

Schele brought up one case in point in regard to the bloodletting ceremony. She stated that in shedding blood Maya kings were fulfilling the female role of nurturer. She pointed out that Chan Bahlum is called, glyphically, the "mother" (T1.I:606:23) of the gods in the Cross

Fig. 2 Temple of the Inscriptions, Palenque, Pier C (after Robertson 1983: fig. 39).

39. Pier C.

Group inscriptions (1978a). Similarly, David Stuart (1988) showed that in a glyphic text from Dos Pilas (Stela 25), the ruler is said to have "given birth" (T740) to the Paddler Gods through the bloodletting act. We might recall that, in ancient Greek mythology, Zeus gave birth to Athena through his skull. Such male parthenogenic acts impute a nonexistent level of creative ability that greatly enhances the illusion of cosmic powers.

Another form of assuming the guise of women can be seen in the male ruler's association with the holding of children. This is infrequently shown in Maya art, though it is much more emphatic in Olmec art, as noted below. Men are shown holding children in their arms at Bonampak (Room I mural), at Palenque (fig. 2) on the

Temple of the Inscriptions piers,[1] and occasionally on polychrome ceramics (fig. 5 below).

The Ceremonial Bar

The image of infant holding is relevant to the image of the ruler holding the ceremonial bar (fig. 3), another form of social impersonation.

The ceremonial bar first appears in recognizable form in Lowland Maya art in the Classic Period, the earliest known examples being Stela 29 from Tikal (292 A.D.) and the Leiden Plaque (320 A.D.; fig. 3). Two methods of holding the bar, either horizontally or diagonally, already appear at this time, as do the flexible and stiff bar,

196

Fig. 3 Leiden Plaque (after Schele and Miller, 1986: pl. 33b).

so it is not clear if one or the other has priority. Many of these early renditions show a flexible bar formed from the body of a serpent, especially in the Early Classic Period. The flexible bar appears on the Leiden Plaque, Calakmul Stelae 9 and 28, and Tulum Stela 1, among

other examples, and is particularly prevalent at Copán, appearing on the earliest stela, Stela 35, as well as on Stelae 1, 2, 3, 4, 5, 6, 7, I, N (north), and P.

The association of the ceremonial bar with serpents seems quite certain. In searching for antecedents to the ceremonial bar in the Guatemala Highlands, where we find many precursors to Lowland Maya art, the best parallel can be found in Abaj Takalik Stela 5, dated by Long Count to 8.4.5.17.11 (Graham, Heizer, and Shook 1978:92 and plate 3). This sculpture is the closest to the Lowland Maya style of any Highland Preclassic sculpture; as can be seen by the date, it is close in time to the earliest Lowland inscriptions. The right-hand figure exhibits the bent arms and "crab-claw" hand position associated with carrying the ceremonial bar, but what he holds is a serpent, which, though lacking detail, is unmistakable.

In Lowland Maya art the flexible bar takes the form of a two-headed serpent with the body bearing serpent markings and/or divided into segments (fig. 3). Polychrome vases show a serpent flowing out of the ends of the rigid ceremonial bar (Robicsek and Hales 1981: vessel 6 and other unpublished examples). The rigid bar sometimes bears sky band markings, an excellent example appearing on Toniná Monument 20 (fig. 4). These data strongly suggest that the ceremonial bar, especially in its beginning "ophidian" stages, was an embodiment of the serpent/sky homophony. This idea seems to be generally accepted by scholars. In more specific terms, Freidel and Schele (1988) suggested that the ceremonial bar drew its inspiration from sky images on Preclassic decorated pyramids (J-scrolls brackets plus serpents). On Stela N from Copán the north side shows a flexible bar with serpent segments and the south side shows a rigid bar. This suggests a substitutional equivalence for the flexible serpent bar and the rigid bar at quite a late date, 9.16.10.0.0.

Now, why would a Maya ruler want to show himself holding the sky? The fact that the sky is held is important to the meaning of the ceremonial bar and distinguishes it from the function of a sky band, which primarily conveys spatial information. The manner in which the bar is held, usually horizontally, lying across both arms, suggests the act of guardianship, reminiscent of the way an infant is held.

The Yucatec Maya make a conceptual distinction between holding a child in the arms, as the ceremonial bar is held, and carrying a child astride the hip. In addition, in Highland Maya languages there are specific words for carrying a child in the arms, notably *chel* in Quiché (Brasseur de Bourbourg 1862:176) and *cheleh tu* in Cakchiquel (Saenz de Santa Maria 1940:85). In Yucatán the distinction is marked by the Hetzmek ceremony, celebrated when a child is three or four months of age. The ceremony marks a rite of passage for the child, who is carried astride the hip and at the same time ritually passes out of a stage of infantile helplessness. As de-

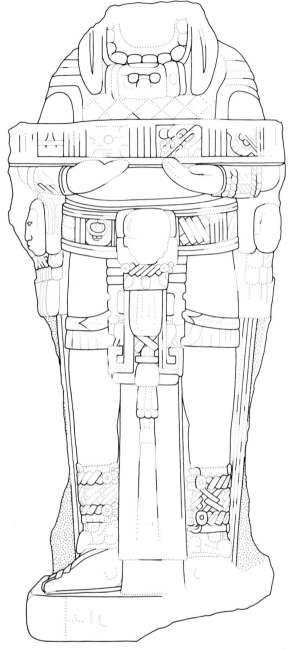

Fig. 4 *Toniná Monument 20 (after Mathews 1983a: fig. 6:54; courtesy Peabody Museum, Harvard University).*

scribed by Redfield and Villa Rojas (1962:189), "The ritual is supposed to awaken the physical and intellectual faculties of the child and make him useful for the future." Objects are placed on a table that will be instrumental in the future life of the child; they vary according to the child's sex. Common objects are a book, pencil, hatchet, food, and money. They are introduced into the child's hand by the godparents, who circumambulate around the room holding the child astride the hip.

Prior to the Hetzmek the child is carried in both arms by the parents. Presumably this manner of support is associated with a "pre-Hetzmek" stage of infantile helplessness. I propose that this association was made by the Maya in carrying the ceremonial bar. The structure of my argument is straightforward. The ruler holds the "sky" in the form of a ceremonial bar in the pre-Hetzmek fashion. He is being portrayed as assuming supreme parental responsibility, essentially for the celestial cosmic order. Creating such a persona for the ruler—guardian of the cosmic order—was a priority of Proto- and Early Classic iconography. Freidel and Schele (1988) showed this to be true in the carved stucco masks of Cerros. Structure 5C-2nd would position the ruler at the top of a pyramid that meshes a symbolic reference to the motion of Venus and the sun with the actual movement of the sun across the heavens.

In the Early Classic we commonly see GI of the Palenque Triad or the ruler dressed as GI, carrying the Quadripartite Monster headdress. Lounsbury (1985) convincingly argued GI's association with Venus, and Schele (1977) showed that the Quadripartite Monster on one level can be identified with the cyclical sun. The GI/ Quadripartite Monster headdress theme is an astronomical paradigm for kingship that portrays the ruler's responsibility as Venus for the safe cyclical passage of the sun. Holding the ceremonial bar in the pre-Hetzmek fashion essentially expresses the same idea, which might be translated into modern vernacular as "he's got the whole world/sky in his hands." We might note, too, that carrying the ceremonial bar is often coupled with GI impersonation. In a sense, carrying the ceremonial bar or sky is a redundant expression of the ruler as GI carrying the Quadripartite Monster.

If we look at the Leiden Plaque (fig. 3), one of the earliest representations of the ceremonial bar, we see God K and the Sun God popping out of the serpents' maws. These two gods (in the case of the Sun God this may take a variety of substitutional forms, such as the Jaguar God of the underworld) are most commonly associated with the ceremonial bar. It is noteworthy that these two gods are also associated with infants and may take an infantile form.

God K appears as a supine infant glyphically in the texts of the Palenque Cross Group and Palace Tablet. On the piers of the Temple of the Inscriptions from Palenque, Pacal holds the child Chan Bahlum, who is impersonating God K, in the manner of a helpless child (fig. 2). Significantly, one of the most common appearances of GIII, the jaguar sun (Lounsbury 1985) is as a supine helpless infant about to be sacrificed (Robicsek and Hales 1981: vessels 19–26). The figure on El Zapote Stela 5 (9.0.0.0.0) holds a supine jaguar contained within a square cartouche, prefixed by the number twelve and the Mexican year sign. Xultun Stela 10 shows a ruler holding both God K and a jaguar.

I think part of the meaning of these gods associated

Stone

with the ceremonial bar, especially considering that they do take an infantile form on many occasions, is again the notion of guardianship. This idea also accords with the fact that GI is the holder of the bar, that is, the guardian of the other two gods. If we consider a correspondence with the Palenque Triad, GI is the oldest brother, and GI is also the name of the Triad's father (Lounsbury 1985). The idea of showing infantile gods recalls Nancy Farriss's (1984:286) statement that "Mesoamerican gods were like extremely powerful infants . . . likely to go into tantrums and eventually expire if neglected."

The supine infant held in the arms, which I claim is a prototype for the ceremonial bar, is a highly charged image in Maya art. It has multiple levels of meaning, one of the most important being sacrifice. The supine infant in Maya art was so strongly associated with the notion of sacrifice that this posture essentially became emblematic of sacrifice.[2] We know from early colonial sources that the Maya were especially fond of sacrificing children, so much so that they would kidnap them from villages for that purpose (Roys 1943[1972:81]). Archaeologically, infant sacrifices are not uncommon in the Maya area. Petroglyph Cave in Belize revealed now a dried up pool of water where six young children had presumably been submerged (Dorie Reents, personal communication, 1980). Maya art is rife with images of infant sacrificial victims, always supine and often lying in bowls.

This strong association between the supine child and sacrifice is further evidence of the highly charged ritual meaning with which this pose is imbued. We see this again in a painted polychrome cylinder that shows a supine helpless child being held by a Death God (fig. 5). The context is clearly one of sacrifice and again we have a male figure holding the child in this manner. Though the two ideas of holding a helpless child and sacrifice may appear to contradict one another, they really do

not. For both sacrifice and an infant embody the idea of fertility and ritual duty. Furthermore, as discussed earlier, it is through the sacrificial complex that the female domain of infant holding becomes transferred to the male.

It might be expected that the Maya would portray women holding infants in their arms, for is this not part of their special role in child-bearing and rearing? Indeed, Wisdom (1940: note 40) reported that among the Chortí only the women would carry the saints in ritual processions "since it is said only women carry infants both before and after birth."

Yet the only instance of which I am aware of a woman holding a supine infant in Maya art is a Jaina figurine that portrays an elderly woman (fig. 6). I have already stated that holding the supine infant had special ritual, sacrificial status, and the fact that this one example of a woman in Maya art is an aged "grandmother" confirms this observation.

There is abundant evidence from the colonial and modern Maya that old women held any ritual status that could be compared with men. Landa mentioned repeatedly that only old women were allowed to enter the temples and participate in ceremonies (Tozzer 1941: 143, 145, 147, 152). Both Landa and Lopez Medel stated that old women baptized the young girls, while the priest baptized the boys (Tozzer 1941:103, 226). In the celebration in the month of Mol, an old woman called Ix Mol administered blows to the young girls (Tozzer 1941:159).

Thompson (1930:62) reported that among the Kekchi old women are major participants in the ceremony called *tzen huitz*, "the feeding of Huitz." They are the only women to take a role in the ritual portion of this ceremony. Vogt (1969:266) stated that elderly women past menopause, *hchik pometik*, serve in a special ritual capacity to the mayordomos of Zinacantan.

Fig. 5   Rollout of Polychrome Vase (photograph copyright Justin Kerr 1985).

Fig. 6 Jaina figurine (courtesy Heye Collection, Museum of the American Indian, New York).

By restricting the holding of infants to males (or old women), by the association of supine infants with sacrifice, and by the holding of the ceremonial bar, female fertility associated with holding infants was absorbed into the masculine office of kingship.

Fertility and Maya Kingship

A superb rationale for the importance of fertility among male elites was offered by Maurice Bloch (1977). The gist of his argument might be summarized as follows: in order to receive compliance from those subjected to authority, they must believe that they are receiving compensation for their obedience and material support of the ruling hierarchy. This compensation often takes an intangible form, channeled through the belief system, of the ruler's blessing of fertility. These mystical powers appear to be god-given and place the ruler at the center of the natural reproduction cycle.

Bloch (1977:330) also raised the point that powers based on associations with cosmic forces often "link up with the process of nature and its beneficial cyclical aspects, fertility and reproduction." Cyclicality in nature is a redundant, self-manifesting statement of "truth."

Thus, rulers who align themselves through ritual and symbol with natural cycles seek corroboration of their (in fact nonexistent) cosmic powers through truth that is perceived through regular redundant acts and not through logical argument. Repetition, seen in codified ritual or natural phenomena, becomes a corroboration of sacred propositions.

Cyclicality and redundancy were central to the strategy of creating the illusion of cosmic power among the Classic Maya. The astronomical, calendrical, and agricultural cycles became the symbolic and ritual vehicles of kingship. Fertility is at the heart of the agricultural and reproductive cycle, and the Maya were clearly trying to confer an exalted fertility status on the male ruler. Impersonation of the female procreative role, to the exclusion of female portrayals of this theme, was one means of achieving this end.

Social Impersonation in Olmec Art

Many of the patterns outlined here are applicable to the Olmec. An important comparison comes in the theme of the adult male holding a supine infant (e.g., La Venta Altars 2, 3, and 5, San Lorenzo Monuments 12 and 20, and the Las Limas Figure). Joralemon (1981: note 5) brought up the possibility that the infant in Olmec art is related to the Olmec ceremonial bar.[3] Similarities between the Olmec and Maya versions of these themes are: (1) this is the exclusive prerogative of males, (2) with exceptions only being found in old women (Joralemon 1981), (3) the supine infant posture had special ceremonial significance, and (4) the supine infant may also be associated with sacrifice for the Olmec. While most of the infants are not well preserved, that of the Las Limas Figure has a limp, lifeless look.

Chalcatzingo Relief 1 (fig. 7) also recalls these ideas. The main figure holds a symbolically marked box much the same size as a child, as noted by Joralemon (1981: note 5). The importance of rain and agricultural fertility in this scene is quite pronounced. The symbolic markings on the bundle and throne are similar to the cloud-like forms that emerge from the symbolic cave in which the figure sits. The figure, be it male, as I believe, or female as others believe (Joralemon 1981: note 5), could be holding a symbolic representation of rain or weather. This idea ties into the fact that the supine baby god, Joralemon's God IV (1971), has been interpreted as a Rain God (Coe 1973a). For the Olmec, holding the baby God IV associated the ruler with the fertility cycle, an idea also espoused by Grove (1973:134). To speculate along the lines of what we have seen for the Maya, the fertility connections with this image are amplified by the idea of holding a supine baby, a traditionally female activity. The Olmec may have participated in a game of female impersonation, not unlike the Maya, and may even have set the precedent for it. The Olmec, like the ancient Maya, lack a significant artistic tradition of showing women as the bearers of the gift of fertility. In-

Fig. 7   Chalcatzingo Relief 1 (after Coe 1965a: fig. 10).

deed, especially in elite art, this role was reserved for the male ruler. Thus, we see the Olmec and Maya sharing in this important strategy of kingship.

Net Skirt-*Xoc* Fish-Shell Costume as a Male Costume

One other point to raise concerns the netted costume with "*xoc* fish" and shell around the waist, often accompanied by the Quadripartite Monster headdress (fig. 8). This costume is generally referred to as a female costume (J. Miller 1974; Marcus 1976:159), yet it is worn by men, some clear examples being Caracol Stelae 1 and 3, the Time Museum Stela, and Chan Bahlum on the Tablet of the Foliated Cross. Schele (1978a) suggested that these instances may reflect a kind of female impersonation related to the nurturing aspect of blood sacrifice.

Yet I think the idea can be advanced that women wearing this costume are impersonating a male image of power, specifically a view of kingship that iconographically condenses the ruler's connection to the cyclical forces of nature. If specific meanings are sought in an iconographical analysis of the costume, the contexts in which they are found feature male protagonists.

The most common depiction of the "*xoc* fish" and shell motif is on *male* dancing figures, especially seen in Holmul-style pottery and on architectural sculpture from Copán. Karl Taube (1985:178) identified the dancing figure as a representation of the "tonsured young lord" who is a Maize God. Thus, the "*xoc* fish" and shell motif seems to have some connection to a maize complex and a male Maize God. It is not found in any specific way associated with women.

A second important iconographic component usually accompanying this costume consists of the Quadripartite Monster headdress. Iconographically the wearing of the Quadripartite Headdress is associated with the Maya deity GI, whom Lounsbury (1985) has identified as Venus, Hunahpu. The connection of GI to the Quadripartite Monster complex is especially evident in the Early Classic period, on cache vessels, on Stela I from Copán, on Stela 2 from Tikal, and on the superb jade head from Río Azul. This complex can be interpreted in essence as Venus carrying the cyclical sun and a sacrificial bowl. It is a theme of responsibility for the cosmos as expressed through an astronomical paradigm. Both Venus and the ruler who portrays him take responsibility for the astronomical cycle. There is no evidence for any special relevance of these ideas to women.

Fig. 8   Naranjo Stela 31 (after Graham 1978:II, pt. 2, fig. 2:83; courtesy Peabody Museum, Harvard University).

Nor are the components of the so-called female costume found in general thematic contexts relating to women. In fact, the opposite seems to be true. Women shown wearing this costume are more often associated with male activities, and they are always women of great importance, often featured in a cameo stela portrait.

Women who wear the complete costume seem to have had enormous power; they appear to be among the most powerful women we have yet identified from the Classic period. We might start with Lady Zac-Kuk of Palenque. Evidence of her enormous power is seen in the inscriptions of Palenque, where she is noted as having acceded to the throne in 9.8.19.7.18, and celebrated katun endings 9.9.0.0.0 and 9.10.0.0.0 (Mathews and Robertson 1985:16). In her portrait on the Oval Palace Tablet she wears, in addition to the net skirt, "xoc fish," and shell costume, a headdress adorned with Jester Gods, a device usually identifying lordly status (Freidel and Schele 1988). In awarding the royal crown to her son, she is clearly fulfilling a role usually assumed by men.

Another important series of female figures wearing this costume comes from Naranjo, Stelae 24, 29, and 31 (fig. 8). The protagonist can be identified as a woman, Lady Six Sky, who carries the Tikal/Petexbatun emblem glyph. She was the mother of an important Naranjo ruler, Smoking Squirrel (Marcus 1976:60; Closs 1985), and seems to have been especially powerful during the early years of his reign. Her own parentage is given on Stela 24 (E7–D13) and she celebrates the lahuntun 9.13.10.0.0 (St. 24, D15–E18) as well as other royal events. The unusually large quantity of pictorial and epigraphic information about Lady Six Sky suggests that she was a woman of exceptional power. Closs (1985:72) believed that on Stela 31 Lady Six Sky is shown acceding to the throne.

On Stelae 24 and 29 she is shown standing on a bound captive, a type of pose generally reserved for portraits of male rulers going back to the Leiden Plaque. It is a militaristic theme that does not seem to be fostering a female context. In fact, many examples of women wearing this costume have a decidedly military flavor.

We see this in the Cleveland Stela where the woman holds a shield (J. Miller 1974: fig. 2). Stela 28 from Calakmul shows a woman standing on a captive and holding a ceremonial bar (Marcus 1976: fig. 5.5).

There is abundant evidence that women shown wearing the net jade skirt, "xoc fish," and shell costume are carrying out tasks typically associated with men and that they are women of enormous prestige, whose power and status are exceptional. If the costume had a general connection to women, it might be found with secondary women and with specifically female themes.

Ironically, one of the primary themes associated with women wearing this costume is holding the ceremonial bar (fig. 8). Here I believe we witness the complexities of the Maya tradition of social impersonation. We can observe a woman impersonating a male image of power by costume who is impersonating a woman by the underlying meaning of holding the ceremonial bar, that is, fertility and duty associated with holding a helpless infant.

Notes

1. Robertson (1983:35) identified the figure on Pier C, wearing a long beaded net skirt, as Lady Zac-Kuk, Pacal's mother, though she admitted, "Long beaded skirts are known to have been worn by both men and women [at Palenque]." A case in point is the series of crypt figures from Pacal's tomb. While most of the figures wear a short skirt, one figure, clearly male, wears a long beaded skirt and cape. A net skirt and cape is also worn by the male protagonist on the side of Altar T from Copán. This costume, then, is not necessarily an identifying feature of women. Robertson argued for a female identification based on the fact that the psychoduct that leads into the crypt begins at Pier C. This she interpreted as an umbilical cord: ergo, the figure is female. Since there is no clear sexual dimorphism or glyphic evidence to make a positive identification of the figure, I feel judgment must be reserved. A male identification could just as easily be suggested by the fact that the figure stands above a stingray spine, an emblem of the male penis perforation rite. According to my view, it would be unlikely to see a woman holding a child in this manner in Maya art—though if the Pier C figure were Lady Zac-Kuk, her extraordinary power might allow such a transgression.

2. This idea is in accord with those of Mary Miller (1985) in her analysis of the Mesoamerican Chacmool.

3. See also Henderson (1979:77).

The Maya "Posture of Royal Ease"

ANNE-LOUISE SCHAFFER
COLUMBIA UNIVERSITY, NEW YORK, AND MUSEUM OF FINE ARTS, HOUSTON

With so much emphasis being placed on the ruling elite in Maya studies today, it is easy to lose sight of the artists who created the monuments and ceramics that are the sources for most of the information being utilized. David Stuart's (1986a) recent decipherment of the glyphs for "scribe" and "to write" has led to his further discovery that at least some of the scribes were of high social rank. It is therefore, perhaps, time to turn our attention to the artists who glorified that elite. Previous work at the level of the individual artist or workshop has been scarce. Robertson (1974) studied various aspects of the stone sculpture of Palenque; Greene Robertson (1977, 1979) studied the painting practices of stucco sculptors at the same site and their change through time; and Cohodas (1979) studied the various workshops, schools, and hands at Yaxchilán. This paper focuses not on the art of a particular site but on a feature that shows up in the art of many different ones, tracing its occurrences over space and time and suggesting possible relationships between them. How did artists get their ideas? How did they interact with each other in the same region or between regions? How mobile were they? While we may never know the full answers to these questions, they are worth considering even at a preliminary level for the possibilities that can be glimpsed. The corpus of Maya art is large enough to provide a suitable pool of information to draw from. This paper attempts a foray into this swampy area. It is also a study in Maya aesthetics. How did artists solve certain problems of composition? How did they use composition to produce a particular effect? A close analysis of key examples of the chosen subject can give us clues to the inner workings of the Maya artist's mind.

The "Posture of Royal Ease"

Scenes of lords and gods seated on thrones in palace settings represent a sizable proportion of the imagery on Classic Maya pottery. A large number of monumental reliefs in stucco and stone show lords seated on thrones as well. While the majority of these figures are seated in cross-legged position, a few rare ones are depicted with one leg hanging down over the throne touching the ground.[1] This would seem to be an obvious, simple variant of the seated position, but it occurs with such rarity in Maya art that, when it does occur, it must have been chosen by the artist for a good reason. To date I have turned up only eleven stone or stucco relief examples, ten on ceramic vessels (both carved and painted), and one terra-cotta figurine. If this number is doubled to account for those that are unknown to me, the total is still under fifty. Given the huge body of Maya art that is known today, this tiny percentage is truly startling.

Aside from its rarity, what makes this particular position worth studying is the fact that only a restricted group of individuals can assume it. Any seated figure can sit cross-legged, be it on the ground or on a raised surface such as a step, platform, or throne. However, only a lord or god is permitted to be elevated above the ground— hence this position is synonymous with rulership and authority (in the case of living mortals) or with sacred status (in the case of immortals). For that reason I am calling it the "posture of royal ease."[2]

Another intriguing aspect of this pose is its restricted distribution in space and time in the Maya area. The monumental examples show up in only three areas: the Usumacinta drainage, the site of Copán, and the northern Yucatán peninsula. Except for three examples from the latter area, these all date to the eighth century A.D. The addition of ceramic vessels and the one terra-cotta figurine to this corpus broadens the area to include the region of northeastern Petén and adjacent Belize and Campeche but does not help in the temporal sphere. While all of them probably fall within the span of years A.D. 600–800, they can be fitted into the chronological framework only roughly using stylistic and other criteria. A brief survey and discussion of the more interesting and typical examples of this posture follows, conducted by region in rough chronological order.

The Usumacinta Drainage

The two earliest datable examples of this pose both come from the site of Palenque. The earliest of these seems to be the legs of the del Río throne (fig. 1), dated by Linda Schele (personal communication, 1985) either to Kan-Xul's reign, 702–711 (9.13.10.6.8–9.13.19.13.3), or to the first part of Chaacal's, 722–726 (9.14.10.4.2–9.14.15.0.0). Now disassembled and the pieces scattered, this throne originally stood in House E of the Palace beneath the Oval Tablet of Pacal the Great. Each leg depicts one of the four Bacabs, lesser gods believed to inhabit the watery underworld and support the four corners of the sky (Schele and Miller 1986:54 and 61, note 62). The water-lily plants that they hold up refer to their natural habitat. They sit on glyphlike thrones in mirror image, facing the center of the actual throne. The right image (fig. 2), which is still in good condition, shows the throne to be a monster mask facing upward; the Bacab's right hand rests on its snout and the glyph for *imix* (T 501) occupies its eye (Greene Robertson 1985: 30–31). The Bacab wears a fringed kilt and a loincloth whose fringed end also rests on top of this throne in order not to cover up the identifying feature of the monster by falling down over its eye. The figures of the Bacabs are crowded into their respective rectangular frames, their images touching all four sides. The resulting visual effect is one of oversized powerful figures bursting the frame, even though the actual reliefs are less than 50 cm high. In addition, the torsos of the figures lean inward as if countering the weight they hold. This feeling of strength and contained power is very appropriate both to the function of the Bacabs in general—as sky-bearers—and to these two in particular—in holding up the heavy stone slab of the throne upon which a living ruler sat. This slab is carved with a glyphic inscription detailing the list of Palenque rulers from Pacal to, presumably, the one who commissioned the throne,

Fig. 2 "Madrid Stela" (throne leg), del Río throne, 47 cm high. Museo de América, Madrid (photo courtesy Merle Greene Robertson).

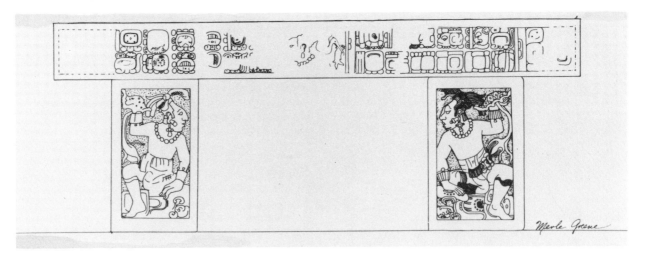

Fig. 1 Del Río throne, House E, Palace, Palenque (reconstruction drawing by Merle Greene Robertson 1985: fig. 92).

so these two Bacabs not only hold up the ruler physically but symbolically as well, by supporting the entire lineage of rulers along with the reigning one.

The second example of this seated pose from Palenque (fig. 3) is the now destroyed "Beau Relief" from the Temple of the Jaguar (or Lion), dated by Linda Schele (1981:112) and Merle Greene (personal communication, 1986) to between 721 and 741 (9.14.10.0.0– 9.15.10.0.0). This oft-ignored stucco relief is the earliest monumental example of the pose in question and the earliest to depict a lord. Its approximate dating overlaps that of the del Río throne, so it is possible that it predates the throne and is the source for later examples. Its size would make it a more obvious choice as a model as well. The lithograph by Frédéric Waldeck, done in 1797 but not published until 1822, seems to be the most accurate of the several versions of this relief known today. It was made after sketches done while the relief was still relatively intact. It shows an unidentified lord sitting on an elaborate cushion placed atop a double-headed jaguar throne reminiscent of that depicted on Pacal's Oval Tablet. A cushion appears on only one other monumental relief at Palenque—The Tablet of the Slaves—where it inconspicuously fills in the gap between Chac-Zutz' (the central figure) and the two slaves that form his throne. In contrast, this cushion is very obvious; it may have been added by the original artist to give extra height to the seated figure in a vertical format. While certain details of the lithograph are clearly influenced by Waldeck's classical European training,[3] many of them are quite accurate, such as the typical Palencano hairdo. The figure's loincloth end is skewed to one side here, as it was in the throne leg, in order to avoid covering the central medallion of the cushion. It then continues beneath the figure's right leg to reappear and fall down over the cushion. Unlike the Bacab, however, this figure is set liberally in space, with plenty of room between him and the frame. The asymmetrical seated pose may have been utilized to keep the composition from becoming a static, symmetrical pyramid of horizontally stacked forms resembling a wedding cake. The slight dip in the figure's right shoulder and the asymmetrical position of the arms help to give a little life to the figure, but it is a far cry from the dynamic naturalism of the Bacabs on the throne legs. The total effect is of a calm, dignified lord at ease with his station in life and removed from the petty concerns of the world around him.

Not long after these two Palenque reliefs were created, in 746, a large relief panel was carved for the site of Kuná-Lacanhá (fig. 4). Probably set into the interior wall of a temple or palace, as was the "Beau Relief," it now rests in the collection of Dumbarton Oaks in Washington, D.C. The subject matter is again a single lord seated on a throne. The inscription indicates that he is a *cah*, or subsidiary lord, of the Bonampak polity (David Stuart, personal communication, 1984) and that he is acceding to some office, symbolized by the large ceremonial bar that he holds. The throne upon which he sits is an upward-facing monster mask reminiscent of that on the del Río throne leg. The loincloth here skews to the left instead of the right, but, like the one in the "Beau Relief," it disappears beneath the figure's leg before emerging to fall over the front of the throne, thereby avoiding the eye of the monster. The figure is set into a rather confined space; like the Bacabs on the throne legs, he and his accoutrements touch all four sides of the space set aside for him. This space is framed on the sides by columns of glyphs that physically and visually contain the central figure, forcing one's attention immediately on him. The horizontal framework with its dominating rectilinearity is broken most effectively by the one strong diagonal of the figure's left leg. This leg leads the eye up to his right hand and thence to his face. From here the figure's gaze leads the viewer to the top left corner of the panel, where the oversized Initial Glyph signals the beginning of the text. Thus, the diagonal that begins as a visibly concrete entity ends up as an implied horizontal direction, cleverly integrating text and figure.

There are enough points of similarity in these three works from the Usumacinta region to convince me that the artists involved knew each other's work and adapted what was useful to their own. The unusualness of the

Fig. 3 "Beau Relief," Temple of the Jaguar, Palenque (lithograph by Frédéric Waldeck, 1797; del Río 1822: frontispiece).

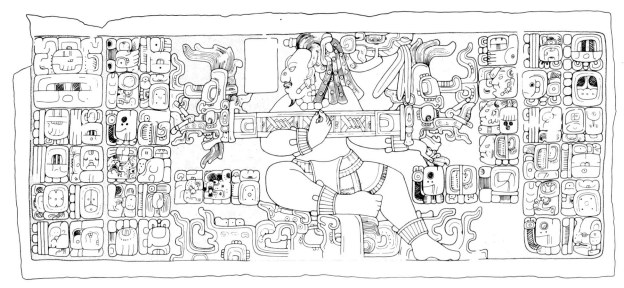

Fig. 4   Panel, Kuná-Lacanhá, 70 cm high. Dumbarton Oaks, Washington, D.C., B-145.MAS (drawing by David S. Stuart).

pose, its use in compositions involving only one figure, and the position of the figures' left leg falling down in front of the throne argue against coincidence. The close temporal placement of these examples—a minimum of twenty years, a maximum of forty-four—makes the possibility of influence likely. Even many of the details correspond. For example, all of the figures are bare-chested, wearing only kilts and simple bead necklaces, and all have their heads turned to left profile. A last feature all of these reliefs have in common is their original placement in private spaces sheltered within buildings.

Totally different from these three examples is the fourth and latest one from the Usumacinta drainage, Stela 12 from Piedras Negras (fig. 5). It is dated 795 (9.18.5.0.0; Schele and Miller 1986:219)—almost fifty years after these first three. This relief is a public outdoor war monument showing the presentation of captives from Pomoná to the ruler of Piedras Negras. Twelve figures are shown on three main levels: eight captives huddled at the bottom, their leader at mid-level, and the Piedras Negras ruler at the top, looking down at them from a position of power and superiority. Two soldiers standing sternly at the sides act as static visual pillars to keep the eye focused inward and upward. All of the other figures in the scene are in a state of movement, not the least of which is the one at the top. He bends downward with one hand on the knee that rests on the top step of a stairway. This is reminiscent of the pose the Bacabs take on the del Río throne legs, except that the bend of the body is in the opposite direction to the resting arm there. Another difference is that the right leg of the ruler hangs down over the step, not the left one as we have seen in each case so far. The ruler is more elaborately dressed as well, wearing a feather cape and an elaborate necklace with a full-figure pendant. His loincloth end, however, disappears beneath his leg and emerges again, as we have seen twice before.

All of these differences point to an independently thought-out approach to the posture of royal ease, created at some remove in time from the other examples known from this region. The multifigural scene and the casualness of the figures' poses come from the tradition of painting on ceramics and walls. Its purpose is narrative and historic, and it is limited to the Late Classic. In contrast, the "Beau Relief" and the Kuná-Lacanhá panel derive from an earlier hieratic tradition of stone carving wherein one monumental figure is presented without context. Piedras Negras Stela 12 is an anomaly among the monumental examples of the corpus of works utilizing this asymmetrical pose.

Copán

The second location where the posture of royal ease shows up is the site of Copán. All four of the stone monuments that display it were carved during the reign of the last named ruler there, Yax-Pac (alias Madrugada and New-Sun-at-Horizon). All but one are associated with Temple 11 and date to the year 775 (9.17.5.0.0; Schele and Miller 1986:122–126). Because they were carved at the same time as part of the same program, and because their styles, compositional devices, and details are so similar, they were probably designed by and executed under the same master artist.

The first of these monuments, Altar Q (fig. 6), has sixteen lords ranged around the four sides of its square block, with a glyphic text on top. It is generally accepted now that the figure to the right of the central date is Yax-Pac, who is receiving the baton of office from an ancestor. This and the other fourteen figures may be his predecessors in office (Schele and Miller 1986:125). All of the figures sit on thrones that consist of glyphs, some or all of which may be their names (Miller 1981: 79–80; Ferguson and Royce 1984:276). For the most

Schaffer

part, they sit in either a cross-legged position or a slight variant of it, but the legs of those on the front side (the top quartet in fig. 6) hang down more than those on the other three sides, and those of Yax-Pac and the figure at the extreme left hang down the most. None of these feet touch the ground as they do in the Usumacinta examples, however. The obvious explanation for this variation in leg positions is adding visual variety to rows of figures of similar size and dress holding similar scepters (Miller 1981:45, 81). Subtle differences in the pose and costume of Yax-Pac—notably his headdress—serve to distinguish him from the other lords.

This same method is used to differentiate Yax-Pac in the row of figures carved on the bench panel of Temple 11 (fig. 7). In this panel he is flanked by nineteen figures, each sitting on a glyphic throne again. Like those

Fig. 5   Stela 12, Piedras Negras. Museo Nacional, Guatemala (drawing by Linda Schele; Schele and Miller 1986: 219, fig. V.8).

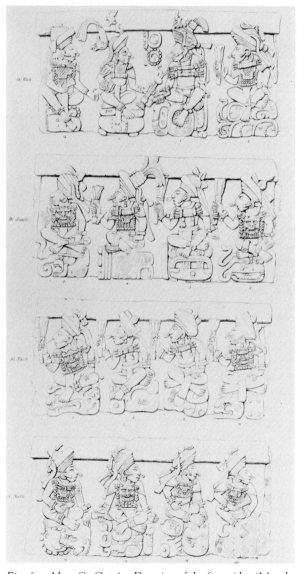

Fig. 6   Altar Q, Copán. Drawing of the four sides (Maudslay 1889–1902:I, pl. 92).

Fig. 7 Bench panel, Temple 11, Copán, ca. 51 cm high. British Museum, London (photo copyright Justin Kerr, 1985).

on Altar Q, they may represent the ancestors of Yax-Pac or previous rulers of Copán or both (Schele and Miller 1986:124–126). However, unlike the thrones on that altar, these glyphs are not names but a continuous running ritual text. As before, Yax-Pac is positioned just right of the central date, but he is depicted awkwardly from the front with both legs hanging down from the throne. Unlike the lords on Altar Q, the majority of these who extend one leg down actually touch the ground. Despite the fact that they share the same costumes, pectorals, headdresses, and scepters with the lords on Altar Q, these exhibit much more variety in their leg positions. The reason for this may be because on the bench relief the entire row of twenty figures is seen at a glance, whereas the row of sixteen on Altar Q is seen only four at a time.

Two other examples of the posture of royal ease occur at the site of Copán. The third (see Schele and Miller 1986: pl. 37, 132) is a fragmentary panel forming part of the cornice decoration above the north door of Temple 11. It depicts Yax-Pac sitting on a now-missing throne holding in front of him a plate with the head of God K on it lying face upward. Beneath the plate and in front of the ruler is a column of glyphs that include his name. Stylistically and in costume he is a carbon copy of any number of figures on Altar Q and the bench panel already discussed. The rest of the cornice decoration is missing, but apparently this panel was one of several that formed a row including hieroglyphic inscriptions and portraits of Yax-Pac.

These examples of the posture of royal ease from Copán differ greatly in context, composition, style, and detail from those we have already seen from the Usumacinta region. Foremost is the fact that they are part of

group scenes and were meant to serve a decorative function on architecture or large-scale "furniture." The replication of rows of similar-sized figures is the favored presentation format. The figures are squat and chunky in comparison to their Usumacinta counterparts. To give some relief to the otherwise monotonous rows, the positions of the loincloth ends, arms, and legs are varied. Thus, sometimes the loincloth end falls over a leg, sometimes it goes under it and reemerges, and sometimes it disappears behind both legs. The legs may be in a tight crossed position, or one may hang down vertically toward the ground, or the dangling leg may be somewhere in between. Additional variety is found in the batons that the figures hold, the chest ornaments that they wear, and the way the turbans are wrapped. The elaborate pectorals and the capes that some of them wear are lacking in the three Usumacinta examples that predate these Copán ones. These figures also wear simple loincloths instead of the more elaborate kilt of the Usumacinta area.

The sudden appearance of rows of seated figures representing ancestors and previous rulers at Copán coincides with the first appearance of the asymmetrical seated pose there as well. While both features may have been the result of a sudden flash of invention by a master artist at Copán, they might also have been the result of outside influence, perhaps from Palenque, where both the pose and rows of similar figures were already in use. The vehicle for this hypothetical transmittal may have been the documented marriage of a Palenque woman to Yax-Pac's father (Mathews 1986). The date of this marriage is unknown, but it likely took place some time between the 730s and 750s (Peter Mathews and William Fash, personal communication, 1986). There is now evidence

Schaffer

that artists were part of the tribute owed to a conquering state,[4] so it is not farfetched to imagine artists being sent as part of dowry as well. The timing of this presumed entourage from Palenque would allow for the artists to have been familiar with the two reliefs from Palenque discussed earlier. In addition, they would also have been familiar with the series of seated figures on thrones on the piers of House C of the Palace, created during Pacal's reign, and the series of portrait busts lining the wall of the eastern corridor of House A, attributed to Chan Bahlum. They might even have heard about the seated and standing guardian-lords on the walls of Pacal's tomb chamber and the busts of his ancestors on the sarcophagus there. Until Yax-Pac's monuments were carved, rows of similar figures do not show up in the sculpture at Copán, not to mention rows of ancestors and rulers and the use of the asymmetrical seated pose. These features may signal an interjection of Usumacinta naturalism and innovation into the representation of humans at Copán. The problem with this proposed theory is the gap in time between the arrival of the artists no later than the 750s and the date of Temple 11's dedication in 775. Were they inactive until Yax-Pac, an innovative ruler of first degree, took over and allowed them free rein? Had they by then forgotten the details of Palenque styling and absorbed the Copán one? What, indeed, was the sculptural style of Palenque from 731 on?

The fourth and last example of the asymmetrical seated pose at Copán comes not from Temple 11 but from Structure 9N-82, the main building of a residential compound of a local lineage head located a kilometer from the Main Plaza (see Schele and Miller 1986: fig. III.7,140). The two-storied facade displays five figures sculpted in the round and tenoned to the wall. Over the central doorway is a fragmentary figure that Fash (1986) read as the historical head of a high-ranking lineage of scribes who lived in the compound. He was apparently deified as God N, the patron of scribes and artists. He and the two figures of scribes that flank him on the second story are seated on *na* glyphs. Because of his huge water-lily headdress, this glyph may refer to *na:ab,* or water lily, which also means "to daub," a possible reference to what scribes do (Schele and Miller 1986:141). This central figure is seated rigidly frontal on the glyph with his left leg hanging down in front. His loincloth end falls in front of his other leg and ends abruptly at the "throne" (to be tucked under his leg?). The posture is a clear reference to the many examples in the Temple 11 complex, but the style is unlike them in being very stiff, formal, and hieratic. The posture of royal ease makes him stand out from the other figures on the facade, who are seated in cross-legged fashion. The inscription associated with this building indicates that it was dedicated by Yax-Pac in 787, twelve years after Temple 11 was dedicated. The facade decoration was almost certainly done by an artist different from the one who worked on the Temple 11 reliefs, one who was very conservative in his use of the motif.

The Northeastern Petén

Neither Copán nor the Usumacinta drainage produced examples of the posture of royal ease on ceramics. This seems to have been the prerogative of the Petén, in particular the area near Tikal and adjacent Belize and Campeche. Of the nine examples known to me, all are polychrome painted cylinder vases except one, which is lightly incised. While none of these can be dated precisely, they seem to fall in the middle of the Late Classic, making them contemporary with the stone and stucco reliefs discussed so far. Given the huge number of decorated vessels known and the freedom of line that is characteristic of the painted medium, one would expect the pose in question to be more numerically visible, but such is not the case; it seems to be as rare in ceramics as it is in the monumental art forms.

On these pots the asymmetrical seated pose appears in multifigural scenes, and, despite the fact that in some cases more than one figure of equal rank is seated on a raised object, only one figure in any scene assumes it. Interior palace scenes are the most common type, representing all but two of the examples. Five of these depict only humans; the other two include a mixture of both humans (mythological heroes?) and gods. One of the latter (Hellmuth 1976: fig. 11) illustrates a decapitation scene being performed by animals in the presence of a lord seated on a large cushion. The other (Robicsek and Hales 1981:108, fig. 9) illustrates an old god being attacked by a strange flying creature while another god and a human, seated on separate thrones, look on; the god is the one seated in the posture of royal ease. There are only two scenes using this pose that clearly take place out-of-doors. One (Hellmuth 1976: fig. 3) shows a deer hunt on one side and a male-female couple, seated on a "throne" of swirling water, on the other; the male is the one seated in this pose. The second outdoors example (Hellmuth 1976: fig. 56) shows a young lord being dressed by two naked women on one side and a canoe carrying another young lord (or the same one) and two gods on the other; the god in the rear, the Jaguar God of the underworld, is the figure in the posture of royal ease.[5] This listing of subjects indicates that the pose in question is used on these ceramics in a wide variety of contexts, in contrast to the much more restricted ones in stone and stucco already discussed.

The forms in which this pose are represented also show innovation and freedom. Five of the ceramic examples depict the figure from the front, four from the side. The side view exists only on this group of pots and not on any monumental sculpture.[6] I take this to be another sign of the greater freedom of form and subject matter allowed to ceramic artists. I present here a typical example of each type to show how the pose is treated in the overall composition of a scene and how it compares to examples in stone and stucco that have already been presented.

The painted vase seen in rollout form in figure 8 is a

Fig. 8 *Polychrome vase, Structure 5C-49, Tikal, 13.2 cm high. Museo Nacional de Arqueología y Etnología, Guatemala City, MAP-004 (photo copyright Justin Kerr 1985).*

Fig. 9 *Polychrome vase, northern Petén(?). Whereabouts unknown (Robicsek and Hales 1981:131, fig. 33).*

typical example of the pose as seen from the front. It comes from Tikal and is dated 750–800 (Gallenkamp and Johnson 1985:158). Though the scene has been overpainted, it is correct in most of its details. Like most of these painted versions, it depicts a lord seated on a throne in a palace setting accompanied by various subsidiary figures. The thrones in these scenes, unlike those seen in the monuments so far, are all normal, realistic ones, as opposed to glyphs or monster masks. The main figure here wears a luxurious white feather cape and a

dark loincloth, whose end disappears beneath his foot and falls in front of the throne, as we have seen in several instances already. Except for his strong gesturing right arm, the form of the lord is remarkably like that of the lord on the Kuná-Lacanhá panel (minus the ceremonial bar, of course), down to the rightward skew of the loincloth. The choice of leg to depict hanging over the throne varies in these pots, but all of them include a forward tilt of the upper body and a lowered right shoulder, as in Piedras Negras Stela 12. In all of the examples

Schaffer

the figure's face is seen in left profile. In this scene the eye of the viewer is caught by the strong forms of the lord's dangling leg and outstretched right arm, which, like the parallel features in the Kuná-Lacanhá panel, lead the eye to the matter at hand—here a seated man holding a small limp jaguar or jaguar pelt.

The rollout of a painted vase from the northern Petén seen in figure 9 is a typical example of the posture of royal ease as seen from the side. It is another indoor palace scene. A lord with lavish body-painting sits on a platform wearing a loincloth whose back fringed end lies atop the platform behind him. He gestures toward a functionary standing in front of him. A different aesthetic is used in these side views, which include both left and right profile figures. The upper torso is always just barely off the absolute vertical, giving a slight hint of lifelike tension to the body. The leg on the throne surface is represented only as the sole of a foot. Usually it is naturally placed flat on the surface next to the knee with only the front part visible, but here it is awkwardly rendered in full on the diagonal. The artist exploits the right-angle bend of the dangling leg to echo the architectural elements in the scene, the arms of the figures, and the glyph block between them.

These painted pots from the Petén form the largest body of examples of the pose in question in the ceramic medium. Their absence from the monumental sculpture of the area may be due to the fact that the major art forms of this region—the stelae, altars, and lintels—exhibit a conservative, hieratic strain throughout its entire history. This, in turn, is probably due to the fact that the hieratic tradition of stone carving mentioned previously stems back the furthest in time in this region. The artists working in stone and wood relief were apparently not free enough to experiment with new figural forms or unusual compositions. This is clearly not true of the artists working in the painted polychrome tradition, where invention of form and subject matter flourished. Narrative scenes were a Late Classic invention and were thus not saddled with centuries of tradition. Ceramic artists may also have had more freedom and opportunity to move around the Maya countryside due to the greater portability of their wares. In traveling they would have been exposed to other styles and ideas or would have spread their own. The posture of royal ease could have been picked up in this way or invented independently and spread out from the Petén to other areas.

The Northern Yucatán Peninsula

The fourth and last area in which the asymmetrical seated pose appears is the Puuc region and at Chichén Itzá. The examples from here are unusual in several respects: they exhibit a wide range of styles; they span the greatest number of years (ca. 600–880), including the only examples from the ninth century; and they cover three different media. These latter include monumental

stone reliefs, carved pottery vessels, and the only example in three-dimensions—a Jaina-style figurine.

Beginning chronologically with the terra-cotta examples, two of them are carved vases of the style called Chocholá, which originates from the Puuc region or the area adjacent to the southwest (Coe 1973b:114; Tate 1985:123–124, 132). These Chocholá ceramics are Late Classic in date, but, since many of the figures depicted on them show the dynamic, complex postures characteristic of the stone monuments from the Usumacinta that date from 751 to 810 (9.16.0.0.0–9.19.0.0.0), at least some of them may be more finely dated to that period (Tate 1985:124). The styles on these vessels vary from the typical northern Yucatán one of simplified, unmodeled forms emphasizing right angles to one that is very fluid and naturalistic, like that of Usumacinta monuments and Petén ceramics.

An example of the former style is the vase in figure 10. One side has a recessed panel with the scene of a lord seated on a mat-topped throne, handing an object toward a kneeling attendant who is holding a bowl (Coe 1973b:113) or basket (Tate 1985:132). The scene takes place indoors, as the swagged curtain overhead indicates. The seated figure is twisted into an impossible position: his lower body faces to our right, his torso itself is frontal, and his face is in left profile. The posture of royal ease is thus depicted in a combined side/front view, the sole of his left foot giving the best clue to what is really going on.

Fig. 10 Carved vase, Jaina Island, Campeche, 20.7 cm high (Kimbell Art Museum, Fort Worth, Texas, APx 74.4).

Fig. 11 Carved vase, Chocholá or Maxcanú, Yucatán, 20.6 cm high. Private Collection, New York City (photo copyright Justin Kerr 1971).

The lord is simply dressed except for his elaborate bird headdress. His loincloth is rendered in a unique fashion with both back and front ends shown falling over the front of the throne. His lowered right shoulder is the only stylistic feature that relates this piece to artistic movements to the south; iconographic details such as the basket may indicate a connection to the Usumacinta region (Tate 1985). The other elements are original and therefore probably indigenous to the area.

The vase in figure 11 exhibits a totally different style. Of the two lords that occupy the recessed panels on this vase, only the one shown sits in the posture of royal ease; the other (Coe 1973b:114) sits in the standard cross-legged position. The depicted lord sits on a simplified cushion out of which curl two elements that almost make it into a monster mask like those on two of the Usumacinta examples that we have seen. In fact, when compared to the Bacab of the del Río throne leg, its similarity is remarkable: the figure is compressed into a rectangular frame, whose four sides it touches; its body forms are fleshy and powerful; it has one arm raised; it is simply dressed; and the hair is tied up with a cloth in the same way. A direct connection between the two works is hard to resist. This figure is not a sky-bearer performing a chore, however, but a lord in a palace setting, moving aside the curtain swag and drape at the upper left corner. One clear difference between them is the treatment of the loincloth end. The odd rigidity of the Chocholá example interrupts the flow of the rest of the image; it falls

down over the lord's right ankle and the front of the cushion, turns abruptly at the edge of the panel, and then runs straight off to the bottom left corner.

Both of these vases, then, exhibit stylistic affinities to the Usumacinta and Petén regions, but in mixed proportions. Iconographically they relate very closely to Petén ceramics (Tate 1985:123). This situation is most explainable by ceramic trade and/or artists' travel. Given the current poor state of knowledge about the relationships between the northern Maya areas and the Petén or Usumacinta during the Late Classic, confirmation on this will have to await further archaeological work in Yucatán and Campeche.

A similar problem arises with the one three-dimensional example of the asymmetrical seated pose, a Jaina-style figurine of the Jaguar God of the underworld with no provenience (fig. 12). Iconographically this deity would be more at home in the Petén or Usumacinta than in Campeche. He rides on the back of a crocodilian monster, holding onto the snout with his right hand (for balance?) and raising an axe in his left one. The piece probably depicts the deity as the Night Sun riding through the underworld on his steed on his nightly journey (Joralemon 1975:64–65). Though made in three dimensions, the figurine is meant to be seen from the front and can be compared to the painted and relief examples

Fig. 12 Terracotta figurine of the Jaguar God of the underworld, Jaina-style, 300–900 A.D., 26 cm high (reproduced by permission from the collection of the Australian National Gallery, Canberra).

Fig. 13 East panel, South Building, Glyphic Group, Xcalumkin (courtesy Peabody Museum, Harvard University. Photograph by Pollack. Copyright © President and Fellows of Harvard College 1935).

already seen, but nothing conclusive turns up. The two raised arms are vaguely reminiscent of those in the "Beau Relief" from Palenque and the vase from the Petén in figure 8. Except for his headdress, which contains a large Venus sign, the god is simply dressed. His loincloth end is especially wide and falls down over his tucked-up left leg. The only other instance where this element is so dominant is in the panel from Xcalumkin (fig. 13), a similarly frontal image discussed next. One must conclude, however, that this unusual depiction of the posture of royal ease owes its inspiration to nothing extant. It is unique and marvelous.

The earliest stone example of this pose from this region comes from Xcalumkin (fig. 13) and dates to approximately 751 (Proskouriakoff 1950:166). It is a small square panel of a seated lord that, along with a similar panel on the opposite side, flanked the inner doorway of the South Building of the Glyphic Group (fig. 14). The matching panel depicts a lord in simple cross-legged position. Both sit on rectilinear stone thrones with curved backs that are similar to those seen on ceramics from the Petén and on the Palace Tablet from Palenque, Kan-Xul's accession monument of 702–711. These thrones are also reminiscent of the del Río throne and its placement in front of the Oval Tablet (fig. 1). Both square panels on the South Building wall contain a column of glyphs on the side nearest the central doorway, leaving only two-thirds of the space for the seated figure. As a result, the figures are wedged tightly into the frame of the panel like the Bacabs of the del Río throne legs, giving the impression of being seated in a recessed niche. The figures exhibit a style that is frequent in the northern Yucatán peninsula, characterized by simple

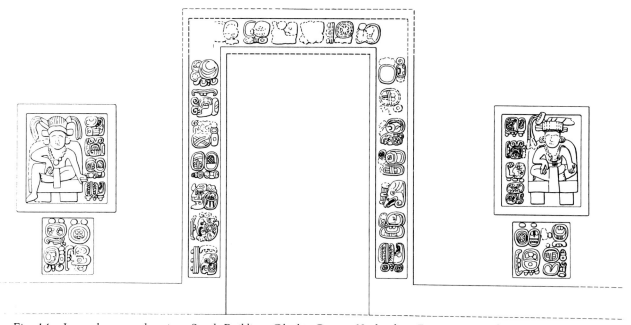

Fig. 14 Inner doorway elevation, South Building, Glyphic Group, Xcalumkin. Reconstruction drawing (courtesy Peabody Museum, Harvard University. Photograph by Pollack. Copyright © President and Fellows of Harvard College 1935).

blocky forms emphasizing right angles and the horizontal and vertical directions. The proportions of the body are chunky like those of the figures associated with Temple 11 at Copán, but without the softening roundness and liveliness. The lord in figure 13 sits rigidly frontal and his right-angled legs fit the quadrilinearity of the composition very well. Details of clothing are deemphasized and simplified so as not to clutter up the basic geometric forms of the panel, which cause the figures to stand out on the wall despite their small size. The loincloth end falls down over the figure's left leg, as happens on Altar Q and the bench panel from Copán, but here it is a wide, straight, rigid form that adds another vertical line to the composition of the panel.

The only other stone examples of the posture of royal ease from northern Yucatán both come from Chichén Itzá. The earliest of the two, dated ca. 869 (10.2.0.0.0) by Kelley (1982:14), is the Watering Trough lintel from Hacienda Chichén Itzá, now in the Museo de Arqueología y Historia, Mérida (Beyer 1937: pl. 6). It is very weather-worn, but the main points of the composition and pose can be made out. A seated lord, with right leg hanging down over a throne, occupies about half of a square framed space. He leans slightly to our left toward a tall vessel next to his right foot. Surrounding him and wedging him tightly into his space are glyph columns at both sides and one row above. Surrounding the entire square panel is a wide frame containing more glyphs of a larger size. The only relevant detail in the figure that can be seen is his loincloth end, which goes beneath his tucked-up left leg and reemerges to fall in front of the throne.

A similar but better-preserved example of this type is the lintel from the inner doorway of Structure 4D1, the Akabdzib or Akatzib or Ak At'cib (fig. 15). Thompson (1937:185) dated it to ca. 870 (10.2.1.0.0), while Kelley (1982:14) preferred ca. 880 (10.2.11.0.0). In either case, it is the latest stone example of this pose from the northern Maya area and also the latest in the entire corpus. Again we see a seated lord in a square format framed partially by columns and a row of glyphs. However, the carving on this lintel is finer and the composition and details more aesthetically pleasing than on the Watering Trough lintel. The style is not the simple, blocky, angular one of the Xcalumkin panel. Instead, the human forms are longer and thinner and the pose less rigid; the profile head and slight tilt of the torso give a small amount of life to the figure. The cushion he sits on, with its curved corners, also helps soften the effect. This cushion is reminiscent of those found on the "Beau Relief" from Palenque and on many painted ceramics from the Petén.

The presence of a tall flaring vessel on the ground is unique to the two lintels from Chichén. In the Akabdzib example it is slightly tilted and sets up a focus for the lord's attention as well as adding more asymmetry to the composition. A nice touch is the upside-down L formed by the glyphs at the left, which echo the bend of the

Fig. 15 *Lintel over inner doorway, Akabdzib, Chichén Itzá (courtesy Peabody Museum, Harvard University. Photograph by Andrews. Copyright © President and Fellows of Harvard College 1939).*

lord's dangling right leg. Both of these are mirrored by his long thin loincloth end, which appears unexpectedly from behind his left knee, falls down over the cushion, and then lies flat on the ground to our left. This treatment is suspiciously similar to that on the Chocholá vase in figure 11, indicating its probable northern Yucatán origin. It has been noted before (Proskouriakoff 1950: 170) that the position of this figure's arms and legs recalls the ruler at the top of Stela 12 from Piedras Negras (fig. 5), though this one is much more erect. Both have their left hands resting on their left legs. The Chichén lord's headdress is unusual for that site; its closest cousins seem to be from the Usumacinta as well, in particular Yaxchilán and Piedras Negras (Lincoln 1982:20). Another possible link to that area may be the sandals that he wears; they are found associated with this asymmetrical pose only on the "Beau Relief." Like the figure on that relief, this one has a moderate amount of space around him, giving him a similar calm, dignified air.

The two lintels from Chichén Itzá are the latest examples of the posture of royal ease that I have found. More than any other reliefs at Chichén, they exhibit the strongest ties in both hieroglyphic writing and sculptural style to the more southern traditions of the Late Classic Maya (Lincoln 1982:20A). Thompson (1937:191–192) felt that this was due to the peripheral location of the site, which allowed archaic elements to survive here long after they had disappeared from the central area. He even suggested that some of the glyphic writing reached Chichén from the Usumacinta area. However, there may be a more concrete historical reason for this

Schaffer

vague reference to southern areas in these two lintels. Both of them were carved during the period of time when Kakupacal, a military captain of the Itzá, held sway over the site—from at least 869 to at least 881 (10.2.0.15.3–10.2.12.2.4; Kelley 1968:264). There is also a Kakupacal mentioned as ruler at Uxmal, who may have been the grandfather or great-grandfather of the one mentioned at Chichén (Kelley 1982:2–3). It has even been suggested that these men were in some way related to the ruling dynasty of Palenque 150 years earlier (Kelley 1982: table 2), but this is highly conjectural. Chichén was a multiethnic polity, a city where ideas from many different areas were brought together, including ideas related to art. Infusions from elsewhere added to the new dynamism of the city. However, the 74-year gap in time between the two Chichén lintels and the nearest other example of the pose—Piedras Negras Stela 12—makes direct influence from elsewhere unlikely, unless artists traveled around to various cities to see their sculptured monuments, as did European artists from the Renaissance on. Though there was another example close by at Xcalumkin, it was totally different in style and approach from these two and could not have served as a model for them.

Sources and Relationships

From the foregoing discussion of these examples of the posture of royal ease, two immediate conclusions can be drawn. First, there are no instances of women assuming it. Second, there is no overt meaning attached to it, only the implied one of elevated status. It appears in several different contexts—especially on polychrome pottery—but the majority are lords seated on thrones and most of these are nonscenic situations; that is, they involve only single, isolated figures or, in two cases from Copán, similar figures lined up in a row. In the few multifigural scenes, only one figure at a time assumes it. When looking for a possible origin for this pose, then, a source incorporating a single, dominant image in a hieratic presentation should be sought. The pose seems to have been primarily an artistic device chosen occasionally by an artist to give a certain effect to the composition and/or to add another dimension to the subject matter depicted. It seems to appear first in the Usumacinta region at a time when dynamic naturalism was popular in Maya art, replacing the earlier stiff formality. Virginia Miller (1981:49) suggested that it was introduced as a compromise between the ubiquitous cross-legged posture and the rare one with both legs hanging down from a raised surface; like the former (and unlike the latter) it could be presented unambiguously in both front and side views. Not only does the pose create a more dynamic and interesting composition because of its asymmetry, but it humanizes the ruler as well. On the physical level, it gives him a more relaxed, approachable look. On the symbolic one, it connects the two dispar-

ate strata of society: the elite lord above on the throne and the commoner below on the ground.[7]

The truly interesting question about this pose is its widely spaced occurrences. Were these flashes in time and space independent inventions, or was there some kind of connecting link between them? In the case of the Usumacinta examples, there is a coherence to the earliest three that points towards actual knowledge of the works by their creators. The Piedras Negras example reflects influence from wall and vase painting. In the case of the Copán examples, there is a possibility that some kind of impetus may have come from Palenque in the form of resident artists from that site. Two different approaches are present, though, indicating two different artists in charge. The Petén examples are the most varied, being part of multifigural painted scenes on pottery. The narrative character of these examples and the freedom of the medium suggest that the motif was independently invented here. Since the vessels involved are not precisely datable, there is always the chance that these—and not the Usumacinta stone monuments—are the earliest examples from which others may have derived. While the portability of the finished product makes this possibility quite feasible, the use of the pose in narrative situations, which were new in the Late Classic, argues against it. In the case of the Puuc and Chichén Itzá examples, not enough is known about connections to the rest of the Maya area to offer more than vague, tantalizing clues as to possible sources. Only stylistic comparisons are available at this time, and they give mixed results.

The earliest extant example of the posture of royal ease in Mesoamerica is to be found far from the Maya area—at Oxtotitlán, Guerrero (fig. 16). Mural 1 here is

Fig. 16 Mural 1, Oxtotitlán, Guerrero (drawing by Mrs. Kent Weeks; Joralemon 1971:52, fig. 150).

a monumental polychrome image painted directly on a cliff face over a cave entrance on a hillside above the site. It belongs to the Olmec culture and dates between 800 and 700 B.C. (Grove 1969:422). The subject matter is a ruler or lord seated on a stylized jaguar throne wearing an elaborate bird costume, including feathers and mask. His arms create a strong diagonal in a composition that is basically static, given his rigidly upright torso and right-angled right leg. As far as I know, this example of the asymmetrical seated pose is unique in Olmec art, though others may once have existed. Its prominent exposure out in the open on such a large scale and with such a vivid color palette must have had repercussions in ancient times. Those seeing it would undoubtedly have been impressed by it. Could this have been the source of the earliest Usumacinta examples? It fits the general type of a single image in a hieratic format postulated as the prototype. The windmill-like arms are similar to those of the Bacabs on the del Río throne, and the stylized jaguar throne is the precursor of the later Maya jaguar throne, such as appears in the "Beau Relief." The Olmec figure also wears a kilt with a loincloth end falling down over it in front, as do the earliest Usumacinta figures.

Obviously this Olmec mural was visible during Late Classic times, as it is today. Did Maya artists travel into that area of Mexico and see it? We know that Olmec sites in the central Highlands were located at strategic points along trade routes for desired raw materials such as stone and, especially, jade (Grove 1969:422, 1970: 33). Like the Olmec, the Lowland Maya did not have deposits of jade within their territories and had to trade elsewhere for it. At least one Late Classic Maya jade (Schele and Miller 1986: pl. 18) is said to have come from Guerrero (museum files), attesting to some trade into this area. Furthermore, in the nearby state of Tlaxcala the murals at Cacaxtla, dating between 700 and 900 A.D. (López and Molina 1980:8), show strong Maya influence in costume, pose, and iconography. During the Early Classic, the ties between the Maya area and Teotihuacán are known to have been exceptionally strong, and Schele (1986a) suggested that Lowland Maya were actually in residence in that Highland city. The transmittal of a pose from one area to another is not as far-fetched as it may sound; Miller (1981:84–85) attributed the presence of two other seated positions that she found in Maya art to foreign intrusion. The old view of the Maya as a solitary, peace-loving people who stayed put

in their tropical homeland has now been replaced by a view of them as warlike, aggressive, and on the move. We now have evidence that they ventured into other parts of Mesoamerica. Within Maya territory itself, we know that in some instances artists were captured along with rulers and taken to the conquering city. It makes sense that they also made voluntary forays outside their home bases. In looking at Maya art now, we should seriously consider interregional connections as well as those with other parts of Mesoamerica.

The mural at Oxtotitlán may *not* have been the origin for the posture of royal ease among the Lowland Maya, but it is certainly a possibility. Other Olmec objects utilizing this pose, such as portable stone carvings, may also have existed; these could have been carried great distances and would have lasted centuries interred in the ground. The alternative to this theory is that the pose erupted independently among the Late Classic Maya. The presence of the pose in both Olmec and Maya art, then, could be attributed to the shared affinity that the Olmec and the Maya had for semiactive, asymmetrical, seated and reclining poses. This affinity has been noted more than once.[8] At this time the search for the origin of this motif produces intriguing but inconclusive results. I hope the future will bring more examples and more information on regional interaction to help fill the many gaps that exist.

Notes

1. This is one variant of Kurbjuhn's "Haltung C" (1980:166) and Miller's "Position III" (1981:30–31).

2. This term was suggested to me by Esther Pasztory's use of it in discussions and lectures on Late Classic Maya art—especially that of the Usumacinta area—a term that she borrowed from Indian art.

3. For example, the arms and fingers seem to have been taken from Jacques-Louis David's "Death of Socrates" of 1787 (Bergh 1985). Waldeck claimed to have studied with David in Paris and was familiar with his work.

4. See Schele and Miller (1986:218–219) for examples from Toniná and Piedras Negras.

5. There is some controversy over the authenticity of this vase (Hellmuth 1976:10).

6. One figure seen from the side on Oxkintok Stela 3 may be in this seated pose, but it is so worn that it is hard to be certain (see Pollock 1980:317, fig. 544b). It dates to ca. 849 (10.1.0.0.0; Pollock 1980:318).

7. Thanks go to Esther Pasztory for this idea.

8. Most recently this was shown in a talk by Kent Reilly (this volume).

The "Holmul Dancer" Theme in Maya Art

DORIE REENTS-BUDET
DUKE UNIVERSITY MUSEUM OF ART

Among the many styles of Late Classic Maya poly-chrome pottery, the Holmul-style vessels painted with the "Holmul Dancer" (Hellmuth 1982) pictorial program provide fertile ground for iconographic studies. Holmul-style pottery (fig. 1) is characterized by a red-and-orange on cream slip palette whose primary pictorial program is that of a male dancing figure accompanied by a dwarf or hunchback, with horizontal and vertical hieroglyphic bands. Scores of vessels painted in this style are known; although most are without archaeological provenience, tandem stylistic and chemical analyses identify the Holmul-Naranjo area as the location of the workshops that created this pottery (Reents 1985).

Vessels painted in this style were first identified during excavations at the site of Holmul in eastern Guatemala (Merwin and Vaillant 1932), and numerous researchers have since discussed the pottery in terms of both style and iconography (cf. Coe 1978; Hellmuth 1982; Reents 1985). In light of recent developments in our understanding of Maya hieroglyphs and iconography, another

look at the pictorial program is in order, particularly the principal figure and his costume.

The "Holmul Dancer" (Hellmuth 1982) was recently identified as a male figure dressed as the Young Corn God (Taube 1985). He is adorned with jewelry, sports a monster headdress with flowing feathers, and wears an elaborate backrack. The figure strikes a dancing pose with outstretched arm, bent knee, and angled torso. Similar dancers are found on stone monuments such as the Dumbarton Oaks Tablet, a scene that Linda Schele (1980) identified as the dead ruler at apotheosis dancing out of the underworld after defeating the netherworld lords. This theme is repeated on many objects in many media, including the so-called Tikal dancer plates (see Coggins 1975: figs. 86, 88) and other styles of pottery (fig. 2; see also Robicsek and Hales 1981: fig. 60), and an incised jade plaque dredged from the cenote at Chichén Itzá (Proskouriakoff 1974: fig. 79-16).

This study focuses on the pottery presentations of the Holmul Dancer theme in which the vessel's pictorial surface is divided into equal sections by two short vertical

Fig. 1   Holmul-style vessel, MS 1374 (photograph copyright Justin Kerr 1976).

217

Fig. 2 A "Holmul Dancer" from a non-Holmul-style vessel, MS 0159 (drawing by Dorie Reents-Budet; vessel in the collection of the Duke University Museum of Art).

texts. Between these texts is found the theme of dancer and accompanying dwarf or hunchback. Minor variations occur in each of the two scenes, such as the presence of a hunchback on one side and a dwarf on the other (V. Miller 1985).

A vase, MS 1374, presents the most detailed ceramic version of the Holmul Dancer (fig. 1).[1] This cylinder vase is unusual for its height and wide diameter, which provide additional pictorial space for the dancer theme

to be repeated three times. These three repetitions exhibit noteworthy iconographic and hieroglyphic substitutions, particularly in the dancers' backracks and the accompanying vertical texts.

Coe (1978:94) first described the backrack's constituent parts, which include the Principal Bird Deity at the top standing on a celestial band that bends to form part of the vertical upright of the backrack. On vessel MS 1125 (fig. 3) the sky band takes the form of a feathered serpent surmounted by a downward-looking feathered monster head, and the second dancer's backrack is composed of an arching serpent surmounted by a feathered Venus sign.

Returning to MS 1374 (fig. 1), the sky band and a plaited ribband create the upright section of the backrack, which terminates with a Cauac Monster head forming the bottom of the backrack. In the concavity created by these elements sits a supernatural zoomorphic character holding a God K head upside down in one hand. A "personified banner" composed of a plaited band, skeletal serpent head, and long quetzal feathers hang below the Cauac Monster and reach to the ground line.

This backrack can be identified as a model of the universe as conceived by the Classic Maya. The Principal Bird Deity marks the zenith above the arch of heaven (Stone 1983), that is, the celestial band (or feathered serpent as on MS 1125) that symbolizes the sky. The Cauac Monster symbolizes the earth below. The supernatural character sits in the space between the earth and the sky above, which can be interpreted as the realm of humans (that is, the earth and the center of the cosmos).

Like the dancer theme, this cosmographic backrack is not restricted to the Holmul-style pottery. It is worn by rulers in many contexts as an integral part of royal costuming. For example, two versions of the backrack are worn by the standing figures on the Initial Series Vase from Uaxactún (fig. 4; compare the righthand figure's

Fig. 3 Holmul-style vessel, MS 1125. Note the feathered saurian backracks (drawing by Dorie Reents-Budet, copyright 1985).

Reents-Budet

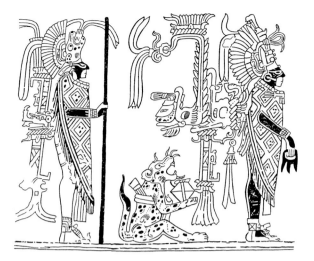

Fig. 4 The Initial Series Vase. The figures wear two versions of the cosmographic backrack (drawing courtesy Stanford University Press, copyright 1983).

backrack with those on MS 1125). The backrack is also part of the royal costumes seen on Late Classic monuments such as Tikal Temple IV Lintel 2 (fig. 5a) and possibly on Stela 11 (Jones and Satterthwaite 1982: fig. 16). The full backrack assemblage is depicted on Dos Pilas St. 17, complete with a water-lily jaguar seated within the cosmic frame (Greene, Rands, and Graham 1972: pl. 93). An unusual rear view of the backrack is depicted on Quiriguá Monument 9 (Stela I; fig. 5b).[2]

An elaborate representation of the backrack imagery is found on Lintel 3 of Temple IV at Tikal (fig. 6). Here

the ruler (Ruler 8) does not wear the backrack but rather is surrounded by the components of its cosmographic imagery. Ruler B sits upon a throne set atop steps that terminate in Cauac Monster heads. Replacing the sky band of the backrack, a feathered serpent arches over the ruler while the Principal Bird Deity perches atop the arching serpent.[3] This imagery recalls the rear of Monument 9 of Quiriguá (fig. 5b) where the ruler also is set within the cosmogram of the backrack, the same space occupied by the supernatural characters on the Holmul-style pottery. In both cases, then, rather than carrying the burden of the universe on their backs, these rulers appear to declare their central position within the cosmos.

The cosmographic backrack worn by the dancers depicted on the Holmul-style pottery appears frequently in Classic Maya art and is an integral part of royal Maya costuming. Its rendition on this pottery is particular to the style group, however, and represents a local iconographic interpretation characteristic of this ceramic tradition.

The Holmul Dancer's Backrack and Hieroglyphic Texts

The uniqueness of the Holmul-style pottery's iconographic interpretation pertains to the presence of three different supernatural creatures seated in the backracks and the accompanying vertical hieroglyphic texts. Returning to vessel MS 1374, a vertical text accompanies each dancer (figs. 1, 7). Coe (1978:96) suggested that the first two glyphs, which are the same in each ex-

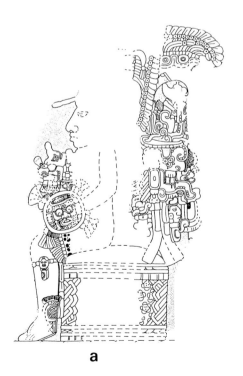

a   b

Fig. 5 (a) Tikal Temple IV Lintel 2. Profile view of the cosmographic backrack (drawing by William Coe; courtesy of The University Museum, University of Pennsylvania, copyright 1982). (b) Quiriguá Monument 9 (Stela I). Frontal depiction of the cosmographic backrack (drawing by Andrea Stone, copyright 1983).

Fig. 6 Tikal Temple IV Lintel 3 (drawing by William Coe; courtesy of The University Museum, University of Pennsylvania, copyright 1982).

ample, refer to the "Young Lords" (the dancers), whom he identifies as the Hero Twins of the Popol Vuh.

Although I agree that these vertical texts are nominal in nature, recent hieroglyphic decipherments suggest a slightly different interpretation. I propose that the first two glyphs in each vertical text function as nominal in-

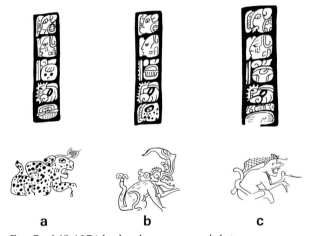

a   b   c

Fig. 7 MS 1374 backrack creatures and their accompanying hieroglyphic texts. (a) the water-lily jaguar (Ix balam); (b) the sky supernatural ("10-sky" Chicchan); (c) the monkey supernatural ("10" Chuen) (drawings by Dorie Reents-Budet, copyright 1985).

troducers (after Schele 1982:191). That is, the first glyph T757 is a general verb that introduces name phrases, and the second glyph T1000b is a head variant of *ahau*, "lord," with a more general connotation than Coe's (1978:96) "Young Lords" (the Hero Twins).

Coe (1978:96) noted that the third and fifth glyphs in each text differ from each other and must refer to the different supernaturals seated within the backracks. He suggested that the third glyph names each creature in the respective backracks. At A3 (fig. 7a), ten.T86.524 (Ix) names the water-lily jaguar. The glyph compound at B3 (fig. 7b), six.T86.561, names the long-snouted furry-bodied zoomorph, and at C3 (fig. 7c), ten.T86.520 (Chuen) names the anthropomorphic monkey. Coe proposed that the final glyph in each text, which is composed of the mainsign of an emblem glyph (Berlin 1958), associates each of the dancer and dwarf pairs with a particular archaeological site. I propose instead that these final glyphs are additional parts of the names of the supernaturals and make no reference to Classic Maya sites.

The nominal concordance is particularly clear in the case of the water-lily jaguar supernatural (fig. 7a). The third glyph at A3 is the day sign Ix, which is associated with the jaguar and the underworld (Thompson 1950: 82). The final glyph T569 depicts bundled or twisted cords, a sign that is also the main component of the Tikal emblem glyph. Here, however, the water-group prefix (T36) and *ah po* (T168) are absent, affixes whose presence is mandatory for the identification of a glyphic compound as an emblem glyph (Berlin 1958). Schele (1985a:63) suggested that T569 is read *balan*, "coiled up, bundled," which is nearly homophonous with *balam*, "jaguar." Therefore, these two glyphs together name the water-lily jaguar as Ix Balam or "(underworld) jaguar-jaguar," a supernatural who figures prominently in underworld scenes on Classic Maya pottery.

Following the pattern established by the water-lily jaguar and its accompanying text, the second backrack creature is a long-snouted furry-bodied supernatural (fig. 7b). He is named by the compounds at B3 and B5, a "6-sky" (six.T86.561) compound, and T25.764 (phonetic *ca* and the day sign Chicchan) or "serpent" (Thompson 1950:75). Similar long-snouted saurians represent the sky on other Classic monuments (e.g., the stucco long-snouted saurian from Palenque House E, east chamber). This visual similarity suggests that the furry-bodied long-snouted supernatural from the Holmul-style vessels, named "6-sky serpent" in the vertical text, is a sky deity.[4] Although Coe (1978:96) noted that T764 is the main sign of the emblem glyph of Calakmul and identified the dancer and dwarf with this site, I suggest that here T764 is part of the name of this sky-related supernatural and makes no reference to Calakmul.

The last of the three backrack creatures is an anthropomorphic simian named by the glyphs at C3 and C5 (fig. 7c). The first nominal is ten.T86.520, whose main component is the day sign Chuen. Thompson (1950:80) noted that the day Chuen is associated with the Monkey God (Hun Chuen and/or Hun Batz from the Popol Vuh), who is associated with the arts. The glyph at C5 is composed of T174:563var, the latter being the main sign of the Machaquilá emblem glyph. As noted above, I do not believe that the reference is to the archaeological site of Machaquilá. Instead, this final

Fig. 8   Holmul-style vessel, MS 0603. Holmul dancer with "6-sky" supernatural seated in his backrack (drawing by Dorie Reents-Budet, copyright 1985).

glyphic compound must be part of the name of the anthropomorphic monkey deity, although I cannot explain the connection.

The fourth glyph in each of these three vertical texts is the same (fig. 7), and bears some resemblance to Coe's "Step glyph" of the Primary Standard Sequence (Coe 1973b:159). However, the affixes are different (T331 in Coe's compound and T166 *akbal* here on the vessel); given the compound's position within a nominal phrase, it is more likely that this glyph functions nominally much like the T1000b *ahau* title in the second position.

These vertical texts, then, function primarily as nominal phrases and name the supernaturals seated in the dancers' backracks. As such, they operate like many of the short texts in the monumental art (cf. Yaxchilán Lintel 8 and the Bonampak murals) that identify the participants. The last glyph in each phrase, composed of the main signs of various emblem glyphs, does not make reference to any Maya site, polity, or dynasty. Instead, these glyphs are additional parts of the supernaturals' names.

Implications for Emblem Glyphs

If the above hypothesis is correct, a logical conclusion is that the emblem glyphs of at least some Maya sites are derived from the names of supernaturals, a pattern consonant with Maya naming practices, wherein the names of supernaturals are incorporated into those of royal individuals, polities, and ruling families.

Many examples can be cited of rulers' names incorporating those of supernaturals. For example, the nominal main sign (T844) of the Early Classic Tikal ruler Curl Snout is the front head of the contemporary Celestial Monster (see the incised tripod cylinder vase in Berjonneau and Sonnery 1985:219). The glyph for the deity God K figures prominently in the name of Curl Snout's son Stormy Sky, and many of the Late Classic rulers of the Petexbatun area include this deity name in their nominals (Johnston 1985). Another example is that of the Early Classic Palenque ruler "Casper" (Schele 1978d) whose name glyph main sign (T628) marks the ear of a supernatural Deer Monster depicted on a Late Classic cylinder. A final example is the second zoomorphic glyph of Lord Smoking Shell's name on Lamanai St. 9. This zoomorphic monster glyph is the same as that found within an isolated glyphic cartouche inscribed on the lid of an Early Classic vessel in the Dumbarton Oaks Maya Photographic Archive (EC-p4-17) and may refer to a supernatural saurian.[5]

The naming of rulers after deities is not restricted to the Classic Period. In the Tizimin and Mani Chronicles of Yucatán (Brinton 1882) we read that the head chief of Chichén Itzá was named Chac Xib Chac (Tozzer 1941:138). David Stuart (in Schele and Miller 1986: 304, 307) identified Chac Xib Chac as the Post-Classic version of the Classic Period deity GI as evening star. The ruler Chac Xib Chac was defeated by Ah Nacxit Kukulcan (Brinton 1882:146), the name Kukulcan being the Maya name for the Mexican deity Quetzalcoatl.

Turning to emblem glyphs, these glyph compounds refer either to a specific Maya site or polity or to its ruling family. Although most remain undeciphered, in the case of the Tikal emblem glyph cited above a reading for the main sign coincides with the name of a jaguar supernatural (Schele 1985a). Additional examples of emblem glyph main signs making reference to supernaturals include what may be an Early Classic version of the Piedras Negras emblem glyph main sign (T585c) incised on the back of an aged supernatural that may name this character (Easby 1966:101). The Copán emblem glyph is composed of the head of a bat (T756) and may refer to the underworld supernatural Camazotz of the Popol Vuh.

Such polity naming practices would be consonant with findings from Late Post-Classic Yucatán, where settlements characteristically had tutelary idols whose names were applied to the towns as well.[6] Bruce Love (1986:160) cited the *Relaciones de Yucatán,* which lists at least eight towns that carried the same name as their respective idol (supernatural). For example, Campeche was named for an idol whose attributes included a coiled snake (*kaan*) with a tick (*pich'*) on its head. It would not be improbable, then, for the Classic Period emblem glyphs, which name sites or their ruling families, to be derived from the names of supernaturals. One could further suggest that these supernaturals or idols would have held a special place in the socioreligious life of the site in question.

In conclusion, the Holmul dancers' backracks contain different supernaturals who are named by the accompanying vertical texts. Their respective names include the main sign of various emblem glyphs that here do not refer to Maya sites or ruling families, but rather are part of the names of the supernaturals. It would appear, then, that at least some emblem glyphs may be derived from the names of supernaturals in a manner similar to that of Post-Classic Yucatán, where the nominals of the towns' tutelary idols were employed to name the towns as well. Given the vertical texts on vessel MS 1374, the emblem glyph main signs of Machaquilá and Calakmul (or Site Q) may be derived from the names of the two supernaturals seated in the dancers' backracks, although their identifications have yet to be made.

Notes

1. When possible, the Holmul-style vessels are referenced by their archival numbers from the Maya Ceramic Archive, Conservation Analytical Laboratory, Smithsonian Institution (e.g., MS 1374).

2. Claude Baudez (personal communication, 1986) brought to my attention the backrack on Copán St. H as another cosmographic image, although here the Cauac Monster is replaced by a sun visage wearing a quadripartite badge headdress.

3. Schele (1985a:142) interpreted this arching serpent on Tikal Temple IV Lintel 3 differently. She identified it as her "Vision Serpent" associated with bloodletting rites, an entity seemingly separate from the cosmographic backrack saurian. Schele also identified the backrack on Tikal Temple IV Lintel 2 as the Vision Serpent, although here a feathered Venus sign replaces the Principal Bird Deity atop the serpent. This feathered **serpent** and Venus symbol motif recalls the dancer's backrack on vessel MS 1125 (fig. 3). In both these examples the Cauac Monster is found below the serpent, and on Tikal Lintel 2 an eroded figure sits inside the backrack, which may be one of the backrack creatures like those from the Holmul-style pottery. Because of these close iconographic and positional similarities, I would identify the backrack from Tikal Temple IV Lintel 2 as the cosmographic backrack like those on the Holmul-style pottery and not as Schele's Vision Serpent.

4. This "10-sky" glyph compound (or "6-sky" in the case of MS 0603; see fig. 8) also names Schele's (1985a) Vision Serpent. I am not certain whether her Vision Serpent is synonymous with or substitutable for the "10/6-sky serpent" backrack supernatural, who in turn resembles the long-snouted sky saurians. It would seem that, although the backrack "10/6-sky saurian" and Schele's Vision Serpent (and possibly the arching feathered serpent with Venus sign of MS 1125 and Tikal Temple IV Lintel 2 as well) are separate entities, some kind of acceptable substitution or convergence exists among these saurian images.

It should be noted that on MS 1374 the creature with the "10-sky" name does not resemble any of the Vision Serpents identified by Schele (1985: figs. 8, 9, 10). Instead, his body is that of a furry zoomorph. This creature appears on another Holmul-style vessel, MS 0603 (fig. 8), whose body is marked with cross-hatching rather than fur. Here he has an elongated snout and his name includes the "6-sky" title. However, the second nominal compound is not the Chicchan glyph but rather is that of an undeciphered title (T606:23.565var?:23) that appears on a third Holmul-style vessel, MS H13, naming another furry-bodied zoomorph (Merwin and Vaillant 1932: pl. 30c).

If one is to suggest that the "10-sky" creature from the MS 1374 backrack and Schele's "6-sky Vision Serpent" are the same creature, one would have to explain their different depictions. For example, on stone monuments Schele's Vision Serpent can appear with a beard and/or feathers. It is possible that these stone monument versions of the serpent are depicted here on the pottery vessels in full detail, the beard being expanded into a furry body and the "serpent" portion referenced by the "10/6-sky" glyph compound and the cross-hatched body of the creature (see MS 0603; fig. 8). Such an explanation may be stretching the point, however, and leads to the conclusion that we do not yet understand the iconographic domains of these various serpents.

5. An equivocal example is the Naranjo Ruler Ah K'ak ("Lord Fire"), whose name glyph main sign (T563a) constitutes one of the nominals of a jaguar being sacrificed on a polychrome vessel (Robicsek and Hales 1981: fig. 22c). On the vessel, however, the wavy line above the T563a in Ah K'ak's name is replaced by a subfixed T61, which may distinguish these compounds as two separate nominals. This "fire" glyph (T563a) repeatedly names the flaming jaguar found on Classic Period vessels, however, and Ah K'ak's name may refer to this underworld supernatural.

6. Bruce Love brought to my attention these idol/town naming practices in Post-Classic Yucatán.

An Investigation of the Primary Standard Sequence on Classic Maya Ceramics

NIKOLAI GRUBE
UNIVERSITY OF HAMBURG

In the corpus of Maya hieroglyphic inscriptions the Primary Standard Sequence can be considered unique in many aspects. No other kind of text is written more often and is more widely distributed throughout the Classic Maya culture than the Primary Standard Sequence. Due to its wide distribution, no other glyph text presents such a large number of glyphic substitution patterns and scribal variations. An investigation of the Primary Standard Sequence contributes to our knowledge of glyphic substitution patterns and offers many insights into the internal structure of the writing system in general. The decipherment of the sequence itself will provide the scholarly community with an understanding of the function of Classic Maya polychrome ceramic in religious and funerary ritual.

The large body of texts now known as the Primary Standard Sequence was discovered by Michael D. Coe in 1973. It is a sequence of glyphs whose elements display highly predictable behavior. The Primary Standard Sequences tend to be written on ceramic vessels, bowls, or plates; only a few single glyphs of the sequence occur in monumental inscriptions. The only interpretation of the Primary Standard Sequence for a long time was that of Coe, who conjectured that the sequence is a "glyphic form of a long hymn which could have been sung over the dead and dying person, describing the descent of the Hero Twins to the Underworld, the various sinister gods and perils which they (and the dead's soul) might encounter there . . ." (Coe 1973b:22). This kind of mortuary interpretation for the Primary Standard Sequence in particular and the painted scenes on ceramics in general has been accepted by many scholars and found additional support in a comparison of the painted scenes with episodes of the Popol Vuh.

The recent progress in Maya hieroglyphic decipherment now begins to open a completely new interpretation of the Primary Standard Sequence. New readings of important glyph compounds of the Primary Standard Sequence indicate that the sequence is not a "hymn for the dead" but refers to the ritual use and manufacture of the ceramics on which it is written. David Stuart discovered

that one of the most frequent glyph compounds in the Primary Standard Sequence can be read as the Maya word for "writing." Stephen Houston and Karl Taube discovered that the sequence contains a glyph that refers to the bowl, plate, or vessel on which the text is written.

This essay shows that there is even more evidence for this less esoteric interpretation of the Primary Standard Sequence. It attempts to outline the new interpretations of the glyphs of the Primary Standard Sequence that result from an analysis of substitution patterns in the sequence and a comparison of the structural parallels between the Primary Standard Sequence and monumental inscriptions.

The Introductory Formula

Primary Standard Sequences usually begin with an introductory formula consisting of the glyphs called "Initial Sign," "Flat-hand Verb," and "God N" by Coe (1973b) (fig. 1). The three glyphs obey strict orders of precedent. Except for "Initial Sign," they are not necessarily part of the introductory statement. Only rarely are all three glyphs employed at the same time. Alternatively, Primary Standard Sequences can start with "Wing Quincunx," the most frequent glyph, discussed further below. Primary Standard Sequences beginning with "Wing Quincunx" are more common in the Early Classic. If the sequence does not begin with "Wing Quincunx," "Initial Sign" must always be present.

"Initial Sign" is regarded as a verbal glyph by Schele (1982:318–320). It appears frequently on monuments, located either between calendric information and verbal glyphs or immediately at the beginning of a text clause. The use of "Initial Sign" on monuments suggests that it is an introductory glyph that highlights the following glyphic information. "Initial Sign" is usually composed of three signs. Most frequently, the main sign is written with T617, the "mirror" grapheme. It is always prefixed by a sign of the *a/ah* substitution set (T228, T229, and T239). The suffix is T126, a grammatical morpheme with the possible reading of *i/ih*. I wonder whether "Ini-

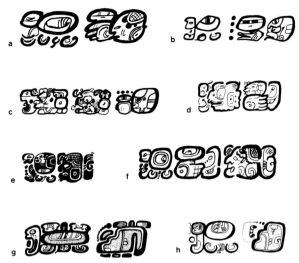

Fig. 1 The introductory formula. (a) von Winning 5662;
(b) "Initial Sign" and "Flat-hand Verb" (after Clarkson
1978: fig. 4); (c) "Initial Sign"—unknown glyph—"Flat-
hand Verb" on a polychrome plate (Robicsek and Hales
1981: fig. 57); (d) "Initial Sign" and "Flat-hand Verb"
(Coe 1975: no. 14); (e) "Initial Sign" and "God N" (von
Winning 6308); (f) "Initial Sign," "Flat-hand Verb," and
"God N" (Hellmuth 1978:197); (g) "Initial Sign" and
"Step" (Hellmuth 1978:195); (h) "Initial Sign" and "Step"
(Coe 1982:38).

tial Sign" reads ah₃-?Vl-ih and refers to Proto-Cholan
*yäli "it said" or "he said it" (3.Sg.Erg.-SAY-compl.-
3.Sg.A; from Proto-Cholan *äl "say," Kaufman and
Norman 1984:116), with the initial y- for the 3.Sg.
ergative pronoun perhaps not represented. This would
render a reading al or Vl for the "mirror" grapheme
T617. T617 can be identified as the main sign form
of affix T24. This affix is used as a suffix in nominal
constructions making a -Vl reading most likely for it.
Dütting (1980:108–112) identified the depiction of a
human eye as the iconic origin of the sign. If the icon
"eye" can stand for the act of "seeing," the value of
T24/T617 was probably derived from Proto-Cholan
*il-ä, "see" (Kaufman and Norman 1984:121). The
suggested reading of the glyph finds support in the fact
that there are spellings of "Initial Sign" in Early Classic
examples with "inverted ahaus" (T178) superponed, read
al or la.

There is no explanation yet for the other signs and
head glyphs that occasionally substitute for T617. At
least some of the head variants seem to be T1011, the
glyph of God I of the Palenque Triad (fig. 1d).

The second glyph in the introductory formula is Coe's
"Flat-hand Verb." From its suffix, T181 can be inferred
to be a verbal glyph. It also occurs in many different contexts on monuments and in the codices. The standard
representation of this glyph in the Primary Standard Sequence is T24:713a.181; however, there are many different spellings. Especially the superfix varies consider-

ably, whereas the "hand" T713a and the verbal postfix
T181 are more constant. The combination of T713a and
T181 is part of a lot of verbal glyphs in stone inscriptions. There is always a superfix, whose form depends on
the context in which the glyph is used. With one of the
superfixes T1030a, T58.522, or T60 the glyph is well attested as part of an accession expression in Palenque
(Schele and Miller 1983:36). If the superfix is T528.116
tun₂-(ni), the glyph indicates the "completion of tun"
(Thompson 1950:190–191). In the Dresden Venus
tables "Flat-hand Verb" appears as the principal event
glyph with the same superfix as in the Primary Standard
Sequence. Its initial position in the texts accompanying
the "spearing scenes" suggests that it is a verbal glyph.
Thompson (1972:65) translated "Flat-hand Verb" in
the Dresden Venus tables as "it appears, is visible or influences . . ." In summary, even if "Flat-hand Verb"
eludes complete decipherment, something of its function can be inferred from the various contexts in which
it appears. They indicate that T713a.181 is a unit and
that only the superfix is directly related to the context.
The superfix seems to carry the bulk of the semantic information of the glyph. T713a.181 functions as some
kind of verbalizer and is possibly used for the derivation
of verbs from nouns. The various forms the glyph has on
Tepeuh 1 and earlier ceramics cannot yet be explained
(figs. 1a, b, c).

The third glyph in the introductory formula shows up
in two different manifestations: the head of the old God
N (fig. 1e, f) or a glyph representing a step (figs. 1g, h).
These signs never occur in the same sequence and substitute for each other. They are allographs representing
the same information. Houston (n.d.:5) shows that
both "God N" and "Step" may dissolve into each other
through the process of glyphic affixation and infixation.
There are glyphs that unite typical features of both "God
N" and "Step" in one sign (fig. 1e).

"Step" and "God N" also occur outside the Primary
Standard Sequence. If T679a is prefixed to them, the
glyphs indicate the completion of tun. Both "Step" and
"God N" can be part of a certain compound on monuments, whose second element is T61.756a°568a (yu-bat;
fig. 2). This seems to be an introductory compound of
minor or incised texts on monuments. Although "Step"/
"God N" are not unfrequent glyphs on the monuments
and in the Primary Standard Sequence, they remain
unexplained.

a   b

Fig. 2 "God N"/"Step" and T61.756a°568a, yu-bat, in
stone inscriptions. (a) Yax. Lnt. 25, 02; (b) Nim Li Punit
St. 2, bottom.

The sequence of "Initial Sign," "Flat-hand Verb," and "Step"/"God N" forms what I call the "introductory formula" of the Primary Standard Sequence. Conceivably, the introductory formula consists of glyphs that serve to introduce a text and to underscore the following information.

Manik Hand

The glyph called "Manik Hand" (fig. 3) is not limited to one single position in the Primary Standard Sequence. Usually it either stands between "Nahal" and "Wing Quincunx" or follows next to the introductory formula, preceding the "U Tz'ib" statement. "Manik Hand" is one of the most regular glyphs of the Primary Standard Sequence. The most common form of it is T18.671 (fig. 3a, b, d, f), the main sign being the hand of the day sign "Manik." The hand T671 is read with the phonetic value *chi*. It is derived formally from the gesture "to eat" (Yuc. *chi-bal, comer carne, pescados o huevos*), which is still used in Yucatec sign language. In the Primary Standard Sequence T671 is sometimes replaced by a deer head (fig. 3e), because it represents the day Manik "deer" logographically and the syllable *chi* phonetically. The

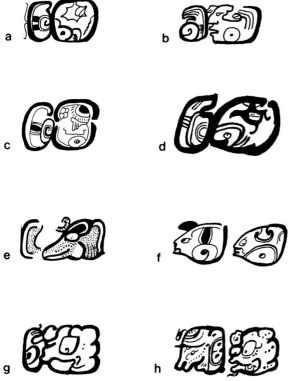

Fig. 3 "Manik Hand." (a) Robicsek and Hales 1981: fig. 57; (b) Museo Popol Vuh 1117; (c) Coe 1982:38; (d) von Winning 5662; (e) deer head for T671 on red-background bowl from Flores(?), Bayly Museum; (f) Clarkson 1978: fig. 4; (g) Robicsek and Hales 1981: fig. 86; (h) T758b replaces T18 as prefix, Kerr Photo no. 2068.

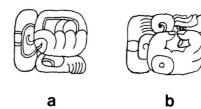

Fig. 4 T18 in glyphs that express a relationship. (a) T18.565a:88, Pal. T. 18 Tab., C14; (b) T18.86:671, Aguat. 1, D6.

Proto-Cholan word for "deer" is *chij* (Kaufman and Norman 1984:118). T18, the prefix, is difficult to distinguish from T17 and T88 of the Thompson (1962) catalog. T18 has a head variant (fig. 3h), the head of a creature with a long nose, which could be the same head as the one Thompson classified as T758b. Sometimes T88 replaces the usual prefix T18 of "Manik Hand." T88 and T18 differ only in one detail: T18 has an infixed curl (similar to the curl of T17) that is absent in T88. T18 and T88 are also distinguished through their distribution. T18 is often preposed to relational glyphs (fig. 4). T88 is a widely distributed verbal suffix in equal distribution with T136 and T246. No reading for any of the affixes T18, T88, and their head form T758b has been offered so far. Combined, the two signs of "Manik Hand" transliterate to ?-*chi*. If the assumptions are valid that "Manik Hand" is a phonetic spelling of a CVC word and that the *i*-vowel of *chi* reflects vowel synharmony, the word behind "Manik Hand" can be reconstructed as C*i*-ch(*i*). This would render in a C*i* or C*e* reading for T18 and the related signs. However, there is as yet no thoroughgoing analysis of this element that could be used to confirm the vowel reconstruction.

Since "Manik Hand" does not occur outside the Primary Standard Sequence, it is difficult to draw any definite conclusion in regard to its meaning or function in the text. The variable position of "Manik Hand" in the Primary Standard Sequence between the introductory formula and "Wing Quincunx" supports evidence that it does not denote essential thematic information.

"U Tz'ib"

The glyph compound called "U Tz'ib" (fig. 5) was first recognized and successfully deciphered as the glyph for "writing" by David Stuart. He also discovered that the "U Tz'ib" compound is an essential part of the Primary Standard Sequence. It occurs in many different forms, employing a large number of interesting substitution patterns.

The core of the "U Tz'ib" glyph compounds are two signs that represent the phonetic values *tz'i* and *b*(V). The length of the "U Tz'ib" compound, however, varies considerably. There are compounds that occupy the space of only a single glyph block; others are extended over four successive glyph blocks.

The analysis of the "U Tz'ib" compound reveals in

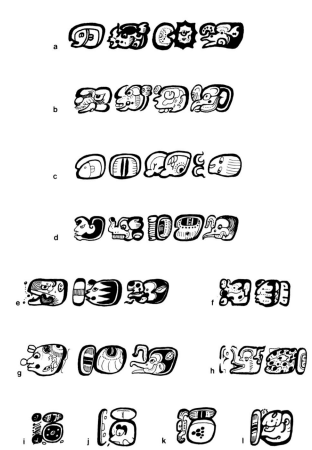

Fig. 5 "U Tz'ib." (a) U-tz'i-?-V1 (Coe 1973:39); (b) U-tz'i-ba(k)-V1 (Robicsek 1978: fig. 146); (c) U-tz'i-?-ul (Smith 1955: fig. 72b); (d) U?-tz'i-ᵇᵃba-V1 (Robicsek and Hales 1981: fig. 32); (e) U-tz'i-ba-V1 (Robicsek and Hales 1981: fig. 57); (f) U₆-tz'i-ba-? (Robicsek and Hales 1981: vase 186); (g) U-tz'i-ba-V1 (Coe 1982:38); (h) U-tz'i-bal(am)-? (Kerr Photo no. 2206); (i) U₆-tz'i-be-V1 (von Winning 6308); (j) U-tz'i-b(e) (Robicsek and Hales 1981: fig. 22a); (k) U₅-tz'i-b(e) (Kerr Photo no. 1837); (l) tz'i-b(e) (Robicsek and Hales 1981: vase 138).

how many different ways the same word can be spelled in Maya hieroglyphic writing. It also helps to throw light on the structure of phonetic constructions in the writing system.

The first part in the "U Tz'ib" compound is the 3.Sg. ergative pronoun *u*. Apparently it is an optional element in the glyph. The pronoun is usually represented by one of the allographic signs T1, T3, T11, T13, T204, T230, and T231 (fig. 5f, h, i, j, k). Additionally the pronoun can be represented by T513 and its head variant, the head of the *xoc*-monster (fig. 5a, b, c, e). Thompson (1944) was the first to regard both signs as members of the same substitution set. They are now read *u*, following a suggestion by David Stuart. Both signs are employed alternatively in the PDI and ADI glyphs in the inscriptions where they spell the word T513/738c:59 *u-t(i)*, "come to pass" (Proto-Cholan *uht; Kaufman

and Norman 1984:135). There are examples for the substitution of T513 and T1 in the stone inscriptions clearly demonstrating that both signs are allographs that can freely substitute for each other. There are even more signs in the position where one would expect the *u*-pronoun than the pronouns discussed above (figs. 5d, g). They appear to be rare allographs of the other *u*-signs. The possible *u*-sign in figure 5g depicts a (female?) head with an infix T171. This affix is Landa's second *u*. In the codices it is infixed into the forehead of the Moon Goddess (T1027), perhaps based on Yucatecan and Cholan *uh*, "moon."

The second position in the "U-Tz'ib" compound is occupied by the set of signs representing the phonetic value *tz'i*. Two signs are used to express this value. The first one is Thompson's T563a "Fire" (fig. 5c, e, g, i, j, k, l). The *tz'i* reading for T563a results from a phonetic spelling of the month name Zotz' on an unprovenanced column altar now in the St. Louis Art museum (Liman and Durbin 1975). At the same time, there is evidence that T563a can substitute for a glyphic doghead (fig. 6a). The Proto-Cholan word for "dog" is *tz'i? (Kaufman and Norman 1984:134). More evidence for the *tz'i* reading comes from two vase texts (fig. 6b, November 60 and Kerr 2286). Both vases depict among other supernaturals(?) a potbellied figure with a hugely swollen belly. The accompanying text to both figures begins with the glyph T57:563a. T57 is part of the month glyph Kayab, read by Fox and Justeson (1984b:67) as *k'anasi*, the documented Cholan name of the corresponding month. They noted that the *k'an* sign (T281) is always present in the month glyphs as an infix of T743, *a* or *ah*, as well as the final *-i* in T126. With these readings clear, Fox and Justeson proposed to read T57 as *si*. The first glyph in the columns accompanying the potbellied figures can be deciphered now. Read together, the signs T57 and T563a result in a word like *si'tz'i*. In Chol (Aulie and Aulie 1978:105) *sits'* means *ganas de comer (carne)*, and *sits'lel* is glossed as *glotonería*. The same basic meaning has the word *sits'* in Yucatec. The potbellied figure appears to have such a hugely swollen belly because of its gluttony.

In place of T563a another glyph, the head of a bat, can be employed to spell the *tz'i* of *tz'ib* (fig. 5a, b, d, f, h). This is Thompson's T756a/b, the same sign that logographically represents the month name Zotz', "bat." The *tz'i* reading of T756a/b is supported by substitutions of the bat head by the head of a dog (*tz'i*) in the "k'in-animal" glyph (fig. 6c). The substitution patterns involving T563a and T756a/b clearly show that T756 has two glyph values: the logographic value *SOTZ'* and a phonetic value *tz'i*. This apparently is supportive evidence for the existence of polyvalence in Maya hieroglyphic writing. The phonetic value *tz'i* can in no way be related to the logographic value *SOTZ'*, "bat."

Next there is the *-b(V)* part of the word *tz'ib*. There are numerous spellings for the final *-b(V)* in the Primary Standard Sequence. Most common are the signs T585a

Fig. 6 *The substitution set tz'i. (a) The replacement of T563a by a dog head. Piedras Negras St. 26, front, Lnt. from the Bonampak area (Mayer 1978 Cat. no. 2, B8); (b) The sitz'-personage with the swollen body (after Kerr Photo no. 2286); (c) The alternation between "dog" and "bat" (Kerr Photo no. 2206; Coe 1973:26).*

be (fig. 5i) and T501 *ba* (fig. 5d, g), whose phonetic values are beyond discussion. The head variants of both signs are also often employed (fig. 5j, l). The phonetic value be can also be represented by a realistic depiction of a human footprint (fig. 5k). This is Landa's first *B* and corresponds to Thompson's T501. Other signs used to write the final -*b*(V) are less frequent and are less well understood. The glyphs occupying the location of the final -*b*(V) on red-background Uaxactún ceramics include a skull (fig. 5b) or a compound glyph consisting of two elements: the first is not included in Thompson's catalog; the second is T528, "Cauac" (figs. 5a, c). The phonetic value of the skull sign could be based on Proto-Cholan *bak*, "bones" (Kaufman and Norman 1984: 116). The words for "skull" in many Lowland languages are derived from a descriptive expression like "bony head" (Chol b∧quel jol∧l calavera, Aulie and Aulie 1978:35). The compound sign used for the writing of the final -*b*(V) on Uaxactún red-background ceramics cannot yet be interpreted.

Another uncommon glyph in the same substitution set is a head sign with black scalloping elements in the left half (figs. 5e, f). Finally a very unusual spelling for the final -*b*(V) has to be mentioned: on a vase in Nebaj style (fig. 5h) "U Tz'ib" is spelled with T751, the jaguar head. This spelling is based on the common Mayan word for "jaguar," which in all Mayan languages begins with *b* (Proto-Cholan *b'ahlām*, "jaguar," Kaufman and Norman 1984:116). This spelling requires an acrophonic interpretation, since at least the -*am* of *balam* has to be dropped for a grammatical correct reading, *u-tz'i-bal(am)*. The existence of acrophony in Maya hieroglyphic writing is still debated, so this spelling could be an argument in favor of it.

Finally, "U Tz'ib" has an optional -V*l* suffix, for which there are at least three different signs. The most frequent of these functionally equivalent signs is "Worm Bird" (fig. 5a, b, d, e, g). As the name implies, it shows the head of a bird carrying a worm in its beak. That this is a -V*l* suffix can be confirmed by the substitution of "Worm Bird" with T82 on Uaxactún red-background ceramics (fig. 5c). The same substitution pattern occurs in other contexts. "Worm Bird" substitutes for T24 and T82 in Glyph D of the Lunar Series (fig. 7). Occurrences of "Worm Bird" in this position are rare but nonetheless in evidence on Site Q glyphic panel 4, now in a private collection in Zürich (Mayer 1978b:no. 48), B4, and on Copán Hieroglyphic Stairway, step 11. T82 is generally acknowledged to represent -V*l* or *ul*. It is perhaps the affix form of main sign T568a, which iconically is a heart and thus originally may have been *ol*. The equivalence of "Worm Bird" with T82 suggests the bird's name perhaps sounding V*l*. A bird V*l* is not known to me. However, if the V*l* logogram may be used also with the corresponding *lV* value, suitable words for a bird can be found. A widely distributed word for hawk (*gavilan[cillo]*) in the Lowland languages is *li?* or *lik* (Proto-Cholan *lik-lik*, Proto-Mayan *li/lik*). The alternations between "Worm Bird" and T82 in some contexts could perhaps result from homophony between the values *il/ul* of T82 and *li/lik* of "Worm Bird." Finally, there are "U

a   **b**

Fig. 7 *The substitution of "Worm Bird" by T82 in Glyph D of the Lunar Series. (a) Site Q Glyphic Panel 4, B4; (b) Site Q Glyphic Panel 3, B1.*

Tz'ib" glyphs that have a suffix T140 or T178 (fig. 5i). This is the la sign, whose reading is now accepted by all scholars. The use of three -Vl signs—all with different vowels—in the same substitution set suggests that the vowel was less important, or that the vowel of each sign was flexible and could change to represent the grammatically required Vl or V'l suffix.

In a number of instances, another compound is set into the position that is otherwise taken by "U Tz'ib"—T61.756°568a (fig. 8b, c). The ceramics on which this compound substitutes for "U Tz'ib" (e.g., Smith 1955: fig. 10s; Coe 1973b:73; Dütting 1974: fig. 8a; Tate 1985: fig. 6; Kerr 2229; Kerr 3199) all have a common feature: they are not painted but carved or incised. Most of them come from northern Yucatán (Xcalumkin or Chocholá) or are very late (Tepeu 3) Petén ceramics. Although the compound T61.756°568a escapes decipherment, a lot more information about it can be inferred from a consideration of its monumental occurrences.

The hieroglyphic lintels of Chichén Itzá contain glyph sequences structurally parallel to the Primary Standard Sequence (fig. 8a). T61.756°568a usually precedes the glyph T1000.181:178 or T23.683b:178, "Nahal," in the Chichén Itzá texts. In the Primary Standard Sequence "Nahal" is the next glyph to "U Tz'ib." On Monjas Lnt. 4 and Four Lintels Lnt. 3 two glyphs precede T61.756°568a that correspond to "Initial Sign" and "Flat-hand Verb" of the Primary Standard Sequence. Even the glyph that follows "Nahal" on Monjas Lnt. 4, Bl, and the Four Lintels, Lnt. 3, A3, are syntactically equivalent to their counterpart in the Primary Standard Sequence, "Wing Quincunx." The glyph next to "Nahal" on the Chichén Itzá lintels can be read U-pa-ka-b(a), "his lintel" (Houston n.d.:12) and refers to the medium on which the text is written. This corresponds clearly to "Wing Quincunx," which also names the artifact on which the glyphs are written, with a 3Sg. ergative pronoun preposed (see below). On Itzimte Lnt.

1 I1–J3 another glyph text is written that corresponds structurally to the Primary Standard Sequence and the Chichén Itzá clauses discussed above (fig. 8d). It includes even the glyph "Manik Hand" as a specific feature of the Primary Standard Sequence. "Manik Hand" precedes T61.756.568a? and a tun_2 glyph in J3, again referring to the medium of the monument.

All these parallels furnish further evidence that T61.756°568a is a glyph that substitutes for "U Tz'ib." Logically, it should refer to the semantic domain of "writing." The Chichén Itzá clauses as well as the first half of the Primary Standard Sequence before "Wing Quincunx" describe the act of writing or the dedication of a glyph text on a certain medium. T61.756°568a is a widely distributed initial compound on small incised secondary texts on stone monuments (fig. 2). It can be assumed, therefore, that its meaning is not "writing" in general, but rather "carving" or "it is incised" and thus introduces minor texts.

"Nahal"

The glyph "Nahal" is only optative in the Primary Standard Sequence (fig. 9). It usually is located between "U Tz'ib" and "Wing Quincunx." Sometimes, but not often, it occupies a different position between the introductory formula and "Wing Quincunx." "Nahal" is a remarkably uniform glyph. It is composed of two signs with a third one not necessarily present: (1) na, spelled by one of the three signs T4, T23 (fig. 9d), or T1000, a female head (fig. 9a, b, c), (2) the moon sign T683b/181, which is read ah, and (3) a sign for the suffix al/la, which does not have to be present. The equivalence of the different na signs was convincingly demonstrated by Lounsbury (1984a). The moon sign T181/683b is read ah because it is employed as the male proclitic particle ah in names and titles and because it can be shown to

Fig. 8 T61.756°568a replacing "U Tz'ib" on ceramics and in stone inscriptions. (a) Chichén Itzá, Monjas Lnt. 4, B5–C1; (b) Primary Standard Sequence on carved vase in Pelling Collection, Tübingen (Dütting 1974: fig. 8); (c) Primary Standard Sequence on a carved bowl in Chocholá-style (Kerr Photo no. 3199); (d) Itzimte, Lnt. 1, I1–J3.

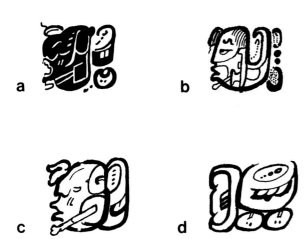

a   b

c   d

Fig. 9 "Nahal." (a) von Winning 6308; (b) Kerr Photo no. 1398; (c) Kerr Photo no. 1383; (d) Robicsek and Hales 1981: table 3e.

a

b   c

Fig. 10 "U lak." (a) Plate in private collection, Austria; (b) Robicsek and Hales 1981: vessel 117; (c) Coe 1982: fig. 38.

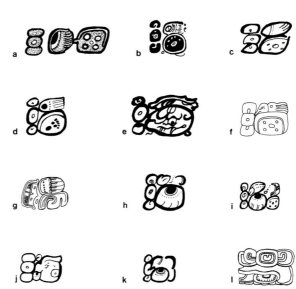

a   b   c

d   e   f

g   h   i

j   k   l

Fig. 11 "Wing Quincunx." (a) T61.77.585a (bowl in the Bayly Museum); (b) T61.77:585a:140 (von Winning 6308); (c) T61.77:585a (Clarkson 1978: fig. 4); (d) T61.77:301 (Robicsek and Hales 1981: vessel 179); (e) T61.77:585aP (Duke University Museum of Art 1978.35.4); (f) T61.236:585a (Tate 1985: fig. 6); (g) T1.77:? (Berjonneau and Sonnery 1985: fig. 351); (h) T61.128:501 (Robicsek and Hales 1981: fig. 22a); (i) T61.128:501.585a (Robicsek and Hales 1981: vessel 184); (j) T61.128P°501 (Robicsek 1978: fig. 156); (k) T61.128P:501 (Kerr Photo no. 1728); (l) T61:128P:501, one of the earliest occurrences of "Wing Quincunx" (Chase and Chase 1986).

express the verbal suffix -ah of the Cholan and Yucatecan languages, and finally because a graphically similar sign is documented in the Landa alphabet for the same value. Although there is some evidence for an ah reading, this reading fails to explain the obvious function of T683b as a moon sign at least in the Lunar Series. I wonder whether the sign just has a Vh value with a variable vowel whose value is determined by the context. This would allow to read the sign ah when it is used as a proclitic particle or as a verbal suffix, and uh, "moon," when it occurs in the Lunar Series.

In the "Nahal" glyph the value of the vowel most likely is a (because of vowel synharmony). The glyph than transliterates as na-ha-(la). It seems no problem to translate the glyph now with the help of dictionaries. However, there are numerous different lexical entries for such a word in the dictionaries of the Chol and Yucatec languages. None of the lexical glosses satisfactorily elucidates the meaning of the glyph. The only conclusion that can be drawn without too much speculation is that the glyph seems to connect the verbal expression for "writing" with the medium on which the text is written.

"Wing Quincunx"

The most important and most frequent glyph of the Primary Standard Sequence is "Wing Quincunx" (figs. 10, 11). This is the core of the whole sequence (Grube 1985:59). The syntactical position of "Wing Quincunx" actually is occupied by two entirely different glyphs in complementary distribution. Stephen Houston and Karl Taube recognized that "Wing Quincunx" never occurs on flat dishes or plates. Instead, there is a compound that reads U-la-k(a), "his dish," in the same position. This compound, however, is restricted to plates and is not written on bowls or vases (fig. 10). This is clear evidence that "Wing Quincunx" and u lak are related to a certain type of ceramic. If u lak is the glyph for flat dishes

or plates, it can be assumed that "Wing Quincunx" is an expression for vessels and bowls. So there are actually two glyphs that are functionally equivalent in the position of Coe's "Wing Quincunx" glyph. The u lak glyph consists of the 3.Sg. ergative pronoun prefix U, main sign T534 for the phonetic value la, and a fish head or affix T25 representing the value ka. The la sign sometimes is merged in a death head with missing lower jaw, perhaps because lah means "to finish, die" in Chol and Yucatec (Proto-Cholan *laj, "v.i. finish," Kaufman and Norman 1984:124, Yucatec *lah, fin, cabo*, Martínez Hernández 1929; fig. 10c).

"Wing Quincunx" is restricted to vessels and bowls. It is usually composed of three signs. The first sign in the reading order always represents the 3.Sg. ergative pronoun. Although there are a few "Wing Quincunx" glyphs that have T1 *ü* as a prefix (fig. 11g), T61 is far more common in this position. T61 is now known to have the value *yu*. It is not only used phonetically but is also employed logographically as prevocalic 3.Sg. ergative pronoun *ÿ/üÿ*. This reading is confirmed by substitution patterns in Chichén Itzá, where T61 and signs of the *u*-set freely substitute for each other in the glyph T61.756°568a studied above (cf. Monjas Lnt. 4, D5 [T61]—Four Lintels, Lnt. 3, A2 [T1]). The sign value perhaps is derived from *uy*, "necklace" (Kaufman and Norman 1984:135). The second element to be read in "Wing Quincunx" is the superfix. Four different signs can be employed here: (1) the "wing" affix T77 (fig. 11a, b, c, d, e, g), (1) the affix T128 (fig. 11h, i); (3) the head variant of T128 (fig. 11j, k, l), and (4) the full-figure representation of a bird, corresponding to T236 (fig. 11f). All these signs are equivalent and perhaps are allographs that have the same phonetic value.

T77 represents a bird's wing. It never occurs outside "Wing Quincunx." However, it is the superfix most found with "Wing Quincunx." T128 is less frequent and seems to be restricted to ceramics of the "Ik site" or "Codex style site D" (Robicsek and Hales 1981:236). T128 also has a head variant. The *be* or *ba* sign that always must be present in "Wing Quincunx" is infixed into the mouth of the head variant of T128. Both T128 and its head variant are found in glyphic contexts outside the Primary Standard Sequence, too. T128 is the usual superfix to Glyph F of the Lunar Series (T128: 60:23). The head variant is also found in this context (e.g., Dos Pilas St. 5, D1, Yax. Lnt. 46, B3). T128 is part of the glyphic expression "end of (month)." There is no evidence for the use of the head variant of T128 or any of the other signs of the substitution set in this expression. The head variant of T128 is the main sign of the name glyph of "Humo-Jaguar," the twelfth ruler of Copán. Humo-Jaguar's name is also seen with T128 replacing the head. Finally, there is a rare substitution pattern that involves T609b, an object consisting of two layers of jaguar skin. An examination of ceramic iconography leads to the identification of this object as a codex, bound in jaguar hide, such as we can find in Robicsek and Hales 1981 (fig. 33a and Vessel 1, in front of the rabbit). The "codex-sign" now can replace T128 and its head variant in Glyph F of the Lunar Series as well as in the name of the Copán lord (Cop. St. E, D13).

The full-figure bird that substitutes for the superfixes on ceramics of the Maxcanú/Chocholá-region (Tate 1985) does not occur in the contexts of Glyph F or the name of Humo-Jaguar. T236 seems to have been a local introduction, perhaps based on a dialect(?) word for a bird species homophone to the phonetic value required

for signs in the substitution class only in that particular language/dialect region.

No reading has been suggested yet for any of the superfixes. The fact, however, that T1 and T204, both with the reading *u*, are sometimes infixed into the head variant of T128 could indicate that the first vowel of T128 and its head variant is *u*. On Tila St. B, A7, *u* is superfixed to the codex sign T609a. I believe that this is a phonetic complement *u* written to indicate the first vowel of the sign. This assumption finds support in the fact that the *u* signs are only optional.

The main sign of "Wing Quincunx" represents the value *b*(V). Both T585a *be* and T501 *ba* occur in this position, including their head variants. In summary, "Wing Quincunx" as the most important and most frequent glyph in the Primary Standard Sequence is a word or metaphorical expression for "bowl," "vessel," or a comparable ceramic artifact. Except for one sign, the glyph can be read *yu/uy-?-b*(V).

Glyphs Following "Wing Quincunx"

"Wing Quincunx" can be regarded as the core of the Primary Standard Sequence. The Primary Standard Sequence continues after "Wing Quincunx" with a clause of relatively nonvariable glyphs. This second half of the Primary Standard Sequence is less well understood than the first half. The number of glyphs in this part of the sequence can vary from one to seven. The glyphs in this part of the Primary Standard Sequence and some of their most obvious substitution patterns are illustrated in figure 12.

The first glyph that can stand after "Wing Quincunx" can be read phonetically as *TI-u-lu* or *TI-u-ul*. The glyph consists of three signs. The prefix is one of the prepositions *ti/ta* (cf. Mathews and Justeson 1984:186: figs. 1h–n). The superfix to the glyph represents either the value *U* (T1, T3, T11, etc.) or *yu* (T61). The main sign is always T568a "Sacrifice," which bears the value *ol* or *ul/lu*. A close inspection of the occurrences of this glyph shows that it is restricted in its distribution. It cannot occur on every kind of ceramic plate or bowl. *TI-u-lu* is written only on bowls whose diameter is considerably larger than its height (cf. Robicsek and Hales 1981: vase 184; table 1i; table 2e; Kerr Photo no. 2226, no. 2358, no. 3025). The bowls on which this glyph occurs usually do not have a scene painted on them, the Primary Standard Sequence being the only painting. This restricted distribution of *TI-u-lu* is clear evidence for the association of the glyph with the form of the bowl. Since *TI-u-lu* always follows "Wing Quincunx," which is a glyph for bowls and vessels, the combination of both glyphs should be translated "his bowl for (*ti*) *u-lu*." The word *u-l*(*u*) perhaps denotes the use or the content for which the specific bowl was designed. It can be assumed, then, that only bowls whose diameter was larger than the height could be used for the *u-l*(*u*) function.

The next glyph can also be read completely *TI/TA-*

yu-ta-(Vl). This glyph has been termed "Serpent Segment" by Coe. The main sign of this glyph is T565a and is read *ta*. It can be used for the prefix with the same phonetic value (Mathews and Justeson 1984). Both the prefix and the superfix are the same as in the *Tl-u-lu* glyph; however, T61 is never replaced by T1 in "Serpent Segment."

The following glyph, "Young Lord," is also prefixed by a preposition *ti* or *ta*. "Young Lord" and the glyph Coe lists as "Spotted Kan" are actually one and the same glyph. "Young Lord" can merge in "Spotted Kan," and "Spotted Kan" sometimes is represented with the facial features of "Young Lord," so there can be no doubt about the unity of both glyphs. The glyph consists of a prefix and a main sign, which can be either T507 ("Spotted Kan") or the nominal glyph of the tonsured young lord, the Maize God of the classic Maya culture (Taube 1985).

The first three glyphs of the second part of the Primary Standard Sequence should be analyzed as a unit because they share the common feature of the preposed preposition. The grammatical functions of cognates of Proto-Mayan *ti* in the Cholan and Yucatecan languages are manifold and should be considered for an interpretation and reading of the three glyphs.

The next glyph to "Young Lord" is Coe's "Muluc." It has a variable superfix, a main sign that is either T513 (without the dot in the left half of the sign shown in Thompson's illustration in the catalog) or the head of the god of the month Pax (Thompson 1950: fig. 23, 18–20) and always the postfix T188 *le*. The glyph has been interpreted as a title by Coe, but there is no clear indication for this.

"Muluc" is followed by "Fish." This is a remarkably nonvariable glyph always composed of a drawing of a fish (sometimes prefixed by T25 *ka*) and the affix T130 *wa* set below or after the main sign. The combined signs read *ka*-*wa*. Again, this is a case of a phonetic reading of a glyph where no translation yet found would fit into the context. "Fish" is one of the most frequent glyphs of the Primary Standard Sequence.

The glyph termed "Rodent Bone" stands next in the sequence. The main sign is the head of a rodent, T758a. There is always a sign prefixed to it, either T111, a bone, read logographically *BAK*, or a skull. If the skull is chosen, another small affix not included in the Thompson catalog is put before. The affix always following the rodent main sign is T110, which Stuart and Grube (1986) read with the phonetic value *ko*. The rodent

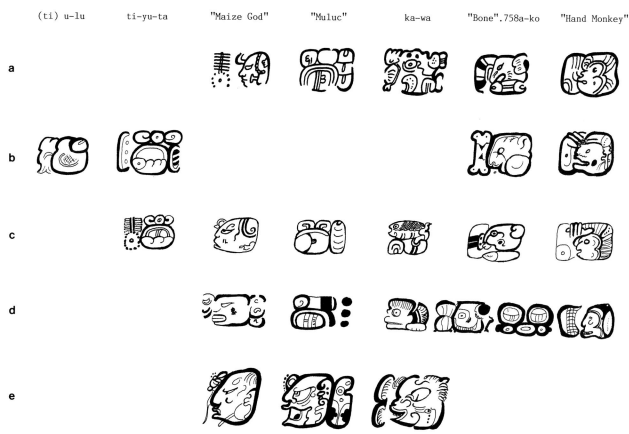

(ti) u-lu	ti-yu-ta	"Maize God"	"Muluc"	ka-wa	"Bone".758a-ko	"Hand Monkey"

Fig. 12   The second half of the Primary Standard Sequence. (a) Holmul plate, Merwin and Vaillant 1932: fig. 32c; (b) Robicsek and Hales 1981: table li; (c) Coe 1978:14; (d) text on vessel from Altun Ha, Mac phase, Pendergast 1982: fig. 34a; (e) Robicsek and Hales 1981: vessel 179.

The Primary Standard Sequence on Classic Maya Ceramics

main sign itself can be replaced by T287, a substitution well known from other contexts—for example, Glyph B of the Lunar Series.

"Hand Monkey" and "Ah Spotted Kan" are the last glyphs in the Primary Standard Sequence. Both glyphs have escaped decipherment. "Ah Spotted Kan" presumably is a title also known from the Palenque inscriptions.

Conclusions

The Primary Standard Sequence is not a hymn or an abbreviated version of the Popol Vuh. It now turns out that the mortuary interpretation that was generally accepted has to be dropped in favor of a less esoteric explanation. The Primary Standard Sequence seems to be in reference to the ritual use and manufacture of ceramics. This interpretation is more consistent with the discovery of the glyph for "writing" in the sequence. The most important glyph of the Primary Standard Sequence records a word for the ceramic on which the text is written. The glyph that refers to "ceramic" is followed by a clause of three glyphs with prepositions. At least one of the glyphs is associated with a certain type of bowls, perhaps in reference to its use or content. It can only be speculated whether other glyphs of the Primary Standard Sequence following "Wing Quincunx" also record the use of the ceramics. Our lack of knowledge about the use of Maya polychrome ceramics turns out to be a major hindrance to the understanding of the Primary Standard Sequence. Additionally, due to the destructive work of looters, the archaeological contexts of Maya polychrome ceramics are lost forever. It will be an important task to gather all ethnohistoric sources and archaeological data on the use of ceramics in order to shed more light on the function of polychrome ceramics in Maya ritual. Such research would also contribute to a deeper understanding of the Primary Standard Sequence.

The Primary Standard Sequence provides one of the most productive areas for the analysis of glyphic substitution patterns. A much more careful and detailed study of them is urgently needed for the decipherment of Maya hieroglyphic writing.

Acknowledgments

This paper has benefited from extensive discussions about the Primary Standard Sequence with Dieter Dütting, Stephen Houston, Kornelia Kurbjuhn, Dorie Reents-Budet, Linda Schele, and last but certainly not least David Stuart. I owe special thanks to Barbara and Justin Kerr for allowing me to use their photographic collection and for their gracious hospitality. This paper could not have been written without the help of Stacy Goodman, Karl Herbert Mayer, Robert Peters, Roberto Rolando Rubio Cifuentes and the Museo Popol Vuh, and Gordon Whittaker, who kindly provided me with data and with stimulating thoughts.

A Study of the Fish-in-Hand Glyph, T714: Part 1

DIANE WINTERS
NEW SCHOOL FOR SOCIAL RESEARCH

Thompson's T714 (1962), an icon consisting of a fish grasped vertically in a hand, was used from the Early through Late Classic Period as well as in the Dresden and Paris codices, and its geographic range encompassed Copán, Palenque, and Chichén Itzá. Its appearance in three distinct syntactic contexts—with *bolon* prefix as G1 of the Nine Lords of the Night, with *hun* prefix as a ruler's name, and most frequently as a verb—led to study from different directions by a number of Mayanists whose work has already resulted in several suggestions regarding a reading, and in the establishment of a connection with both bloodletting events and ancestral lineage. My interest has been to explore more fully the avenues already opened. This paper presents the initial results of my study, focusing primarily on the glyph itself in its textual and associated visual contexts and on possible readings. Work will continue on aspects of meaning to be gleaned from a better understanding of its verbal affixation patterns, and on the specific nature of the "fish-in-hand event" and its role in the lives of the individuals involved in its performance.

Though by no means rare, the fish-in-hand is not a common glyph. I gathered fifty-eight clear or probable examples, listed in the appendix to this paper. As archaeological work and publication of existing materials continue, more will undoubtedly surface. Nonetheless, compared with many glyphs of as geographically widespread usage, there are not a great number.

The fish-in-hand glyph is iconically remarkably intact, nearly always having the same form (fig. 1a–e). One exception is the example on Quiriguá Stela J (fig. 1f), which shows the hand grasping what appears, in the drawing published by Maudslay, to be something with fishlike parts, as though two fish tails had been joined end to end by a curving bar with three or four adjacent beads—perhaps a decorative rendition of the number nine, which prefixes the compound. While this object may conceivably be some sort of scepter, the glyph clearly functions as a fish-in-hand. Not within the scope of this paper are several occurrences of glyphs depicting an item or items with T44 prefix in a grasping hand.

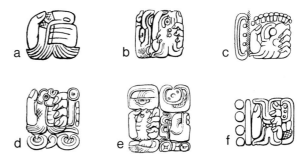

Fig. 1 "Fish-in-hand" glyphs from (a) Early Classic conch shell; (b) Palenque, Tablet of the Foliated Cross at C9; (c) Tikal, Temple I, Lintel 3; (d) Copán, Stela 6; (e) Copán, Stela I; (f) Quiriguá, Stela J. (1a: drawing by Diane Winters; 1b–f: after Maudslay 1889–1902; courtesy Milpatron Publishing Corp).

The fish is always held in the left hand. That this may be significant is suggested by its depiction on the face of Yaxchilán Lintel 25, whose entire text was carved in mirror-image form (fig. 2). Although this reversal forces God K's glyphic head to face right instead of left and presents Shield Jaguar's own name with components reversed, Jaguar Shield, the fish-in-hand is *not* reversed. If mirrored, the glyph would have presented a right hand, though whether the scribe was ruled by this consideration is a matter of speculation.

Association with Bloodletting and Ancestry

Proskouriakoff (1973), focusing only on the verbal fish-in-hand and its associated compounds and sculpted motifs, noted the affinity, most evident at Yaxchilán, with women, evidence of blood sacrifice, serpent visions and serpent bars inhabited by various personages, and the T712 glyph. She also pointed out the fact that some of the recorded fish-in-hand events occurred on dates considerably earlier than the execution of the monument

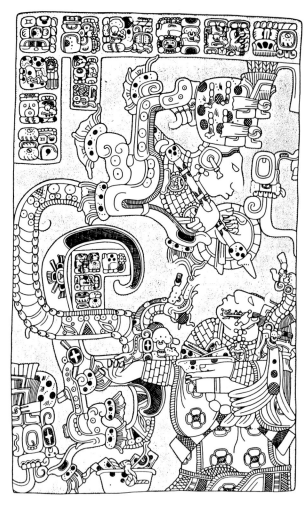

Fig. 2   Yaxchilán, underside of Lintel 25 (drawing by Ian Graham; courtesy Peabody Museum, Harvard University).

and, considering implications of the entire constellation of associated material, proposed the now accepted view that the fish-in-hand glyph is also connected with lineage and ancestry.

Joralemon's work on ritual bloodletting (1974) and Schele's subsequent work on human sacrifice (1984a) shed light on the prevalence and forms of blood sacrifice among the Classic Maya and concomitant instruments and iconography. T712 is identified as representing an obsidian bloodletting instrument. It occurs in five of the assembled fish-in-hand clauses and is depicted twice in associated visual scenes at Yaxchilán among the contents of bloodletting bowls on Lintels 13 and 14. The two bowls on Lintel 25 at that site contain as substitutes a stingray spine and two implements identified by Schele as shell bloodletters. Additionally, the bowls on Lintels 15 and 25, as well as Stela 32, include the ropes drawn by women through holes pierced in their tongues (figs. 2 and 3).

A flint connection with the fish-in-hand glyph ap-

pears to exist as well. Tikal's Lintel 3 of Temple I tells us that a fish-in-hand event occurred on 12 Etz'nab 11 Zac (9.13.3.9.18), forty days after the "war" event recorded in the preceding clause on 11 Etz'nab 11 Ch'en. That preceding clause contains a compound, T1.245:642, "his flint shield," nearly identical to the T245.642 "flint shield" compound immediately following the fish-in-hand on Copán Altar X. The Copán event occurred, not incidentally I suspect, on 11 Etz'nab 1 Kankin (Long Count position uncertain but probably 9.8.12.7.18 or possibly 9.5.19.12.18). However, no other fish-in-hand events occurred on the day Etz'nab, nor have I been able to detect any reliably significant pattern of favored days, numerical coefficients, "months," or even seasons, beyond a slight predilection for the period Zip through Mol. Another flint connection is perhaps provided on an incised Early Classic conch shell (Coe 1982). There the fish-in-hand glyph is immediately followed by a vertical hand with fingers upright holding three sharply pointed objects, which Robicsek and Hales (1984) believed to be flint knives. Finally, the Machaquilá ruler known as One-Fish-in-Hand writes his name I/714/257, the T257 representing a flint blade.

However, lest the autosacrifice and war connections lead to precipitous conclusions, I want to put the matter into perspective on two counts. First, the only explicit sacrificial scene associated with the fish-in-hand glyph is one depicted on a codex style vase (fig. 4), photo-

Fig. 3   Yaxchilán, Lintel 15 (drawing by Ian Graham; courtesy Peabody Museum, Harvard University).

Fig. 4 Codex-style vase (rollout photograph no. 1370; copyright Justin Kerr 1980; vessel 22 in Robicsek and Hales 1981:23).

graphed by Justin Kerr (no. 1370) and published by Robicsek and Hales (1981: vessel 22). Below a very brief text ending T714.181, the youthful "werejaguar" (Xbalanque) lies atop a Cauac Monster altar. At one end shell-eared God GI of the Palenque Triad (Hunahpu) appears on the verge of sacrifice with Cauac-head blade and axe in hand, while 1-Death at the other end squats with outstretched greedy arms. In this scene, however, as in the Popol Vuh's episodes of the brothers' sacrificial "dance" in Xibalba, Xbalanque's impending death is presumably not permanent, and he is ultimately recon-

stituted. The theme appears to be not mortal sacrifice, but regeneration and the triumph over death.

Second, while the implication of bloodletting certainly does envelop the occurrence of the fish-in-hand glyph, the bloodletting act itself is not as directly bound to the glyph as is sometimes implied. A survey of the oft-cited Yaxchilán monuments demonstrates this point (see table 1). Evident is the fact that, at Yaxchilán, fish-in-hand texts are most closely allied with the presence of serpent visions and serpentine bars, and to some extent with bloodletting implements and bowls of *already* blood-

Table 1. Bloodletting, Serpents, and T714 in Yaxchilán Monuments

Monument	Gender (M/F)	Bloodletting		T714 Fish-in-Hand	Serpentine		
		Act	Implements		Vision	or	Bar[a]
Lintel 13	M&F		X	X	X		
Lintel 14	M&F		X	X	X		
Lintel 15	F		X	X	X		
Lintel 17	M&F	X	X				
Lintel 24	M&F	X	X				
Lintel 25	F		X	X	X		
Stela 32[b] front	F		X	X	X		
Stela 32[b] back	F	X	X				
Lintel 38	F			X			X
Lintel 39	M			X			X
Lintel 40	F			X			X
Lintel 42	2M			X			
Lintel 43	M&F		X				
HS3, Step III	[M]			X			
HS3, Step V	[M]			X			

[a] This "bar" is longer and more flexible (plus asymmetrically so) than the flexible serpent bars on, for example, the Copán stelae. Although its emergent busts are those of God K instead of "persons" of probably historical identity, deified ancestors, I have treated it as akin to the serpents of the "visions."
[b] This stela found in 1983 at Structure 21 was reported in *Mexicon* 9/21/84 with the designation Stela 32; however, that designation had previously been given, at least in Ian Graham's *Corpus of Maya Hieroglyphic Inscriptions,* to a plain stela associated with Structure 66, and I am now uncertain about the official numbering.

A Study of the Fish-in-Hand Glyph, T714

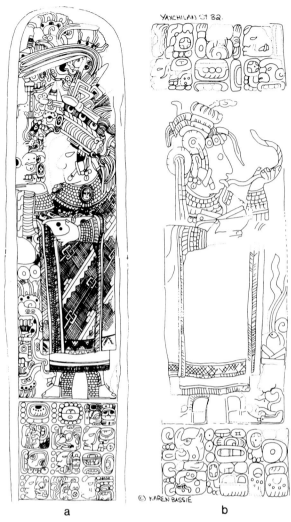

YAXCHILAN St 32.

(c) KAREN BASSIE

a   b

Fig. 5 Yaxchilán, new stela of Structure 21: (a) front; (b) back (drawing courtesy Karen Bassie; copyright 1986).

Bloodletting and blood of ancestry are concepts inextricably intertwined. It is, however, probable that most of the occurrences of T712 in fish-in-hand texts do indeed signal the bloodletting implement, indicating that such an act had occurred.

As G1 of the Nine Lords of the Night

With *bolon* (nine) prefix the fish-in-hand glyph was known to substitute on Piedras Negras Stela 36 (9.10.6.5.9) for the usual G1 Lord of the Night, the *bolon*-prefixed compound composed of the God C head with "water group" affix held in the T670 hand (another left hand, by the way). That the correlation is valid and also not confined to one site can now be confirmed by its use as Glyph G of the Supplementary Series on a small lintel dated 9.4.6.14.9, bearing the Bonampak emblem glyph (exhibited in 1973 at the Dayton Art Institute, Dayton, Ohio, and in 1984 in New York as part of the Wray Collection) and on an altar at Toniná dated 9.12.0.0.0. The Toniná example is listed in Thompson's catalog (1962) as T714?, apparently due to its somewhat eroded condition, and was considered a dubious identification by Proskouriakoff (1973). It occurs with a head prefix as the first of a pair of compounds between the day (with head variant prefix) and the haab position in a Calendar Round date linked by a clear Distance Number to the dedicatory date. This derived secondary date, 9.12.4.0.1, is also one on which G1 ruled as the Lord of the Night, so the head is no doubt the variant of number nine. What Toniná thus offers *is* a T714, as Glyph G of the Supplementary Series with either a companion Glyph F or a "lunar series" in very abbreviated form.

The fish-in-hand with *bolon* prefix does occur on two occasions in noncalendric material, presumably as a verb, and is in those instances seemingly unrelated to the G1 Lord of the Night aspect. On Quiriguá Stela J and a nearly parallel passage on the central upper Step III of Structure 44 at Yaxchilán the associated dates were ruled respectively by the Lords of the Night G7 and G8. *Bolon* as prefix to a verb is puzzling, unless perhaps it is not to be read aloud, but serves purely as a visual clue to the word intended.

The fish-in-hand substitution as G1 provided the first auspicious avenue toward a reading of the glyph. Based on Thompson's identification of G1 Lord of the Night as the deity Ah Bolon Tz'acab, de Gruyter (1946) suggested reading the fish-in-hand version as *bolon tzac kab,* since *tzac* in Yucatec is "a small fish" and *kab* is "hand." He also considered the word *tz'a*, "to give, hand over, place, concede" and *tz'aac*, "that which is given." Kelley (1976) favored the latter proposal; he was averse to compromising the distinction made by the Maya between glottalized and nonglottalized consonants, although he was willing to accept the possible relevance in this case of the "fish" gloss. The deity's name, as Kelley noted, has usually been interpreted as involving the word *tz'akab,* or

spattered bark strips. But when the act itself is depicted, the fish-in-hand glyph is absent. The clearest case for this argument is made by the new Stela 32 of Structure 21 (fig. 5). On the back, where Lady Ik-Skull Sky draws a rope through her tongue, the verbal phrase does not include the fish-in-hand; on the front, however, above a fish-in-hand text, the vision serpent is encountered. It seems that our glyph has more to do with either the aim or what ensues from this particular autosacrificial act, the connection through the serpent with lineage concerns, and perhaps symbolic communion with ancestors, mythical or historical.

One further caution with respect to equating the fish-in-hand glyph with the bloodletting act per se involves the interpretation of T712 in fish-in-hand clauses. This glyphic element, as Schele (1984a) pointed out, also serves as the main sign of a compound used as a metaphor for the relationship between child and parent.

"generations." While several very interesting glosses exist for the words *tzak* and *tzak'*, the present paper is confined to words that retain the glottal pattern of *tz'akab*.

Dictionary Entries

Pursuing the possibilities of a Maya reading based on the initial clue provided in Ah Bolon Tz'acab, the dictionaries offer a number of words that may be implicated and should be considered. As orthographic systems vary considerably, particularly with respect to the glottalized and nonglottalized *tz* and *k* sounds crucial here, reproducing those words as the various lexicographers published them would blur distinctions I wish to keep clear. I have therefore taken the liberty of translating the entries into a uniform system that employs *tz* and *tz'*, *k* and *k'*.

In Yucatec, the Cordemex dictionary lists:

(Ah) Bolon Tz'akab, "el-nueve-gran-fecundador" [nombre de una diedad prehispánica]
bolon tz'akab, cosa perpetua
bolon tz'akabil, perpetuidad, eternidad
bolon, nueve y cuenta de nueve; also especie de abeja muy pequeña, no pica y se enreda en el pelo, la llaman "vieja"
tz'akab, abolorio, casta, linaje o generación [several cited sources further specify por vía recta de la parte de la madre] also descendiente así en linaje, orden de generación

Since the glyphic texts record events occurring on specific dates, these words are of no immediate help. They may, however, provide a background to our understanding of the nature of the event. The secondary meaning of *bolon* as a kind of tiny stingless bee called "old one" or "ancient one" is included here in light of Thompson's (1950:84–86) discussion of several Maya beliefs associating flying insects, variously flies or bees, with the spirits of the deceased, in some cases dead relatives, returning to visit the earth after first having become stars.

There are apparently at least two roots *tz'ak*, revealed by numerous word entries listed in the Cordemex. The first includes:

tz'ak, para siempre, and the related tz'akah, atesorar, acaudalar [guardar, conservar]
tz'ak, grados de parentesco [to which another cited source adds por parte de la madre]
-tz'ak, cuenta de grados y escalones y otras cosas que van unas encima de otras [a numerical classifier]
tz'ak, aumentar, añadir and grada de escala, nudo de caña
tz'ak, contar [equated with xok]
tz'ak, medida general para las milpas

The other main root encompasses:

tz'ak, medicina and remedio
tz'ak, curar and medicinar, and the reflexive tz'akba, curarse
tz'ak, chupar como panal [a bee's honeycomb] o piñuelas

tz'ak, emponzoñar and emponzoñarse con bebida
tz'ak kay, envenenar peces con la corteza de ciertos árboles para cogerlos [kay being Yucatec for "fish"]

The tree referred to in this last entry may well be of the genus *Erythrina*, called the coral bean tree or *colorín*, of which Clark (1972) said, "[i]ts wood is so poisonous that, thrown into water, it kills fish; Indians have been known to employ it as an aid to fishing."

Also, in view of the seemingly contradictory *curar* and *emponzoñar* glosses above, it may be worth noting the mention by Schultes (1976) that *Erythrina* species seeds, which resemble mescal beans and are sometimes sold mixed with them in herbal markets, may be used as hallucinogens in some parts of Mexico; but, although they contain alkaloids that elicit biochemical activity resembling that of arrow poisons, no alkaloids presently known to possess hallucinogenic properties have yet been identified. No analysis of *Erythrina* bark is reported to have been made. On this particular subject the following information is intriguing, but I do not intend any implication that it applies to the Maya. Schultes discussed in some detail the well-studied use of *Virola* tree bark by various Indians of Colombia, Venezuela, and northern Brazil. The bark yields a bloodred resin used in some tribes mainly by shamans as a hallucinogen believed to aid them in their curing ceremonies. Among the Waika it is used both as an arrow poison and hallucinogenically by males in an annual ceremony to memorialize those who have died in the previous year (the ashes of whose calcined bones are added to a fermented banana beverage consumed during the ritual). Its hallucinogenic effects include increased excitability, numbness in the limbs, lack of muscular coordination and macropesia, the sensation of seeing things greaty enlarged.

Notwithstanding the possible use of hallucinogens by the Maya, at present unconfirmed, evidence for some form of intoxication in connection with the fish-in-hand event may occur on a codex-style vase (Kerr photograph no. 1973; fig. 6). The reclining Water-Lily Jaguar in white shawl wears Hellmuth's "enema bib" and holds before his open mouth a vaguely conch-shaped, though seemingly soft, object. A flow of material, probably liquid, to or from the far end joins the body of one of the God K heads emerging on serpent body from a Cauac Monster head.

Further glosses among the *tz'ak* entries are:

(Ah) Tz'ak, embebedizo, ponzoña que mata; also listed with this entry is the word kab, which the Cordemex elsewhere glosses as abeja en general, colmena and ponzoña de algún insecto [not to be confused with k'ab, in the present orthographic system, for "hand"]

(Ah) Tz'ak, médico en general y cirujano [equated with (Ah) Tok', which under its own entry is also sangrador] and Ah Tz'ak Yah, médico que lo tiene por oficio y de ordinario se toma en mala parte por hechicero que cura con palabras malas y de idólatras

Fig. 6   Codex-style vase (rollout photograph no. 1973; copyright Justin Kerr 1983).

None but the last entry above connects with the circumstantially established association of bloodletting with the fish-in-hand glyph.

In Tzotzil, Laughlin (1975) provides many words derived from the root *tz'ak*, which he glossed as "know, complete, set /bone/, graft," "boundary marker, boundary line," and "units joined horizontally." The derived words and terms generally imply the concept of joining or linking successively (as in the nodes of a cane stem, mules tied one behind the other); even the curative aspect, bone mending, seems allied here. Similar Tzeltal words reported by Slocum and Gerdel (1976) are *tz'akal, cabal, completo; ta'akawil, coyuntura;* and *tz'aquel, añadir, unir.*

The Chol dictionary of Aulie and Aulie (1978) includes the following entries, in which I have imitated Kaufman and Norman in replacing the "inverted v" sixth vowel with an *ä*:

tz'ak, medicina, remedio
tz'äkal, recaudo and *medicina* [with an indication that this noun is always preceded by a possessive pronoun]
tz'äkan, curar
tz'äkäbil, tratado (con medicina) [the sample sentence provided involves potato plantings treated with insecticide, suggesting a simultaneous association with poison]
stz'äkaya, curandero, hierbatero, brujo
tz'äkäl, completo, and *tz'äktesan, completar*

The reconstructed proto-Cholan word list produced by Kaufman and Norman (1984) offers **tz'äk* as both "complete, whole, enough" (which in Yucatec is *tz'akan*) and "medicine, fish poison."

I am indebted to Joanne Spero (personal communica-

tion, 1986) for supplying additional examples of *tz'ak* as "medicine" in Mopan, Itzá, Lacandón ("medicine, liquor, spice"), Chontal, Chortí ("remedy, remedial herb, narcotic, poison"), and Choltí. The verb in Choltí is *tz'aka,* and in all of these languages practitioner "curer" or "herbalist" forms, with slight variations in spelling, occur as well. In Tzeltal, terms that may involve a cognate are *h-tzak k'abal* and *h-tzak chi,* both glossed as *el brujo.* Spero also suggested the possible relevance of the various Mixe-Zoquean language group words for curing and witchery from the root *tzo'k.*

Throughout the Yucatecan and Cholan-Tzeltalan realms at least, several meanings for *tz'ak* recur. In Quiché, according to the dictionary compiled by Pontious (1980), only one of the common threads is to be found—in *tz'akat completo, cabal,* and *u tz'akatil, una parte de ello.*

Affixes of Possible Phonetic Assistance

Now the problem arises of determining which, if any, of the assembled words may apply to the fish-in-hand glyph. Some assistance might first be sought in those of its affixes that are less likely to be serving as grammatical particles, or in portions of affixes that may incorporate phonetic clues. Affixes to the fish-in-hand are listed in table 2, along with tentative transliteration possibilities based on Kelley (1976), and on articles by Fox and Justeson (1984b) and MacLeod (1984), and Justeson (1984a) listing glyph interpretations by a number of epigraphers.

At Chichén Itzá the inscription on the mid-wall of Casa Colorado has the compound T714:25:136 (fig. 7).

Fig. 7   Chichén Itzá, portion of inscription on the middle wall of Casa Colorada (after Maudslay 1889–1902; courtesy Milpatron Publishing Corp.).

T25 is certainly *ka*, and suggests the presence of an un-glottalized *k* in the fish-in-hand. Were T25 the beginning of an entirely separate syllable, T714 would be left as a CV form, too short I believe to allow it to stand alone for *tz'akab* when used in the G1 Lord of the Night context. For T136, Lounsbury suggested a phonetic *lo* and Kelley a phonetic *-b* ending, possibly derived originally from a formation indicating plurality. T136 does occur as suffix in a Bacab title (T501.25:501:136) at Bonampak and occurs elsewhere on a number of occasions similarly suffixed in *u cab* agency expressions. However, after examining a number of occurrences of T136 suffixed in other compounds, I see plausible arguments for each of these suggestions, so the door must be left open on the final consonant here.

On Copán Stela I the fish-in-hand appears in the compound T679af:714:?, followed by T683b graphically prefixed in the subsequent compound, but probably serving as a T181-equivalent verbal suffix to the fish-in-hand (fig. 1e). The suffix directly below T714 is damaged but was transcribed by Thompson as T130? and by Schele as T24. If T24, it may indicate either a grammatic or phonetic *-il* or *-Vl* before the final verbal *-ah* (if that is T683's function). Neither of the endings proposed for T24 would phonetically complement *tz'akab* or any of the verb roots already presented, but either might operate grammatically.

While T24 does not occur elsewhere affixed to the fish-in-hand, T130 shows up as a suffix on four other occasions, at Copán, Palenque, and Yaxchilán (table 2). However, in none of those instances is it followed by what might be an *-ah* suffix. T130 is usually read phonetically as *wa* or as a final *-w*, although Kelley (1976:176, 181, 214) instead considered *aan* to be correct. Meanwhile, Fox and Justeson (1984b) proposed polyvalence for T130, with a probable alternative value of *-ab'*, or at least *-Vb'*, representing an instrumental suffix and perhaps also (at least in some codical occurrences) the Yucatec passivizer *-ab'*. The Cordemex spelling of both the instrumental and passive suffixes is *-ab*, without the final glottal used by Fox and Justeson. If the fish-in-hand is meant to stand for the full word *tz'akab*, as derived from a verb *tz'ak*, a *-Vb* derivational suffix could be serving as a reinforcing element. However, if the fish-in-hand is *tz'ak*, and T130 here is indeed *-ab*, the suffix is performing one of its grammatic functions. More recently, MacLeod (personal communication, 1986) postulated a different grammatic function for some T130 suffix occurrences, as an antipassive marker *-wa*.

On Yaxchilán Lintel 25, at M1, the fish-in-hand bears a T246 suffix, apparently used as a verbal affix and indicator of the anterior fish-in-hand event at B1a. Lounsbury read it as *-b'ih*. As T246 is generally understood to be a conflation of T136 and T126, with the elements graphically represented in that order, Lounsbury's reading may be compatible with Kelley's reading of T136 as a *-b* ending.

Among proposals for the suffixes discussed, the most

frequently recurring consonantal elements are the *-l*, *-n*, and *-b* endings. If the *-b* components proposed for T136, T130, and T246 were eventually to be substantiated in other contexts, a reading as the full word *tz'akab* for the fish-in-hand would gain some strength. I suspect that that is unlikely. More probable is that only the *k*, from Chichén Itzá's T25, applies to the word represented by T714.

Transitive or Intransitive Verb: God K as Patient or Agent

The obvious major drawback with *tz'akab* is that the dictionaries do not report a verbal usage, while that seems to be the fish-in-hand's primary use in the texts. Most of its affixes are verbal inflections or their phonetic values. It may, therefore, have been read slightly differently, by one of the verb roots listed previously, when occurring as a verb. However, the relative dearth of affixed phonetic complements, given its broad, sparse use geographically, implies that the glyph could be properly read fairly easily on its own by the (literate) Maya. If it could serve as *tz'akab* in the deity's name but, alternatively, be read merely as *tz'ak*, "to cure, poison," "to count, add," or in some manner "complete," the verbal usage would have to involve more than the generalized action of the verb as glossed. The icon must signal some more specific association between the verb and the deity or his role, his cosmic function.

Dütting (1978) suggested one such association by treating the fish-in-hand glyph as a reference to "'grasping of fishes/human embryos' for rebirth by god K." I do not know the basis for his interpretation, but I do see compelling reasons for entertaining it as a possibility, perhaps with some modification. As discussed below, there are implications of God GI of the Palenque Triad's involvement as an actor in connection with the fish-in-hand and of procreatively sexual connotations in the bloodletting act with which it is associated. A careful examination, however, of the fish-in-hand's verbal grammar seems to diminish the notion of God K as an agent in the fish-in-hand event.

God K, often considered a god of lineages and sometimes referred to as Bolon Tz'akab due to the numeral nine frequently prefixed to his glyphic head (T1030a–d), follows T714 in at least thirteen of the fish-in-hand texts, in eleven instances in the immediately succeeding position (see table 2). The sites at which this pattern occurs are Quiriguá and Copán (where "God K" is known to have been either a title or possibly an office held by some rulers) and Yaxchilán. An additional example occurs on a codex-style vase (Kerr photograph no. 1383). Because a human agent usually appears later in these clauses, the question arises as to whether God K may here be the object/patient of the fish-in-hand verb.

At first glance the pronominal and verbal inflection pattern in conjunction with the summaries of subsequent clause text seems to reveal nontransitive verbal

Table 2. Occurrences of T714, the "Fish-in-Hand" Glyph

Location	Use	Compound	Event Date		Agent	"Dedication Date"
??Caracol	St.21, A3b	v	714?:?	9.13.10.0.0 +/− ?.19.12.4	7 Ahau 3 Cumku or	?	9.13.10.0.0
Chichén Itzá	C. Colorada Mid-Wall, Maudslay's glyph #20b	v	714:25:136	10.2.0.15.3 to 10.2.12.2.4?	(per Kelley)	Kakupacal?	10.2.?.?.?
?Chichén Itzá	C. de Monjas L.7, E2a	?	714?	10.?.?.?.?		?	10.0.?.?.?
Copán	Alt.X, A2	v	714	9.8.12.7.18 or 9.5.19.12.18	11 Etz'nab 1 Kankin " "	eroded	9.8.15.0.0 or 9.6.0.0.0?
Copán	Alt.Y, F2	?	1.714	9.8.13.16.6 9.6.1.3.6 9.7.1.7.6 9.9.14.2.6	6 Cimi 19 Zip ? or " " ? or 6 Cimi 19 Uo ? or " " ?	local ruler	9.7.5.0.0??
Copán	St.I, C1	v	679af:714:130?/ [↑ followed by 683]	9.12.3.14.0	5 Ahau 8 Uo	Knot-Skull? or Smoke-Jaguar?	9.12.5.0.0 or 9.13.0.0.0?
Copán	St.6, D5[6?]	v	714.?:125	9.12.10.0.0	9 Ahau 18 Zotz	18-Rabbit	9.12.10.0.0
?Copán	St.H, C1	v	714?:125??	9.14.19.5.0	4 Ahau 18 Muan	18-Rabbit? or his consort??	9.15.0.0.0
Copán	St.8, B2	v	1:714:130	9.17.12.6.2 9.16.19.2.17??	9 Ik 15 Zip or 9 Caban 15 Zip	New-Sun-at-Horizon	9.17.15.0.0
Machaquilá	St.5, B1	NP	I:714.257	10.0.10.17.5	13 Chicchan 13 Cumku	I-Fish-in-Hand	10.0.10.0.0
Machaquilá	St.6, A4b	NP	I:714:?	10.0.5.16.0	8 Ahau 13 Cumku	I-Fish-in-Hand	10.0.5.0.0
Machaquilá	St.7, E1b	NP	I:714:257?	10.0.0.14.15	3 Men 13 Cumku	I-Fish-in-Hand	10.0.0.0.0
Machaquilá	St.8, B3	NP	I:714	9.19.15.13.0	1 Ahau 3 Cumku	I-Fish-in-Hand	9.19.15.0.0
?Naranjo	Alt.1, B8 and C11	v v	679af.714?.181 714?	7.2.4.5.14 7.4.17.0.14	13 Ix 12 Xul or " "	?	9.8.0.0.0
Palenque	TFC, C9	v	204.714	2.0.0.0.0	2 Ahau 3 Uayeb	Lady Beastie (ancestral goddess)	9.13.0.0.0
Palenque	TFC, M10	v	105.714.35	9.12.18.5.19	5 Cauac 17 Mol	Chan Bahlum II	9.13.0.0.0
Palenque	TC, 09	v	11:714:130	9.12.18.5.19	5 Cauac 17 Mol	Chan Bahlum II	9.13.0.0.0
Palenque	TS, 013	v	714:130.138 [↑ "water group" version]	9.12.18.5.19	5 Cauac 17 Mol	[Chan Bahlum II]	9.13.0.0.0
Palenque	Pal.House E above Oval Tablet	?	714	?		?	9.14.10.0.0??
Piedras Negras	St.36, A5	G1	IX.714	9.10.6.5.9	8 Muluc 2 Zip	n/a [Glyph G, Supplementary Series]	9.11.15.0.0
Piedras Negras	L.2, M1	v	1.714	9.11.6.2.1 or 9.9.19.6.13	3 Imix 19 Ceh 8 Ben 1 Xul ??	[Ruler 2 - "Turtleshell"] ?	9.11.15.0.0
Quiriguá	Alt.L, A2	v	?.714.?	9.11.0.11.11 9.12.0.17.0	9 Chuen 14 Zec or 12 Ahau 3 Xul	?	9.12.0.0.0
Quiriguá	St.J, G5	v?	IX.714.181	9.14.13.4.17	12 Caban 5 Kayab	Two-Legged Sky	9.16.5.0.0
Quiriguá	Zoom.P, R2b1 and R2b2	?? ??	714.? 714:125?	?		?	9.18.5.0.0
Tikal	TI L.3, C3		11.12?:714 [↑ T12 var.?]	9.13.3.9.18	12 Etz'nab 11 Zac	Ah Cacao [Ruler A]	9.15.0.0.0
Tikal	MT 32 (bone)	v	714	9.12.14.3.11	12 Chuen 9 Yaxkin	"Ahpo-Kin"	9.15.0.0.0
Tikal	MT 33 (bone)	v	714	9.12.17.3.11	13 Chuen 14 Xul	18-Rabbit	9.15.0.0.0
Tikal	MT 36 (bone)	v	714	9.13.2.4.11	13 Chuen 9 Xul	18-Rabbit	9.15.0.0.0
Toniná	Altar, B	G1	head.714 [↑ probably var. of number 9]	9.12.4.0.1	8 Imix 9 Xul	n/a [Glyph G, Supplementary Series]	9.12.0.0.0

Table 2. (continued)

Location		Use	Compound	Event Date		Agent	"Dedication Date"
Yaxchilán (c.u.)	Str.44 HS 3 III, C12	?	IX.714	9.12.9.8.1	5 Imix 4 Mac	[Shield Jaguar I]	9.15.0.0.0
Yaxchilán	L.25, B1a	v	1:714:130	9.12.9.8.1	5 Imix 4 Mac	Shield Jaguar I	9.15.0.0.0
Yaxchilán	L.25, M1	v	714:246	[9.12.9.8.1	5 Imix 4 Mac	Shield Jaguar I]	9.15.0.0.0
Yaxchilán (nw.u.)	Str.44 HS 3 V, D7a	v	714–683.23	9.15.0.15.3	8 Akbal 11 Yaxkin	?	9.15.0.0.0
Yaxchilán	L.14, D2	v	714.181	9.15.10.0.1	4 Imix 4 Mol	Lady Great-Skull	9.16.5.0.0
Yaxchilán	St.32[a], A2	v	714.181	9.15.10.0.1	4 Imix 4 Mol	Lady Ik-Skull Sky	9.16.5.0.0?
Yaxchilán	L.39, A2	v	714	9.15.10.0.1	4 Imix 4 Mol	Bird Jaguar IV	9.16.15.0.0
Yaxchilán	L.40, A2	v	1.714	9.15.15.6.0 9.16.7.0.0?	12 Ahau 18 Ceh or 13 Ahau 18 Zip ??	Lady Balam	9.16.15.0.0
Yaxchilán	L.13, D1	vn	92?.714?	9.16.0.14.5	1 Chicchan 13 Pop	Lady Great-Skull	9.16.5.0.0?
Yaxchilán	L.42, F3	?	568.714	9.16.1.2.0	12 Ahau 8 Yaxkin	Bird Jaguar IV	9.16.5.0.0
Yaxchilán	L.38, A2	v	1.714:?	9.16.12.5.14	3 Ix 7 Mol	Lady of Ik site	9.16.15.0.0
Yaxchilán	L.15, A2	v	714.181	9.16.17.2.4	4 Kan 12 Zip	Lady of Ik site?	9.16.18.0.0
Yaxchilán	L.15, F2	v	679af.714	9.16.17.2.4	4 Kan 12 Zip	Lady of Ik site?	9.16.18.0.0
Vase (Kerr photo 1370)[b]		v	714.181	?	7 Cib 4 Kayab		
Vase (Kerr photo 1382)[b]		v	714.181	?	13 Muluc? 18 Pax		
Vase (Kerr photo 1383)		v	714.181	?	7 ? 12 Cumku or Mac?	Río Azul ruler or his "mother"	
Vase (Kerr photo 1973)		v?	?.714:?	?	7 Cib 19 Pop or Kayab??		
Conch shell trumpet Tikal area, Peten, T714 at C5		v?	714	Early Classic		?	Early Classic
Costa Rica Jade Balser (1974), pl.XIV		v	1.714	9.0.11.0.0? or 9.3.16.0.0??	3 Ahau 17[18] Chen 3 Ahau 17[18] Zac?	?	9.0.11.0.0 or 9.3.16.0.0
Wray Collection lintel Bonampak area ??, T714 at A5		G1	IX:714	9.4.6.14.9	5 Muluc 12 Zac	n/a [Glyph G, Supplementary Series]	
?Relief fragment, publ. by K. H. Mayer, 1978; Pomona, Tobasco ?, T714 at A5a		v?	head?.714?	9.18.10.0.0?	10 Ahau 8 Zac?	a local ruler	9.18.10.0.0?
Motul de San José 1, A4		NP	I.714.121?				
Dresden Codex, 65a		v	1.714	n/a		a Chak	12th-century copy of earlier text
Paris Codex, 5d		v	714	n/a		God E?	15th(?)-cent. copy of earlier text
Paris Codex, 7d			714	n/a			"
Paris Codex, 8c			III:714	Katun 3 Ahau		God [VI affixed]?	"
?Paris Codex, 9d			714?	n/a			"

Note: v = verb; vn = verbal noun; NP = nominal phrase; G1 = G1 Lord of the Night; n/a = not applicable.

[a] This stela found in 1983 at Structure 21 was reported in *Mexicon* 9/21/84 with the designation Stela 32; however, that designation had previously been given, at least in Graham's *Corpus of Maya Hieroglyphic Inscriptions*, to a plain stela associated with Structure 66, and I am now uncertain about the official numbering.

[b] Two of these four vases listed have been published in Robicsek's *The Maya Book of the Dead: The Ceramic Codex* as Vessels 12 (No. 1382) and 22 (No. 1370) and are from codex-style Site A (possible El Perú).

Fig. 8   Palenque "fish-in-hand" clauses from (a) Tablet of the Foliated Cross at L10-L14; (b) Tablet of the Cross at 08-015 (after Maudslay 1889–1902; courtesy Milpatron Publishing Corp.).

behavior. Briefly, that is suggested by: (a) the presence of only twelve instances of preposed ergative pronouns (excluding the T92 before the T714 verbal noun on Yaxchilán Lintel 13) and the fact that in those instances God K shows up in less than half of the clauses; (b) the near absence of coincident ergative pronouns with completive aspect markers, if that is indeed what T181 and T130 are, and assuming the Classic writing used a split-ergative system; and (c) the absence of *any conceivable* stated direct object or patient on, at the very least, eight occasions, probably more.

Particularly in light of the instances in which no direct object occurs, it is initially tempting to view T714 as an intransitive root and to suggest that, when the God K glyph does appear, the named human agent may be impersonating him or acting on his behalf, somewhat similar to the concept of acting in the capacity of "God K" title-holder. In five instances the God C head with "water group" affix muddies the stream by appearing (usually in clauses whose verb carries the ergative pronoun) in the intervening text between T714 and the human agent—seemingly substituting for God K. This is not so surprising when the same "water group" God C's role in the G1 Lord of the Night glyph is recalled. In one additional case the substitution is by a head-variant numeral six with "water group" prefix. If the "water group" + God C glyph is in fact substituting for, or at least parallel to, the God K glyph, comparison of two Palenque clauses (fig. 8) might reinforce an argument that God K is not the patient of the fish-in-hand verb. On the Tablet of the Foliated Cross, with T232 initial prefix (perhaps semantically equivalent to T1), the function is titular, while on the Tablet of the Cross, with T11 prefix, it directly follows the *u*-prefixed fish-in-hand as does God K on Yaxchilán Lintel 25 (fig. 2). It may be that, in one or more instances, the God K glyph is in fact intended as part of the nominal phrase of the agent.

I had at one point thought that a fair number of passive constructions might be reflected in table 2. Agency expressions, theoretically to be expected in passive constructions, are not as prevalent as might be wished, but

the ubiquitous *u cab* does appear between the God K glyph and named human protagonist in the texts of two Yaxchilán monuments, Stela 32 and Lintel 39, and possibly on Copán Stela I. On the other hand, the possibility that some antipassive constructions may be present would also help account for the semblance of intransitive inflections. Viewing the fish-in-hand's verbal usage as transitive in nature, despite the relative infrequency of preposed ergative pronouns and the occasional deletion of the hence implied patient, is in complete accord with Schele's observations (1982:11–12) regarding the distribution pattern of constructions for the root transitive verb *chuk,* "to capture." A transitive interpretation also obviates the need to view the *u*-prefixed examples as indicating incompleteive action, as is the case with intransitive verbs. This is particularly helpful with respect to Lady Beastie's fish-in-hand event, recorded on the Palenque Tablet of the Foliated Cross as having occurred on 2.0.0.0.0. T714 is thus presumably either a derived or root transitive verb, and the God K glyph (and perhaps the God C with "water group" affix), when present in the fish-in-hand texts, does not generally represent the agent. It represents the patient either as God K, the deity himself, or as the spiritual force he embodies.

God GI of the Palenque Triad

A deity with attributes of GI of the Palenque Triad, on the other hand, does make several appearances, in contexts directly or indirectly relevant to the fish-in-hand, which appear to imply an agency role. He is the perpetrator of the sacrificial act depicted on the vase in figure 4. The associated text, however, presents a grammatic anomaly in that the verb, T714.181, occurs in the clause-final position. As this text is directly above the jaguar-child and directly in front of 1-Death's head, it is likely that one of them represents the deleted subject of the clause. This makes sense if viewed as a passive construction, the implied agent being either GI or, if the youth is the passive verbal subject, conceivably 1-Death.

At Copán, God GI or the guise of a ruler impersonating him appears as the frontal figure of Stela I. The inscription on the back records a fish-in-hand event on 9.12.3.14.0, the same as its Initial Series date. Since intervening text records two much earlier dates, 8.6.0.0.0 and 8.6.0.10.8, it is not entirely clear whether the personified GI figure refers to the agent's role in the fish-in-hand event or represents an antecedent person or event. He wears atop his headdress the head of the Quadripartite God, featured again on Stela H as the central back-rack element above the inscription recording another fish-in-hand event.

The third relevant depiction of GI is on the incised bone MT51 from Tikal's Burial 116 of Ruler A beneath Temple I (fig. 9). While its text does not include the fish-in-hand glyph, T714 occurs at Tikal only in connection with Ruler A: on Temple I's Lintel 3 and on incised bones MT32, MT33, and MT36, all from Burial 116. Both sides of MT51 depict three deities with GI attributes engaged in catching fish by hand. These deities share with GI of the vase in figure 4 the diagnostic shell-ear, crossed-bands headpiece, T121 body markings, and elaborately knotted sash. The fish being caught are rendered with similar attention to detail. All but the largest on MT51B appear to be basically the same type, generally identifiable by dark body markings, usually two short vertical bars on the back and, in one case, additional small spots along the side, as well as an outlined definition of the area on the top of the head. These are not the same fish that in other contexts float about nibbling water-lily buds. They are, however, the same fish that appear in the fish-in-hand glyph, when sufficient specificity is provided (see figs. 1a–e and 8a). (A fellow student has tentatively suggested that they are Cichlids,

whose range includes the Petén and Usumacinta River region. She has work in progress on the fish depicted by the Maya, so I offer only a few remarks here. Cichlid species exhibit considerable variability in their markings, but included are dark vertical stripes, a lateral row of spots, or in some instances a single dark spot on the side. Dominant individuals, usually males, tend to develop a prominent hump at the top of the head, which results in a profile not typical of most other fish. One Cichlid species does occur in the Yucatán peninsula, but it does not have the distinctive head shape.)

The text on MT51 consists of a verb, God GI's head (T1011), T11.501:102, and a nominal phrase (probably that of Ruler A), roughly equivalent to the syntax encountered in the fish-in-hand clauses that have agency expressions. If T11.501:102 here is interpreted as "captive of," the implication is of GI's having been caught rather than doing any catching. Even if some more generalized agency expression is involved, GI as the recipient of verbal activity does not square with his image in the illustration as an actor upon his environment. This is not the only puzzle for which I have no present solution. The God GI head of the MT51 text does appear glyphically in two fish-in-hand clauses at Yaxchilán: in preceding text on Lintel 42, and in following text on Lintel 25 (in skeletalized form, fig. 2). It is the second of a recurring pair of compounds, the first of which involves T122:563a or its personified version T1035. The God GI glyph has in both instances a T279 prefix and T102 suffix. The function of this compound pair remains unclear. On the central upper Step III of Structure 44 at Yaxchilán, however, the compound pair occurs with what appears to be God K instead of the GI head.

Fig. 9 Drawing from Tikal incised bone MT51A&B (courtesy of The University Museum, University of Pennsylvania).

Connotations of Procreativity and Rebirth

On yet another vase photographed by Kerr (no. 1382) the fish-in-hand occurs in text above a scene in which an old male deity, possibly the aged sun, emerges from a serpent's jaw to approach a female, possibly the young Moon Goddess, and appears to touch her naked breast (fig. 10). Meanwhile, a male figure sits before, perhaps communicating with, a trussed and bundled creature whose head appears to be that of God GI of the Palenque Triad, or perhaps his father. Depictions of the serpent/ old god with the young goddess on certain other vases suggest that, while the meaning may be metaphorically celestial, the encounter as illustrated is sexual in nature. Vegetal fertility is implied by the ear of corn attached to the top of the serpent's head.

Human and vegetal fertility are very closely mingled concepts, and fish have for some time been seen as symbolic of the fertility inherent in raised field agriculture. There are several indications that fish and also the auto-sacrificial acts of bloodletting associated with the fish-in-hand event have connotations of human procreative potential as well as its cyclic manifestation, successive generations.

T608 (fig. 11) is listed in Thompson's catalog as occurring at Chichén Itzá and in the Madrid and Dresden codices. In the codices it is frequently affixed by T149, which is interpreted as depicting both eggs and testicles. T608 is considered by Fox and Riese (see Justeson and Campbell 1984, app. B, p. 347) to depict a penis, *ton* in Yucatec, and is read by Riese as its near homophone *tun* for "drum" in the Madrid Codex. Since *eel, yel,* and *he'* in Yucatec can all be both eggs and testicles, the association of T608 with a penis is entirely plausible. However, although I find no Yucatec words standing dually for "fish" and "penis," nor any indication in any Mayan languages of "fish" as a euphemism for the male organ, I

agree with Kelley that T608 seems clearly to depict a headless fish (see Tikal MT51 in fig. 9, detail in fig. 11). The male act of autosacrificial bloodletting most frequently illustrated or circumstantially implied involves the perforation of the penis with a stingray spine or sharp instrument of bone. Women, on the other hand, are disposed to draw a rope or cord through a hole pierced in the tongue. That the tongue in this case may be an anatomically displaced equivalent or surrogate for the penis is suggested by the fact that the Yucatec word for tongue, *ak'*, is also glossed in the Cordemex as *la crica de la mujer* (from the Motul dictionary) and *clítoris* (modern Yucatec).

Of the examples of T608 listed by Thompson from Chichén Itzá, one occurs on the mid-wall inscription of Casa Colorada in a phrase that includes the fish-in-hand glyph (fig. 7, detail fig. 11). Here what can be seen is actually not a headless fish, but a whole fish, bent over and seeming to nibble what may be a water-lily bug. This fish has on the side of its body the % symbol of death, and the glyph is suffixed by T188 below. Although T188 may be a purely phonetic *el/le,* I am inclined to believe that in this instance it is *le* for "lineage." Such an interpretation prompts speculation that the fish is in some instances involved with the death aspect of successive regeneration. At Machaquilá the fish that nibbles the water lily on the headdress of One-Fish-in-Hand (as well as that of his predecessor) is depicted in skeletalized form, suggesting the same notion.

The fish may also be involved with the aspect of rebirth. The south end of Altar O at Copán shows an adult male standing beside a boy (fig. 12). A fish hovers above the boy to nibble rather voraciously either his hair or a water lily atop his head. On the north end of the same altar a frog or toad, used in one of the glyphs for birth, "swims" downward, one hand nearly touching ground level of the altar, perhaps enacting the idiom for

Fig. 10 Codex-style vase (rollout photograph no. 1382; copyright Justin Kerr 1980; vessel 12 in Robicsek and Hales 1981:19).

Fig. 11 Glyph T608: (a) archetype; (b) fish from Tikal MT51; (c) Chichén Itzá glyph transcribed as T608 by Thompson (11a: after Thompson (1962); 11b: detail of fig. 9; 11c: detail of fig. 7).

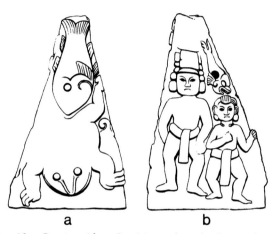

Fig. 12 Copán, Altar O: (a) south end; (b) north end (after Maudslay 1889–1902; courtesy Milpatron Publishing Corp.).

birth, "to touch the earth." From above, swimming deep into the space between the frog/toad's spread legs, is a fish. The fit is so snug that the fish seems on the verge of either entering or merging with the frog. The Yucatec word for "embryo," *balnak,'* is also the word for "glutton, gluttonous," which would not be entirely out of order in characterizing the fish above the boy's head, although this may be merely coincidental. A frog's own visible embryonic stage is, of course, a very fishlike tadpole.

Summary

The fish-in-hand glyph does not in my view represent the act of bloodletting, but involves rather some sort of conjuring and communication, or communion, with deceased ancestors or ancestral deities, for which purpose certainly bloodletting and possibly an intoxicated state are implicated. At present I think that the verb should probably be read as *tz'ak* (or a Cholan language group form), either in its sense of "counting and augmenting" the lineage or for its "poison/cure" methods, or both. "Know, complete" in the context of spiritual union is plausible as well. Underlying the fish-in-hand event is contact with that other "world axis" that is not of the spatial universe, but the temporal line: gods and grandfathers whose powers and pedigrees feed and are in turn fed by the present rulership, and the real and symbolic rebirths necessary to continue and preserve the order of the world.

Jaws II: Return of the *Xoc*

TOM JONES
HUMBOLDT STATE UNIVERSITY

In 1944, in what was to become one of his most cele-brated contributions to Maya studies, J. Eric S. Thompson proposed a demonstration of Maya use of rebus writing in the hieroglyphic inscriptions.[1] The previous year Thompson had identified what he called "directional counting glyphs," the main signs of which were the glyph for the day Muluc and a head variant that appeared to be an anthropomorphized fish, and had suggested a meaning such as "count" or "counting" (Thompson 1943). In the meantime, pursuing the possibility that the fish-head might function as a rebus, Thompson (with the assistance of Ralph Roys) found linguistic evidence in a number of Yucatec sources to show that the word *xoc*, meaning "count," also applied to a "poorly defined group of large fish," including sharks. Though he was unable to find *xoc* with the meaning "count" in any other Maya language and could locate but one non-Yucatec source that defined the word as a fish (*tiburón* in a seventeenth-century Pokomchi dictionary), Thompson proposed that the anthropomorphized fish-head employed in directional counting glyphs through-out the Classic Maya world represented a rebus. *Xoc*, a fish, served to convey the semantic value of a pho-netically identical verb meaning "count," which, when considered with the constant suffix *ti* (T59) provided a reading of *xoc ti*, "count to" or "count from" (fig. 1).

While convinced that the Muluc sign and the fish-head were interchangeable within the general meaning of "count," Thompson did not suggest that the specific reading of *xoc* should be extended to include the former. Nor did he later explicitly argue such an extension, though his wording regarding the water connections with Muluc sometimes seemed to encourage such an in-ference (Thompson 1954[1966:191]; 1971:163). How-ever, following out substitution patterns in both Initial Series and Distance Number introductory glyphs, in the "double imix" glyphs, and in the glyphs for Mac and for a phrase at Palenque that we now read as Pacal's name, Thompson noted the interchangeability of the fish-head glyph with the "nicked bracket" prefix (T1),

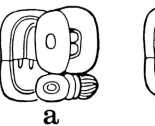

a   **b**

Fig. 1 Directional counting glyphs with T59 suffix and main signs: (a) Muluc; (b) fish-head (drawings by Tom Jones).

the "dotted bracket" prefix (T11), the "comb" (T25), and the "fish-head" prefix (T204) and concluded that "all these elements therefore must have the same mean-ing or meanings so close to one another that they could be interchanged at will" (fig. 2a–d). Acknowledging that the "bracket" and "comb" affixes probably had alter-native meanings in contexts that did not require count-ing, he nevertheless attempted to accommodate Landa's *ca* for the "comb" by stressing its phonetic proximity to *cai*, the Yucatec word for "fish," suggesting that the "comb" be recognized as a conventionalized dorsal fin. "Presumably," he wrote, "*ca* could represent fish in gen-eral and *xoc* in particular." By extension, the *ca* glyph could apparently participate in the *xoc* pun to carry the meaning "count" where such a need was felt out-side the context of directional counting glyphs. Hence Thompson's conclusion: "In all probability the various fish symbols should be read as *xoc* 'count.'"

In addition to proposing the above reading for the verb in the directional counting glyphs, Thompson's study seemed to identify the creature portrayed in the fish-head variant as the classic Maya ancestor of the mythological Chac Uayeb Xoc ("the great [or red] de-mon shark or whale") of the Book of Chilam Balam of Tizimin. He observed, "The glyph in question does not resemble a shark, but that is hardly surprising when one considers how little the inhabitants of the cosmological

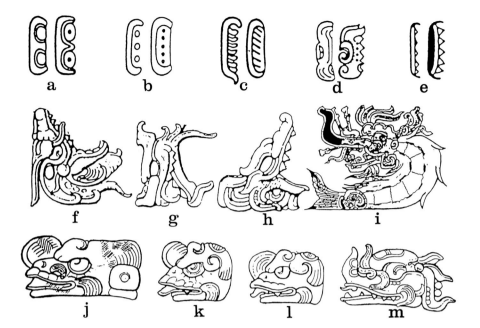

Fig. 2 Prefixes: (a) T1; (b) T11; (c) T25; (d) T204; (e) T10 (a–e modified by Tom Jones from J. Eric S. Thompson); fish-head prefixes (f–h) Quiriguá Zoomorph B (modified by Tom Jones from Maudslay); mythological fish (i), Dumbarton Oaks polychrome vessel (modified by Tom Jones from Diane Griffiths Peck); patron of Zotz': (j–l) Copán Stela 7 and (m) Copán Stela 6 (modified by Tom Jones from Maudslay 1889–1902).

and mythical worlds of the Maya resemble their counterparts in nature. The *xoc* was probably a large mythological creature with no immutable characteristics, and with a tendency to become anthropomorphized" (p. 17). His pursuit of substitution patterns of the "bracket" prefixes provided Thompson with a "full-figure" version of the *xoc* in Glyph C of the lunar series on Zoomorph B at Quiriguá (fig. 2f). "This fantastic creature is clearly a fish because of its bifurcated tail. The ornament at the back of the head is present, there is a sweeping curve around the nose, and what are presumably the barbels are shown as a bearded tuft on the extremity of the lower jaw" (p. 5).

This is the same creature that Thompson believed served as the patron of Zotz' in the Initial Series introductory glyph (fig. 2j–m), where it had nothing to do with the concept of counting and thus served no rebus function but was rather intended to convey the meaning of the fish itself. Of this Zotz' patron he wrote, "In some cases the nose is prolonged to become an elongated and upturned snout, such as is typically found in Maya presentations of reptiles. This is not a constant feature. Perhaps, if our identification of this creature as a fish is correct, it represents the elongated snout of the shark. Serrated teeth are prominent" (p. 4). Thus, if the primary consequence of Thompson's study was that the verb *xoc*, meaning "count," entered the lexicon of Maya hieroglyphic readings, a secondary result was that a recognizable mythological *xoc*-fish was added to the iconography of classic Maya art—and both depended upon the rebus reading of the directional counting glyphs.

The forty years that followed saw almost universal acceptance of Thompson's reading. The *xoc* became, for Maya scholars, the classic example of rebus usage in the hieroglyphs, whether in formal academic treatment (Kelly 1976:123; Schele 1980:17) or when presenting findings to the public (G. Stuart 1975:789). This is not to say that Thompson's elaboration of ramifications of his rebus theory went unchallenged. It was argued, for example, that there were at least two fish present in the inscriptions. One appeared in the directional counting glyphs and was pronounced *xoc*, but another substituted for the "comb" glyph in a variety of contexts, and, like the latter, carried Landa's phonetic value *ca*, derived, as Thompson had suggested, from the Yucatec word for "fish" (Kelly 1976:123). With respect to the directional counting glyphs themselves, the *xoc* reading of the fish-head variant was left untouched, while a completely different sound and slightly different meaning emerged for the Muluc sign for which the fish-head substituted. In recognition of the fact that the equivalent of the Yucatec day Muluc in three of the Maya languages was Mulu and that the word *mul* was defined in a Quiché source as "time, turn, rotation, revolution," it was proposed that the Muluc sign should be read *mul* with the idea of the turning of time being related to the counting of time (Kelly 1976:123). This reading was subsequently strengthened by observations that the Muluc sign represented a vase, several words for which contain the root *mul* in a number of Maya languages, and that *mul* and its cognates turn up in phrases pertaining to time and counting (Schele and Miller 1983:51–52), and by the suggestion of a hypothetical preclassic compound **mul-ta*, meaning "accumulation" or "accumulate," from which **mul*, "to heap up," derived (Justeson and Norman 1983). At the Fifth Palenque Round Table in 1983, invoking Occam's razor and emphasizing the function of the *xoc* as one of the omens named in the Chilam Balam of Kaua for the day Muluc, I argued against the idea that the fish-head variant and the Muluc sign represented two separate verbs in favor of their phonetic and semantic identity as *xoc,* meaning "to count" (Jones 1985: 215). The rebus reading thus remained unchallenged.

The following year, David Stuart presented a brilliantly compelling argument that the fish-head and Muluc sign of the directional counting glyphs, as well as several other glyphs that substitute for them (a sacrificial head, a monkey, and Thompson's "nicked bracket" and "fish-head" prefixes), at times all carried the phonetic value *u.* The use of these glyphs in contexts known to require that sound was demonstrated in an exceptionally rigorous examination of their distribution. With a commitment to the full implications of the Maya system of substitutions that would have done William of Occam proud (if not Thompson, as well), Stuart rejected the possibility of the phonetic polyvalency of these glyphs, and thus denied both the *xoc ti* and *mul ti* renderings of the directional counting glyphs. He concluded instead that the *u* and *ti* values of the latter should be read *ut,* a verbal stem in Cholan languages for "to finish," "to happen," or "to occur" (Stuart 1984b). It seems clear, then, that Thompson was in error in believing that a pun had led to the use of the fish-head as a rebus for the verb *xoc.* No such verb had ever been involved in the directional counting glyphs.

However, as emphasized earlier, not only this verb but also the mythological *xoc*-fish depended upon the validity of the rebus thesis. If there was no rebus, then there was no pun. And if there was no pun, then there is no reason to identify a mythological fish of classic Maya art with the *xoc* of the Chilam Balams and dictionaries of the colonial era. It would appear that the question of the identification of the ancient fish has been thrown wide open. Either the term "*xoc*-fish" should be abandoned or, if scholars are to continue to refer to it, then a case for that appellative must be built anew from entirely different foundations. But is that possible? Without reference to Thompson's 1944 rebus thesis and quite apart from its phonetic value as employed in the hieroglyphs, is it possible to show that the fish portrayed in the directional counting glyph, the "fish-head" prefix, and the Initial Series introductory glyph as the patron of Zotz' and represented on painted ceramic vessels and sculptured panels by a piscatorial monster that shares its features—is it possible to show that this creature may have been known to Maya of the Classic Period as *xoc*? Was the word *xoc* in the lexicon of those who painted the vases and shaped the monuments of Palenque, Copán, and Yaxchilán? If so, can the word be shown to have meant "shark"? And, if these two requirements can be met, can either the word or the shark be tied directly to the iconography of the creature portrayed in the directional count glyph? What follows is an attempt to make that tie and thereby reinstate the *xoc*-fish to a place in the art and mythology of the ancient Maya world.

It will be remembered that Thompson, following Roys,

perceived the Yucatec *xoc* to refer to a poorly defined group of large fish. Though this group included several small whales, it seems clear that Thompson preferred to think of the *xoc* as a shark. This was the definition preserved in the Vienna dictionary and also in the only non-Yucatec source that he could locate, the previously mentioned Pokomchi dictionary. Thus, "shark" would seem to be the most appropriate meaning of the word. Certainly those living close to the shores of the Yucatán peninsula would have been thoroughly familiar with sharks, whose ubiquity was brought to the attention of Europeans as early as 1566 by Bishop Landa (Landa 1959 [1982:123]). The same cannot be said regarding whales. Nor have the latter been reported in the inland waters of the Maya region. On the other hand, it has been shown that a particular species of shark, the bull shark or cub shark (*Carcharhinus leucas;* fig. 3), notorious the world over for its spectacular fresh-water excursions (as much as 3,500 km up the Amazon), is found in most of the rivers that flow into the Gulf of Mexico or Caribbean Sea from the region of ancient Mesoamerica, with sightings well up the rivers of the Maya area in particular (Jones 1985:217).[2] There is, then, reason to assume that, like their coastal neighbors, the ancient inhabitants of Palenque, Piedras Negras, Yaxchilán, Quiriguá, and other inland sites were familiar with the shark.

Indeed, it is this assumption of familiarity with the river shark that prompted the suggestion that Roberto Bruce's rendering of the Lacandón name for the Usumacinta River, Xokla', as "Water of the *Xok*" (Bruce S. 1976:143), should be extended to include the Yucatec and Chontal words for "river" (*x-ocola'* and *xocel haa,* respectively), the sixteenth-century name of the river-town known today as Mamantel (recorded variously as Xoquelha, Xocola, Cocolha, and Jocola), the name of the river that flows into the Usumacinta below Piedras Negras on the Mexican side (Chocolja), and, finally, the name of the Manche Chol town on the Polochic River that flourished into the first half of the seventeenth century (Xocolo), and that his rendering should be translated "water of the shark" (Jones 1985:216–217). The presence of these cognates in Lacandón, Yucatec,

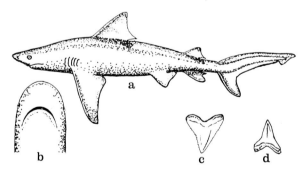

Fig. 3 Bull shark or cub shark, Carcharhinus leucas: *(a) lateral view; (b) underview of head; (c) upper tooth; and (d) lower tooth (drawings by Tom Jones).*

Jones

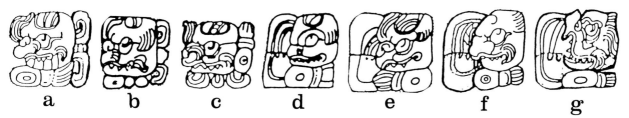

Fig. 4 Directional counting glyphs with fish-head: (a) Palenque Palace Tablet; (b) Palenque Temple of the Sun; (c) Palenque Temple XIV; (d) Palenque Temple of the Cross; (e) Palenque Temple of the Inscriptions; (f) Palace Tablet (drawings by Linda Schele); and (g) Chinikiha Throne 1 (drawing by Thompson).

Chontal, and Chol suggests a common ancestry in Classic times, as it also suggests that the word contained within them, *xoc*, known also in Pokomchi, was a pan-Maya name for the shark.

It remains, of course, to connect the word and meaning with the pisciform being that is the focus of this inquiry. A description of the latter would seem the place to start. The head of the fish found in the directional counting glyphs, which occasionally appears where one would normally expect one of the *u* prefixes, can be identified by a cluster of frequently encountered features, none of which is found in every example. The general appearance is that of the profile of a fantastic zoomorphic monster, only slightly anthropomorphized (fig. 4). Teeth are usually present, typically numbering from one to four or, rarely, five,[3] forming a short, serrated row of triangles projecting from beneath the upper lip at the side of a usually closed mouth and terminating in a single snaggle tooth at the front to reveal a sometimes severe overbite. Occasionally, a curl emerges from inside the corner of the mouth to curve downward and backward over the lower jaw. The jaw, the teeth of which are hidden, is at times marked with a pattern suggestive of the belly scales of a snake. The upper lip protrudes forward of the mouth to shape the base of a bulbous or blunted, downturned snout, sometimes articulated by a line rising from the upper lip to a point forward of the center of the lower edge of the eye and thence forward to a nasal curl that usually rests directly in front of the eye. The latter, somewhat lemon-shaped, is marked by a curved line that descends from its upper edge and hooks toward the front of the face. Occasionally, the curve rises from the bottom to hook forward.

At times a double line decorated very rarely with three beadlike pendants traces the lower edge of the eye and continues horizontally from the back of the eye to the rear of the head, separating the latter into clearly defined upper and lower zones. The back of the head rises vertically, making a squarish turn to form a flattened or moderately curved top within which is usually set a double-edged oval mirror sign. The forehead slopes downward, sometimes undulating toward a swollen point directly above the nasal curl to shape a frown to the upper line of the eye. Finlike appendages sprout from predictable points on the head. Most consistent is the one that rises from the top of the nose to complement

the line of the forehead or turn out from it. A second fin originates from the side of the nose to sweep downward in front of the eye, at times intruding upon it slightly, touching or overlapping the upper lip. A third fin hangs from the back of the head like a shock of hair, sometimes curving forward toward the eye. This fin can also be swept upward and is often split to include both this sweep and the hanging, shocklike form. A fourth fin springs from near the corner of the mouth, from the corner itself, from the upper lip, or from the cheek. A fifth fin is occasionally seen growing from behind the eye near the hinge of the jaw.

Examples of this same fish, identifiable by their flowing fins, eye mark, and serrated teeth, appear in the position of *u* prefixes in the full-figure glyphs of Zoomorph B at Quiriguá. In contrast to the blunt-nosed version just described, these have pointed muzzles that tend to turn upward, a beardlike growth that flows from their chins, and gaping jaws that suggest the origin of the *u* brackets they displace (T204, T10, etc.; fig. 2f–h). Extremely rare instances of this open-mouth form with the snout turned sharply upward occur in the directional counting glyphs (fig. 4g). As noted by Thompson, this form and the blunt-nosed version are both also found functioning as the patron of Zotz' in the Initial Series introductory glyphs (fig. 2j–m). It is this long-nosed rendition that seems to have been preferred by artists for non-glyphic representations of the fish, the diagnostic feature of which is the fin sweeping before the eye (fig. 2i).

Because of the distribution of fins on its portrait glyph, GI of the Palenque Triad has long been associated with fish (fig. 5a–e).[4] Though the strong jaw, thickly shaped lips, and well-defined Roman nose of GI leave a clear anthropomorphic impression, nevertheless, the regular feature of one fin rising from the upper bridge of the nose and following the sloping line of the forehead, a second fin growing variously from the cheek or line at the corner of the mouth, and a third falling from the back of the head (sometimes obscured by an ear ornament assemblage) suggest a close connection with the previously discussed fish-head. Moreover, both the single tooth at the front of GI's usually open mouth and the eyes, though somewhat squarish, are similar. But there are clear distinctions between the two glyphs. GI never displays the serrated row of teeth of the fish, nor does he possess the fin that grows from the side of the fish's nose

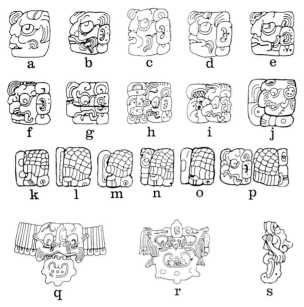

Fig. 5 Spondylus shell supernaturals. GI portrait glyphs: (a), (c–e) Palenque Temple of the Inscriptions; (b) Palenque Temple of the Foliated Cross; Chac Xib Chac portrait glyphs: (f–g) Temple of the Inscriptions; with GIV (h) Palenque Palace Tablet and (i) Palenque Temple of the Foliated Cross; and in directional counting glyph (j), Yaxchilán Hieroglyphic Stair 5 (drawing by Ian Graham); substitutions in u:678:130 phrases: (k–p) Temple of the Inscriptions; fish-head belts: (q) Naranjo Stela 24 (drawing by Ian Graham); (r) Cleveland Stela (drawing by Jeffrey Miller); and (s) Palenque Palace House D, Pier d (uncited drawings by Linda Schele).

past its eye and toward its mouth. Conversely, the latter never wears the *Spondylus* shell ear ornament that is GI's characteristic adornment. As is now well known, GI and GIII of the Palenque Triad have been identified as Classic Period prototypes of the Hero Twins of the Popol Vuh, Hunahpu and Xbalanque, respectively. Not only does GI, to whom the Temple of the Cross is dedicated, share his name with his father in the inscriptions of that building, exactly as in the Popol Vuh, but his name glyph has been read Hunahpu, while that of his brother, GIII, whose portrait in the Temple of the Sun identifies him as the Jaguar God of the underworld, contains the sound for "jaguar" (*balam* or *balan*), approximating the name of Hunahpu's twin, Xbalanque (Schele 1984b:103).

GI is not alone in wearing the *Spondylus* shell. A similar deity, zoomorphic in appearance and wearing the same ear shell, is named as the fifth of an expanded list of seven deities that includes the Palenque Triad as the first three in hieroglyphic passages from the Palace Tablet and the Temple of the Foliated Cross. In both inscriptions he shares a glyph-block with the fourth-named deity, who has been read Ek Balam Ahau (Schele 1985c:82; fig. 5h, i). On an incised bone from Tikal he is shown pulling a fish from the water and carrying a second in a bag strapped to his back. Identified phonetically as Chac Xib

Chac, he appears on polychrome vases waving an axe in scenes where he is paired with a reclining baby jaguar, or with a jaguar with water-lily foliage atop his head, enacting sacrificial scenes in the underworld that seem to anticipate passages in the Popol Vuh (Schele and Miller 1986:49). Thus two recognizable fish-related deities, sharing the sign of the *Spondylus* shell, are paired with jaguar supernaturals in contexts which invite comparison with the Hero Twins, Hunahpu and Xbalanque.

The same shell turns up on the front of a belt worn by women, and by men dressed as women for ritual purposes (Schele and Miller 1986:71), where it serves as the lower jaw of a version of the directional counting glyph fish identical to that portrayed as the patron of Zotz on Stela 6 at Copán (fig. 2m), implying a connection with the *Spondylus* shell deities. This possibility is strengthened by the observation that, in the inscriptions, the zoomorphic form of the latter can substitute for the fish-head as phonetic *u* both in a noncalendric context (fig. 5p) and as the main sign of the directional counting glyph itself (fig. 5j). A similar substitution is detectable in the art. The Palace Tablet from Palenque shows three figures seated upon three thrones adorned with zoomorphic heads representing the Palenque Triad (Schele 1978b:58). The single heads to the right and left are recognizable as the snake and the jaguar associated with GII and GIII, respectively. The two heads of the central throne, assumed to symbolize GI, possess all of the traits associated with the long-nosed variety of the fish in question and none that are not (fig. 6b). Insofar as GI and GIII can be regarded as twins, the fish is here paired with the jaguar.

A more explicit pairing is found on a Late Classic vessel that shows an underworld temple; on the roof are crouched two Water-lily Jaguars in profile, flanking a frontally presented long-nosed fish (with a second implied behind it, facing away from the viewer; fig. 6c). In front of the temple, a sacrificial ceremony is carried out by two axe-wielding figures, one wearing a jaguar-paw mask and the other linked iconographically to GI, Chac Xib Chac, and yet another antecedent of Hunahpu, Hun Ahau of the so-called Headband Twins (Schele and Miller 1986:286–287).

A fourth duo of importance to this inquiry is what have been called the "Paddler Gods" shown on incised bones from the burial under Temple 1 at Tikal escorting the departed lord Ah Cacau into the underworld by canoe (Mathews 1977; Stuart 1988). These deities appear on carved stelae throughout the Maya world in connection with blood sacrifice with both their name and portrait glyphs recorded in the inscriptions (fig. 7). The first of these Paddlers has easily been identified with the jaguar, whose ear he possesses and whose facial traits he sometimes shares. At times he wears a jaguar head as a hat. The second Paddler presents a problem. Because his profile is frequently characterized by a pronounced chin, and because his most consistent characteristic is a stingray spine that pierces his nose horizontally at its base,

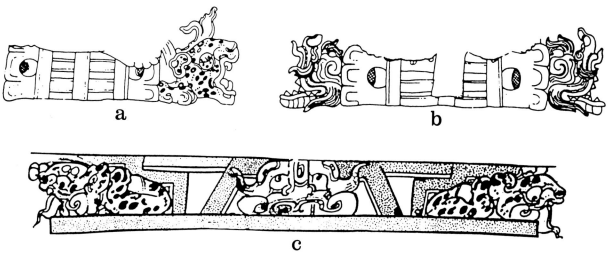

Fig. 6 *Jaguar-fish pairings: (a–b) Palenque Palace Tablet (drawing by Linda Schele); (c) Grolier ceramic vase 42 (modified by Tom Jones from Michael Coe).*

passing behind the alar walls of the nostrils to press against his cheeks, he is referred to as the "Old Stingray God." But his iconography involves more than stingray spines. On Stela 1 from Sacul this deity wears as a head-piece what may very well be the jawless head of the fish with which this study is concerned. In any case, an in-disputable representation of that fish serves as the cap of this second Paddler Deity in the inscription on Stela P at Copán. Its features include a sharply upturned snout, a lemon-shaped eye, and fins rising from the bridge of its nose, falling in double shocks from the back of its head, and sprouting from the corner of its mouth. Two tri-angular teeth show at the side of its upper jaw, while a single snag-tooth protrudes from its front. Of as much significance as the presence of this piscine headpiece is the absence of the telltale stingray spine from the nose of

the deity upon whose head it rests. The saw-toothed fish, in fact, substitutes for the spine. Thus, the fish of the directional counting glyphs has once again been paired with the jaguar.

This same partnership can be shown to have survived both the Classic Maya collapse and the Spanish con-quest. It has long been thought that the Chilam Balam of Kaua contained information important to an under-standing of the substitution of the Muluc sign and fish-head in the directional counting glyphs (Thompson 1971:78). This belief, of course, rested upon the convic-tion that the presence of the fish indicated the "count" meaning of the word *xoc*. Thus, the naming of the *xoc* as the animal associated with the day Muluc in the Kaua document seemed to provide a key to the substitution problem. But in concentrating upon the "count" reading

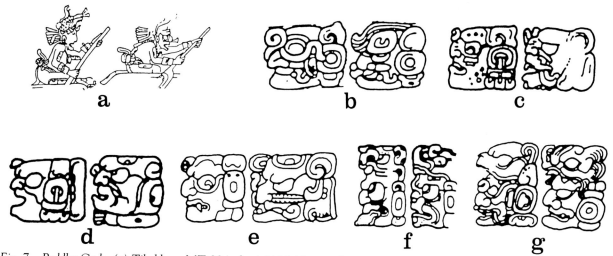

Fig. 7 *Paddler Gods: (a) Tikal bone MT-38A, burial 116 (drawing by Linda Schele); (b) Tikal Stela 31 (drawing by William Coe); (c) Dos Pilas Stela 8; (d) Ixlu Altar 1; (e) Quiriguá Stela C; (f) Sacul Stela 1; and (g) Copán Stela P (modified by Tom Jones from Linda Schele; uncited drawings by Ian Graham).*

of the *xoc*, it was generally overlooked that the Chilam Balam of Kaua names *two* animals as the *anuncios* for Muluc. The *prognóstico* for that day, as rendered in *El Libro de los libros de Chilam Balam* (Barrera Vásquez and Rendón 1948:193), reads: "Muluc: Ah Xoc, El-tiburón, y Ah Balam, El-jaguar, son su anuncio. Devorador de sus esposas. Devorador de sus hijos. Mortecinos niños. Mortecinas esposas. Rico. Matador de zarigüeyas también."[5] Approaching this passage with no concern for the concept "count," but, instead, with the conviction that *xoc* was a pan-Maya word for "shark" in Classic times, and with the knowledge that a fish-head that substituted for the Muluc sign in predictable contexts in the hieroglyphs was also repeatedly paired with jaguars and jaguarlike beings in the art and inscriptions of the period, the conclusion seems inescapable that the latter was the visual image of the former. Whatever phonetic value the Maya may have assigned to the hieroglyphic usage of its portrait, the creature was the *xoc*.

Certainly the serrated dentition and consistent overbite of the glyph contribute an iconographic confirmation of its identity as a shark. Perhaps the eye-hook is a vestige of the nictitating membrane characteristic of the carcharhinid sharks.[6] Beyond that, however, taxonomy becomes problematic. It will be recalled that the *xoc*-monster has two major forms. There are both long-nosed and blunt-nosed varieties. Thompson suggested that the former might be supposed to represent the elongated snout of the shark. Indeed, it was in recognition of this very feature of the profile of many sharks that the family to which the species inhabiting the rivers of the Maya area belongs was named Carcharhinidae ("sharp-nosed"; fig. 3). Interestingly, when viewed from above, the river shark reveals a nose so blunted that it has generated popular names that draw upon images of flat-nosed mammals.[7] The English bull shark and cub shark have their Mexican equivalent in *tiburón toro*. Fishermen have nicknamed the same shark *chato*, glossed in dictionaries as "flat," "flattened," or "flat-nosed."[8] It is conceivable that the two versions of the *xoc* reflect the two perspectives of the fish's snout. It is just as possible that they represent a lumping together of *C. leucas* with truly sharp-nosed carcharhinids found on the coasts. This possibility receives support of a sort if one attempts to account for the fins that flow from around the mouth or the sides of the nose of the *xoc* as "barbels" (Thompson 1944:3). None of the carcharhinids have barbels, though there are sharks on the Yucatán coast that do have them, most notably the nurse shark, *Ginglymostoma cirratum*. Again, the implication is that, less concerned with speciation than we are, the Maya drew from a number of less familiar sharks to elaborate upon an image inspired by a creature close at hand—or it may well have been the other way around. The coastal sharks may have generated a mythological creature whose image passed to the interior, where it was nourished and sustained by the presence of *C. leucas*. The difficulty of resolving these questions becomes even more apparent in the light of accumulating evidence that the Maya may have inherited their *xoc*-monster from an antecedent Olmec shark deity (Reilly this volume).[9] The presence of sharks in the Olmec area in the Coatzacoalcos River near San Lorenzo Tenochtitlán, some 90 km from the sea (Coe and Diehl 1980:122), suggests that, in the Olmec area too, *C. leucas* may have been the primary source for this shark deity, though I have no doubt that other sharks contributed to its iconography.[10]

Whatever the difficulties surrounding its origin, the glyph in question portrayed a shark known as Ah Xoc. Mythologized and anthropomorphized, Ah Xoc survived the conquest to become the Yucatec Chac Uayeb Xoc, or the Chac Xoc of the Lacandón today (Jones 1985:217), descendant of a classic Maya *xoc*-monster, itself perhaps of Olmec ancestry. The latter, teamed with a jaguar supernatural, evolved a number of variously anthropomorphized pairs culminating in the Hero Twins of the Popol Vuh. That one of these is called the Old Stingray God is perhaps a trifle misleading. It might more accurately reflect his shark-head and stingray spine substitution pattern if the companion of the Jaguar Paddler were perceived as a "selachian" paddler.[11]

Linking the word *xoc* with the meaning "shark" to the fish associated with the supernatural pairs of the jaguar deities suggests the possibility that further meaning of the fish can be derived from its specific occurrences on the belts of women and as the headdress of the Selachian Paddler. Before the validity of Thompson's "count" rebus was called into question, it had been proposed that the positioning of the *xoc* over the pelvis on the center of belts worn by women might be intended to refer to a woman's waist, since in Yucatec *xoc* included the meaning "waist" or "hips," and in eight other Maya languages *ixoc* and its cognates mean "woman" or "lady" (Miller 1974j:154). In this connection, the *xoc'ojaw* recorded in the sixteenth century by Las Casas as the title of legitimate wives of the lords of Utatlán and the *xokajaw*, *ucab ixok*, and *rox ixok* recorded in our own century as the titles of wives of the *alcalde*, *ucab achi*, and *rox achi* in the *cofradías* of Santa Cruz del Quiché (Carmack 1981:150, 358) might have had their Classic Period prototypes in the *xoc* glyphs that appear in name phrases of women at Yaxchilán (fig. 8). These glyphs are invariably followed by a suffix (T102) for which the phonetic value *c(i)* has been postulated (Fox and Justeson 1984b), which could serve as a phonetic complement for *xoc* to distinguish it from its usual value of *u*. If this turns out to be the case, then not only is the *xoc* glyph polyvalent, but it is also functioning as a rebus in name phrases of females.[12]

But there may have been more than femininity involved in the wearing of the *xoc*-head belt. The same belt was worn by men, but only in bloodletting rituals, where, symbolizing the role of rulers as nourishers of the gods, it could substitute for a belt with the personified lancet employed in drawing the blood (Schele and Miller 1986:71). This substitution perfectly parallels that of

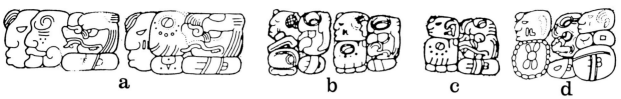

Fig. 8 *Yaxchilán name phrases: (a) Lintel 25; (b) Lintel 24; (c) Lintel 25; and (d) Lintel 23 (drawings by Ian Graham).*

the *xoc*-head for the stingray spine in the portrayal of the Selachian Paddler on Stela P at Copán. In both cases, the *xoc*-head replaces a bloodletting instrument—not that such an instrument is thereby lacking; the *xoc* is equipped with his own. Indeed, the shark-tooth and stingray spine are not only interchangeable, but merge to become indistinguishable.[13] They range from the realistically portrayed spines held by participants in bloodletting ceremonies, through the stylized central element that rises from the sacrificial bowl in the headdress of the Quadripartite Monster, to the tooth that projects from the front of the upper jaw of the *xoc* and other zoomorphic dragons. This last is, as well, the tooth of GI, sometimes filed to a geometrically shaped T. All of these, whether presented frontally or in profile, can share a set of Early Classic iconographic traits, allowing them to be seen as one and the same thing (fig. 9). It is impossible to determine whether the glyph that derives from them is intended to be a tooth or a spine. The edges that run from the cusp of the structure are finely scored, reflecting their selachian origins in the serrated weapons of the stingray and the bull shark. At the wide end are a pair of rounded projections or recurved flares—again, vestiges of the swollen bases of batoid spines and carcharhinoid dentition. The center of this base is marked by a U-shaped form set within a circular enclosure. Descending from the cusp toward the base, and increasing in size, is a row of up to a dozen dots. Given the context, the latter are surely symbolic of sacrificial blood.[14] A striking version of this spine-tooth, carved from shell, protrudes from the mouth of a beautiful fuchsite mask of GI from Río Azul. In place of the descending dots and U-form, a deep groove runs from the cusp of the denticle to its base, apparently as a channel for the flow of sacrificially drawn blood (fig. 9g). On the forehead of GI is the quadripartite emblem, the central element of which displays the blood drops and U-form missing from the tooth below. Of equal interest are the large stucco masks of the Early Classic temple facade of Kohunlich. Atop the ear ornaments at the sides of each mask rests a *xoc*-head in profile, its lower jaw missing and a large spine-tooth mounted near the tip of the upper jaw. In addition, from the mouth of the mask itself another tooth projects. Of considerable size, flattened at its cutting edge, and filed in the shape of a T, the tooth possesses all of the selachian traits described above, including the blood drops and U-form, adapted to the geometry of its new form (fig. 9h).

The substitutions of the *xoc*'s tooth or head for known bloodletters throws light upon an unusual use of *xoc*-heads on a sculptured monument at Tikal. Three late classic stelae at that site (nos. 19, 21, and 22) portray rulers supporting by one arm an instrument with two diamond-shaped forms separated and flanked by the three knotted cloths symbolic of the personified lancet, and wearing on their ankles the portrait of the latter. On a fourth monument, Stela 16, the ruler Ah Cacau wears similar anklets and holds the same instrument. The bloodletter portrait, however, is on the instrument and in its place on the anklets are paired heads of the *xoc*-monster, alluding, it would seem, to a bloodletter of selachian derivation. But there may be more to it. In Ah Cacau's headdress are symbols of the planet Venus, whose presence has been explained as referring to a first appearance of the planet as evening star that occurred on the dedication date of the monument, 9.14.0.0.0, or 1 December 711 A.D. (Lounsbury 1982:156). If one recalls the association of Venus with Hunahpu (Thompson 1971:218), this extraordinary occasion of the planet's heliacal rising occurring on a Period Ending may ac-

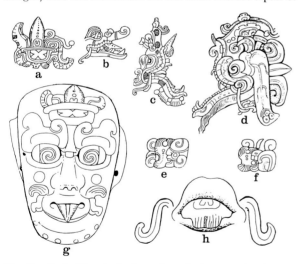

Fig. 9 *Early Classic shark-tooth and stingray spine iconography: (a–c) incised tripod bowl (modified by Tom Jones from Lin Crocker-Deletaile); (d) incised ceremonial plate (modified by Tom Jones from Lin Crocker-Deletaile); (e–f) Yaxchilán Lintel 35 glyphs (drawing by Ian Graham); (g) Río Azul fuchsite mask (drawn by Tom Jones from a photograph by J. Taylor); and (h) Kohunlich temple mask (drawn by Tom Jones from a personal photograph).*

count for the unique appearance of the Hero Twin's *nagua* on Ah Cacau's ankle as a substitute for the personified lancet. Following the wake of the *xoc* as bloodletter, we are brought back, once again, to Hunahpu, twin of the Jaguar-Hero, Xbalanque.

The pairing of the shark and the jaguar in the Chilam Balam of Kaua can be viewed as a mytho-zoological analogue of the pairing of the Hero Twins, Hunahpu and Xbalanque, in the Popol Vuh. Both descended from Precolumbian prototypes who manifested themselves in a variety of ways, spawning a series of paired supernaturals with overlapping features, functions, and behaviors. The frequent appearance of jaguar traits as markers on figures portrayed in Maya art and the happy circumstance of the word for "jaguar" appearing in Xbalanque's name meant that the identification of his animal correlate could be established with some confidence. The identification of Hunahpu's faunal form was less clear. His name offered no clue, nor was there any episode in the Popol Vuh to suggest a line of inquiry. Once his fish features were recognized from his association with GI, the only specific form that he was given, the Yucatec *xoc*, seemed to depend upon a pun that had nothing to do with the Popol Vuh. The pairing of another Jaguar counterpart of Xbalanque with an old deity with a stingray spine stuck through his nose made a specific identification of Hunahpu's zoological form seem even less promising. Then came the abandonment of the *xoc* rebus, necessitating a fresh inquiry into the legitimacy of its offspring, the *xoc*-monster. Such has been the purpose of this study. If there is merit to it, then it appears that there was indeed a sharklike being called *xoc* who was as familiar and important to the ancient Maya as the jaguarlike being called *balam*. Thus, although the rebus theory upon which it was originally predicated can no longer be accepted, the *xoc*-fish seems to have earned an important entry in any study that pretends to include a complete Maya bestiary. If Thompson was like most of us, he was probably enamored of his rebus and would have been disappointed with its abandonment.[15] But perhaps he would also have taken some satisfaction in the observation that his intuition regarding the identity of his fish, even if for the wrong reasons, may well have been correct. Nor would he have been indifferent to the possibility that a second pun had accompanied the return of the *xoc*.

Notes

1. Unless otherwise indicated, Thompson references are to Thompson 1944.

2. In addition to the shark sightings reported in Jones 1985, I have been informed by boatmen (July 1986) that small sharks (*tiburones chicos*) have been caught a few kilometers south of the bridges at Boca del Cerro above the rapids near Linda Vista on the Usumacinta River, and by Ausencio Cruz Guzman (July 1986), who has fished for sharks on the Tulijá River near Salto de Agua, that sharks are usually taken there during the dry season—he has caught specimens up to 3m in length.

3. There are examples with even more.

4. Thompson calls T1011 "the Fish god" in his catalog (Thompson 1962:318).

5. "Muluc: Ah Xoc, the shark, and Ah Balam, the jaguar, are its omens. Devourer of his children. Devourer of his wives. Deathly children. Deathly wives. Rich. Killer of opossums also."

6. The presence of this same eye-mark on a number of Maya supernaturals might be attributed to their having derived from birds or mammals that also possess such a membrane. Having its origin in several faunal forms, the hook may have evolved as a mark to distinguish mortals from divinities.

7. "The bull shark has an *extremely short snout* (much shorter than the width of the mouth) . . ." (Castro 1983:135). "The species is distinguished from possibly all other carcharhinids except the lemon shark, *Negraprion brevirostris*, and the whitetip, *Carcharhinus longimanus*, by its very short, very broadly rounded snout . . ." (Lineaweaver and Backus 1984:84). "Diagnostic features: . . . Snout very short and bluntly and broadly rounded; internarial width 0.7 to 1 times in preoral length . . ." (Compagno 1984:479).

8. Moises Morales informed me that *chato* is a nickname in Chiapas for people with flattened or gently rounded noses (personal communication, 1983).

9. Independently, Kent Reilly proposed that the iconographic traits by which the Olmec shark can be recognized include an eye shaped to reflect the shark's nictitating membrane.

10. At the Sixth Palenque Round Table, Rosemary Joyce showed several Olmec ceramic pieces with zoomorphic forms that she identified as sharks (Joyce et al. this volume) among which at least one sported not only the triangular tooth traceable to *C. leucas*, but a second tooth that appears to me to owe its origin to another carcharhinid, *Galeocerdo cuvieri*, the tiger shark.

11. *Webster's New Universal Unabridged Dictionary* defines "selachian" as "a member of the Selachii," which, in turn, is defined as "an order of fishes including the sharks, dogfishes and rays; now sometimes restricted to the division of this order containing the sharks and dogfishes." My use of this term is intended to reflect both the iconographic substitutions mentioned and the ambiguity involved in its usage by zoologists.

12. Among the more interesting examples outside of Yaxchilán are those of two women named on the Grolier Panel, in both of whose name phrases the *xoc*-head (admittedly, without the T102 suffix) is the final glyph, suggesting a titular structure parallel to the *ucab ixoc* and *rox ixoc* titles of the Quiché.

13. This may be viewed as an interesting recognition on the part of the Maya of the modern zoologist's view that both the shark's tooth and the stingray's spine have a common evolutionary source in the dermal denticle of ancestral selachians.

14. Rosemary Joyce proposed an analogous sacrifical use for shark's teeth among the Olmec (Joyce et al. this volume).

15. Charles Darwin's undying attachment to his wholly untenable theory of pangenesis ("my beloved child") comes to mind (Darwin 1869:1871).

Acknowledgments

I am grateful to Linda Schele and David Stuart for valuable criticism at the presentation of this material at the Sixth Palenque Round Table and am indebted to Carolyn Young for reading, commenting upon, and volunteering to type the text.

Classic and Modern Relationship Terms and the "Child of Mother" Glyph (TI:606.23)

NICHOLAS A. HOPKINS
INSTITUTE FOR CULTURAL ECOLOGY OF THE TROPICS

Among the more culturally interesting and historically informative glyphs in the inventory of deciphered Mayan hieroglyphs are those referred to as "relationship glyphs," which typically occur in "parentage statements." The phrases known as parentage statements were first interpreted as such by Christopher Jones (1977:41–44), who noted a pattern in the inscriptions of Tikal in which the name phrase of the text's protagonist was followed, after certain intervening glyphs, by the name of another man and often that of a woman. The man whose name followed in such a text was the ruler who preceded the protagonist in office. Jones's interpretation of this kind of text, later accepted by other scholars and confirmed in the inscriptions of many other sites, was that the pair of persons named after the protagonist are the parents of the protagonist; in other words, these texts record the genealogy of the protagonist of the text (Schele and Mathews, 1983:2).

Three of the glyphs that stand between the name phrases in these texts, now called "relationship glyphs," were also identified by Jones (1977:42; see fig. 1a–c). Further work by Jones and other scholars led to the recognition of variants of these glyphs and to the identification of at least one more relationship glyph (fig. 1d). These glyphs appear to represent kin terms, and they are usually taken to be terms for "child" (Schele 1983:32; Mathews 1985b:27–28). Some scholars, including Jones (1984:17), reserved their opinion on this point, or argued that the relationship glyphs may mean "father" and "mother" rather than "child." However, most epigraphers currently accept that the grammar and syntax of the expression, as well as their phonetics, support the gloss of "child."[1]

Relationship Glyphs

Schele and Mathews (1983), in a major unpublished paper on the parentage expressions, presented the four most common relationship glyphs (fig. 1; note that the initial element in most of these compounds, T1, T3 or T11, but not T126, is the third person possessive prefix,

u-, "his or her"). Of these glyphic compounds, two are glossed as "child of mother"—the name following the relationship glyph identifies the mother of the person named before the relationship glyph. The compounds glossed "child of mother" are T1.1.606.23 and T126.19:670 and their variants.[2]

A third compound, T3.122:535, is glossed "child of father"—the name phrase following identifies the father of the person previously named. The last parentage expression treated by Schele and Mathews is the compound T1.757:59.712:81 and its variants. This compound is more general in its meaning glossed "child of (either) parent," and may be followed by the name of either the mother or the father. These glyph compounds are referred to below as the 606, 670, 535, and 712 compounds, respectively, following the usage established by Schele and Mathews (n.d.).

As the glosses indicate, the terms, insofar as they specify sex, are specific for sex of the parent, not for sex of the child. This is in agreement with the pattern of kin terms in many of the Mayan languages, where a distinction is made in the terms for children by male and female speakers (Romney 1967:222–235). Such distinctions usually correlate with unilineal kinship systems, where membership in the kin group is transmitted to children by only one parent—where the child is a member of the father's lineage, but not of the mother's, or vice versa. Thus, in Chalchihuitán Tzotzil (Hopkins 1969), a man's child is a member of the man's own lineage, and is called his *nich'on*. A woman's child, not a member of her own lineage but of the father's lineage, is the woman's *ol*.

Parentage Statements

The syntax of a parentage statement is illustrated by the parentage statement of Bird Jaguar on Yaxchilán Stela 11 (fig. 2). Bird Jaguar's name (at F1) is followed by his titles (E2–F4) and the statement that he is the child (G1) of Lady Ik-Skull (H1; her titles follow at G2–G3), and the child (H3–G4) of Shield Jaguar (I1; his titles

a. The 606 Compound

T 1. I:606.23   T 3. I:606:23   T 11. I:606:Lady Zac Kuk

b. The 670 Compound

T 126:178(=534):670:?   T 126.19:670:?   T 126.584:670:140

c. The 535 Compound

T 3. (122):535

d. The 712 Compound

T 1:757:59.712:81

Fig. 1 The four most common relationship glyphs: the 606, 670, 535, and 712 compounds. Redrawn by Nicholas Hopkins from the following sources: (a) first example, Tikal, Lintel 3 (Temple I), underside, E-1 (Jones 1977: fig. 1; original drawing by William R. Coe); second example, Palenque, Tablet of the 96 Glyphs, I-8 (original drawing by Linda Schele); third example, Palenque, Temple of the Inscriptions, sarcophagus lid, Glyph 54 (Schele 1983:64; original drawing by Merle Greene Robertson); (b) first example, Yaxchilán, Lintel 10, A-2 (Graham and von Euw 1977:31; original drawing by Ian Graham); second example, Tikal, Stela 17, H-5 (Jones and Satterthwaite 1982: fig. 25; original drawing by W. R. Coe); third example, Tikal MT 43, Glyph 7 (Jones 1977: fig. 8; original drawing by A. Seuffert); (c) first example, Tikal, Stela 19, B-7 (Jones 1977: fig. 20; original drawing by W. R. Coe); second example, Palenque, Temple of the Inscriptions, sarcophagus lid, Glyph 52 (Schele 1983:64; original drawing by Merle Greene Robertson); (d) Tikal, Lintel 3 (Temple I), F-4 (Jones 1977: fig. 1; original drawing by W. R. Coe).

precede and follow his name, at H4 and I2–I4). Parentage statements may identify one or both parents; here the mother is identified first, but some other parentage statements name the father before the mother.

In the parentage statement of Bahlum Kuk on the Tablet of the 96 Glyphs, Palenque (fig. 3), Bahlum Kuk's name (at J3) is followed by his titles (I4–J4) and the statement tha the is the child of Chaacal (I5–I7) and the child of Lady X-Ahau, Lady Cahal (I8–K1).

The somewhat unusual relationship glyphs in this expression occur at I5–J5 and at I8.

It should be noted that "parentage statements" are not in fact syntactically independent "statements," but parts of complex noun phrases that occur as subjects of sentences. These phrases name and identify the actor in an event, often the protagonist of an accompanying scene. Thus, the essential statement on Stela 11 of Yaxchilán is that Bird Jaguar took an office on a particular date (9.16.1.0.0, 11 Ahau 8 Tzec). The "parentage statement" is merely a part of Bird Jaguar's elaborate name phrase. Changing the Mayan verb-object-subject sentence order (VOS) to English order (SVO) and adding emphasis to mark the parentage statements, the text from Stella 11 reads as follows (lunar data omitted from the Initial Series):

On 9.16.1.0.0, 11 Ahau 8 Tzec
    Bird Jaguar,
        Captor of Ah Cauac,
        3 Katun Lord,
        Batab,
        Lord of Yaxchilán,
        child of Lady Ik-Skull,
            Lady of Sky Title and God C Title, Lady Bacab,
        child of the 5 Katun Lord Shield Jaguar,
            Captor of Ah Ahual,
            Lord of Yaxchilán, Bacab,
    took office as Lord of the Succession.

Proposed Readings

Readings have been accepted by most epigraphers for some of the relationship glyphs (table 1). These readings are discussed below. Following this discussion, a new reading for one of the "child of mother" glyphs is proposed.

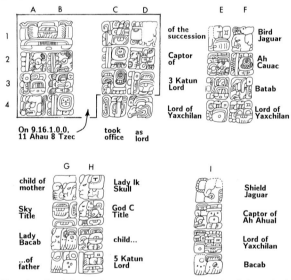

Fig. 2 Bird Jaguar's parentage statement, Yaxchilán, Stela 11, front, G1–I4 (after Schele 1985:38; drawing by Linda Schele).

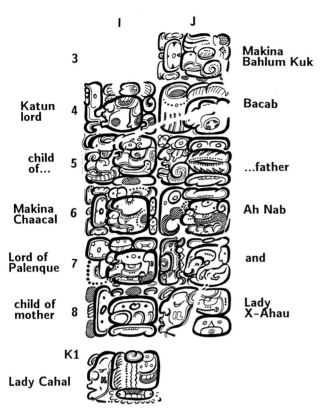

Makina
Bahlum Kuk

Bacab

...father

Ah Nab

and

Lady
X-Ahau

3

Katun
lord   4

child
of...   5

Makina
Chaacal   6

Lord of
Palenque   7

child of
mother   8

K1

Lady Cahal

I   J

Fig. 3   Bahlum Kuk's parentage statement, Palenque, Tablet of the 96 Glyphs, I4–K1 (after Schele 1985:99; drawing by Linda Schele).

The 535 Compound

T122:535, which is called "capped Ahau" or "decorated Ahau" (Thompson 1962:150) and glossed as "child of father," is read *ahau*. This is perhaps the most common relationship glyph. Its reading as *ahau*, "child of father," does not conflict with the reading of T535 elsewhere as *ahau*, "lord," although Jones (1984:17) took this as evidence that, rather than meaning "his child," the glyph (with its possessive prefix) is "perhaps more properly, 'his father . . . ,'" since *ahau* has the meaning of "lord'" (Jones

1977:41). However, the coincidence of terms for "lord" and "child" is a widespread Mesoamerican phenomenon (Hopkins 1984). The "baby-faced" royal figures of Olmec political art suggest an origin in a Preclassic Mixe-Zoquean metaphor or word play. At any rate, the equivalence between terms for "lord" and for "child" is also attested in Colonial Yucatec *almehen*, "noble, child," Mixtec *iya*, "lord, child," and Nahuatl *pilli*, "lord, child," so the phenomenon has considerable geographical extension as well as chronological depth.

The 670 Compound

T126.19:670, called "inverted Ahau in the palm" (Jones 1984:17), is glossed "child of mother" and read *al*. This is the most common relationship glyph for recording the female parent. The reading *al* corresponds to a widespread term in Mayan languages for "child (of female)" that may ultimately derive from the Proto-Mayan root *'a(h)l*, "heavy." That is, this may be another metaphor: a woman's child is her "burden."[3]

In origin, the "inverted Ahau in the palm" may be ideographic: the *ahau*, "child of father," sign, placed in a hand to indicate it is a "burden," and then inverted to distinguish it from other Ahau-in-hand glyphs meaning "to take office," based on the act of holding the God K scepter (cf. Schele 1983:41). Whatever its origins, the "inverted Ahau" becomes one of the most common *phonetic* signs, having the phonetic values *al* and *la* or *l(a)*, as in the final syllable of Pacal's name when spelled out, *pa-ka-l(a)*.

The 712 Compound

T1.757:59.712:81, a complex expression usually called a "bloodletting expression" (Schele and Mathews 1983), is glossed "child of (either) parent," and currently has no accepted reading. This parentage expression involves an auxiliary verb construction, *u*- Aux + *ti* + Verbal Noun, marked by the string T 1.757:59 and its equivalent T1.580:59, and furthermore has to do with a bloodletter, T712. Josserand, Schele, and Hopkins (1985) explained these verbal constructions featuring *ti* and showed that,

Table 1. The Four Major Relationship Glyphs: Catalog Numbers, Common Names, Glosses, and Readings (see also fig. 1)

Glyph Compound	Common Name	Gloss	Reading
The 606 Compound (fig. 1a): *u*- I 606 23	"the 'shell' glyph with numeral 1"	"child of mother"	(see text)
The 670 Compound (fig. 1b): 126 { 178/534 / 19 / 584 } 670 140/?	"inverted Ahau in the palm"	"child of mother"	*al*
The 535 Compound (fig. 1c): *u*- (122) 535/533	"capped Ahau" or "decorated Ahau"	"child of father"	*ahau*
The 712 Compound: (fig. 1d): *u*- Aux *ti* 712 81	"bloodletting expression"	"child of (either) parent"	(see text)

although the auxiliary carries the verbal marking, the "semantic" verb—the part that specifies the action—follows the particle *ti*. Schele (1985c:101) suggested this verbal expression "is not a specific kinship term, but a metaphorical reference to the offspring as the blood of his parents." Note that the stingray spine, a common bloodletter, appears in a variant of this 712 compound in Bahlum Kuk's parentage statement on the Tablet of 96 Glyphs, J5 (see fig. 3, above).

The 606 Compound

TI:606.23, called "the 'shell' glyph with numeral 1" (Jones 1984:17), is usually glossed "child of mother," without assigning a specific reading. Fox and Justeson (1986) proposed a radically different interpretation (discussed below), again without arguing for a specific reading. That is, this is an extremely common glyph compound whose meaning is disputed, and for which no reading—no association with words or phrases in the relevant Mayan languages—has been generally accepted

by epigraphers. After discussing the current issues, I present evidence for a reading of this compound that supports the gloss "child of mother."

TI.606.23, "Child of Mother"

The 606 compound, glossed as "child of mother," consists of three rather stable signs. These are:

(1) the numeral "one" (TI), read *hun*, as a prefix or superfix;
(2) a main sign (T606) for which no reading has been proposed; and
(3) a suffix or postfix (T23) usually read *-na*.

A concordance of T606 drawn from Thompson's (1962) glyph catalog (table 2, from Hopkins 1973; see also Hopkins 1968) indicates that T606 occurs in a limited number of combinations with other glyphs. The overwhelming majority of its occurrences are in this relationship compound, as TI:606.23 (Thompson 1962:

Table 2. Occurrences of T606, from a Concordance of Thompson's Glyph Catalog

			Glyph String					Source Inscription
TI:606.23								
			I	606	23			Cop. H.S., Step G
		1	I	606	23			Pusil. M, C7; Nar. 24, D8
		3	I	606	23			Tik. L. 3, H5; L. 4, E1; Pal. 96 Gl., I8
		11	I	606	23			Pal. Fol. N17
		11	I	606				Pal. Sarcoph., Gl. 55
		191	I	606	23			Pal. Insc. W A1; M F7
		204	I	606	23			Pal. Cross, E. Pan. B1; Yax. 10, H1
		232	I	606	23			Pal. Ruz I, D14
125	669b	130	I	606	23			Pal. Insc. W S11
T606:23 (without the prefixed numeral I)								
				606		23		Pal. Sun C2; Ruz I, C6, D4; T. 18, detached stucco; Calak. 51, F4; Yax. L. 25, M2, I8, C1; Ixkun 2, D4; Yax. L. 25, T2
		44	110	606		23		Pal. Sun, P5
		110	44	606		23		Pal. Cross, S2
				606		23	(74)	173	(variants of Half-Period glyph)
T606 with 59 or 24 and 23								
				606	59	23		Yax. L. 32, G1
				606	24	23		Yax. L. 25, T2
Other occurrences of T606								
	16	713	61	606				Cop. 9, F10
	110	168	44	606				Pal. Fol. E9
			89	606	181			Pal. Fol. E9
				606	248			Uaxac. sherd 4781
				606	[508]			P.N. Thr. 1, I1, F'6
				606	[508]	23		P.N. Thr. 1, F'1

Source: Hopkins 1973, from Thompson 1962:229–230, 303. Glyph strings marked as variants (v) or questions (?) were not included in the concordance. Nevertheless, these do not seem to introduce significant new combinations. Thompson (1962:230) remarked, "The many occurrences of this glyph with a coefficient of one present an interesting problem."

229–230). In the concordance, these are recorded with prefixed *u-* (T1, 3, 11, 204, etc.).

The set T606:23, without the initial numeral 1 (TI), occurs in other contexts, with preposed T44 and T110 (in either order) or with postposed T173, or with postposed T74 and T173. These compounds have variously been described as referring to Period Endings divisible by five, or as Half-Period Endings (Thompson 1962:230, Schele 1984b:73).

A third set of examples has T606 with postposed T24 or T59 (*ti*), both followed by T23 (*-na*); two examples occur at Yaxchilán (Lintel 25, T2; Lintel 32, G1; Thompson 1962:230).

Apart from these three repeating combinations, there are scattered other occurrences of T606 that, together with the more common contexts, constitute the evidence that must ultimately be explained in order to support a reading for T606. The present paper considers only the first set of examples, all of which have the prefix TI ("one").

While most epigraphers accept a gloss of "child of mother" for the 606 compound, Fox and Justeson (1986) proposed a radically different glossing, which not only has a bearing on the possible readings for this glyph, but has broad implications for Classic Mayan social organization and political succession as well. This proposal must be dealt with before any readings can be proposed for the 606 compound.

Fox and Justeson's Proposal

Fox and Justeson (1986) argued that the 606 compound should be glossed not as "child," but as "nephew/niece." They analyzed TI:606.23 as the numeral "one" (TI) plus a kinship term (T606:23), identified it as referring to collateral rather than direct, lineal, relatives, and argued for a sweeping reanalysis of Classic Mayan patterns of political succession based on the concept of a ruling matriline. Motivated by their interpretation of the 606 compound and citing an unpublished reconstruction of early Mayan kin terms, they argued that "linguistic evidence . . . indicates the existence of a Greater Lowland Mayan subsystem of kin terms designating aunts, uncles, nephews and nieces . . . of which the 1-T606:23 [*sic*] glyphic term was a part . . . [it] designated at least a woman's sister's child, and it may have designated a woman's sibling's child. We cannot yet read the compound phonetically" (Fox and Justeson 1986:14; a footnote suggests T606:23 could be *ihtz'in*, "younger sibling," shifted to mean "child," and its use in Half-Periods might be as a metaphor derived from "child" or "younger sibling," and meaning "half, portion"). Terms prefixed by "one" are found in Tzotzil, where a woman's child is her *ol* (cognate with Yucatec *al*, "child of woman"); her *hun-'ol*, with a prefixed number "one," is her nephew. Likewise, one's father is one's *tot*; one's uncle (father's brother) is one's *hun-tot* (Hopkins 1969). However, these combinations do not occur with sibling terms such as *itz'in*, "younger sibling."[4]

Since the 606 compound occurs as a relationship glyph that connects rulers to women, presumably the wives of the previous rulers, and since they interpret these relationship glyphs as "(woman's) nephew/niece" rather than as "child," Fox and Justeson (1986:16) argued that, in Classic Maya society, rule "did not normally pass from father to son." Rather, they hypothesized that "royal succession was founded upon regularly maintained dynastic alliances; that systematic matrilateral parallel-cousin and/or patrilateral cross-cousin marriage joined ruling families, with a *ruler's son-in-law the heir to his throne* and fraternal nephew the heir at a politically affiliated site; and that at the core of these alliances at each site was a *single royal matriline whose husbands ruled*" (Fox and Justeson 1986:7, emphasis added).

In order to explain this pattern of political succession, Fox and Justeson invoked their reconstruction of Mayan kinship and posited a ruling matriline. That is, the ruling family at Piedras Negras (and, by implication, at other sites) would be composed of a line of women and their descendants, the husbands of these women being the actual rulers (fig. 4). A particular ruler would be ruler because he had married a woman of the ruling family. Their son would not become the next ruler; rather, the man who married their daughter would become the next ruler. A ruler is "nephew" to the wife of the preceding ruler because an heir apparent would marry his mother's sister's daughter in order to succeed: "a ruler succeeded his uncle, his aunt's husband" (Fox and Justeson 1986:15).

Thus, Fox and Justeson proposed that it is the line of descent traced through the women—woman to daughter to granddaughter—that determines who is to rule, rather than the line of descent traced through the men, as has been proposed by other scholars. However, the rest of

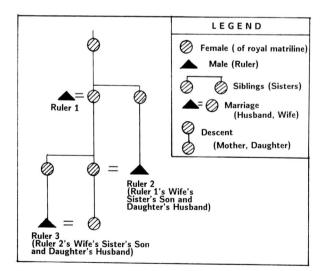

Fig. 4 Classic Maya succession patterns according to Fox and Justeson (1986). Only relevant female members of the matriline are displayed.

society, apart from the ruling family, is said to have been *patrilineally* organized, so that rule (by males who marry into ruling matriline) passes from patrilineage to patrilineage, satisfying the political interests of these descent groups through marriage alliances with the ruling matrilineage.

The linguistic evidence that leads Fox and Justeson to propose such a unique social system cannot properly be evaluated until more details of their reconstruction of Mayan kinship are available for scrutiny. However, other lines of evidence can be brought to bear on the evaluation of key elements in their proposals. The ethnohistoric evidence, derived from early reports of relatively unacculturated Mayan societies, is relevant to the question of matrilineal organization, as is the ethnographic evidence, derived from more recent reports. The epigraphic evidence, involving the interpretation of Classic Maya writing, is equally relevant to the question. I believe that this evidence fails to support the proposals of Fox and Justeson. Furthermore, with specific regard to the relationship glyph TI:606.23, I believe there is overwhelming evidence that the gloss "child of mother" is correct, and I support this statement by proposing a new reading for the 606 compound.

Ethnohistorical Evidence

Fox and Justeson's sweeping reanalysis of Classic Mayan patterns of political succession was based on the concept of a ruling matriline. In support of this concept, they appealed to the ethnohistorical interpretations proposed by Ralph Roys as evidence of matrilineality among the Maya. Roys's writings have been a constant support for scholars proposing matrilineal organization for the Classic Maya (e.g., Joyce 1981; P. C. Thompson 1982). Roys (1939, 1940) believed that the Maya had elements of matrilineal organization because of three observations (cited in Tozzer 1941:98–99):

(1) In the kinship terminology, a man called his own son and his brother's son by the same term, *mehen*. But a woman called her own son and her *sister's* son by the same term, *al*. Roys took this to be evidence of the importance of both matrilineal and patrilineal descent.

(2) The Yucatec Maya term for "noble" was *almehen*, composed of the terms *al*, "child of woman," and *mehen*, "child of man." Thus, according to Roys, a noble was someone of royal descent in *both* the female and the male lines, implying that matrilineal descent was as important as patrilineal descent.

(3) There are two terms in Maya dictionaries sometimes glossed "lineage"; Roys translated *ch'ibal* (⟨*chibal*⟩) as "descent in direct line through the father" and *tz'akab* (⟨*dzacab*⟩) as "descent in direct line through the mother." These translations imply the presence of patrilineal and matrilineal descent, respectively.

But while Roys believed these phenomena were evidence of matrilineal organization, in fact this is not the case. First, the lumping of one's own and one's same-sex sibling's children in the fashion described is characteristic of patrilineal systems as well as matrilineal ones and simply does not constitute evidence of matrilineal principles of organization.

Second, the term *almehen*, a typical Mayan compound noun, does not imply that a "noble" is of royal descent through both mother and father, as Roys assumed. The term is parallel to such terms as Tzotzil *totil-me'il* ("father-mother"), which means "ancestors." Such compounds refer to a superordinate category (e.g., ancestors) by juxtaposing the contrasting subordinate categories (fathers, mothers). Thus, *al-mehen* ("child of woman"-"child of man") simply means "descendants" or "children." Its use as "noble" is an example of the Mesoamerican metaphor "child" = "lord" discussed above, and has no implications for matrilineal organization.

Third, the definitions of the terms *ch'ibal* and *tz'akab* in the Mayan dictionaries are by no means adequate evidence for matrilineal organization. The Motul dictionary (Martínez Hernández 1929) makes no reference to patri- or matrilineality, glossing *ch'ibal* as *casta, linage, genealogía por linea recta* (155 r.) and *tz'akab* as *abolorio, casta o linage o generación* (124). References to "mother's side" in the later Spanish-Maya inversion of the Motul and other sources (most notably, Roys himself) as compiled in the Cordemex dictionary (Barrera Vázquez et al. 1980) are vague. At best they are ambiguous. There is little reason to think that they refer to anything other than mother's *patriline* rather than a hypothetical matriline. In patrilineal societies, mother's patriline is always important and is called by a term distinct from that used for one's own (i.e., one's father's) patriline.

With Roys's interpretations removed as evidence for matrilineality, there is no *ethnohistoric* support to be found for the principle of matrilineal descent among the Maya.

Ethnographic Evidence

Put briefly, there is no ethnographic evidence to support the notion of matrilineality in Mayan societies, as I have argued at length elsewhere (Hopkins 1984). On the other hand, there is a great deal of support both in the colonial sources and in the ethnographic record for the institutions of patrilineages and patrilineal descent. Nutini (1961) interpreted Landa's description of Yucatec society and Las Casas's reports from Alta Verapaz as clear evidence of patrilineal social organization, and a number of other scholars have agreed with this evaluation. The evidence makes it clear that a system such as that proposed by Fox and Justeson would be totally without precedent in the Mayan area, or for that matter in Mesoamerica. That is, as with the ethnohistorical evidence, there is no *ethnographic* evidence to be found that supports their proposals of matrilineality.

Epigraphic Evidence

The only remaining line of evidence that could provide support for the Fox and Justeson hypothesis is *epigraphic*: their interpretation of the 606 compound as "nephew."

I would like now to suggest a different interpretation of this compound, one that would not require the postulation of abnormal and otherwise unattested systems of kinship and political succession for the Classic Maya.

Fox and Justeson's argument hinged on the interpretation of the 606 compound as a collateral, rather than direct, kin term (i.e., "nephew" rather than "child"), and this interpretation is based on the occurrence of the number "one" before the main sign. They offered no specific reading, other than suggesting the possibility of *hun-itz'in, "one-younger brother," motivated by the initial hun and final -n(a). Nonetheless, they assumed, on the model of the Tzotzil terms discussed above, that TI:606.23 is composed of a basic kin term T606:23 plus a preposed number "one" (TI) that marks it as a collateral term. However, there is no evidence of a kin term written T606:23. The occurrences of T606:23 without prefixed TI are Half-Period and Period-Ending signs, not kin terms.

Furthermore, according to the reconstruction of these compound kin terms by Kaufman (1972) for the ancestor of Tzotzil and Tzeltal, the order of elements in ancient times was not the same as the order of the elements in modern Tzotzil: numeral + kin term. Rather, Kaufman reconstructed terms with the elements ordered kin term + numeral, as in Tzeltal. This is also the order of elements in Chol kin terms, which use a modifier instead of a numeral—for example, p'ene(l)-jel, "son-substitute," "nephew." While such reconstructions are admittedly hypothetical, the probability that Tzotzil has innovated by reversing the order of elements in these compounds means that there is no evidence to support the hypothesis of an ancient term with the numeral + kin term order supposed by Fox and Justeson to be represented in the Classic period by TI:606.23, which they interpreted as "one + child."

A Proposed Reading for TI:606.23

Epigraphically, the TI:606.23 compound has three stable elements, the first of which is the numeral "one," phonetically hun in the relevant Mayan languages. The main sign is unidentified. The last sign is phonetic -na (perhaps -n, since final vowels of the syllabary are often suppressed). Thus, we are dealing with a kin term, most likely "child," which begins something like hun, ends something like n(a), and has something in between. That is, we may look for terms of the general form hun . . . n(a).

Linguistic Evidence

It happens that an appropriate term is attested in most Western Mayan languages. Tzeltal, Tzotzil, Tojolabal, Chuj, Kanjobal, Jacaltec, and Motocintlec, as well as Chortí and Chol, have terms of the shapes une', unen, or unin, with a meaning of "child" (table 3). These terms begin with the required (h)un and end with the

Table 3. Words Meaning "Child" Loaned from Mixe-Zoquean to Mayan and Other Language Families

Language / Group	Term	Gloss
Mixe-Zoquean:		
Proto-Zoque	*une	"child"
Proto-Mixe	*unak	"child"
Popoluca	una'k	"child," diminutive suffix
Cholan:		
Chol	une'	"small child who cries a lot"
Chortí	u'nen	"son of male"
Proto-Cholan	*une'/unen	"child"
Tzeltalan:		
Tzeltal	uhnen	"tender"
Tzotzil	unen	"baby"
	unin	"small, young, unripe, new"
Proto-Tzeltal-Tzotzil	*unin	"tender"
Kanjobalan:		
Chuj	une'	"child (son/daughter) of female," diminutive
	unin	"son of male"
Jacaltec	unin	"child/grandchild of female"
Other language families:		
Xinca	one	"child, immature"
Otomí	uEne	"baby"
Nahua?	kone-tl	"child"

Data from Campbell and Kaufman 1976, Clark 1981, Aulie and Aulie 1978, Wisdom 1940, Slocum and Gerdel 1980, Laughlin 1975, Kaufman 1972, Hopkins 1967a, and Day 1971.

required n(a), and I conclude that the 606 compound is to be read with some variant of this set of terms.[5]

In an article that demonstrates the association of Mixe-Zoquean languages with the Preclassic Olmec culture, Campbell and Kaufman (1976) noted that all these Mayan terms are loans from a Mixe-Zoquean original. They report the Mixe-Zoquean loans to be found in Tzeltal, Tzotzil, Tojolabal, Chuj, Kanjobal, Jacaltec, Choltí (sic, but it is surely Chortí that is meant) and Mam; Kaufman and Norman (1984:135) deleted Mam and added Motocintlec (also known as Mochó).

Kaufman reconstructed the forms *'une (Proto-Zoque) and *'unak (Proto-Mixe), with the meaning "child" (Campbell and Kaufman 1976:86). Modern Popoluca, for instance, a Mixe-Zoquean language, has una'k, "child," which when suffixed to other nouns becomes the diminutive (Clark 1981:62).

The Mixe-Zoquean term passed not only to Mayan languages, but also to more southerly Xinca (one, "child, immature") and on the north to Otomí (uEne, "baby") and perhaps also to Nahua (kone-tl, "child," which has no Uto-Aztecan cognates and cannot thus be native

Nahua). Campbell and Kaufman (1976:86) speculated that "perhaps the importance of infants in Olmec art motifs, and therefore presumably also in Olmec religion, contributed to the wide-spread borrowing of this term from Mixe-Zoquean languages." I would add to this speculation that the later association of "child" with "noble, lord" in widespread Mesoamerican languages also suggests an Olmec origin for this metaphor, and this association may also have had to do with the spread of the Mixe-Zoquean term for "child."

In Chol, the Mixe-Zoquean loan survives only as *une'*, "small child who cries a lot" (Aulie and Aulie 1978:126). No Chontal evidence is known, but in Chol's next nearest relative, Chortí, Wisdom (1940:262) reported the term *u'nen*, "son of male ego."

In Tzeltal and Tzotzil, the borrowed terms have the double meaning also found in the cited Popoluca forms: "child" and "diminutive." Tzotzil (Laughlin 1975) has *unen*, "baby," varying with *unin*, "small, young, unripe, new," while Tzeltal (of Bachajón; Slocum and Gerdel 1976) has *uhnen*, "tender." Kaufman (1972:120) reconstructed **unin*, "tender," for Proto-Tzeltal-Tzotzil.

In Chuj (Hopkins 1967a) two versions of the loan exist. The form *une'* is "child (son or daughter) of female," while *unin* is "son (only) of male." A common diminutive formation in Chuj is to use *y-une'* (literally, "its child") before the term to be diminished: for example, *yune choñap*, "Little Town" (literally, "child of

town"), a place name. Finally, in Jacaltec, *unin-e* is the term for "child or grandchild of female" (Day 1971).

The existence of the borrowed terms in Chol and Chortí is enough to allow the reconstruction of a term **une'/unen*, "child," for Proto-Cholan (Kaufman and Norman 1984:135), that is, for the language of most of the Classic Maya Lowlands. Thus, the term (perhaps in both forms) was present in a major language of the Classic period in the Classic area and, given its phonetic similarity to the forms suggested by the epigraphic evidence, *unen* is a likely reading for the TI:606.23 compound.

Historical Implications

The distribution of the *une(n)* terms in Mayan languages has important chronological implications. The loans occur in virtually all of the Western Mayan languages and almost no others (fig. 5). Therefore, the loan is most likely to have come into Mayan *after* Western Mayan existed as a distinct variety; otherwise, the loan would be found in other branches of the family as well. The borrowing most likely dates to the period of an early, unified Western Mayan, *before* Western Mayan diversified to form the multitude of modern languages in the Western branch of the Mayan family.

The time frame indicated (see fig. 5) would be from about 1600 B.C. (when Western Mayan became distinct from other varieties) to about 1000 B.C. (when Western languages had begun to spread and diversify). This is an

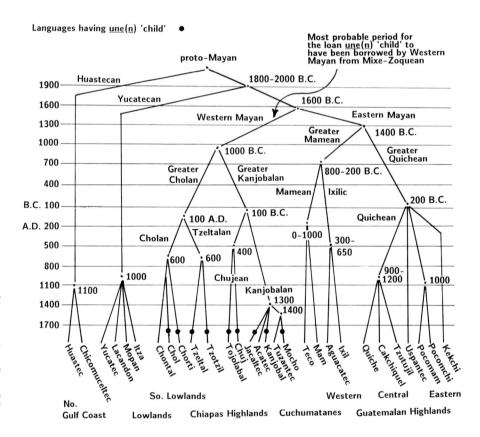

Fig. 5 Mayan classification and diversification and the occurrence of une(n) (⟨Mixe-Zoquean). Languages having the loan are marked with dots; the most probable time for this loan to have entered Western Mayan is between approximately 1600 B.C. and 1000 B.C., after Western had separated from other Mayan, and before it diversified.

appropriate time to expect Mixe-Zoque (Olmec) influence on other languages. The geographical area occupied by Western Mayan at that time has not been established, but all current proposals would place Western Mayan in a reasonable place for Olmec contact—either along the foothills of the Cuchumatanes in western Guatemala, further east along the foothills above the Classic Lowlands, or as far east as Chalcuapa in El Salvador.

The Meaning of the Borrowed Term

The meaning of the borrowed kin term may be determined from its meanings in the various languages that show the loan. The Chol term is simply "small child who cries a lot" (i.e., "cry-baby"). In Chortí the meaning is "child of male." In Tzotzil and Chuj it is "child of (either) parent." And in Jacaltec it is "child of female." It thus appears that the term borrowed was not strongly marked for sex of parent. In Mixe-Zoquean, there seems to be no sex-of-parent association with the term.

Kathryn Josserand (personal communication) suggested that perhaps the T23 -na suffix on the TI:606.23 compound is in fact the term for "woman," so that the glyph reads une, "child" + na, "woman," or unen + na. In that case the compound could be used for "child of woman" only, even though 'une(n) might mean "child" without regard to sex of parent.

In a sample taken from Thompson's catalog (Hopkins 1973), TI.606 occurs without T23 in only one parentage statement, on the sides of the sarcophagus lid (at Glyph 54a; Thompson 1962:229, Lounsbury 1974:15–16). There a personage is described as the child of Lady Zac-Kuk with the expression TI:606, without T23 (see fig. 1a, third example). However, the following name is written with a large initial "Lady" (i.e., na), with Zac and Kuk below.

Support for the Proposed Reading

After I had suggested reading TI:606.23 as a variant of unen, David Stuart (personal communication), called my attention to a paper of his that gives strong support to the reading. Stuart (1985a) identified a new relationship glyph, on Tikal Stela 31, which substitutes for "capped Ahau" and therefore glosses "child of father," but for which he was not prepared to offer a reading. The main sign of the glyph in question (fig. 6a) is a representation of a jaguar tail, with the possessive prefix T61/62/65, u-/hu-/yu- (Justeson 1984:320). Since the term for "tail" in the relevant Mayan languages is ne, a reading of u-ne or yune is reasonable. It is immediately apparent that this must be the kin term une(n). This discovery of a variant glyphic spelling thus supports my reading of TI:606.23 as unen, by confirming that the term was used in the Classic inscriptions.

Stuart did not treat the jaguar tail glyph as equivalent to the 606 compound, since the jaguar tail occurs as "child of male," while TI:606.23 occurs as "child of fe-

Fig. 6 *Two Additional Glyphs for* une, *"Child." (a) Stuart's (1985: fig. 1) "jaguar tail" relationship glyph: yu + "tail," yu-ne (redrawn by Nicholas Hopkins from Jones and Satterthwaite 1982: fig. 52, Tikal, Stela 31, right side, M-3; original drawing by W. R. Coe); (b) Aguateca, Stela 1, Glyph D8b, "bead" + "tail," u-ne (redrawn by Nicholas Hopkins from Johnston 1985: fig. 4; original drawing by Ian Graham, 1967).*

male." But if Josserand's suggestion is correct, then this is just what we would expect: une, "child of male," and une-na, "child of female." At any rate, the evidence from comparative Mayan vocabulary argues for a term not strongly marked for sex of parent.

Once the relationship glyph based on "tail" has been defined, it is not difficult to recognize other instances of its use. Aguateca Stela 1, for instance, has an apparent example at D8b (fig. 6b), which appears to be composed of a large bead and a jaguar tail (i.e., u, "bead," plus ne, "tail," une). This third spelling variant further supports my hypothesis by indicating that the initial element in these glyphs does not represent the numerical value "one" but the phonetic value u.

Stuart's evidence suggests that the term une, "child (of male)," was current in the Classic Period. Other glyphic evidence presented suggests that a similar term ending in n(a) was also current, meaning "child (of female)" (TI:606.23). It therefore seems reasonable on epigraphic grounds to posit une and une-na as the readings of Stuart's jaguar-tail glyph and TI:606.23, respectively. However, the evidence of comparative Western Mayan vocabulary argues for a final -n even when the meaning is not "child *of female*." Pending the compilation and evaluation of further glyphic evidence, it seems appropriate at this point to accept a range of possibilities, including une, "child of male," unen, "child of (either) parent", and une(n)-na, "child of female."

Readings for T606

Regardless of whether T23 is to be read as final -n or as na, "lady," all of the proposed readings of TI:606.23 limit the possibilities for the phonetics of the main sign T606. Any of the readings e, ne, or nen would give unen(a) according to the known rules of Mayan syllabics:

(h)un-*e*-n(a)
(h)un-*ne*-n(a)
(h)un-*nen*-n(a).

A vague similarity between T606 and Landa's *e* is probably spurious and gives the least attractive of these three potential patterns. At least in Stuart's jaguar-tail glyph the spelling of the kin term is with *ne*, "tail," and *(h)un-ne-n(a)* is a possible analysis for TI:606.23. The last possibility for T606, *nen*, is a widespread term for "mirror," but none of the mirror signs are known to substitute for T606, or vice versa (however, see the discussion of the 712 compound below). The best guess for T606, then, appears to be *ne*. What object T606 represents visually, if any, is not clear; it does not appear to be "tail."

Some Further Considerations

A matter that may bear exploration in the future is the relationship glyph "child of parent," T1.757:59.712:81 (see fig. 1d), which is not just a noun phrase, but is a rather complex verbal expression. T1.757:59 is the Auxiliary Verb + *ti* construction (Josserand, Schele, and Hopkins 1985). The main sign that carries the verbal meaning (T712) has been glossed as "bloodletter" (Schele and Mathews n.d.). But this sign bears the "shine" of a mirror (i.e., *nen*) and is often prefixed *u-* (as in Bahlum Kuk's parentage statement on the Tablet of the 96 Glyphs, at J5b—see fig. 3). It is possible that the 712 compound could contain the term *unen*, and be read something like "follows as a child of" or "follows in the descent of."

Assigning readings to the T535 compound "child (of male)," now read *ahau*, and the T606 compound "child (of female)," here read *unen*, was retarded by the fact that modern Mayan terminologies, specifically those of Yucatecan and Cholan, do not generally use terms for "child" cognate with *ahau* and *unen*. Chortí, which uses the latter term, has it with the meaning "child (of male)," but the major source for Chortí kin term data (Wisdom 1940) gave a mistaken etymology for the term, deriving it from Spanish *nene*, "baby." Thus, none of the languages closely related to hieroglyphic writing seemed to furnish direct evidence of the reading. Only the comparative data from the rest of Western Mayan make it clear that the term must have existed in Classic times.

Finally, the Colonial Yucatec replacement for *ahau*, recorded in the Motul dictionary (Martínez Hernández 1929) and elsewhere, is *mehen*, "child (of male)." The current Chol term is *p'enel*, "child (of male)." Both these terms also mean "semen, sperm" in their respective languages. It is apparent that we have here another metaphorical expression, "man's child" = "his semen," which occurs across languages, as did the Classic metaphor "child" = "lord."

Conclusions

In summary, there is considerable evidence that the relationship glyph TI:606.23, the 606 compound meaning "child of mother," can be read with the Proto-Cholan term *une(n)*, "child." This term is a loanword with an

Olmec (Mixe-Zoquean) origin, which most likely came into Western Mayan in the Late Preclassic.

This interpretation allows us to escape the implications of Fox and Justeson's interpretation of TI:606.23 as a collateral kin term, "nephew," which would require wholesale reanalysis of political succession, to say nothing of kinship systems, among the Maya. More importantly, it instructs us that at least two of the terms used in the statement of royal relationships critical to political succession were based on Olmec models. The "child of mother" term *une(n)* is an actual foreign word, borrowed by the Maya from the Olmec. The "child of father" term *ahau* may use native vocabulary, but appears to be influenced by an (unattested) Olmec metaphorical model, equating "child" with "lord." In this regard it should be kept in mind that while **'ahaw* is reconstructed for proto-Mayan, its bisyllabic shape is atypical, and the possibility that it is a loan must remain open.[6]

In the last few years, it has become apparent that the Maya of the Late Preclassic acquired the trappings of royalty from the Olmec, as expressed in the iconography of rule and rulers. It is also increasingly apparent that the Maya acquired from the Olmec at least the basic elements of the writing system with which they began to record the dynastic affairs of rulers. Now it appears that the Maya made use of Olmec terminology to express the relationship between rulers and their children. It is important to note that the introduction of foreign terminology may imply the introduction of new principles of kinship organization as well, and this possibility should be taken into account in evaluating the data pertaining to the development of Late Preclassic, Proto-Classic, and Early Classic Mayan societies.

Notes

1. The term "gloss" means an approximate translation to English. "Readings" assign to a glyph a specific syllable, word, or other element from an appropriate Mayan language (e.g., *ahau*).

2. In Thompson's transcription system, T1 is the prefix *u-*, "third person pronoun," but TI is the dot numeral *hun*, "one."

3. One of the signs Jones first identified as "child of mother" (fig. 2b, third example) has in the hand the sign for the day name Ben rather than *ahau*, and Jones described it as "*u*, hand holding *ben*, dots" (1977:41). This variant may be accounted for by Lounsbury's (1973) interpretation of the Ben glyph as *ah* in some contexts (e.g., in the *ah-po* or Ben-Ich superfix of emblem glyphs), that is, as part of a spelling of *al*. But Lounsbury noted that, while the day corresponding to Ben is Ah in certain Highland languages, in languages normally more closely tied to the Lowland Classic Maya (Yucatec, Tzeltal, Tzotzil, and Chuj), the day name is Ben (Been, Be'en, etc.). The Chuj day name has glottalized *p'*, that is, *p'e'en*, with a regular reduction to *p'en*. This raises the interesting possibility that the day name in Chol might also have been *p'en*, and that there might be some relation between this day name, the Ben variant of the "child of mother" glyph, and the modern Chol term for "child" (of father), *p'en-el*.

4. Evidence that the prefix on these Tzotzil kin terms is "one" and not some other word *hun* is the fact that there is another set of kin terms prefixed by *cha*, "two." These compounds are terms for step-relatives: *cha'-tot*, "step-father," *cha'-me*, "step-mother," *cha'-bankil*, "step-elder brother," *cha'-wix*, "step-elder sister," *cha'-nich'on*, "step-child (of male)," and *cha'-ol*, "step-child (of female)" (Hopkins 1969:99). There is no attested **cha'-itz'in*, "step-younger sibling."

5. The initial *h* in *hun*, like initial glottal stops (', not written here) would be absorbed or replaced by the prefixed person marker *uy-*. Since kin terms are always possessed, they never occur without the prefix. Thus a word that did not begin with an *h* but with a glottal stop could be written with an *h*-initial element such as *hun*, since neither the *h* nor the glottal stop would be pronounced after the possessive prefix *uy-*.

6. To my knowledge, no one has suggested *ahau* might be an Olmec loanword, and a quick search of Mixe-Zoquean sources turns up no likely source—similar Mixe-Zoquean terms have not been reported. Nonetheless, the CVCVC shape (counting the unwritten initial glottal stop) is suspicious, along with the apparent lack of other terms based on a native *'ah* root, unless it is related to the masculine agentive prefix. (Note that the Proto-Mayan forms should properly be written *'ajaw* and *'aj*, since *h* contrasts with *j* in Kaufman's reconstruction.)

Acknowledgments

This material is based upon work supposed by the National Science Foundation under Grant BNS-8305806, administered by the Institute for Cultural Ecology of the Tropics. Any opinions, findings, and conclusions or recommendations expressed in this publication are those of the author and do not necessarily reflect the views of the National Science Foundation or of ICET. In the preparation of this material, I have benefited from the constructive criticism and numerous substantive contributions of Kathryn Josserand.

I am grateful to Victoria B. Bricker, Brian Stross, and Martha Macri for reading this paper following its presentation, and for their comments. Bricker (personal communication, 1986) noted that TI.606:23 appears on Piedras Negras Stela 3, at C7, with the prefix *na*, reading *na-unen* and referring to the daughter of Ruler 3. Stross (personal communication, 1986) noted that my figure 1d, as drawn, shows T580, not T757, a regular substitution. He also adds the following Tenejapa Tzeltal data for table 3: *unin*, "young, tender"; *une(')*, "sound of a baby crying"; *uneh*, "to carry (a baby)." Martha Macri anticipated the reading of TI.606:23 as *une(n)* in a paper published in 1985 (Macri 1985:223–224), although she treated as a whole the phrase T1.757 1.1:606:23, and took the compound to read *u ba [hun] unen* (3-POSS first-born #1 child), that is, *u ba unen*, "her first-born child" (reading the superfixed number as a semantic determinative, not to be read phonetically).

Prepositions and Complementizers in the
Classic Period Inscriptions

MARTHA J. MACRI
UNIVERSITY OF CALIFORNIA, DAVIS

The Mayan languages most commonly considered relevant to Mayan hieroglyphic studies include languages in the Yucatecan, Cholan, and Tzeltalan families. There is a group of particles found in these languages—*ti, ti7, ta, tä,*—used variously as prepositions and complementizers. The primary purpose of this paper is to describe and compare these particles and their functions across languages and to show how such comparison is relevant to the study of language/dialect variation in the inscriptions of the Classic Period.

Both complementizers and prepositions are morphemes that indicate that what immediately follows is in an oblique relationship to the main verb of the sentence—that is, what follows is neither a subject nor a direct object of the main verb but is related to it indirectly. The difference between them is that while a complementizer introduces an embedded sentence, a preposition introduces only a noun phrase. For example, in the sentence "Anna showed that Mary was right" the word "that" is a complementizer introducing the embedded sentence "Mary was right" and it indicates that "Mary" is not the object of the main verb "showed," but, rather, the subject of the verb "was" in the embedded sentence.

In the sentence "He arrived for the game at 8:30" "for" and "at" are both followed by noun phrases that stand alone in oblique relationship to the verb "arrived." Prepositions that indicate spatial relationship such as "in," "on," "under," and "behind" are called locatives. Locative prepositions frequently are extended semantically to include location in time, such as "*in* two days," "*at* five o'clock," "*on* Friday." Prepositions are sometimes used in partitive constructions, such as "three pieces *of* candy," "the second day *of* April."

Complementizers and Prepositions
in Mayan Languages

Figure 1 shows a map of the Maya area that contains a table of complementizers and prepositions in various Mayan languages. The table represents a simplification of the actual situation, which for some languages is more complex. I have not listed every complementizer or every preposition, only those that are most common and are related to this discussion. In addition, the words given as complementizers often have certain nonlocative prepositional functions.

In both modern and Classical Yucatec *ti7* is a general preposition with a number of uses, including location: *té7 ti7 a k'aano7,* "there in your hammock"; time: *oxlahunte ti katun,* "13 katuns"; substance: *ti7 ce7,* "with wood"; source: *ti7 in-maamah,* "from my mother."

The particle *tii7, entonces,* is uncommon in modern Yucatec, but is used as a complementizer in the following example from the Book of Chilam Balam of Chumayel (Roys 1933[1967:49]): **Tii** *ualac u u cutob, oxlahun cut-hi u cutob lae,* "**While** they were settled, thirteen were their settlements."

In Chol the particle *ti* can be used as either a preposition: *7i mi k'otel ti yotot,* "He went **to** his house" (Cruz G. et al. 1980:117); or a complementizer: *Che7 wolis i kax ti tik'an,* "When it begins **to** cook."

It is significant that of the two languages most commonly cited in glyphic studies, Chol and Yucatec, Chol does not differentiate between the two functions of complementizer and preposition, and modern Yucatec does not typically use a complementizer at all. Furthermore, in Classical Yucatec the difference between the complementizer *tii7* and the preposition *ti7* is one of vowel length, a phonetic distinction that has not yet been observed in the hieroglyphic writing system.

Modern Chontal and Tzeltal have *tä* and *ta,* respectively, used only as prepositions. They do not have complementizers as such; thus the particle cognate with *ti* in Yucatec and Chol has only a single function.

The third language most commonly referred to in relationship to the hieroglyphic script is Acalán Chontal, known from a seventeenth-century document (Scholes and Roys 1968).[1] The Acalán document has both *ti* and *ta.* According to Smailus (1975:216), *ti* and *ta* are

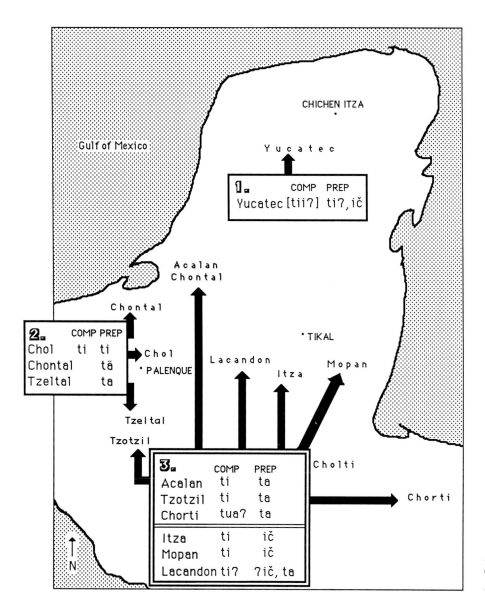

CHICHEN ITZA

Gulf of Mexico

Yucatec

1.	COMP	PREP
Yucatec	[tii?]	ti?, ič

Acalan
Chontal

Chontal

2.	COMP	PREP
Chol	ti	ti
Chontal		tä
Tzeltal		ta

Chol

• PALENQUE

• TIKAL

Lacandon

Itza

Mopan

Tzeltal

Tzotzil

Cholti

3.	COMP	PREP
Acalan	ti	ta
Tzotzil	ti	ta
Chorti	tua?	ta
Itza	ti	ič
Mopan	ti	ič
Lacandon	ti?	?ič, ta

Chorti

N

Fig. 1 Map: Prepositions and Complementizers in Greater Lowland Mayan

probably in free variation, and he glossed them both as "*en, a, hacia.*" However, upon more careful examination, a distinction in functions can be observed (see table 1). In 127 occurrences *ta* is followed by a geographical place name 50% of the time, by locations, such as "on the road," "in the canoe," in 13% of the examples. *Ta* is followed by possessed body parts, in typical Mayan relational noun constructions, 9% of the time. All of these are locative expressions, and they account for 75% of all occurrences.

There is one occurrence of *ta* cited by Mathews and Justeson (1984:190) as a complementizer: *koti ta tectelob ta tuxakhaa* (Smailus 1975:47), "They went to establish themselves at Tuxakha."

Of 15 occurrences of *k'oti* in the Acalán document, it is followed by *ta* 8 times. In all of the other cases, how-

Table 1. *Ta* in Acalán Chontal

ta followed by:		Times	Approx %
geographical place names	LOCATIVE	64	50%
locations	LOCATIVE	16	13%
relational noun constructions	LOCATIVE	12	9%
TOTAL LOCATIVE		92	72%
time expressions	TEMPORAL	16	13%
name of office	STATUS	9	7%
manner of speaking, writing	MANNER	6	5%
undetermined		5	4%
TOTAL		128	100%

ever, *ta* introduces a location or an expression of time. Although *ta* does appear here where one would expect a complementizer, it may be that its presence is dictated by the fact that the verb *k'oti*, "arrived," is a verb of motion and is thus frequently followed by the location *ta*, since *ta* is not used anywhere else as a complementizer.

The remaining uses of *ta* include time expressions, such as "in January"; manner of speaking or writing, for example, "in writing"; status in phrases such as "as lord," "as governor"; and three instances of undetermined uses. In Acalán Chontal, then, *ta* can be characterized primarily as a locative preposition with several other specific uses.

There are far fewer examples of the particle *ti*, only 15, but the uses are varied and more complex. Twice it is used with numbers, once in a partitive construction following a number in "50 *ti* soldiers," and once before the number "*ti* 80 people." *Ti* is also used before the word "cacao" in *chol pakal yithoc utz ti cacau*, literally, "field(s) cultivated and good with/of cacao." *Ti* is also used as a benefactive "for someone." Most significantly, *ti* is used several times before a verb or verbal noun to introduce a dependent clause: *utz xach **ti** bix ic on* (Smailus 1975:53), "it is good **that** I go"; *ti y-ol* Dios (Smailus 1975:75), "**as** God wishes"; *utz **ti** ta-c-than çut-lec-et-ix* (Smailus 1975:78), "it is good **that,** in my words, you return . . ."

There are only two examples in which the functions of *ti* appear to overlap with *ta*, that is, following *ui*, "here," before the word *cah*, "town" (twice), and once before *cab*, "land." Here is a contrasting pair: *ui ta cah Tixchel* (Smailus 1975:23); *ui ti cah Tixchel* (Smailus 1975:111). Presumably both expressions mean "here in the town of Tixchel." Either the two particles are indeed here used here in free variation, or there is a scribal error, or there is a difference in meaning that, lacking sufficient contexts and any native speakers, is beyond our capabilities to discover.

What emerges from this discussion is that the two particles do indeed have different primary functions, *ta*, as a locative, and *ti*, as a complementizer and nonlocative preposition. We find, then, that Acalán Chontal made a distinction between the two functions in contrast to a lack of distinction in Chol and Yucatec. However, when the other Yucatecan and Cholan languages are examined, this distinction proves to be present in a majority of the Lowland languages.

Chortí differentiates between the two functions of preposition and complementizer. As in Acalán Chontal, the preposition is *ta*. The complementizer, *tua7*, may not be phonologically cognate with the *ti* complementizer in other languages, but it does serve to make the same distinctions between the two types of particles.

In modern Tzotzil there is also a clear distinction between the functions of *ta* and *ti*. *Ta* was glossed by Laughlin (1975:327) as a preposition meaning "among, as, at, before, by, from, in, to." In other words, it functions as a locative preposition with a number of other

functions, similar to *ta* in Acalán Chontal. *Ti* is a particle meaning "the, that, the fact that," that is, it introduces complement clauses, and indicates certain other oblique relationships, as does *ti* in Acalán. (There is at least one other complementizer in Tzotzil, *li*, but that does not concern us here.)

The Yucatecan languages Itzá, Mopan, and Lacandon also differentiate between complementizers and prepositions. *Ti* is the complementizer, and the most common preposition is *ich*. *Ich* is also found in Yucatec with a more limited meaning and use than the Yucatecan preposition *ti7*. Lacandon uses *ti7* as a benefactive "for him" and as a complementizer. *Ich* is a preposition, but *ta* is used as the preposition in relational noun constructions (e.g., *ta pach*, "at one's back," "behind").

It is significant that the languages that differentiate between complementizers and prepositions are numerous and widespread, and are members of the Cholan, Yucatecan, and Tzeltalan families. The languages that do not differentiate are in the minority. Yucatec and Chol, our standard linguistic sources, turn out to be atypical. This fact has important implications for the study of the ancient Maya script.

Glyphic Evidence of Contrasts

In the glyphs there are several affixes that relate to this discussion. The first is T59, given by Landa as the syllable *ti*, T51/53, *ti* or *ta*, T103, T113, T565, all read *ta*, T89/90/91/92, *tu* from *ti + u* (fig. 2) and T747, the vulture head with a T59 prefix, which sometimes replaces T59.[2] Mathews and Justeson showed that these glyphs substitute for one another in various contexts (1984: 193ff).

The complementizer/preposition contrast that exists in some modern Mayan languages can be an important

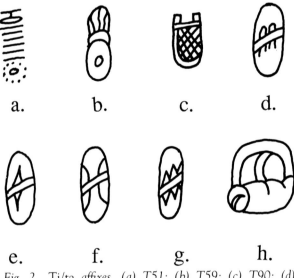

Fig. 2 Ti/ta affixes. (a) T51; (b) T59; (c) T90; (d) T102; (e) T103; (f) T113; (g) T245a; (h) T565.

diagnostic in determining linguistic variation among the ancient Maya. In the glyphic texts a *ti/ta* affix can tentatively be identified as a locative preposition if it occurs before locations such as "house" or "sky." It is a preposition with more general uses if it occurs before titles, "he was seated as lord, in lordship," or before time periods "on 5 Ahau." A particle is a complementizer if it occurs before another verbal form such as a verbal noun. That is, the particle T59 following T757, the jog glyph, and preceding a verbal noun can be called a complementizer. When observing any of these affixes in the inscriptions it is important to note when the functions are contrastive, and when certain signs are consistently substituted for each other.

Because of potential language/dialect differences, it is not sufficient to compare these affixes indiscriminately across sites and time periods. If dialectical variation does exist, it will only be detected by comparing patterns at multiple levels: single text, texts from a single period, texts within a site or within a given geographical area. Also, it is crucial in such an investigation to frame the proper question. The object is not simply to try to find which modern language is closest to the ancient language recorded at a particular site. Neither is it simply to choose between Yucatecan or Cholan as the language family for various Classic Maya groups. The question is, rather, what patterns of variation did exist, and what were their temporal and geographic limits?

To test whether or not preposition/complementizer contrasts (or, more properly, extended locative preposition vs. nonlocative preposition and complementizer) would provide interesting information about dialect groups, I examined *ti/ta* affixes in texts from sixteen Classic Period sites. I tallied occurrences of these affixes in the following contexts:

1. as a phonetic complement in the anterior and posterior date indicators,

2. in *ti*-constructions (following T1.60.757 or T516),
3. as a main sign,
4. before the "Half-Period marker,"
5. occurrences of T89/90/91/92 (hereafter referred to as T89),
6. preceding offices or titles such as Ahau and Batab,
7. as miscellaneous prefixes,
8. as suffixes,
9. as locatives, before "sky," "house,"
10. as temporal markers, before "day," before the coefficients of day names, and
11. in partitive constructions, between coefficients and day names.

The glyphs recorded were T51/T53 (hereafter referred to as T51), T59, T89, T102, T103, T113, T245a, T565, and T747. The sites included Ixkun, Naranjo, and Tikal from the Petén, Seibal, Machaquilá, Aguateca, Tamarindito, Itzán, and Dos Pilas from the Petexbatun region, the Usumacinta site of Yaxchilán, Caracol in Belize, Copán and Quiriguá in the east, and the western sites of Palenque, Bonampak, and Tortuguero. Many important sites were not considered, and not all inscriptions at the included sites were available. This was a preliminary foray into the data to test the hypothesis that complementizer/preposition differences can be diagnostic of dialect differences, and to find out what patterns might prove the most helpful.

Table 2 gives some of the results of this pilot survey. The presence of a glyph in a particular category is significant, but due to the accidents of preservation, the paucity of texts at some sites, and the speed with which the data were scanned, the absence of a given item is not necessarily significant. I would like to begin discussion of the findings with those features that offer the clearest results, and then to mention several of the categories that were looked at, but were not included in table 2.

The most universal use of T59 is in the anterior and

Table 2. *Ti/ta Affixes*

SITE	*uti*	as Ahau, etc.	*ti*-const	locative	PE	temporal	partitive
PAL	59	51,102,103, 113,245a,565		113,565		113	
TRT		51,113,565				51	
BPK	59	59,565					
NAR	59		59	113	59	51,113,565	59
CPN	59,747	59			59	59	51,59
QRG	59,747						59
YAX	59	59	59	59		51,59	
MQL	59					59	
CRC	59				59		
AGT	59		59				
ITN	59	59				59	
DPL	59	59					
SBL	59	59	59				
IXK	59						
TAM	59						
TIK		59 (as Batab)					

posterior date indicators. David Stuart suggested that T59 is a phonetic complement in a reading of *ut(i)*, "it happened," "it came to pass" for the combination of a phonetic sign for *u* + T59 (+T126) (fig. 3a). The only two sites for which I found any substitution for T59 were Copán and Quiriguán, where the *ti*-vulture head, T747, occurs at least six times.

The second category in table 2 is the occurrence of a prefix before Ahau or Batab (fig. 3b), both titles or offices known from ethnohistorical sources, and still used in some modern languages. Also included is the phrase at Palenque read by Schele as *ta och le*, "as enterer of the succession" (fig. 3c; Schele 1984:95). T59 is found at seven of the sites that have these title expressions. At Palenque and Tortuguero there are various examples of the *ta* group of affixes, and none of T59. Bonampak has one example of T59 (St.2:C2; fig. 3d) and one of T565 (Stone 1:A2; fig. 3e). The two inscriptions are dated by Peter Mathews (1980:72f) as about 100 years apart, and are done in very different glyphic styles, so it is possible that the use of the two prefixes reflects linguistic variation within a single site. All three sites having glyphs other than T59 to introduce titles are on the western edge of the Maya area.

The next category is that of *ti*-constructions, defined for purposes of this study as a verb, either T1.60:757, the general verb (fig. 4a), or T516:103 (fig. 4b) followed by a *ti/ta* affix followed by another glyph, which may be a noun, a verb, or a verbal noun. There is some question whether all of these are complementizer constructions,

a.

c.   d.

Fig. 4 Examples of ti/ta *affixes. (a) Naranjo, St. 24 A1–4 (after Graham and von Euw 1975). (b) Yaxchilán Lnt. 53 B2–C2 (after Graham 1979). (c) Palenque TFC L8 (after Schele 1984). (d) Copán St. 6 A6 (after Maudslay 1889–1902).*

or whether some are simply prepositional phrases following a verb. The glyphs that were used in locative phrases have some bearing on this issue.

In the texts examined there were *ti/ta* affixes before "sky" and "house" (fig. 4c), presumably as locative prepositions. At Yaxchilán T59 occurs in this context. T565 occurs at Palenque, and T113 occurs at both Palenque and Naranjo. The best argument in favor of the *ti*-constructions being complement clauses is that at Naranjo on a single stela, Stela 24, T59 is used following T1.60:757 (A4) and T113 is used as a locative (D5), and in a calendrical expression (A2) as well. T59 and T113 substitute for each other in similar contexts at different sites, but I do not yet know of an instance of them substituting for each other within a single site. The fact that they are found in different contexts at Naranjo suggests that this site recorded a language that distinguished between a complementizer/preposition and an extended locative preposition, and that the *ti*-phrase following T757 is indeed more than just a prepositional phrase. This argument is not necessarily relevant to the *ti*-phrases that follow T516:103.

a.   b.

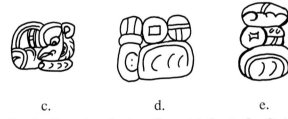

c.   d.   e.

Fig. 3 Examples of ti/ta *affixes. (a) Copán St. C A7 (after Maudslay 1889–1902). (b) Tikal St. 21 A11 (after Jones and Satterhwaite 1982). (c) Palenque TFC G2 (after Schele 1984b). (d) Bonampak St. 1 C2 (after Mathews 1980). (e) Bonampak Mon. 1 A2 (after Mathews 1980).*

There are at least three sites at which T59 precedes the glyph for the Half-Period Ending (fig. 4d). It would appear to be a temporal preposition except for the fact that at Naranjo other temporal markers are T51, T113, and T565, while T59 appears before the half-period. It is possible that instead of "at/on the Half-Period" it means "because of/on the occasion of the Half-Period," or it may be a phonetic complement.

Seven of the sixteen sites that have one of the affixes occurring either before a *k'in* "day" sign or before the co-efficient of a day in the Sacred Calendar. Those sites that have T103, T113, T565, and so forth, have them as temporal markers. Those sites that have T59 consistently have T59 in temporal expressions as well.

There are three sites at which T59 occurs after the coefficient of the day and before the day sign, usually (always?) Ahau. Besides the fact that these phrases differ in word order from the temporal constructions, Naranjo gives us additional evidence that they are different. T59 is used in these, contrasting with T51, T113, and T565 in the temporal expressions. It is very possible that this phrase is cognate with the Yucatec expression given above, *oxlahunte ti katun*, "13 katuns," literally, "13 of katuns."

There are a number of categories for which data were collected, but which were not included in table 2. Examples of the affixes that used prefixes, suffixes, and main signs in miscellaneous contexts were dropped since they did not seem to add any significant information about pattern variation. Status markers for "as Ahau," "as Batab," and so forth, were subsumed into a single category. Finally, examples of T89 were found at several sites, but their presence did not seem to correlate with any of the *ti/ta* differences that were observed.

In the course of this pilot study it became apparent that, in addition to finding some categories superfluous, others might usefully be added. One of these is the number of times an affix occurs in a particular context at each of the sites, as well as some estimate of the size of the corpus for the site. This would allow for a comparison of relative frequency of occurrence and would show whether a particular pattern was unique or fairly common. Although the miscellaneous prefix and suffix categories were deleted in order to simplify the material, each of these occurrences needs to be recorded with its context. It goes without saying that the count needs to be done on a corpus of the Classic inscriptions that is as complete as possible, that is, including all possible sources of inscriptions at every known site.

Summary

Is it possible to sort out functions and phonetic readings for the *ti/ta* affixes? Based on the data of this preliminary study, it is possible to make some tentative generalizations about phonetic readings for certain of the *ti/ta* affixes. If we scan across the columns of table 2 it is evident that T59 and T747 do not substitute in the same contexts as the *ta* group of affixes (T103, T113, T565, etc.), which seem to be equivalent with each other. If we scan down the columns, we see that those sites that do not have any of the *ta* group of affixes in prepositional contexts have T59 in the corresponding columns.

At Palenque, where T59 is used phonetically, but not prepositionally, we can conclude that the preposition used, which was written with members of the *ta*-group, was not pronounced *ti*, but probably *ta* or *tä*. Likewise, at Tortuguero, only *ta* affixes are found. Bonampak, however, is the only site at which T59 and any of the *ta* group of affixes are found in similar contexts. As mentioned above, the separation of two occurrences by almost a century and differences in carving style allow for the possiblity that this may reflect actual language differences.

There is one other glyph that occurs in contexts both with T59 and with the *ta*-group. T51 is used with T59 in temporal constructions at Yaxchilán, and in partitive constructions at Copán. These sites do not have *ta*-group prepositions. However, at Palenque and Tortuguero T51 occurs in the same contexts as the *ta* prepositions and is presumably equivalent with them.

If we attempt to assign phonetic readings to the prepositional affixes, one solid piece of evidence is that T59 was read *ti* by Yucatec speakers at the time of Landa. However, at those sites that have only T59 in prepositional contexts there are several possible readings: (1) T59 is always *ti*; (2) T59 is *ti* phonetically, but *ta* or *tä* logographically, when used as a preposition; or (3) T59 was read *ti* or *ta* depending on the context (phonetic complement, preposition, complementizer).

At those sites that have only *ta* affixes prepositionally, but use T59 phonetically for *ti*, the preposition was probably pronounced *tä* or *ta*. The unusual distributional patterns of T51 may indicate one of two things: (1) it was always read *ta*, so, at those sites where it substitutes with T59, T59 was also read *ta*, or, (2) it was bivalent, *ti* at sites with only *ti*, and *ta* at sites with *ta*.

At the site of Naranjo, where contrasts exist within a single monument, it appears that there were two distinct particles, one of which, *ti*, functioned as a complementizer with some additional uses, and *ta*, which was a preposition.

Those sites with only one particle are similar to modern Yucatec, Chol, Chontal, and Tzeltal (fig. 1). Palenque and Tortuguero, with only *ta* or *tä*, are similar to Tzeltal and Chontal. Naranjo, with both *ta* and *ti*, would pattern with modern Tzotzil and colonial Acalán Chontal.

It is important to remember that the *ti/ta* patterns represent only one diagnostic feature among many that are available in determining the nature and extent of language differences among the Classic Maya. Many of the observations about site groupings made here have been apparent to epigraphers for some time and are supported by the presence and absence of other types of constructions, use of particular glyphs, choice of subject matter, and differences in artistic style and craftsmanship.

As more data are processed, some of these generalizations will be confirmed; others, particularly those based on negative evidence, will have to be revised. In many ways the Classic Period inscriptions represent a *grapholect*, that is, a transdialectal language that is an artifact of the commitment of a culture to writing (Ong 1982:8, 106–108). Even though the sounds, vocabulary, syntactic constructions, and formulaic expressions of a Highland Scotsman and a Texan are quite distinct, many of the differences disappear when they write formal English; if they are literate, they can be expected to read formal English equally well. Language differences are much more obvious in a conversation between the two than in their ability to comprehend written English.

In the same way, it would appear that, while the Classic inscriptions were understandable to literate people throughout the area, the glyphic texts give clues about the language differences of the scribes who composed them. And although some phonetic differences are known, in a logo-syllabic script shared by languages with a high percentage of cognate vocabulary, subtle phonetic contrasts can be difficult to detect. On the other hand, syntactic differences, such as preposition/complementizer contrasts, can provide important clues to language variation during the Classic Period.

Notes

1. I would like to express appreciation to William Ringle for providing some of the statistical information on the Acalán data cited in this section.

2. Phonetic readings given in this paper are consistent with the interpretations listed in Justeson 1984a unless otherwise noted.

Aspects of Polyvalency in Maya Writing: Affixes T12, T229, and T110

DIETER DÜTTING
MAX PLANCK-INSTITUT FÜR ENTWICKLUNGSBIOLOGIE, TÜBINGEN, FRG

Recent attempts at decipherment of the Maya script are characterized by an unbalance between an advanced elucidation of its phonetic component and a delayed semantic analysis of its major constituents, the logograms or word-signs. Several graphemes turned out to be both, logographic (type CVC) and phonetic signs (type CV). But since logographic readings are less easily proved than phonetic ones, the weight of the research was on the phonetic signs. The intricate interrelation of the two components becomes apparent on the following pages, which are concerned with a contextual analysis of affixes T12, T229, and T110.[1]

Complete exchangeability of affixes T12 and T229 by means of their likely primary value *ah* (male prefix/agentive in name or title glyphs) is not given. The initial glyph of glyph sequences on pottery rims, T229.617:126 in its most common form, never substitutes affix T12 for its prefix T229. Likewise, I know only one case of T229 replacing suffix T12 of the Distance Number introducing glyph T1.573:12 (Naranjo Stela 13, G14). I supposed an additional complementary meaning of these affixes, for T12 a secondary value *xul*, "end, death," for T229 a secondary value *ac*, "set in," or *ak*, "new, fresh" (Dütting 1985b:112). Affixes T12 and T229 are also rarely used to represent the perfective verbal suffix *-ah* of action glyphs for which other affixes exist, in particular T181, *ah/Vh?*, and T126/125, *ah/ih*.

T229, *ah*, and *ac/ak*

The turtle head T743, with primary value *ac*, "turtle," substitutes for affix T229, and its Chichén Itzá variant T228, but never for affix T12 (fig. 1). Among the additional meanings of *ac* in Yucatec, I mention the verb root *ac-*, "to set in." Examples of the substitution are the compounds T743°516b.181:102 and T229.516b.181:102, Yaxchilán Lintels 2 (K1) and 7 (A2), or the name glyphs of the Palenque Lord Chaacal, T1010b.743°528:178 and T1010a.229:528:178 (Schele and Mathews 1979: nos. 434 and 518). At Chichén Itzá, Temple of the

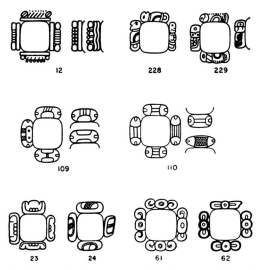

Fig. 1 Principal affixes discussed (redrawn by Dieter Dütting after Thompson 1962).

Four Lintels, we recognize the exchange in the compounds T743.87?.515–44:112 and T228.87?.515–44: 112, Lintel I (G5) and Lintel II (H1, G2) (Beyer 1937: figs. 175/176).

The "turtle" head T743 is Landa's first, T238 his second, and T228 his third A (Tozzer 1941:170). Therefore, one could argue that the replacement is not based on the *ac* value, but on the value *a(h)* of both, T228/229 and T743. The Yaxhá emblem compound T16.743, *yax-(h)a*, and the glyph of the Yucatecan month Kayab, termed *Kanazi* in Kekchi/Chol and Pokom month name lists, T743°281:57:126, *kan-a-zi-i(h)*, are examples of T743, *a* (see Stuart 1985c).

Yax.ha or *yax.ac* is mentioned in a passage of Naranjo Stela 23, left side (fig. 2a). This stela refers in E13–F16 to the marriage of a princess of Tikal,[2] T1000a.168a:569, to Lord Fire-Squirrel of Naranjo, T122.765v:117, on the Vernal Equinox and Full Moon date 9.13.18.4.18, 8 Etz'nab 16 Uo, 19 Mar 710, moon age 15[d] (Dütting

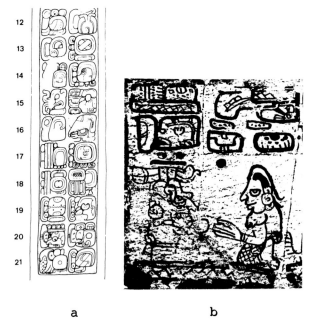

a   b

Fig. 2 Passages concerned with marriage. (a) Naranjo Stela 23, left side, glyphs E12–F21 (drawing by Ian Graham); (b) Madrid Codex 91d, col. 1 (photograph by Dieter Dütting).

1970:204, 1984:67). After a DN of 97^d (E17) the text continues:

F17, E18   (9.13.18.9.15) 1 Men 13 Yaxkin
F18   202:630.151, *pa.zih.uh = paz.ih.uh*, "it emerges the grandchild, the necklace"³
E19   1.570°109:24?, *u.bac.(chac).il*, "his (long) bones"
F19   1.1040, *u.tzek?*, "his skull(s)"
E20   16.IX:103b, *yax.bolon.tz'acab?* (reference to God K or God K-title of lord of Yaxhá)
F20   16.168a:743, *ahau.yax.ha/ac*, "owner of the freshwater/green turtles," or "lord of Yaxhá"
E21   710.59:511:117, *xab?.ti.toh.wi'?*, scattering event.

Bones and skull are linked on Tikal Altar 5 with the Goddess T1001 (Dütting 1985b:266), on this stela with God K. In both instances, these deity glyphs could address the divinities themselves or could be titles of historical persons, on Stela 23 of a lord of Yaxhá. The text might refer to a divination ritual, to the throwing of seed-kernels in divination, or to the shedding of blood in self-castigation, on 9.13.18.9.15, 1 Men 13 Yaxkin, 24 June 710, a day under the patronage of the Moon Goddess, perhaps performed to assure a good fortune of the expected parturition of the Tikal princess.

At Chichén Itzá, Temple of the Four Lintels, we find on Lintel I (D2–C4) a passage in which T228 could be the "grass," *ac*, pulled through the mutilated penis (T608, *toon*) in self-castigation (cf. Barthel 1955: 20):T33.568:228, *ku.(h)ol.ac*, "(shedding) the divine (blood) by piercing and (pulling) grass"—608°134v.188,

toon.kik?-el, "through the penis, stained with blood"—130:136, *ahan.may*, "the gift for the *elotes*," or "*elotes* are the gift." In a slightly modified passage of Lintel I, Temple of the Three Lintels, T33.568–228.608:188v–130.506, the blood is said to be for the "desired (506 = *kan*) *elotes* (130)."⁴

A typical primary standard glyph sequence of pottery (PSS) is that of Vessel 184 (Robicsek and Hales 1981: 200; fig. 3). In my opinion this sequence gives information on at least two levels, the deeper, more esoteric level being concerned with the fate of the deceased in the underworld, the other more profane level with the manufacture and ritual use of the vessel itself (see N. Grube, this volume). On the first level, the four initial glyphs of the PSS, Vessel 184, can be read: T229.617: 126, *ah.il.ih = a.hil-ih?*, "he came to rest"/1014a.18, *mam.yih?*, "(in the realm of) the aged Grandfather (= God N)"/1.563a:585a, *u.tz'i-b(e)?*, "her painted/spotted one"/100b.181, *ix.uh*, "Lady Moon." The deceased may be marked with the spots of the Jaguar God when coming to rest in the underworld.⁵ Proto-Chol * *hil = descansar(se)*; Chol (Aulie) *jijlel = descansar; jilel = terminarse*; Yucatec (Motul) *helel = descansar, descanso, hacer jornada*; Kekchi (Sedat) *hilanc = descansar*. The translation of the first glyph makes use of the Chorti/Choltí *a* set of pronominals, which employs *a* for third person sing. and plur. instead of *u* (MacLeod 1984:258). Some PSS miss the God N glyph (see examples in Robicsek and Hales 1981: tables 1, 2, 15, 16):T229.617:126, "he came to rest"?/563a:585a(P), "the painted/spotted one"?/1000b.181, "(of) Lady Moon."

A secondary value *ac* of T229 is of no advantage for the interpretation of T229.617:126. Previously I assumed (Dütting 1980:112) a reading *ak.hil-ah*, "a new one is resting" (in the realm of God N), with T229 being the Yucatecan and Kekchi *ak*, "new, fresh" (*ach'* in Chol). For this to be acceptable, T229 should have the secondary values *ac* and *ak*. Since the *c/k* distinction probably was less strictly observed in word-final position (Furbee and Macri 1985:412), this is not impossible. Grube (1985:79) presented the compound T229.507P from the PSS of the Blom Plate, which could denote *ah.tzih*, "new/renewed one," or *ak.ixim*, "fresh seedcorn." T507, which in some PSS is substituted by

Fig. 3 Pottery standard glyph sequence, Vessel 184 (from Robicsek and Hales 1981), glyphs A–E.

T1006b, the head of the Maize God, could be bivalent for the values *tzi(h)* and *ixim*. In C. Dresden 30b/31b, col. 2, the gift of Zac Xib Chaac are T528.559–506.136:130, "turkey tamales," and T109.507, *chac.ixim?*, "boiled corn." Grube also mentioned three PSS (1985:95) in which T229 is prefixed to the head T1000a,b of the Moon Goddess. This argues for a reading of T229 different from its primary value *ah*.

Main sign T563a can be replaced by the "bat" head T756a (see Grube, this volume). On Vase no. 5 of the November Collection (Robicsek and Hales 1982:26), the initial glyphs of the PSS are written T229.683b: 142, *ak.kal-om?*, "a new one is enclosed"/1014a.18, *mam.yih?*, "(in the realm of) the aged Grandfather"/ 1.756a–501.7, *u.tz'i -ba(l).uh?*, "the spotted one of the Moon"?/62.77:585a, *hol?.xi(k).be*, "end of the frightening/dangerous road."[6] The PSS of Vase no. 2206 of J. Kerr replaces the T501 of this sequence by the "jaguar" head T751a, *bal*. The phonetic value *tz'i* of T756a may be derived from Yucatec *tz'iic*, "left, sinister, malevolent," which would be an appropriate title of the bat-demon.

The only example of T12.617:126 known to me occurs in the PSS of Vessel 58, Pearlman Collection (Coe 1982:103), but somewhere toward the end of the sequence. The three initial glyphs A–C are T229.G506: 126/331.843v/563a.585a (G506 of N. Grube is an allograph of T617; the "step" glyph T843v substitutes for God N). The final glyph of the partly destroyed sequence is the phonetic compound for "earth," T25:501, *ca-b(a)*, followed by affix T12, probably to indicate the "end" of the sequence.

Compounds related to the initial glyph of PSS are part of some IS and CR dates. On Tikal Stela 31, T229.617a: 125:360 (fig. 4) is inserted in A12 between the IS date 9.0.10.0.0(including its Lunar Count glyphs) and the event glyph T846°520.59. I prefer a reading *ah.il-ih* = *a.hil-ih*, "it came to rest (the count)," but a statement *a(h).al-ih* = *a.(h)al-ih*, "it is said," cannot be excluded. Sacchana Stela 2 (Mayer 1978: plate 11) records the Summer Solstice and New Moon date 10.2.10.0.0, 2 Ahau 13 Ch'en, 22 June 879. The date is followed in C1/D1 by T13.617a:713a:87–528P.116, a glyph that probably refers to the erection of a stela at the end of the tun period. According to Schele and Stuart (1985), the Chorti name of the stelae of Copán is *te.tun*, "tree-stone." One could consider a reading T617a, *(h)al*, "to speak," and T13.617a:713a:87–528.116, *u-al.cun.te-tun.(n)*, "the tree-stone stands upright/was set up." Note Mopan (Ulrich, deUlrich) *wa'cuntic* = *de pie, erecto, parado*; Yucatec (Motul) *wacunah* = *poner en pie o enhestar alguna cosa*; Proto-Chol (Kaufman, Norman) **wa?* = *parado*. The hand T713a could then function as verbalizer *-cun*, contrary to T713b which could be *lah*, "end, completion."

Main sign T617 and affix T24 are probably allographs with respect to their likely value *il*, "see, take care of." As a noun suffix in word-final position, T24 may be a

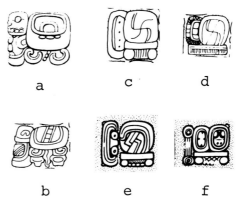

Fig. 4 *Glyphs used in counting. (a), (b) T229.617:126 (Quiriguá St. J, G1; Tikal St. 31, A12); (c), (d) T11/1.573:12 (Palenque Sun-Tablet, N7; Tikal St. 31, F15); (e), (f) T1.664:12 and T1v.544.504:12 (Dos Pilas St. 8, F10, and F23). (Redrawn by Dieter Dütting, A. P. Maudsley [a], W. R. Coe [b, d], Linda Schele [c], and Ian Graham [e, f].)*

more general ending *-Vl*, since it can be replaced by suffix T82, *ul/Vl*, which in turn is related iconically to main sign T568, *ol/ul* and *lu* (see note 4). Lounsbury's (1984a) T617 and T24, *ne(n)*, derived from Yuc/Chol *nen*, "mirror," would demand a T82, *nel/-en?*, but with such a reading T82 cannot be related easily to T568.

As a noun suffix, T24 is replaced in some compounds by affix T23, Barthel's *al*, read *na* by most other researchers. Examples are the "child of father" glyph T1.535:(24/23), interpreted by Lounsbury (see Justeson 1984a:341) as *u.mehen.(ne/na)*, "his son," the glyph T126.552:(23/24), read *ya-tan.(na/ne)*, "his wife," and the name glyph of God D of the codices, T152.1009c: (23/24), read as *tzim.na/(i)tzam.na*. Suffixes T24/23 are regarded as phonetic complements in cases 1 and 2, but as spoken morphemes in case 3. A reading T24, *il*, could explain the compounds T1.535:24 as *u.mehen-il*, "his son," and T126.552:24 as *ya-tan-il*, "his wife," but the introduction of suffix T23, *al*, would result in a change in meaning as in T1.535:23, *u.mehen.(n)al*, "his tender *elote*" (as metaphor for "son"). T24, *il/Vl*, and T23, *al*, would suggest a reading *itzam.al* of God D's name glyph. There are other compounds that cannot be reconciled with T24, *ne*, like the glyph for "drought," T544: 528.548:24, *kin.tun.yaab.il*. They are discussed in Fox and Justeson (1984b:53) and in Dütting (1986).

Lounsbury's reading T535, *mehen*, "son," demands that the "child of father" indicatory glyph always addresses a male child. This is not clear on the Glyph Panel, Grolier no. 3 (Coe 1973b:28), which refers to birth and accession of an individual, regarded by Coe as female, but by Mathews (see Mayer 1980:53) as male. The birth clause D1–C4 is followed by references to her/his "mother" and "father," the "child of father" indicatory glyph C7 being T122.535v:24, the "child of mother" indicatory glyph D4 being T126.747°747, a small vulture head placed within a vulture's beak. This may be a variant of T126.534:670, interpreted by me as "throwing out (of the womb) in pains (126.670 = ya.pul?) the child (534 = al)." Clearly, the "vulture emerging from the vulture" indicates "noble offspring." The difficulty with the child's sex could be avoided by reading T535, almehen, "noble one."

T12, ah, and haw

Affix T12 (fig. 1) resembles the "death-collar" worn by underworld deities (see Vase no. 60 of the Pearlman Collection; Coe 1982:109), and was regarded by Thompson (1950:189) as a sign for "end, death," hitz'. Later readings proposed were tz'oc, "end" (Barthel 1966:113), and xul, "end, death" (Dütting 1978:41), all derived from Yucatec. In 1980 I suggested a bivalency of T12 for the values ah and xul (Dütting 1985b:112).

Variants of the "Distance Number introducing glyph" (DNIG) (fig. 4) are T1.573:12 (standard form), T1:573:25:12 (e.g., Copán Stela I, F5), T1.664:12 (e.g., Dos Pilas Stela 8, F10), and on the 96 Glyph Tablet, Palenque, compounds that replace T573, hel, "change" (Yuc/Chol), or T664, hal, "change" (Quichéan languages), by alternating natural phenomena: T1.544P.504P:12 (day and night, C2), T1.human head.skull:12 (life and death, D8), T1.2.683b:12 (stars and moon, E7), and T1.503.501P:12 (air and water, G6). A possible reading of T1.573:12 could be u.hel.ah = u.hel.lah, "its change comes to an end/is completed." Unusual DNIGs on Itzán Stela 17 (G13,I12,L10), T13/1.664:1v, replace suffix T12 by what seems to be an affix T1 variant. I am inclined to relate this T1v to the Proto-Cholan *uht, "finish, come to pass." If true, this would argue for a meaning "end, finish" of affix T12. The variant T1:573:25:12 could denote "the change (573) of the power (25 = cal?) comes to pass (12)" (Yuc cal = fuerza y poder para hacer algo). The compound T573:25 resembles T573:21, probably hel.t'an, "change of the command." The substitution T573/T664, hel/hal, argues against my previous T1.573:12, u.kex.xul = u.kexul, "its change" (Dütting 1978:48).

There are two contexts that strongly support a secondary value haw-, "cease, end; lie face up," of affix T12. They occur in the Rain God almanac 70, Dresden Codex 65b–69b, cols. 2 and 11, discussed in Barthel (1953) and Thompson (1972:83). The structure of these texts is best understood if we analyze first the text of col. 1, p. 65b (fig. 5a), which shows the Rain God Chaac paddling a canoe:

T238.667:23, a-yan.(na)?, "he is there"/
552°95.526:251, tan.cab.(ba), "in the midst of the earth"/
668.103, Chaac/III.567:130, ox.oc-aan?, "abundance has entered"?/
IX.506:130, bolon.kan.ahan/ (wah), "much desired elotes/ (bread)"
1.1038b, u.p'a-chi'?, "(are) his promise/offering"?

a   b   c

Fig. 5   Dresden Codex 65b–69b, almanac 70. (a) col. 1, p. 65b; (b) col. 2, p. 65b; (c) col. 11, p. 68b (photograph by Dieter Dütting).

Independent of its precise reading, the compound TIX.506:130 in position 5 is one of Chaac's gifts for men.

Col. 2, p. 65b (Fig. 5b), shows Chaac walking in sand or clouds, armed with spearthrower and spears. The text above reads:

T238.667:23, a-yan.(na)?, "he is there"/
96.296:613, ta? . . . men, "in . . ." / 668.103, Chaac/
115.648:140, ya.kaz-al, "harm and misery"?[7]/
12.671:136.130, haw.(wa).ceh.(h), "deers lying face up/dead deers"/
1.1038b, u.p'a-chi'?, "his promise/gift."

The compound T115.648:140 suggests that Chaac is at an evil place, that his gift for men is negative, most likely inedible "carrion/carcass of deer," as already surmised in Barthel (1953:98). The postfix T130 of T12.671:136.130 could be a phonetic complement wa of T12, haw, but one could consider also a reading T12.130 = ha-wa = haw. The glyphs T12.671:136 and T12.671 of the "deer-hunt" almanacs, Madrid Codex 40–41, on the other hand, seem to refer to the "deer-hunter," ah.ceh.(h) or ah.chih.(h), and not to "dead deer." In Dresden Codex 19c–20c, almanac 50, col. 1, the Moon Goddess bears the T648-demon on her back, a burden related in the text above to the negative God Q, a god of war and sacrifice (Thompson 1972:59).

Col. 11, p. 68b (fig. 5c), presents the reclining young Moon Goddess and Chaac on a mat, where they embrace in the act of coition, the final event of their wedding ceremony. The text above is:

Dütting

T238.667:23, *a-yan.(na)?*, "he is there"/
12.238.552°95:23, *haw?.a(h)-tan.(na)*, "to conclude the wedding (ceremony)," or "it lies face up the wife (of)"/[8]
668.103, *Chaac*/115.734:116, "place (115 = *ti?*) of . . ."/
283:563b.104:731, "joined? (563b) bodies? (283 = *bak*) . . ."/
1.1038b, *u.p'a-chi?*, "his promise/offering."

Note Yucatec (Motul) *haual atancil = cerrarse velaciones.*
    Previously I interpreted the compound T238.552°95:23 as *ah.tan-al*, "sinner," or as *ah.kat-al*, "the one who asks" (bridegroom), and its prefix T12 as *xul*, "digging-stick," as a possible metaphor for the groom's "penis" (Dütting 1978:43). The main sign T552 probably is bivalent for the logographic values *kat* and *tan*. Madrid Codex 94b shows gods with their wives seated on a mat, a scene that indicates "marriage." The text above does not distinguish between T552 and its blackened version T552°95. Here the initial glyphs T238.552 and T238.552°95 most likely denote *a(h)-tan*, "wife." Marriage is also the subject of Madrid Codex 91d, col. 1, where a divine couple on a mat is accompanied by the text (fig. 2b):

T563a.558:192, *zi-ba.pop?*, "the gift of the mat"/
115.192:601, *y(o).otoch.(cho)*, "his house"/
24.1016c, *ku-l(i)*, "divine one"/162:506.501, "choice? of food and drink."

One particular emblem glyph of the Palenque inscriptions argues for a secondary meaning "end, finish" of affix T12. The genealogical record of Chan Bahlum's ancestors on the Tablet of the Cross Temple is divided into a mythological and a historical section. The mythological section ends with the record of birth and accession of a mythical lord named T11.212:764, *u?.kix.chan*, "serpent-spine" (see Lounsbury 1985:45). The emblem glyph that follows his name and accession date 5.8.17.15.17 is the only one of the entire corpus of Palenque inscriptions that is suffixed by T12, probably to indicate the *end* of an era important for Palenque (F15–Q3, fig. 6):

1.6.7.13/740:246, (birth)/11.212:764/679a.58:522:713a–89.204:757, (inauguration)/11.212:764/(5.8.17.15.17) 11 Caban 0 Pop/38.168a:570:*12*.

No emblem glyphs are given in the record of the historical lords on the Cross-Tablet, but on other tablets this type of emblem glyph is written T38.168a:570:178.130 (East Tablet, Temple Inscriptions, J1/Q9), or simply T38.168a:570, with the compound T570:178 denoting *baac-al*. The reading T12, *haw-*, is appropriate here, this because of Yucatec (Pérez) *haw = unida a un numeral sirve para contar cosas partidas por mitad; la mitad de una cosa dividida en dos; hawal = la otra mitad de una cosa partida en dos.*
    Kix-Chan's inauguration on 5.8.17.15.17 lies precisely 26,550 lunations (of 29ᵈ.53059) after 13.0.0.0.0, 4 Ahau 8 Cumku, the beginning of the current era, 17,222

Fig. 6 Temple Cross-Tablet, Palenque, glyphs F15–F17 and P1–Q3 (drawing by Linda Schele).

lunations after 1.18.5.3.2, the birth of God GI of the Palenque triad of deities. It precedes the birth of Lord Pacal on 9.8.9.13.0 by 1,569 tropical years (of 365ᵈ.2422) and Pacal's inaugural date 9.9.2.4.8 by 989 Venus Periods (of 584ᵈ). Kix-Chan's birth (on 5.7.11.8.4) is said to have preceded his accession by 1.6.7.13 = 9513ᵈ, ca. 26 years. It precedes Pacal's birth on 9.8.9.13.0 by 1,595 Julian years (of 365ᵈ.25).
    In the long inscription of the Early Classic Stela 31 of Tikal, affix T12 appears only in the DNIG T1.573:12. This glyph precedes the dates 8.18.0.0.0 (F15/E16), 8.19.10.0.0 (H6/G7), 9.0.0.0.0 (H9–H14), and 9.0.3.9.18 (H24–H27). The last date, the only one preceded by a DN, lies 2322ᵈ = 85 sidereal lunar months (of 27ᵈ.32166) before 9.0.10.0.0, the IS date of Stela 31, which is the 1 Katun anniversary of Lord Stormy-Sky's inauguration on 8.19.10.0.0. These early examples of affix T12 consist of a "bar with a row of short hairs underneath." No flanking "death eyes" are present. Only affix T125 is used on Stela 31 as prefix of title glyphs (B23, C23, L1), as the "male prefix/agentive" *ah*. Affixes T229 and T12 occur only in glyphs connected with counting, T229.617a:125 (see above) and T1.573:12 (fig. 4). Strikingly, T229 appears in these glyphs in the prefix, T12 in the suffix position. This positional peculiarity is found again in the glyphs T229.187:743:12 (La Amelia Stela 1) and T?:229.503:12 (Yaxchilán Stela 21; Proskouriakoff 1964: fig. 3).
    The inscription of the Right Lintel of the Initial Series Building at Xcalumkin presents the clause: T61:756a.568:12:689–630.60b:23/187:513.229/68:679c. A variant of this clause is recorded on an unpublished vase from the Xcalumkin area (fig. 7): T61.756a.568:24?/12P.689–630.60b:23P / 187:513:229 / 99.110:565aP:?/III.bird's head°524:178/68:679c.59/12.1.756a.568.

Fig. 7 Xcalumkin Vase, the vertical glyph columns with part of the rim inscription.

Here the name glyph following the initial action glyph replaces the T12 superfix by a head variant that represents a "victim's head" (see Mathews and Justeson 1984: fig. 21). According to recent ideas by D. Stuart, N. Grube, and others, the glyph T61:756.568 could refer to the action of carving the lintel, the carver being named by the glyph T12:689–630.60b:23. The third glyph T187:513.229 is understood as *u.kaba.(a)*, "his name," with T187 being a logogram for *kaba*, "name," and T513 being a phonetic *u*.

If there existed a vowel contraction rule i + u → u that allowed to contract *tz'i* and *ul* to *tz'ul*, "foreigner" in Yucatec (such a rule is known from modern Chontal; Knowles 1984:57), one could consider the following alternative interpretation: T61.756a.568:24?, *hol?.tz'(i)-ul.il = hol.tz'ulil*, "chief of the foreigners"[9]/12P.689–630.60b:23P, *hau.pa-cah (= pac-ah). kax-an?*, "death is the recompense for the tied one"[10]/187:513.229, (name of captive?)/. . ./12.1.756a.568, *hau.(u).tz'(i)-ul = hau.tz'ul*, "it lies face up/dies the foreigner." The vase depicts an enthroned Maya lord and in front of him a strange-looking individual with a submissive gesture, probably a captive. In the glyph column to the left of this scene a date is given, XIV.528:116–VIII:113.533:130, "in the 14th Tun of (Katun) 8 Ahau (= 9.13.0.0.0)," that is, 9.12.14.0.0.

The reading *kax-an* of the collocation T60b:23 raises two questions: (1) can T23 in suffix position be the Yucatecan past participle *-an* in addition to having the value *na*? and (2) the "multi-stranded knot" T60b, *ha*, and affix T136, *hi*, previously interpreted *may*, "gift, offering," substitute for each other in the event glyph T190:25.757:136 or 60b of the three CR dates on Step VII, Hieroglyphic Stairway 2, Yaxchilán Structure 33 (A2, C1). They could function as phonetic complement *ha/hi: bat.cah.bah. (ha/hi)*, "the fighting begins, the hit-

ting." T136 could be also a phonetic complement in the "deer" glyph T671:136 of Madrid Codex 40, 41, which could denote *chih.(hi)* or *ceh.(hi)* instead of *chih-may* (see above). The compound T60b:528 could be *(ha).haab*, "year," instead of *kax.haab*, "bound are the years."

The Compound T606:23

Recently N. Grube (personal communication) and N. Hopkins (this volume) proposed a reading *une(n)*, "baby," for T606, a term of the Cholan/Tzeltalan languages derived from Proto-Zoque * '*une*, "baby, child." They interpret the "child of mother" compound T1.I: 606:23 as *u.(hun).une.n(a)*, "her baby," with the number I (*hun*) and suffix T23 (*na*) regarded as phonetic complements. On the other hand, the numeral I, *hun*, could be included in a phonetic spelling, T1.I: 606:23, *u.hun.in/en.na = uh.unin/unen.na*, "the necklace, the baby/tender one of the mother," or *uh.unin/unen.(n)a(1)*, "the necklace, the tender child." Note Proto-Chol (Kaufman, Norman) *une . . . =* "baby." Proto-Tzeltal/Tzotzil (Kaufman) * *unin = tierno*. Tzeltal (Domingo de Ara) *unin alal = niño*. A reading T606, *in/en*, would allow as additional interpretation *u.hun.in-nah = u.hun.inah*, "her unique seed."[11] Any reading of T606 has to be tested in its use as constituent of half-period glyphs like T606:23.173°552 (Thompson 1950: figs. 32–50), which I would interpret as "(the katun's) decline (173°552.23 = *me-tan.[na]*) up to the mid-point (606 = *xin*)."[12]

On an Early Classic incised conch-shell (Schele and Miller 1986:84: pl. 27A), the compound T585a°606, *bin/ben-?*, "to go," occurs. On Piedras Negras Throne I, right leg, we find the clause T606°585a:23–599:23, *bin.nah–tan.(na)*, "it goes the first one—in front/in the midst." The Men glyph of the date 9 Men 13 Kayab, Dos Pilas Stela 8 (I17b/H18a) may have inscribed in its cartouche T606, *en*. The "shell fist" T672 is a hand with infixed T606, possibly *kuben*, *encomendar*, *dar a guardar*, *encargar*, and *koben*, *cocina o hogar* (Yucatec).

The short inscriptions of codex-style Vessels 3 and 20 (Robicsek and Hales 1981:16, 22) present on Vessel 3 the clause T1030d/58°520.1016°582:23?, on Vessel 20 the variant clause T1030a/58°520.606:23. The eye of the God C head T1016 in T1016°582:23? is replaced by T582, which is a phonetic *mo*, but could also be a logogram for "blood." I regard T1016°582 as a variant of T33.1016, interpreted as *ku/ch'u*, "he/she of divine (blood)." In the codices a T582 sign is set into the beaks of hummingbirds that symbolize the "spine" used in drawing blood for self-castigation (Seler 1923:574ff.). The emblem glyph of Río Azul is essentially a knotted T1008 (*xib*) head with T582 covering the mouth (Houston 1986:5). It misses a T168 superfix and one of the "noble blood" prefixes T32–T40. Here T582 may substitute for the "noble blood" prefix. This argues for a semantic basis of the exchange T1016°582:23?/606:23, probably found among terms for "blood-descendants; seed."

A problem for any interpretation of T606:23 is the "era clause" P1–Q2 of the Vase of the Seven Gods (Grolier no. 49; Coe 1973b:109) : (13.0.0.0.0) 4 Ahau 8 Cumku/ 573.181:126, *hel/kex.ah.i(h)*, "to be changed is"/95.1: 606:23, "the darkness (95 = *ek*) of their (1) blood-descendants/seed (606:23 = *in-[n]ah?*)." This text continues with the reference (P3–R10) to six ancestor(?) deities, entitled T501-35.1016°582, probably *ba.ku*, "first one of divine blood." The second glyph connects them with zenith, T86:561a:23.178, . . . *caan. (n)a.l(a)*, "place (86) there on high," and nadir, T526.178, *cabal*, "(place) below," and with the four cardinal directions represented by TIX.765a:87 (*Bolon Yocte*, east?), TIV?.653°568?:59 (north?), T151.87:671 (west?), and T1018c (*Jaguar God*, south).

Compare the zenith/nadir glyphs of this text with Dresden Codex 56a:T1.561c:23, *u.caan.(n)a(l)*, "above is"/17.676/1.526:23, *u.cab-al?*, "below is"/64:790v. Whereas T561:23, *caanal*, can be reconciled with T23 *na* and *al* (the final -*l* is unimportant and lost in the spoken language), T526:23, *cabal*, demands the *al* reading (a reading *cab-an* is unlikely). We encounter here the controversy about affix T23 (see below), which is not solved in favor of *na* by always regarding main signs suffixed by T23 as logograms for terms ending in -*n*. In previous papers I used the reading T606:23, *cux-(t)al*, "life," a reading based on Barthel's T23, *al*.

The final glyphs S11–T12 of the West Tablet, Inscriptions Temple, Palenque (fig. 8a), could denote: T125:669b:130, *ya-ka-w(a)*, "he offered to"/I:606:23, *hun.in-(n)ah?*, "the unique seed/descendant"/IX.78: 514.4, "the great one (IX = *bolon*) of the Temple of the Inscriptions (78:514)"/11:187:1016, *u?.pazel?.ku*, "he at the shelter of the divine ones"/1:1040:24, *u.cim-il*,

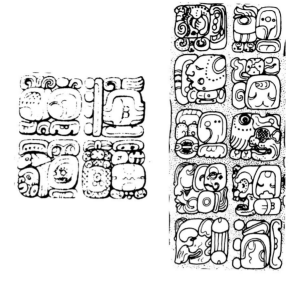

a   b

Fig. 8 *T606:23 in two different contexts at Palenque. (a) West Tablet, Inscriptions Temple, glyphs S11–T12; (b) Palace-Tablet, glyphs C4–D8 (after A. P. Maudslay and Merle Greene Robertson).*

"his death"/74:184:624a, Mah Kina Pacal/11:168a: 570:178, "ruler of Palenque."

On the Palace-Tablet, Palenque, T606 compounds occur in a passage referring to the birth of Lord Kan-Xul II (fig. 8b):

C4 T740.181:126, *poc?.ah.ih*, "washed (at birth) is the descendant/grandchild"?

D4 115:506:178, "the beloved (506 = *kan?*) offspring (115–178 = *ya-al*)"—606:24, *(x)in-il*, "in the middle"?/

C5 16.1003b:173°606?, "the first (16) son? (1003b) . . ."

D5 122.244:522°188, "(he of) the lineage (188 = *le*) . . ."?

C6 16:44:110, *yax.to(c).coh?*, "first seizing the dear one"[13]—606:23, *in.(n)ah?*, "the seed/blood-descendant"

D6 501:178.115:765a, *ba-l(a).y(o).oc*, "the one who was hidden/rolled up entered"

C7, D7 1058a.19.230:59—230.521:102

C8 758.110, *tz'u(b).coh?*, "the sucking dear one"?

The text continues with two titles of the newborn Kan-Xul II. T506 in D4 cannot be read *wah*, "bread." The likely phonetic value *co* of T110 (Grube and Stuart 1987) can be extended to a logographic *coh*, "dear, beloved" in Yucatec (*choh* in Chorti). If T758:110 entitles an adult ruler, a reading (restricted to Yucatec), "dear one (110 = *coh*) in the middle/center (758 = *tz'u'*)," might be appropriate.

Affix T110 and the Compounds
T758:110 and T44:110

In texts that follow the birthdates of lords, the compound T758.110 or its variant T287:110 occasionally addresses the newborn noble child, while the future ruler's actual name is used only after his accession. Examples are El Cayo Lintel 1 (A10/B10), Piedras Negras Altar 2, south support (A2–B3), and Palenque Temple XVIII-Jambs (B13/A14a), besides the mentioned passage of the Palace-Tablet. The central figure of Piedras Negras Wall Panel 2 (Schele and Miller 1986:149), Lord Turtleshell (P.N. Ruler 2), is accompanied by a smaller, youthful warrior, his successor Ah Cauac (Ruler 3) who is entitled T287:110 in K'3. Long ago T. Proskouriakoff (in a letter of 10 May 1973) wrote to the author: "My observations indicate that T758 with the 110 sign may mean 'son' or 'offspring,' but of this I am not entirely sure."

I based my recent reading T758, *tz'u(b)* (Dütting 1984:24; 1985b:274), (1) on Mopan (Ulrich, de Ulrich) *tz'ub, joven, muchacho, niño,* (2) on the strong resemblance of the T758 rodent to the cotuza or serec, termed *tzub* in Yucatec, *chüctzub* in Mopan, and (3) on its substitute T287, which I read as *tz'u(h),* "drip; drop (of water)" (Dütting 1974:11). Some examples of T287 resemble "eyes," but these are the eyes of the Rain God Tlaloc, which may have been associated with "drops of water," with "tears." T758 could also represent the pizote, *äh.ts'u'ts'u'* in Lacandon, but *chiic* in Yucatec/Choltí. In the inscriptions of the Naj Tunich cave, Group IV, j, an example of T758:110 was found, the T758 head of which strongly resembles the head of a "rat" or "mouse," *ch'o(h)* in Yucatec/Chol. A possible Early Classic form of T758:110 occurs on Yaxchilán Lintel 18, B2/B3/B4. These rodent heads are ratlike in presenting whiskers, but are atypical with respect to their ears.

By making use of the latter findings, N. Grube (personal communication) and S. Houston now interpret the preaccession title T758:110 as *ch'o-c(o)* = *ch'oc,* which is the Cholan term for "young child; unripe." Note also Chontal (S. Knowles) *ch'oc* = "small, young; son or daughter, child." They regard T287 as the widely opened eyes of a rat and refer to Chol *ch'uc,* "watch." Such a reading does not account for the T758:110 title of an adult ruler. For instance on Yaxchilán Stela 7, passage C2–D5 (fig. 9), Shield Jaguar II, captor of Tah Moo, is entitled by the final glyphs C5/D5: T38:168b:562–32:168b:511:142, "he of noble blood (38/32), ruler/lord (168) of Yaxchilán (562/511)"/758:110, *tz'u'.coh,* "dear one in the middle"?/501:25:501, *ba.ca-b(a),* "first one of the land/world."

Some occurrences of T758, in particular the main sign of the month Xul glyph, cannot be explained with a reading *tz'u(b)* or *ch'o(h).* The Palace-Tablet, Palenque (Greene Robertson 1985b: figs. 257/258), clearly distinguishes the rodent head of T758.110 (C8, C17, E11, K8, K13) from that of the Xul glyph T758:116 (N15,

Fig. 9   Yaxchilán Stela 7, glyphs D2–D5 (photograph by Dieter Dütting).

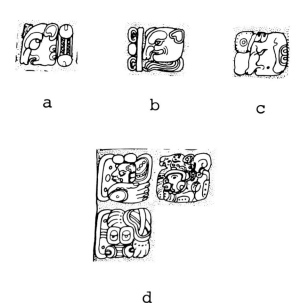

Fig. 10   Variants of T758 from the Palace-Tablet, Palenque. (a) T758a.110 (K8); (b) VI.758c:116 (N15); (c) ?.758b (F19); (d) glyphs 2C, X2, B of Lunar Count (A16–A17). (Redrawn by Dieter Dütting after Merle Greene Robertson.)

Q5; fig. 10a, b). The former is characterized by a large eye and a T7 (darkness?) infix, the latter by a small eye and the absence of a T7 infix. A third variant of T758, Thompson's 758b, the likely head variant of affixes T136/88, is distinguished by T7 infixes and an elongated ear. For an example, see Palace-Tablet F19 (fig. 10c). These head graphemes are certainly different logograms. On the other hand, in the Venus Tables of the Dresden Codex the main sign of the Xul glyph has a T504 (darkness) infix, while the main sign of T758.110 in C. Dresden 20b, almanac 43, has none. I am inclined to in-

Fig. 11 Dresden Codex 5b–6b, almanac 15, cols. 1 and 2 (p. 5b) (photograph by Dieter Dütting).

terpret the Xul glyph of the Dresden Venus Table, T758°504:116, as *xul.kin*, "end of the sun/days," and its variant T765b:116 (C. Dresden 61/63) as *ockin*, "it enters the sun (the underworld)." There is evidence that the solar year of the Maya, the Haab of 365^d, once started with the month Yaxkin, T16:544:116, *yax.kin.(n)*, "new sun/day," and ended with the month Xul, T758:116 (cf. Tozzer 1941:158, note 808).[14]

In Dresden Codex 5b–6b, almanac 15, four deities are shown drilling a new fire: a positive deity starts the drilling, a negative one terminates it, for example, cols. 1 and 2 (fig. 11):

T589.765b, *hoch'.oc*, "the drilling begins"/1.671:671, *u.chi-ch(i)*, "his force"/XI.1005b, God R/168b:573.130, *ahau.(wa).hel*, "lord successor (in office)";

T589.758°504, *hoch'.xul*, "the drilling ends"/13.671:671, *zat?.chi-ch(i)*, "lost is the force"[15]/name glyph God A'/1.648:25, *u.kaz.cah*, "his doing evil," or *u.muk.cah*, "their suffering begins."

The problem of Glyph B of the Lunar Count, either T1.187:758:110 or T1.187:287:110, cannot be solved without reference to the preceding Glyphs C and X. Figure 10d presents Glyphs 2C, X2, B of the Lunar Count that follows the IS date 9.10.11.17.0, 2 Nov 644, of the Palace-Tablet. A very tentative meaning might be: two lunations in the cycle of six have passed (2C), the rule has God X2 who joined the Moon Goddess in the location B, "the heavenly shelter (187 = *pazel?*) from where the children/sucking ones (758:110) descend."

My previous reading T110, *chic/chec/chac*, "appear, be visible" (Dütting 1984:24) was not without problems.[16] T110 (fig. 1) functions not only as a logogram, but also as a phonetic sign in compounds like T33:

568.110:110:502 (Chichén Itzá, Akab Dzib, a, E2). Here logographic values of T110 do not work, but with T110, *co*, Grube and Stuart (1987) derived a meaning "he of the blood (33:568) of the *Co-co-m(a)* (110:110:502)."[17] According to them, the glyph T110:501.228, *co-ba-a*, of Cobá Stela 18, D11, and Panel C, Ball Court, Group D, top side, could be the name of the place.

An additional argument for T110, *co*, is provided by Vase no. 11 of the Pearlman Collection (Coe 1982:35) with its vivid representation of the Mesoamerican ball game. Directly above the rubber ball and stepped platform between the two players, we recognize a L-shaped panel of five glyphs. The final T110:753 could designate the "ball" as *co-tz'i'*, "circular, round"; cf. Yucatec (Motul) *cotz'il* = *circulo o redondéz*; *cotz'-* = *arrollar*. T753, a dog's head, may correspond to the Cholan, *tz'i'*, "dog."

In Dresden Codex 38b–41b, almanac 61, col. 9 (p. 40b), the compound T1.49:110 refers to the "flaring torch" in the paw of a heavenly dog diving earthward from a sky band and may designate the lightning (fig. 12a): T1.49:110, *u.to-c(o)*, "its burning/fire"[18]/ 559.568b.561c, *tzu-l(u).caan*, "dog in the sky"/172.1016c, *numya?.ku*, "woe to those of divine blood"/172.85:115v.663.115v, "woe (172) to the maize-seed (85:663)."

In Paris Codex 21, T110:49, *co-to* = *cot*, "resound"

a   b

Fig. 12 T44:110 in two different contexts. (a) Dresden Codex 38b–41b, almanac 61, col. 9, p. 40b (drawing by Ian Graham); Yaxchilán Structure 44, Hieroglyphic Stairway 3, Step I (tread), glyphs A3/B3 (photograph by Dieter Dütting).

(Yuc), or *coh.lem*, "flash of lightning"(?), with *coh* used instead of *hatz'*, is set into water streaming down from a sky band, next to a long-nosed Sun Monster head that suspends from a system of twisted (umbilical?) cords. Note Yucatec *coh* = *batir, mazoncar, golpear con mazo o cosas así; lemba* = *resplandor, brillo, relámpago*; Proto-Chol **lem* = *brilliante*; Tzeltal (Domingo de Ara) *cogh* = *golpe*.

Yaxchilán Structure 44, Hieroglyphic Stairway 3, Step I (tread), presents in A3/B3 the clause (fig. 12b): T281:23.44:110:568a:102, *kan.(na).to-c(o).yol.ci?*, "the precious one is seized, the heart, the exquisite one"/756a: 25:4?, *zotz'.cay. . . .*, "bat who kills . . ."?/168b:513: 130, "respected (513 = *tzic/xoc*) lord (168–130)." The compound T281:23 refers to "precious liquid" (blood) in the caption next to a prisoner with bleeding fingers on the north wall of Room 2, Bonampak Murals (Miller 1986: plate 47): T281:23, *kan.(n)a(l)*, "the precious liquid"/44.580, *(l)em?.bol*, "comes down, the payment"/ ?.?/501.44:669a, *nab.lem.kab*, "besmeared glistening hand" (= sacrificial knife), or *nab.to-k(a)*, "besmeared flint-knife."[19] Both readings of T23, *na* and *al*, can be reconciled here with the "precious liquid" interpretation of T281:23.

In Pre-Classic times, when—according to a plausible hypothesis—Mixe/Zoque speakers initiated the development of the glyphic script, affix T23 may have been the sign for (Proto)-Mixe/Zoque *na'*, "water, liquid." Later, when speakers of Mayan languages continued this development, this meaning of the term *na'* got lost ("water" is *ha'* in the Mayan languages), and may have been replaced by an additional logographic value *(y)al*, "liquid," of T23. A possible bivalency of T23 for *na'* and *(y)al*, which would solve many problems (see Dütting 1985b:108), could be explained in this way.

Affixes T44/49 must have a logographic value in addition to the phonetic *to*. Of the possible candidates I prefer *lem*, "shiny, flashing," contrary to *toc*, "burn." On Vessels 39 and 40 (Robicsek and Hales 1981:28) a jaguar entwined by a rattlesnake, with T2 (star) signs attached to his body (seven on Vessel 39), is referred to by the glyphs T49:673:140.2/524.140.609v. On Vessel 40 (and on Vessel 8), T49 is also attached to the serpent's body (note Mopan *leet'* = *ondas; le'leet'* = *ondas, ondulaciones*). Probably we have here a reference to the Pleiades. T673 might refer to something "piled up or clustered," *much'/moch'*. Proto-Chol (Kaufman, Norman) **much'* = "piled up"; **moch'* = "squeeze in hand" (T673 is a hand squeezing T552). Yucatec *much'tal* = *amontonarse*. Kekchi *moch'* = *puñado; mochoc* = *recoger, juntar, encoger*. The compound T49:673.2 thus might denote *lem.much'.ek*, "glistening/brilliant clustered stars." The readings T49, *to* and *toc* ("burn"), make no sense. Note Tzeltal (Ara) *leblon ec* = *estrella o lucero resplandeciente*.

One of the lord's attendants in the scene of J. Kerr Vase no. 2914 is accompanied by the glyph T673:110.130:?, "piling up (673 = *much'*) grains (110 = *co[h]*) of tender

ears of corn (130 = *ahan?*) . . ." This glyph reminds of "scattering" compounds like Ixtutz Stela 4 (B2), T1:33v:670:110:130, "his (1) throwing (33v:670 = *pul?*) grains (110) of *elotes* (130)"—93:758b, *ch'a.h(i)*, "and pellets of *ch'ah* incense" (Love 1987), into a brazier for burning.

A problem is the interpretation of T49:112 in the "fire-drilling" scene of Madrid Codex 38c: T589.93, *hoch'.ch'ah* = *hoch'ah*, "it is drilled"[20]/49:112, *lem/toc. (tok)*, "that which gleams/burns (on stone)." This in contrast to Madrid Codex 38b, where the fire is kindled on wood: T589.93, "it is drilled/he drills"/1.122:563a, *u.kak.(zi')*, "his fire (on wood)." If T49:112 would be just *(to).tok*, "flint," the relationship T49/T122 would be lost.

The Early Classic variant T287:G13 of T287:110 can be identified as face of the Teotihuacán Rain God, the later Tlaloc (Grube 1985:108). T287 are the "encircled eyes" of Tlaloc, G13 his "teeth," the "maize-kernels" (T851), *co(h)* in Yucatec, as seen by comparing examples of T287:G13 on Early Classic pottery (Robicsek and Hales 1981:135, fig. 39A; Coe 1975a:11, Vase no. 2, glyph F3) with the Tlaloc face on the right side of Tikal Stela 31 (warrior's shield). Affix T110 is present in Early Classic inscriptions (e.g., Tikal Stela 31, L2) independently of G13, and therefore must have had an independent development. While having different icons and therefore originally different meanings, G13 and T110 probably converged on the common value *co(h)*, the basis of the later substitution. For the icon of T110, Yucatec *coo, corteza así sacada del árbol*, might be of interest.

Inside of the cartouche incised on Peccary Skull 1 from Tomb 1, Copán, two lords are seated in front of a stela and a death's head altar. Above the stela a clause is inscribed: 1 Ahau 8 Ch'en (9.10.3.11.0 or 9.7.10.16.0)/ 528.116:713a, "the stone/stela (528.116) is set up? (713a)"/115v.535.115v, (germinating grain of corn). The glyph T74:110, *mah.coh*, "the lord who strikes," incised above the cartouche, might refer to the Death God incised underneath the cartouche, blowing a conch-trumpet.

On Copán Stela A, G1–G2, a comparable reference to the Death God is made: T114:566:23, "(in) the north"/74:110:74, *mah.coh.ma(n)*, "the lord who strikes passed by"/60v.1040v, Death God.

In Dresden Codex 31b–35b, almanac 59, Chaacs of the four colors and directions enter the scene bearing torches and axes, their "entering" being described by the compound T765b.103, *oc.(ci)*, in cols.2,3, and by T765b.110, *oc.(co)*, in col.1. My previous interpretation was:

col. 1   T765b.110, *oc.chac*–668.103, *chaac.(cV)*, "it entered the red Chaac";

col. 2   765b.103, *oc.(cV)*–58.668, *zac.chaac*, "it entered the white Chaac";

col. 3 115.765b:103, *y(o).oc.(cV)*–95.668:103, *ek.'chaac.*
(cV), "it entered the black Chaac";

col. 4 281.668, *kan.chaac*–115.726, *y(o).oc?* "the yellow
Chaac entered."

These passages are preceded by a directional glyph and
by the compound T588b:140.181. It follows a positive
or negative augury for the maize. The new interpretation
of T765b.110 (Grube and Stuart 1987) deletes the color
"red" in col. 1.

Conclusion

This paper has provided further arguments for a context-
dependent polyvalency in Maya writing, established
in papers delivered at conferences in 1979 (Fox and
Justeson 1984b) and 1980 (Dütting 1985a). We con-
stantly encountered the problems created by the interaction of the phonetic and the logographic component of
the script. The restricted number of phonetic syllabic
spellings and the uncertainty of most logographic assignments make the decipherment of the Maya script such a
difficult job. There should be more research on semantic
aspects of the glyphs. The texts and scenes on codex-
style polychrome vases demonstrate how limited our
"understanding" actually is and leave us with a feeling of
admiration and despair. Presently there is no way to
bridge the large gap that separates the Classic and Early
Classic Maya world from the declining Post-Classic society and the remnants of it at the time of the conquest,
the main source of our knowledge. All our attempts to
penetrate this lost world are therefore a long process
with many setbacks that may never come to an end.

Notes

1. Hieroglyphs are transcribed by Thompson's (1962) code numbers. The infixing is indicated by a degree sign in front of the infixed
grapheme (e.g., T671°544 instead of the former T671[544]). Maya
words are written with the phonemes of Classical Yucatec as defined in
the Motul dictionary (*c* for *k*, *k* for *k'*, *z* for *s*, *x* for *š*). The dictionaries
of Mayan languages used are those cited in Dütting (1981) and previ-
ous papers. I am indebted to Nikolai Grube (Hamburg) and Thomas
Barthel (Tübingen) for helpful discussions.

2. The "marriage" clause (E13–F16) may denote:

T17?.565a:136?, *ye-ta-h(i)?*, "the companion"?/
126.552:23, *ya-tan.(na)*, "his wife"/
1000a.168a:569, princess of Tikal/
1.526:246, "his being in charge of the land"?/
122.765a:117–561a23.1030b, Fire- or Smoking Squirrel/
38?.1016–747a:130, . . . *ku/ch'u.ahau. (wa)*, "lord of divine
  blood—head-chief."

3. One could also read *pa.zah.uh = paz.ah.uh*, "it emerges the (one
with the) necklace." See note 10 for a discussion of T630. Postfix
T151, *uh*, "necklace," replaces affix T181, *-ah/-Vh*, including *uh*.

4. I extend the reading *ol/ul* of T568 to *hol/hul*, "pierce; hole"; cf.
Yucatec (Motul, under H simple) *hol = agujero; hol, ah = agujerear,
horadar*. Ironically T568 might represent a "heart," *yol* (Justeson
1984a:344). T568, *ol/ul* (besides phonetic *lu*), is strongly supported by
the Palenque Temple XVIII stucco glyph T87.601°568:528.1068
(Schele and Mathews 1979: nos. 475/492), the initial part of which
may denote *chu-c(u)-ul-te*, "captive." At Chichén Itzá, Temple of the

Four Lintels, Lintel II, E6/F6, we recognize the "cenote" compound
T13.561inv:568, *u.tam.hol?*, "its deep hole"/53:33, "place of shedding
blood." Affix T96, previously read *yol*, may be *ta(n)*, "amidst"; T96
replaces T552 (*tan/kat*) of the month glyph Uo, T95:552, in the Uo
variant T95:96 of C. Dresden 62 (bottom).

A reading T130.506, *(wa).wah*, "bread, food," would mean that the
blood is spent for the prepared tortillas rather than for its prerequisite,
the growth of the maize plants. The icon of affix T130 does not resemble a "prepared food" and is easier to reconcile with Knorozov's
T130, *ahan*, "*elote*, tender ear of corn," than with T130, *wah*, "bread"
(Mathews and Justeson 1984:205). A problem is that both *ahan, elote*,
and *kan*, "desired, beloved," are Cholan/Tzeltalan terms, not found in
Yucatec, where *elote* is *nal*. Texts like those of Chichén Itzá and the
Dresden Codex, on the other hand, are basically Yucatec. The likely
use of Cholan and Yucatecan terms in the (sacred) language of the
script also suggests a certain flexibility with respect to the expression of
grammatical functions. In its function as a verbal suffix, I regard T130
therefore as polyvalent with values *-wa(n)* and *-aan/-ahan* (Dütting
1985b:106, 112). One could give the "seating" compound T644b:
130.116:125 a Cholan and a Yucatecan interpretation, *chum-wan.
(n).ih/ cum-aan.(n).ih*, "seated was"/113.168a:513:188, *ta.ahau.tzic.
le/el*, "in the line of the respected rulers"/74.184.624a:178, *Mah Kina
Pacal* (East Tablet, Inscriptions Temple, Palenque, R10–R11), with
T130.116 being the Cholan verbal ending *-wan.(n)* and the Yucatecan
-aan.(n). The verbal suffix T130 appears not only in inscriptions attributed to Cholan speakers, but also in the Chichén Itzá texts, whose
language was Yucatec.

5. The "painted/spotted one" could be one of the Hero Twins of
the Popol Vuh in his role as representative of a deceased human lord
(cf. J. Kerr Vase no. 1004; Robicsek and Hales 1982:40). I regard
T563a as a logographic *zi'*, "firewood; gift," and—following D. Stuart
and N. Grube—as a phonetic *tz'i*. The "Lady Moon" glyph is also written T1000a.181:178 (J. Kerr Vase no. 2914) or T4.683b:178 (J. Kerr
Vase no. 2730), which suggests a reading *na-ha-l(a); na.hal*, "mother
who weaves" (among other meanings), could be a reference to the
Moon Goddess.

6. Note Kekchi (Sedat) *xic'* = (1) *ala*, (2) *resbaloso, peligroso (el
camino), mal paso; xic'obal* = *horrible*. Yucatec (Motul) *xik* = *ala de
cualquier ave; xikbal* = *volar, vuelo*.

7. Instead of *kaz*, "evil" (Thompson 1950:268), T648 could also
denote *muk*, "suffering." Affix T115 represents a "leaf" iconically.
I derived my former T115, *ual*, "leaf," from Yucatec. D. Stuart's reading *yo* can be related to the Cholan *yopol*, "leaf." I am inclined to extend a T115, *yo*, to *y(a)*. The earliest known ruler of Yaxchilán is
entitled T115.608:751a, either *(to).toon.balam* or *y(a)-at.bahläm*,
"penis/progenitor jaguar," on a newly discovered lintel of Structure 12.

8. Bricker (1986:107) interprets the T12 prefix as T13, as possessive pronoun *uy*, and reads *uy.a-tan.(na)*, "his wife." I follow Zimmer-
mann (1956:125) in transcribing T12. The prefix cannot be distinguished from the first T12 prefix in the column above the enthroned
Death God in Dresden Codex 53a.

9. I do not extend Barthel's (1966) T61/62, *hol/hool*, "head, chief,
top, end," to Yucatec *hol*, "pierce." The initial *h* is the *h recia* in the
first, the *h simple* in the second case (see Motul dictionary).

10. T689 is the Xcalumkin variant of T586/602, *pa*. The reading
makes use of Lounsbury's T630, *cah*. My reading T630, *zih*, does not
work well in this context. An interpretation with T689, *pac* (in addition to *pa*), and T630, *zah*, might be possible: *hau.pac*, "death is the
recompense"/*zah.kax-an?*, "for the tied one who is afraid."

My earlier reading T630, *tzem*, "chest; to faint," besides *tzen*, "sustenance, sustain" (Dütting 1972:221), would make sense here, but
cannot be reconciled with the name clause of Lord Dawn of Copán.
The phonetic version of its "dawn" constituent, T16:602.630.(181),
demands a value of T630 beginning with *z* like *zi(h)* or *za(h)*, if one
wants to apply the Cholan term *paz-*, *salir (el sol)*, to explain the
T602.630 compound (Dütting 1985b:268).

Further evidence for T630, *zih*, is a title of the Moon Goddess mentioned in the Ritual of the Bacabs (p. 107; Roys 1965:37), and on
the Vase of the 88 Glyphs, November Collection no. 11 (Robicsek
and Hales 1982:38; Dütting, 1986), S5/T1, T1000b.181–630.23,
ix.uh.zih-na(l), "lady moon who gives birth." Main sign T630 re-

sembles T563a, but while the elements of T563a are set into a cartouche, those of T630 are not. This is shown by pottery texts displaying both graphemes (J. Kerr Photo nos. 772 and 791). A problem is the title T630–181:178 and its head variant T1004–181°178, Lounsbury's *ca(h)-ha-l(a)* = *cahal,* "native of town/province; fellow citizen." The Yucatec terms *zihul/zihnal, nativo de un lugar* (Pérez dictionary), perhaps derived from an earlier *zihal,* have essentially the same meaning as *cahal.* Kuná-Lacanhá Lintel 1 and El Cayo Lintel 1 record the "seating" to the *rank* of T630–181:178, perhaps to "one who is in charge of a town/country."

11. This discussion owes much to a continuous exchange of ideas with Nikolai Grube. Note Yucatec (Motul) *(h)inah* = *semilla, simiente de la generación.* Proto-Chol (Kaufman, Norman) * *(h)inaj* = "seed." Chorti (Wisdom) *hinah* (written *xinax*) = "seed, sprouting maize"; *hinih* (written *xinih*) = "come forth, issue, sprout."

12. I extend Grube's reading T173/163, *mi* (personal communication), to *me,* and interpret T173°552 as *me-tan,* "lie down, decline"; cf. Chol (Aulie) *metan* = *acostarse (sobre); xin* = *en medio.* Chortí (Wisdom) *metwan* = "lie down, fall prone." At Palenque, the X2 glyph "deer's head": 138.1016. "serpent jaws" in the Lunar Count of the IS date 9.10.11.17.0 of the Palace-Tablet (see fig. 10d) substitutes a deer's head ("deer" = *me'* in Chol) for the usual superfix T173 (*mi/me*).

13. Or *yax.lem.coh,* "first resplendent dear one."

14. I regard T116 as a phonetic *n(e)* and a logographic *kin.* On J. Kerr Vase no. 2572 the glyph T74.184.671:116, *mah.kina.chi-kin,* "lord of the west," occurs. The main sign does not have an infixed T544.

15. Affix T13 consists of two forms, T13a/Z2 and T13b = T13°153. Both can function as third pers. sing. pronoun replacing T1, *u,* but T13a may have in addition a meaning *zat,* "lose, disappear, exhaust," related to its iconic aspect, to the "death eyes" it represents (Dütting 1974:36).

16. This reading was derived, among others, from supposed substitutions of T110 for T109, *chac,* in the month Ceh compounds T109:528 of Copán Stelae 2 and 13 and of Altar U. These substitutions turned out to be errors of Maudslay's and Morley's drawings, recently corrected by new drawings of the Copán Project artists.

17. If this reading is correct, the Cocoms, one of the ruling (Toltec?) families of Post-Classic Yucatán, must have been settled there already in A.D. 870, the date 10.2.0.15.3 of the Casa Colorada inscription, in which the same glyph occurs.

18. Previously I considered a reading T1.49:110, *u.lem.chac,* "his (flash of) lightning," but the *chac* (better *chaac*) of this expression should be related to the Cauac sign T528 and its derivative T530, *pec.chac?,* and not to T110 as substitute for T109, *chac* (cf. Choltí *chahac* = *rayo; u lem chahac* = *relámpago*).

19. An alternative reading of T44.580 could be *to-pol* = *topol, entrarse como la espina* (Yucatec, Pérez). For T44:669a, *lem.kab,* see Düttingh (1985b:110).

20. The reading T93, *ch'a(h)* (Love 1987), argues for a reading T589, *hoch',* instead of *hax.* Both are Yucatec terms for "drilling." Phonetic readings are also possible: T589.93, *ho-ch'(a),* T589.758, *ho-ch'(o),* and (less reasonable) T589.765b, *ho-(o)ch* (see discussion of Dresden 5b–6b given above).

Faunal Offerings in the Dresden Codex

VICTORIA R. BRICKER
TULANE UNIVERSITY

T he middle register of pages 29 to 31 of the Dresden Codex contains two ritual almanacs of 260 days. The first almanac is composed of five periods of 52 days, which are further divided into four intervals of 13 days (fig. 1). The second almanac consists of four intervals of 65 days (fig. 2). Although the numerical structures of these almanacs are very different, the hieroglyphic texts associated with them are thematically similar.

The clauses in each almanac seem to refer to the motion of the Rain God Chac toward one of the four world directions—east, north or zenith, west, and south or nadir—and to some faunal offering—tortoise, fish, iguana, turkey, or deer. The 13-day interval between the events described in the first almanac closely approximates the periodicity of the chachac, or rain-making ceremonies, as they are performed today by the Maya in the western part of the Yucatán peninsula. The distance numbers associated with the four clauses in the second

almanac, 65 days, imply that they refer to the Burner ceremonies, for which there are ethnographic parallels in eastern Yucatán. Moreover, the chachac, and Burner ceremonies both involve offerings of animals to each of the four world directions. This means that the modern versions of these ceremonies may be useful in deciphering the hieroglyphic texts in the ritual almanacs on pages 29b to 31b of the Dresden Codex.

Let us look, first, at the almanac in the middle of pages 29 and 30 (fig. 1). Each clause begins with a verbal collocation composed of a main sign (T588) and two suffixes (T140 and T181). The main sign looks like a head variant of the syllabic sign tze in collocations for the month Tzec on other pages (compare fig. 3a and b). The first suffix is a variant of T178 (la; Kelley 1976:201); the second represents the past tense or perfective suffix -ah (Bricker 1986). The collocation can therefore be read as tze-la-ah or tzel-ah. The positional verb root tzel meant "to skirt" or "to sidle" in Classical Yucatec (Pío

29b   30b

Fig. 1 Pages 29b and 30b of the Dresden Codex (redrawn by Victoria R. Bricker after Villacorta C. and Villacorta 1930 [1976:68, 70]).

285

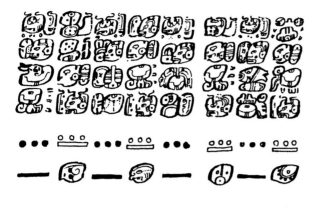

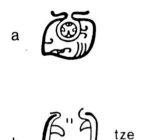

30b   31b

Fig. 2   Pages 30b and 31b of the Dresden Codex (redrawn by Victoria R. Bricker after Villacorta C. and Villacorta 1930 [1976:70, 72]).

a

b   tze

ca

Fig. 3   Relationship between T588 and T521. (a) T588; (b) codical spelling of Tzec (D. 46c) (a: redrawn by Victoria R. Bricker from Thompson 1962:453; b: redrawn by Victoria R. Bricker from Thompson 1950 [1960: fig. 1652]).

Pérez 1866–1877:363), and *tzel-ah* can be translated as "he sidled" or "he moved sideways."

The second collocation in the first clause on page 29b represents the codical spelling of *lakin*, "east" (Bricker 1983:347); *tzelah lakin* means "he sidled east." The same slot in the other three clauses in that almanac is filled by the collocations for north or zenith, west, and south or nadir (Bricker 1983). Thus, the first two collocations in each clause refer to lateral movement in one of the four world directions.

The third collocation in the first clause is composed of three signs: T283, T558, and T25. T283 resembles a sign that Floyd Lounsbury (1948b; see also Mathews and Justeson 1984:212–213) showed can be read as *ca* or *cah* (compare fig. 4b and c). That sign is half of a glyphic compound coded by Thompson (1962:246) as T630 (fig. 4a). The signs differ only in the treatment of the severed edge, which is ragged in the codical variant (compare fig. 4b and c). However, the fact that T283 occasionally represents the syllable *ca* in collocations based on T526 (*cab*; e.g., fig. 4d) suggests that this difference is not significant. T558 represents the syllable *ba*, and T25 is the codical variant of Landa's grapheme for *ca* (fig. 6a and e). The collocation can be interpreted as a phonetic

spelling of *cah bac*; it is followed by a collocation representing *chac*, "rain" (Fox and Justeson 1984; see fig. 1); *cah bac* is similar to *cahi baac*, which is translated as "if only . . ." or "it's about time!" in the Motul dictionary (Martínez Hernandez 1929:167). The exclamation *cahi baac be* meant "if only it were like this!" in Classical Yucatec (Martínez Hernández 1929:167; Michelon 1976:44). *Be*, "thus," can be replaced by *chac*, "rain," in this expression, yielding *cahi baac chac*, "if only it would rain!" or "it's about time for rain!" Since the root of *cahi* is *cah*, it seems reasonable to conclude that *cah baac chac* had the same meaning in Precolumbian times.

The four *cah baac* collocations contain some interesting substitution patterns. The syllable *ba* is represented by four different signs: T558, T757, T251, and T556 (fig. 6a–d). T558 and T556 are both codical variants of T501. The main sign in the second *cah baac* collocation is the codical allograph of T757 (compare fig. 6b with f), which substitutes for T501 in *bacab* and *bate* collocations in monumental inscriptions (Proskouriakoff 1968a; Closs 1984b; cf. fig. 5g and p). T251 is frequently suffixed to T526 in the codices, where it functions as a phonetic complement indicating that the logogram should be read as *cab* instead of *caban* (fig. 5a–c). And T103 (*ci*) substitutes for T25 (*ca*) in the last three clauses (compare fig. 6c with 6f–h).

The fifth collocation in each clause depicts an offering (fig. 1). The nature of the offering in the first clause is unclear; Thompson (1972:98) thought it might be a turtle, but it also resembles an offering of a fish in the picture on page 27b of the same codex (compare fig. 7b with d). In both cases, the head and the feet or fins of the animal are shown emerging from a Kan sign. The offering mentioned at the end of the second clause is cer-

a

b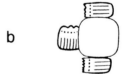

Fig. 4   Relationship between T283 and T630. (a) T630 (Cop. A, H10); (b) T283; (c) cah (Cop. T. 11, cornice) (a and c: redrawn by Victoria R. Bricker after Maudslay 1889–1902:I, pls. 7, 30; b: redrawn by Victoria R. Bricker from Thompson 1962:450).

c      ca

ah

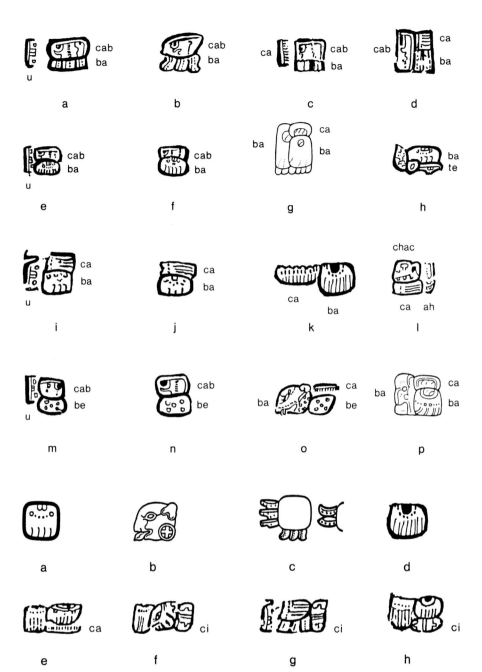

Fig. 5 Alternative spellings of cab and other words employing the same signs. (a) M. 104c; (b) D. 24; (c) M. 69b; (d) M. 77; (e) M. 103b; (f) M. 104b; (g) Yax. L. 27, G2b; (h) M. 40a; (i) M. 42c; (j) M. 42c; (k) M. 46a; (l) M. 41a; (m) M. 110c; (n) M. 104a; (o) D.74; (p) Nar. 24, E18 (a–f, h–o: redrawn by Victoria R. Bricker after Villacorta C. and Villacorta 1930 [1976:58, 304, 306, 308, 316, 362, 380, 430, 432, 444]; g redrawn by Victoria R. Bricker after Graham and von Euw 1977:59; p redrawn by Victoria R. Bricker after Graham and von Euw 1975:64).

Fig. 6 Alternative spellings of baac. (a) T558; (b) T757; (c) T251; (d) T556 (M. 46a); (e) D. 29b; (f) D. 29b; (g) D29b; (h) D. 30b (a, b, and c: redrawn by Victoria R. Bricker from Thompson 1962:251, 452, 455; d, e, f, g, and h: redrawn by Victoria R. Bricker after Villacorta C. and Villacorta 1930 [1976:68, 70, 316]).

tainly a fish (fig. 1). The fifth collocation in the third clause depicts an iguana draped over a Kan sign, and the fourth clause ends with a picture of a turkey head peering out of a Kan sign.

In spite of its brevity, the hieroglyphic text associated with the almanac on pages 29b and 30b contains sufficient information to link it to the kind of rain-making ceremony I witnessed in Hocabá, Yucatán, on 18 July 1971. Four such ceremonies are performed in Hocabá every summer, the first on the eastern side of town, the second in the north, the third in the west, and the

fourth in the south. They usually take place on alternate Sundays in June and July. The one I saw was the last in the sequence for that year and was located at the southern end of town.

There is a striking relationship between the timing and the location of the modern ceremonies and the Distance Numbers and the sequence of directions mentioned in the alamanac on pages 29b and 30b. In both cases, the ceremonies begin in the east and move counterclockwise. The almanac mentions a distance of 13 days between ceremonies; the ceremonies occur at 14-

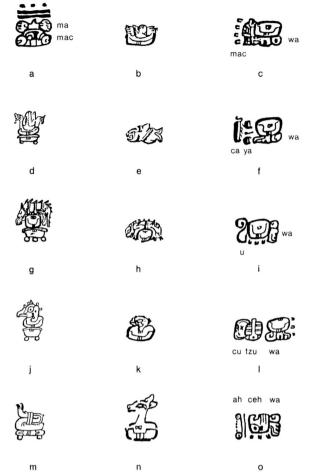

Fig. 7 *Alternative representations of offerings in the Dresden and Madrid codices. (a) D. 69; (b) D. 29b; (c) D. 67b; (d) D. 27b; (e) D. 29b; (f) D. 67b; (g) D. 43c; (h) D. 29b; (i) D. 68b; (j) D. 28c; (k) D. 30b; (l) D. 30b; (m) D. 28c; (n) M. 78d; (o) D. 65b (redrawn by Victoria R. Bricker after Villacorta C. and Villacorta 1930 [1976:64, 66, 68, 70, 96, 140, 144, 146, 148, 378]).*

day intervals in Hocabá. This suggests that the fortnight has become the functional equivalent of the *trecena* in the Precolumbian calendar.

The people of Hocabá make several types of offerings during rain-making ceremonies. One of them, called *x yaacħ*, seems to be depicted in the last collocation in each clause on pages 29b and 30b of the codex. *X yaacħ* means "squeezings" or "lees." It is prepared by mixing maize dough with water and forming cakes from the material that sinks to the bottom of the container. The cakes resemble large tortillas in shape, but they have a fibrous texture. After the maize cakes have been baked in an earth oven, they are broken up and mixed with chicken broth and giblets. The cooked heads and feet of the chickens used in making the broth are then placed upright in the porridgelike mass, and the dish is placed on the altar as an offering.

Similar offerings have been described for rain-making ceremonies in other parts of the Yucatán peninsula. In Chan Kom, however, only the legs of the chickens are inserted in the porridge (Redfield and Villa Rojas 1934:136). And the people of Tusik in Quintana Roo usually sacrifice a deer instead of several chickens in their rain-making ceremonies, substituting deer hooves for drumsticks in the porridge (Villa Rojas 1945:114). The maize cakes from which the porridge is made are called *nabal wah* in these communities (Redfield and Villa Rojas 1934:136; Villa Rojas 1945:109).

The use of animal heads and/or feet in offerings is also depicted in the ritual almanac on pages 29b and 30b of the Dresden Codex (fig. 1). They are further evidence that the hieroglyphic text on these pages refers to the need for rain and the measures necessary to alleviate the situation. Some clues to the names that were used for these offerings in Precolumbian times appear in the next almanac in the middle of pages 30 and 31, to which we now turn.

The clauses in the second ritual almanac begin in the same way as the first, with "sidling" and directional collocations (fig. 2). The third collocation in each clause contains a prefix representing the color associated with the previously mentioned direction: red (*chac*) for east, white (*zac*) for north, black (*ek'*) for west, and yellow (*kan*) for south. The fourth collocation in the last three clauses refers to the Rain God Chac. I assume that there is an error in the first clause—that the *chac* collocation in the sixth position really belongs in the fourth. The clauses end with a fuller description of offerings than the one provided in the previous almanac.

The second almanac seems to be concerned with the same kinds of offerings as the first (fig. 2). The fifth collocation in the first clause depicts the head of a deer rising from a Kan sign. The same position in the third clause is occupied by an iguana draped over a Kan sign. And the fourth clause mentions a fish in the same place. Only the second clause is different, providing a syllabic spelling of *cutz*, "wild turkey," instead of a picture of a turkey head emerging from a Kan sign, in that slot (compare fig. 7k with l).

The seventh position in the first clause and the sixth position in the other three clauses is occupied by a Kan sign complemented by T130 (*wa*; fig. 2). The phonetic complement indicates that the Kan sign is to be read as *wah*, "bread," in this context (John S. Justeson, personal communication). This means that the offering mentioned by the fifth and sixth collocations in the second clause was called *cutz wah*, "wild turkey bread," in Precolumbian times (fig. 7l).

We turn now to the last collocation in each clause, which contains the main sign T1038b. The distinguishing feature of this glyph is a cranium with an almond-shaped eye, but without the mandible. It differs from another glyph classified by Thompson (1962:458) as T1038a only in the addition of antennae (compare fig. 8a and b). Several clues to the reading of T1038a appear

a

b

Fig. 8 Variants of T1038. (a) T1038a; (b) T1038b; (c) D. 28b (a and b: redrawn by Victoria R. Bricker from Thompson 1962: 458; c: redrawn by Victoria R. Bricker after Villacorta C. and Villacorta 1930 [1976:66]).

c

can tuy-otoch

Fig. 9 Page 28b of the Dresden Codex (redrawn by Victoria R. Bricker after Villacorta C. and Villacorta 1930 [1976:66]).

on page 28 of the same codex (fig. 9). The middle register on that page depicts the Death God seated in his house. The caption above the picture contains T1038a with a coefficient of "4" (four dots), followed by a "house" collocation. The context implies that the collocation with T1038a refers to the Death God. The word for "death" was *cim* in Classical Yucatec (Pío Pérez 1866–1877:50); the final nasal in that word assimilates to the following consonant, so that *cim* becomes *cin* before dental consonants, as in *cinsic*, the verb meaning "to kill"; *cim* is cognate with Cholan *chAm* (Aulie and Aulie 1978:52), Tzeltalan *cham* (Slocum and Gerdel 1971:131), and Quichean *cam* (Edmonson 1965:55). The word for "4" was *can* in Classical Yucatec (Pío Pérez 1866–1877:42); it is cognate with Cholan *chAn* (Aulie and Aulie 1978:52) and Tzeltalan *chan* (Slocum and Gerdel 1976:131). If the documentable shift of /a/ to /i/ in the word for "death" in the Yucatecan languages postdated the surviving version of the Dresden Codex, then the four dots representing *can*, "four," could have served

as a phonetic complement for T1038a, indicating that it was read as the *can*-allomorph of *cam*, "death." The word is *can* rather than *cam* because the house collocation that follows it was probably read as *tuy-otoch*, "in his house" (Lounsbury 1984a; see fig. 9), and the nasal would have assimilated to the dental consonant at the beginning of that prepositional phrase.

Can was also a word for "gift" or "offering" in Classical Yucatec (Pío Pérez 1866–1877:41). This suggests that the antennae that differentiate T1038b from T1038a have a semantic function, indicating that the former refers to *can*, "gift, offering," instead of the *can*-allomorph of *cam*, "death." Thompson would then be justified in classifying them together as semantic variants of the same phonetic sign.

The offering collocation, which I read as *u-can*, "his offering," also appears at the end of clauses in the almanac at the bottom of pages 65 to 69, along with alternative representations of the words for tortoise, iguana, fish, deer, and wild turkey. The fifth collocation in the second clause on page 67b refers to a tortoise offering as *mac wah* (fig. 10). The *mac* reading is provided by the prefix T626, which represents the carapace of a tortoise and occasionally appears as the main sign in collocations for the month Mac (fig. 7a). *Mac* was the word for tortoise in Classical Yucatec (Pío Pérez 1866–1877:210). The *wah* reading for the Kan sign is signaled by the phonetic complement T130 (*wa*; fig. 7c). *Mac wah u-can* can be translated as "tortoise bread is his offering" in Classical Yucatec.

Another possible example of *mac wah u-can*, in abbreviated form, appears in the third clause on the next

Fig. 10 Page 67b of the Dresden Codex (redrawn by Victoria R. Bricker after Villacorta C. and Villacorta 1930 [1976:144]).

a

mac

b

ma

Fig. 11 Alternative spellings of mac, "tortoise"?
(a) D. 67b; (b) D. 68b
(redrawn by Victoria R.
Bricker after Villacorta C.
and Villacorta 1930 [1976:
144, 146]).

Fig. 12 Page 68b of the Dresden Codex (redrawn by Victoria R. Bricker after Villacorta C. and Villacorta 1930
[1976:146]).

page (figs. 11 and 12). Here the Kan sign is preceded by
T74, Landa's grapheme for ma, and could represent the
first syllable in a phonetic spelling of mac. This would
be an example of the orthographic principle of conso-
nant-deletion, of which there are other examples in the
Mayan script (Bricker 1984; Lounsbury 1984b).

The fifth collocation in the third clause on page 67b
also contains a Kan sign complemented by T130 (wa;
fig. 10). The first prefix is T10, which is usually considered to be a codical variant of the third person pronominal prefix u- (Bricker 1986). In this context, however, it may represent a variant of Landa's grapheme for
ca. I have argued elsewhere (Bricker 1986) that the second prefix, which is the codical allograph of T126,
should be read as ya. Other epigraphers (e.g., Fox and

Justeson 1985b:54–62; Smith-Stark 1981:74) read it as
y or i. Either interpretation for T126, combined with a
ca reading for T10, yields a phonetic spelling of cay, the
word for fish in Classical Yucatec (Pío Pérez 1866–
1877:45; fig. 7f). This reading is supported by the picture below the clause, which shows a fish flanked by two
seashells swimming in water (fig. 10). Cay wah u-can
would have meant "fish bread is his offering" in Classical
Yucatec.

We continue with the fifth collocation in the first
clause on page 68b (fig. 12). Here, again, the Kan sign
is complemented by T130 (wa). The spiral prefix resembles Landa's second grapheme for u (compare fig. 13a
and b). The word for iguana was huh in Classical Yucatec (Pío Pérez 1866–1877:145). According to John
Justeson (1978:88, 298), who has made a comparative
study of forty-eight different writing systems, /h/ belongs
to a class of "glide" or "weak" consonants that are frequently underrepresented in logosyllabic scripts. It is
therefore possible that the prefix in question represented
huh, "iguana," instead of the third person pronominal
prefix u-, in this context. Huh wah u-can would have
meant "iguana bread is his offering" in Classical Yucatec.

We now turn to the fifth collocation in the second
clause on page 65b (fig. 14). A similar collocation appears at the end of the second clause on page 40b of the
Madrid Codex, above the picture of a captured deer (fig.
15). The clause begins with a collocation that represents
the perfective passive inflection of the verb for capture,
chucah, "it was captured." It is followed by a syllabic
spelling of matan, another word for "gift" in Classical
Yucatec (Pío Pérez 1866–1877:216; see Lounsbury
1984a for evidence that T537 was read as na). Matan is
the general term for offering in the Yucatán peninsula
today (cf. Sullivan 1983:88–90). The nature of the
offering is specified by the last collocation in that clause,
which contains signs representing the agentive prefix
ah- and the day named Deer in many Mesoamerican calendars. It would have been read as ah-ceh, "hunter"
(literally, "deerslayer"), in Classical Yucatec (Martínez
Hernández 1929:77) and must refer to the man shown
tying up the deer in the picture below the clause. The
fifth collocation in the second clause on page 65b of the
Dresden Codex contains the same two signs followed by
T130 (wa) and an u-can collocation (fig. 14). Ah-ceh
wah u-can can be translated as "deerslayer bread is his
offering" in Classical Yucatec.

a

u

b

Fig. 13 A phonetic glyph for huh,
"iguana"? (a) Landa's grapheme
for u, (b) D. 68b (a: redrawn by
Victoria R. Bricker from Tozzer
1941:170; b: redrawn by Victoria
R. Bricker after Villacorta C. and
Villacorta 1930 [1976:146]).

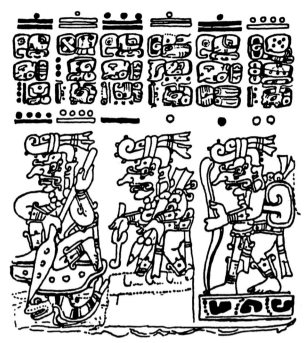

Fig. 14 Page 65b of the Dresden Codex (redrawn by Victoria R. Bricker after Villacorta C. and Villacorta 1930 [1976:140]).

chuc-ah ma

tan
na
ah-ceh

Fig. 15 Page 40b of the Madrid Codex (redrawn by Victoria R. Bricker after Villacorta C. and Villacorta 1930 [1976:304]).

I am now in a position to offer phonetic readings for all of the faunal collocations on pages 29b to 31b of the Dresden Codex. The first almanac on those pages refers to four types of animals in the following order: tortoise, fish, iguana, and wild turkey (fig. 1). I assume that the first offering is a tortoise because the second is clearly a fish, and it is unlikely that the same kind of offering would be mentioned twice in adjacent clauses. The second clause on page 67b implies that the offering was called mac wah, "tortoise bread" (fig. 7c). The second

offering collocation depicts a fish without a Kan glyph (fig. 1). The third clause on page 67b implies that it was called cay, "fish" (fig. 7f). An iguana is shown draped over a Kan sign in the third offering collocation (fig. 1). The first clause on page 68b refers to an iguana offering as huh way, "iguana bread" (fig. 7i). A syllabic spelling of the fourth offering collocation as cutz wah, "wild turkey bread," appears in the second clause on page 30b (fig. 7l).

The second almanac refers to all but one of the same animals in a different order: deer, wild turkey, iguana, and fish (fig. 2). A phonetic spelling of the first offering as ah-ceh wah, "deerslayer bread," appears in the second clause on page 65b (fig. 7o). The syllabic spelling of the second offering as cutz wah, "wild turkey bread," has already been discussed, as has the huh wah, "iguana bread," reading for the third (fig. 7i and l). The fourth offering is referred to as cay ci wah, "fish flesh bread" (fig. 2). The Yucatecan Maya apply the word ci to the main part of a meal, usually meat, reserving wah for breadstuffs. A meatless meal or a sandwich without a filling is said to be without flesh or substance (minaan u ciil). Thus, the expression cay ci wah refers to an offering with fish as its meat or filling. Alternatively, it is possible that the ci suffix had a purely semantic function (Fox and Justeson 1984b:34) and that the collocation in question was read as cay wah, "fish bread."

Figure 16 provides a morpheme-by-morpheme transcription of the hieroglyphic text on pages 29b and 30b. The first clause makes three statements: (1) tzelah lakin, "he sidled east"; (2) cah baac chac, "it's about time for rain!"; (3) mac wah, "tortoise bread." What we have here are brief stage directions for performing a rainmaking ceremony, not a connected text. The other

Fig. 16 Morphemic transcription and translation of the text on pages 29b and 30b of the Dresden Codex (redrawn by Victoria R. Bricker after Villacorta C. and Villacorta 1930 [1976:68, 70]).

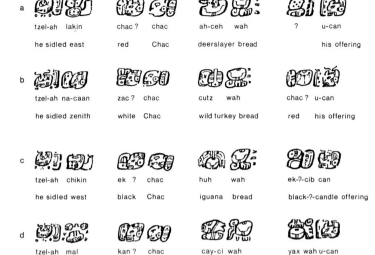

a	tzel-ah	lakin	chac ?	chac	ah-ceh	wah	?	u-can
	he sidled east		red	Chac	deerslayer	bread		his offering

b	tzel-ah	na-caan	zac ?	chac	cutz	wah	chac ?	u-can
	he sidled zenith		white	Chac	wild turkey	bread	red	his offering

c	tzel-ah	chikin	ek ?	chac	huh	wah	ek-?-cib can	
	he sidled west		black	Chac	iguana	bread	black-?-candle offering	

d	tzel-ah	mal	kan ?	chac	cay-ci	wah	yax wah u-can	
	he sidled nadir		yellow	Chac	fish-food	bread	first bread his offering	

Fig. 17 Morphemic transcription and translation of the text on pages 30b and 31b of the Dresden Codex (redrawn by Victoria R. Bricker after Villacorta C. and Villacorta 1930 [1976:70, 72]).

three "clauses" are equally terse, telling the reader only that ceremonies are to be held at 13-day intervals in other parts of town with different offerings.

The ritual almanac that follows, on pages 30b and 31b, contains a more detailed set of instructions for ceremonies performed every 65 days (fig. 2). It must refer to the *tupp kak,* or fire-extinguishing rites, which occurred at the same intervals and on days with the same names (Oc, Men, Ahau, and Chicchan) in colonial times (Tozzer 1941:162–164; Edmonson 1982:180). A transcription of most of the hieroglyphic text appears in figure 17.

The two almanacs refer to a type of offering that is still in use today, not only in rain-making ceremonies, but also in the "milpa-food" (*u-hanli col*) and "town-sacrifice" (*loh cahtal*) rites (Judith P. Dides, personal communication; Redfield and Villa Rojas 1934:136; Villa Rojas 1945:117). The names of the offerings have changed, the wild turkeys have been replaced by domesticated chickens, and the number of species used for this purpose has been reduced from five to two. It is, nevertheless, clear that when the modern Maya place the nead and/or feet of chickens or deer in the dish that they call *x yaach* or *nabal wah,* they are continuing an ancient tradition, for which some instructions are given on pages 29b to 31b of the Dresden Codex.

A Text from the Dresden New Year Pages

BRUCE LOVE
DUMBARTON OAKS

This paper presents an analysis of the hieroglyphic writing on the Dresden Codex, page 26 (fig. 1), the second page of the Dresden New Year pages (fig. 2). First a transliteration of each glyph block is presented, then there is a discussion of each glyph block that summarizes up-to-date knowledge about the constituent glyphs in the blocks. Wherever applicable, ethnographic and ethnohistorical data are brought to bear on specific readings of glyphs.

Transliteration by Glyph Block

In the following analysis, glyphs in each block are first listed according to their Thompson (1962) and Zimmerman (1956) catalog numbers, after which a transliteration is given. Slightly modified transliteration conventions proposed by Fox and Justeson (1984a) are followed:

×   Glyph is illegible.

*   Glyph has been reconstructed based on parallel texts elsewhere.

Capital letters are for logographic usage.

Lowercase spellings are for phonetic usage. "Phonetic" is used in contrast to "logographic" (following Kelley 1962:277 and elsewhere, and Fox and Justeson 1984a:363) in that "phonetic" is used for submorphemic phonetic values while "logographic" is used for glyphs whose readings are whole morphemes.

- Hyphens join signs forming single words.

( ) Parentheses mark parts of morphemes not pronounced; thus, ma-m(a) is read mam.

" Quotation marks indicate interpretations that are not actual transliterations; for example, "God K."

? Question marks attached to the front of a reading means "unsure reading"; a doubled question mark (following Thompson 1962) means "very unsure"; for example, ??WAYEYAB. A question mark in place of a reading means "unknown reading"; for example, U ?-k(a).

: Colons within a reading (this does not refer to catalog numbers) indicate fused glyphs—two glyphs have been conflated to form one glyph; for example, po:m(o) at block C4.

VII, 7 Numbers are readings of Maya bar-and-dot numbers in the glyph blocks (e.g., for block C4, VII is written in the transcription to catalog numbers so as not to be confused with the Arabic catalog numbers, but 7 is written in the transliteration).

Orthographic Conventions

Maya words follow the spellings of the Cordemex Dictionary (Barrera Vásquez 1980) and are in italics. Angle brackets mark words presented in the orthography of the original sources, such as ethnohistorical sources or colonial dictionary entries (e.g., ⟨uah⟩ compared to modern wah). In some cases the original orthography is maintained without the angle brackets, as in quotes or well-known names of gods or idols (e.g., Uac Mitun Ahau) and calendar names (e.g., the day Kan).

Discussion by Glyph Block

Dresden Page 26, Top

A1–B1   Illegible

A2   T109.130:572.47/Z1368.76:1307.74   CHAK ??WAYEYAB RED WAYEYAB. There is a choice between "red" and "great" as translations of CHAK. In this case "red" is the appropriate choice because the glyph here alternates with a known color glyph in the same position on page 28 (fig. 2). On page 28 the glyph is EK', "black." Although the parallel positions on pages 25 and 27 are illegible, it is likely that four different colors appear on the four pages. Thompson (1972:92) and Kelley (1976:252) reconstructed "yellow" on page D27 and Kelley went one further and reconstructed "white" on page D25.

T130 is now secure as phonetic wa, leading to an expected reading for the main sign that begins with wa- and has color associations in the context of New Year

Transliteration

Gly blk	Catalog # (T = Thompson, Z = Zimmerman)	Transliteration
Dresden 26, Top (fig. 3)		
A1	×	×
B1	×	×
A2	T109.130:572.47 Z1368.76:1307.74	CHAK (wa)-??WAYEYAB-?
B2	T1.74:557 Z1.75:1361	U ma-m(a)
A3	T112.548:24 Z31.1340:80	TOK' HAB-IL
B3	T524.58/60:548 Z1334.21:1340	BALAM ? HAB
A4	T544:548:142.528 Z1341:1340:?.1339	K'IN-TUN-(-n)-HAB
B4	T1.528:87:601 Z1.528:82:1363	U ku-(ch-)-ch(u)
C1	×	×
D1	×	×
C2	×	×
D2	×	×
C3	T277.523:102 Z29.1331:61	(wi)-WINIK-(ki)
D3	T1.×:25 Z1.×:81	U ?-ka
C4	VII.T687b VII.Z1316	7 po:m(o)
D4	XVI.T93:682b XVI.Z85:147	16 ch'a-h(a) TE
D26, Middle Row		
E	T168:573.130 Z42:1319.76	? AHAW-(wa)
F	T168:544.130 Z42:1341.76	K'IN AHAW-(wa)
G	T166.1006 Z27.126	?ITS'-"GOD E"
H	III.T567:130 III.Z1330:76	OX OCH WAH
I	T172.109:800 Z4.20:710	AH CHAK BOLAY
J	T162:506.558 Z55:1324.1360	? WAH ?IXIM
D26, Bottom Row		
K	T68:592.181 Z?21:1305.60	?-?-AH
L	T16.1009:87 Z24/1344.146:82	NOH ?-TE/CHE
M	T74:136.16.136 Z75:65.24/1344.65	MAH/NOH-? NOH-?
N	T16:506.548:24 Z24/1344:55.1340:80	NOH WAH HAB-IL
O	T1020.1006 Z742.126	"GOD K" "GOD E"

in the monuments included in Thompson's (1962:158) catalog. This infrequency makes it impossible to analyze the glyph based on substitution patterns. The suffix T47 occurs frequently in the codices but needs further study in those contexts.

B2 T1.74:557/Z1.75:1361 U MAM ITS/HIS MAM. On D27 and 28 the compound is T1.74:74, U ma-m(a). Here, at B2 on page 26, T557 substitutes for T74. The substitution of T557 for T74 *ma* in this compound lends support for the generally accepted interpretation of T557 as phonetic *ma*.

The reading U MAM has been given by others, notably Knorozov (1967:49) and Kelley (1976:177). Kelley argued that the Mams refer to the opossum actors in the top scenes on these pages. In turn, I think a good case can be made for the identification of Mam with the Wayeyab idols described in Landa. By comparing three ethnohistorical accounts of the Wayeb rites—Landa (Tozzer 1941:139–148), Cogolludo (1867–68[1954: I,353]), and Pío Pérez (Stephens 1843[1963:I,281])—it can be seen that the principal idol in one, Landa's, was the Wayeyab idol, while the main idol in the other two accounts was Mam. In Landa, the Bolon Dzacab, Kinich Ahau, Itzamna, and Uac Mitun Ahau idols were important, but these gods changed every year and were worshiped only every fourth year. The Wayeyab idols were venerated every year. In another place in Landa (Tozzer 1941:166), the celebration of the five days preceding the New Year was referred to as "the festival of the idol U Uayeyab." Thus, it is clear that the Wayeyab idols were the principal idols of these yearly rites.

In Cogolludo the chief idol of the Wayeyab celebrations was a wooden figure "dressed like those figures of boys made of straw that are used in bull fights . . ." (1867–68[1954:I, 353], translation by Tozzer 1941:139). The idol was called Mam.

In a document passed on to John Lloyd Stephens by Pío Pérez, there was a description of a Wayeb festival that contained the following line: "these five days were assigned for the celebration of the feast of the god Mam" (Stephens 1843[1963:I, 281], translation by Tozzer 1941:139).

If Mam is the outstanding idol in two accounts and Wayeyab is the main idol in another account, then Mam and Wayeyab might be cognate idols, or at least closely associated. This argues against Mam being identified with the opossum actors and supports the readings at A2–B2 on Dresden pages 26–28 as CHAK/K'AN/EK' WAYEYAB U MAM, "red/yellow/black Wayeyab is the Mam." Some additional support that Mam is the idol rather the performer in these scenes comes from the Morán (1695[1935]) Choltí dictionary gloss for "idol," which is Mam.

A3 T112.548:24/Z31.1340:80 TOK' HABIL FLINT BLADE YEAR. T112 may be read logographically as TOK', "flint," as proven by phonetic substitutions

Fig. 1 Dresden page 26 (from Villacorta and Villacorta 1930).

ceremonies. Such a word is ⟨uayeyab⟩, given by Landa (1959) as the names of the idols or statues that were the principal idols of these ceremonies. Fox (personal communication, 1985) suggested that WAYEYAB be read here based on the phonetic *wa-* prefix and the appropriateness of the reading in the context of New Year rituals.

The spotted main sign, T572, which appears in this position and on page 28, appears nowhere else in the Maya codices (Zimmerman 1956:82) and only two times

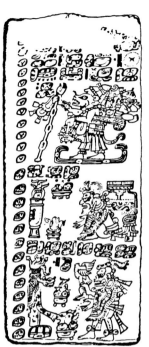

Fig. 2   Dresden New Year pages, 25–28 (from Villacorta and Villacorta 1930).

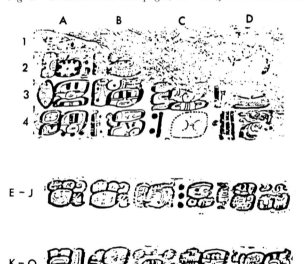

Fig. 3   The text from Dresden page 26 (after Thompson 1972).

pointed out by Houston (1983) in "flint-shield" compounds. This is an appropriate augury for "jaguar years" (see next compound) that are filled with warfare and bloodshed.

B3 T524.58/60:548/Z1334.21:1340 BALAM HAB JAGUAR YEAR.   T524, as the day sign *Ix (Hix)*, is generally accepted as a reference to "jaguar" (Thompson 1971:82, 89; Kelley 1976:109), but here I am proposing that it be read specifically BALAM. T58, SAK,

"white," before the HAB sign is enigmatic. The reading for the compound without the SAK sign, BALAM HAB, is supported by the frequent occurrence (pointed out by Thompson 1971:297) of ⟨balam haab(il)⟩ as an augury or prognostication in the books of Chilam Balam (1971:300–301), translated by Thompson "jaguar year" or "jaguar rain."

A4 T544:548:142.528/Z1341:1340:?.1339 K'INTUN HAB DRY YEAR.   This is another variant of the ⟨kintunyaabil⟩, "drought" augury. The suffix under the TUN sign is different than the other cases (cf. D25 O, D27 M). Recently, Grube (1986) proposed word-final *-m* or *-n* as a reading for this often-overlooked glyph. The readings for the glyphs in this well-known compound (proposed by Thompson 1971:269–271) are discussed in detail by Fox and Justeson (1984b:52–53).

B4 T1.528:87:601/Z1.528:82:1363 U KUCH ITS/ HIS BURDEN.   This reading is generally accepted, meaning "its load, cargo, or burden." This compound appears on all four pages of the New Year pages. On pages 26–28 the T87 glyph is present; on page 25 it is absent, which argues for T87 being optional in this context. Lounsbury (1973:119) suggested that the presence of T87 could distinguish between a *cho* and a *chu* reading for T601. The way I have transliterated this compound uses T87 as a phonetic complement *ch(e)* prefixed to T601 *chu*.

C1–D2   Illegible

C3 T277.523:102/Z29.1331:61 WINIK Unknown translation.   *Winik*, usually glossed "20-day period, person," is based on Fox and Justeson's (1984b:29–47) reading of T102 as phonetic *ki* and T277 as phonetic *wi* (Justeson 1984a:334).

D3 T1.×:25/Z1.×:81.   The main sign is illegible, but based on the suffix T25 *ka,* it ends with *-ak,* or, more cautiously, *-Vk.*

C4 VII.T687b/VII.Z1316 UUK POM SEVEN POM. This lacks the *il* suffix found in position C3 on page 25. The *pom* reading was worked out by Lounsbury (1973). The *-il* reading was first advanced by Thompson (1971:269–271). *Pomil* is a variant of *pom* "copal incense" (Barrera Vásquez 1980:665).

D4   XVI.T93:682b/XVI.Z85:147)   WAKLAHUN CH'AH SIXTEEN DROPLETS.   On pages 27 and 28 this same compound, with different number coefficients, takes a T87 suffix and is read *CH'AH TE.* The absence of T87 here indicates that it is optional. There is an offering in Landa that has specified numbers associated with it and ends in *-te.* This is ⟨chahalte⟩, the incense described as follows: "And when they come (*sic*) there the priest incensed it [the idol] with forty-nine grains of maize ground up with their incense, and they distributed it in the brazier of the idol and perfumed him. They call the ground maize alone *sacah* and that of the lords *chahalte*" (Tozzer 1941:140–141).

Later, in the same ceremony but for a different year, Landa reported: "On arriving there, the priest perfumed it with fifty-three grains of ground maize and with their incense, which they call *sacah.* The priest also gave to the nobles more incense of the kind we call *chahalte,* to put in the brazier . . ." (Tozzer 1941:144).

The generally accepted phonetic value *ha* for the main sign (T682b) can serve as a phonetic complement to T93 if T93 is logographic CH'AH, transliterated **CH'AH-(ha),** or it can serve as phonetic *-h(a)* to complete a CVC morpheme if T93 is phonetic *ch'a,* producing the transliteration **ch'a-h(a).** Either way, the reading *ch'ah* for the compound results.

Ch'ah is glossed as a droplet of liquid in the Motul and other dictionaries (Barrera Vásquez 1980:121), but, in addition, in the Vienna dictionary (1972:113r), it means drops of tree resin. *Ch'ah te,* or as Landa called it ⟨chahalte⟩, is a good reading for incense offerings of tree resin, which in this text are paired with *pom* offerings, another incense made from tree resin.

D26, Middle Row

E T168:573.130/Z42:1319.76 ?AHAW ?LORD. T168 has been read as AHAW ever since Lounsbury's (1973) "ben-ich" article appeared. A complete discussion of the T168 AHAW prefix and its commonly suffixed phonetic complement T130 *wa* is given by Mathews and Justeson (1984:203–205). I am proposing the reading order here Main Sign Ahaw, rather than Ahaw Main Sign, in accordance with Mathews and Justeson's (1984:213–215)

reading order for "numbered Katun Ahaw." This reading order also works for compound F on Dresden 26 (see below) where the K'IN AHAW reading is supported by the ethnohistorically known ⟨Kinich Ahau⟩.

Here in the Dresden New Year pages, however, T168 AHAW is suffixed by T130 *wa* only one time in four parallel occurrences at glyph block E. The T130 *wa* suffix appears in the first compound of the middle row on page 26 only. In the first compound of the middle row on pages 25 and 27, T116 *ne* is the suffix. In the same location on page 28 there is no suffix. The most likely explanation for the affix substitution (suggested by Peter Mathews, personal communication, 1985) is that when T130 *wa* is present it serves as a phonetic complement to T168 AHAW, but when T116 *ne* is present, it works as a phonetic complement for the main sign, T573. This, of course, could be tested if the linguistic value of the main sign was known. This compound, with AHAW above and *ni/ne* following, also occurs on pages 68b and 72b of the Madrid Codex and page 24 of the Paris Codex.

Riese (1984a) did a thorough review of the occurrences of T573 (generally referred to as the "hel" glyph) and found support for its semantic interpretation (following Thompson) within the general range of "change, termination, time" (1984:284), but it remains without an accepted phonetic reading at this time.

F T168:544.130/Z42:1341.76 K'IN AHAW SUN LORD.   The AHAW reading is secure for T168.130 and the K'IN reading is secure for the main sign T573. The ethnohistorical material suggests that it might be read K'INICH AHAW because ⟨Kinich Ahau⟩ is given by Landa as the idol in the principal's house in one of the New Year ceremonies (Tozzer 1941:144).

G T166.1006/Z27.126 ?ITS "GODE" Unknown translation.   The prefix to God E here is undeciphered but *its,* suggested by Riese (Justeson 1984a:328), seems reasonable. The same sign is found as the top part of T159, the prefix in Itsamna's name compound (see page 27, F). Barrera Vásquez (1980:271) wrote:

El morfema *its* de *itsa'* forma parte de una familia de variantes existentes en las lenguas mayences; en cakchiquel aparece sin o con modificación. *its*: hechicería, brujería, encantamiento; *ah-its*: hechicero; en el maya yucateco aparece en la variante *its'*.

(The morpheme *its* from *itsa'* forms part of a family of variants extant in the Mayan languages; in Cakchiquel it appears without or with modification. *its*: sorcery, witchcraft, enchantment; *ah-its*: sorcerer; in Yucatec Maya it appears as the variant *its'*.)

There are some ten deity names beginning with *Its'* listed in the Cordemex dictionary.

The main sign is Schellhas's God E, the "Maize God," which does not have a reading at this time (Taube 1985).

H III.T567:130/III.Z1330:76 OX OCH WAH ABUN-

DANCE (OF) PROVISIONS. This compound was recently read by Fox (Morley et al. 1983:540) and Fox and Justeson (1984b:67) as OX OK WAH. T567 is the sign for the day Ok, given by Landa, and T130 is secure as phonetic *wa*, in this case serving as logographic WAH. The support for this reading is an augury in the Chilam Balam of Tizimin, ⟨y oc noh wah⟩ "germinate the big food," and an entry in the Motul dictionary, ⟨oc vah⟩, "wedding party." *Ox* was interpreted as "abundance" by Luis Romero Fuentes and William Brito Sansores in a discussion of the etymology of Oxcutzcab presented in the Cordemex dictionary (p. 612). Thompson (1971: 129) said *ox* has an "intensificatory value" that adds emphasis to a phrase. The whole phrase then, in Fox and Justeson's view, means something like "big feast."

While this reading is reasonable, there is another reading that also works here—it is OX OCH WAH, "abundance (of) provisions." The San Francisco dictionary (Michelson 1976:271) has the following entry: "Och uah; och; och hanal; och haa: mantenimiento, sustento, comida."

The Motul dictionary (Martínez-Hernández 1929: 709–710) has the following entries:

Och: sustento o comida, mantenimiento o provisión de comida.
Och hanal: provisión de comida, mantenimiento, y sustento que uno tiene para si y para su casa.
Och ixim: provisión o sustento de maíz que uno tiene para si y para su casa o viage.
Och keyem/koyem: mantenimiento y provisión de masa de maíz para el camino o viage.

There is support in the ethnohistorical sources for the appropriateness of the reading OCH WAH. There are accounts of ritual sacrifices in sixteenth-century Yucatán in the Diego Quijada papers (Scholes and Adams 1938) that include the prayers offered by the Ah K'inob. The prayers are not given in their Maya form; the gist of the prayers is given in Spanish. The two most important things prayed for by the priests were rain and food. One priest's testimony said that sacrifices were made so that the gods would provide *bastimentos* (vol. 1, p. 89). *Bastimentos*, "supply (of provisions)" (Collins 1974:71), is identical to the Motul dictionary glosses for *och hanal* and *och ixim*, "supply of food" and "supply of maize"; and it is very close to the San Francisco dictionary gloss for *och wah*, "food in general."

The OCH reading for T567 also depends upon accepting an OCH/OK polyvalence. This polyvalence has been demonstrated by Schele (1984c:300–305) in heir-designation phrases at Palenque where *och* means "enter (into office)" and by Justeson et al. (1985:61) in a case where T567 takes a *chi* phonetic complement, resulting in a reading *och*, on Tortuguero Monument 6.

Summarizing then, Fox and Justeson's reading of OX OK WAH is reasonable and appropriate, but OX OCH WAH also works well.

I T172.109:800/Z4.20:710 ?AH CHAK ?BOLAY HE (THE) FIERCE JAGUAR. T172 is a frequent prefix to apparent deity names (Justeson 1984a:328) that could possibly be read AH. T109 is either CHAK, "great," or CHAK, "red." Thompson (1972: see hieroglyphic glossary under T800, p. 153) reads the compound T109.800 as "chac bolay." AH CHAK BOLAY is a reasonable reading, given the occurrence of ⟨chac bolay⟩ in the Motul dictionary (Martínez-Hernández 1929:292) as *tigre bermejo y bravo* (reddish, fierce jaguar). There are priests of this name in the Tizimin (Edmonson 1982: lines 267, 1812, 3022), spelled ⟨Chac Bol Ai⟩, one of whom, Edmonson pointed out (note to line 1812), is always involved in war.

J T162:506.558/Z55:1324.1360 ? WAH ?IXIM ? BREAD (OF) MAIZE. This group has often been referred to as an augury; Thompson (1972:91–93) read it

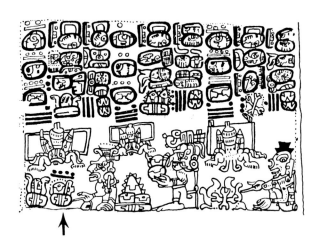

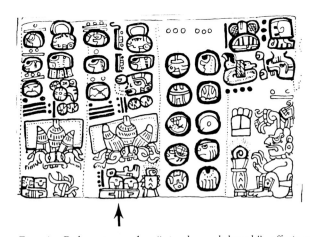

Fig. 4 Bolon tas wah, *"nine-layered bread,"* offerings from Madrid 103b and 106c.

"abundance of maize." Zimmerman (1956: table 8) listed it with other compounds he called attributive glyphs. The T506.558 compound could possibly be read WAH IXIM, "bread of maize." The WAH reading is secure, but IXIM is speculative.

The arguments for the WAH reading for T506 are presented in detail elsewhere (Love, in press; Taube 1989). The arguments in Love, briefly, are (a) the reading *bolon tas wah* for the offerings on Madrid 103b and 106b (fig. 4) is strongly supported by ethnographic and ethnohistorical data; (b) T506 is frequently (24%) affixed with phonetic *wa* (T130) in the codices (e.g., fig. 6); (c) Mathews and Justeson (1984:205; Justeson 1984a:338) read T506 as logographic WAH when suffixed *or* prefixed with T130, *wa;* (d) T130 directly substitutes for T506 in compounds at Chichén Itzá (fig. 5; Beyer 1937:53, figs. 86–91, pointed out to me by David Stuart); and (e) phonetic spellings of WAH, using both T130, *wa*, and T181, *ha*, are found on Dresden 13b– 14b (fig. 6) and Madrid 65ab–72ab (fig. 7).

The IXIM reading for T558 was proposed by Cyrus Thomas (1882:156) over a century ago based on its phonetic similarity to the day name Imix and its juxtaposition with T506 (in the same compounds discussed here). In the ceremonies to avert calamities in the coming new years described by Landa (Tozzer 1941:145), there is mention of ceramic dogs with bread on their backs, *pan en las espaldas* (Landa 1959:66 for the Spanish version). A pictorial representation of this on Madrid page 35 (fig. 8) has T506 and T558 together on a dog's back, suggesting that the whole compound might be "bread" of some

sort. In the Solís Alcalá dictionary (1949:553) *tortilla de maíz, pan de maíz* is given as ⟨U uah ixim⟩.

In order for WAH IXIM to make sense in the New Year pages, however, it needs to be more than just a lexical item like maize bread; it needs to be an augury or attribute. Such an example (although with the order reversed) is ⟨yxim [l] uah⟩, found in the Chilam Balam of Kaua (Barrera Vásquez 1943[1976:14], pointed out by Thompson 1971:71) as an *atributo prognóstico* for the day Imix.

No other students have accepted the IXIM reading to date and the arguments for it are not conclusive—hence the question mark in the transliteration—but, given the arguments just presented, the reading is a reasonable suggestion.

D26, Bottom Row

K T68:592.181/Z?21:1305.60 There are no known readings for the prefix and main sign at this time. The suffix is generally accepted as logographic AH and phonetic *a* or *ha.* T68:592, without the T181 suffix, but with T1 U, initiates three texts with bee ceremonies on Madrid 112c.

L T16.1009:87/Z24/1344.146:82 NOH ? TE/CHE GREAT ??. In the second glyph block of the bottom row on each of the four New Year pages in Dresden (fig. 2), the same main sign and suffix, T1009 and T87, occur. On pages 26–28, these glyphs are prefixed by T16, commonly read as YAX. On page 25 the prefix is T109 CHAK. This substitution pattern suggests that the two

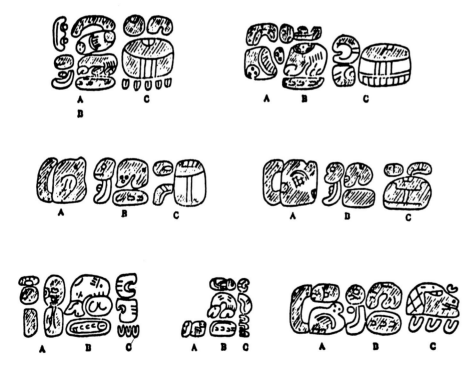

Fig. 5 Substitutions of T130 for T506 (at compound marked "C") at Chichén Itzá (from Beyer 1937: figs. 86–91).

Fig. 6 Dresden 13b–14b. Substitutions of wa- and -h(a) phonetic complements on T506 WAH (from Villacorta and Villacorta 1930).

Fig. 8 Madrid 35, bread on the back of a dog (from Villacorta and Villacorta 1930).

Fig. 7 Madrid 72ab, showing a possible spelling of NOH wa-h(a) at the sixth position of each t'ol (from Villacorta and Villacorta 1930).

prefixes are within the same semantic range. Glyphs that substitute for each other in otherwise parallel texts can indicate phonetic substitutions, morphemes within the same semantic range, or a change in grammatical structure. There is no suggestion anywhere that either T16, YAX, or T109, CHAK, is used phonetically or as a grammatical affix. This leaves semantic interpretations.

The most obvious interpretation is that they both fall into the semantic range "color." Glyphs for various colors have long been known, including *chak,* "red," *k'an,* "yellow," *ek',* "black," *sak,* "white," and *yax,* "blue/green" (see Kelley 1976:53–59 for a review of color glyphs). The two alternating prefixes in the second glyph blocks of the bottom rows are both "color glyphs," T109 CHAK, "red," and T16 YAX, "blue-green." The fact that both glyphs are known as colors, coupled with the ethnohistorical data indicating that certain colors associated with particular directions played an important role in Maya ritual, has led students of these pages to assume the glyph blocks deal with colors.

The problem, of course, is that in all the ethnohistorical accounts the colors change with each year and each direction; so it is very difficult to explain why there is blue/green on three pages and red on one page. This problem can be solved by putting the two prefixes in a different semantic range—instead of "color," they can both mean "great," *noh* in Yucatec.

That T109, CHAK, can mean "great" is simple to argue because *chak*, "great," and *chak*, "red," are homonyms in Yucatec. It means "great," for example, in the compound for Venus (T109.510b), CHAK EK', "great star," also known as *noh ek'*, "great star."

Yax can also mean "great," but only indirectly. Its primary meaning, in composition with nouns, is "first thing" or "first time" (Barrera Vásquez 1980:971). *Yax* can mean "great" in the sense that "first" can also mean most important or foremost; for example, *yax mehen*, *hijo primero*, *primogénito*, "first son, first-born" (Barrera Vásquez 1980:971) is cognate to *noh mehen*, *hijo primogénito*, "first-born" (Barrera Vásquez 1980:574). Generally speaking, though, *yax* and *noh* would not be considered synonyms. In the second part of the Cordemex dictionary, where the Yucatec entries are listed under their Spanish glosses, *noh* and *chak* are both given below Spanish *gran* and *grande*, but *yax* is not found there.

There is a strong suggestion that T16 YAX is read NOH in the compound for the direction "south" (glyph block M, below) which in Yucatec is *nohol*. As far as I know the only published phonetic transliteration of the "south" compound is Fox and Justeson's (1984b:45). They suggested "*noh* 'great' + -*ol*." Lounsbury (personal communication, 1986) also reads T16 as NOH in the "south" compound. So here is at least one case in which T16 is very probably read NOH.

There is another context in which T16 substitutes with T109 CHAK and reads better as NOH than as YAX. In the middle scene and the bottom scene on Dresden page 26 (fig. 2), there are pictures of vessels—one with a double Kan sign, and one with a single Kan sign. Above the Kan signs are *T109*, CHAK, in one case and T16 in the other. The Kan signs can now be read as WAH, "bread/tamale" (see compound J, above) giving the reading NOH WAH, which accords very well with ethnographic accounts of ceremonial breads in which *noh wah* is sometimes given as the name of the principal bread offering. In the Becanchen Wahil Kol ceremony (Love 1984b), for example, one special bread of thirteen layers was made for god. It was referred to as *noh wah*. In a rather complete review of ceremonial breads (Love, in press) it was found that *noh wah* was often cited as a principal offering, but there was no mention of breads called *yax wah* (although there is a ceremonial bread called *yaxche' wah*, "ceiba tree bread" in Redfield and Villa Rojas 1934:129).

A reading NOH WAH instead of YAX WAH also makes more sense on Dresden page 27, C3 (fig. 2). Here the context may be offerings, or it could be auguries or prognostications. In either case, NOH WAH fits well. NOH WAH fits in the sense of offering, as just de-

scribed, and it also happens to be an augury in the Chilam Balam of Tizimin (pointed out to me by Justeson) and in the Pérez manuscript (summarized by Thompson 1971: 300–301).

Finally, the reading NOH for T16 works perfectly on Madrid 65–72 (fig. 8), where T16 as a main sign accompanies a phonetic spelling of **wa-h(a),** the whole compound reading NOH WAH in an unconventional but not unprecedented reading order, T130:16.130, **NOH wa-h(a).**

There is no secure reading for T1009, the "God D" head main sign, at this time. The T87 suffix may be semantic "tree or wood product," logographic TE/CHE, or phonetic *te/che*.

M   T74:136.16.136/Z75:65.24/1344.65   NOHOL SOUTH.   A discussion of this glyph is included in the argument for reading T16 as NOH, "great," in N, above. The compound does not transliterate well, given the small U-shaped elements. The whole compound may be a fossilized convention with the reading *nohol*. T74, Landa's MA in ⟨ma i n ka ti⟩, is apparently derived from Mixe-Zoquean *mah*, "big" (Justeson et al. 1985:44, 66) from which the Maya borrowed the phonetic *ma* value for the sign but may also have borrowed the "great" value and read the sign NOH (Lounsbury 1984a:181). In the "south" compound, T74, MAH or NOH, may be semantically reinforcing a NOH reading for T16, the "yax" sign.

N   T16:506.548:Z24/1344.55.1340:80   NOH WAH HABIL   GREAT BREAD YEAR.   The arguments for the reading NOH WAH are given above. This is apparently an augury for the year.

O   T1020.1006/Z742.129   "GOD K" "GOD E"   Unknown translation.   The name glyphs for these two gods appear side-by-side in the glyph block. Readings for these are not known, although Bolon Dzacab has been mentioned as a possibility for God K (Zimmerman's God 8). As Kelley pointed out (1976:65), the glyph does not have *bolon*, "nine," prefixed here in the codex but it does have it at Chichén Itzá, Copán, and Palenque.

Conclusion

This paper has presented several new readings for Maya epigraphers to scrutinize. The three most secure readings, in my opinion, are WAH for T506 (also arrived at independently by others), NOH for T16 (suggested by others for the *nohol*, "south," compound, but here shown to work in other contexts as well), and CH'AH or *ch'a* for T93. Other more tentative readings are found throughout the analysis above. They include CHAK WAYEYAB at A2 (suggested by Fox), TOK' HABIL, BALAM (SAK?) HAB, and NOH WAH HABIL at N; OX OCH WAH at H; and WAH IXIM at J. Another contribution of this paper has been the discussion of the Mams (spelled phonetically at B2), showing, I think, that the Mams are not the opossum actors but, based on ethnohistorical accounts, are idols.

Acknowledgments

Part of this work was performed while a Junior Fellow at Dumbarton Oaks. I thank all the Maya epigraphers who have discussed these various ideas with me over the last year or so. I especially want to thank Jim Fox and John Justeson, who critically read this paper for me when it was still part of my dissertation. Of course, I am responsible for the content, and I know Fox, for one, disagrees with me on more than one reading, but I am very grateful for his time and work in reviewing this with me.

Codex Dresden: Late Postclassic Ceramic Depictions and the Problems of Provenience and Date of Painting

MERIDETH PAXTON
UNIVERSITY OF NEW MEXICO

Codex Dresden is one of only four surviving legible Maya manuscripts commonly accepted as pre-Conquest.[1] Painted on lime-coated bark paper, the screenfold document is one of the most comprehensive extant accounts of the religious ritual and astronomical knowledge of these people. Unfortunately, no colonial records pertaining to the provenience and date of this important ethnohistorical source are known prior to its 1739 acquisition in Vienna for the Dresden Royal Library (Förstemann 1880:1–2). This study is part of a more general investigation of the Codex Dresden illustrations and hieroglyphic text, conducted for the purpose of determining the pre-Hispanic cultural context of the manuscript.

The origin of the codex has thus far not been established through chemical testing. The date of the bark paper has not been determined by the carbon-14 process; identification of the tree from which it was made is not helpful because the distribution is common throughout Yucatán (Standley 1917:20; von Hagen 1977:67). Therefore, theories on the provenience and date of the codex must be based on inferences made from its contents and on comparisons with other pre-Conquest Maya paintings, sculpture, and ceramics.

The generally accepted view concerning the origins of Codex Dresden is that of J. Eric S. Thompson.[2] In the most comprehensive study of the manuscript published to date, Thompson (1972:16) suggested that the codex was probably painted in the vicinity of Chichén Itzá around A.D. 1200–1250, or toward the end of the Postclassic occupation of the site. This theory was based on hieroglyphic similarities with the Chichén Itzá texts,[3] as well as correlation of some of the pottery depictions with excavated ceramics.

The Thompson commentary did not include detailed study of the Codex Dresden ceramics. Rather, the incensarios painted on pages 25b, 26b, 27b, and 28b of the manuscript were generally associated with the early part of the Hocabá period (A.D. 1200–1300; R. E. Smith 1971: part 2, p. 173) and cited (Thompson 1972:15, 90) as evidence supporting the proposed A.D. 1200–1250 date of painting. Because Thompson believed that Late Postclassic Maya culture was incapable of producing such a high-quality manuscript, and Hocabá ceramics were regarded as transitional between the successive florescences of Chichén Itzá and Mayapán, he associated this work with the end of the primary (A.D. 1000–1200) occupation of Chichén Itzá (Thompson 1972:15–16). However, it is possible that religious conservatism resulted in the inclusion of antiquated ritual objects in the manuscript illustrations. Moreover, Thompson did not consider certain iconographic motifs in Codex Dresden that are otherwise known only from the Late Postclassic. The codex motifs also occurring on Chen Mul Modeled figure effigy incensarios of the Mayapán Tases period (traditionally dated between A.D. 1300 and 1450; R. E. Smith 1971: part 2, p. 173) could be interpreted as evidence of a post-Hocabá painting date. To understand better whether the painting of Codex Dresden is more closely related to the Postclassic occupation of Chichén Itzá or the Late Postclassic occupation of Mayapán, more extensive analysis of the codex pottery is needed. It is appropriate to identify specific examples of excavated ceramics corresponding to the Dresden illustrations and study their archaeological contexts.

The Problem of Naturalistic Representation

In relating the Codex Dresden incensarios to ceramics from the archaeological sites, the first consideration must be the degree of accuracy that can reasonably be expected. Comparison of the securely identified Dresden plant forms with their living counterparts has shown (Paxton 1986:596–600) that artistic convention was far more important than precise reproduction of characteristic shapes. Certain illustrated elements were evidently based on the characteristic forms, but the overall designs were the result of imaginative interpretation. So, although it may still be possible to relate the Codex Dresden pottery to existing ceramic types, it is unlikely that the correspondence will be exact in every detail. Further study of the Dresden pottery in relation to iconographic depictions is also important (see below).

Cehac-Hunacti Composite-Type Censers from Mayapán

In comparing the Codex Dresden illustrations with ceramics reported in the archaeological literature, I have not identified pottery in the manuscript that can be directly related to excavated types exclusively postdating the Hocabá period. The latest ceramic forms illustrated in Codex Dresden are apparently the incensarios cited by Thompson to support his date for the painting of the manuscript.

The reconstructed vessel that most closely resembles the Codex Dresden censers used in the Thompson dating argument is a Cehac-Hunacti Composite-Type urn from lot C-90 at Mayapán that parallels the spiked form on page 26b, left (fig. 1a, b). Like the Dresden incen-

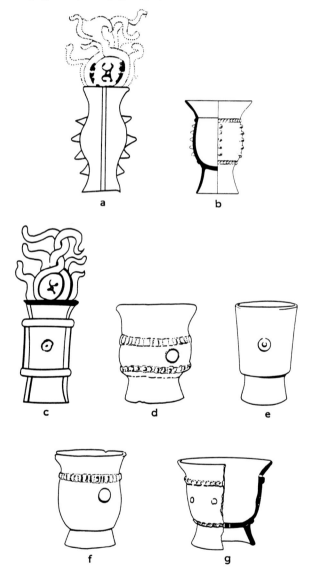

a   b

c   d   e

f   g

sario, the Mayapán censer has a pedestal base, globular body, and flaring neck, as well as widely spaced rows of appliqué spikes. This Mayapán form seems to be the only one that significantly resembles the Dresden page 26b incensario. The Mayapán urn was excavated from one of the few deeply stratified deposits at the site, a deposit that apparently represents most of its occupational history (Shook and Irving 1955:145, 152). The C-90 level was the first in which figure effigy incensarios occurred and hence is transitional between the Hocabá and Tases periods. According to the R. E. Smith (1971: part 1, p. 255, part 2, p. 173) chronology, the date of the transition is c. A.D. 1300.

Two other Cehac-Hunacti Composite-Type censers from the C-90 lot at Mayapán can be related to the Codex Dresden illustrations. These urns have pedestal bases, flaring necks, and sparse appliqué disk decoration like the Dresden forms seen on pages 25b, 25c, and 28b (fig. 1c, d; R. E. Smith 1971: part 2, fig. 62c). One notable difference is the shape of the middle sections of the incensarios: the Dresden drawings show cylindrical forms, whereas the bodies of the Cehac-Hunacti censers are characteristically globular (R. E. Smith 1971: part 1, p. 74). The only pedestal base urn having similar appliqué disk decoration and a cylindrical body is apparently that found with Chen Mul Modeled-style figure effigy fragments in a late deposit at Chichén Itzá (fig. 1e).[4] The dissimilarity in this instance is the lack of a flaring neck. On the whole, the Mayapán Hocabá-Tases level button appliqué censers discussed above, along with similar late examples from Chichén Itzá, present the greatest resem-

Fig. 1 Comparison of Codex Dresden Censers with Excavated Urns from Mayapán and Chichén Itzá.

(a) Codex Dresden, page 26b (redrawn by Meredith Taylor from the 1972 Thompson facsimile).

(b) Mayapán, Mayapán Unslipped Ware, Cehac-Hunacti Composite-Type censer, Middle lot C-90 (redrawn by Meredith Taylor from R. E. Smith 1971: part 2, fig. 31b; see also R. E. Smith 1971:48 and Miller 1982: fig. 96).

(c) Codex Dresden, page 25b (redrawn by Meredith Taylor from the 1972 Thompson facsimile).

(d) Mayapán, Mayapán Unslipped Ware, Cehac-Hunacti Composite-Type censer from Middle lot C-90 (redrawn by Meredith Taylor from R. E. Smith 1971: part 2, fig. 62a; see also p. 94).

(e) Chichén Itzá (redrawn by Meredith Taylor from E. H. Thompson 1938: fig. 13b).

(f) Mayapán, Mayapán Unslipped Ware, Cehac-Hunacti Composite-Type censer from Middle lot A-530 (redrawn by Meredith Taylor from R. E. Smith 1971: part 2, fig. 62b; see also p. 94).

(g) Chichén Itzá, unslipped censer found at the Caracol. Attributed by Brainerd (1958:312) to the Middle Mexican or Late Mexican stages, which correspond with R. E. Smith's (1971: part 2, p. 173) Hocabá and Tases periods (redrawn by Meredith Taylor from Brainerd 1958: fig. 97c).

blance to the Codex Dresden disk-decorated urns. The lack of agreement in the body shapes may well be explicable in terms of the same artistic license observable in the depictions of the Dresden plants.

Yet another Dresden-like Mayapán Cehac-Hunacti incensario with disk decoration, whose chronological position is not so well fixed, is that recovered near the shrine of elite residential structure Q-244b (fig. 1f). The ceramic lot to which the Q-244b censer belongs was designated by R. E. Smith (1971: part 1, p. 10; part 2, p. 94) as middle, a term he used in referring to the residue of the ceramic material that was not definitely early or late. In considering the general Mayapán collection of 1,301 sherds from pedestal base Cehac-Hunacti censers with spike or disk appliqué decoration, it can be seen that 52 percent (671 sherds) are assigned to this middle Hocabá-Tases category. Only 8 percent (109 sherds) of the collection was clearly Hocabá, and 40 percent (521 sherds) was unequivocally Tases (calculated from R. E. Smith 1971: part 2, table 37). Hence, it is easily possible that a Cehac-Hunacti Composite censer like the Q-244b example could date from the latest period of the Mayapán occupancy. In fact, the typical shapes cited by R. E. Smith (1971: part 1, p. 213, figs. 31a–c, 62a–c) to illustrate his discussion of the Tases Cehac-Hunacti censers include the same vessels compared above with Codex Dresden. So it is evident that a Hocabá period *terminus ante quem* for the painting of the codex is not implied by the page 25–28 incensario illustrations. Even without considering the possible presence of archaic motifs associated with religious conservatism, a Tases period painting date is feasible.

It would naturally be of great interest to compare the Dresden versions of the Cehac-Hunacti censers with representations in the painting and sculpture of Mayapán. It is indeed unfortunate that so few examples of these arts were found in the ruins; regrettably, the surviving paintings and carvings do not include pottery censers as motifs.

Cehac-Hunacti Composite-Type Censers from Chichén Itzá

The only incensarios from Chichén Itzá that resemble the codex depictions are from apparently postconstruction deposits. Other Cehac-Hunacti censers with button decoration, one of which shows reasonably close resemblance to the codex examples (fig. 1g), have been found at the Caracol and the Sacred Cenote. These urns are thought to date from the Hocabá or Tases period because of their similarity to Mayapán incensarios (Brainerd 1958:312; R. E. Smith 1971: part 2, p. 173). The only other Chichén Itzá pedestal base incensario that resembles the codex illustrations is the previously mentioned urn with a straight neck, found in a late deposit at the High Priest's Grave.

The only pedestal base form in the Sotuta Ceramic Complex, characteristic of the primary occupation of

Chichén Itzá, is the hourglass shape, known from Chichén Itzá Unslipped Ware (R. E. Smith 1971: part 1, p. 172).[5] Predictably, it is also the hourglass censer, not the Dresden-like Cehac-Hunacti Composite-Type incensario, that is depicted in the art of Chichén Itzá (cf. Ruppert 1935: figs. 168–69; personal photograph). The illustration in Codex Dresden of Cehac-Hunacti Composite-Type censers suggests that if the codex was painted at Chichén Itzá, it was as part of the Mayapán-related secondary occupation of the site and that the work could have occurred during either the Hocabá or Tases periods. Unfortunately, the possibility of Late Postclassic painting of Codex Dresden at Mayapán, or at Chichén Itzá during the Mayapán-related secondary occupation, can not be thoroughly investigated due to the scarcity of surviving painting and sculpture. Also pertinent to the problems of the provenience and date of painting of Codex Dresden are iconographic similarities to the art of several other Late Postclassic Maya sites. As well as supporting the association of Codex Dresden with the fully developed (Tases equivalent) Late Postclassic, these comparisons also suggest other proveniences for the manuscript.

Other Late Postclassic Comparisons

Various motifs in the Dresden illustrations are otherwise known only from Maya art associated with the late phase of the Late Postclassic culture (Paxton 1986:129–149). Of particular interest is the necklace—whose distribution is, with one possible exception, limited to these sources—worn by the figure at the top of page 26a. This necklace form consists of a long rectangular braided section, usually suspended from a horizontal bar, with pointed oval decoration and tassels along the sides (fig. 2a). The necklace on page 26a of Codex Dresden is the same as necklaces worn by the figures attached to Mayapán Chen Mul Modeled-Type effigy incensarios (fig. 2b, c), which are characteristic of the Tases Period occupation of the site (A.D. 1300–1450; R. E. Smith 1971: part 2, p. 173). The use of such figure effigy incensarios, including examples with similar braided necklaces (cf. Gann 1900: pl. 32; Anders 1963: Tafel 19; Bullard 1970: fig. 22, left; Pendergast 1981: fig. 27), was widespread in the Maya area during the Late Postclassic. Indeed, the incensarios are accepted as a marker of the Late Postclassic Maya cultural horizon.

The Dresden page 26a braided necklace can also be found in the Late Postclassic frescoes of Tulum (fig. 2d) and Santa Rita Corozal (fig. 2e), as well as a Kabah painting known from a late nineteenth century drawn copy (figs. 2f, 3). The Kabáh painting is presently undated. Because the other dated examples of the braided necklace are attributable to the Late Postclassic, and because this painting is iconographically unrelated to the art now known from Kabáh, it is possible that the painting occurred during a Late Postclassic reoccupation of the previously abandoned site.[6] However, further ar-

Fig. 2   The Rectangular Braided Necklace Motif.

(a) Codex Dresden, page 26a (redrawn by Meredith Taylor from the 1972 Thompson facsimile).

(b) Mayapán, Mayapán Unslipped Ware, Chen Mul Modeled-Type figure effigy incensario (redrawn by Meredith Taylor from a personal photograph; see R. E. Smith 1971: part 2, fig. 67e).

(c) Mayapán, Mayapán Unslipped Ware, fragment from a Chen Mul Modeled-Type figure effigy incensario (redrawn by Meredith Taylor from R. E. Smith 1971: part 2, fig. 73c, p. 1).

(d) Tulum, Structure 16, fresco on north end of west facade of inner building (redrawn by Meredith Taylor from a personal photograph; see Miller 1982: pl. 38, upper left).

(e) Santa Rita Corozal, Mound 1, fresco from east half of north wall, figure 3 (redrawn by Meredith Taylor from Gann 1900: pl. 29).

(f) Kabàh, painting found on principal (rear?) wall of Structure 2C2, Room 24 (redrawn by Meredith Taylor from de Rosny 1872: atlas, pl. 20; see also fig. 3, below).

Fig. 3 Painting Found at Kabah, Structure 2C2, Room 24. From de Rosny's (1872:I, p. 178) description, it is apparent that this is the same Kabàh painting referred to by Charnay (1888:382–383) and Pollock (1980:181). Hatched pattern indicates pale yellow color; scale approximately 15.5 percent of painting size (redrawn by Meredith Taylor from de Rosny 1872: atlas, pl. 20).

chaeological excavation, which has thus far been minimal at Kabah, is necessary before the context of the painting, as well as its relationship to Codex Dresden, can be understood. At present, the iconographic similarity between the Kabah painting and the manuscript is useful only as an indicator of another possible area of origin for the codex.[7]

Codex Dresden as a Prototype

The illustration of the Cehac-Hunacti Composite-Type incensarios on pages 25–28 of Codex Dresden can be interpreted as evidence that the painting of the manuscript was done during the Hocabá or Tases periods of the Late Postclassic. Furthermore, the presence in the codex of a group of iconographic motifs otherwise unique to the fully developed Late Postclassic Maya culture could mean that Codex Dresden is more properly associated with the Tases-equivalent late phase than the early part of the Hocabá transition. Hence, the provenience of the manuscript could be assigned to Tases Period Mayapán, or to contemporary occupations of Chichén Itzá, Santa Rita Corozal, Tulum, or, possibly, Kabah. However, before reaching such a conclusion, the possibility that Codex Dresden served as a model that was broadly influential in the development of Late Postclassic Maya art must be considered. The manuscript could have functioned, as did European prints during the Spanish colonial era, as an easily portable source of images.

If the existence of iconographic forms unique to Codex Dresden and the Tases period Late Postclassic Maya art is explained by such a prototypical relationship (Quirarte 1982:54), then the manuscript must be the only known survivor from some earlier group of art works that also used these motifs. Future excavation at certain sites, such as Kabah, may clarify this possible prototypical relationship. However, it must be noted that complete images corresponding with counterparts in the codex are not found at the Late Postclassic Maya sites, and that the shared motifs are not exact duplicates. It is more plausible, according to present information, to deny the prototypical relationship and accept the idea that Codex Dresden was painted during the Tases, possibly at Mayapán, Chichén Itzá, Tulum, Santa Rita Corozal, or Kabah.[8]

Absolute Dating of the Comparative Sources

The chronology for Yucatán followed thus far is that published in 1971 by R. E. Smith. Since the appearance of the Smith report, which focused on the stratigraphy of Mayapán, several significant developments have occurred (see Andrews 1981:335–336). While detailed discussion of revised initial dates for the Mayapán Hocabá and Tases periods, as well as for related sequences in other areas, is beyond the scope of the present discussion, it must be noted that shifts in the earlier direction appear justifiable. The Cream Kukula Group of Peto Cream Ware, which served as the basis for the A.D. 1200–1300 alignment of the Hocabá Period, and for the founding date of Mayapán, is now known from earlier contexts (Andrews 1981:335; Connor 1983:255). The founding of Mayapán could easily have occurred around A.D. 1100/1200 (Robles C. 1980:47–48; Paxton 1986: 627–631).[9] Additionally, I have argued elsewhere (Paxton 1986:612–622) that the Chen Mul Modeled-Type figure effigy incensarios, which are characteristic of the Tases Period at Mayapán, developed from Tohil Plumbate Ware. Consequently, the initial date of the occurrence of these urns, as well as that of the related figure effigy incensarios that generally mark the Late Post-

classic Maya horizon, should probably also be revised accordingly, perhaps to around A.D. 1150/1250.

Conclusions

It has been shown that the archaeologically known censers most closely resembling the Codex Dresden illustrations on pages 25b, 25c, 26b, and 28b are Cehac-Hunacti Composite-Type incensarios, produced at Mayapán during both Hocabá and Tases periods. The urns on pages 25b, 25c, and 28b are also comparable to incensarios found at Chichén Itzá, which have been assigned to the same periods on the basis of their similarity to the Mayapán forms (Brainerd 1958:312). Present information argues against the use of Codex Dresden as a model for the Late Postclassic Maya art. Therefore, it is reasonable to interpret certain motifs known only from the codex and Maya art contemporary with the Mayapán Tases as indications that the painting of the manuscript is more properly associated with this later period. However, it is likely that the initial dates of both the Hocabá and Tases periods, as well as related sequences from other areas, should be revised to a position earlier than that proposed by R. E. Smith (1971). Thus, the painting of Codex Dresden could have occurred during the full Late Postclassic florescence (Tases equivalent; A.D. 1150/1250[?] to 1450/Spanish contact) at Mayapán, Chichén Itzá, Tulum, Santa Rita Corozal, or, possibly, Kabah.

Notes

1. Various illegible fragments are known as well. See, for example, R. E. Smith (1937:216, pl. 5c) for discussion of the codex remains found in Pyramid C at Uaxactún.

2. In a summary article on Maya calendrics, Linton Satterthwaite (1965:618–619) expressed the view that the latest clearly written Long Count position in Codex Dresden, 10.17.13.12.12 4 Eb (5 Pax), or 1178 A.D., according to the Goodman-Martínez-Thompson correlation of Maya and Christian calendars, could be interpreted as an early limit for the painting date. Satterthwaite (1965:625) additionally commented that the Dresden Venus table would have been useful for predicting the behavior of the planet until 11.10.0.17.0 1 Ahau 18 Pax, or 1422 A.D., following the G-M-T correlation.

The Satterthwaite interpretation of the eclipse table also included in Codex Dresden was consistent with his proposed period of use of the manuscript (A.D. 1178 to 1422). Three possible Long Count bases, all falling within this period, were suggested for this table (Satterthwaite 1965:625, 629). However, the Satterthwaite view is not universally accepted (Lounsbury 1978:814), and the prevailing theory on the origins of the codex is that of Thompson (1972; see also Bricker and Bricker 1983).

3. One of the most important hieroglyphic traits cited by Thompson (1972:16, 89) in his association of Codex Dresden with the inscriptions of Chichén Itzá is their common use of the Akbal-Lamat-Ben-Etz'nab year-bearers. At the time the Thompson commentary was written, the year-bearers of the Late Postclassic East Coast Maya culture were unidentified. Through the recording of a 1376 A.D. painted text at Playa del Carmen, Quintana Roo (Mayer 1978a; Riese 1978; see also Hartig 1979), it has been possible to show that the Akbal-Lamat-Ben-Etz'nab year-bearers were also in use at this site (Paxton 1983).

4. This is evidently the same urn from the Peabody Museum collection as is illustrated by Brainerd (1958: fig. 97d). E. H. Thompson (1938:42, fig. 4b) mentioned finding fragments of effigy figures, comparable to the Chen Mul Modeled-style incensario in figure 20 of the same report, with the disk-decorated urn.

5. A terraced ringstand form is also known (Brainerd 1958: fig. 104c, p. 1).

6. Some support for this theory is provided by Ball's (1979:30) observation that numerous Late Postclassic figure effigy incensarios, reportedly found in such contexts in the Puuc zone, are now in private collections.

7. Notwithstanding iconographic similarities, present calendrical evidence would discourage acceptance of Kabah as the area of origin for Codex Dresden. Proskouriakoff and Thompson (1947:146) identified Kabah as one of the sites at which there was a shift of year-bearers from the Akbal-Lamat-Ben-Etz'nab series followed in Codex Dresden to the Kan-Muluc-Ix-Cauac set. The text cited in support of this usage at the Puuc site is an inscription from the carved north jamb of Room 21 of the Codz Poop (Structure 2C6; Proskouriakoff 1950: fig. 103b). The date, whose probable Long Count position is unknown due to the apparent lack of tun and katun notations, is 2 Chuen 3 Muan. Use of the Akbal-Lamat-Ben-Etz'nab year-bearers would have resulted in the recording of 4 Muan as the solar year position. So, for Codex Dresden to have been painted at Kabah, it would be necessary to postulate a carving error or complex glyphic usage, such as concurrent use of different year-bearers.

The several iconographic similarities between the Kabah fresco and Codex Dresden are of considerable interest to the problems of the provenience and date of painting of the manuscript. When further archaeological excavation is conducted at the site, it may be possible to determine if the wall painting referred to here is an isolated occurrence, attributable to a late reoccupation, or part of a larger group of artistic works that encompasses the manuscript.

8. There are obvious stylistic dissimilarities between Codex Dresden and the Late Postclassic Maya artworks discussed here; these could result from differences in scale and function (Schapiro 1953:294; see Paxton 1986 for additional discussion).

9. On the basis of preliminary information from Cobá and his interpretation of recent Tancah data, Ball (1979:33–34, fig. 17) also suggested the possibility of an earlier founding date for Mayapán, as well as an earlier alignment of the Hocabá sequence.

Acknowledgments

I would like to thank E. Wyllys Andrews V, Flora S. Clancy, Jeremy A. Sabloff, and Mary Elizabeth Smith, for their comments on this paper; however, I am solely responsible for any errors in content. I also sincerely appreciate the research permits and courtesy extended to me by the Mexico City and Mérida offices of the Instituto Nacional de Antropología e Historia. Prof. Angel García Cook, Director de Monumentos Prehispánicos, Lic. Javier Oropeza y Segura, Director de Asuntos Jurídicos, and Arql. Norberto González Crespo, Director del Centro Regional del Sureste, were particularly helpful while the fieldwork for this project was being conducted. During that phase, discussions with Alfredo Barrera Rubio were informative as well. The accompanying illustrations were drawn by Meredith Taylor. Funding was provided by a Fulbright-Hays grant, a University of New Mexico Challenge Assistantship, and awards from the Student Research Allocations Committee of the Graduate Student Association of the University of New Mexico.

The Real Venus-Kukulcan in the Maya Inscriptions and Alignments

ANTHONY AVENI
COLGATE UNIVERSTIY

This paper is dedicated to the proposition that to know the Maya is to see what they saw, to hear what they heard, to feel what they felt, to taste what they tasted, and to smell what they smelled. Understanding the symbolism of a culture often begins by bearing witness to the complex behavior of the things and phenomena of that segment of the world view we call "natural." For Maya symbolism specifically, this means we are obligated to know the life cycle of the toad, the stingless bee, and the maize plant, to name but a few of the entities that we, in our unfortunate wisdom, separate from the rest of nature and relegate to the zoological and botanical realms. We must also be able to follow the course of the sun, the stars, and the intricate movement of Venus, matters that we choose to label astronomy.

My proposition rests on the assumption that the Maya integrated and interrelated the properties of things they captured in their universe of senses and that they applied them to the course of their lives, the unfolding of their history (however they conceived it), their politics, their social relations, their concept of creation, and the afterlife—in short, to every phase and component of human activity. I further assume that the processes of interrelation, which are manifest in so many aspects of the material remains of the Maya, were sophisticated, complex, well thought out, and in nearly all cases very different from our positivist taxonomies, cause-effect explanations, and functional principles of association. I believe their acuity in sensing the phenomena they transformed into their symbolism was sharper than our own, and that it was capable of revealing patterns of behavior in nature not yet known to us, for they were conditioned by a lifetime of immersion in particular sights, smells, and sounds that nourished their sensual appetites, a lifetime unencumbered by the dulling of direct sensual perception that results from the intervention of technology.

Specifically, I further suggest that sky phenomena that we, because of a cultural-environmental bias, may tend to regard as universal could have had little or no fascination or applicability in their world view. While my proposition has the effect of making the truth much more difficult to uncover, given what we know of the Maya mentality I feel quite safe operating under the umbrella of this proposition and its corollaries and I shall continue to do so until my proposition, which I regard as a humbling fact of modern life, is disproven.

The Real Venus

Venus is a very special luminary. After the sun and the moon, it is the brightest celestial object. Its movement across the sky is unique and its visual relationship to the sun is special. Except for Mercury, which is difficult of access (though it was also probably observed), Venus is the only object that remains close to the sun, always becoming visible a few hours either before sunrise over the place where the sun will come up or after sunset over the place where it went down. Its full cycle of movement, from first appearance in the predawn sky through its two intervals of appearance as morning and evening "star," each punctuated by a pair of intervals of disappearance, unfolds over an interval of time (584 days) that is commensurate with the length of the seasonal year in the ratio of 5 to 8. To the eye, this means that any visible aspect of Venus relative to the sun will be repeated after 8 years—that is, Venus behaves seasonally. Two full cycles of this motion are exactly equivalent to two Calendar Rounds (two cycles that represent the shortest interval of time that embraces a complete matching set of day names in the 260- and 365-day cycles). We already recognize that the 365-day Haab is a count of the days that corresponds to the annual cycle of movement of the sun. Not so well known is the fact that the count of 260 days is a fair approximation to either of the mean intervals of appearance of Venus (Gibbs 1977: 33–34; Aveni 1980:86 and note 15). I calculated a mean interval of appearance of Venus as morning star of 263 days based upon predicted dates of disappearance and reappearance published over a 20-year period in *Sky and Telescope* magazine. More recently, Schaefer (n.d.)

developed a model based upon his own naked-eye observations that yields a range of apparition intervals lying between 253 and 265 days (avg. 259 days).

In effect, then, we can say that the Calendar Round synthesizes the primary solar and Venus intervals. An ethnohistoric account of the connection between Venus and the 260-day cycle in Central Mexico was given long ago by Nuttall (1940), who referred to the manuscript of Serna (1892):

. . . here is explained the calendar or table of the star named Hesper, or, in the language of the Indian, Hueycitlalin [lit. the Great Star] or Totonametl [lit. the Shining One]. The table given here can be designated as the calendar of the Indians of New Spain, which they counted by a star which, in the autumn, begins to appear, toward evening, in the west with a clear and resplendent light. Indeed, those who have good eyesight and know where to look for it can perceive it from midday on. This star is that we call Lucifer, etc. . . . As the sun goes lower and the days grow shorter the star seems to rise—thus each day it appears a little higher until the sun seems to reach it and pass it in the summer and spring when it sets with the sun and is visible through its light. And in this land the duration of time from the day when it first appears to when after rising on high it loses itself and disappears amounts to 260 days, which are figured and recorded in said calendar or table . . . the sign cipactli is the first day of the 260 and of all days. . . . This count is not that of the course of the sun or the year, nor is it in respect [the sun] that it is named and the signs exist, but it is from contemplation of the star. They named this count Tonalpoualli . . . which means the count of the planets or heavenly bodies which illuminate or give light, and by this they did not only signify the planet named Sun.″ . . . They also name the star Citlaltona, or "the star of light." . . . Next to the sun they adored and made more sacrifices to this star than to any other celestial or terrestrial creature. The astronomers knew on what day it would appear again in the east after it had lost itself or disappeared in the west, and for this first day they prepared a feast, warfare, and sacrifices. The ruler gave an Indian who was sacrificed at dawn, as soon as the star became visible. . . . In this land the star lingers and rises in the east as many days as in the west—that is to say for another period of 260 days. Some add thirteen days more, which is one of their weeks. They also kept account, like good astrologers, of all the days when the star was visible. The reason why this star was held in such esteen by the lords and people, and the reason why they counted the days by this star and yielded reverence and offered sacrifices to it, was because these deluded natives thought or believed that when one of their principal gods, named Topiltzin or Quetzalcoatl, died and left this world, he transformed himself into that resplendent star . . .

Of all the visible subintervals that one can identify within the cycle of Venus (Closs 1979: table 2, p. 154), the most fundamental would appear to be those that are demarcated by the events of apparition or disappearance of the planet. Unlike the stationary points, greatest elongation or inferior conjunction, which are accorded great importance in western astronomy, the dates of heliacal rise and set serve as precise definitive time markers that delineate the two intervals of appearance

and separate them from the two disappearance intervals that lie in between.

To see what Venus really does, let us follow its path in the sky referred to the local horizon background during a series of actual morning and evening star apparition intervals over a full 8-year cycle (fig. 1). This sort of motion, referred to the local horizon rather than to the stars, seems especially noteworthy for Venus, as opposed to the other planets, for at least two reasons: first, this particular planet always lies relatively close to the horizon; second, it is visible when the sky is very bright, lying closer to the horizon when the celestial background is darker—therefore, usually, but not always, few stars are conveniently visible in the vicinity of Venus to which one can refer its position. (I am indebted to O. Gingerich and B. Welther [assisted by B. Collea], Smithsonian Astrophysical Observatory, for providing these plots, which they graciously generated from computer programs at the request of Arthur Schlak, who has employed similar curves in another study.) These particular curves are computed for the period A.D. 933–941 at the latitude of north Yucatán. The position of Venus is given at 5-day intervals at the beginning or end of twilight.

Consulting figure 1, we note that over the approximately 260-day course of its interval of appearance Venus moves on a serpentine curve that can variously be described as a figure 7 (E4), a figure 7 with a small loop (E1), a broad open curve (W), or a large loop (E5). Often the shape of the curve is intermediate between these forms. Most important of all, if we follow the temporal sequence of the shapes of the curves Venus executes on successive morning and evening sky apparitions, proceeding in the order E1, W2, E2, W3 . . . W7 we find that an orderly transformation of shapes occurs (as fig. 1 illustrates). Not surprisingly, the interval between the execution of a pair of sky paths of similar form is 8 years (2,920 days or 5 Venus cycles). Thus, compare E1 and E6 or W2 and W7. For example, curve E1 begins on 21 Apr 933 while its next exact duplicate, E6 commences on 19 Apr 941. This set of visual perceptions offers one sound empirical reason for the Maya habit of counting Venus cycles in groups of 5.

There are a few other obvious Venus phenomena the Maya may have noted that can aid us in interpreting their celestial symbolism. We notice that the speed of Venus along its looped track changes with time (recall that the dots forming the curves in fig. 1 are spaced at equal time intervals). Viewed as morning star on a succession of days, Venus bursts on the scene: it comes flying out from below the horizon and almost immediately rises to a crescendo of brilliance. Very soon after, it slows suddenly to its turnaround point (highest point in the sky) and then, also slowly, it begins to descend toward its disappearance point, gaining speed as it goes. Evening star apparition is exactly the reverse. Much fainter in general throughout this period of the cycle,

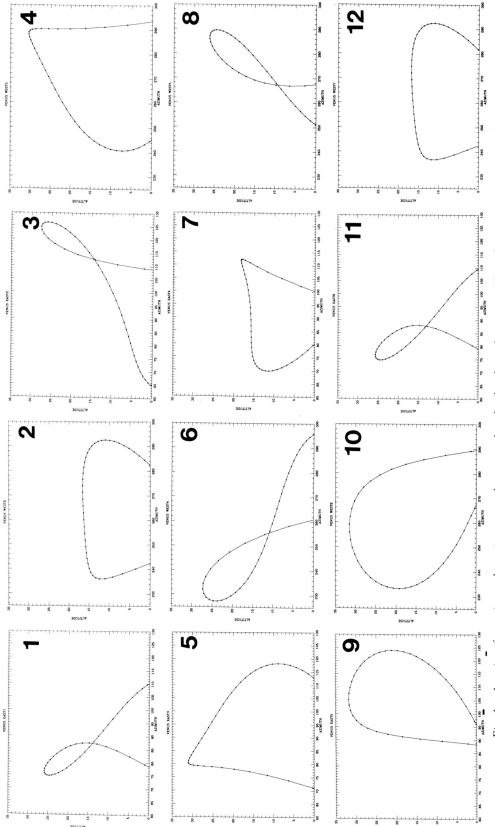

Fig. 1 A series of morning and evening star paths executed in the sky above the eastern (E) and western (W) horizons by the planet Venus, each over the course of approximately 260 days. Note that five consecutive sets of curves span a total of eight years (courtesy O. Gingerich and B. Welther, Smithsonian Astrophysical Observatory).

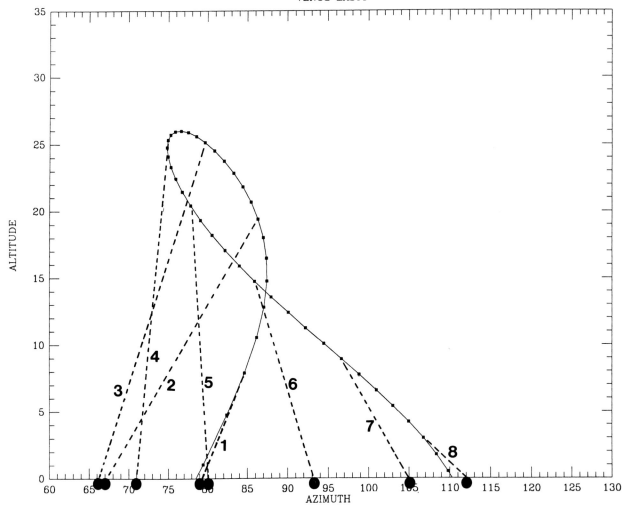

Fig. 2 Motion of Venus relative to the sun (dotted lines) drawn on two of the charts of fig. 1 (courtesy O. Gingerich and B. Welther, with additions by Anthony Aveni).

Venus makes a more labored ascent to its maximum height above the western horizon at twilight, but once it begins its return toward disappearance it plummets like a falling stone.

To demonstrate the movement of Venus with respect to the sun, I have indicated in figure 2, by solid circular markers on the horizon, the place of the sun at monthly intervals during the period of appearance of Venus in the evening and morning sky on two of the selected charts. This relative motion is rather like that of a yo-yo or, perhaps even better, a ball on the end of an elastic string. As the ball (Venus) gets farther away from the point about which it pivots (the sun), it moves more slowly. Furthermore, the line connecting the sun with Venus (dotted in each diagram) twists and turns as the two move together, Venus appearing alternately to the left and right of the sun. However, we must realize that the two are never readily visible in the sky at the same time. With the eye, this particular relationship can be per-

ceived only by connecting Venus, via an imaginary line, with the glow that remains over the place where the sun has recently departed or will shortly appear.

Finally, we must remind ourselves that the curves plotted in figure 1 actually represent a series of "time lapse shots" taken at mid-twilight over the course of approximately 260 days. On every one of those days, Venus, along with everything else in the sky, would be seen to move either from a given point on its evening star curve along a steeply inclined *daily* path downward to its setting point (illustrated in fig. 3 by heavy arrows in one of the charts of fig. 1), or from its rising point up to a given point on its morning star curve. Each of these steeply inclined daily motions occurs in two hours or less, depending on the height to which Venus is enabled to climb or from which it can descend; either of these parameters in turn depends upon how far in the sky Venus appears from the sun. The farther apart they are, the longer one sees Venus in the sky on a given night.

Aveni

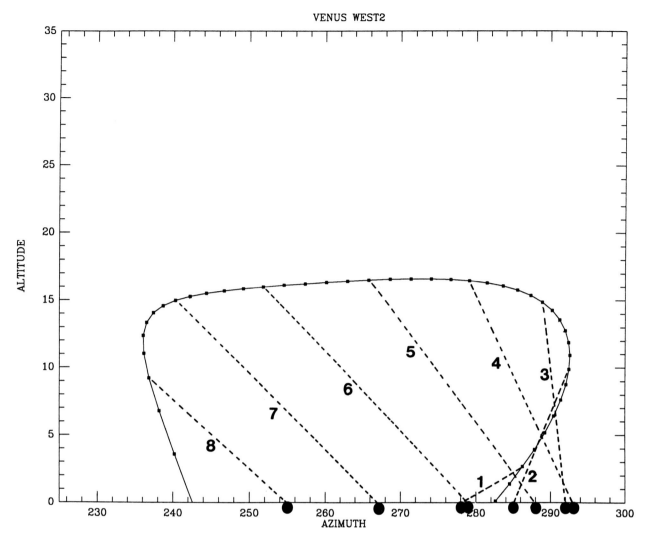

Fig. 2 (continued)

At this point, it may be worth a brief digression to discuss the danger of assuming that all Venus phenomena are visible with equal facility. Take, for example, the greatest elongation, or maximum angular distance between Venus and the sun. Unlike first or last appearance of the planet (the so-called heliacal events), the date of greatest elongation is very difficult to pinpoint. As is the case with planetary conjunctions, one must question the success with which either the subject or the investigator could employ the elongation phenomenon as a time-marking event. To illustrate the problem, consider the extreme upper right portion of the Venus morning star path depicted in figure 2a. Recall that the dots indicate Venus's position at the onset of morning twilight plotted at 5-day intervals.

Around the time of greatest elongation, as Venus stretches to its most remote position from the sun in the sky, it is situated at an altitude of approximately 22° in a relatively well backlighted sky. Note that at this time

the planet takes about 25 days (almost 10 percent of its total interval of visibility as morning star) to move back and forth over a 1° long segment of the sky. This is about double the diameter of the disk of the full moon; however, there is no fixed object such as a nearby horizon for reference; furthermore, one must assume that Venus will first be sighted at precisely the same apparent solar time each evening (or morning) if an accurate fix on the planetary position is to be established. It is difficult to believe that this amount of movement relative to the sun could actually be detected unless one were to postulate the existence of some sort of instrument or tool to facilitate measurement. Perhaps a sighting of the object off the corner of a building from a fixed position such as a temple doorway would help. In any case, the matching of a Maya date with an elongation event, taken by itself, means little as far as the human senses are concerned. Like the celebrated lunar limits of Stonehenge, the elongation may be an artifact of western astronomy, an

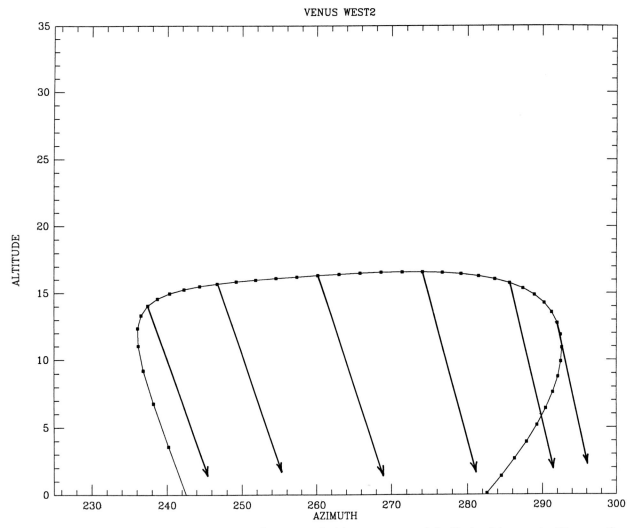

Fig. 3 *Motion of Venus in the sky on a given night in its cycle (choose any one of the black solid arrows). (Courtesy O. Gingerich and B. Welther, with additions by Anthony Aveni.)*

item in our own stock inventory of supposed universal celestial phenomena that we search out in the Maya astronomical inscriptions simply because it has a certain importance in the astronomical background of our own culture and consequently appears in our modern textbooks of astronomy.

Another directly observable Venus phenomenon consists of the positions of appearance and disappearance of Venus at the horizon. Thus, we find not only that the planet executes an annual horizontal oscillating motion in a period very much in tune with that of the sun but also that the limits it attains along the horizon are exactly repeatable at 8-year intervals (Aveni 1980:93).

The length of the disappearance intervals of Venus may be correlated with the season of the year during which they occur (Aveni 1983) and consequently with the place of disappearance of Venus at the horizon (see fig. 4). This plot is intended to correct the falsehood,

rather commonly held, that Venus always disappears for 8 days prior to its reappearance in the east as morning star. In fact, the graph reveals that when Venus disappears during our month of February it is likely to be gone from view for only a few days prior to heliacal rise. Under extreme conditions, it is even possible to view Venus as evening and morning star *on the same day*. On the contrary, in August a disappearance interval can be up to 20 days long; however, averaged over the entire year, the mean disappearance interval of Venus is precisely 8 days, in perfect agreement with the canonic interval assigned to that particular aspect of the planet in the Venus table in the Dresden Codex.

This horizon cycle provides the discerning Maya astronomer with a rather precise predictive capacity. He could use the time of year and the position of Venus at the horizon, which itself varies with the season of the year, to predict how long it would be before Venus would

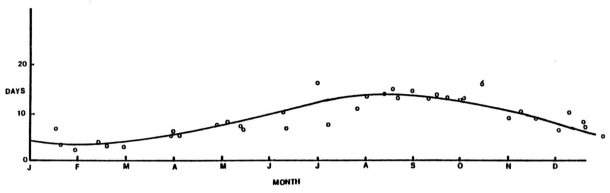

Fig. 4 Length of disappearance interval of Venus around inferior conjunction plotted as a function of the season of the year.

return once it had vanished, as well as where it could be seen when it did return.

In summary, the behavior of the real Venus may be characterized as follows: it moves on a sinuous curve as it guards the sun closely, twisting and turning about it, alternately darting toward and flying away from it—never very far ahead or behind it. Whether it is followed by marking the place on the horizon where Venus appears or disappears or by counting the intervals of disappearance and appearance as in a calendar, all of its activity functions in perfect tempo with the seasonal solar cycle in 5/8 time. If our goal is to view Venus through Maya eyes, a privilege not reserved for astronomers alone, then we must begin by witnessing, appreciating, and understanding all of these phenomena.

Maya Venus Iconography

The previous section indicated what can be seen of Venus in the sky. Some of the perceptions described are known to have been important in the astronomies of various cultures (e.g., the disappearance interval and the commensurability of the Venus and solar "years" were known to the Babylonians as well as the Mayas); but certain other aspects of the planet, equally apparent if one cares to look for them, have never really been discussed before in the literature (e.g., the 8-year oscillation of Venus at the horizon and the seasonality of its disappearance intervals).

Was any or all of this motion and change witnessed by the Maya and did they accord it any significance that can be revealed to us through the record that survives them? We can attack this far more difficult question first at the most general level by focusing on the fivefold nature of the condition of Venus. As we have seen, the "fiveness" of the real Venus is directly visible in the repeatability of numerous Venus phenomena, in sequences of 5 cycles of 584 days, including the limits it marks along the horizon, and the recurrence of the shape and direction of its path on the sky.

No one doubts that the Maya attributed a "fiveness" to the changing aspect of Venus. In their inscriptions we

see it in the quincunx structure of the Venus-Lamat symbol (T510, esp. 510 a and b), in the five pages of the Venus table and the five sets of pictured intervals therein. In architecture it appears in the arrangement of the Chac masks bearing Venus symbols that are stacked vertically in groups of five on the upper frieze of the Palace of the Governor at Uxmal or horizontally in the Nunnery at Chichén Itzá.

To be more specific, let us look at some of the detail about Venus obtainable from the Dresden Codex (pp. 24, 26–50; J. Thompson 1972; Lounsbury 1978; Aveni 1980:184–195). I will not review the contents of this exquisite artifact that has offered us a rare glimpse of the true depth of Maya astronomical and mathematical ingenuity except to say that a consideration of the format of the table ought to remove any doubts that the Maya conceived of five forms of Venus.

Incidentally, some of the numbers appearing in the table that represent the Venus intervals but do not agree with astronomical reality may have resulted from Maya attempts to fit the movements of Venus and the moon together in the same table (Aveni 1983). Their rationale may have resulted from the recognition of certain obvious coincidences between lunar and Venus cycles. For example, the 263-day mean apparition interval of Venus is close to nine lunations (265.7 days). The 260-day cycle was tied to the human gestation period in Central Mexico in the Serna manuscript (see Nuttall:495 for a discussion) and more recently among contemporary Maya (Earle and Snow 1985). Closs (in press) and Bricker and Bricker (1986) also summarized linguistic and inscriptional evidence suggesting that the Maya related Venus to the moon.

At a more detailed level, the four canonic station intervals tabulated in the Dresden document, three of which are greatly corrupted from reality, are fairly precise multiples of the lunar phase cycle (90 days = 3 lunar synodic months; 236 days = 8 lunar synodic months and 250 days = 8 1/2 lunar synodic months). Recently, I demonstrated that the Venus table actually can be used to predict lunar eclipses visible in the area inhabited by the Classic Maya (Aveni 1983) and furthermore that the correction mechanism suggested by Lounsbury (1983), when applied to the table, would result in a device that is a better predictor not only of the Venus apparitions but also of the eclipses as well. It is as if the creators of the table were attempting to discover a rhythm that would enable the moon to march in Venus time. Unlike western astronomers, they were not concerned with isolating the motion of Venus from that of the moon any more than they cared to separate the activities of the sun and Venus. The epitome of Maya astronomy lay in producing a predictive temporal scheme that wove together the observed actions and interactions of these heavenly bodies.

Both Lounsbury (1978, 1983) and Closs (1979) capably summarized the hieroglyphic forms associated with the planet Venus. Symbolic assignation is based principally upon the occurrence of combinations of glyphs found in the Dresden Venus Table, which taken together can mean Chac Ek = Great Star or Red Star. These forms are either T109:510 or T109:1/2(T510), the latter often being confused with T2, the variable element in the Initial Series Introductory Glyph. The symbol we call "1/2(T510)," by virtue of its occurrence in the Dresden Venus Table, should more appropriately be termed a variant of T510. (It is not illustrated in Thompson's 1963 catalog.) It is formed from T510 by dividing the latter in half by a horizontal line and utilizing only the bottom portion. One or another combination of this pair appears on each page of the Dresden Venus Table at line F14 and at several places in the "preamble" (p. 24). It also occurs in each column of calculations on Dresden 46–50 (i.e., cols. A through D, lines 18 and 23). The exceptions are page 48, l. 3, where the signs are omitted altogether, and page 47, D18, where 1/2 (T510) appears alone. The halved form of the Venus sign again occurs by itself in the headdress of Lahun Chan = Venus (Thompson 1950 [1960:219]) in the middle picture on page 47. In this case, it lies in very close proximity to the right of the 1/2 (T510) symbol at position D18 in the table. Kelley (1976:38) erroneously stated that in all cases the great or red prefix precedes the word for star in the table. This is his basis for drawing the unwarranted conclusion that, taken by itself, the symbol simply means star. In fact every "star" compound known to have been deciphered unambiguously is known to refer to Venus (Closs: personal communication, 1986).

More recently, Lounsbury's (1982) study of the sky scenes above the mural paintings in Room 2 of Bonampak singled out the 1/2 (T510) form and identified it with specific dates given in the associated inscriptions. These dates match heliacal rise dates of the planet Venus visible from Bonampak. Lounsbury concluded that the appearance of the planet was associated with the conduct of war ritual or in the initiation of actual battles, a function that, perhaps only coincidentally, is also mentioned in the Serna manuscript.

The solitary (prefixless) form of the Venus glyph ap-

pears in many instances in sky bands together with the sun and the moon (Closs 1979:148); finally, there is linguistic evidence that Ek taken by itself can mean either star or Morning Star = Venus = Lucifer. I conclude, with Lounsbury and Closs, that the main component of the combination 109:510 or 109:1/2(510) "can be taken in either of two senses: either in a general sense as 'star' or in a specific sense as 'THE star' or 'Venus'" (Lounsbury 1982:144). Closs, who articulated additional iconographic associations with Venus to which the interested reader may refer, went even further, concluding that "when qualifying affixes are absent it should be interpreted as a Venus symbol" (1979:164).

Recently, Justin Kerr kindly provided me with rollouts of a number of vases that contain Venus symbols. In certain cases (Kerr nos. 1230, 1652, which correspond to vessels no. 40 and 39, respectively, in Robicsek and Hales 1981, and no. 2234), the symbols adorn the back of a sinuous serpent who courses through the scene in much the same way that I describe Venus as moving across the sky during its morning and evening star apparitions.

Venus Orientations in the Architecture

Archaeoastronomy seeks to interpret the role of astronomy in ancient cultures through the study of inscriptions in all forms as well as iconography, architectural alignments, and the ethnographic and ethnohistoric record. Sound explanations in this interdiscipline are those that draw pieces of evidence from more than one study or discipline and combine them in such a way that they converge harmoniously.

Our understanding of the significance of the planet Venus for the Maya has been enhanced by the discovery that physical alignments toward the planet at its extremes on the horizon were registered in Maya architecture. Two salient points about the alignments that I postulate are worth underlining. First, they are reasonable in the context of what we know about Venus in the written record. Such alignments include the directions to Venus that we might anticipate given the type of predictions and information that the Maya were dealing with in the Dresden Codex. Second, the alignments are found to occur in buildings that possess, in their structure and/or iconography, characteristics that can be related specifically to Venus. As if to betray their response to environmental motivating forces, the buildings containing these alignments often possess peculiar shapes and/or orientations relative to neighboring structures. Here I cite three examples of Venus-oriented buildings: the Caracol of Chichén Itzá, the Palace of the Governor at Uxmal, and Temple 22 of Copán, briefly mentioning some tentative possibilities for Venus orientation at Palenque. The discussion of the first two case studies is brief, since all of the arguments and associated data already have been published (see Aveni 1980: ch. V for a detailed summary and references). Temple 22 is discussed at somewhat greater length since there is new information to add to the arguments already published (Closs et al. 1984).

The Caracol and the Palace of the Governor

In the Caracol of Chichén Itzá, an oddly oriented, highly asymmetric building containing a central cylindrical element, we find four alignments pointing to the 8-year Venus extremes. Two of these consist of diagonal sight lines taken through the windows at the top of the turret. A third perhaps even more fundamental alignment connects the exact center of the round core of the Maya-Toltec structure with the center of the stairway of the lower platform, which itself is aligned with the northerly extreme of Venus. Though no Venus symbolism can be found in the iconography of the building, a set of five Chac masks, with 1/2 (T510) symbols under the eyes, is situated on the NE facade of the Nunnery facing the Caracol at a distance of approximately 100 m. Finally, the circular or cylindrical character of the Caracol has been linked symbolically with one form of Kukulcan-Venus (Tozzer 1941:23–26).

A more purely Toltec manifestation of Venus at Chichén Itzá may be found in the year-bundle symbol adjoined by eight dots appearing on a carved stone in the Mérida Museum, said to have come from the Platform of Venus. Long ago Seler (1902–1903 [1961:386]) commented about this symbol: "it denotes 8 long periods of 52 years, that is 416 years, which corresponds exactly to 13 × 20 Venus periods (of 584 days each)." The star symbol attached to the year-bundle is reminiscent of the image associated with Quetzalcoatl in the Central Mexican Codices (e.g., in the Vienna, where he is seen holding up the sky, which is lined with an array of these symbols).

The Palace of the Governor is noticeably disoriented relative to the other buildings at Uxmal and faces outward from the site, a very uncommon trait among Puuc structures (Aveni and Hartung in press). A line perpendicular to its central doorway passes through the largest structure at Nohpat, a neighboring center located at a distance of 6 km that was once connected to Uxmal by a *sacbe*. This alignment of the facade of the Governor's Palace fits the southerly extreme of Venus rather precisely. The iconographic record offers strong support that the alignment between the two Maya cities incorporated a deliberate Venus orientation. The facade of the Palace contains a large number of Chac masks, which, except for those on the facade of the Nunnery of Chichén Itzá, are the only ones known in the Maya world to possess Venus symbols (the 1/2[T510]) symbols are located under the eyes). The masks are nearly always arranged in groups of five. Finally, excavations on the NE and (very recently) NW corners of the platform of this structure revealed "cornerstone" Chac masks with the number eight appearing over the eyebrows. Whether this was intended to indicate the 8-year cycle or the 8-day disappearance of Venus one cannot say. I favor the latter possibility because the temporal currency of the Maya

seems always to have been the day rather than the year. Another Venus orientation at the site has been proposed (Aveni 1975: table 5) but there is no evidence to support it beyond the mere equivalence of architectural alignment and Venus direction.

Venus at Palenque?

There is circumstantial evidence for a Venus orientation at Palenque. At the entrance to the upper stairway of the tower, on the upper part of the S wall, is the well-known painted red 1/2 (T510) Venus symbol. Furthermore, House E, adjacent to the patio of the tower on its west side, contains a stucco bicephalic serpent along the top of the north wall where the corbeling commences. Venus symbols adorn the sky bands that make up the segmented body of this serpent and are also infixed into the ear and eye of the front head of the Celestial Monster on the west side of House E. On the other hand, the rear head (on the eastern wall) contains the glyphic kin sign. This same directional-iconographic arrangement occurs on the bicephalic serpent carved on the altar at the base of the south side of the Palace group. Schele and Miller (1986:45) interpreted the iconography of the bicephalic serpent to mean "sun follows Venus," which, as seen from the earlier discussion, actually happens when the two appear in the morning sky. The imaging is symbolic of the opposition between these two bodies and their journey in tandem across the sky from east to west.

Now, House E is a west–east facing building. Though the view to the western horizon today is partially blocked by the tower, we can be sure that the tower was a later addition. The western facade of House E is aligned 15°34′N of W and the eastern facade 15°34′S of E (Aveni and Hartung 1979:174), a direction that might not appear to be what we would have chosen if we desired a Venus orientation (i.e., it does not correspond to one of the Venus horizon extremes). On the other hand, the view to the west passes over the last visible segment of the distant horizon before it begins to give way to the elevated hills to the south and in the immediate vicinity (behind the Temple of the Inscriptions).

The inscriptions may offer a further clue. Long Count dates at Palenque that deal with Venus include a katun-ending date on the Middle Panel of the Temple of the Inscriptions and another date on the Initial Series Pot. Both refer to evening star observations (i.e., Venus above the western horizon) according to Closs (1981:40). So there is little doubt the Maya at Palenque were paying some attention to Venus. Unfortunately, the extant evidence provides none of the details. The general northwest-facing direction of the building, the associated iconography, and Venus dates that correspond to a western horizon are suggestive of some relationship worthy of further exploration.

Venus, the Sun, and Copán, Temple 22

Closs et al. (1984) argued that the worship and observation of the planet Venus may have been a special feature of Temple 22 at Copán, one of three structures at the site with associated iconography possessing Venus symbols. The key to the astronomical part of this argument, however, rests upon an observational relationship between the position of the planet on the horizon and the direction of the single narrow window located on the west side of the structure. Looking through this window, one could have sighted Venus above the western horizon during the months of April and May while it was on its way to or returning from one of its 8-year horizon extremes. Specifically, at the time of the building of Temple 22, in the year prior to a great extreme, the first day of visibility of Venus always fell within or very close to an 8-day period ranging between 25 April and 3 May; in a year following a great extreme, the last day of visibility of Venus possessed essentially the same property. These extremes occurred at the same time of the year as the traditional period associated with the onset of the rainy season and I have used the ethnohistoric and ethnographic record to demonstrate a coherent pattern connecting rain, maize planting, and Venus. I posited that the window could have served as a structure to aid in marking the time when Venus would reappear in the sky following its last appearance in the west during the rainy season.

In my 1986 paper, I called attention to the Venus symbolism, in the form of the prefixless 1/2 (T510) on the bicephalic serpent that overhangs the doorway of Temple 22. W. Fash (personal communication, 1986) reported the discovery of additional Venus symbols on fragments of stucco discovered on the west side of Temple 22. It is a well-known fact that other 1/2 (T510) symbols exist at Copán, namely, on the altar of St. M. and on Altar G1, where in each case they occur on the live side of a bicephalic monster. In the case of Temple 22, the symbol appears three times—once over the live head of the monster and twice at its knees.

It can be argued that a special relationship between Temple 22 and Venus is negated by the appearance of Venus symbols in the iconography of bicephalic serpents elsewhere. However, I would consider this to be a weak argument—is it reasonable to expect that every building with Venus iconography would also possess a functional Venus orientation? Such a guiding assumption seems unwarranted. For example, we know of many Maya stelae that possess the "kin" symbol but are not oriented toward the sun. On the other hand, we already know of a building (at Uxmal) that possesses a good deal of Venus iconography (specifically the 1/2 [T510] symbol) and that also happens to be skewed out of line from its neighbors and oriented toward Venus.

Reasoning from a different perspective, ought we impose the dictate that all round temples should be demonstrably Venus-oriented before we can give credence to the possibility that the Caracol was so oriented deliberately? A more reasonable assumption would be that for the Maya different Venus-related buildings possessed different functions, one of which may have involved orientation. Other possible functions might include the presentation of dates on which important Venus phenomena occurred, or more general considerations such as war imagery.

The contents of the 32-glyph text of Str. 22 offers us yet another Venus indication for that building. The day names used in this text are the same ones that are known to have been emphasized in marking the stations of Venus in the sky. The text begins with 5 Lamat and ends (260 days later) with 5 Eb. (I have already pointed out that one of the elements logically underpinning the origin of the Tzolkin is the interval of appearance of Venus in the evening/morning sky.) Now, Lamat and Eb are two of the ten day names associated with Venus stations in the Dresden Codex. Moreover, they are two of the four day names employed most frequently (three times each) in that table.

Concerning the existence of a Venus cult at Copán in general, Closs (1979:164) specifically related, by the appearance of the great star compound glyph, two Copán Long Count dates, one on Altar R, the other on T11, to the Long Count Venus dates in the Dresden Codex. The Altar R text ties Venus to the inaugural date of New-Sun-at-Horizon (Kelley 1977:70), but yields no Venus position in the sky of obvious significance. The Temple 11 date, for which no ritual significance is posited, coincides with the time of termination of Venus's retrograde motion. In both instances, Venus was clearly visible as evening star. Elsewhere, Closs (1981:39–40) has argued that glyphic forms exist (G8 and G9 from the Middle Panel of the TI at Palenque) that suggest that the directions that refer to the movement of Venus are intended to refer specifically to the position of the sun. Finally, Schele and Miller (1986:122–123) tied Venus events to episodes in the lives of Copán ruler Yax-Pac, as represented in the iconography of Temple 11.

On architectural grounds, one might find fault with my Venus orientation hypothesis, again by appealing to the necessity of establishing uniqueness. For example, it is possible that the western window of Temple 22 may not be the only one originally built into the structure and, furthermore, that the view from that window, even if it had been intended to look through, could have been clocked, for a portion of time, by the upper structure of the adjacent Temple 22A. Accordingly, it could be argued that any apertures located within the building were simply intended for ventilation. In fact, there is no solid archaeological evidence that there now exists or ever existed any other windows in the building, though Hohmann and Vogrin (1982: Abb. 314) indicated the appearance of a niche at the north side on the west side of the structure, as did Marquina (1951:598), after Trik (1939). However, that this or any other niches ever might have possessed narrow slits connected with the outside of the building is pure extrapolation, as Hohmann and Vogrin (1982:50) themselves admitted. There is also some evidence in the Hohmann and Vogrin plan that the west side of T22 may once have contained a passageway that later was built over to incorporate the window.

The fact that Str. 22A was built against the platform of Temple 22 argues against absolute contemporaneity of the two structures. Like Str. 21A, which also leans against Temple 22, on its opposite side, it probably was intended as an annex. There is no proof that Str. 22A ever blocked the view from the window for a significant period of time. One needs but a few generations to see a number of Venus cycles unfold. Moreover, the structure and function of Maya buildings often were altered by succeeding generations. Concerning the use of the window as a visual aperture rather than as an air passage, Hohmann and Vogrin referred to the fact that the mat motif carved on T22A would have been visible from the window, thus supporting the idea that the slit still may have functioned as a window even after the view of the horizon had been blocked.

Temple 22 may not have been the only structure on the acropolis with a built-in slitlike aperture. Four tall and narrow slits are visible in the plan of Temple 20 (reconstruction by Hohmann and Vogrin 1982: Abb. 178—the building is now destroyed, having fallen into the Copán River). A fifth lay at the back of the building. These bear little relation in either form or dimension to the window in Temple 22. The mere existence of other apertures, whether of the same or of a different kind, does not change the specific functional relationship that exists between the window of Temple 22 and the Venus events at the western horizon that we have posited. In fact, the existence of these other apertures could conceivably be used to bolster the case for a Venus relation: the four that were located symmetrically about the doorway of Temple 20 also face the same direction as the window of Temple 22, insofar as one can determine their alignments with any reliability from the Hohmann and Vogrin map.

Precisely what were the events that transpired on or near Temple 22 at the times when Venus was ritualized? Miller (1984) interpreted the Main Acropolis of Copán, and particularly Temple 22, to be the ritual palace of the royal family. She argued that the ruler literally sat over the glyphic text of Temple 22, elevated and framed by the bicephalic dragon as he appeared within the interior chamber of the temple. Here youthful rulership is celebrated and symbolized as one of the stages of the growth of the maize plant. (The maize component in the cosmic monster of Temple 22 as well as in other contexts has been explicated by Stone 1985.) The ruler enters through the mouth of the monster represented by the doorway of Temple 22, which Miller suggested was not unlike the typical Chenes facade. He becomes enthroned as if planted like a kernel of corn; then the Maya ruler sprouts and grows. This metaphor of maize as the flourishing career of the sun-god ruler is consistent with the hypothesis (Closs et al. 1984) that attempted to connect celestial representations of this king with the act of sowing maize and of the apparition of Venus in

Temple 22 with the time of maize planting. Recalling the way it was employed at Bonampak, Miller (1984:27) argued that the Venus imagery associated with the Jaguar Staircase suggests that the building might have been employed as a place for ceremonies related to the sacrifice of captives, a setting in which the image of Venus itself could well have played a role.

The bond between the sun and Venus, both in the sky and in the iconography of Temple 22, offers a logical explanation for the observed fact that the alignment of the window of Temple 22 also marks the place where the sun set on precisely the same dates that it set along the solar-related baseline between Stelae 12 and 10, which are located on opposite sides of the Copán valley. Furthermore, the dates indicated by the 12-10 baseline also fit ideally into an orientation calendar consisting of 20-day periods symmetrically pivoted about the dates of passage of the sun across the zenith (Aveni 1977: fig. 1.5). It is no coincidence that this 7 km baseline also lies parallel to and cuts across the south end of the acropolis where Temple 22 and its associated structures are located. Actually, I had demonstrated this fact in an earlier work before I ever realized the possibility that Venus might have played a role in the orientation problem (Aveni and Hartung 1976). Indeed, Stela 10, at the western horizon, would have been visible in the window of Temple 22 in the ceremonial center, from which one would have sighted Venus on the same evening that one viewed the sunset from the periphery of the site. Thus, there is an implied physical connection between the sun and Venus, and between Temple 22 and the baseline. They are connected by a concrete set of observations and were probably accompanied by an attending ceremony.

I should point out that the astronomical hypothesis relating Stelae 12 and 10, taken by itself, can be attacked on the grounds that there are other outlying stelae and that they were used as boundary markers to indicate the limits of Copán polity. On the other hand, of all the stela groups lying in the environment of Copán *only St. 10 and St. 12 are intervisible over some considerable distance* and they are the only pair that interconnect points at or very near the horizon (Stelae 2, 3, 5, and 6 are all located on the valley floor of Copán and St. 23 is on the valley floor in Santa Rita; St. 13, on the east side of the valley, is not visible from St. 10, which is located in the west; nor is St. 19, further west, visible from St. 10. From St. 12 in the east one cannot see St. 19 or St. 23. From either St. 19 or 13 no other outlying stela is visible.) Therefore, only this particular pair could reasonably be postulated as a functional baseline regardless of how many outliers exist.

That these outliers could have functioned as spatial/territorial boundary markers and calendrical markers at the same time seems not incompatible. Ethnohistoric data strongly imply that mnemonic schemes such as the ceque system of Cuzco served a multiplicity of functions. In that case, we have clear evidence that the ceque lines used to divide up the Inca capital were boundary markers for water rights, lines indicating the delineation of kinship groups, and astronomical sight lines used in the partition of the seasonal calendar (Aveni 1980: ch. V).

To discount the importance of the baseline further, on the grounds that one element of it (namely, Stela 10) is not located precisely at the horizon, I should point out that I have demonstrated (Aveni 1977: fig. 4) that in fact it is very close to the horizon, only about 1/2° below it. We must be careful not to require the Maya to align their stelae the way we would if we had possessed the desire to invent their calendar.

I conclude that this baseline, above all others that can possibly be constructed among the outliers, is the very one that works—that is, it fits with the calendar as we know it and it fits quite precisely. Finally, it is worth remembering that Stela 10 is the only one that would have been visible at the horizon *as seen from Temple 22.* Any suggestion that the sun would not have been visible at the beginning of the Milpa because of weather conditions at this time is unfounded. Eternal cloudiness is not a precondition anywhere in the Maya world in any season. Given generally bad weather at this time, I believe the Maya would have had a significant need to anticipate this time of year by establishing a solar baseline that marked a time well in advance of the start of the rainy season for the attending ritual ceremonies. This appears to be exactly what the Copanecos did by establishing the baseline to mark the 12 April date, which falls about 20 days (one uinal) in advance of (and in the same month as) the average date of the first rainfall. The importance to the Maya of doing things on the proper day is reflected in the very existence of the codices, which were intended to be carried from place to place by the priests. It was their function to give the correct date for a civic, social, or agricultural ceremony or event based on what was happening in the natural world. And we know that the codices are based at least in part upon real astronomical observations.

In a situation not unlike that which Schele and Miller (1986:106) advocated for Cerros 5C-2nd, Temple 22 seems to have been related to the reenactment and reaffirmation of kingship, though I would suggest the hierophany is a bit more complex. The ceremony, like the calendar of which it is a part, has both its public and private aspects and it is interesting that the Venus glyph, complete with its Chac prefix, appears in the Copán hieroglyphs in the chain of appellations associated with ascension to rulership. That part of the scheme visible to the public consists of the king on his throne, Venus in the sky, and the sun coming to the horizon. We have, on the one hand, in real time, the visual phenomenon of the sun attached to Venus as the two are observed twisting about in the western sky and, on the other hand, in mythological time, the Venus and sun symbols appearing in stucco carvings at opposite ends of the bicephalic monster. The eye, viewing at the appropriate time, is confronted with two different kinds of visual imagery that, for the Maya, conveyed identical notions of

reality. Additional knowledge, perhaps known only to the priests, is encapsulated in the view that appeared to them through the window of the temple and along the sight line between Stelae 12 and 10. The invention of a scheme associating the baseline with the temple was a brilliant stroke of Maya genius relating center and periphery, sun and Venus, king and deity, all at the same time. The ceremonies attending the astronomical observations, whatever they might have been, would surely have impressed anyone standing in the East Court of the Copán Acropolis a millennium and a half ago.

Postscript

Today we stand at a crossroads in Mesoamerican archaeoastronomical research. Many ideas and methodologies are beginning to give converging results about the practical use of the heavens by very real people. But in formulating ancient astronomical interpretations and intentions one often confuses symbolism and function. It would be dangerous to postulate that people adhered strictly to observations of the heavens in the regulation of the planting cycle. In this sense I believe the 12-10 baseline and the window of Temple 22 at Copán did not function as *precise* astronomical observatories. Rather, they were more likely intended as symbolic triggering mechanisms that played a role in ritual enactments of Maya principles and beliefs related to agricultural fertility. Understanding architecture, like astronomy, to possess a multitude of levels of meaning in the Maya mentality, I see no conflict between the use of the Stela 12-10 baseline as a time marker and in a broader sense as part of a group of outlying monuments intended to mark the limits of the Copán polity.

The study of possible astronomical orientations at Copán and elsewhere offers us an opportunity to examine what constitutes evidence in archaeoastronomy and what types of evidence take priority in arguing a case. To understand astronomical evidence and the possible impact of astronomical phenomena upon the Maya world view, this paper has tried to emphasize that we must witness the celestial events that the Maya actually saw in the sky over Copán. By doing so, one begins to realize the dialectical nature of the sun-Venus relationship and the magnitude of the visible events associating these two luminaries. Even if one were to reject the iconographic arguments altogether, one cannot ignore the fact that the Venus and solar orientations in the architecture fit together in a way that evokes not only the most vital period of the agricultural season but also the very type of calendar (counting by twenties relative to solar zenith passage) that we know the ancient Maya once practiced and that their descendants continue to employ.

Now these interconnected, convergent, internally consistent arguments, substantially backed by dates that appear in the Copán inscriptions, must be reflected against the purely archaeological evidence concerning the probable sequence of construction of buildings and the laying out of subsidiary monuments. But what is bothersome about the use of archaeological evidence is that too often its practitioners accord it a certain priority, especially when it is employed in a reductionist-type argument that tries to combat explanations for human behavior derived from other ways of thinking and dealing with other kinds of evidence. Such reductionist arguments, which emanate from the domain of normal scientific thinking, can become too preoccupied with the professionally necessary task of setting limitations upon hypotheses, but this often occurs with the imposition of the dictate that those other explanations must employ a given archaeological datum uniquely—for example, the idea that the existence of more than one window or baseline or Venus glyph reduces astronomical arguments to pure coincidence. These are the sorts of objections that pay no regard whatever to the astronomical evidence that, as real as the buildings the archaeologist has exhumed from the ground, appears in the sky above them. While it is true that man built the buildings but did not construct the sky, he did erect all of the sky symbols, inscriptions, and arrangements that served to connect sacred space to the natural environment. These symbols provide the link in explaining how the Maya interpreted what they saw, and every investigator is obligated to pay attention to them as well as to the structures they adorn.

One category of evidence ought not take priority over another. The best hypothesis becomes the one that is both internally self-consistent and externally relatable or interpretable in light of *all* the evidence. And the safest guiding assumption in our search for the answers is always that the Maya probably did not operate the way we do.

Acknowledgments

I am indebted to Horst Hartung, Victoria and Harvey Bricker, Mary Miller, Linda Schele, Justin Kerr, Tom Jones, Claude Baudez, and Michael Closs for invaluable discussions on the problem dealt with in this paper; to the officials of INAH Mexico and the Government of Honduras for granting permission to work at the sites; and to the OSCO Fund for supporting the research program.

Artificial Intelligence Meets Maya Epigraphy

JORGE L. OREJEL OPISSO
UNIVERSITY OF TEXAS AT AUSTIN

This paper presents a research project involving a novel application of Artificial Intelligence (AI) techniques to the problem of deciphering the Maya hieroglyphic inscriptions.

One goal of AI is to understand the nature of intelligent behavior from a computational point of view; the intention is to implement, in terms of computer programs, the fundamental processes underlying intelligence. AI researchers have been working for a number of years on problems including machine vision, natural language understanding, knowledge representation, and commonsense reasoning. A result of such researches is a body of computational tools finding application in fields other than AI itself, as exemplified by commercial AI-based systems ranging from database management to computer-aided design and manufacturing (Winston and Prendergast 1984).

Maya epigraphy attempts to unravel the meaning of the hieroglyphic inscriptions that the Maya carved on their monuments and wrote in their religious books. The goal is a better understanding of Maya thought as revealed by the content of their writing. Here, too, a number of scholars have devoted their efforts to areas including grammar, phonology, iconography, and religion.

The one feature that AI and Maya epigraphy have in common is their attempt to solve quite difficult problems. AI strives to explain intelligence, while Maya epigraphy attempts to decipher a language for which to date no Rosetta stone has been found. This paper shows that the decipherment of Maya inscriptions can be approached by using AI techniques and tools developed within the areas of machine vision, knowledge representation, natural language understanding, and commonsense reasoning.

Issues Involved in the Decipherment of Maya Inscriptions

This section is an appraisal of the major issues involved in the problem of deciphering Maya hieroglyphic inscriptions.

Methodology

One of the problems faced by any novice attempting to study Maya inscriptions is that the knowledge amassed throughout years of research is scattered in a number of books (some out-of-print), journals, doctoral dissertations (some unpublished), workshops, and conference proceedings. The problem is further aggravated by the fact that knowledge about the Maya is fragmentary, sometimes highly speculative and even contradictory.

The use of drawings has long been the standard way to study Maya hieroglyphic inscriptions. Several researchers have done remarkable reproductions, the most notable examples being Maudslay's plates (1889–1902) and Schele's drawings (1978c). The quality of these works of art is such that they are often borrowed by other researchers to report their investigations.

Aside from the fact that copying glyphs from the actual inscriptions takes much time that could otherwise be devoted to their interpretation, it is often the case that the misidentification of glyphs leads to errors of interpretation. Recognizing this, several scholars have reported their results with drawings made on the basis of high-quality photographs (Schele 1974); yet there have been complaints regarding the lack of graphic material to aid in the interpretation of the inscriptions (Closs 1984a). To alleviate this, some researchers are working on the compilation of inscriptions from all the major sites in the Maya area (Graham et al. 1975–1983), and of hieroglyphs and their variants (Morell 1986), presumably with their meanings in specific contexts.

An example of the methods used to decipher Maya inscriptions is the one followed by Linda Schele and David Stuart, called "patterning out" (Morell 1986:56). This involves gathering all the known glyphs related to a given subject and studying and drawing them a countless number of times "until a pattern shows up." However, it would be interesting to figure out an effective procedure (that is, an algorithm) to achieve such patterning out. Also, it is questionable whether one has to draw the glyphs many times in order "to pay attention to the smallest detail that might give a clue toward their interpretation."

Language Components

The decipherment of Maya inscriptions, dealing with the understanding of a language, involves lexical, syntactic, and semantic analyses. Another important aspect is the pragmatism involved in the everyday use of language.

Lexical Analysis

This aspect concerns the identification of the basic tokens, or lexical units, of a language. In the case of the inscriptions on the monuments, a given cartouche is composed in general by an arrangement of elementary units: prefixes, postfixes, superfixes, subfixes (all denoted by the term "affixes"), and main signs. The graphic nature of the glyphs makes lexical analysis a very hard problem in pattern recognition, for in many respects it is identical to the problem of recognizing handwritten words: any given letter may be written in an infinite number of ways. During recognition, humans somehow compensate for the variations; it seems that they compare the actual letter with an "ideal" model of it. The variations that are readily apparent in the hieroglyphic inscriptions include scaling, rotation, stretching and shrinking in various directions, slanting, and slight differences in the rendering of a given lexical unit.

A nice illustration of the way epigraphers perform pattern matching at the lexical level is presented by Morley and Brainerd (1983:530) in their explanation of Knorozov's approach to the decipherment (fig. 1): "Noting the similarity of our first glyph in the compound for turkey [fig. 1a] to the glyph over Landa's *cu* [fig. 1b] (they both have the X-shape inside, for example), we hypothesize that this glyph is indeed the syllabic sign for *cu*, and the word being spelled in the codices is *cutz*." It is not hard to see that the glyphs considered are quite different (for one thing, the glyph for *cu* is upside-down with respect to the corresponding glyph in the compound). Nevertheless, the matching was carried out suc-

cessfully. Figure 1c shows a more striking example of the glyph for *cu* embedded in a glyph group on page 19 of the Dresden Codex. Note that in this case the matching has to be done on the basis of general resemblance, rather than pairing of specific features.

Syntax

Syntactic analysis concerns the valid ways in which the lexical units can be put together to form a sentence of the language. In the case of Maya texts, there are certain orders of reading of glyph blocks (fig. 2), but no justifications have been given as to why they are in effect. Presumably, these orders are supported by the fact that they "work" in the sense of leading to a successful interpretation, or by evidence from the syntax of spoken Maya languages. However, the orders of reading say nothing about specific meanings associated with lexical units.

Semantics

Semantic analysis is the crux of the decipherment problem, for it deals with the denotation (meaning) of sentences of the language. In this case, there are some examples illustrating glyph groups constituting semantic units including dates, names and titles, parentage relationships, and historical events (fig. 3).

The use of dictionaries of Maya languages is valuable for assigning meanings to glyphs, by interpreting them either logographically or phonetically, and then finding their meaning on the basis of the meanings associated to surrounding glyphs. Nevertheless, the dictionaries from the colonial period pertain to Maya languages that may be quite different from the one spoken by the Classic Maya (Morley and Brainerd 1983:510). Aside from this, Marta Foncerrada de Molina has pointed out (personal communication, 1986) the weaknesses inherent to the unsystematic use of words from just about *any* Maya dialect with the sole purpose of providing a plausible interpretation for a given glyph.

Even though research has reached a point where complete inscriptions can be read (Morley and Brainerd 1983), much remains to be done. First, it is necessary to reach a consensus on the meanings of glyphs; for instance, the catalogs of phonetic interpretations of Maya glyphs often list the various phonetic values assigned by different scholars (Justeson and Campbell 1984; Ayala 1985). Regarding the partial Maya syllabary, Fox and Justeson (1984b) determined that a large number of Maya glyphs are polyvalent in that they have the same phonetic value. However, little is known about semantic polyvalence, the denotation of several concepts by the same glyph as a function of the context. An example of semantic polyvalence is the glyph for *zotz'*, which can mean either "bat" or "to write" (Morell 1986). On the other hand, the case of synonymy, the assignment of the same semantic referent to different glyphs, has scarcely been investigated.

The status of the understanding of Maya inscriptions is evidenced by the somewhat cryptic or obscure nature

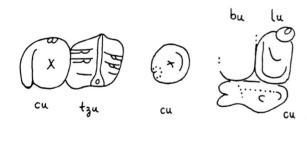

a   **b**   **c**

Fig. 1 (a) Glyphic compound for the word "turkey"; (b) Glyph for syllable cu *in Landa's "alphabet"; (c) Glyph group containing the glyph for* cu *(drawings by Jorge L. Orejel Opisso, adapted from Morley and Brainerd 1983: 530–531).*

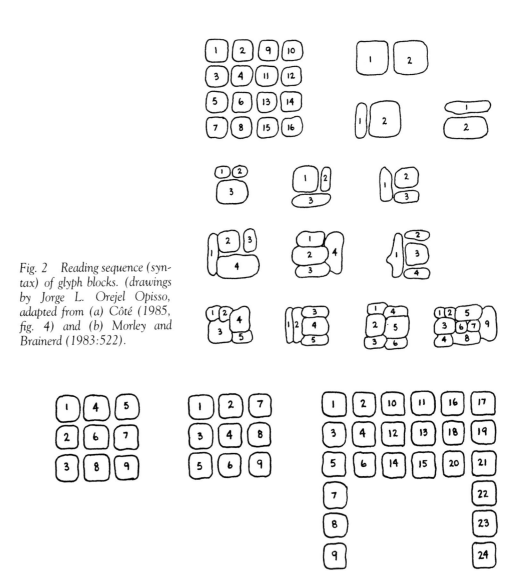

Fig. 2 Reading sequence (syntax) of glyph blocks. (drawings by Jorge L. Orejel Opisso, adapted from (a) Côté (1985, fig. 4) and (b) Morley and Brainerd (1983:522).

b

of their readings, for quite often researchers introduce additional words in order to make the texts more understandable. This conciseness suggests a pragmatic use of the glyphs to convey a given concept. In everyday use of language, people make elisions of words for the very reason that they know what they are talking about, so that their use of language is devoid of most of the formalities enforced by a grammar. It may be the case that Maya scribes wrote their texts in such a cryptic way just because they knew that anyone living in that time should understand them. Therefore, of the three aspects involved in understanding Maya inscriptions, lexical and semantic analyses are of prime importance; a rigid syntax can be dispensed with.

The Application of AI to the Decipherment Problem

This section outlines the way AI tools and techniques can be applied to the problem of deciphering the Maya hieroglyphic inscriptions.

Machine Vision

Early work on AI had to do with machine vision, the endeavor of making computers able to "see" (Winston 1970; Waltz 1972). A related research area, called pattern recognition, dealt with the use of syntactic and semantic information about picture elements to identify objects in a visual scene.

An example of the work on pattern recognition is that

Orejel O.

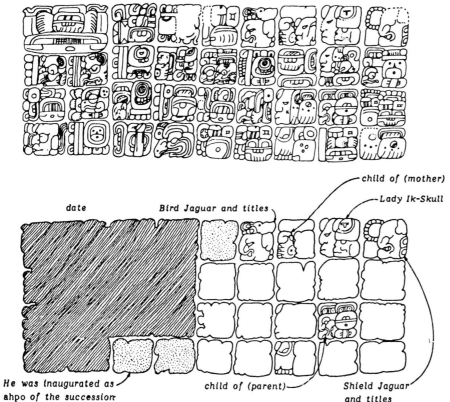

date   Bird Jaguar and titles

child of (mother)

Lady Ik-Skull

He was inaugurated as
ahpo of the succession

child of (parent)

Shield Jaguar
and titles

Yaxchilan Stela 11, front lower register

Fig. 3   Identification of meaningful units (semantics) in hieroglyphic inscriptions (drawings by Linda Schele 1982:31).

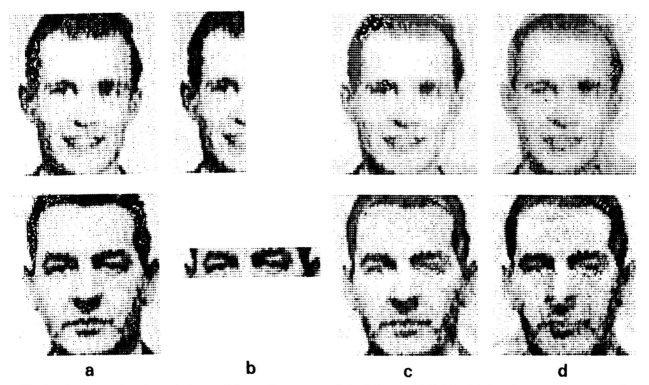

a   **b**   **c**   **d**

Fig. 4   Demonstration of associative recall from a linear system (after Kohonen 1978:21). (a) Samples of original images; (b) key patterns; (c) recall from a memory with 160 stored images; (d) recall from a memory with 500 stored images.

of Kohonen (1978), who showed that humanlike pattern recognition could be achieved with the aid of associative memories, that is, memories accessed by their content rather than specific addresses. The main result was the demonstration that techniques of associative recall could be employed to recognize complete images, such as faces, from the presentation of fragmentary information, such as a region surrounding the eyes (fig. 4).

The discussion of any details concerning associative recall is outside the scope of this paper; suffice it to say that such a mechanism avoids the problems involved in brute-force sequential search for an item stored in memory. The recollection takes a constant amount of time, independent of the number of items stored, a feature that makes associative memory a good vehicle for retrieving digitized images of any kind.

The first interesting application of pattern recognition and machine vision to the decipherment of Maya inscriptions is the implementation of a computerized database of glyphs, such as those in Thompson's *Catalog* (1962).[1] The implementation of the database requires the use of a digitizer to store digital representations of glyphs in memory. During the storage of glyphs, additional information associated with them could also be introduced in order to constitute a *knowledge base* (fig. 5a). This additional information would include names and meanings of individual glyphs and their interrelationships, as well as complete inscriptions and their interpretations.

The most trivial use of such a database would be facilitating the access to hieroglyphic inscriptions and individual glyphs. Instead of going through either a printed

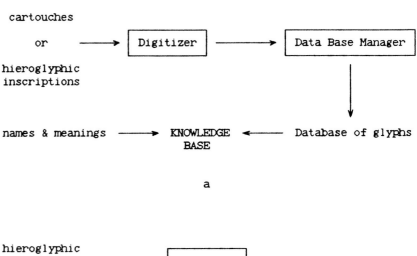

a

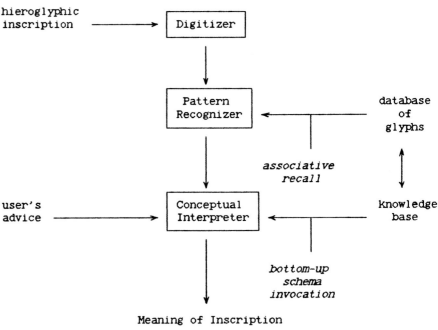

Fig. 5 (a) Implementation of a database of digitized hieroglyphs; the hieroglyphs plus associated information (names, meanings, etc.) constitute a knowledge base; (b) organization of a system for computer-aided decipherment of Maya inscriptions.

b

catalog or scores of publications, researchers would simply issue a query (possibly in natural language) to the computer, and a query interpreter would recall from memory the inscriptions or glyphs needed. With present-day computer technology, it is possible to build a database equivalent to the expected contents of Graham's *Corpus*; the requirements are sharp photographs of the inscriptions, a digitizer, a program implementing the mechanism of associative mapping, a query interpreter, and a graphics program to depict the digitizations on the computer screen.

Natural Language Understanding

A second, far more interesting application of the database is the interpretation of inscriptions by the computer. A system could be implemented not only to help researchers in the decipherment, but also to attempt decipherments on its own, that is, to suggest possible meanings for some inscriptions. The major components of such a system would be a pattern recognizer and a conceptual interpreter (fig. 5b).

The pattern recognizer would identify the glyphs comprising an inscription, by matching their digital representations against those stored in the database. By means of the mechanism of associative recall, it would retrieve all the glyphs matching a given glyph within the inscription.

The recognition of glyphs by computer entails the solution of certain problems. One of them is the partitioning of the image from a cartouche in order to identify its constituents (main sign and affixes). To this end, it will be necessary to use one or more of the techniques for image segmentation (Pavlidis 1977) and edge detection (Hildreth 1980; Canny 1983) that have emerged from AI research.

Another problem is the identification of glyphs in spite of variations such as scaling, rotation, perspective distortion, and stretching and shrinking, which by itself is a very hard problem in pattern recognition. These variations can be viewed as transformation operations on an "ideal" glyph, and they can be mathematically accounted for (i.e., reproduced) by means of homogeneous transformations (Roberts 1965), matrix operators that transform a given matrix representation of an object into another.

Gerald Sussman pointed out (personal communication, 1986) that the key issue is knowing just which transformation to apply for matching an idealized glyph with the actual glyph under consideration, but it may be the case that a reduced number of transformations were actually "applied" by the Maya scribes. Support for this hypothesis comes from the statement that "[the] visual symbol system in Maya art worked like a language, [in such a way] that individual taste and creative expression had to be subordinated to the imperative of communication" (Schele and Miller 1986:41). Given that Maya inscriptions are considered an artistic expression, the "conservativism of Maya iconography" would entail few

stylistic variations in the rendering of hieroglyphs within the inscriptions. In any event, the work of Leung and his colleagues (1985) on the generation of Chinese characters from "standard" versions of them could help to characterize the variations present in Maya inscriptions.

The function of the conceptual interpreter would be receiving information about identification of glyphs by the pattern recognizer and then trying to figure out a meaning for the unknown portions of the inscription. To achieve such a task, the interpreter has to have access to a huge amount of information, which would be used to establish a context of interpretation for the given inscription. This information has to be represented in some form within the database; hence, any successful implementation of the interpreter depends on an efficient knowledge-representation mechanism.

Knowledge Representation

The work of Tatiana Proskouriakoff (1960, 1963, 1964) has been recognized as a major breakthrough toward the decipherment of Maya inscriptions; based on pure commonsense reasoning, her approach led to the association of glyphs to concepts dealing with historical events. The main result was Proskouriakoff's definition of some sort of "conceptual schema" for identifying phrases of historical content (italics added): "It seems safe to say that glyphs which immediately follow dates and especially those that tend to combine with the 'lunar' postfix make reference to *actions*, events or ceremonies, and are essentially predicate glyphs. Following them *we can expect* to find substantives referring to the *protagonists* of the events, and if the representations are historical, some of these would be *appellatives* identifying the persons involved."

Proskouriakoff also showed that certain inscriptions associated with portraits of personages could be interpreted as narratives. An example is Lintel 8 at Yaxchilán, which depicts the capture of Jeweled Skull by Bird Jaguar (Stuart 1975:788; Morell 1986:55–56). It is remarkable that about seven glyphs were enough for the Maya to render a concept as complicated as the capture of an enemy in battle. It is tempting to say that the Maya used the glyphs as some sort of *conceptual representation* of stereotypical situations; this view is supported by the observation that Maya texts were highly abbreviated, even to the point of being telegraphic or mnemonic (Morley and Brainerd 1983:539).

In the realm of AI, the problem of understanding natural language has followed various paths. One of them is called the conceptual approach, whereby language is understood by relating concepts to each other in the most reasonable way. A fundamental feature of this approach is that syntax plays only a minor role (if any) in the understanding process; rather, it is semantics that guides the interpretation. Several computer programs have implemented one part or another of this *conceptual dependency theory* (Schank and Riesbeck 1981), on the basis of knowledge-representation mechanisms known as *scripts,* which capture "chunks" of knowledge (i.e., concepts) in a way that can be used by these programs to understand stories about stereotypical situations.

Scripts have been replaced by more elaborate mechanisms such as *schemata,* which are also data structures representing generic concepts (Rumelhart 1980). In general, schemata contain knowledge and information about how to use it. A schema has *variables* that can be associated with different aspects of the environment of a story (protagonists, objects, etc.); it also enforces *constraints* on the typical values taken by the variables and on their possible interrelationships.

Schemata have *default assignments* for their variables; such values are used when the environment (i.e., the context) does not provide specific values for some variables. Usually, a schema is activated upon the recognition of specific *keywords* in the text, as exemplified by the mechanism known as *bottom-up schema invocation* (Granger 1980). Finally, schemata can *embed* within each other—that is, a complex schema can usually be defined in terms of simpler schemata, thereby enabling the activation of a schema when any one of its constituent subschemata gets activated.

With regard to story understanding, a reader is said to have understood a given text when finding a configuration of hypotheses (i.e., schemata) that accounts for the various aspects of the story. This accounting for the meaning of a story is usually demonstrated by the ability of the understander to paraphrase the story, to answer specific questions about it, or to *fill in* any details left unsaid in the story.

The theory about schemata fits very well with Proskouriakoff's approach. Schemata can represent in a concise yet expressive way the knowledge pertaining to the decipherment of the inscriptions. For instance, the skeleton for one of Proskouriakoff's schemata could be the following:

Trigger:	dates and glyphs combined with "lunar" prefix.
Reference:	birth, accession to power, commemoration, death.
Quality:	lineage personages.
Expectations:	names of rulers, sites, and parentage relationships.

The symbolic information contained in a schema can be expressed in terms of Lisp-like data structures.[2] Figure 6 shows the definition of a schema for identifying the components of the Initial Series, along with an application of it to a representation of Stela A at Copán, Honduras. In the schema, names preceded by "?" and "*" denote *pattern variables* that match, respectively, a single glyph or an indefinite number of glyphs (including none) when the schema is successfully applied to an inscription. Names preceded by ">" denote constants whose value is defined outside of the schema; all other names denote either a glyph or a subschema. The assignment of values to pattern variables is indicated by writing their names inside the region containing the glyphs that matched with it.

Figures 7 through 9 show the definition of most of the schemata pertaining to the "birth event," along with their application to sample inscriptions (see the assignments to pattern variables) in the Tablet from the Temple of the Cross, Palenque (Schele 1978c). Note that almost all the schemata are defined in terms of simpler subschemata; for instance, the first version of the schema for *Birth* (fig. 7) is defined in terms of a schema for the *Calendar Round Date,* a schema for a *Name Phrase,* and a schema for *Place Identification.* In most cases, schemata also contain constant information, specific patterns of glyphs that "trigger" them during the interpretation of inscriptions. Once a schema is activated, all the *predicates* stated in the section named "constraints:" are tested in order to see if the values for pattern variables

Fig. 6 (a) Definition of a schema for identifying the Initial Series; (b) representation of Stela A at Copán, Honduras. Assignments to pattern variables are indicated by writing them inside the glyph group matching each one: "pattern:" describes the components of the inscription; "LongCountDate," "260DayCount," "God-Name," "phrase," "Lunar-Series," and "365DayCount" are subschemata comprising the schema; "constraints:" indicates the restrictions (predicates) imposed on the values taken by pattern variables.

```
(DefSchema InitialSeries
    (pattern:
        ?ISIG
        (LongCountDate   *a)
        (260DayCount     *b)
        (GodName         *c)
        (phrase          *d)
        (LunarSeries     *e)
        (365DayCount     *f))
    (constraints:
        (?ISIG   (and (infixed ?MG)
                      (in ?MG >MonthPatrons)))))


(setq MonthPatrons
    '(pop uo zip zotz tzec xul yaxkin mol
      chen yax zac ceh mac kankin muan
      pax kayab cumku uayeb))
```

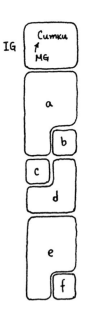

```
(DefSchema Birth
    (version: 1)
    (pattern:
        (CalendarRoundDate  *v1)          v1 = (A16 B16)
        "740.181:126"
        (NamePhrase         *v2)))        v2 = (B17 C1)

(DefSchema CalendarRoundDate
    (pattern:
        (260DayCount        *v1)          v1 = (A16)
        (365DayCount        *v2))         v2 = (B16)
    (suggests:
        InitialSeries
        Birth
        Death
        Accesssion
        Burial))

(DefSchema 260DayCount
    (pattern:
        ?coeff                            coeff   = (prefix A16)
        ?DayName)                         DayName = (main A16)
    (constraints:
        (?coeff    (in >TzolkinNumbers))
        (?DayName (in >TzolkinDays))))

(DefSchema 365DayCount
    (pattern:
        ?coeff                            coeff     = (prefix B16)
        ?MonthName)                       MonthName = (main B16)
    (constraints:
        (?coeff       (in >HaabNumbers))
    (suggests:
        CalendarRoundDate))
        (?MonthName (in >HaabMonths))))

(DefSchema NamePhrase
    (pattern:
        (ProperName         *v1)          v1 = (B17 C1)
        (Titles             *v2)          v2 = ()
        (EmblemGlyph        *v3)))        v3 = ()
```

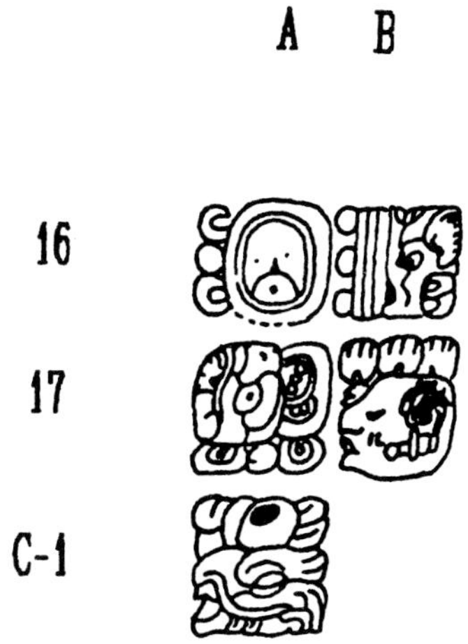

Fig. 7   First version of a schema for identifying the "birth event." The schema Birth is defined in terms of two subschemata (CalendarRoundDate and NamePhrase), plus a constant glyph group ("740.181:126"). The subschema CalendarRoundDate is defined in terms of two subschemata (260DayCount and 365DayCount), while NamePhrase is defined in terms of three subschemata (ProperName, Titles, and EmblemGlyph). "Suggests:" signals the names of the schemata that would be triggered upon the activation of the Birth schema. Assignments to pattern variables correspond to the application of the schemata to a portion of the Tablet of the Temple of the Cross, Palenque (drawing by Jorge L. Orejel Opisso, adapted from Schele 1978:16).

are allowed. If a schema is successfully activated, then it will cause the activation of all the schemata mentioned in the section named "suggests:."

After the activation of schemata, the interpreter (either human or machine) is expected to "zero in" on the meaning of the inscription by deleting all the schemata that really are irrelevant. Evidently, this "zeroing in" requires a great deal of reasoning by the interpreter.

Figure 8 shows the second version of a schema for Birth, while figure 9 illustrates the definition of a schema, named *BirthToAccession*, that accounts for a narrative about the time span between the birth of a ruler and his accession to power.

Deductive Systems, Data Dependencies, and Belief Revision

The conceptual interpreter, being a reasoning system, is bound to make deductions; in a typical situation, portions of a given inscription suggest schemata that enable the interpreter to deduce the meaning of glyphs. The minimum requirement for such a deductive system is the ability to keep track of the logical dependence of facts.

```
(DefSchema Birth
    (version: 2)
    (pattern:
        (RelativeDate    *v1)          v1 = (E10 F10 E11 F11 E12 F12)
        "?pre.740"
        (NamePhrase      *v2)))        v2 = (F13 E14 F14 E15)


(DefSchema RelativeDate
    (pattern:
        (DistanceNumber     *v1)       v1 = (E10 .. F11)
        "ADI.126:59"
        (CalendarRoundDate *v2))       v2 = (F12)
    (suggests:
        Birth))


(DefSchema DistanceNumber
    (pattern:
        ?DNIG
        (Kins       *v1)               v1 = (prefix-main E10)
        (Uinals     *v2)               v2 = (superfix-main E10)
        (Tuns       *v3)               v3 = (F10)
        (Katuns     *v4)               v4 = (E11)
        (Baktuns    *v5))              v5 = (F11)
    (constraints:
        (?DNIG     (match "11.12.?ms:12")))
    (suggests:
        Birth
        BirthToAccession
        BirthToBirth))


(DefSchema NamePhrase
    (pattern:
        (ProperName     *v1)           v1 = (F13)
        (Titles         *v2)           v2 = (E14 F14)
        (EmblemGlyph    *v3)))         v3 = (E15)
```

10

11

12

13

14

15

Fig. 8   Second version of a schema for the "birth event." The schema Birth is defined in terms of two subschemata (Relative-Date and NamePhrase) plus a pseudo-constant glyph group ("?pre.740") that allows for variations in the prefix position. Assignments to pattern variables result after applying the schemata to a portion of the Tablet from the Temple of the Cross, Palenque (Schele 1978:19).

Data dependencies were developed to enable AI reasoning systems to record the logical antecedents of deduced facts (de Kleer et al. 1977, 1978), in such a way that these systems are capable of explaining their "train of thoughts" from a conclusion back to its premises. Another advantage of data dependencies is the possibility of introducing *assumptions* on the basis of lack of knowledge.[3] Assumptions are important because any reasoning system must use them in order to make hypotheses with regard to the meaning of a text that provides only partial information.

Data dependencies are also useful for performing belief revision upon the detection of contradictions. The simplest case of the occurrence of a contradiction is when a reasoning system asserts (i.e., believes) both a fact and its negation; however, there exist more subtle examples of contradictions, such as the case where two *semantically opposite* facts are simultaneously asserted by the reasoner. To the best of my knowledge, to date no AI system is capable of dealing with such cases of logical inconsistency.

It is likely that during the interpretation of an inscription the conceptual interpreter will introduce incorrect assumptions about the meaning of portions of the inscription, either because the text is too general or because some "low-level" schemata misled the interpreter to a certain interpretation. After detecting a contradiction, the interpreter must invoke a *dependency-directed backtracker* (Stallman and Sussman 1976), a module responsible for retracting (i.e., making the system disbelieve) an incorrect assumption in order to remove the contradiction. This process, known as *truth maintenance*

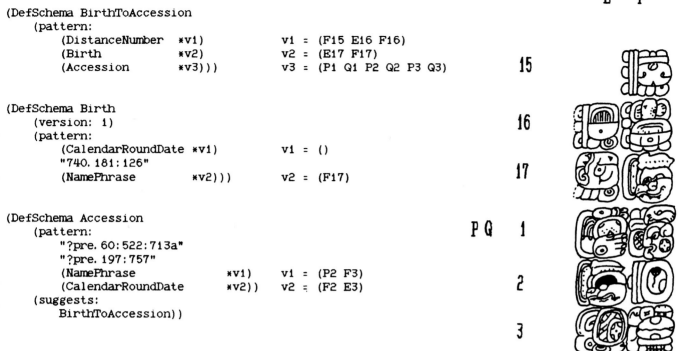

```
(DefSchema BirthToAccession
    (pattern:
        (DistanceNumber    *v1)           v1 = (F15 E16 F16)
        (Birth             *v2)           v2 = (E17 F17)
        (Accession         *v3)))         v3 = (P1 Q1 P2 Q2 P3 Q3)

(DefSchema Birth
    (version: 1)
    (pattern:
        (CalendarRoundDate *v1)           v1 = ()
        "740. 181:126"
        (NamePhrase        *v2)))         v2 = (F17)

(DefSchema Accession
    (pattern:
        "?pre. 60:522:713a"
        "?pre. 197:757"
        (NamePhrase        *v1)           v1 = (P2 F3)
        (CalendarRoundDate *v2))          v2 = (F2 E3)
    (suggests:
        BirthToAccession))
```

Fig. 9 *Definition of schemata* BirthToAccession *and* Accession *for identifying (in conjunction with the schema for birth) a historical record of the time span between the birth of a ruler and his accession to power. Assignments to pattern variables result after applying the relevant schemata to a portion of the Tablet of the Temple of the Cross, Palenque (drawing by Jorge L. Orejel Opisso, adapted from Schele 1978:20).*

(Doyle 1978) or reason maintenance (Charniak and McDermott 1985), enables the reasoning system to believe in a well-founded set of deducted facts, in such a way that each fact has some reason to be believed.[4]

There is, however, a problem related to the introduction of assumptions: too many assumptions at different stages of the reasoning process may prevent the backtracker from retracting those assumptions that are directly responsible for the occurrence of the contradiction. This phenomenon has been called *assumption screening* (Orejel 1984) and its solution entails the implementation of a dependency-directed backtracker that uses domain-dependent knowledge to select the assumptions that most likely caused the contradiction. In addition, the schema-based conceptual interpreter has to use world-knowledge in order to judge the relevance of schemata in a given situation; to work properly, it must know what things can be done, what constitutes a coherent behavior, and what features characterize individuals, objects, and situations.

AI systems intended to understand natural language have worked on modern languages like English. Given that our world is quite complex, the designers of these programs often circumscribe themselves to "microworlds," that is, worlds that incorporate some simplifying assumptions. The reason is that at present there is no general formalism for representing and managing knowledge in an efficient way inside the memory of a computer.

In proposing the design of a system for interpreting the Maya hieroglyphic inscriptions, I am making the fundamental assumption that understanding the Maya language requires far less world-knowledge than is required to understand modern languages; by necessity, life and culture in the Classic Maya Period were much simpler than their modern counterparts. The key to success is capturing in the knowledge base the state of affairs in the Maya area around A.D. 600.

Conclusions and Future Work

It has been shown that AI technology can help in the decipherment of the Maya hieroglyphic inscriptions, in particular regarding their historical content. A reasoning system was proposed to attempt decipherments of the inscriptions, on the basis of schemata containing information about glyphic compounds; however, the implementation of the modules comprising the system was described in very general terms.

Our present research efforts involve the implementation of the digitizer, to build the database of digital representations of individual glyphs and complete inscriptions. Essentially, it is a parallel version of a digitizer designed to work on the basis of a dynamic random-access memory that can provide a digital readout after being exposed to light from an image (Ciarcia 1983a, 1983b). To date, the implementation is halfway toward completion.

Regarding the conceptual interpreter and associated modules, the most challenging and difficult part is the pattern recognizer, for it is the module responsible for identifying glyphs and their constituents; this module has not been implemented yet because it depends on the completion of the digitizer. Other modules, such as a deductive data-retrieval system, a reason maintenance system, and a discrimination net manager, have already been implemented, on the basis of those designed as part of a story understander called WATSON (Orejel 1984).[5] However, it is certain that some of these modules will have to be extended and refined in a number of ways; for instance, the reason maintenance system will need a domain-dependent dependency-directed backtracker.

The import of this research project is twofold. Artificial Intelligence will help to broaden our understanding of Maya thought, and it will provide a more systematic approach to the investigation of the content of the Maya hieroglyphic inscriptions. On the other hand, the decipherment problem will point out many weaknesses in current AI technology and will suggest ways to improve it.

Notes

1. It is interesting to note previous efforts to use computers in Maya epigraphy. The work of Michael McCarthy and Rosalie Robertson dealt with the implementation of a computerized glyph catalog. Quite remarkably though, their paper was not included in the proceedings of the conference in which it was presented (Justeson and Campbell 1980).

2. The programming language Lisp (McCarthy et al. 1980) has long been the workhorse of AI research.

3. In the AI jargon, this technique is called *default reasoning*, or the assumption of a fact on the lack of evidence that its negation holds.

4. Data dependencies have been used, with modest success, by AI reasoning systems for analyzing and synthesizing electronic circuits (Stallman and Sussman 1976; de Kleer and Sussman 1980), for learning to prove theorems (O'Rorke 1984), and for understanding natural language (O'Rorke 1983; Orejel 1984).

5. Currently, these modules run on an IBM Personal Computer, and are written in the Lisp dialect known as IQLISP (Integral Quality, 1983).

Acknowledgments

I am indebted to Marta Foncerrada de Molina and to Augusto Molina for their constant encouragement, and for being my mentors at the Sexta Mesa Redonda de Palenque. I appreciate all the suggestions and comments of Pedro Molina Foncerrada (a former student and a colleague of mine at the Instituto Tecnológico de Monterrey) on the various drafts of this paper. I am also indebted to Merle Greene Robertson for her encouragement and for accepting my paper for presentation at the Mesa Redonda. Last, but not least, thanks to my wife, Irma, and to my daughter, Raquel, for their love, patience, and encouragement.

Bibliography

Ackerman, Diane
1988 A Reporter at Large: Crocodilians. *The New Yorker* October 10:42–48.

Adams, Richard E. W.
1971 *The Ceramics of Altar de Sacrificios*. Papers of the Peabody Museum of Archaeology and Ethnology 63(1). Cambridge, Mass.: Harvard University.
1973 Maya Collapse: Transformation and Termination in the Ceramic Sequence at Altar de Sacrificios. In *The Classic Maya Collapse*, edited by T. Patrick Culbert, pp. 133–163. Albuquerque: University of New Mexico Press.
1984 Rio Azul Project Report, Number 1. Final 1983 Report. Center for Archaeological Research, University of Texas at San Antonio.
1986 Rio Azul: Lost City of the Maya. *National Geographic* 169(4):420–451.
n.d. A Reevaluation of Maya Militarism. MS.

Anders, Ferdinand
1963 *Das Pantheon der Maya*. Graz, Austria: Akademische Druck- und Verlagsanstalt.

Anderson, A. H.
1958 Recent Discoveries at Caracol Site, British Honduras. In *Proceedings of the 32nd International Congress of Americanists*. Copenhagen.
1959. More Discoveries at Caracol, British Honduras. In *Actas del 33rd Congreso Internacional des Americanistas*. Costa Rica.

Andrews IV, E. Wyllys
1970 *Balankanche, Throne of the Tiger Priest*. Middle American Research Institute Publication no. 32. New Orleans: Tulane University.

Andrews IV, E. Wyllys, and E. Wyllys Andrews V
1980 *Excavations at Dzibilchaltun, Yucatan, Mexico*. Middle American Research Institute Publication no. 48. New Orleans: Tulane University.

Andrews V, E. Wyllys
1981 Dzibilchaltun. In *Supplement to the Handbook of Middle American Indians*. Vol. 1, *Archaeology*, edited by Victoria R. Bricker and Jeremy A. Sabloff, pp. 313–341. Austin: University of Texas Press.
1982 Some Comments on Puuc Architecture of the Northern Yucatan Peninsula. In *The Puuc: New Perspectives*, edited by Lawrence C. Mills, pp. 1–17. Scholarly

Studies in the Liberal Arts Publication no. 1. Pella, Iowa: Central College.

Angulo V., Jorge
1987 The Chalcatzingo Reliefs: An Iconographic Analysis. In *Ancient Chalcatzingo*, edited by David C. Grove, pp. 133–158. Austin: University of Texas Press.

Attinasi, John J.
1979 Chol Performance: Do Not Talk to Dogs, They Might Talk Back to You. In *Mayan Texts II*, edited by Louanna Furbee-Losee. IJAL-NATS Monograph 3:3–17.

Aulie, H. Wilbur, and Evelyn W. de Aulie
1978 *Diccionario Ch'ol-Español, Español-Ch'ol*. Serie de Vocabularios y Diccionarios Indigenas Mariano Silva y Aceves, tomo 21. Mexico, D.F.: Instituto Lingüístico de Verano.

Aveni, Anthony F.
1975 Possible Astronomical Orientations in Ancient Mesoamerica. In *Archaeoastronomy in Pre-Columbian America*, edited by Anthony F. Aveni, pp. 163–190. Austin: University of Texas Press.
1977 Concepts of Positional Astronomy Employed in Ancient Mesoamerican Architecture. In *Native American Astronomy*, edited by Anthony F. Aveni, pp. 3–20. Austin: University of Texas Press.
1980 *Skywatchers of Ancient Mexico*. Austin: University of Texas Press.
1983 The Moon and the Venus Table in the Dresden Codex: An Example of Commensuration in the Maya Calendar. Paper presented at the Conference on Ethnoastronomy, Washington, D.C.

Aveni, Anthony F., and Horst Hartung
1976 Investigación Preliminar de las Orientaciones Astronómicas de Copan. *Yaxkin* 1(3):8–13.
1979 Some Suggestions About the Arrangement of Buildings at Palenque. In *Tercera Mesa Redonda de Palenque*, edited by Merle Greene Robertson and Donnan Call Jeffers, pp. 173–177. Palenque: Pre-Columbian Art Research Center.
1986 Maya City Planning and the Calendar. *Transactions of the American Philosophical Society* 76(pt. 1):1–81.

Ayala Falcon, Maricela
1985 *El Fonetismo en la Escritura Maya*. Mexico, D.C.: Universidad Nacional Autonoma de Mexico, Centro de Estudios Mayas.

Ball, Joseph W.

1974 A Coordinate Approach to Northern Maya Prehistory: A.D. 700–1200. *American Antiquity* 39(1):85–93.

1979 Ceramics, Culture History, and the Puuc Tradition: Some Alternative Possibilities. In *The Puuc: New Perspectives*, edited by Lawrence C. Mills, pp. 18–35. Scholarly Studies in the Liberal Arts publication no. 1. Pella, Iowa: Central College.

Balser, Carlos

1974 *El Jade de Costa Rica*. San Jose, Costa Rica: Lehmann.

Bardawil, Lawrence W.

1976 The Principal Bird Deity in Maya Art: An Iconographic Study of Form and Meaning. In *The Art, Iconography & Dynastic History of Palenque, Part 3*, edited by Merle Greene Robertson, pp. 195–209. Pebble Beach, Calif.: Robert Louis Stevenson School.

Barrera, Marciano

1965 Apuntes sobre los rios de Usumacinta. *Periódico Oficial del Departamento de Yucatan*, Merida.

Barrera Vasquez, Alfredo

1943 Horoscopos Mayas o el Prognostico de los 20 Signos del Tzolkin, segun los Libros de Chilam Balam, de Kaua y de Mani. *Registro de Cultura Yucateca* 6, Merida (reissued in 1976, with a new appendix by José Diaz Bolio).

1980 *Diccionario Maya Cordemex: Maya-Español, Español-Maya*. Merida, Mexico: Ediciones Cordemex.

Barerra Vasquez, Alfredo, and Silvia Rendon

1948 *El Libro de los Libros de Chilam Balam*. Mexico City: Fondo de Cultura Económica.

Barthel, Thomas S.

1953 Regionen des Regengottes (zur Deutung der unteren Teile der Seiten 65–69 in der Dresdener Mayahandschrift). *Ethnos* 18:86–105.

1955 Versuch uber die Inschriften von Chich'en Itza Viejo. *Baessler-Archiv*, N.F. Band 3:5–33.

1966 Mesoamerikanische Fledermausdamonen. *Tribus* 15:101–124.

Basauri, Carlos

1931 *Tojolabales, Tzeltales y Mayas: Breves Apuntes Sobre Antropología, Etnografía y Lingüística*. Mexico, D.F.: Talleres Graficos de la Nación.

Bassie, Karen

1986 The Relationship Between Text and Image. Pt. 2, The Group of the Cross at Palenque. MS.

In preparation The Relationship Between Text and Image. Pt. 1, Yaxchilan.

Baudez, Claude F.

1983 (editor) *Introducción a la arqueología de Copan, Honduras*. 3 vols. Tegucigalpa: Instituto Hondureño de Antropología e Historia.

1984 Le Roi, La Balle et le Mais: Images du Jeu de Balle Maya. *Journal de la Société des Americanistes* 70:139–152.

1985 The Knife and the Lancet: The Iconography of Sacrifice at Copan. In *Fourth Palenque Round Table, 1980*, edited by Elizabeth P. Benson (Merle Greene Robertson, General Editor), pp. 203–210. San Francisco: Pre-Columbian Art Research Institute.

1988 Solar Cycle and Dynastic Succession in the Southeastern Maya Zone. In *The Southeast Classic Maya Zone: A Symposium at Dumbarton Oaks*, edited by Elizabeth H. Boone and Gordon R. Willey, pp. 125–148. Washington, D.C.: Dumbarton Oaks.

In press The House of the Bacabs: An Iconographic Analysis of Structure 9N-82, Copan. In *The House of the Bacabs*, edited by David Webster. Washington, D.C.: Dumbarton Oaks.

Baudez, Claude F., and A. S. Dowd

1983 La Decoración del Templo. In *La Estructura 10L-18: Capitulo X*, edited by Marshall J. Becker and Charles D. Cheek, pp. 447–473. Vol. 2 of *Introducción a la Arqueología de Copán, Honduras*. Tegucigalpa: Instituto Hondureño de Antropología e Historia.

Beadle, George

1977 The Origins of Maize. In *The Origins of Agriculture*, edited by Charles Reed, pp. 615–635. The Hague: Mouton Publishers.

1978 The Origin of *Zea mays*. In *Cultural Continuity in Mesoamerica*, edited by David L. Bowman, pp. 23–42. The Hague: Mouton Publishers.

Becerra, Marcos E.

1980 *Nombres Geográficos Indígenas del Estado de Chiapas*. Tabasco, Mexico: Consejo Editorial del Gobierno del Estado de Tabasco. (First edition Tuxtla Gutiérrez: Imprenta del Gobierno, 1930.)

Becquelin, Pierre, and Claude F. Baudez

1982 Tonina, une cité Maya du Chiapas (Mexique). *Etudes Mesoamericaines* 6(2). Paris: Mission Archeologique et Ethnologique Française au Mexique. Tomes 2, 3.

Beetz, Carl P., and Linton Satterthwaite

1981 *The Monuments and Inscriptions of Caracol, Belize*. University Museum Monograph no. 45. Philadelphia: The University Museum, University of Pennsylvania.

Benson, Elizabeth P.

1971 *An Olmec Figure at Dumbarton Oaks*. Studies in Pre-Columbian Art and Archaeology, no. 8. Washington, D.C.: Dumbarton Oaks.

Bergh, Susan E.

1985 An Analysis of the Drawings of the "Beau Relief." Seminar paper. Columbia University, New York.

Bergman, John F.

1959 The Cultural Geography of Cacao in Aboriginal America and Its Commercialization in Early Guatemala. Ph.D. diss., Department of Geography, University of California, Los Angeles.

Berjonneau, Gerald, and Jean-Louis Sonnery

1985 *Rediscovered Masterpieces of Mesoamerica: Mexico-Guatemala-Honduras*. Boulogne: Editions Arts.

Berlin, Heinrich

1955 News from the Maya World. *Ethnos* 20:201–209.

1958 El glifo "emblema" en las inscripciones mayas. *Journal de la Société des Americanistes* 47:111–119.

1963 The Palenque Triad. *Journal de la Société des Americanistes* 52:91–99.

Bernal, Ignacio

1969 *The Olmec World*. Berkeley: University of California Press.

Beyer, Hermann

1937 Studies on the Inscriptions of Chichén Itzá. *Contributions to American Archaeology* 4(21). Carnegie Institution of Washington Publication no. 483. Washington, D.C.

1969 Relaciones entre la civilización Teotihuacana y Azteca. In *Cien años de arqueología Mexicana*, pp. 245–272. El Mexico Antigua, tomo XI. Sociedad Alemana Mexicanista.

Bloch, Maurice
  1977 The Disconnection Between Power and Rank as a Process: An Outline of the Development of Kingdoms in Central Madagascar. In *The Evolution of Social Systems*, edited by J. Friedman and M. J. Rowlands, pp. 303–340. London: Duckworth.
Blom, Frans
  1923 *Las Ruinas de Palenque, Xupá y Finca Encanto.* Mexico, D.F.: Instituto Nacional de Antropología e Historia.
  1953 La Selva Lacandona y Tierras Colindantes, Chiapas, Mexico. San Cristobal de las Casas, Chiapas.
Blom, Frans, and Oliver La Farge
  1926 *Tribes and Temples.* 2 vols. New Orleans: Tulane University.
Bolles, John S.
  1977 *Las Monjas: A Major Pre-Mexican Architectural Complex at Chichén Itzá.* Norman: University of Oklahoma Press.
Borhegyi, Stephen F.
  1959 The Composite or "Assemble-it-Yourself" Censer: A New Lowland Maya Variety of the Three-Pronged Incense Burner. *American Antiquity* 25:51–58.
  1965 Archaeological Synthesis of the Guatemalan Highlands. In *Handbook of Middle American Indians* (Robert Wauchope, General Editor). Vol. 2, *Archaeology of Southern Mesoamerica*, edited by Gordon R. Willey, pp. 3–58. Austin: University of Texas Press.
  1969 The Pre-Columbian Ballgame: A Pan-Mesoamerican Tradition. *Proceedings of the 38th International Congress of Americanists* 1968(1):499–515. Munich.
Borhegyi, Stephen, and Suzanne Borhegyi
  1963 The Rubber Ball-Game of Ancient America. *Lore-Leaves* (Milwaukee Public Museum) 8.
Bove, Frederick J.
  1981 The Evolution of Chiefdoms and States on the Pacific Slope of Guatemala: A Spatial Analysis. Ph.D. diss., University of California, Los Angeles. (Available from University Microfilms, Ann Arbor, Michigan.)
  1989a Settlement Classification Procedures in Formative Escuintla, Guatemala. In *New Frontiers in the Archaeology of the Pacific Coast of Southern Mesoamerica*, edited by Frederick J. Bove and Lynette Heller. Anthropological Research Papers, no. 19. Tempe: Arizona State University.
  1989b Dedicated to the Costeños. Introduction. In *New Frontiers in the Archaeology of the Pacific Coast of Southern Mesoamerica*, edited by Frederick J. Bove and Lynette Heller. Anthropological Research Papers, no. 19. Tempe: Arizona State University.
Brainerd, George
  1958 *The Archaeological Ceramics of Yucatan.* University of California Anthropological Papers, no. 19. Berkeley.
Brasseur de Bourbourg, Charles E.
  1862 *Gramatica de la Lengua Quiche.* Vol. 2, pt. 2 of *Collections de Documents dans les Langues Indigenes*, edited by A. Beltrand. Paris.
Breton, Adela C.
  1907 Wall Painting at Chichén Itzá. *Proceedings of the 15th International Congress of Americanists*, pp. 165–169. Quebec.
Bricker, Harvey M., and Victoria R. Bricker
  1983 Classic Maya Predictions of Solar Eclipses. *Current Anthropology* 24(1):1–23.

Bricker, Victoria R.
  1973 *Ritual Humor in Highland Chiapas.* Austin: University of Texas Press.
  1974 The Ethnographic Context of Some Traditional Mayan Speech Genres. In *Explorations in the Ethnography of Speaking*, edited by Richard Bauman and Joel Sherzer, pp. 368–388. Cambridge: Cambridge University Press.
  1981 Las Ceremonias de Año Nuevo en los Monumentos Clasicos Mayas. Paper presented at the 15th Mesa Redonda de la Sociedad Mexicana de Antropología, June 21–27, San Cristobal de las Casas, Chiapas, Mexico.
  1983 Directional Glyphs in Maya Inscriptions and Codices. *American Antiquity* 48:347–353.
  1984 The Last Gasp of Maya Hieroglyphic Writing in the Books of Chilam Balam Chumayel and Chan Kan. Paper presented at the Colloquium on the Language of Writing in the Maya Region, April 23–24, University of Chicago.
  1985 A Morphosyntactic Interpretation of Some Accession Compounds and Other Verbs in the Mayan Hieroglyphs. In *Fourth Palenque Round Table, 1980*, edited by Elizabeth P. Benson (Merle Greene Robertson, General Editor), pp. 67–85. San Francisco: Pre-Columbian Art Research Institute.
  1986 *A Grammar of Mayan Hieroglyphs.* Middle American Research Institute Publication no. 56. New Orleans: Tulane University.
Bricker, Victoria R., and Harvey M. Bricker
  1986 Archaeoastronomical Implications of an Agricultural Almanac in the Dresden Codex. *Mexicon* 8(2): 29–35.
Brinton, Daniel G.
  1882 *The Maya Chronicle.* Brinton's Library of Aboriginal American Literature, no. 1. Philadelphia.
Bruce S., Roberto D.
  1976 *Textos y Dibujos Lacandones de Naja.* Collección Científica Lingüística, tomo 45. Mexico City: Instituto Nacional de Antropología e Historia.
  1979 *Lacandon Dream Symbolism: Dream Symbolism and Interpretation Among the Lacandon Mayas of Chiapas, Mexico.* Vol. 2. Mexico, D.F.: Ediciones Euroamericanas Klaus Thiele.
Brundage, Burr C.
  1979 *The Fifth Sun: Aztec Gods, Aztec World.* Austin: University of Texas Press.
Bullard, William R.
  1965 Ruinas Ceremoniales Mayas en el Curso Inferior del Rio Lacantun, Mexico. *Estudios de Cultura Maya* 5: 41–51.
  1970 *Topoxte: A Postclassic Maya Site in Peten, Guatemala.* Papers of the Peabody Museum of Archaeology and Ethnology 61(3):245–276. Cambridge, Mass.: Harvard University.
Campbell, Lyle, and Terrence S. Kaufman
  1976 A Linguistic Look at the Olmecs. *American Antiquity* 41(1):80–89.
Canny, John
  1983 Finding Edges and Lines in Images. Technical Report 720, Massachusetts Institute of Technology AI Lab. Cambridge, Mass.
Carlson, John B.
  1986 The Iconography of Rio Azul Tomb 12. Paper presented at the Sexta Mesa Redonda de Palenque, Mexico.
Carmack, Robert M.
  1981 *The Quiché Mayas of Utatlán: The Evolution of a*

Highland Guatemala Kingdom. Norman: University of Oklahoma Press.

Carmack, Robert M., and James L. Mondloch
  1983 *El Titulo de Totonicapan*. Mexico, D.F.: Universidad Nacional Autonoma de Mexico.

Castro, Jose I.
  1983 *The Sharks of North American Waters*. College Station: Texas A&M University Press.

Cervantes, Maria Antonieta
  1969 Dos elementos de uso ritual en el arte olmeca. *Anales del Instituto Nacional de Antropología e Historia, 1967–1968*. Epoca 7, Tomo 1:37–51. Mexico.

Charnay, Desire
  1885 *Les anciennes villes du Nouveau Monde: Voyages d'explorations au Mexique et l'Amerique Centrale*. Paris.
  1888 *Ancient Cities of the New World*. New York: Harper and Brothers.

Charniak, Eugene, and Drew V. McDermott
  1985 *Introduction to Artificial Intelligence*. Reading, Mass.: Addison–Wesley.

Chase, Arlen F.
  1976 Topoxte and Tayasal: Ethnohistory in Archaeology. *American Antiquity* 41:154–167.
  1983 A Contextual Consideration of the Tayasal-Paxcaman Zone, El Peten, Guatemala. Ph.D. diss., University of Pennsylvania.
  1984 Organizational Aspects of Classic Period Santa Rita Corozal, Belize. Paper presented at the 83rd annual meeting of the American Anthropological Association, Denver.
  1985a Archaeology in the Maya Heartland: The Tayasal-Paxcaman Zone, Lake Peten, Guatemala. *Archaeology* 38(1):32–39.
  1985b Contextual Implications of Pictorial Vases from Tayasal, Peten. In *Fourth Palenque Round Table, 1980*, edited by Elizabeth P. Benson (Merle Greene Robertson, General Editor), pp. 193–201. San Francisco: Pre-Columbian Art Research Institute.
  1985c Postclassic Peten Interaction Spheres: The View from Tayasal. In *The Lowland Maya Postclassic*, edited by Arlen F. Chase and Prudence D. Rice, pp. 184–205. Austin: University of Texas Press.
  1985d Troubled Times: The Archaeology and Iconography of the Terminal Classic Southern Lowland Maya. In *Fifth Palenque Round Table, 1983*, edited by Virginia M. Fields (Merle Greene Robertson, General Editor), pp. 103–114. San Francisco: Pre-Columbian Art Research Institute.
  1986 Time Depth or Vacuum: The 11.3.0.0.0 Correlation and the Lowland Maya Postclassic. In *Late Lowland Maya Civilization: Classic to Postclassic*, edited by Jeremy A. Sabloff and E. Wyllys Andrews, pp. 99–140. Albuquerque: University of New Mexico Press.

Chase, Arlen F., and Diane Z. Chase
  1987a *Glimmers of a Forgotten Realm: Maya Archaeology at Caracol, Belize*. Orlando: University of Central Florida.
  1987b *Investigations at the Classic Maya City of Caracol, Belize: 1985–1987*. Pre–Columbian Art Research Institute Monograph no. 3. San Francisco.
  In press El Norte y el Sur: Politica, Dominios, y Evolución Cultural Maya. In *Los Mayas del Norte de Yucatan*, edited by M. Rivera and F. Jimenez. Madrid: Sociedad Española de Estudios Mayas y Instituto de Cooperación Ibero-americana.

Chase, Arlen F., Diane Z. Chase, and Harriot W. Topsey
  1988 Archaeology and the Ethics of Collecting. *Archaeology* 41(1):56–60, 87.

Chase, Diane Z.
  1981 The Maya Postclassic at Santa Rita Corozal. *Archaeology* 34(1):25–33.
  1982 Spatial and Temporal Variability in Postclassic Northern Belize. Ph.D. diss., University of Pennsylvania.
  1985a Between Earth and Sky: Idols, Images, and Postclassic Cosmology. In *Fifth Palenque Round Table, 1983*, edited by Virginia M. Fields (Merle Greene Robertson, General Editor), pp. 223–233. San Francisco: Pre-Columbian Art Research Institute.
  1985b Ganned But Not Forgotten: Late Postclassic Archaeology and Ritual at Santa Rita Corozal, Belize. In *The Lowland Maya Postclassic*, edited by Arlen F. Chase and Prudence M. Rice, pp. 104–125. Austin: University of Texas Press.
  1988 Caches and C. Meaning from Maya Pottery. In *A Pot for All Reasons: Ceramic Ecology Revisited*, edited by L. Lackey and C. Kolb. Philadelphia: Temple University Press.

Chase, Diane Z., and Arlen F. Chase
  1982 Yucatec Influence in Terminal Classic Northern Belize. *American Antiquity* 47:596–614.
  1986 *Offerings to the Gods: Maya Archaeology at Santa Rita Corozal*. Orlando: University of Central Florida.
  1988 *A Postclassic Perspective: Excavations at the Maya Site of Santa Rita Corozal, Belize*. Pre-Columbian Art Research Institute Monograph no. 4. San Francisco.

Ciarcia, Steve
  1983a Build the Micro D-Cam Solid-State Video Camera. Pt. 1, The IS32 Optic Ram and the Micro D-Cam Hardware. *BYTE* (September).
  1983b Build the Micro D-Cam Solid-State Video Camera. Pt. 2, Computer Interfaces and Control Software. *BYTE* (October).

Clark, Lawrence E.
  1981 *Diccionario Popoluca de Oluta*. Serie de Vocabularios y Diccionarios Indígenas Mariano Silva y Aceves, tomo 25. Mexico, D.F.: Instituto Lingüístico de Verano.

Clark, Phil
  1972 *A Flower Lover's Guide to Mexico*. Mexico City: Minutiae Mexicana, S.A. de C.V.

Clarkson, Persis
  1978 Classic Maya Pictorial Ceramics: A Survey on Content and Theme. In *Papers on the Economy and Architecture of the Ancient Maya*, edited by Raymond Sidrys, pp. 86–141. Institute of Archaeology Monograph no. 8. Los Angeles: University of California.

Clavijero, Francisco Javier
  1968 *Historia Antigua de Mexico*. Colección Sepan Cuantos 29, Editorial Porrua, Mexico.

Closs, Michael
  1979 Venus in the Maya World: Glyphs, Gods, and Associated Astronomical Phenomena. In *Tercera Mesa Redonda de Palenque*, edited by Merle Greene Robertson and Donnan Call Jeffers, pp. 147–165. Palenque: Pre-Columbian Art Research Center.
  1981 Venus Dates Revisited. *Archaeoastronomy Bulletin* 4(4):38–41.
  1984a The Dynastic History of Naranjo: The Early Period. *Estudios de Cultura Maya* 15:77–96.

1984b   The Maya Glyph *batel,* "warrior." *Mexicon* 6(4): 50–52.

1985   The Dynastic History of Naranjo: The Middle Period. In *Fifth Palenque: Round Table, 1983,* edited by Virginia M. Fields (Merle Greene Robertson, General Editor), pp. 65–78. San Francisco: Pre–Columbian Art Research Institute.

In press   Cognitive Aspects of Mayan Eclipse Theory. In *World Archaeoastronomy,* edited by Anthony F. Aveni. Cambridge: Cambridge University Press.

Closs, Michael, Anthony F. Aveni, and B. Crowley

1984   The Planet Venus and Temple 22 at Copan. *Indiana* 9:221–247.

Cobean, Robert H., Michael D. Coe, Edward A. Perry, Jr., Karl R. Turekian, and Dinkar P. Kharkar

1971   Obsidian Trade at San Lorenzo Tenochtitlan, Mexico. *Science* 174:666–671.

Codex Dresden

1880   *Die Maya-Handschriften der Koniglichen Bibliothek zu Dresden.* Edited by E. Forstemann. Leipzig: A. Naumann'scen Lichtdruckerei.

Coe, Michael D.

1965a   *The Jaguar's Children: Preclassic Central Mexico.* New York: Museum of Primitive Art.

1965b   The Olmec Style and Its Distribution. In *Handbook of Middle American Indians* (Robert Wauchope, General Editor). Vol. 3, *Archaeology of Southern Mesoamerica,* edited by Gordon R. Willey, pt. 2, pp. 739–775. Austin: University of Texas Press.

1965c   A Model of Ancient Community Structure in the Maya Lowlands. *Southwestern Journal of Anthropology* 21(2).

1966   *An Early Stone Pectoral from Southeastern Mexico.* Studies in Pre-Columbian Art and Archaeology, no. 1. Washington, D.C.: Dumbarton Oaks.

1968   *America's First Civilization.* New York: American Heritage (in association with the Smithsonian Institution, Washington, D.C.).

1972   Olmec Jaguars and Olmec Kings. In *The Cult of the Feline: A Conference in Pre-Columbian Iconography,* edited by Elizabeth P. Benson, pp. 1–18. Washington, D.C.: Dumbarton Oaks.

1973a   The Iconology of Olmec Art. In *The Iconography of Middle American Sculpture,* edited by Ignacio Bernal et al., pp. 1–12. New York: The Metropolitan Museum of Art.

1973b   *The Maya Scribe and His World.* New York: The Grolier Club.

1975a   *Classic Maya Pottery at Dumbarton Oaks.* Washington, D.C.: Dumbarton Oaks.

1975b   Death and the Ancient Maya. In *Death and Afterlife in Pre–Columbian America,* edited by Elizabeth P. Benson, pp. 87–104. Washington, D.C.: Dumbarton Oaks.

1977a   Olmec and Maya: A Study in Relationships. In *The Origins of Maya Civilization,* edited by R. E. W. Adams, pp. 183–196. Albuquerque: University of New Mexico Press.

1977b   Supernatural Patrons of Maya Scribes and Artists. In *Social Process in Maya Prehistory: Essays in Honour of Sir J. Eric S. Thompson,* edited by Norman Hammond, pp. 327–347. London: Academic Press.

1978   *Lords of the Underworld: Masterpieces of Classic Maya Ceramics.* Princeton: Princeton University Press.

1982   *Old Gods and Young Heroes: The Pearlman Collection of Maya Ceramics.* Jerusalem: The Israel Museum.

Coe, Michael D., and Elizabeth P. Benson

1966   *Three Maya Relief Panels at Dumbarton Oaks.* Studies in Pre-Columbian Art and Archaeology, no. 2. Washington, D.C.: Dumbarton Oaks.

Coe, Michael D., and Richard A. Diehl

1980   *In the Land of the Olmec.* 2 vols. Austin: University of Texas Press.

Coe, William R.

1965   Artifacts of the Maya Lowlands. In *Handbook of Middle American Indians* (General Editor, Robert Wauchope). Vol. 3, *Archaeology of Southern Mesoamerica* edited by Gordon R. Willey, pp. 594–602. Austin: University of Texas Press.

1967   *Tikal: A Handbook of the Ancient Maya Ruins.* Philadelphia: The University of Museum, University of Pennsylvania.

Coggins, Clemency C.

1975   Painting and Drawing Styles at Tikal: An Historical and Iconographic Reconstruction. Ph.D. diss., Harvard University. (Available from University Microfilms, Ann Arbor, Michigan.)

1979   A New Order and the Role of the Calendar: Some Characteristics of the Middle Classic Period at Tikal. In *Maya Archaeology and Ethnohistory,* edited by Norman Hammond and Gordon R. Willey. Austin: University of Texas Press.

1980   The Shape of Time: Some Political Implications of a Four-Part Figure. *American Antiquity* 45:727–739.

1983a   An Instrument of Expansion: Monte Alban, Teotihuacan, and Tikal. In *Highland-Lowland Interaction in Mesoamerica: Interdisciplinary Approaches,* edited by Arthur G. Miller, pp. 49–68. Washington, D.C.: Dumbarton Oaks.

1983b   *The Stucco Decoration and Architectural Assemblage of Structure 1-sub, Dzibilchaltun, Yucatan, Mexico.* Middle American Research Institute Publication no. 49. New Orleans: Tulane University.

1986   A New Sun at Chichén Itzá. Paper presented at the Second Oxford International Conference on Archaeoastronomy, January 1986, Merida, Mexico.

Coggins, Clemency C., and Orrin C. Shane III

1984   *Cenote of Sacrifice: Maya Treasures from the Sacred Well at Chichén Itzá.* Austin: University of Texas Press.

Cogolludo, Diego Lopez de

1867–68   *Historia de Yucatan.* 2 vols. Merida, Mexico: Manuel Aldana Rivas. (4th edition. Merida: Talleres Graficos del Gobierno, 1954.)

Cohen, Abner

1974   *Two-Dimensional Man: An Essay on the Anthropology of Power and Symbolism in Complex Societies.* London: Routledge and Kegan Paul.

Cohodas, Marvin

1975   The Symbolism and Ritual Function of the Middle Classic Ball Game in Mesoamerica. *American Indian Quarterly* 2(2):99–130.

1978a   *The Great Ballcourt at Chichén Itzá Yucatan, Mexico.* New York: Garland Publishing.

1978b   Diverse Architectural Styles and the Ball Game Cult: The Late Middle Classic Period in Yucatan. In *Middle Classic Mesoamerica: A.D. 400–700,* edited by Esther Pasztory, pp. 85–107. New York: Columbia University Press.

1979   The Identification of Workshops, Schools, and Hands at Yaxchilan, a Classic Maya Site in Mexico. *Actes du Congres International des Americanistes* 7:301–313.

Collins, William, Sons and Co.
 1974 *Collins Spanish–English, English–Spanish Dictionary.* Glasgow: Press of the Publishers.

Compagno, L. J. V.
 1984 *FAO Species Catalogue.* Vol. 4, *Sharks of the World: An Annotated and Illustrated Catalogue of Shark Species Known to Date.* Pt. 2, *Carcharhiniformes.* Rome: United Nations Development Program, Food and Agriculture Organization.

Connor, Judith
 1983 The Ceramics of Cozumel, Quintana Roo, Mexico. Ph.D. diss., University of Arizona.

Côté, Manon Robyn
 1985 Mayan Words Spoken and Written: A Linguistic and Epigraphic Approach. *Haliksa'i* 4(Spring):15–42.

Covarrubias, Miguel
 1957 *Indian Art of Mexico and Central America.* New York: Knopf.

Cruz Guzman, Ausencio, J. Kathryn Josserand,
 and Nicholas A. Hopkins
 1980 The Cave of Don Juan. In *Third Palenque Round Table, 1978, Part 2,* edited by Merle Greene Robertson, pp. 116–123. Austin: University of Texas Press.
 1986 *T'an ti Wajali: Tales of Long Ago.* MS. (Chol texts, translated and annotated).

Culbert, T. Patrick
 1973 The Maya Downfall at Tikal. In *The Classic Maya Collapse,* edited by T. Patrick Culbert, pp. 63–92. Albuquerque: University of New Mexico Press.
 1977 Early Maya Development at Tikal, Guatemala. In *The Origins of Maya Civilization,* edited by R. E. W. Adams, pp. 27–43. Albuquerque: University of New Mexico Press.

Dahlin, Bruce H.
 1983 Climate and Prehistory on the Yucatan Peninsula. *Climatic Change* 5:245–263.
 1984 A Colossus in Guatemala: The Preclassic Maya City of El Mirador. *Archaeology* 37(5):18–25.

Darwin, Charles
 1869 Pangenesis: Mr. Darwin's reply to Professor Delphino. *Scientific Opinion: A Weekly Record of Scientific Progress at Home & Abroad* 2:426.
 1871 Pangenesis. *Nature: A Weekly Illustrated Journal of Science* 3:502–503.

Davoust, Michel
 1977 *Les Chefs Mayas de Chichen Itza.* Angers.
 1986 Nuevas lecturas de los textos Mayas de Chichen Itza. Paper presented at the Sexta Mesa Redonda de Palenque, June 1986, Palenque, Chiapas, Mexico.

Day, Christopher C.
 1971 *Un Diccionario de Jacalteco.* Computer printout, Department of Anthropology, University of Rochester.

De Gruyter, W. J.
 1946 *A New Approach to Maya Hieroglyphics.* Amsterdam.

De Kleer, Johann, and Gerald G. Sussman
 1980 Propagation of Constraints Applied to Circuit Synthesis. *International Journal of Circuit Theory and Applications* 9:127–144.

De Kleer, Johann et al.
 1977 AMORD, Explicit Control of Reasoning. Memo 427, Massachusetts Institute of Technology AI Lab. Cambridge, Mass.
 1978 AMORD, a Deductive Procedure System. Memo 435, Massachusetts Institute of Technology AI Lab. Cambridge, Mass.

De la Fuente, Beatriz
 1968 *Palenque en la Historia y el Arte.* Mexico, D.F.: Fondo de Cultura Economica.

De Long, Richard A.
 1986 Chiasmus in Mesoamerican Writing. Paper presented at the Sexta Mesa Redonda de Palenque, June 1986, Palenque, Chiapas.

Demarest, Arthur A., ed.
 1984 Proyecto El Mirador de la Harvard University 1982–1983, un informe preliminar. *Mesoamerica* 5(7).

Deutsche Gesellschaft fur Volkerkunde
 1983 Resolución. October 11. Freiburg.

De Vos, Jan
 1980 *Fray Pedro Lorenzo de la Nada, Misionero de Chiapas y Tabasco.* Chiapas, Mexico: Chilon.

Doebley, John F., and Hugh H. Iltis
 1980 Taxonomy of *Zea* (*Gramineae*). Pt. 1, A Subgeneric Classification with Key to Taxa. *American Journal of Botany* 67(6):982–993.

Doyle, Jon
 1978 Truth Maintenance Systems for Problem Solving. Technical Report 419, Massachusetts Institute of Technology AI Lab. Cambridge, Mass.

Drucker, Philip
 1952 *La Venta, Tabasco: A Study of Olmec Ceramics and Art.* Bureau of American Ethnology Bulletin no. 153. Washington, D.C., Smithsonian Institution.

Drucker, Philip, Robert Heizer, and Robert Squier
 1959 *Excavations at La Venta, Tabasco, 1955.* Bureau of American Ethnology Bulletin no. 170. Washington, D.C.: Smithsonian Institution.

Duran, Fray Diego de
 1965 *Historia de las Indias de Nueva Espana e Islas de Tierra Firme.* Tomo 2. Mexico, D.F.: Editora Nacional.
 1971 *Book of the Gods and Rites and the Ancient Calendar,* translated by F. Horcasitas and Doris Heyden. Norman: University of Oklahoma Press.

Dütting, Dieter
 1970 On the Inscription and Iconography of Kuna-Lacanha Lintel 1. *Zeitschrift für Ethnologie* 95:196–219.
 1972 Hieroglyphic Miscellanea. *Zeitschrift für Ethnologie* 97:220–256.
 1974 Sorcery in Maya Hieroglyphic Writing. *Zeitschrift für Ethnologie* 99:2–62.
 1978 "Bats" in the Usumacinta Valley: Remarks on Inscriptions of Bonampak and the Neighboring Sites in Chiapas, Mexico. *Zeitschrift für Ethnologie* 103:1–56.
 1980 Aspects of Classic Maya Religion and World View. *Tribus* 29:106–167.
 1981 Life and Death in Mayan Hieroglyphic Inscriptions. *Zeitschrift für Ethnologie* 106:185–228.
 1984 Venus, the Moon, and the Gods of the Palenque Triad. *Zeitschrift für Ethnologie* 109:7–74.
 1985a On the Astronomical Background of Mayan Historical Events. In *Fifth Palenque Round Table, 1983,* edited by Virginia M. Fields (Merle Greene Robertson, General Editor), pp. 261–274. San Francisco: Pre-Columbian Research Institute.
 1985b On the Context-dependent Use of Bi- and Polyvalent Graphemes in Mayan Hieroglyphic Writing. In *Fourth Palenque Round Table, 1980,* edited by Elizabeth P. Benson (Merle Greene Robertson, General Editor),

pp. 103–114. San Francisco: Pre-Columbian Art Research Institute.

1986 The Vase of the Eighty-eight Glyphs: Implications for the Decipherment of the Maya Script. *Tribus* 35: 83–103.

Earle, Duncan, and Dean Snow

1985 The Origin of the 260-day Calendar: The Gestation Hypothesis Reconsidered in Light of Its Use Among the Quiche People. In *Fifth Palenque Round Table, 1983*, edited by Virginia M. Fields (Merle Greene Robertson, General Editor), pp. 241–244. San Francisco: Pre-Columbian Art Research Institute.

Earle, Timothy K.

1978 *Economic and Social Organization of a Complex Chiefdom: The Halelea District, Kauai, Hawaii.* Anthropological Papers, no. 63. Ann Arbor: University of Michigan, Museum of Anthropology.

Easby, Elizabeth K.

1966 *Ancient Art of Latin America: From the Collection of Jay C. Leff.* Brooklyn: The Brooklyn Museum.

Easby, Elizabeth K., and John F. Scott

1970 *Before Cortes: Sculpture of Middle America.* New York: Metropolitan Museum of Art.

Edmonson, Munro S.

1965 *Quiche-English Dictionary.* Middle American Research Institute Publication no. 30. New Orleans: Tulane University.

1971 *The Book of Counsel: The Popol Vuh of the Quiche Maya of Guatemala.* Middle American Research Institute Publication no. 35. New Orleans: Tulane University.

1982 *The Ancient Future of the Itza: The Book of Chilam Balam of Tizimin.* Austin: University of Texas Press.

1984 Human Sacrifice in the Books of Chilam Balam of Tizimin and Chumayel. In *Ritual Human Sacrifice in Mesoamerica*, edited by Elizabeth Boone, pp. 91–100. Washington, D.C.: Dumbarton Oaks.

1985 The Baktun Ceremonial of 1618. In *Fourth Palenque Round Table, 1980*, edited by Elizabeth P. Benson (Merle Greene Robertson, General Editor), pp. 261–265. San Francisco: Pre-Columbian Art Research Institute.

Ekholm, Susanna

1969 *Mound 30a and the Early Preclassic Ceramic Sequence of Izapa, Chiapas, Mexico.* Papers of the New World Archaeological Foundation, no. 25. Provo, Utah.

Ekholm-Miller, Susanna

1973 *The Olmec Rock Carving at Xoc, Chiapas, Mexico.* Papers of the New World Archaeological Foundation, no. 32. Provo, Utah.

Farriss, Nancy M.

1984 *Maya Society Under Colonial Rule: The Collective Enterprise of Survival.* Princeton: Princeton University Press.

1987 Remembering the Future, Anticipating the Past: History, Time, and Cosmology among the Maya of Yucatan. *Comparative Studies in Society and History* 29:566–593.

Fash, William L.

1982 A Middle Formative Cemetery from Copan, Honduras. Paper presented at the annual meeting of the American Anthropological Association.

1983 Maya State Formation: A Case Study and Its Implications. Ph.D. diss., Harvard University, Cambridge, Mass.

1986 A New Look at the Early Classic Maya: Iconography, Inscriptions, and Archaeology. Paper presented at Maya Art and Civilization: The New Dynamics, May

16–18, Kimbell Art Museum, Fort Worth, Texas.

1986a La fachada esculpida de la Estructura 9N-82: Contenido, forma, iconografía. In *Excavaciones en el Area Urbana de Copan*, edited by William J. Sanders, pp. 319–382. Tegucigalpa: Instituto Hondureno de Antropología e Historia.

In press The Sculpture Facade of Structure 9N-82: Content, Form, and Meaning. In *The House of the Bacabs*, edited by David Webster. Washington, D.C.: Dumbarton Oaks.

Fash, William L., Ricardo Agurcia, and Elliot M. Abrams

1981 Excavaciones en el Sitio CV36, 1980–1981. *Yaxkin* 4(2):111–132.

Fash, William L., and C. Rudy Larios

In press The Restoration and Hypothetical Reconstruction of a Maya Nobleman's Palace. *Archaeology*

Fash, William L., and Sheree Lane

1983 El Juego de Pelota B. In *Introducción a la Arqueología de Copan*. Vol. 2, pp. 502–562. Tegucigalpa: Secretaria de Estado en el Despacho de Cultura y Turismo.

Ferguson, William M., and John Q. Royce

1984 *Maya Ruins in Central America in Color: Tikal, Copan, and Quirigua.* Albuquerque: University of New Mexico Press.

Fields, Virginia M.

1989 The Origins of Divine Kingship Among the Lowland Classic Maya. Ph.D. diss., University of Texas at Austin.

Flannery, Kent V.

1968 The Olmec and the Valley of Oaxaca: A Model for Interregional Interaction in Formative Times. In *Dumbarton Oaks Conference on the Olmec*, edited by Elizabeth P. Benson, pp. 79–117. Washington, D.C.: Dumbarton Oaks.

1972 The Cultural Evolution of Civilizations. *Annual Review of Ecology and Systematics* 3:399–426.

1973 The Origins of Agriculture. *Annual Review of Anthropology* 2:271–310.

1976 Contextual Analysis of Ritual Paraphernalia from Formative Oaxaca. In *The Early Mesoamerican Village*, edited by Kent V. Flannery, pp. 333–345. New York: Academic Press.

Förstemann, E.

1880 (editor) *Die Maya-Handschrift der königlichen Bibliothek en Dresden.* Leipzig: A. Naumann'schen Lichtdruckerei.

Fought, John G.

1965 A Phonetic and Morphological Interpretation of Zimmerman's Affix 61 in the Maya Hieroglyphic Codices. *Estudios de Cultura Maya* 5:253–280.

1976 Time Structuring in Chorti (Mayan) Narratives. In *Mayan Linguistics*. Vol. 1, edited by Marlys McClaren, pp. 228–242. Los Angeles: American Indian Studies Center, University of California.

1985 Cyclical Patterns in Chorti (Mayan) Literature. In *Supplement to the Handbook of Middle American Indians*. Vol. 3, *Literatures*, edited by Victoria R. Bricker and Munro S. Edmonson, pp. 133–146. Austin: University of Texas Press.

Fox, James

1984 The Hieroglyphic Band in the Casa Colorada. Paper presented at the American Anthropological Association, November 17, Denver, Colorado.

Fox, James A., and John S. Justeson

1984a Conventions for the Transliteration of Mayan Hieroglyphs. In *Phoneticism in Mayan Hieroglyphic Writing*, edited by John S. Justeson and Lyle Campbell, pp. 363–366. Institute for Mesoamerican Studies Publication no. 9. Albany: State University of New York.

1984b Polyvalence in Mayan Hieroglyphic Writing. In *Phoneticism in Mayan Hieroglyphic Writing*, edited by John S. Justeson and Lyle Campbell, pp. 17–76. Institute for Mesoamerican Studies Publication no. 9. Albany: State University of New York.

1986 Classic Maya Dynastic Alliance and Succession. In *Supplement to the Handbook of Middle American Indians*. Vol. 4, *Ethnohistory*, edited by Victoria R. Bricker and Ronald Spores, pp. 7–34. Austin: University of Texas Press.

Fox, John W.

1985 The Postclassic Highland Maya Ballgame: Its Spatial, Sociopolitical and Mythic Connotations. Paper presented at the Symposium on the Native American Ballgame: Regional Contexts and Comparative Interpretations, Tucson, Arizona.

Freidel, David A.

1979 Culture Areas and Interaction Spheres: Contrasting Approaches to the Emergence of Civilization in the Maya Lowlands. *American Antiquity* 44:36–54.

1981 Civilization as a State of Mind: The Cultural Evolution of the Lowland Maya. In *The Transition to Statehood in the New World*, edited by Grant D. Jones and R. R. Kautz, pp. 188–227. Cambridge: Cambridge University Press.

1983 Polychrome Facades of the Lowland Maya Preclassic. In *Painted Architecture and Monumental Sculpture in Mesoamerica*, edited by Elizabeth Boone, pp. 5–27. Washington, D.C.: Dumbarton Oaks.

1986 The Monumental Architecture. In *Archaeology at Cerros, Belize, Central America*. Vol. 1, *An Interim Report*, edited by Robin A. Robertson and David A. Freidel, pp. 1–22. Dallas: Southern Methodist University Press.

Freidel, David, and Linda Schele

1985 Knot-Skull, the Shining Seed: Death, Rebirth, and Heroic Amplification in the Lowland Maya Ballgame. Paper presented at the International Symposium on the Mesoamerican Ballgame and Ballcourts, Nov. 20–23, Tucson, Arizona.

1988 Symbol and Power: A History of the Lowland Maya Cosmogram. In *Maya Iconography*, edited by Elizabeth P. Benson and Gillett G. Griffin, pp. 44–95. Princeton: Princeton University Press.

Furbee, Louanna, and Martha J. Macri

1985 Velar and Alveopalatal Consonants in the Maya Hieroglyphs. *Journal of American Linguistics* 51(4):412–416.

Furst, Peter T.

1976 Fertility, Vision Quest, and Auto-Sacrifice: Some Thoughts on Ritual Blood-Letting Among the Maya. In *Segunda Mesa Redonda de Palenque*, edited by Merle Greene Robertson, pt. 3:181–193. Pebble Beach, Calif.: Robert Louis Stevenson School.

Gallenkamp, Charles, and Regina Elise Johnson, eds.

1985 *Maya: Treasures of an Ancient Civilization*. New York: Harry N. Abrams (in association with The Albuquerque Museum).

Gann, Thomas

1900 *Mounds in Northern Honduras*. Bureau of American Ethnology 19th Annual Report. Pt. 2:655–692. Washington, D.C.: Smithsonian Institution.

1918 *The Maya Indians of Southern Yucatan and Northern British Honduras*. Bureau of American Ethnology Bulletin no. 64. Washington, D.C.: Smithsonian Institution.

Garber, James F.

1983 Patterns of Jade Consumption and Disposal at Cerros, Northern Belize. *American Antiquity* 48(4):800–807.

Garcia Moll, Roberto

1975 Primera Temporada Arqueologica en Yaxchilan, Chiapas. *Boletín INAH* 12, epoca 2:3–12.

1985 *Palenque 1926–1945*. Mexico: INAH-SEP.

1986 El "Planchon de las Figuras" en Chiapas, Nuevo Reconocimiento Arqueologico. *Antropología, Nueva Epoca* (Instituto Nacional de Antropología e Historia, Mexico, D.F.) 7:23–25.

Gay, Carlo

1971 *Chalcacingo*. Graz, Austria: Akademische Druck-u. Verlagsanstalt.

1972 *Chalcacingo*. Portland: International Scholarly Book Services.

1974 *Xochipala: The Beginnings of Olmec Art*. Princeton: The Art Museum, Princeton University.

Gibbs, S.

1977 Mesoamerican Calendars as Evidence of Astronomical Activity. In *Native American Astronomy*, edited by Anthony F. Aveni, pp. 21–35. Austin: University of Texas Press.

Gillespie, Susan D.

1985 Ballgames and Boundaries. Paper presented at the International Symposium on the Mesoamerican Ballgame and Ballcourts, November 20–23, Tucson, Arizona.

Goldman, Irving

1970 *Ancient Polynesian Society*. Chicago: University of Chicago Press.

Gordon, George B.

1896 *Prehistoric Ruins of Copan, Honduras: A Preliminary Report of the Explorations by the Museum 1891–1895*. Peabody Museum Memoirs 1(1). Cambridge, Mass.: Harvard University.

Gould, Stephen J.

1984 A Short Way to Corn. *Natural History* 93(3):12–20.

Graham, Ian

1976 Archaeological Explorations. In *El Peten, Guatemala*. Middle American Research Institute Publication no. 33. New Orleans: Tulane University.

1978 *Naranjo, Chunhuitz, Xunantunich*. Vol. 2, pt. 2, of *Corpus of Maya Hieroglyphic Inscriptions*. Cambridge, Mass.: Peabody Museum of Archaeology and Ethnology, Harvard University.

1979 *Yaxchilan*. Vol. 3, pt. 2, of *Corpus of Maya Hieroglyphic Inscriptions*. Cambridge, Mass.: Peabody Museum of Archaeology and Ethnology, Harvard University.

1986 Looters Rob Graves and History. *National Geographic* 169(4):452–461.

Graham, Ian, and Eric Von Euw

1975 *Naranjo*. Vol. 2, pt. 1, of *Corpus of Maya Hieroglyphic Inscriptions*. Cambridge, Mass.: Peabody Museum of Archaeology and Ethnology, Harvard University.

1977 *Yaxchilan*. Vol. 3, pt. 1, of *Corpus of Maya Hieroglyphic Inscriptions*. Cambridge, Mass.: Peabody Museum of Archaeology and Ethnology, Harvard University.

Graham, Ian, Eric Von Euw, and Peter Mathews
1975–83 *Corpus of Maya Hieroglyphic Inscriptions.* 6 vols. Cambridge, Mass.: Peabody Museum of Archaeology and Ethnology, Harvard University.

Graham, John A., Robert F. Heizer, and Edward M. Shook
1978 Abaj Takalik 1976: Exploratory Investigations. In *Contributions to the University of California Archaeological Research Facility* 36:85–109. Berkeley: University of California.

Granger, Richard H.
1980 Adaptive Understanding: Correcting Erroneous Inferences. Technical Report 171, Computer Science Department, Yale University. New Haven, Conn.

Greene, Merle, Robert L. Rands, and John A. Graham
1972 *Maya Sculpture from the Southern Lowlands, the Highlands and the Pacific Piedmont: Guatemala, Mexico, Honduras.* Berkeley, Calif.: Lederer, Street, and Zeus.

Greene Robertson, Merle
1974 The Quadripartite Badge—A Badge of Rulership. In *Primera Mesa Redonda de Palenque, Part 1,* edited by Merle Greene Robertson, pp. 77–92. Pebble Beach, Calif.: Robert Louis Stevenson School.

1977 Painting Practices and Their Changes Through Time of the Palenque Stucco Sculptors. In *Social Process in Maya Prehistory: Studies in Honour of Sir Eric Thompson,* edited by Norman Hammond, pp. 297–326. London and New York: Academic Press.

1979 A Sequence for Palenque Painting Techniques. In *Maya Archaeology and Ethnohistory,* edited by Norman Hammond and Gordon R. Willey, pp. 149–171. Austin: University of Texas Press.

1983 *The Sculpture of Palenque.* Vol. 1, *The Temple of the Inscriptions.* Princeton: Princeton University Press.

1985a *The Sculpture of Palenque.* Vol. 2, *The Early Buildings of the Palace and the Wall Paintings.* Princeton: Princeton University Press.

1985b *The Sculpture of Palenque.* Vol. 3, *The Late Buildings of the Palace.* Princeton: Princeton University Press.

Greene Robertson, Merle, Edward Kurjack,
and Ruben Maldonado C.
1985 Ball Courts of the Northern Maya Lowlands. Paper presented at the Symposium on the Native American Ball Game: Regional Contexts and Comparative Interpretations, Tucson, Arizona.

Griffin, Gillett G.
1981 Olmec Forms and Materials Found in Central Guerrero. In *The Olmec and Their Neighbors,* edited by Elizabeth P. Benson, pp. 209–222. Washington, D.C.: Dumbarton Oaks.

Grove, David C.
1968 Chalcatzingo, Moreles, Mexico: A Reappraisal of the Olmec Rock Carvings. *American Antiquity* 33(4): 486–491.

1969 Olmec Cave Paintings: Discovery from Guerrero, Mexico. *Science* 164(3878):421–423.

1970 *The Olmec Paintings of Oxtotitlan Cave, Guerrero, Mexico.* Studies in Pre–Columbian Art and Archaeology, no. 6. Washington, D.C.: Dumbarton Oaks.

1973 Olmec Altars and Myths. *Archaeology* 26(2): 128–135.

1981 Olmec Monuments: Mutilation as a Clue to Meaning. In *The Olmec and Their Neighbors,* edited by Eliza-beth P. Benson, pp. 48–69. Washington, D.C.: Dumbarton Oaks.

1984 *Chalcatzingo: Excavations on the Olmec Frontier.* London: Thames and Hudson.

1987a Comments on the Site and Organization. In *Ancient Chalcatzingo,* edited by David C. Grove, pp. 420–433. Austin: University of Texas Press.

1987b "Torches," "Knuckledusters," and the Legitimization of Formative Period Rulership. *Mexicon* 9(3):60–65.

Grove, David C., and Susan Gillespie
1984 Chalcatzingo's Portrait Figurines and the Cult of the Ruler. *Archaeology* 37(4):27–33.

Grove, David C., and Louise I. Paradis
1971 An Olmec Stela from San Miguel Amuco, Guerrero. *American Antiquity* 36(1):95–102.

Grube, Nikolai
1985 Die Struktur der Primaren Standardsequenz auf Keramiken der Klassischen Mayakultur. Master's thesis, Altamerikanische Sprachen und Kulturen, University of Hamburg.

1986 *A Note on the Reading of Affix T142.* Research Reports on Ancient Maya Writing, no. 4. Washington, D.C.: Center for Maya Research.

Grube, Nikolai, and David Stuart
1987 *Observations on T110 as the Syllable ko.* Research Reports on Ancient Maya Writing, no. 8. Washington, D.C.: Center for Maya Research.

Guiteras Holmes, Calixta
1961 *Perils of the Soul: The World View of a Tzotzil Indian.* New York: The Free Press of Glencoe.

Hagen, Victor W. von
1977 *The Aztec and Maya Papermakers.* New York: Hacker Art Books. (Originally published in 1944.)

Hardy Gonalez, Arnulfo
1985 *Palenque: Pasado y Presente.* Tuxtla Gutiérrez: Gobierno del Estado de Chiapas.

Harrison, Peter D.
1974 Precolumbian Settlement Distributions and External Relationships in Southern Quintana Roo. Pt. 1, Architecture. *Atti degli XL Congreso Internazionale degli Americanisti* 1:479–486.

Hartig, Helga-Maria
1979 Datieres Lintel in Playa del Carmen. *Mexicon* 1(1): 5–6.

Haviland, William A.
1978 On Price's Presentation of Data from Tikal. *Current Anthropology* 19(1):180–181.

In press From Double Bird to Ah Cacao: Dynastic Troubles and the Count of the Katuns at Tikal, Guatemala. In *Papers of the 1987 Maya Weekend.* Philadelphia: The University Museum, University of Pennsylvania.

Hellmuth, Nicholas M.
1976 (editor) *Tzakol and Tepeu Maya Pottery Drawings: Portfolio of Rollout Drawings by Barbara van Heusen, Persis Clarkson, Lin Crocker.* Guatemala City: Foundation for Latin American Anthropological Research.

1978 *Tikal Copan Travel Guide: A General Introduction to Maya Art, Architecture, and Archaeology.* Guatemala City and St. Louis: Foundation for Latin American Anthropological Research.

1982 The Holmul Dancer and the "Principle Young Lord" in Maya Art. MS. Foundation for Latin American Anthropological Research, Guatemala City.

Helms, Mary W.
1979 *Ancient Panama*. Austin: University of Texas Press.
Henderson, John S.
1979 *Atopula, Guerrero, and Olmec Horizons in Meso-america*. Yale University Publications in Anthropology, no. 77. New Haven.
Herald, Earl S.
1964 *Fishes of North America*. New York: Doubleday.
Hermitte, Esther
1970 *Poder Sobrenatural y Control Social*. Instituto Inter-americano Ediciones Especiales, tomo 57. Mexico, D.F.
Hildreth, Elen
1980 Implementation of a Theory of Edge Detection. Technical Report 579, Massachusetts Institute of Technology AI Lab. Cambridge, Mass.
Hohman, Hasso, and Annegrete Vogrin
1982 *Die Architektur von Copan (Honduras)*. Graz, Austria: Akademische Druck- und Verlagsanstalt.
Holmes, William L.
1895–97 *Archaeological Studies Among the Ancient Cities of Mexico*. Field Columbian Museum Anthropological Series 1(1). Chicago.
Hopkins, Nicholas
1967a The Chuj Language. Ph.D. diss., University of Chicago.
1967b Some Aspects of Social Organization in Chalchihuitan, Chiapas, Mexico. *Anthropology Tomorrow* 2(2):13–33.
1968 A Method for the Investigation of Glyph Syntax. *Estudios de Cultura Maya* 7:79–83.
1969 A Formal Account of Chalchihuitan Tzotzil Kinship Terminology. *Ethnology* 8(1):85–102.
1973 Concordance of Glyph Strings from Thompson's Glyph Catalog. Computer printout, Department of Anthropology, University of Texas at Austin.
1982 Classic-area Maya Kinship Systems: The Evidence for Patrilineality. Paper presented at the Taller Maya 6, July, San Cristobal de las Casas, Mexico.
1984 Classic Maya Kinship Systems: Epigraphic and Ethnographic Evidence for Patrilineality. Paper presented at the annual meeting of the American Anthropological Association, Denver (revised version in press, *Journal of Mayan Linguistics*).
Hopkins, Nicholas, and J. Kathryn Josserand
1985 The Story of Lak Mam. Paper presented at the Third Annual Advanced Workshop on Maya Hieroglyphic Writing, March 11–16, the University of Texas at Austin.
1986 The Characteristics of Chol (Mayan) Traditional Narrative. Paper presented to the 25th Conference on American Indian Languages: Mayan Discourse, annual meeting of the American Anthropological Association, December, Philadelphia.
Houston, Stephen D.
1983 A Reading for the Flint-Shield Glyph. In *Contributions to Maya Hieroglyphic Decipherment*, edited by Stephen D. Houston, pp. 13–25. New Haven: Human Relations Area Files.
1986 *Problematic Emblem Glyphs: Examples from Altar de Sacrificios, El Chorro, Rio Azul, and Xultun*. Research Reports on Ancient Maya Writing, no. 3. Washington, D.C.: Center for Maya Research.
n.d. Notes on the Primary Standard Sequence. MS.
Houston, Stephen D., and Peter Mathews
1985 *The Dynastic Sequence of Dos Pilas, Guatemala*. Pre-Columbian Art Research Institute Monograph 1. San Francisco, Calif.: Pre-Columbian Art Research Institute.
Houston, Stephen, and Karl Taube
1987 Name-Tagging in Classic Mayan Script: Implications for Native Classification of Ceramics and Jade Ornament. *Mexicon* 9(2):38–42.
Hurley Vda. de Delgaty, Alfa, and Augustin Ruiz Sanchez
1978 *Diccionario Tzotzil de San Andres con Variaciones Dialectales*. Vocabularios Indígenas 22. Mexico, D.F.: Instituto Lingüístico de Verano.
Iltis, Hugh H.
1983a Lecture. November 2, University of Texas at Austin.
1983b From Teosinte to Maize: The Catastrophic Sexual Transmutation. *Science* 222(November 25):886–894.
Iltis, Hugh H., and John F. Doebley
1980 Taxonomy of *Zea* (*Gramineae*). Pt. 2, Subspecific Categories in the *Zea mays* Complex and a Generic Synopsis. *American Journal of Botany* 67(6):994–1004.
Instituto de Antropología e Historia de Guatemala
1985 Reconocimiento, Rescate e Investigación de la Ribera del Rio Usumacinta, 1985–2000.
Integral Quality, Inc.
1983 IQLISP Reference Manual. Seattle.
Johnston, Kevin
1985 Maya Dynastic Territorial Expansion: Glyphic Evidence from Classic Centers of the Pasion River, Guatemala. In *Fifth Palenque Round Table, 1983*, edited by Virginia M. Fields (Merle Greene Robertson, General Editor), pp. 49–56. San Francisco: Pre-Columbian Art Research Institute.
Jones, Christopher
1977 Inauguration Dates of Three Late Classic Rulers of Tikal, Guatemala. *American Antiquity* 42(1):28–60.
1984 *Deciphering Maya Hieroglyphs*. Workshop notebook. Philadelphia: The University Museum, University of Pennsylvania.
Jones, Christopher, and Linton Satterthwaite
1982 *The Monuments and Inscriptions of Tikal: The Carved Monuments*. University Museum Monograph no. 44, Tikal Report no. 33, pt. A. Philadelphia: The University Museum, University of Pennsylvania.
Jones, Larry B., and Linda K. Jones
1984 Verb Morphology and Discourse Structure in Mesoamerican Languages. In *Theory and Application in Processing Texts in Non-Indoeuropean Languages*, edited by Robert E. Longacre, pp. 25–58. Hamburg: Helmut Buske.
Jones, Linda K., ed.
1979 *Discourse Studies in Mesoamerican Languages*. Vol. 1, *Discussion*. Vol. 2, *Texts*. Summer Institute of Linguistics, Publications in Linguistics, no. 58.
Jones, Tom
1985 The Xoc, the Sharke, and the Sea Dogs: An Historical Encounter. In *Fifth Palenque Round Table, 1983*, edited by Virginia M. Fields (Merle Greene Robertson, General Editor), pp. 211–222. San Francisco: Pre-Columbian Art Research Institute.
Joralemon, Peter D.
1971 *A Study of Olmec Iconography*. Studies in Pre-Columbian Art and Archaeology, no. 7. Washington, D.C.: Dumbarton Oaks.
1974 Ritual Blood-Sacrifice Among the Ancient Maya, pt. 1. In *Primera Mesa Redonda de Palenque*, pt. 2, edited by Merle Greene Robertson, pp. 59–75. Pebble Beach,

Calif.: Robert Louis Stevenson School.

1975 The Night Sun and the Earth Dragon: Some Thoughts on the Jaguar God of the Underworld. In *Jaina Figurines: A Study of Maya Iconography*, edited by Mary E. Miller, pp. 63–66. Princeton: The Art Museum, Princeton University.

1976 The Olmec Dragon: A Study in Precolumbian Iconography. In *Origins of Religious Art and Iconography in Preclassic Mesoamerica*, edited by H. B. Nicholson, pp. 27–72. Los Angeles: UCLA Latin American Center.

1981 The Old Woman and the Child: Themes in the Iconography of Preclassic Mesoamerica. In *The Olmec and Their Neighbors: Essays in Memory of Matthew W. Stirling*, edited by Elizabeth P. Benson, pp. 163–180. Washington, D.C.: Dumbarton Oaks.

Josserand, J. Kathryn

1984 Discourse Analysis of Chol and Mayan Hieroglyphics. Lecture, 3rd Advanced Seminar on Maya Hieroglyphic Writing, University of Texas at Austin.

Josserand, J. Kathryn, and Linda Schele

1984 Discourse Analysis of Narrative Hieroglyphic Texts. Paper presented at the annual meeting of the American Anthropological Association, Denver.

In press Discourse Analysis of Narrative Hieroglyphic Texts. In *Hieroglyphic Studies in Memory of Marshall Durbin*, edited by J. Kathryn Josserand and C. A. Hofling. *Journal of Mayan Linguistics* (special issue).

Josserand, J. Kathryn, Linda Schele, and Nicholas A. Hopkins

1985 Linguistic Data on Mayan Inscriptions: The *ti* Constructions. In *Fourth Palenque Round Table, 1980*, edited by Elizabeth P. Benson (Merle Greene Robertson, General Editor), pp. 87–102. San Francisco: Pre-Columbian Art Research Institute.

Joyce, Rosemary A.

1981 Classic Maya Kinship and Descent: An Alternative Suggestion. *Journal of the Steward Anthropological Society* 13(1):45–57.

Justeson, John S.

1978 Mayan Scribal Practice in the Classic Period: A Test Case of an Explanatory Approach to the Study of the Writing System. Ph.D. diss., Stanford University. (Available from University Microfilms, Ann Arbor, Michigan.)

1983 Mayan Hieroglyphic "Name-Tagging" of a Pair of Rectangular Jade Plaques from Xcalumkin. In *Contributions to Maya Hieroglyphic Decipherment*, edited by Stephen Houston. New Haven: Human Relations Area File.

1984a Interpretations of Mayan Hieroglyphs. In *Phoneticism in Mayan Hieroglyphs*, edited by John S. Justeson and Lyle Campbell, pp. 315–362. Institute for Mesoamerican Studies Publication no. 9. Albany: State University of New York.

1984b Subscript Designations for Mayan Hieroglyphs. In *Phoneticism in Mayan Hieroglyphic Writing*, edited by John S. Justeson and Lyle Campbell, pp. 367–370. Institute for Mesoamerican Studies Publication no. 9. Albany: State University of New York.

Justeson, John S., and Lyle Campbell, eds.

1984 *Phoneticism in Mayan Hieroglyphic Writing*. Institute for Mesoamerican Studies no. 9. Albany: State University of New York.

Justeson, John S., and William M. Norman

1983 A Reinterpretation of Some "Auxiliary Verb" Constructions in Mayan Hieroglyphic Writing. Paper pre-

sented at the Fifth Palenque Round Table, Palenque, Chiapas, Mexico.

Justeson, John S., William M. Norman, Lyle Campbell, and Terrence Kaufman

1985 *The Foreign Impact on Lowland Mayan Language and Script*. Middle American Research Institute Publication no. 53. New Orleans: Tulane University.

Kaufman, Terrence S.

1967 *Preliminary Mocho Vocabulary*. Working Paper no. 5, Laboratory for Language-Behavior Research. Berkeley: University of California.

1972 *El Proto-Tzeltal-Tzotzil: Fonología Comparada y Diccionario Reconstruido*. Centro de Estudios Mayas Cuaderno 5. Mexico, D.F.: Universidad Nacional Autonoma de Mexico.

Kaufman, Terrence S., and William Norman

1984 An Outline of Proto-Cholan Phonology, Morphology, and Vocabulary. In *Phoneticism in Maya Hieroglyphic Writing*, edited by John S. Justeson and Lyle Campbell, pp. 77–166. Institute for Mesoamerican Studies Publication no. 9. Albany: State University of New York.

Kelley, David H.

1962 Fonetismo en la Escritura Maya. *Estudios de Cultura Maya* 5:93–134.

1968 Kakupacal and the Itzas. *Estudios de Cultura Maya* 7:255–268.

1976 *Deciphering the Maya Script*. Austin: University of Texas Press.

1977 Maya Astronomical Tables and Inscriptions. In *Native American Astronomy*, edited by Anthony F. Aveni, pp. 57–76. Austin: University of Texas Press.

1982 Notes on Puuc Inscriptions and History. In *The Puuc: New Perspectives*, edited by Lawrence W. Mills, pp. 1–18. Scholary Studies in the Liberal Arts Publication no. 1. Pella, Iowa: Central College.

1983 The Maya Calendar Correlation Problem. In *Civilization in the Ancient Americas: Essays in Honor of Gordon R. Willey*, edited by Richard Levanthal and Alan Kolata. Albuquerque: University of New Mexico Press (with the Peabody Museum, Cambridge, Mass.).

1984 The Toltec Empire in Yucatan. *Quarterly Review of Archaeology* 5(1):12–13.

Kerr, Justin

n.d. Collection of roll-out photographs of Maya vases. New York.

Kidder, A. V.

1947 *The Artifacts of Uaxactun, Guatemala*. Carnegie Institution of Washington Publication no. 576. Washington, D.C.

Kim de Bolles, Alejandra

1972 *Stories my Mother Was Told Long Ago: Stories and Songs in the Mayan Language*. Komchen, Yucatan.

Knauth, Lothar

1961 El Juego de Pelota y el Rito de la Decapitación. *Estudios de Cultura Maya* 1:183–198.

Knorozov, Yurii V.

1967 *Selected Chapters from the Writing of the Maya Indians*. (Translated by Sophie Coe.) Russian Translation Series, no. 4. Cambridge, Mass.: Peabody Museum of Archaeology and Ethnology, Harvard University.

Knowles, Susan M.

1984 A Descriptive Grammar of Chontal Maya (San Carlos Dialect). Ph.D. diss., Tulane University, New Orleans. (Available from University Microfilms, Ann Arbor, Michigan.)

Kohonen, Teuvo
  1978 *Associative Memory, A Systems Theoretical Approach.* Berlin: Springer-Verlag. (Corrected printing of the first edition.)

Kowalewski, Stephen, Gary Feinman, Laura Finstein, and Richard E. Blanton
  1985 Prehispanic Ballcourts from the Valley of Oaxaca. Paper presented at the Symposium on the Native American Ball Game: Regional Contexts and Comparative Interpretations, Tucson, Arizona.

Kowalski, Jeffrey K.
  n.d. A Reference to a Historical Figure in the Hieroglyphic Texts from the Cemetery Group and a Probable Tun-Ahau Date from the Glyphic Monument of the Nunnery Triangle. MS.

Krickeberg, Walter
  1966 (1948) El Juego Mesoamericana y su Simbolismo Religioso. *Traducciones Mesoamericanistas* (Sociedad Mexicana de Antropología) 1:191–313.

Krochock, Ruth
  1985 A Reconsideration of Reading Orders from Selected Monuments at Chichén Itzá. Paper presented at the Workshop for Maya Hieroglyphic Writing, University of Texas at Austin.
  1986 A Possible Link Between Parentage and Sacrifice in the Hieroglyphic Inscriptions and Iconography of Chichén Itzá. Paper presented at the Sexta Mesa Redonda de Palenque, Palenque, Chiapas, Mexico.

Kubler, George
  1961 Chichén Itzá y Tula. *Estudios de Cultura Maya* 1:47–80.
  1962 *The Art and Architecture of Ancient America: The Mexican, Maya and Andean Peoples.* Baltimore: Penguin Books.
  1973 The Clauses of Classic Maya Inscriptions. In *Mesoamerican Writing Systems*, edited by Elizabeth P. Benson, pp. 145–164. Washington, D.C.: Dumbarton Oaks.
  1974 Mythological Ancestries in Classic Maya Inscriptions. In *Primera Mesa Redonda de Palenque, Part 2*, edited by Merle Greene Robertson, pp. 22–43. Pebble Beach, Calif.: Robert Louis Stevenson School.
  1976 *The Art and Architecture of Ancient America.* 2d ed. London: Penguin Books.
  1977 *Aspects of Classic Maya Rulership on Two Inscribed Vessels.* Studies in Pre-Columbian Art and Archaeology, no. 18. Washington, D.C.: Dumbarton Oaks.

Kurbjuhn, Kornelia
  1980 Die Sitze de Maya. Eine ikonographische Untersuchung. Ph.D. diss., Eberhard-Karls-Universitat, Tübingen, West Germany.
  1985 Man in the Turtle, Man in the Snail: A Study of Occupants of Turtle and Snail Shells in Maya Art. In *Fifth Palenque Round Table, 1983*, edited by Virginia M. Fields (Merle Greene Robertson, General Editor), pp. 159–169. San Francisco: Pre-Columbian Art Research Institute.

Lacroix Gonzalez, Domingo
  1976 *Gotas de recuerdo.* Villahermosa, Mexico: Fondo de Cultura Tabasquena.

La Farge, Oliver, and Douglas Beyers
  1931 *The Year Bearer's People.* Middle American Research Institute Publication no. 8. New Orleans: Tulane University.

Landa, Fray Diego de
  1959 *Relación de las Cosas de Yucatan.* Mexico, D.F.: Editorial Porrua.
  1966 *Relación de las Cosas de Yucatan.* Biblioteca Porrua, tomo 13, Mexico, D.F.: Editorial Porrua. (12th ed. published in 1982.)

Laporte, Juan P., and W. Fialko
  1987 La Ceramica del Classico Temprano desde Mundo Perdido, Tikal: Una Reevaluación. In *Maya Ceramics*, edited by Prudence M. Rice and Robert J. Sharer, pp. 121–181. British Archaeological Reports International Series, no. 35. Oxford.

Larios, C. Rudy, and William L. Fash
  1985 Excavación y Restauración de un Palacio de la Nobleza Maya de Copán. *Yaxkin* 8 (1):111–134.

Larráinzar, Manuel
  1875–78 *Estudios sobre la historia de America, sus ruinas y antigüedades.* 5 vols. Villanueva, Mexico: Imprenta de Villanueva.

Laughlin, Robert M.
  1969 The Tzotzil. In *Handbook of Middle American Indians* (Robert Wauchope, General Editor). Vol. 7, *Ethnology*, pt. 1, edited by Evon Z. Vogt. Austin: University of Texas Press.
  1975 *The Great Tzotzil Dictionary of San Lorenzo Zinacantan.* Smithsonian Contributions to Anthropology, no. 19. Washington, D.C.: Smithsonian Institution.

Lee, Thomas A., Jr.
  1969 *The Artifacts of Chiapa de Corzo, Chiapas, Mexico.* Papers of the New World Archaeological Foundation, no. 26. Provo, Utah.
  1985 (editor) *Los Codices Mayas.* Edición Conmemorativa X Aniversario. Universidad Autonoma de Chiapas.

Leung, C. H., Y. S. Cheung, and K. P. Chan
  1985 A Distortion Model of Chinese Character Generation. In *Proceedings of the IEEE International Conference on Systems, Man, and Cybernetics*, pp. 38–41. Tucson.

Liman, Florence F., and Marshall Durbin
  1975 Some New Glyphs on an Unusual Maya Stela. *American Antiquity* 40(3):314–320.

Lincoln, Charles
  1982 The "Total Overlap" Model of Chichén Itzá as a Terminal Classic Maya Site: A Discussion of Monumental Sculpture. Seminar paper, Harvard University, Cambridge, Mass.
  1985 The Chronology of Chichén Itzá: A Review of the Literature. In *Late Lowland Maya Civilization: Classic to Postclassic*, edited by Jeremy A. Sabloff and E. Wyllys Andrews V, pp. 141–196. Albuquerque: University of New Mexico Press.

Lineaweaver, Thomas H., and Richard H. Backus
  1984 *The Natural History of Sharks.* New York: Nick Lyons Books.

Lizardi Ramos, Cesar
  1936 Los Secretos de Chichén Itzá. *Excelsior* (Mexico, D.F.), Dec. 21.
  1937 New Discoveries of Maya Culture at Chichén Itzá. *Illustrated London News* July 3:12–15.

Longacre, Robert E.
  1979 Introduction. In *Discourse Studies in Mesoamerican Languages*, edited by Linda K. Jones, vol. 1, pp. vii–ix.

Summer Institute of Linguistics. Publications in Linguistics, no. 58.

Longyear, John M., III

1952 *Copan Ceramics: A Study of Southeastern Maya Pottery.* Carnegie Institution of Washington Publication no. 597. Washington, D.C.

Lopez de M., Diana, and Daniel Molina F.

1980 *Cacaxtla: Guía Oficial.* Mexico, D.F.: Instituto Nacional de Antropología e Historia.

Lothrop, Samuel K.

1952 *Metals from the Cenote of Sacrifice.* Memoirs of the Peabody Museum of American Archaeology and Ethnology 10(2). Cambridge, Mass.: Harvard University.

Lounsbury, Floyd

1973 On the Derivation and Reading of the "Ben-Ich" Prefix. In *Mesoamerican Writing Systems,* edited by Elizabeth P. Benson, pp. 99–143. Washington, D.C.: Dumbarton Oaks.

1974 The Inscription on the Sarcophagus Lid at Palenque. In *Primera Mesa Redonda de Palenque, Part 2,* edited by Merle Greene Robertson, pp. 5–20. Pebble Beach, Calif.: Robert Louis Stevenson School.

1976 A Rationale for the Initial Date of the Temple of the Cross at Palenque. In *The Art, Iconography & Dynastic History of Palenque, Part 3,* edited by Merle Greene Robertson, pp. 211–224. Pebble Beach, Calif.: Robert Louis Stevenson School.

1978 Maya Numeration, Computation, and Calendrical Astronomy. In *Dictionary of Scientific Biography,* vol. 15, supp. 1, edited by C. C. Gillespie, pp. 759–818. New York: Scribner's.

1980 Some Problems in the Interpretation of the Mythological Portion of the Hieroglyphic Text of the Temple of the Cross at Palenque. In *Third Palenque Round Table, 1978, Part 2,* edited by Merle Greene Robertson, pp. 99–115. Austin: University of Texas Press.

1982 Astronomical Knowledge and Its Uses at Bonampak, Mexico. In *Archaeoastronomy in the New World,* edited by Anthony F. Aveni, pp. 143–168. Cambridge: Cambridge University Press.

1983 The Base of the Venus Table of the Dresden Codex and Its Significance for the Calendar Correction Problem. In *Calendars in Mesoamerica and Peru: Native American Computations of Time,* edited by Anthony F. Aveni and Gordon Brotherston, pp. 1–26. British Archaeological Reports International Series, no. 174. Oxford.

1984a Glyphic Substitutions: Homophonic and Synonymic. In *Phoneticism in Maya Hieroglyphic Writing,* edited by John S. Justeson and Lyle Campbell, pp. 167–184. Institute for Mesoamerican Studies Publication no. 9. Albany: State University of New York.

1984b Positional Analysis of Glyph Substitutions. Paper presented at the Colloquium on the Language of Writing in the Mayan Region, April 23–24, University of Chicago.

1985 The Identities of the Mythological Figures in the Cross Group Inscriptions of Palenque. In *Fourth Palenque Round Table, 1980,* edited by Elizabeth P. Benson (Merle Greene Robertson, General Editor), pp. 45–58. San Francisco: Pre-Columbian Art Research Institute.

n.d.a Letter on the inscriptions of Copan to William Fash, 1975.

n.d.b The Slaves Tablet: Notes on the Text. Class hand-

out, Maya Hieroglyphic Writing, Yale University, 1976–1977. MS.

Love, Bruce

1984a Ethnographic Analogy and Maya Glyph Studies. Paper presented at the 83rd annual meeting of the American Anthropological Association, Denver.

1984b Wahil Kol: A Yucatec Maya Agricultural Ceremony. *Estudios de Cultura Maya* 15:251–300.

1986 Yucatec Maya Ritual: A Diachronic Perspective. Ph.D. diss., University of California, Los Angeles.

1987 *Glyph T93 and Maya "Hand-scattering" Events.* Research Reports on Ancient Maya Writing, no. 5. Washington, D.C.: Center for Maya Research.

In press Yucatec Sacred Breads Through Time. In *The Cultural Content of Mayan Glyphs: Language, History, and Representation,* edited by William Hanks and Don Rice.

Lowe, G. W., T. A. Lee, Jr., and E. Martinez

1982 *Izapa: An Introduction to the Ruins and Monuments.* Papers of the New World Archaeological Foundation, no. 31. Provo, Utah.

McCarthy, John et al.

1980 *LISP 1.5 Programmer's Manual.* 2d ed. Cambridge: Mass.: The MIT Press.

MacCleod, Barbara

1983 Remembrances of Cycles Past: T669b in Palenque Katun Histories. In *Contributions to Maya Hieroglyphic Decipherment,* edited by Stephen Houston. New Haven: Human Relations Area Files.

1984 Cholan and Yucatecan Verb Morphology and Glyphic Verbal Affixes in the Inscriptions. In *Phoneticism in Mayan Hieroglyphic Writing,* edited by John S. Justeson and Lyle Campbell, pp. 233–262. Institute for Mesoamerican Studies Publication no. 9. Albany: State University of New York.

McDonald, Andrew J.

1983 *Tzutzuculi. A Middle Preclassic Site on the Pacific Slopes of Chiapas, Mexico.* Papers of the New World Archaeological Foundation, no. 47. Provo, Utah.

Macri, Martha J.

1985 Formulaic Patterns in the Maya Script. In *Proceedings of the Eleventh Meeting of the Berkeley Linguistics Society,* edited by Mary Niepokuj et al., pp. 216–225. Berkeley: Berkeley Linguistics Society.

Madrid Codex

1967 *Codex Tro-Cortesianus (Codex Madrid).* Einleitung und Summary von F. Anders. Graz, Austria: Akademische Druck-und Verlagsanstalt.

Maler, Teobert

1901–03 *Researches in the Central Portion of the Usumatsintla Valley.* Memoirs of the Peabody Museum 2 (1, 2). Cambridge, Mass.: Harvard University.

Mangelsdorf, Paul C.

1974 *Corn: Its Origin and Improvement.* Cambridge, Mass.: The Belknap Press of Harvard University Press.

1986 The Origin of Corn. *Science* 225:80–86.

Marcus, Joyce

1973 Territorial Organization of the Lowland Classic Maya. *Science* 180:911–916.

1976 *Emblem and State in the Classic Maya Lowlands: An Epigraphic Approach to Territorial Organization.* Washington, D.C.: Dumbarton Oaks.

Marquina, Ignacio

1951 *Arquitectura Prehispanica.* División de Monumentos

Prehispanicos Memoirs, tomo 1. Mexico, D.F.: Instituto Nacional de Antropología e Historia. (2d ed. published in 1981.)

Martinez Donjuan, Guadalupe
1982 Teopantecuanitlan, Guerrero: un sitio Olmeca. *Revista Mexicana de Estudios Antropologicos* 28.

Martínez Hernández, Juan, ed.
1929 *Diccionario de Motul, maya-español, atribuido a Fray Antonio de Ciudad Real y Arte de la lengua maya por Fray Juan Coronel*. Merida, Mexico: Talleres de la Compañía Tipográfica Yucateca.

Matheny, Raymond T.
1978 Northern Maya Lowland Water-Control Systems. In *Prehispanic Maya Agriculture*, edited by P. D. Harrison and B. L. Turner, pp. 195–210. Albuquerque: University of New Mexico Press.
1980 *El Mirador, Peten, Guatemala: An Interim Report*. Papers of the New World Archaeological Foundation, no. 45. Provo, Utah.
1986 Investigations at El Mirador, Peten, Guatemala. *National Geographic Research* 2(3):332–353.

Matheny, Raymond T. et al.
1983 *Investigations at Edzna, Campeche, Mexico*. Vol. 1, pt. 1, *The Hydraulic System*. Papers of the New World Archaeological Foundation, no. 46. Provo, Utah.

Mathews, Peter
1977 The Inscription on the Back of Stela 8, Dos Pilas, Guatemala. Paper presented at the International Meeting on Maya Iconography and Hieroglyphic Writing, Guatemala City, Guatemala.
1979 The Glyphs on the Ear Ornaments from Tomb A-1/1. In *Excavations at Altun Ha, Belize, 1964–1970*, edited by David Pendergast, vol. 1. Toronto: Royal Ontario Museum.
1980 Notes on the Dynastic Sequence of Bonampak, pt. 1. In *Third Palenque Round Table, 1978*, edited by Merle Greene Robertson, pp. 60–73. Austin: University of Texas Press.
1983a *Corpus of Maya Hieroglyphs*. Vol. 6, pt. 1, *Tonina*. Cambridge, Mass.: Peabody Museum of Archaeology and Ethnology, Harvard University.
1983b Palenque's Mid-life Crisis. Paper presented at the Fifth Palenque Round Table, Palenque, Chiapas, Mexico.
1984 A Maya Hieroglyphic Syllabary. In *Phoneticism in Mayan Hieroglyphic Writing*, edited by John S. Justeson and Lyle Campbell. Institute for Mesoamerican Studies Publication no. 9. Albany: State University of New York.
1985a Maya Early Classic Monuments and Inscriptions. In *A Consideration of the Early Classic Period in the Maya Lowlands*, edited by Gordon R. Willey and Peter Mathews, pp. 5–54. Institute for Mesoamerican Studies Publication no. 10. Albany: State University of New York, Albany.
1985b Maya Hieroglyphic Workshop Notebook. Department of Anthropology, University of Southern California, Los Angeles.
1986 Late Classic Maya History and Site Interaction as Recorded in the Inscriptions. Paper presented at Maya Art and Civilization: The New Dynamics, May 16–18, Kimbell Art Museum, Fort Worth, Texas.

Mathews, Peter, and John S. Justeson
1984 Patterns of Sign Substitution in Mayan Hieroglyphic Writing: "The Affix Cluster." In *Phoneticism in Mayan Hieroglyphic Writing*, edited by John S. Justeson and Lyle Campbell, pp. 185–231. Institute for Mesoamerican Studies Publication no. 9. Albany: State University of New York.

Mathews, Peter, and Merle Greene Robertson
1985 Notes on the Olvidado, Palenque, Chiapas, Mexico. In *Fifth Palenque Round Table, 1983*, edited by Virginia M. Fields (Merle Greene Robertson, General Editor), pp. 7–18. San Francisco: Pre-Columbian Art Research Institute.

Mathews, Peter, and Linda Schele
1974 Lords of Palenque—The Glyphic Evidence. In *Primera Mesa Redonda de Palenque, Part 1*, edited by Merle Greene Robertson, pp. 63–76. Pebble Beach, Calif.: Robert Louis Stevenson School.

Maudslay, Alfred P.
1889–1902 *Archaeology: Biologia Centrali-Americana*. 5 vols. London.

Mayer, Karl H.
1978a Ein Inschriftenfund in Playa del Carmen, Mexico. *Ethnologia Americana* 15(87):859–860.
1978b *Maya Monuments: Sculptures of Unknown Provenance in Europe*, translated by Sandra L. Brizee. Ramona, Calif.: Acoma Books.
1980 *Maya Monuments: Sculptures of Unknown Provenance in the United States*. Ramona, Calif.: Acoma Books.
1984 *Maya Monuments: Sculptures of Unknown Provenience in Middle America*. Translated by Sally Robinson and Karl H. Mayer. Berlin: K. F. von Flemming.

Merwin, Raymond, and George Vaillant
1932 *The Ruins of Holmul, Guatemala*. Memoirs of the Peabody Museum of American Archaeology and Ethnology 3(2). Cambridge, Mass.: Harvard University.

Michelon, Oscar, ed.
1976 *Diccionario de San Francisco*. Graz, Austria: Akademische Druck- und Verlagsanstalt.

Miller, Arthur G.
1974 West and East in Maya Thought: Death and Rebirth at Palenque and Tulum. In *Primera Mesa Redonda de Palenque, Part 2*, edited by Merle Greene Robertson, pp. 45–49. Pebble Beach, Calif.: Pre-Columbian Art Research Institute.
1977 Captains of the Itza: Unpublished Mural Evidence from Chichén Itzá. In *Social Process in Maya Prehistory*, edited by Norman Hammond, pp. 197–225. New York: Academic Press.
1982 *On the Edge of the Sea: Mural Painting at Tancah-Tulum, Quintana Roo, Mexico*. Washington, D.C.: Dumbarton Oaks.

Miller, Jeffrey
1974 Notes on a Stelae Pair Probably from Calakmul, Campeche, Mexico. In *Primera Mesa Redonda de Palenque, Part 1*, edited by Merle Greene Robertson, pp. 149–161. Pebble Beach, Calif.: Robert Louis Stevenson School.

Miller, Mary Ellen
1984 The Main Acropolis at Copan: Its Meaning and Function. Paper presented at the Dumbarton Oaks Conference on Copan, Quirigua, and the Southeastern Maya Periphery, Washington, D.C.
1985 A Re-examination of the Mesoamerican Chacmool. *The Art Bulletin* 67(1):7–17.
1986 *The Murals of Bonampak*. Princeton: Princeton University Press.

Miller, Virginia

1981 Pose and Gesture in Classic Maya Monumental Sculpture. Ph.D. diss., University of Texas at Austin.

1985 The Dwarf Motif in Classic Maya Art. In *Fourth Palenque Round Table, 1980*, edited by Elizabeth P. Benson. (Merle Greene Robertson, General Editor), pp. 141–154. San Francisco: Pre-Columbian Art Research Center.

Moholy-Nagy, Hattula

1966 Mosaic Figures from Tikal. *Archaeology* 19(2): 84–89.

Moholy-Nagy, H., F. Asaro, and F. H. Stross

1984 Tikal Obsidian: Sources and Typology. *American Antiquity* 49:104–117.

Molina Montes, Augusto

1978 Palenque—The Archaeological City Today. In *Tercera Mesa Redonda de Palenque*, edited by Merle Greene Robertson and Donnan Call Jeffers, pp. 1–8. Palenque: Pre-Columbian Art Research Center.

Molloy, John P.

1985 Ball Courts and the Oaxaca Codices. Paper presented at the Symposium on the Native American Ball Game: Regional Contexts and Comparative Interpretations, Tucson, Arizona.

Montejo, Victor

1984 *El Kanil, Man of Lightening*. Translated by Wallace Kaufman. Carrboro, N.C.: Signal Books.

Moore, S. F., and B. G. Myerhoff

1977 *Secular Ritual*. Amsterdam: Van Gorcum.

Moran, Fray Francisco

1935 *Arte y Diccionario en Lengua Cholti Quiere Decir Lengua de Milperos. Vocabulario en Lengua Cholti*. (Facsimile of 1695 manuscript. Edition by William Gates.) Baltimore: The Maya Society.

Morel, V.

1986 The Lost Language of Coba. *Science 86* (March): 48–57.

Morley, Sylvanus G.

1938 *The Inscriptions of Peten*, vols. 2, 5. Carnegie Institution of Washington Publication no. 437. Washington, D.C.

1948 *Checklist of the Corpus Inscriptionum Mayarum*. Washington, D.C.: Carnegie Institution of Washington, Division of Historical Research.

Morley, Sylvanus G., George W. Brainerd,
and Robert J. Sharer

1983 *The Ancient Maya*. 4th ed. Stanford: Stanford University Press.

Morris, Earl H., Jean Charlot, and Ann A. Morris

1931 *The Temple of the Warriors at Chichén Itzá, Yucatan*. 2 vols. Carnegie Institution of Washington Publication no. 406. Washington, D.C.

Morris, Walter F., Jr.

1985 Flowers, Saints, and Toads: Ancient and Modern Maya Textile Design Symbolism. *National Geographic Research* Winter: 63–79.

Mulleried, Federico K. G.

1927 El Llamado Planchon de las Figuras, en el Estado de Chiapas. *Revista Mexicana de Estudios Historicos* 6:235–243.

Muse, Michael, and Terry Stocker

1974 The Cult of the Cross: Interpretations in Olmec Iconography. *Journal of the Steward Anthropological Society* 5(2):67–98.

Nash, June

1970 *In the Eyes of the Ancestors: Belief and Behavior in a Maya Community*. New Haven: Yale University Press.

Navarette, Carlos

1971 Algunas Piezas Olmecas de Chiapas y Guatemala. *Anales de Antropología* (Instituto de Investigaciones Historias, Universidad Nacional Autonoma de Mexico, Mexico, D.F.) 8:69–82.

Navarette, Carlos, and Eduardo Martinez

1977 *Cueva de los Andasolos*. Tuxtla Gutiérrez: Universidad Autonoma de Chiapas.

Nicholson, Henry B.

1971 Religion in Pre-Hispanic Central Mexico. In *Handbook of Middle American Indians* (Robert Wauchope, General Editor). Vol. 11, *Archaeology of Northern Mesoamerica*, edited by Gordon F. Ekholm and Ignacio Bernal, pp. 395–446. Austin: University of Texas Press.

1976 Preclassic Mesoamerican Iconography from the Perspective of the Postclassic: Problems in Interpretational Analysis. In *Origins of Religious Art and Iconography in Preclassic Mesoamerica*, edited by Henry B. Nicholson, pp. 157–175. Los Angeles: University of California Press.

Nicholson, Irene

1967 *Mexican and Central American Mythology*. London: Paul Hamlyn.

Norman, Garth

1976 *Izapa Sculpture*. Pt. 2, *Text*. Papers of the New World Archaeological Foundation, no. 30. Provo, Utah.

Norman, J. R., and H. Greenwood

1963 *A History of Fish*. New York: Hill and Wang.

Norman, William

1980 Grammatical Parallelism in Quiche Ritual Language. *Berkeley Linguistics Society* 6:387–399.

Nutini, Hugo

1961 Clan Organization in a Nahuatl-speaking Village of the State of Tlaxcala, Mexico. *American Anthropologist* 63(1):62–78.

Nuttall, Zelia

1940 The Periodical Adjustments of the Ancient Mexican Calendar. *American Anthropologist* 6:486–500.

Ong, Walter J.

1982 *Orality and Literacy: The Technologizing of the Word*. London: Methuen.

Orejel, Jorge L.

1984 Story Understanding with WATSON, a Computer Program Modeling Natural Language Inferences Using Nonmonotonic Dependencies. Report T-146. Urbana: University of Illinois at Urbana-Champaign.

O'Rorke, Paul

1983 Reasons for Beliefs in Understanding: Application of Data Dependencies to Story Processing. In *Proceedings of the National Conference on Artificial Intelligence*, pp. 306–309. Washington, D.C.

1984 Generalization for Explanation-based Schema Acquisition. Draft report. Coordinated Science Laboratory, University of Illinois at Urbana-Champaign.

Palacios, Enrique Jean

1945 Guía Arqueológica de Chacmultún, Labná, Sayil, Kabah, Uxmal, Chichén Itzá, y Tulum. In *Enciclopedia Yucatanese*, vol. 2, pp. 405–554. Mérida: Gobierno de Yucatán.

Paradis, Louise I.

1981 Guerrero and the Olmec. In *The Olmec and their*

Neighbors, edited by Elizabeth P. Benson, pp. 195–208. Washington, D.C.: Dumbarton Oaks.

Paris et al.
1939 Ruins of Piedras Negras, Department of Peten, Guatemala. Map. Philadelphia: The University Museum, University of Pennsylvania.

Parsons, Jeffrey A.
1971 *Prehistoric Settlement Patterns in the Texcoco Region, Mexico.* Memoirs of the Museum of Anthropology, no. 3. Ann Arbor: University of Michigan.

Parsons, Lee A.
1969 *Bilbao, Guatemala: An Archaeological Study of the Pacific Coast Cotzumalhuapa Region*, vol. 2. Milwaukee Public Museum Publications in Anthropology, no. 12. Milwaukee: Milwaukee Public Museum.
1981 Post-Olmec Stone Sculpture: The Olmec-Izapan Transition on the Southern Pacific Coast and Highlands. In *The Olmec and Their Neighbors: Essays in Memory of Mathew W. Stirling*, edited by Elizabeth P. Benson, pp. 257– 288. Washington, D.C.: Dumbarton Oaks.
1986 *The Origins of Maya Art: Monumental Stone Sculpture of Kaminaljuyu, Guatemala, and the Southern Pacific Coast.* Studies in Pre–Columbian Art and Archaeology, no. 28. Washington, D.C.: Dumbarton Oaks.

Pasztory, Esther
1972 The Historical and Religious Significance of the Middle Classic Ballgame. *Sociedad Mexicana de Antropología, XII Mesa Redonda:* 441–455.
1978 Artistic Traditions of the Middle Classic Period. In *Middle Classic Mesoamerica:* A.D. 400–700, edited by Esther Pasztory, pp. 108–142. New York: Columbia University Press.

Pavlidis, T.
1977 *Structural Pattern Recognition.* Berlin: Springer-Verlag.

Paxton, Merideth
1983 Codex Dresden: Glyphic Evidence Concerning Provenience and Date. Paper presented at the annual meeting of the American Society for Ethnohistory, November 3–6, Albuquerque, New Mexico.
1986 Codex Dresden: Stylistic and Iconographic Analysis of a Maya Manuscript. Ph.D. diss., University of New Mexico.

Pendergast, David M.
1971 Evidence of Early Teotihuacan–Lowland Maya Contact at Altun Ha. *American Antiquity* 36:455–460.
1981 Lamanai, Belize: Summary of Excavation Results, 1974–1980. *Journal of Field Archaeology* 8(1):29–53.
1982 *Excavations at Altun Ha, Belize, 1974–1980.* Vol. 2. Toronto: Royal Ontario Museum.

Pina Chan, Roman
1955 *Chalcatzingo, Morelos.* Dirección de Monumentos Prehispanicos Informes 4. Mexico, D.F.: Instituto Nacional de Antropología e Historia.
1975 *Historia, Arqueología y Arte Prehispanico.* Sección de Obras de Antropología. Fondo de Cultura Economica, Mexico.
1981 *Quetzalcoatl Serpiente Emplumada.* Sección de Obras de Antropología. Fondo de Cultura Economica, Mexico.

Pina Chan, Roman, and Luis Covarrubias
1964 *El Pueblo del Jaguar (Los Olmecas Arqueologicas).* Mexico, D.F.: Consejo para la planeación e instalación del Museo Nacional de Antropología.

Pio Perez, Juan
1866–77 *Diccionario de la Lengua Maya.* Merida, Mexico: Imprenta Literaria de Juan F. Molina Solis.

Pires-Ferreira, Jane W.
1976 Shell and Iron Ore Exchange in Formative Middle America, with Comments on Other Commodities. In *The Early Mesoamerican Village*, edited by Kent V. Flannery, pp. 311–328. New York: Academic Press.

Pollock, H. E. D.
1980 *The Puuc: An Architectural Survey of the Hill Country of Yucatan and Northern Campeche, Mexico.* Memoirs of the Peabody Museum of Archaeology and Ethnology, no. 19. Cambridge, Mass.: Harvard University.

Pontius, David Henne
1980 *Diccionario Quiche-Español.* Guatemala: Instituto Lingüístico de Verano.

Prensa Libre
1983 Fahsen Comenta Posibilidad de Construir Hidroelectrica. 9 de Noviembre, p. 12.

Pring, Duncan C.
1977 The Dating of Teotihuacan Contact at Altun Ha: The New Evidence. *American Antiquity* 42:626–628.

Proskouriakoff, Tatiana
1946 *An Album of Maya Architecture.* Carnegie Institution of Washington Publication no. 558. Washington, D.C.
1950 *A Study of Classic Maya Sculpture.* Carnegie Institution of Washington Publication no. 593. Washington, D.C.
1960 Historical Implications of a Pattern of Dates at Piedras Negras, Guatemala. *American Antiquity* 25(4): 454–475.
1962 The Artifacts of Mayapan. In *Mayapan Yucatan Mexico*, edited by H. E. D. Pollock et al., pp. 321–438. Carnegie Institution of Washington Publication no. 619. Washington, D.C.
1963 Historical Data in the Inscriptions of Yaxchilan, pt. 1. *Estudios de Cultura Maya* 3:149–167.
1964 Historical Data in the Inscriptions of Yaxchilan, pt. 2. *Estudios de Cultura Maya* 4:177–201.
1968a The Jog and Jaguar Signs in Maya Writing. *American Antiquity* 33:247–251.
1968b Olmec and Maya Art: Problems of Their Stylistic Relations. In *Dumbarton Oaks Conference on the Olmec*, edited by Elizabeth P. Benson, pp. 119–130. Washington, D.C.: Dumbarton Oaks.
1970 On two inscriptions at Chichén Itzá. In *Monographs and Papers in Maya Archaeology*, edited by W. R. Bullard, Jr., pp. 457–467. Papers of the Peabody Museum of Archaeology and Ethnology, 61. Cambridge, Mass.: Harvard University.
1973 The "Hand-grasping fish" and Associated Glyphs on Classic Maya Monuments. In *Mesoamerican Writing Systems*, edited by Elizabeth P. Benson, pp. 165–178. Washington, D.C.: Dumbarton Oaks.
1974 *Jades from the Cenote of Sacrifice.* Memoirs of the Peabody Museum of American Archaeology and Ethnology 10(1). Cambridge: Mass.: Harvard University.

Proskouriakoff, Tatiana, and J. Eric S. Thompson
1947 *Maya Calendar Round Dates such as 9 Ahau 17 Mol.* Carnegie Institution of Washington, Division of Historical Research, Notes on Middle American Archaeology and Ethnology Publication no. 79. Washington, D.C.

Puleston, Dennis E.
1976 The People of the Cayman/Crocodile: Riparian Ag-

riculture and the Origin of Aquatic Motifs in Ancient Maya Iconography. In *Aspects of Ancient Maya Iconography*, edited by Francois-August de Montequin, pp. 1–26. St. Paul: Hamline University.

1977 The Art and Archaeology of Hydraulic Agriculture in the Maya Lowlands. In *Social Process in Maya Prehistory: Studies in Honor of Sir Eric Thompson*, edited by Norman Hammond, pp. 449–469. New York: Academic Press.

1979 An Epistemological Pathology and the Collapse, or Why the Maya Kept the Short Count. In *Maya Archaeology and Ethnohistory*, edited by Norman Hammond and Gordon R. Willey, pp. 63–711. Austin: University of Texas Press.

Quirarte, Jacinto

1974 Terrestrial/Celestial Polymorphs as Narrative Frames in the Art of Izapa and Palenque. In *Primera Mesa Redonda de Palenque*, edited by Merle Greene Robertson, pp. 129–136. Pebble Beach, Calif.: Robert Louis Stevenson School.

1982 *The Santa Rita Murals: A Review.* Middle American Research Institute Occasional Paper no. 4, pp. 43–58. New Orleans: Tulane University.

Rands, Robert L., Ron L. Bishop, and G. Harbottle

1979 Thematic and Compositional Variation in Palenque Region Incensarios. In *Tercera Mesa Redonda de Palenque, Part 1*, edited by Merle Greene Robertson and Donnan Call Jeffers, pp. 19–30. Palenque: Pre-Columbian Art Research Center.

Rands, Robert L., and Barbara C. Rands

1955 *Some Manifestations of Water in Mesoamerican Art.* Bureau of American Ethnology Bulletin no. 157, pp. 265–393. Washington, D.C.

1959 The Incensario Complex of Palenque, Chiapas. *American Antiquity* 25(2):225–236.

1961 Excavations in a Cemetery at Palenque. *Estudios de Cultura Maya* 1:87–106.

Rappaport, Roy A.

1971 The Sacred in Human Evolution. *Annual Review of Ecology and Systematics* 2:23–44.

Rathje, William

1971 The Origin and Development of Lowland Classic Maya Civilization. *American Antiquity* 36:275–285.

1972 Praise the Gods and Pass the Metates: A Hypothesis of the Lowland Rainforest Civilizations in Mesoamerica. In *Contemporary Archaeology*, edited by Mark Leone, pp. 365–392. Carbondale: Southern Illinois University Press.

1977 The Tikal Connection. In *The Origins of Maya Civilization*, edited by R. E. W. Adams, pp. 373–382. Albuquerque: University of New Mexico Press.

Recinos, Adrian

1950 *Popol Vuh: The Sacred Book of the Ancient Quiche Maya*, translated by Delia Goetz and Sylvanus G. Morley. Norman: University of Oklahoma Press.

Recinos, Adrian, and Delia Goetz

1953 *Tha Annals of the Cakchiquels and the Title of the Lords of Totonicapan.* Norman: University of Oklahoma Press.

Redfield, Robert, and Alfonso Villa Rojas

1934 *Chan Kom, a Maya Village.* Carnegie Institution of Washington Publication no. 448. Washington, D.C.

1962 *Chan Kom: A Maya Village.* Chicago: University of Chicago Press.

Redmond, Elsa M.

1983 *A fuego y sangre: Early Zapotec Imperialism in the Cuicatlan Canada, Oaxaca.* Memoirs of the Museum of Anthropology, no. 16. Ann Arbor: University of Michigan.

Reents, Doris J.

1985 The Late Classic Maya Holmul Style Polychrome Pottery. Ph.D. diss., University of Texas at Austin. (Available from University Microfilms International, Ann Arbor, Michigan.)

Reilly, F. Kent

1987 The Ecological Origins of Olmec Symbols of Rulership. Master's thesis, University of Texas at Austin.

1988 Olmec Conceptions of the Sacred Mountain as Underworld Entrance. MS. Institute of Latin American Studies, University of Texas at Austin.

Ricketson, Oliver G., and Edith B. Ricketson

1937 *Uaxactun, Guatemala, Group E—1926–1931.* Carnegie Institution of Washington Publication no. 177. Washington, D.C.

Riese, Berthold

1978 Stellungname zur Inschrift. *Ethnología Americana* 15(87):859–861.

1984a Hel Hieroglyphs. In *Phoneticism in Mayan Hieroglyphic Writing*, edited by John S. Justeson and Lyle Campbell, pp. 263–286. Institute for Mesoamerican Studies Publication no. 9. Albany: State University of New York.

1984b Kriegsberichte der Klassichen Maya. *Baessler-Archiv*, Beitrage zur Volkerunde 30(2):255–321.

In press The Inscriptions of the Sculptured Bench in Copan Valley Structure 82. In *House of the Bacabs*, edited by David Webster. Washington, D.C.: Dumbarton Oaks.

Roberts, L. G.

1965 Homogeneous Matrix Representations of N-Dimensional Constructs. Document MS1045. Massachusetts Institute of Technology Lincoln Lab. Lexington, Massachusetts.

Robertson, Donald

1974 Some Remarks on Stone Relief Sculpture at Palenque. In *Primera Mesa Redonda de Palenque, 1973, Part 2*, edited by Merle Greene Robertson, pp. 103–124. Pebble Beach, Calif.: Robert Louis Stevenson School.

Robertson, Merle Greene. *See* Greene Robertson, Merle.

Robertson, Robin

In press *Archaeology at Cerros, Belize, Central America.* Vol. 2, *The Ceramics.* Dallas: Southern Methodist University Press.

Robertson, Robin A., and David A. Freidel

1986 *Archaeology at Cerros, Belize, Central America.* Vol. 1, *An Interim Report.* Dallas: Southern Methodist University Press.

Robertson-Freidel, Robin A.

1980 The Ceramics from Cerros: A Late Preclassic Site in Northern Belize. Ph.D. diss., Harvard University, Cambridge, Mass.

Robicsek, Francis

1972 *Copan: Home of the Mayan Gods.* New York: Museum of the American Indian, Heye Foundation.

1978 *The Smoking Gods: Tobacco in Maya Art, History, and Religion.* Norman: University of Oklahoma Press.

1979 The Mythical Identity of God K. In *Tercera Mesa Redonda de Palenque, Part 1*, edited by Merle Greene

Robertson and Donnan Call Jeffers, pp. 111–128. Palenque: Pre-Columbian Art Research Center.

Robicsek, Francis, and Donald M. Hales
1981 *The Maya Book of the Dead: The Ceramic Codex.* Charlottesville: University of Virginia Art Museum.
1982 *Maya Ceramic Vases from the Late Classic Period: The November Collection of Maya Ceramics.* Charlottesville: The Bayley Museum, University of Virginia.
1984 Maya Heart Sacrifice: Cultural Perspectives and Surgical Techniques. In *Ritual Human Sacrifice in Mesoamerica,* edited by Elizabeth Boone, pp. 49–90. Washington, D.C.: Dumbarton Oaks.

Robles, C., J. Fernando
1980 La Sequencia Ceramica de la Región de Coba, Quintana Roo. Master's thesis, Escuela Nacional de Antropología e Historia, Mexico, D.F.

Robles C., J. Fernando, and Anthony P. Andrews
1986 A Review and Synthesis of Recent Postclassic Archaeology in Northern Yucatan. In *Late Lowland Maya Civilization: Classic to Postclassic,* edited by Jeremy A. Sabloff and E. Wyllys Andrews, pp. 53–98. Albuquerque: University of New Mexico Press.

Rock, Miles
1895 *Mapa de la Republica de Guatemala,* Guatemala, 2 de enero.

Romney, A. Kimball
1967 Kinship and Family. In *Handbook of Middle American Indians* (Robert Wauchope, General Editor). Vol. 6, *Social Anthropology,* edited by Manning Nash, pp. 207–237. Austin: University of Texas Press.

Rosney, Leon de
1872 *Archives Paleographiques de l'Orient et de Amerique.* Vol. 1. Paris: Maisonneuve.

Roys, Ralph L.
1933 *The Book of Chilam Balam of Chumayel.* Carnegie Institution of Washington Publication no. 505, Washington, D.C. Reprint, Norman: University of Oklahoma Press, 1967.
1939 *The Titles of Ebtun.* Carnegie Institution of Washington Publication no. 505. Washington, D.C.
1940 *Personal Names of the Maya of Yucatan.* Carnegie Institution of Washington Contributions to American Anthropology and History, no. 31 (Publication no. 523). Washington, D.C.
1943 *The Indian Background of Colonial Yucatan.* Carnegie Institution of Washington Publication no. 548. Washington, D.C. Reprint, Norman: University of Oklahoma Press, 1972.
1965 *Ritual of the Bacabs.* Norman: University of Oklahoma Press.

Rumelhart, David
1980 Schemata: The Building Blocks of Cognition. Chap. 2 in *Theoretical Issues in Reading Comprehension,* edited by R. J. Spiro, B. C. Bruce, and F. Weber. Hillsdale, New Jersey: Lawrence Erlbaum Associates.

Ruppert, Karl
1935 *The Caracol at Chichén Itzá, Yucatan, Mexico.* Carnegie Institution of Washington Publication no. 454. Washington, D.C.

Ruz, Mario Humberto
1982 *Los Legítimos Hombres: Aproximación Antropologica al Grupo Tojolabal,* vol. 2. Mexico, D.F.: Universidad Nacional Autonoma de Mexico, Centro de Estudios Maya.

Ruz Lhuillier, Alberto
1969 *Guía Oficial de Uxmal.* Mexico: Instituto Nacional de Antropología e Historia.

Sabloff, Jeremy A.
1973 Continuity and Disruption During Terminal Late Classic Times at Seibal: Ceramic and Other Evidence. In *The Classic Maya Collapse,* edited by T. Patrick Culbert, pp. 107–132. Albuquerque: University of New Mexico Press.

Saenz de Santa Maria, Carmelo
1940 *Diccionario Cakchiquel-Español.* Guatemala: Sociedad de Geografia e Historia de Guatemala.

Sahagun, Fray Bernardino de
1950–71 *The Florentine Codex. A General History of the Things of New Spain,* translated by J. O. Anderson and C. E. Dibble. Santa Fe: School of American Research in cooperation with the University of Utah.
1981 *Historia General de las Cosas de Nueva España.* Mexico: Editorial Porrua.

Sahlins, Marshall
1958 *Social Stratification in Polynesia.* Seattle: University of Washington Press.

Salazar, Ortego Ponciano
1952 El Tzompantli de Chichén Itzá, Yucatan. *Tlatoani* 1(5/6):36–41.

Sanders, William T.
1972 Population, Agricultural History, and Societal Evolution in Mesoamerica. In *Population Growth: Anthropological Implications,* edited by B. Spooner, pp. 101–153. Cambridge, Mass.: The MIT Press.
1973 The Cultural Ecology of the Lowland Maya: A Reevaluation. In *The Classic Maya Collapse,* edited by T. Patrick Culbert, pp. 325–365. Albuquerque: University of New Mexico Press.
1974 Chiefdom to State: Political Evolution at Kaminaljuyu, Guatemala. In *Reconstructing Complex Societies,* edited by C. B. Moore, pp. 97–121. Supplement to the Bulletin of the American School of Oriental Research, no. 20. Chicago.
1977 Ethnographic Analogy and the Teotihuacan Horizon Style. In *Teotihuacan and Kaminaljuyu: A Study in Prehistoric Culture Contact,* edited by William T. Sanders and Joseph W. Michels, pp. 397–410. College Park: Pennsylvania State University Press.
1989 Household, Lineage, and State at Eighth Century Copan. In *House of the Bacabs,* edited by David Webster. Washington, D.C.: Dumbarton Oaks.

Sanders, William T., and Joseph W. Michels, eds.
1977 *Teotihuacan and Kaminaljuyu: A Study in Prehistoric Culture Contact.* Monograph Series on Kaminaljuyu. College Park: Pennsylvania State University Press.

Sanders, William T., J. R. Parsons, and R. S. Santley
1979 *The Basin of Mexico: Ecological Processes in the Evolution of Civilization.* New York: Academic Press.

Sanders, William T., and Barbara J. Price
1968 *Mesoamerica: The Evolution of a Civilization.* New York: Random House.

Sanders, William T., and David Webster
1978 Unilinearism, Multilinealism, and the Evolution of Complex Societies. In *Social Archaeology: Beyond Subsistence and Dating,* edited by C. E. Redman et al., pp. 249–302. New York: Academic Press.

Santley, Robert S.
1983 Obsidian Trade and Teotihuacan Influence in Meso-

america. In *Highland-Lowland Interaction in Mesoamerica: Interdisciplinary Approaches*, edited by Arthur G. Miller, pp. 69–124. Washington, D.C.: Dumbarton Oaks.

Satterthwaite, Linton

1951 Reconnaissance in British Honduras. *University Museum Bulletin* (University of Pennsylvania) 16:21–37.

1954 Sculptured Monuments from Caracol, British Honduras. *University Museum Bulletin* (University of Pennsylvania) 18:1–45.

1958 *The Problem of Abnormal Stela Placements at Tikal and Elsewhere.* University Museum Monograph no. 15, Tikal Report no. 3, pp. 61–83. Philadelphia: The University Museum, University of Pennsylvania.

1965 Calendrics of Maya Lowlands. In *Handbook of Middle American Indians* (Robert Wauchope, General Editor). Vol. 3, *Archaeology of Southern Mesoamerica*, edited by Gordon R. Willey, pp. 603–631. Austin: University of Texas Press.

Scarborough, Vernon

1985 Courting the Maya Lowlands: A Study in Pre-Hispanic Ball Game Architecture. Paper presented at the Symposium on the Native American Ball Game: Regional Contexts and Comparative Interpretations, Tucson, Arizona.

Schaefer, B.

n.d. Heliacal Rise Dates. MS.

Schank, Roger, and Christopher Riesbeck

1981 *Inside Computer Understanding: Five Programs Plus Miniatures.* Hillsdale, New Jersey: Lawerence Erlbaum Associates.

Schapiro, Meyer

1953 Style. In *Anthropology Today*, edited by Alfred L. Kroeber, pp. 287–312. Chicago: University of Chicago Press.

Schele, Linda

1974 Observations on the Cross Motif at Palenque. In *Primera Mesa Redonda de Palenque, Part 1*, edited by Merle Greene Robertson, pp. 41–61. Pebble Beach, Calif.: Robert Louis Stevenson School.

1976 Accession Iconography of Chan Bahlum in the Group of the Cross at Palenque. In *The Art, Iconography & Dynastic History of Palenque, Part 3*, edited by Merle Greene Robertson, pp. 9–34. Pebble Beach, Calif.: The Robert Louis Stevenson School.

1977 The House of the Dying Sun. In *Native American Astronomy*, edited by Anthony Aveni, pp. 42–56. Austin: University of Texas Press.

1978a An Odd Kinship Expression and the Classic Bloodletting Rite. Paper presented at the 26th Annual Meeting of the American Society for Ethnohistory, Austin, Texas.

1978b Genealogical Documentation of the Tri-Figure Panels at Palenque. In *Tercera Mesa Redonda de Palenque*, edited by Merle Greene Robertson and Donnan Call Jeffers, pp. 41–70. Palenque: Pre-Columbian Art Research Center.

1978c *Notebook for the Maya Hieroglyphic Writing Workshop at Texas.* Austin: Institute of Latin American Studies, University of Texas at Austin.

1978d Preliminary Commentary on the Tablet of the Cross at Palenque. MS. University of Texas at Austin.

1979 The Puleston Hypothesis: The Water Lily Complex in Classic Maya Art and Writing. MS.

1980 *Notebook for the Maya Hieroglyphic Writing Workshop.*

Austin: Institute of Latin American Studies, University of Texas at Austin.

1981 Sacred Site and World-View at Palenque. In *Mesoamerican Sites and World Views*, edited by Elizabeth P. Benson, pp. 87–117. Washington, D.C.: Dumbarton Oaks.

1982 *Maya Glyphs: The Verbs.* Austin: University of Texas Press.

1983 *Notebook for the Maya Hieroglyphic Writing Workshop at Texas.* Austin: Institute of Latin American Studies, University of Texas at Austin.

1984a Human Sacrifice Among the Classic Maya. In *Ritual Human Sacrifice in Mesoamerica*, edited by Elizabeth Boone, pp. 6–48. Washington, D.C.: Dumbarton Oaks.

1984b *Notebook for the Maya Hieroglyphic Writing Workshop at Texas.* Austin: Institute of Latin American Studies, University of Texas at Austin.

1984c Some Suggested Readings for the Event and Office of Heir-Designate at Palenque. In *Phoneticism in Mayan Hieroglyphic Writing*, edited by John S. Justeson and Lyle Campbell, pp. 287–305. Institute for Mesoamerican Studies Publication no. 9. Albany: State University of New York.

1984d The Maya Inscriptions: A Window into World View. Paper presented at The Language of Writing in the Maya Region, a conference sponsored by the Center of Latin American Studies, April, 1984, University of Chicago.

1985a *Balan Ahau: A Possible Reading of the Tikal Emblem Glyph and a Title at Palenque. In *Fourth Palenque Round Table, 1980*, edited by Elizabeth P. Benson (Merle Greene Robertson, General Editor), pp. 59–66. San Francisco: Pre-Columbian Art Research Institute.

1985b The Hauberg Stela: Bloodletting and the Mythos of Maya Rulership. In *Fifth Palenque Round Table, 1983*, edited by Virginia M. Fields (Merle Greene Robertson, General Editor), pp. 135–149. San Francisco: Pre-Columbian Art Research Institute.

1985c *Notebook for the Maya Hieroglyphic Writing Workshop.* Austin: Institute of Latin American Studies, University of Texas at Austin.

1986a *Notebook for the Maya Hieroglyphic Writing Workshop at Texas.* Austin: Institute of Latin American Studies, University of Texas at Austin.

1986b The Tlaloc Heresy: Cultural Interaction and Social History. Paper presented at Maya Art and Civilization: The New Dynamics, May 16–18, Kimbell Art Museum, Fort Worth, Texas.

1988 The Xibalba Shuffle: A Dance After Death. In *Maya Iconography*, edited by Elizabeth P. Benson and Gillett G. Griffin, pp. 294–317. Princeton: Princeton University Press.

Schele, Linda, and Peter Mathews

1979 *The Bodega of Palenque, Chiapas, Mexico.* Washington, D.C.: Dumbarton Oaks.

Schele, Linda, Peter Mathews, and Floyd Lounsbury

1977 Parentage Statements in Classic Maya Inscriptions. MS.

Schele, Linda and Peter Mathews

1983 Parentage Statements in Classic Maya Inscriptions. MS. (Rev. ed. of Schele, Mathews, and Lounsbury 1977.)

Schele, Linda, and Jeffrey Miller

1983 *The Mirror, the Rabbit, and the Bundle: "Accession"*

Expressions from the Classic Maya Inscriptions. Studies in Pre-Columbian Art and Archaeology Series, no. 25. Washington, D.C.: Dumbarton Oaks.

Schele, Linda, and Mary E. Miller
  1986 *The Blood of Kings: Dynasty and Ritual in Maya Art.* Fort Worth: Kimbell Art Museum.

Schele, Linda, and David Stuart
  1985 Te-tun *as the Glyph for Stela.* Copan Note no. 1. Copan, Honduras.

Scholes, France V.
  1938 *Don Diego Quijada: Alcalde Mayor de Yucatan, 1561–1565.* Biblioteca Historica Mexicana de Obras Ineditas, vols. 14 and 15. Mexico: Porrua e Hijos.

Scholes, France V., and Eleanor B. Adams
  1938 *Don Diego Quijada: Alcalde Mayor de Yucatán, 1561–1565.* Vols. 14 and 15 of *Biblioteca Histórica Mexicana de Obras Inéditas.* Mexico: Porrúa e Hijos.

Scholes, France V., and Ralph L. Roys
  1968 *The Maya Chontal Indians of Acalan-Tixchel.* Norman: University of Oklahoma Press.

Schultes, Richard Evans
  1976 *Hallucinogenic Plants.* New York: Golden Press.

Secretaria de Agricultura y Recursos Hidraulicos
  1983 *Problematica Regional de la Selva Lacandona.* Chiapas, Mexico: Subsecretaria Forestal.
  1984 *Programa de Desarrollo Integral de la Selva Lacandona.* Chiapas, Mexico: Subsecretaria Forestal.

Secretaria de Recursos Hidraulicos
  1976a *Atlas del Agua de la Republica Mexicana.* Mexico.
  1976b Comportamiento de Presas Construidas en Mexico. Contribucion al XII Congreso Internacional de Grandes Presas, Universidad Nacional Autonoma de Mexico, Mexico.

Sedat, Guillermo S.
  1955 *Nuevo Diccionario: de las Lenguas K'chi y Española.* Alta Verapaz, Guatemala: Chamelco.

Séjourné, Laurette
  1966 *Arqueologia de Teotihuacan.* Mexico: Fondo de Cultura Economica.

Seler, Edward
  1902–23 *Gesammelte Abhandlungen zur Amerikanischen Sprach- und Altertumskunde.* 5 vols. Berlin. Reissued, Graz, Austria: Akademische Druck- und Verlagsanstalt, 1961.
  1904–09 *Codex Borgia: Eine altmexikanische Bilderschrift der Congregation de Propaganda Fide.* 3 vols. Berlin.

Serna, J. de la
  1892 Manual de Ministros de Indios. Collección de Documentos Ineditos para la Historia de España, 114:1–267. Madrid.

Sharer, Robert J.
  1977 The Maya Collapse Revisited: Internal and External Perspectives. In *Social Process in Maya Prehistory: Essays in Honour of Sir J. Eric S. Thompson,* edited by Norman Hammond, pp. 532–552. New York: Academic Press.

Sheets, Payson D.
  1976 *The Ilopango Volcanic Eruption and the Maya Protoclassic.* University Museum Studies, no. 9, Carbondale: Southern Illinois University.
  1979 Environmental and Cultural Effects of the Ilopango Eruption in Central America. In *Volcanic Activity and Human Ecology,* edited by Payson D. Sheets and Donald Grayson, pp. 525–564. New York: Academic Press.

Shook, E. M.
  1957 The Tikal Project. *University Museum Bulletin* (University of Pennsylvania) 21(3).
  1965 Archaeological Survey of the Pacific Coast of Guatemala. In *Handbook of Middle American Indians* (Robert Wauchope, General Editor). Vol. 2, *Archaeology of Southern Mesoamerica,* edited by Gordon R. Willey, pp. 180–194. Austin: University of Texas Press.

Shook, E. M., and Robert F. Heizer
  1976 An Olmec Sculpture from the South (Pacific) Coast of Guatemala. *Journal of New World Archaeology* 1(3).

Shook, Edwin M., and William N. Irving
  1955 *Colonnaded Buildings at Mayapan.* Carnegie Institution of Washington Current Reports, no. 22. Washington, D.C.

Slocum, Marianna C., and Florencia L. Gerdel
  1976 *Vocabulario Tzeltal de Bachajon.* 3d ed. Serie de Vocabularios Indígenas Mariano Silva y Aceves 13. Mexico: Instituto Lingüístico de Verano.

Smailus, Ortwin
  1975 *El Maya-Chontal de Acalan: Análisis Lingüístico de un Documento de los Años 1610–12.* Centro de Estudios Mayas Cuadernos 9. Mexico, D.F.: Universidad Nacional Autonoma de Mexico.

Smith, A. Ledyard
  1950 *Uaxactun, Guatemala: 1931–1937.* Carnegie Institution of Washington Publication no. 588. Washington, D.C.

Smith, Robert E.
  1937 *A Study of Structure A-I Complex at Uaxactun, Peten, Guatemala.* Carnegie Institution of Washington Publication no. 456. Washington, D.C.
  1955 *The Ceramic Sequence at Uaxactun, Guatemala.* Middle American Research Institute Publication no. 20. New Orleans: Tulane University.
  1971 *The Pottery of Mayapan.* 2 pts. Papers of the Peabody Museum of Archaeology and Ethnology, 66. Cambridge, Mass.: Harvard University.

Smith-Stark, Thomas C.
  1978 The Origin of Corn. In *Codex Wauchope: A Tribute Roll,* edited by M. Giardino, B. Edmonsen, and W. Creamer, pp. 57–60. New Orleans: Tulane University.
  1981 A Commentary on the Dynastic History of the City of Crossed Bands. MS.

Solis Alcala, Ermilo
  1949 *Diccionario Español-Maya.* Merida, Mexico: Editorial Yikal Maya Than.

Sosa, John R., and Dorie J. Reents
  1980 Glyphic Evidence for Classic Maya Militarism. *Belizean Studies* 8(3):2–21.

Spence, Michael W.
  1981 Obsidian Production and the State in Teotihuacan. *American Antiquity* 46:769–788.

Spinden, Herbert G.
  1913 *A Study of Maya Art.* Memoirs of the Peabody Museum of American Archaeology and Ethnology, no. 6. Cambridge, Mass.: Harvard University.

Stallman, Richard, and Gerald G. Sussman
  1976 Forward Reasoning and Dependency-Directed Backtracking in a System for Computer-Aided Circuit Analysis. Memo 380, Massachusetts Institute of Technology AI Lab. Cambridge, Mass.

Standley, Paul C.
  1917 The Mexican and Central American Species of

Ficus. *Contributions from the United States National Herbarium* 20:1–35.

Stephens, John Lloyd
1963 (1843) *Incidents of Travel in Yucatan*. New York: Dover Publications.

Stern, Theodore
1948 *The Rubber Ball Games of the Americas*. Monographs of the American Ethnological Society, no. 17. New York.

Stirling, Matthew W.
1943 *Stone Monuments of Southern Mexico*. Bureau of American Ethnology Bulletin no. 138. Washington, D.C.: Smithsonian Institution.

Stocker, Terrance, and Michael Spence
1973 Trilobal Eccentrics at Teotihuacan and Tula. *American Antiquity* 38(2):195–199.

Stone, Andrea
1983 The Zoomorphs of Quirigua, Guatemala. Ph.D. diss., University of Texas at Austin. (Available from University Microfilms, Ann Arbor, Michigan.)
1985 Variety and Transformation in the Cosmic Monster Theme at Quirigua, Guatemala. In *Fifth Palenque Round Table, 1983*, edited by Virginia M. Fields (Merle Greene Robertson, General Editor), pp. 39–48. San Francisco: Pre-Columbian Art Research Institute.

Stone, Andrea, Dorie Reents, and Robert Coffman
1985 Genealogical Documentation of the Middle Classic Dynasty of Caracol, El Cayo, Belize. In *Fourth Palenque Round Table, 1980*, edited by Elizabeth P. Benson (Merle Greene Robertson, General Editor), pp. 262–275. San Francisco: Pre-Columbian Art Research Institute.

Strecker, Matthias
In press Cuevas Mayas en el Municipio de Oxkutzcab (III): Una mascara de madera proveniente de una cueva. *Boletin ECAUDY* (Merida).

Strömsvik, Gustav
1941 *Substela Caches and Stela Foundations at Copan and Quirigua*. Contributions to American Anthropology and History, no. 37. Washington, D.C.: Carnegie Institution of Washington.
1947 *Guide Book to the Ruins of Copan*. Carnegie Institution of Washington Publication no. 577. Washington, D.C.
1952 *The Ball Courts of Copan, with Notes on Courts at La Union, Quirigua, San Pedro Pinula and Asuncion Mita*. Carnegie Institution of Washington Publication no. 596 (Contributions to American Archaeology and History, no. 55). Washington, D.C.

Stross, Brian
1986 Bloodletting Iconography on an Olmec Vase and a Maya Plate. MS. Department of Anthropology, University of Texas at Austin.

Stuart, David
1978 Some Thoughts on Certain Occurrences of the T565 Glyph Element at Palenque. In *Tercera Mesa Redonda de Palenque*, edited by Merle Greene Robertson and Donnan Call Jeffers, pp. 167–171. Palenque: Pre–Columbian Art Research Center.
1984a A Note on the Hand-Scattering Glyph. In *Phoneticism in Mayan Hieroglyphic Writing*, edited by John S. Justeson and William M. Norman, pp. 307–310. Institute for Mesoamerican Studies Publication, no. 9. Albany: State University of New York.
1984b A Reconsideration of Directional Count Glyphs. Paper presented at the annual meeting of the American Anthropological Association, November 1986, Denver, Colorado.
1984c Epigraphic Evidence of Political Organization in the Usumacinta Drainage. MS.
1984d Name-Tagging on Tikal Bones? MS.
1984e Royal Auto-Sacrifice Among the Maya: A Study in Image and Meaning. *Res* 7/8:6–20.
1985a *A New Child-Father Relationship Glyph*. Research Reports on Ancient Maya Writing, no. 2. Washington, D.C.: Center for Maya Research.
1985b The "Count of Captives" Epithet in Classic Maya Writing. In *Fifth Palenque Round Table, 1983*, edited by Virginia M. Fields (Merle Greene Robertson, General Editor), pp. 97–101. San Francisco: Pre-Columbian Art Research Institute.
1985c *The Yaxha Emblem Glyph as Yax-ha*. Research Reports on Ancient Maya Writing, no. 1. Washington, D.C.: Center for Maya Research.
1986a The Classic Maya Social Structure: Titles, Rank, and Professions as Seen from the Inscriptions. Paper presented at Maya Art and Civilization: The New Dynamics, May 16–18, Kimbell Art Museum, Fort Worth, Texas.
1986b The "Lu-Bat" Glyph and Its Bearing on the Primary Standard Sequence. Paper presented at the First World Conference for Maya Epigraphy, Guatemala City, Guatemala.
1988 Blood Symbolism in Maya Iconography. In *Maya Iconography*, edited by Elizabeth P. Benson and Gillett G. Griffin, pp. 175–221. Princeton: Princeton University Press.

Stuart, David, and Nikolai Grube
1986 A Reading for the Affix T110. MS.

Stuart, George
1975 The Maya: Riddle of the Glyphs. *National Geographic Magazine* 148(6):768–791.

Stuart, George E., and S. Jeffrey K. Wilkerson
1985 Las Figuras de Planchon de las Figuras, Chiapas. Album Fotográfico. Instituto Nacional de Antropología e Historia (INAH), Mexico.

Sullivan, Paul R.
1983 Contemporary Yucatec Maya Apocalyptic Prophecy: The Ethnographic and Historical Context. Ph.D. diss., Johns Hopkins University.

Tate, Carolyn
1980 The Maya Cauac Monster: Formal Development and Dynastic Implications. Master's thesis, University of Texas at Austin.
1985 The Carved Ceramics Called Chochola. In *Fifth Palenque Round Table, 1983*, edited by Virginia M. Fields (Merle Greene Robertson, General Editor), pp. 123–133. San Francisco: Pre-Columbian Art Research Institute.
1986 The Language of Symbols in the Ritual Landscape at Yaxchilan, Chiapas. Ph.D. diss., University of Texas at Austin.

Taube, Karl
1985 The Classic Maya Maize God: A Reappraisal. In *Fifth Palenque Round Table, 1983*, edited by Virginia M. Fields (Merle Greene Robertson, General Editor), pp. 171–181. San Francisco: Pre-Columbian Art Research Institute.
1988 A Prehispanic Maya Katun Wheel. *Journal of Anthropological Research* 44(2):183–203.

1989   The Maize Tamale in Classic Maya Diet, Epigraphy, and Art. *American Antiquity* 54(1):31–51.

Taylor, Dicey
1978   The Cauac Monster. In *Tercera Mesa Redonda de Palenque*, edited by Merle Greene Robertson and Donnan Call Jeffers, pp. 79–89. Palenque: Pre–Columbian Art Research Center.

Tedlock, Dennis
1985   *Popol Vuh: The Definitive Edition of the Mayan Book of the Dawn of Life and the Glories of Gods and Kings.* New York: Simon and Schuster.

Thomas, Cyrus
1882   A Study of the Manuscript Troano. *Contributions to North American Ethnology* (U.S. Department of the Interior) 5:1–237.

Thompson, Edward H.
1895   Ancient Tombs of Palenque. *Proceedings of the American Antiquarian Society* 10:418–442.
1938   The High Priest's Grave, Chichén Itzá, Yucatan, Mexico. *Field Museum of Natural History* 27(1).

Thompson, J. Eric S.
1927   The Civilization of the Mayas. Field Museum of Natural History Anthropology Leaflet no. 25. Chicago.
1930   *Ethnology of the Mayas of Southern and Central British Honduras.* Field Museum of Natural History Publication no. 274 (Anthropological Series). Chicago.
1937   *A New Method of Deciphering Yucatecan Dates, with Special Reference to Chichén Itzá.* Carnegie Institution of Washington Publication no. 483 (Contributions to American Archaeology and History, no. 22). Washington, D.C.
1943   *Maya Epigraphy: Directional Glyphs in Counting.* Carnegie Institution of Washington, Division of Historical Research, Notes on Middle American Archaeology and Ethnology, no. 20. Washington, D.C.
1944   *The Fish as a Symbol for Maya Counting and Further Discussion of Directional Glyphs.* Carnegie Institution of Washington Theoretical Approaches to Problems, no. 2. Washington, D.C.
1950   *Maya Hieroglyphic Writing: An Introduction.* Carnegie Institution of Washington Publication no. 589. 2d ed. Norman: University of Oklahoma Press, 1960.
1954   *The Rise and Fall of Maya Civilization.* 2d ed. Norman: University of Oklahoma Press, 1966.
1958   (editor)   *Thomas Gage's Travels in the New World.* Norman: University of Oklahoma Press.
1962   *A Catalog of Maya Hieroglyphs.* Norman: University of Oklahoma Press.
1970   *Maya History and Religion.* Norman: University of Oklahoma Press.
1972   *A Commentary on the Dresden Codex, a Maya Hieroglyphic Book.* Memoirs of the American Philosophical Society, no. 93. Philadelphia.
1977   The Hieroglyphic Texts of Las Monjas and their Bearing on Building Activities. In *Las Monjas*, by John Bolles. Norman: University of Oklahoma Press.

Thompson, Philip C.
1982   Dynastic Marriage and Succession at Tikal. *Estudios de Cultura Maya* 14:261–287.

Toops, Connie M.
1979   *The Alligator: Monarch of the Everglades.* Homestead, Fla.: The Everglades Natural History Association.

Torquemada, Fray Juan
1969   *Monarquía Indiana.* Biblioteca Porrua 42, vol. 2. Mexico: Editorial Porrua.

Townsend, Paul G.
1980   Couplets in Ixil Maya Poetic Genre. In *Ritual Rhetoric from Cotzal*, compiled by Paul G. Townsend et al., pp. 49–62. Guatemala: Instituto de Lingüístico de Verano.

Townsend, Paul G., with Te'c Cham and Po'x Ich' (compilers)
1980   *Ritual Rhetoric from Cotzal.* Guatemala: Instituto de Lingüístico de Verano.

Townsend, Richard
1979   *State and Cosmos in the Art of Tenochtitlan.* Studies in Pre-Columbian Art and Archaeology, no. 20. Washington, D.C.: Dumbarton Oaks.

Tozzer, Alfred M.
1930   Maya and Toltec Figures at Chichén Itzá. In *Proceedings of the 23rd International Congress of Americanists*, pp. 155–164. New York.
1941   *Landa's Relación de las Cosas de Yucatan: A Translation.* Papers of the Peabody Museum of American Archaeology and Ethnology 18. Cambridge, Mass.: Harvard University.
1957   *Chichén Itzá and Its Cenote of Sacrifice: A Comparative Study of Contemporaneous Maya and Toltec.* Memoirs of the Peabody Museum of Archaeology and Ethnology, nos. 11 and 12. Cambridge, Mass.: Harvard University.

Tozzer, Alfred M., and G. M. Allen
1910   *Animal Figures in the Maya Codices.* Papers of the Peabody Museum of American Archaeology and Ethnology 4(3). Cambridge, Mass.: Harvard University.

Trik, Aubrey S.
1939   *Temple XXII at Copan.* Carnegie Institution of Washington Publication no. 509 (Contributions to American Archaeology and History, no. 27). Washington, D.C.
1963   The Splendid Tomb of Temple I at Tikal, Guatemala. *Expedition* 6(1):2–18.

Ulrich, Mateo, and Rosemary de Ulrich
1976   *Diccionario Bilingue: Mopan y Español.* Guatemala: Summer Institute of Linguistics.

Vienna Dictionary
1972   *Bocabulario de Mayathan.* Graz, Austria: Akademische Druck- und Verlagsanstalt.

Villacorta C., J. Antonio, and Carlos A. Villacorta R.
1930   *Codices Mayas* (2d ed. published in 1976). Guatemala: Tipografía Nacional.

Villa Rojas, Alfonso
1945   *The Maya of East Central Quintana Roo.* Carnegie Institution of Washington Publication no. 559. Washington, D.C.

Vogt, Evon Z.
1966   H?iloletik: The Organization and Function of Shamanism in Zinacantan. In *Summa Antropologica en Homenaje a Roberto J. Weitlaner.* Mexico: D.F.: Instituto Nacional de Antropología e Historia.
1969   *Zinacantan: A Maya Community in the Highlands of Chiapas.* Cambridge: Belknap Press.
1981   Some Aspects of the Sacred Geography of Highland Chiapas. In *Mesoamerican Sites and World Views*, edited by Elizabeth P. Benson, pp. 119–142. Washington, D.C.: Dumbarton Oaks.
1985   Cardinal Directions and Ceremonial Circuits in

Mayan and Southwestern Cosmology. *National Geographic Society Research Reports* 21:487–496.

Walker, Debra S.
   1986   A Context for Maya Ritual at Cerros, Belize. Paper presented at the Maya Hieroglyphic Workshop, March 21, 1986, University of Texas at Austin.

Waltz, David
   1972   Generating Semantic Descriptions from Drawings of Scenes with Shadows. Technical Report 271. Massachusetts Institute of Technology AI Lab. Cambridge, Mass.

Watanabe, John
   1983   In the World of the Sun: A Cognitive Model of Mayan Cosmology. *Man* 18(4).

Webster, David L.
   1977   Warfare and the Evolution of Maya Civilization. In *The Origins of Maya Civilization*, edited by R. E. W. Adams, pp. 335–372. Albuquerque: University of New Mexico Press.

Webster, David, ed.
   1989   *The House of the Bacabs.* Washington, D.C.: Dumbarton Oaks.

Webster, David, and Elliott M. Abrams
   1983   An Elite Compound at Copan, Honduras. *Journal of Field Archaeology* 10:285–296.

Webster, David, William L. Fash, and Elliot M. Abrams
   1986   Excavations en Conjunto 9N-8, Patio A (Operacion VIII). In *Excavaciones en el Area Urbana de Copan*, edited by William T. Sanders, pp. 156–315. Tegucigalpa: Instituto Hondureno de Antropología e Historia.

Welsh, W. B. M.
   1988   *An Analysis of Classic Lowland Maya Burials.* British Archaeological Reports International Series, no. 409. Oxford.

Whittaker, Arabelle, and Viola Warkentin
   1965   *Chol Texts on the Supernatural.* Norman: Summer Institute of Linguistics, University of Oklahoma.

Wicke, Charles R.
   1971   *Olmec: An Early Art Style of Pre-Columbian Mexico.* Tucson: University of Arizona Press.

Wilkerson, S. Jeffrey K.
   1983   *Archaeological and Ecological Implications in Guatemala and Mexico of Proposed Hydroelectric Projects on the Rio Usumacinta.* Papers and Report Series, no. 1. Tampa:

Institute for Cultural Ecology of the Tropics.
   1985   The Usumacinta River, Troubles on a Wild Frontier. *National Geographic Magazine* (October): 514–543.
   1986   Exploring the Usumacinta Wilderness. *Panorama* (July). Milan.

Willey, Gordon R.
   1974   The Classic Maya Hiatus: A Rehearsal for the Collapse. In *Mesoamerican Archaeology: New Approaches*, edited by Norman Hammond, pp. 417–444. Austin: University of Texas Press.
   1977   The Rise of Maya Civilization: A Summary View. In *The Origins of Maya Civilization*, edited by R. E. W. Adams, pp. 383–423. Albuquerque: University of New Mexico Press.

Willey, Gordon R., Richard M. Leventhal, and William L. Fash
   1978   Maya Settlement in the Copan Valley. *Archaeology* 31(4):32–43.

Willey, Gordon, A. Ledyard Smith, Gair Tourtellot III, and Ian Graham
   1975   *Excavations at Seibal: Introduction.* Memoirs of the Peabody Museum of Archaeology and Ethnology 13(1). Cambridge, Mass.: Harvard University.

Winston, Patrick H.
   1970   Learning Structural Descriptions from Examples. Technical Report 231. Massachusetts Institute of Technology AI Lab. Cambridge, Mass.

Winston, Patrick H., and Karen Prendergast, eds.
   1984   *The AI Business: Commercial Uses of Artificial Intelligence.* Cambridge: The MIT Press.

Wisdom, Charles
   1940   *The Chorti Indians of Guatemala.* Chicago: University of Chicago Press.

Wright, Henry T.
   1977   Recent Research on the Origin of the State. *Annual Review of Anthropology* 6:379–397.

Zavala, Lauro Jose
   n.d.   Informe personal exploraciones arqueologica segunda temporada 1950. MS. Centro de Estudios Maya. Mexico, D.F.

Zimmerman, Gunter
   1956   *Die Hieroglyphen de Maya-Handschriften.* Hamburg: Cram, de Gruyter.

Index

Abaj Takalik Stela 5: 197
Acante/Acantun: 175
Ahau: 74, 78
Ahau altars: 35, 41
Akbal: 60, 61, 62, 65, 66, 67
Alligator. *See* Gar
Altar de Sacrificios: 34, 55, 127
Ancestors: 8, 10, 12, 68, 78, 79–80, 103, 109, 150, 188, 193; and Cauac Monster, 186–87; communication with, 157–59, 166; and fish-in-hand glyph, 233–34, 245
Archaeoastronomy, in Mesoamerica: 316, 320–21
Architecture, masks on: 151–52. *See also* Chac, as architectural mask
Artists: 203, 209, 211, 215, 216
Atlihuayan "Blind Shaman": 155
Avian zoomorph: 154–55
Axis mundi. *See* World Tree

Bacabs: 84, 93, 95, 100, 204–205
Backrack: 217–22
Bahlum Kuk (Palenque), parentage statement: 256–57, 264
Balakbal: 35
Balberta: 136–42
Ball court: 53, 59–67, 69; glyph for, 41
Ball-court markers, at Copán: 63–64, 67
Ball game: 53–57, 62–67; glyph for, 56
Beard: 97–99, 101
Becan: 55, 135, 141
Bicephalic Monster. *See* Celestial Monster
Bird-in-nest (glyph): 47
Bird Jaguar III (formerly II) (Yaxchilán): 107, 112, 116
Bird Jaguar IV (formerly III) (Yaxchilán): 103, 106, 110, 116, 117; parentage statement, 255–56
Bloodletter: 143, 144–45, 146, 147, 148, 149, 150, 156, 158, 252, 253, 254
Bloodletting: 103, 106, 109, 143–44, 150, 156, 157, 158, 164, 169, 170, 174; and fish-in-hand glyph, 233–36, 238, 244–45; and Olmec iconography of, 143–50; at Santa Rita Corozal, 89–96
Bolon, and fish-in-hand glyph: 233, 236–37
Bolon Tz'acab: 236–39
Bonampak: Sculptured Stone 1, 167; Stela 1, 184–85
Bone: 60, 61, 62, 65, 66, 67

Bread, as offering: 301
Burials, at Santa Rita Corozal: 89, 90, 91, 92, 96
Burner ceremonies: 285, 288, 292

Cacao: 136, 137–39
Cache: 89, 96, 183; at Copán, 81, 88; at Santa Rita Corozal, 91, 93, 94–95, 96
Cabal (title): 7, 9–10
Calakmul: 34, 37; emblem glyph, 221, 222; Stela 28, 202
Calendar Round: 310
Cancuén: 127, 129
Caption texts. *See* Hieroglyphic texts
Captives: 155, 156, 159, 166, 176, 178
Caracol: 32–42; Altar 21, 33, 35, 38–41
Cartouche: 103–105
Cauac Monster: 95, 175, 176–77, 184–87, 190, 218, 219, 235
Causeway: 33, 136
Caves: 184, 187, 188, 189–90, 193, 195
Celestial Bird Deity: 177. *See also* Principal Bird Deity
Celestial Monster: 84, 181, 317, 318, 320
Celt: 168–69, 170, 189. *See also* Humboldt Celt
Censer: 303–308; and stacking, 178–81
Ceramics: Holmul style with hieroglyphic text, 217–22; Usulutan, 141. *See also* Chocolá-style ceramics
Cerro de las Mesas: Stela 8, 171
Cerros: censers at, 178–83; Structure 5C-2nd, 151–52, 181–82, 198
Chaacal III (Palenque): 6–9, 28
Chac (god): 285, 288; as architectural mask, 97, 100, 315, 317
Chac Uayeb Xoc: 246–47, 252
Chac Xib Chac: 176–77, 178, 250
Chac-Zutz' (Palenque): 6–11, 27–30
Chalcatzingo: 144, 145, 149, 157, 158, 163–66, 186, 187, 200–201; Relief 1, 158, 186, 187, 200–201
Chan Bahlum I (Palenque): 22
Chan Bahlum II (Palenque): 6, 9, 12, 23–25
Chiapa de Corzo: 135, 141
Chichén Itzá: 51, 53–57, 214–15, 238–39, 244, 317, 318; architectural style of, 57–58; censers at, 303, 304, 305, 307; emblem glyph, 56; Great Ball Court stone,

51–58; hieroglyphic lintels, 43–50, 228–29, 230
Chilam Balam: 175, 248, 251, 253
"Child of mother" glyphs: 255–65, 278–79
Chixoy (Salinas): 118, 119, 127
Chocolá-style ceramics: 211, 212, 214
Chol language: 12–15
Cichlid: 243
Cleft: 83, 157
Cleveland Stela: 202
Cobá: 35, 36
Coe, Michael D.: 223
Colha: 55
Collapse, Classic Maya: 32, 37
"Computer print-out": 75
Conch shell: 74, 75
Copán: 34, 37, 78, 81–88; Altar O, 244–45; Altar Q, 206–208; Altar R, 318; Altar W, 78, 79; Altar X, 234; ball courts, 59–65, 69; peccary skull, 186–87, 282; Stela 1, 239, 242–43; Stelae 10 and 12, 319–20; Stela A, 85, 87–88, 282; Stela B, 88; Stela N, 76; Stela P, 251, 253; Structure 9N-82, 7, 8, 10, 68–80, 209; Temple 11, 81–85, 206, 207–208, 318–19; Temple 22, and Venus, 316, 317–320
Copán Mosaics Project: 59
Cortés, Hernan: 118
Costume, *xoc*-shell: 201–202, 252–53
Couplet: 14, 15, 16–17
Crocodilian: 147–48, 149, 160, 161–63, 165, 166, 212
Cross: 109; pattern and ritual, at Copán, 81–88
Crossed bands: 145, 146, 147, 149, 156, 160
Curl Snout (Tikal): 175–76, 221

Death god: 288
Decapitation: 54–56
Dedication ceremonies, at Chichén Itzá: 43, 47, 48, 49
Deer, as offering: 285, 288, 289, 290, 291, 292
Directions, world: 83, 87–88
Distance Number Introducing Glyph: 273, 275–76
Diving god: 94
Dresden Codex: page 26, 293–302; pages 29b–31b, 285–92; pages 65b–69b, 276–77, 289–92; censers depicted in,

303–307; New Year pages, 293–302; origin of, 303, 305, 306–307; Venus tables, 315–16; 318
Dumbarton Oaks: Jade pectoral, 170; Panel, from Palenque, 166
Dwarf: 217, 218, 220
Dzibilchaltun: 81, 84, 85, 87, 135

Earth Lord: 184, 186, 187, 189, 193
Edzna: 135, 141
819-day count: 15
18 Rabbit (Copán): 62, 64, 67, 85
El Kanil, Man of Lightning (tale): 189
El Mirador: 34, 135, 141, 151
El Perú: 37
El Sitio, hacha: 168
El Zapote, Stela 5: 198
Emblem glyph: at Calakmul, 221, 222; and deity names, 220, 221–22; at Machaquilá, 221–22
Erythrina: 237

Fauna, as offering, in Dresden Codex: 285–92
Feathered serpent: 218–19
Figurines: 140
Fish: as offering, 285, 286, 288, 291; as zoomorph, 145–48, 149, 150
Fish-head (glyph): 246–49, 252
Fish-in-hand (glyph): 150, 233–45
"Flat-hand Verb" (glyph): 223–24
Flint: 234
Floating figures: 148, 150, 157–59
Formative: Middle, and Olmec influence on Classic Maya, 151–52, 166; Terminal, and transition to Early Classic, 135–36, 140–42
Fortifications: 135, 141
Fox and Justeson: 259–61, 264

G1 (Lord of the Night), and fish-in-hand glyph: 233, 236–37, 239, 242
GI: 19, 143–44, 150, 181, 190, 198–99, 201, 235, 249–50, 253; and codex-style vases, 190–93; and fish-in-hand glyph, 239, 242–43
GIII: 181, 190, 193, 198, 250
Gar: 160, 161, 164. *See also* Crocodilian
García Moll, Roberto: 110, 125
Giralda (Escuintla): 140
Glyphs, computerized database of: 326–27, 331–32. *See also* Thompson numbers *and* under names of specific glyphs
God IV (Olmec): 200
God C (glyph): 109, 190–91
God K: 198, 239, 242
Graffiti: 84–85
Great Ball Court stone at Chichén Itzá: 51–58
Grolier Panel: 275–76
Guatemala, South Coast: Late Terminal Formative to Early Classic, 135, 136, 141–42

Hallucinogenic drugs: 237
Hand-crossed bands (glyph): 46–47
Hauberg Stela: 150
Headdress: Jester God, 157, 167–68, 169, 170, 171, 173; Olmec, 153; Quadripartite Monster, 198, 201
Hel (glyph): 14
Hero Twins: 67, 104, 220, 250, 252, 254

Hetzmek ceremony: 197–98
"Hiatus, Maya": 35–36, 37
Hieroglyphic texts: caption (secondary) texts, 13, 23–25; computer-aided decipherment, 322–32; discourse features of, 15–28; narrative structure of, 12–15
Hieroglyphic writing: couplet, 14, 15, 16–17; polyvalence, 273–84; *ti/ta* affixes, 266–72; word order, 15–16, 19–20
Hocabá, Yucatán: 287–88
"Holmul Dancer": 217–22
House, glyph for: 47
Humboldt Celt: 149
Hunahpu: 253–54
Hunchback: 217, 218

Iguana, as offering: 285, 287, 288, 290, 291
Ik-Skull, Lady (Yaxchilan): 116–17, 236
Impersonation: 194–96, 200–202
Incensario. *See* Censer
Infant, supine: 198–201
Initial Series Vase: 218–19
Itzá: 32
Izapa: 135, 141, 142; Stela 5, 170

Jade: 173, 216
Jaguar, and *xoc*: 250, 251, 252, 254
Jaguar God of the Underworld: 196, 209, 212, 250
Jester God: 167–68, 170–71, 174
J-scroll-and-bracket: 182, 197

Kabah, paintings at: 305–306, 307
Kakupacal (Chichén Itzá): 49, 56–57, 215
Kaminaljuyu, and Teotihuacán: 140, 141, 142; Stela 11, 179, 182
Kan cross: 60, 61, 62, 65–66, 67
Kan-Xul II (Palenque): 6–9, 10, 20
Katun 8 Ahau. *See* Time, cyclical
Kawak, in modern usage: 187–93. *See also* Cauac Monster
Kinich Kakmo: 64, 65
Kinship systems: 259–61, 264
Kin terms. *See* Relationship, glyphs for
Kix-Chan (Palenque): 277
Knife, sacrificial: 91, 93
Knuckleduster: 145, 148–49, 150
Kohunlich: 253
Komchen: 135, 141
Kuk (Palenque): 27
Kuná-Lacanhá Panel: 205–206, 211

Lacondón Forest: 118
Lacondóns: 3
Lady Beastie: 9, 15, 17, 19, 21
Lamanai: 34
Lancet, obsidian: 89, 91, 93
La Pasadita, Lintel 2: 16–18
Las Limas Figure: 145, 154, 200
Las Sepulturas. *See* Copán, Structure 9N-82
La Venta: 151; Altar 5, 153; Monument 6, 162; Stela 2, 170
Leiden Plaque: 12, 16, 17, 170–71, 196–97, 198, 202
Lightning: 184, 187, 189, 190, 193
Lightning men: 189, 190, 192–93
Lintels, wooden, at Chichén Itzá: 57
Lorenzo de la Nada, Pedro: 3–5
Lowlands, Southern, models of development: 33–34, 37
lu-bat (glyph): 43

Macaw: 60, 61, 62, 64–65, 67
Machaquilá, emblem glyph at: 221–22
Madrid Codex: 83, 84, 85, 175, 290–91, 299, 300
Maize: 171–74, 319; iconography of, 60, 61, 62, 66, 67, 167–70, 173–74
Maize god: 174, 201
Mam: 295, 301–302
"Manik Hand" (glyph): 225, 228
Mask, face: 195; Olmec, 154–55
May (cycle): 32
Mayan languages, prepositions and complementizers: 266–72
Mayapan, censers at: 303–305, 306, 307
Merlon, double: 156, 157, 158, 159
Metropolitan Museum Pot: 190
Miraflores Tablet: 9
Monuments, stone, image and text: 13
Muluc: 246, 247–48, 251–52

Naguales: 188, 189, 192, 193
Nahal: 44, 228–29
"Name-tagging," of lintels, at Chichén Itzá: 44–45, 48
Naranjo: 35, 36; Stela 23, 273–74; Stela 31, 201, 202
Narratives: comparison of hieroglyphic texts and modern Chol, 12–15
Necklace: 305
New Year ceremonies: 87, 293, 295; at Santa Rita Corozal, 93–94, 96
Nohpat: 317

Obsidian: 189; green, 139–40, 141
Offerings: 89–91, 93, 96, 175, 178, 182–83; faunal, in Dresden Codex, 285, 286–92
Olmec ceramics, and crocodilian and fish iconography: 147–48
"Olmec Dragon": 146, 147, 149
Olmecs: 171–73; and Earth Lord, 186
Olmec sculpture, and symbols of Maya rulership: 151–66
One-Fish-in-Hand (Machaquilá): 234, 244
Opossum: 295, 302
Ordoñez y Aguiar, Ramón: 3, 5
Orientation, of architecture, and Venus: 316–21
"Otolum": 5
Oxkintok: 34
Oxotitlán, Mural 1: 215–16

Paddlers: 250–51, 252, 253
Palenque: 3, 5, 7–8, 12–13, 35, 37; Beau Relief, 205–206, 213, 214; Creation Tablet, 187–88; del Río throne, 204–206, 213; emblem glyph, 277; Group IV, 7–8, 10; Group of the Cross, 12, 23–25; House E, 317; Oval Palace Tablet, 250, 251, 279; Palace Tablet, 250, 251, 279; Sarcophagus, 166, 176–77; Tablet of the Cross, 13, 15, 17, 19–26; Tablet of the Foliated Cross, 66, 170, 174, 176–77, 184–85; Tablet of the 96 Glyphs, 6, 20–21, 23, 25–27; Tablet of the Orator, 9, 10, 195; Tablet of the Scribe, 9, 10, 195; Tablet of the Slaves, 6–10, 17, 27–30; Temple 18 jambs, 6, 9; Temple of the Inscriptions piers, 196, 198, 202n.1. *See also* Bahlum Kuk; Chac-Zutz'; Chan Bahlum I; Chan Bahlum II; Palenque, village of; Palenque Triad; *and* Zakkuk, Lady

Palenque, village of: 3–5
Palenque Triad: 250. See also GI, GIII
Parentage statement: 255–56, 257, 264
Pauah Tun, at Copán: 73–74, 75–76, 78, 79
Peccary skull, from Copán: 186–87, 282
Period Endings: at Copán, 81, 88; at Yax-
  chilán, 102–109
Piedras Negras: 34, 118, 119; Stela 12,
  206–207, 210; and Usumacinta dam, 121,
  124–25
Pilzintechuhtli: 65–66
Planchón de las Figuras: 127
Popol Vuh: 63, 64, 65, 190
Posterior Event Indicator (PEI): 14–15,
  19–20, 26, 27, 28
Posture, asymmetrical seated: 203–16
Preclassic. See Formative
Primary Standard Sequence: 223–32,
  274–75
Principal Bird Deity: 218, 219, See also
  Celestial Bird Deity
Proskouriakoff, Tatiana: 327, 328
Pusilha: 35

Quadripartite Monster: 198
Quash: 90, 91
Quatrefoil: 64, 186–88
Quiriguá, Stela J: 233, 236

Rain-making ceremonies: 285, 287–88, 291,
  292
Rands, Barbara: 7–8
Rands, Robert: 7–8
Rebirth, and fish-in-hand glyph: 244–45
Relationship, glyphs for: 255–59, 261–65,
  275–76, 278–79
Río Azul: 55, 95, 143, 253
Río de la Pasion, archaeological sites on:
  119, 127
Río Lacantun, archaeological sites on: 119,
  127, 131
Rising Sun (Copán). See Yax-Pac (Copán)
"Rodent Bone" (glyph): 231–32
Rulers: and deity names, 221–22; and imper-
  sonation of women, 195–202
Rulership: 151, 156, 158, 163, 166, 178,
  194–95, 320

Sacrifice: animal, 89–91, 93–94; human,
  53–55, 56, 89–90, 155–56, 199–200
Sacul, Stela 1: 251
San Antonio (Escuintla): 136
San Lorenzo: 153, 171, 172, 173
San Miguel Amuco, stela: 169, 173
Santa Rita Corozal: 89, 90–96, 305, 307;
  censers at, 179–80, 182–83
Scepter: 158–59
Scribes: 79; patron of, 75–76
Seibal: 55, 127, 128
Serna, J. de la: 310, 316
Serpent: 55, 61, 74, 89, 197, 218–19
Serpent wing: 61, 65
Shamanism: 158
Shark: 246–49, 252

"Shark's tooth": 145, 149, 150, 180, 253
Shell-star event: 40–41
Shell-wing dragon: 160
Shield Jaguar I (Yaxchilán): 107–108, 110,
  112, 116, 117
Six Sky, Lady (Naranjo): 202
Sky: 197–98
Sky band: 103–104, 218, 219, 316, 317
"Slim" (Middle Formative Olmec-style sculp-
  ture): 152–66
S motif: 144, 146, 149
Soconusco region: 135
Sorcery. See Witchcraft
Spindle whorl: 140
Spondylus: 92, 159, 250
Stacking (vertical iconography): 175–83
Stelae: in Guatemala, South Coast, 141,
  142; Period Endings, at Yaxchilán,
  102–109
Stingray spine: 89, 92–93, 95, 96, 143, 144,
  149, 150, 250–51, 252, 253, 254, 257–58
Stormy Sky (Tikal): 221
Strömsvik, Gustav: 59–60, 61
Succession, political: 259–60, 264
Sun, and Venus, at Copán: 319, 320

Tamale: 174
Tayasal: 32
Teosinte: 172
Teotihuacán: 33, 34, 37; and Guatemala's
  South Coast, 135–36, 140, 141, 142
Textile, early production of: 140
Thompson numbers: T12, 273, 275–78;
  T16, 299–302; T23, 69, 70, 73; T59,
  268–71; T82, 227; T93, 297, 301; T110,
  281–82; T128, 230; T130, 239; T136,
  239; T229, 273–76, 277; T506, 298–99,
  301; T535 (T122:535), 255, 257, 264;
  T563a, 43, 226; T565, 230; T567,
  297–98; T568, 230; T569, 220–21; T573,
  14; T606, 255, 256, 257–59, 260,
  261–65, 278–80; T608, 244; T609, 230;
  T617, 223–34, 275; T670, 255, 257;
  T671, 225; T673, 46–47; T712, 143, 150,
  236, 255, 257–58, 264; T714, See Fish-in-
  hand glyph; T756, 43; T758, 280–81;
  T764, 221; T1038, 288–89
Three-knotted band: 143, 144, 145, 150, 156
Throne: 203, 204, 205, 210, 211, 213, 214,
  216
Thunder: 184, 187
Ti construction: 22
Tikal: 34–37, 81, 85, 87, 135, 141, 234; in-
  cised bones, 243, 244; Stela 4, 175–76;
  Stela 16, 253–54; Stela 22, 17, 18;
  Temple IV, lintels, 219, 220; and
  Teotihuacán, 141–42; and war with Car-
  acol, 35, 40
Time, cyclical: 32–38
Ti/ta affixes: 266–72
Tlaloc (Mexica god): 100; sculpture, at Ux-
  mal, 97–100, 101
Toniná: 32, 35, 84, 197, 198
Torch: 145, 148, 150, 156, 157, 158, 169

Torch Macaw: 65
Tortoise, as offering: 285, 289, 291
Tres Islas: 127, 129
Tro-Cortesianus Codex. See Madrid Codex
Tulum: 305, 306, 307
Turkey, as offering: 285, 287, 288, 289, 291
Turtle: 95; as offering, 286
Tzibanche: 32
Tzutzuculi: 151–52

Uaxactun: 34, 35, 151; censers at, 179–81
Uayeb days. See New Year ceremonies
Underworld: iconography of, 64, 65, 66, 67;
  portals of, 83, 157, 158, 159
Usumacinta River: basin, 118–19; dam
  project, 118–34
"U Tz'ib": 43, 225–28
Uxmal: Palace of the Governor, 316, 317;
  Tlaloc sculpture at, 97–101

Vase of the Seven Gods: 185, 279
Venus: 181; and architectural orientation,
  309–21; iconography of, 315–16, 317,
  318, 319, 320; glyphs for, 316
Vision Serpent: 89, 90, 175, 177, 182, 183,
  222nn.3–4, 234–35

Waldeck, Frédéric: 205
Warfare: 135, 140–41, 142, 234, 318
Water lily: 73, 74, 75, 76, 79, 84
Water-lily Jaguar: 177, 178, 220–21, 237
Weapons, and cauac (glyph): 188–89, 193
"Wing Quincunx" (glyph): 223, 228,
  229–30
Witchcraft: 189, 190, 193
Women, status of: 199–202
World Tree: 109. 163, 166
"Worm Bird" (glyph): 227
Writing: gods of, 75, 79; glyphs for, 43, 223,
  225–28, 232

Xbalanque: 235, 250, 254
Xcalumkin: 213–14, 288–78
Xoc: 246–49, 251–52, 253, 254
Xocfish Monster: 247–48, 252, 253, 254
Xochicalco: 65; Stela 2, 101
Xochipala: 195
Xultun: 35; Stela 10, 198

Yaxchilán: 34, 100, 101, 110–17, 235;
  Lintel 15, 234; Lintel 25, 233, 234, 239,
  242; Period ending stelae, 102–109; Stela
  3, 103, 104, 106–107, 110, 112, 114,
  116; Stela 19, 107–108; Stela 32, 234,
  236, 242; Structure 8 and tablet, 110, 112,
  115–17; and Usumacinta dam, 119,
  125–27
Yaxhá: 35, 273–74
Yax Naab Chak: 192–93
Yax-Pac (Copán): 76–78, 206–208, 209
Year sign: 97, 98, 99, 100, 101, 317
Yula: 49, 56, 57

Zak-Kuk, Lady (Palenque): 202